This book is dedicated to the memory of my father
Douglas Charles Richards
A gentle, loving, patient man
who would not mind sharing with the following members
of the rising generation

Sarah and Rachel Clark
Megan and Tom Clements
Michael Dollo
Cassia and Hannah Gaden
Eva Herle Schaffer
Matty Man
Callum Mearns-Theodorson
Anna Perkins
Josey Russell
Grace Williams
James Yardley
and all their friends
(OK – and their friends' friends too)

'Everybody ought to treat a stranger right'

Blind Willie Johnson

'Race', Racism and Psychology

Towards a reflexive history

Graham Richards

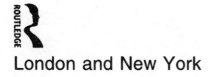

London and New York

First published 1997
by Routledge
11 New Fetter Lane, London EC4P 4EE

Simultaneously published in the USA and Canada
by Routledge
29 West 35th Street, New York, NY 10001

© 1997 Graham Richards

Typeset in Monotype Ehrhardt
by BC Typesetting, Bristol
Printed and bound in Great Britain by
Mackays of Chatham PLC, Chatham, Kent

British Library Cataloguing in Publication Data
A catalogue record for this book is available from the British Library

Library of Congress Cataloging in Publication Data
A catalogue record for this book has been requested

ISBN 0–415–10140–9
ISBN 0–415–10141–7 (pbk)

Contents

Preface

Writing a concise historical review of Psychology's involvements with 'race' and racism seemed a simple enough proposition when I embarked on this project in 1992. This optimism soon proved misplaced. The topic evidently required far more comprehensive coverage if any sense was to be made of it. As will become apparent, the existing secondary literature was inadequate on several counts and its usual portrayal of Psychology as an inveterately racist discipline was something of a caricature. It also often failed to explore the historically situated nature of racial 'knowledge' or the reflexive dimensions of the issue, both ideas which authors otherwise seemed to endorse. The present work is not intended as a defence of the discipline, but does attempt to take these into account. Some important gaps remain nonetheless, notably that I have largely ignored the French (excepting Lévy-Bruhl) and Italian fascist literature, while the German coverage is avowedly sketchy and introductory. Coverage of the rise of Black Psychology is far briefer than the topic deserves and I have also had to set aside a surprisingly substantial corpus of pre-World War II Chinese and Japanese work. There is thus much left to do.

I have been greatly assisted, and my morale sustained, by a host of colleagues, friends, correspondents and second-hand book dealers (these not being mutually exclusive categories!). They include Colin Berry, Ian Bild, Clare Crellin, Mrs Thomas Garth, Howard Gruber, Karen Henwood, Anita Herle, Dennis Howitt, Sabrina Izzard, Nadine Jackson, Eric Korn, Henrika Kuklick, Sandie Lovie, Nancy E. Mann (of the University of Denver Library), Harriet Marshall, Jerry Martin, Mary and Geoff Midgley, Jim Munves, Ann Phoenix, Marian Pitts, Martin Roiser, Barbara Ross, Simon Schaffer, Bernard Spilka, William H. Tucker, Mark Westwood, Anthony Whittaker, Robert Wozniak and Alexandra Yardley. Any omissions from this list are quite inadvertent. The libraries used were primarily the British Library, the University of London Library at Senate House, Cambridge University Library, the Wellcome Institute for the History of Medicine Library and Staffordshire University Library, whose various staffs continue striving to meet our needs with goodwill despite the forces of demoralisation. It would have been impossible to complete this work without substantial funding from the Renaissance Trust, for which I will be ever grateful. Then there are those who, in the deep dreamtime of the early 1960s, first enlightened me on, among many other things, the issue in question: Bert Commissiong, Ron Chandran-Dudley, Phil Hughes, my workmates in Peak Freans, Cadby Hall and the Small Electric Motors Ltd factories and the 424 Camden Road gang. I'm sure there were others too.

Notwithstanding our generally shared abhorrence of racism, none of those just acknowledged is responsible for my sundry interpretations, readings, theories, speculations and detailed conclusions. These, along with any errors of fact, can only be laid at my own door.

Finally, as ever, Maura has been a tower of loving strength even while pursuing her own demanding career.

Venceremos!

Tunbridge Wells
September 1996

Introduction

This book offers a historical overview of how Psychology[1] has engaged the 'race' issue. This is a central aspect of the history of 'race' and racism for it has largely fallen within Psychology's province to address such matters as whether 'race differences' of a psychological kind exist, the nature of racial attitudes and 'race prejudice', and, more recently, the extent to which unacknowledged ethnocentrism distorts theory and practice in the human sciences.

Any authors venturing on these turbulent waters must begin by making their own position explicit, for it is this which determines the character of their work. In fact each of the terms in my title warrants some preliminary consideration in this respect. Without at this stage justifying them in any detail, my positions on these are as follows.

'RACE'

Races as objectively existing biological entities do not exist. The traditional concept of 'race' cannot be reconciled with current understanding of the genetic nature of human diversity. The concept emerged in Western thought in its modern sense around 1800 and has owed its popularity to a variety of, often ideological, cultural factors. By the late 1930s its scientific utility was already being contested by leading geneticists. While seemingly irremovably ensconced in popular usage, and the names of organisations such as the Campaign for Racial Equality, it now has no clear scientific meaning. At most it continues as a convenient short-hand term for something like 'large transiently stabilised and relatively isolated human gene pool'. The criteria commonly used to ascribe 'racial' identity are social and cultural rather than biological. If Africans rather than Europeans had colonised North America and Europeans rather than Africans been enslaved, then presumably anyone with an eighth or a sixteenth white ancestry would have been classified as 'white' in anti-mixed marriage laws designed to maintain the 'purity' of the black 'race'. (And demographers, instead of ascertaining the proportion of 'mulattos' in the 'Negro' population, would have counted them as a proportion of the 'white' population.) The term 'ethnic group' has been proposed as an alternative to 'race', this being understood to refer to cultural rather than biologically defined groups. This is increasingly problematic since the cultural distinctiveness of second and third generation descendants of immigrants from, for example, the Caribbean to Britain may actually be fairly marginal. Many writers are now focusing on the problem of 'racialised discourse' as such, arguing that our very assumption that construing human affairs in terms of distinct 'races', 'ethnic groups' and so on needs to be abandoned – and that applies to much 'anti-racist' as well as 'racist' discourse.

'RACISM'

Racism has proved an extremely difficult concept to define and most authorities now identify a variety of 'racisms'. At its broadest, as Goldberg (1993) defines it, racism may be taken as any practice which, intentionally or not, excludes a 'racial' or 'ethnic' minority from enjoying the full rights, opportunities and responsibilities available to the majority population. There is now wide agreement that Psychology's earlier tendency to view racism as an individual-level quasi-psychopathology was, however well meant, inadequate.[2] Indeed, such a position may well avert attention from more pertinent social and economic factors. The nature of racism is a highly contested issue among social scientists and, as P. Cohen (1992) has shown, most theories contain covert assumptions and 'narra-tives' which constrain their scope. Goldberg's more pragmatic and operational position thus has much to recommend it. While disinclined, therefore, to play the definitional game here, for the purposes of the present work there is one distinc-tion which I believe is helpful, and will be used throughout the book. The term 'racism' will be used to refer to attitudes and practices which are explicitly hostile and denigratory towards people defined as belonging to another 'race'. This implies some level of emotional psychological involvement on the racist's part. The term 'racialism' will refer to a theoretical or ideological belief in the reality of races and the scientific validity of analysing human affairs and human diversity in terms of racial differences. Many racialists are also racists and racialist doctrines provide a rationale for racism, but many racists are not racialists in this sense, their racism not being based on any articulated theory or belief system. With very few exceptions virtually all European and North American scientists of the 19th century were to some degree racialist in this sense, but not all were racist. I return to this point shortly. I am, I stress, adopting this distinction purely pragmatically for the job in hand and not recommending its general adoption. It is needed here in order to differentiate between, for example, S.D. Porteus and T.R. Garth (lead-ing US Race Psychologists, discussed in Chapter 4), the former of whom would be 'racist' and the latter only 'racialist' according to my usage. It is not helpful, for example, in dealing with institutional and cultural racism, which are included in Goldberg's definition, or for those analysing the phenomenon from a sociological direction. (One problem is that these terms only came into use in the 20th century and one risks anachronism in applying them retrospectively.)

Part of this book's intended message is that in relation to 'race', as in most other respects, psychological change occurs over time. While it would be absurd to deny racism's very deep roots in Western culture, extending back to the Middle Ages, it would be equally absurd, and unduly pessimistic, to see it as somehow a fixed, unchanging phenomenon. Elizabethan 'racism' was different from 18th century 'racism' and both were fundamentally different from late 19th century 'Scientific Racism'. Goldberg argues that racism is highly parasitic in nature, latching onto and adapting to changed cultural and intellectual circumstances in a highly versatile fashion. For the historian, especially a white one, the task is to strike the balance between appearing to absolve the racism of previous eras and evaluating it in unrealistically modern terms. Plenty of people at the time knew quite well that slavery was a crime and there is no way that slavers can be excused. On the other hand even white anti-slavery campaigners themselves could not escape prevailing attitudes which to us are clearly racist.

At a time when understanding of the whole 'race' issue is in constant flux it would be highly pretentious to pose as having arrived at an entirely satisfactory and comprehensive standpoint. This book is a contribution to the debate, not an attempt to close it. While clear enough in my own mind that 'race' remains, in Ashley Montagu's (1942) phrase, a 'dangerous myth', and that, this being so, it necessarily follows that 'race differences' are equally mythical, and racism to be fought tooth and nail, I also acknowledge that many related questions remain open. One in particular should be mentioned here. How are we to integrate the competing imperatives to both deny and affirm difference? (This does not apply to 'race' questions alone of course.) The affirmation of the value and distinctiveness of one's group (however defined) is frequently an absolutely necessary aspect of liberatory struggles. The denial of essential differences is equally part of such struggles. This dilemma will resurface at several points.

PSYCHOLOGY

The author's view of the nature of Psychology has recently been outlined elsewhere.[3] For present purposes I should emphasise that I do not see it as a conventional natural science. Psychology's central unique feature, from which much else follows, is its necessarily reflexive character. It is not outside its subject matter regarding it objectively, but a direct expression of that subject matter. Psychologists articulate, reflect upon and participate in the psychological lives of their host societies. In studying how Psychology has addressed racial issues we are therefore not simply examining an episode in the history of science, but also part of our collective *psychological* history. That is to say, there are not objective scientists on the one hand engaged in an on-going study of a separately existing set of 'race-related' phenomena on the other. On the contrary, Psychology is one of the arenas (and a quite important one) in which the whole issue *exists*. It is within this discipline (although not only there) that representatives of the various psychological 'constituencies' in European, North American and colonial societies have debated, defined, wrangled about and proclaimed what the 'race question' actually *is*. Some such constituencies have of course until recently been effectively excluded. In short, Psychology participates in the collective psychological lives of the societies wherein it is practised, it does not, and logically *cannot* simply observe them.

This view should not be taken as simple 'social constructionism', although I would in many respects accept that label. As Roy Bhaskar points out, two kinds of question need to be differentiated.[4] In the physical sciences we have (a) the scientist's account of a phenomenon X. But we also have (b) the question of why this account takes the form it does. The former does not entail that X itself is socially constructed – this would lead us to such absurd conclusions as that dinosaurs did not exist before the 19th century. 'X' exists in what Bhaskar terms an 'intransitive' sense, it is 'transfactual' – existing independently of specific 'scientific facts' which may be asserted of it at a given time and place. But 'the scientist's account', being a social phenomenon (a communication in a specific language at a specific socio-historical juncture) *is* necessarily socially constructed, as are the 'facts' it asserts. While dinosaurs existed before the 19th century, 'dinosaurs' did not. What one cannot claim (and I cannot think of a contemporary philosopher of any school who would want to) is that the scientist's account is as it is simply because that *is* what X is like, that is, the account merely reflects the reality. Were this so science would stand still and all scientific propositions be incorrigible. When we turn to the human and social sciences however, and especially Psychology, the situation becomes more complex for the reasons just sketched. To come to the point, it is not clear that there *is* a 'transfactual' phenomenon 'race' at all. There is only a vast range of human physical diversity in addition to gender differences which, until fairly recent times, was clearly correlated with geographical location. The opening remarks on 'race' state the 'scientific' understanding of this diversity as held by most present-day geneticists.

Why should we be scientifically interested in this diversity? At the physical level it may help us understand (a) the genetic evolution and history of our species – a matter many find genuinely intrinsically interesting, and (b) it might have some bearings on matters of medical importance such as sickle cell anaemia. At the *psychological* level however its interest is far less clear. Only by making the question-begging assumption that physical 'race' differences do correlate directly with psychological phenomena can it be made pertinent. Now there may be all kinds of historical and cultural reasons why 19th century white scientists made this assumption, but the present genetic picture renders it entirely obsolete – along with the old essentialist 'race' concept itself. The question then shifts to 'why do some people *want* this to be psychologically relevant?'.

The concept 'race' thus sits uneasily astride Bhaskar's 'transitive' and 'intransitive' divide. It indeed arose in relation to the 'transfactual' reality of human physical diversity but it now appears as if there was never any 'transfactual' phenomenon to which the term itself referred. For Psychology then, the angle of interest becomes that of addressing the question just posed. (Other human sciences naturally have their own angles, we are not in competition here.) That is, we are concerned with the ineluctably moral question of the psychological nature of the 'race' concept as a psychological phenomenon in its own right. What functions does adoption of this 'racial discourse' framework serve? What are the consequences of adopting it? And how has all this manifested itself historically within Psychology itself? My earlier distinction between 'racialism' and 'racism' may thus be recouched as one between 'necessary' and 'contingent' racism. 'Necessary' racism (my 'racialism') occurs because, given Psychology's reflexive nature, psychologists who are members of culturally and psychologically racist communities will *necessarily* share that community's psychological character in some degree (although unusually recalcitrant and heretical figures may appear on the fringe). *Even the most self-consciously 'anti-racist' people may appear retrospectively racist in this sense.* This was the situation in Europe and the USA during the latter 19th century. 'Contingent' racism (my 'racism') is something over and above this, an active, self-conscious, advocacy of the doctrines of race supremacy, hatred of persons of other 'races', and so on. Again I must stress that this distinction is being made here specifically for the purposes of this book and would not be appropriate in all other contexts, such as sociological level analyses or for everyday campaigning purposes.

Rudimentary though they are, these 'position statements' will hopefully suffice for the reader to gauge roughly from whence I am coming. Since they clearly indicate that I am operating from a specific ideological position, with an agenda derived from that, some may query whether the result can be more than a political tract masquerading as an academic treatise. 'History' should really be included among the problematic terms. There are still, apparently, even some academics who believe history can be written in a detached, even 'scientific', fashion. Certain fundamental misunderstandings are abroad here which can easily lead to us all talking at cross-purposes. The historian's head does not rest in some state of blissful indifference. The enterprise only becomes a masquerade when ideological positions are cloaked with the rhetoric of objectivity. And claiming, even if honestly, to be detached and objective does not mean that one is. However well-intentioned, one simply cannot transcend one's historical situation, temperament, gender and ethnicity when writing about human experience. What, in fact, would it mean to do so? Does anyone really think that, were these all cancelled out, some neutral objective Truth would be revealed? Would it not rather amount to a cancellation of one's own identity as a human being? The intellectual and imaginative efforts we engage in when striving for the 'objective' perspective of the proverbial Martian only extend our humanity, they do not release us from it. We write in the present identifying with peers with whom we broadly share a common worldview, values and priorities. Nor is this a purely 'in-house' matter, since this peer group generally represents a broader psychological constituency in the community at large. Others write with different affiliations and often the ensuing debates comprise part of the very cultural life of the community. What perhaps tends to mislead people is an assumption that the 'truth' always lies between extremes, and that firm beliefs and convictions are a source of 'bias' – a seductive, but unreliable metaphor.

At this point the reader may reasonably feel apprehensive, suspecting that this leaves the door open for extreme relativism and arbitrariness. There is, however, nothing in it which undermines the basic criteria of good scholarship – such things as striving to deal justly with one's sources, not ignoring evidence inconvenient to one's thesis, acknowledging debts owed to others and so on. The rationality of the task is more of a judicial than a 'scientific' kind. In the present case, to pursue this analogy, Psychology stands widely charged with promoting racism and blatant ethnocentrism, and against this charge various defences have been offered. We therefore sift the evidence in relation to the charge as comprehensively as possible. In the event, which is where the analogy fails, historical enquiry reveals a picture rather more complex than can be captured in a simple 'guilty' or 'not guilty' verdict. A better analogy at this point might be clinical diagnosis, with the discipline as suffering patient rather than in the dock. Where my 'ideology' enters is in the choice of questions to address and the underlying values I endorse and seek to promote, in seeing 'racism' as a 'charge' against Psychology rather than a virtue. The same is true, consciously or by default, of every historian and psychologist.

In a world already buried in books a further question arises – is your book really necessary? Those familiar with the relevant literature will, I believe, see that it is. Existing historical coverage of my topic is of two main kinds. First, the Psychological side of the story figures incidentally in other genres of history. Although racism and scientific theories of race have received much historical attention, Psychology is rarely the primary focus. Other disciplines such as biology, anthropology and genetics have tended to dominate, and Psychology most commonly appears only in relation to eugenics, especially in US Psychology during and just after World War I. Secondly, introductory historical accounts have appeared in several books addressing the present situation in the discipline from an openly anti-racist campaigning direction. Psychologists directly engaged in research on the contemporary scene quite understandably cannot undertake detailed historical research. Unfortunately, as a result, they have tended to play 'spot the racism', gathering together miscellaneous collections of quotes from historically diverse sources, often lumping psychiatrists and philosophers in with psychologists, to create the image of a discipline hitherto incorrigibly and universally racist. There are a few works less easy to categorise in this way, but as yet none has appeared which tries, as the present work does, to cover the general topic of Psychology's involvements with 'race' and 'racism'.[5] This absence has meant that the historical image, such as it is, is both distorted and incomplete, and that a number of interesting aspects of the story have been overlooked. The issue is naturally seen in terms of the aftermaths of the Holocaust and the 'Race and IQ' controversy as revived by Arthur Jensen in 1969. Attention has thus concentrated on two issues: first, the role of Psychology in the US immigration panic of the early 1920s, which was underpinned by eugenicist and Nordicist fears of inferior European 'races', including East European Jews; secondly, the meaning of IQ-score differences between African Americans and US whites. Some attention, but not that much, has also been given to the rise of 'race prejudice' and attitude studies in US Social Psychology between the wars. While these are undeniably important, they do not in themselves define the range of the topic, as we will see. In short, there is a genuine gap in the historical literature. Supplying this deficit is essential for a fuller understanding of Psychology's complex role in the modern history of the 'race' issue in Western culture and Western psychology.

I also need to say something about language. Since language provides the very terms in which we understand the world, especially the social world, it becomes one of the principal arenas in which attempts to alter that understanding (and that world) are fought. Those in power necessarily have a built-in, but not always over-whelming, advantage. Nowhere has this been more evident in recent decades than in the fields of racial and gender discourse. In a fairly brilliant manoeuvre, the phrase 'political correctness' has been deployed as a put-down of attempts at changing the terms in which this discourse is conducted. Marxist terminology ('bourgeois', 'proletariat', 'exploitation' etc.) eventually proved generally unusable not because the concepts themselves were 'disproved' but because using them enabled a negative stereotype to be imposed on the user. Something similar seems to be under way with 'feminist' terminology. Mainstream political language is of course equally laden with its own ritualised terminology ('the free market', 'con-sumer choice', 'the deterrent', 'deregulation', 'privatisation' etc.) but this is heard as 'normal' and somehow ideologically neutral. 'Race'-related language remains in considerable flux. This poses a problem for any writer on the topic. In the present work the following policies have been adopted. When discussing earlier work the language of the sources has been preserved, since to do otherwise would be to dis-tort the terms in which these writers understood the matter. When writing in my own capacity and/or referring to the present, I have to some extent played it by ear, trying to use the terminology currently preferred by the people in question. I have tried to avoid 'non-white' since it implies that 'white' is the default condi-tion (perhaps 'whites' should try 'non-black' to see how it feels), though in some contexts it still seems the easiest and most appropriate term. Similar difficulties may arise with 'Non-European'. 'African American' and 'black' (especially in non-US contexts) currently seem unobjectionable. For some reason 'Amerindian' does not appear to have been widely adopted. United States writers often just use 'Indian', since the risk of ambiguity is small, but this clearly would not work for a British readership. 'Native American' remains, as far as I can gather, fairly accept-able, although the word 'native' in itself is highly dubious. 'Aborigine' is more succinct than 'indigenous Australian' and has not acquired quite the pejorative connotations of 'native'; it is also very specific. I have thus continued to use it, but apologise in advance if, unbeknownst to me, it has ceased to be acceptable. In Britain the expression 'black women' is preferred over the US favoured 'women of colour'. 'White' has been retained, however much of a misnomer it really is, and sometimes 'white European' (since nowadays many Europeans are not white). I have rarely used 'Caucasian', the term introduced by Blumenbach around 1800, because for me its Scientific Racist connotations are too strong.

So, just to spell it out, I do not believe 'the Negro' ever physically existed – the Negro was a mythical being invented by white Europeans at the end of the Renaissance, more a psychological symbol of all that white Europeans believed they were not, than a real human type. (Though the word was dropped by African Americans around 1968, the African American Howard University still, curiously, publishes the *Journal of Negro Education*.) Current British use of 'black' often extends to all 'non-whites', although consensus on this is incomplete. Obviously this issue will remain unsettled for some time, and present usages may in due course be abandoned. The heart of the difficulty is that we are still operating in a cultural context where racialised discourse is inescapable, while simultaneously trying to transcend this. Our linguistic difficulties therefore signify both the contradictions inherent in this situation and the problems we face in trying to resolve it.

Finally, I ask the reader's indulgence as I attempt to find a liberating way of reflecting on what is itself a hall of distorting mirrors. If future readers see this book as telling them more about how the race issue appeared to a white male British academic of the 1990s than about the history of Psychology or the natures of 'race' and 'racism', so be it, there is no outflanking this possibility. At the present historical juncture however, it is essential that anti-racist psychologists conscious of the reflexive nature of their discipline should acquaint themselves with, and develop ways of constructively utilising, the history of its entanglements in the 'race' and 'racism' issues. This book is aimed at setting the ball rolling before it goes the way of all texts.

NOTES

1 In this, as in my other writings, I differentiate between the discipline senses of Psychology/Psychological, and subject matter senses 'psychology'/'psychological' by using upper-case for the former.
2 How widespread this view actually was is reconsidered in Chapter 8.
3 G. Richards (1996).
4 This is a general feature of Bhaskar's 'critical realism'. See Bhaskar (1991) esp. pp. 8–13 for a technical exposition in the context of a critique of Richard Rorty. I am simplifying a very dense philosophical argument here.
5 William H. Tucker (1994), an invaluable study, is perhaps the nearest, but he is explicitly concerned with identifying and exposing the ideological character of pro-race differences research, and naturally focuses on the eugenics side of the story.

Chapter 1

The pre-evolutionary background and the roots of Scientific Racism

The Psychological story proper begins with the rise of Spencerian and Darwinian evolutionary theory in the 1850s, when Herbert Spencer and Darwin's cousin Francis Galton opened the Psychological discussion. This chapter is confined to identifying some relevant aspects of the topic's previous history, necessary for an understanding of Spencer's and Galton's views. For fuller coverage readers are referred to the numerous histories of the topic which have appeared in recent decades.[1]

THE CHRISTIAN VIEW

In traditional Christian cosmology, 'Mankind's' basic unity was an article of faith: we are all descendants of Noah's sons and daughters-in-law. This seemingly explained the main varieties of physique and colour with which Europeans were familiar – white Europeans, brown Asians and black Africans.[2] Since the Bible reports that Ham was cursed (for seeing his drunken father naked) our 'common humanity' was reconcilable with the view that Ham's descendants (those with black skin) were eternally ordained to be inferior 'hewers of wood and drawers of water'.[3] This argument was used by Christian racists down to recent times (for example, among sections of the South African Dutch Reform Church). Religious belief systems do not simply determine attitudes, their complexity often supplies a resource for justifying them. 'Christian' arguments can be deployed to oppress as well as humanise.

Prior to Linneaus (founder of modern biological taxonomy in the 1730s), typo-logical classification barely extended beyond this tripartite division. From the early 16th century writers tried to fit the indigenous peoples of the New World into this scheme (for example, Sir Walter Raleigh[4]). Their efforts were never satis-factory, but this was seen as due to human inability to interpret the biblical account correctly.[5] The savagery of 'savages' and barbarity of 'barbarians' was usually viewed in cultural rather than biological terms as arising from ignorance, wickedness, folly and lack of exposure to the message of holy scripture, although the humanity of South American Indians was questioned in Spain late in the 16th century.[6] Excepting the numerous legendary dog-headed cynocephali, tailed, air-eating or one-footed peoples whom nobody had ever closely encoun-tered, biological features (such, notably, as blackness of skin) symbolised rather than caused their possessors' inferiority. They had, as it were, fallen further since the Fall. Most authorities agree that the negative symbolic association of blackness with sin and death in Christian cultures was a factor in pre-modern European attitudes towards Africans. It is largely anachronistic to ascribe the kinds of 'racial' concepts which later become commonplace to anyone prior to the late 18th century. These require more complex political and biological notions of human equality, classification and human–animal relations which only emerged later. Africans and indigenous Americans were cast as bestial cannibalistic savages, Asians as jaded barbarians and Europeans became in some sense 'racially conscious', but no racialist rationale underlay all this.

THE NOBLE SAVAGE

The 18th century also saw the advent of a new image, the 'Noble Savage', spontaneously generous, happy and sin-free, ignorant of civilisation's corrupting pleasures, pains, and temptations and in harmony with a beneficent Nature supplying all life's wants.[7] Combined with a general philosophical assumption of universal psychological uniformity, this promoted a fairly open-minded and tolerant attitude towards other cultures among many (but not all) European intellectuals and travellers until the latter end of the century. Only with a subsequent shift towards 'diversificationism' among natural historians, bolstering a zoological classificatory approach to human variety, did the human status of Africans and other 'savages' become a matter of widespread controversy. While Lord Monboddo (who had never seen one) was prepared to grant this status to the orangutan, his contemporary, Lord Kames, denied it to blacks.[8] David Hume was also contemptuous of Africans. While many devout Christians and Enlightenment social philosophers previously supported egalitarianism, new developments in 'scientific' anthropology and zoology slowly undermined the credibility of the orthodox Christian classification and the creationist 6,000-odd year time scale. The 'Noble Savage' nonetheless persisted in early 19th century anti-slavery rhetoric.

WHITE SUPERIORITY

By 1800 the broader European perspective had fundamentally altered. Imperial expansion, and accelerating technological sophistication, gave ideas of intrinsic European superiority ever more credibility. The Enlightenment notion of history as progressive and directional made it inevitable that differences between peoples and cultures would eventually be construed evaluatively as reflecting relative levels of advancement. Yet the most influential late Enlightenment writer on race, Baron J.F. Blumenbach, was far from sharing such sentiments, writing in 1806:

> there is no so-called savage nation known under the sun which has so much distinguished itself by such examples of perfectibility and original capacity for

scientific culture, and thereby attached itself so closely to the most civilized nations of the earth, *as the Negro*.

(1865, p. 312, italics in original)[9]

Respect for even the complex literate civilisations of India and China waned after the 1820s. Convinced of the objective rectitude of their own beliefs and values, the presence of anything warranting the name of 'culture' among native Americans, Africans or Aborigines became simply invisible to Europeans. Such 'lesser breeds' possessed nothing of value but their worth as potential labour and the material resources of their lands – which they either could not use, did not appreciate or did not know existed. Even the most humanitarian anti-slavery campaigners rarely defended the cultures of those they championed, and few seriously argued that Africans and American Indians were the intellectual, aesthetic or emotional equals of Europeans. Their case relied primarily on religious and moral arguments, a reliance which became a major weakness from the mid-1840s when confronting the growing weight of ostensibly 'scientific' evidence being invoked by the opposition.

CONFUSION OF VIEWS OF RACE

At any period between 1500 and 1800 we can identify antecedents of later divisions between humanitarians and exploiters, egalitarians and inegalitarians, monogenists (holding humanity to be a single species) and polygenists (holding races to be separate species), enslavers and liberators. The conceptual frameworks which structured European thought were all, nevertheless, radically different from those which have dominated the last century and a half. Heredity, time-scale, methods of cross-cultural study, and zoological classification appear in retrospect matters on which even the most sophisticated natural philosophers were utterly confused. Their data were restricted, their methodologies crude, their grasp of underlying conceptual issues hazy. Not that this was how savants saw their condition, far from it – they saw themselves as hacking progressively through the jungle of ignorance as effectively as their fellow empire builders were similarly hacking away (and not only at foliage) for real.

The roots of the racial thinking which subsequently developed lie not in 'scientific' texts alone but in the settings in which they were produced. Proto-racism certainly infused European perceptions of Chinese, Indians and native Americans, but the epicentre of the entire issue was the 'Negro' and the moral issues constellating around slavery.[10] The most cited British proto-racist text is the Jamaican planter Long's *History of Jamaica* (1774) in which the possibility that Africans are a different species is enthusiastically advocated, followed in 1799 by Charles White's *Account of the Regular Gradation in Man*. Their immediate influence appears nonetheless to have been limited, and Long's position contrasts with the American Professor of Moral Philosophy, S. Stanhope Smith's[11] *An Essay on the Causes of the Variety of Complexion and Figure in the Human Species* (1965, 1st edn 1787), which offered a thoroughly environmentalist account. The legacy of the slavery issue has largely continued to determine the agenda, especially in the

USA, now supplemented by that of Nazi anti-semitism and, in Britain and other ex-colonial European countries, immigration from former possessions. While racial thinking may be directed towards virtually any non-European people (and indeed some European ones as well, such as the Irish or Slavs), Africans have, historically, occupied centre-stage, and it is interesting that anti-Jewish racism acquired a separate name, 'anti-semitism', as if it were somehow important to differentiate it from racism in general.[12] Whites' attitudes to Africans were primarily a function of their view of slavery, which, as such things usually are, were in turn a function of economic and cultural circumstance.

THE 'RACISM' QUESTION

Although mentioned in the Introduction, a little more should be said about 'racism' prior to 1850. It would be pure sophistry to deny that prior to 1850 Europeans oppressed and denigrated others on grounds of colour and/or physiognomy, rationalising such behaviour on all kinds of grounds which seem to us spurious. To all practical intents and purposes this was clearly racism. Yet simply to assimilate this behaviour into the modern category 'racism' obscures the extent of historical change in how human differences have been conceptualised and explained. It gives a misleading impression of stasis, masking the degree to which current racisms are very specific products of late 19th and 20th century economic, cultural and scientific history. Ironically the unchangeability of human nature is a common racist dogma; we all allegedly possess an instinctive and legitimate dislike of people of other 'races', and if we do not we are *ipso facto* degenerate mongrels. One can then see the danger: if we perceive no differences between Elizabethan, Enlightenment, and modern 'racisms' we may come to view 'racism' as some inherent feature of white human nature – a not unracist conclusion in itself, entailing perhaps unwarranted gloom regarding the possibility of its elimination.

While it would sidetrack us too far to discuss the matter in detail here, it should be noted that as far as 18th and early 19th century Britain is concerned the historical picture is far from clear-cut. While slavery officially persisted legally until the Somersett case of 1772, and *de facto* to some extent for a long time thereafter, there is, for example, surprisingly little evidence that inter-marriage was viewed with any special horror, as later became the case. It has in fact proved rather difficult to disentangle the roles of race and social class in determining the black person's lot during this period. The number of black people in Britain was probably well into five figures (in a population rising from c .7 to 10 million by 1800). Some managed to achieve a degree of social success.[13] It is easy to get bogged down in the precise details of the level of 'racism' in Georgian Britain. My point here is that however 'racist' white treatment of blacks obviously was, it would be anachronistic to say that most whites, at this time, actually saw blacks (or anybody else) as a 'race' in the modern sense. Rather they saw them as a strange exotic 'tribe', as the cursed descendants of Ham, or as Noble Savages. The African, the Turk, the Indian, the Chinese, the 'Moor' – all elicited reactions in accord with the multitude of long-standing myths, stereotypes, folk-lore and traveller's tales which had accreted to them over a millennium. Each bore their unique blend of exotic vices and virtues, habits and character traits – and insofar as these were negative, whites reacted accordingly. But if exotic, they were, for the English, only further out along the same scale of social distance whereon the Irish, French, Italians, Spanish and Russians were also located.

That it is from this matrix that more explicit, self-conscious, racism and racialism developed is not in dispute. What I query is whether, before 1800 at least, we have anything like genuine 'racial' thinking such as came so rapidly to the fore in the 1840s. Racism is an absolutist doctrine if nothing else; in countering it prudence surely dictates that we stress the extent to which it arises from ultimately transient constellations of cultural and economic forces. Joel Kovel (1988) hints at, but does not explore, a curious sense in which racist racialism *replaced* slavery as a means of maintaining African American subjugation. While naked force backed with a blend of legalistic arguments around the nature of 'property', theological casuistry and straightforward scaremongering were sufficient to sustain white hegemony there was no need for racialist theory. Only when these ceased to prevail did a quasi-scientific theory centred on the 'race' concept become necessary to rationalise white supremacy in a way which whites could find morally acceptable.[14] The period from around 1800–1850 is the gestation phase of that first form of 'Scientific Racism' which swept to dominance immediately prior to, and following, the American Civil War.

Whether we should deploy the term 'racism' in writing about the pre-1850 period cannot then be empirically decided. It genuinely depends on what you mean (or want to mean) by 'racism', which will vary with the goals and circumstances of your discourse. If defined so as to cover every case of someone's treatment being negatively affected by their ethnicity or genetically determined visible physical traits (other than those related to gender and health), it ceases to tell us very much and the distinctive features of modern white racism are lost sight of.[15] But if we define it too narrowly we may easily be read (especially if we are white) as trying to excuse, deny or evade the true historical depth and scale of the problem. That modern racism has deep historical roots is not in question, but this is different from claiming that its forms have remained constant or always presented themselves as something we can sensibly call racism in the modern sense. This line appears to be consistent with Goldberg's insistence on a pragmatic rather than essentialist definition of racism.

THE SYMBOLIC MEANING OF BLACKNESS

An issue of particular Psychogical interest is the common argument that the deep-rooted symbolic meanings of blackness in Western culture have played a central role in determining European perceptions of Africans. In the European mind blackness, it is said, symbolises (ultimately for profound psychodynamic reasons) sin, the Devil, dirt, faeces and death, and Europeans projected these connotations onto peoples with highly melanised skin. This thesis (to which we return in Chapter 10) is of considerable importance because it has become something of a cliché. Both historical evidence and Psychological theory suggest it might be a serious oversimplification. Eighteenth century writers such as Long could certainly wax paranoid about the staining of the purity of the white race by 'mongrel-isation', and even Blake's famous quatrain accepts that blackness is a stigma con-cealing the pure white soul of the African child.[16] For those seeking little black servant boys – and among army regiments seeking black musicians – blackness was, on the contrary, positively valued aesthetically much as it might be in a horse or dog; Shyllon (1977) quotes a 1771 advertisement offering for sale a 'Negro Boy' ten or eleven years old which ends '. . . and for colour, an excellent fine black' (p. 13). While wishing to possess a black boy as a fashion accessory hardly be-tokens absence of racism, it suggests an attitude both less intense and more blasé than either the 'dominative' or 'aversive' positions identified by Kovel. Among the commonest Enlightenment epithets for human blackness are 'sable', 'dusky' and 'ebon' – none of them negative and two being positive equations of blackness with aesthetically valued natural materials. These surely suggest an effort to avoid the negative connotations. If it is suggested that such usages betray, by their very effeteness, a reaction-formation against an underlying disgust, then a no-win situation is created: negative descriptions of blackness proving the point, positive ones proving it too since they are clearly repressing feelings of the opposite kind. In fact 'sable', 'dusky' and 'ebon' are typical 18th century literary usages, not signifying, as they would today, that the user was unusually hung-up about the matter.[17] Nor is white necessarily good, it too can symbolise death (and, espe-cially, sickness) as easily as black can (and Death's horse is, traditionally, 'pale'). In short, European culture has long acknowledged a 'black' aesthetic as well as a 'white' one, esteeming the beauty of jet, ebony, sable fur, the velvety night, and fascinating dark eyes and hair.[18]

The symbolic meaning in European cultures of 'black vs. white' has thus never been *simply* equivalent to 'bad vs. good'. Blackness is, in itself, a great facilitator of projection – we 'see things in the dark' – suggesting that blackness as such is more akin to the screen than the film. Projection, moreover, will only occur if the pro-jector has a prior need to engage in it. We must therefore ask why any projection – negative or positive – occurs in the first place. Discussion of this must, though, be postponed until we consider modern Psychological theories of racism.[19] I merely suggest here that explaining anti-black racism in terms of the negative symbolic meanings of blackness for non-black Europeans raises the question of why such a projection mechanism is initially activated – on which Kovel actually has much to say.

The very notion of 'projection' is, furthermore, a product of modern Psychol-ogy (originating in psychoanalysis). This actually changes the psychological situa-tion, and it is arguable that the application of the category to behaviour prior to its own invention is in some degree anachronistic. 'Projecting' is part of our modern psychological repertoire, used in everyday life to refer to certain kinds of ideas and behaviours. The psychological situation was different when the concept was un-available. If behaviour which, in retrospect, looks like 'projection' did occur (and it certainly did) it could *never* have been recognised, which renders it a different phenomenon. 'Projection' only becomes in any sense culpable in the light of our present possession of the concept, which casts our failure to know we are doing it as a lapse in self-insight for which we are responsible.

THE 'SUBHUMANITY' QUESTION

Another assumption which needs re-examining is that Europeans typically saw Africans and other 'lower races' as 'subhuman'. Technically this question translates into assessing the degree of acceptance of 'polygenism'. We noted earlier that polygenists such as Edward Long and Charles White exerted little influence in Anglophone cultures until the slavery issue came to a head in the 1850s and 1860s.[20] During the 1840s polygenism began to gather popularity in the USA following the work of S.G. Morton. Its fortunes had been better in France from about 1800, being favoured by such writers as Bory de St Vincent, Pruner Bey, J.J. Virey, Paul Broca and Du Chaillu.[21] After about 1870 the wider acceptance of evolutionary thought and a much extended time-scale rendered the polygenist vs. 'monogenist' debate obsolete, at least in its original terms. The enduring ideological authority of Christianity always limited polygenism's broad cultural acceptance however, even in the US South.[22] Europeans did not think that blacks and whites were equal, on the contrary, but then most did not think whites were equal among themselves. Even among slave owners and traders, polygenism only made headway in slavery's final years as a last ditch justification for the 'peculiar institution'. Such polygenist arguments as the existence of a natural repugnance to sexual contact between black and white would have been ludicrous hypocrisy among those who had been happily sexually 'contacting' their black women slaves for decades (as well as lynching black men supposedly lusting after white womanhood). It has also been observed that nobody would want their dinner served by a paw[23] – as would be the case if you genuinely saw your black slaves as animals. Exercise of raw social (and sexual) power over other humans is what gives slave-owning its kick.

The question of belief in the 'subhumanity' of black people during the earlier period is not a straightforward one, particularly in the USA, since an oscillation in perceptions on this score is very much one of the hallmarks of the fundamentally conflicted attitudes engendered by slavery. A more accurate description of the commonest British view (prior to the 1850s) would be that humanity in general comprised a hierarchy ranging from inferior to superior individuals, and that the inferior were more highly represented among non-Europeans, most so among Africans and other 'primitive' or 'savage' peoples. From this it was easy to move to saying, in an unqualified way, that blacks were inferior, but this meant inferior humans not subhumans. I am not, I think, splitting hairs here. That some people are somehow 'inferior' is accepted in all communities – they may be of low intelligence or ability, they may be deficient in social or moral virtues, they may simply be children. They may also evoke fear, pity, contempt, or amusement, but are still classified as humans. A 'subhuman' is something quite different, not merely 'inferior' but quite separated from this continuum of human quality. While some, no doubt, viewed blacks in this way, they were exceptional. The long-established image of the black as subadult, that is, childlike, was far more widespread, and persisted even in some scientific circles until recently.[24]

Besides monogenism and polygenism a minority of writers (notably the Duke of Argyll)[25] argued that modern 'savages' were degenerate descendants from originally civilized peoples. This theory did not long survive the advent of Darwinism, but both Darwin (1871) and Lubbock (1912, 1st edn 1865) felt it necessary to spend time carefully refuting it. In orthodox Christian terms, 'bestial savages' had, as noted earlier, 'fallen' further than Europeans from the original Adamic state, not failed to achieve human status in the first place.

Again we must beware of anachronism. Our term 'subhuman' derives its meaning from an evolutionary perspective we tend to take for granted – denoting a being like the (wrongly) stereotyped Neanderthal: stooping, shambling, slow-witted, semi-articulate, violent, malicious. The subhuman is less evolved, more simian, an 'ape-man'. How then is it to be applied to views predating acceptance of the evolutionary perspective? Since the OED's earliest cited use of 'subhuman', in the sense used here, is from 1957, we should be particularly wary of deploying it to characterise pre-modern racism.[26]

BIOLOGY AND CULTURE

One central theoretical issue which was especially confused, and remains a matter of debate in some quarters, is the relationship between biology and culture. From the 1770s to the 1850s physiognomical and phrenological ideas enjoyed wide popularity and a degree of scientific acceptance. The low brow, the prognathous jaw and the like directly signified moral and psychological character.[27] Scientific Racism clearly has some of its origins in this doctrine which implied that peoples possess the psychological character signified by their physiognomy, which in turn underlies their culture. While phrenology waned, this rooting of culture in biology gained increasing momentum from the 1850s, being reinforced by evolutionary writers such as Spencer. Indeed, what might be termed 'physiognomical essentialism' enjoyed a new lease of life from about 1870–1900 under the aegis of evolution-inspired degenerationist theorising, as we will see in the next chapter. The present point is that a clear differentiation of biology and culture eluded many evolutionary thinkers and the subordination of the latter to the former became a common feature of Scientific Racism. One immediate effect of this 'biologising of culture' was to render oxymoronic the notion of a 'black gentleman'. This had not previously been so, high-class African visitors to Britain for example were treated as such.[28] Biology's higher scientific status, as against sociology, reinforced this tendency and the belief that culture expressed innate racial character remained powerful well into the present century.[29]

ORIGINS OF SCIENTIFIC RACISM

Finally we need to pull together the factors involved in the birth of the doctrine now called 'Scientific Racism', which provided the framework within which psychologists first addressed the topic. This coincided with, and arose from, several mid-19th century socio-cultural and economic developments: the emergence of a more rigid class structure in Britain as industrial culture entrenched itself; the Europe-wide decline of egalitarian radicalism after the numerous unsuccessful revolutionary risings in 1848; science's rising authority vis-à-vis religion, and, in the USA, a growing anti-slavery movement. By the mid-1850s the ever-inflating conviction of the inherent superiority of European peoples and culture over their increasingly numerous subject peoples was shared by anthropologists, ethnographers, travellers and biologists alike.[30] Prior to Darwin's *Origin of Species* (1859) there was, as already mentioned, an upsurge in polygenist thinking, along with widespread sympathy for the Southern States. This yielded numerous texts establishing what would become the commonplaces of European scientific perceptions of non-Europeans, and particularly 'the Negro', to the end of the century and well beyond.[31] They also generated a widespread belief in the racial nature of history, international affairs being the surface level of an aeon-long competition between racial stocks – and this applied within Europe as well as globally. The next chapter will show how evolutionary theory reformulated and consolidated, but did not fundamentally alter, the racial views of earlier Victorian scientists.

Scientific Racism intensified the conflation of the biological and the cultural as biological level explanations came to be considered more fundamentally 'scientific'. Cultural traits, good and bad, were interpreted as direct expressions of innate racial character, a message seductively packaged in several ways, one being the constant invocation of physiological differences allegedly discovered by trustworthy doctors and anatomists. Adopting European anatomy and physiology as the norm, any deviation became quasi-pathological and described accordingly.[32] Secondly the growing corpus of writings by colonial administrators, missionaries, doctors, traders and travellers provided extensive 'authentic' first-hand evidence of the moral, temperamental, intellectual and physical failings of non-Europeans. And who could presume to quibble with their gentlemanly testimony? Home-based writers such as Thomas Carlyle eagerly lent their support.[33] All of this could, finally, be cast as a scientific refutation of the delusions of misplaced philanthropy. The rhetorical resources on which proto-Scientific Racists could draw were, initially at least, nigh on overwhelming.

The faults heaped upon the 'Negro' were unique but in degree, the nether end of a scale of which bovine Slavs and violent, porcine, Irish Celts were the starting point.[34] The Morant Bay insurrection in Jamaica (1865) and the Indian Mutiny (1857) only reinforced such perceptions. The US Civil War (1862–5) ended slavery, but in its aftermath the long-traumatised ex-slave population – socialised into submission, culturally disinherited, and mostly illiterate – were as vulnerable as ever. Segregation, *de facto* disenfranchisement and the Ku Klux Klan effectively maintained their continued subjection following the failure of 'Reconstruction'.[35] In this climate Scientific Racist arguments for their innate inferiority would inhibit policies for the fundamental improvement of the African Americans' lot for nigh on a century. The roles of Psychology in both reinforcing and eroding such arguments will concern us over the next four chapters.

In Europe meanwhile the racial political doctrines of Count Gobineau, Wilhelm Marr, and their like, centred on supposed intra-European racial differences and nourished by the tangled musings of the doyens of Scientific Racist anthropology, were weaving a pernicious web of pseudo-scientific political fantasising which it would take eight decades and millions of lives to break. Ironically, it was a game in which oppressed as well as oppressors could participate, providing Irish Home

Rulers, US 'Back to Africa' black movements and Zionists alike with a racial as well as moral and cultural rationale for their aspirations.

Let us now turn then to the more direct effects of Scientific Racism on Psychological thought.

NOTES

1 See e.g. P.D. Curtin (1964), D.B. Davis (1966), J.S. Haller Jr (1971), D.A. Lorimer (1978), N. Stepan (1982), F. Shyllon (1974, 1977), J. Walvin (1982).
2 Somewhat surprisingly Banton and Harwood (1975) fail to mention this.
3 The biblical account is in Genesis 9.
4 See his *History of the World* (1614) which contains much brain-racking on this matter. For early anthropological views see M.T. Hodgen (1964).
5 The earliest serious challenge to the scheme was Isaac de la Peyrère's *A Theological Systeme upon that Presupposition that Men were before Adam* (1655), which led to the author's imprisonment for heresy and forced recantation.
6 Notably by the historian and theologian Juan Ginez de Sepulveda, in a controversy with Bartolomé de Las Casas in 1550. See D.B. Davis (1966) p. 169 ff.
7 See e.g. Curtin (1964).
8 Views proposed respectively in Monboddo's *The Origin and Progress of Language* (6 vols) (1773–92) and Kames's *Sketches of the History of Man* (1774).
9 This is the final sentence of a brief essay 'Of the Negro in particular' which had appeared in his *Contributions to Natural History* (1806) first published in German. The translation is in J.F. Blumenbach (trans. T. Bendyshe) (1865).
10 See J. Walvin (1982) for a number of monographs on British involvement with slavery and the anti-slavery movement.
11 Professor at the College of New Jersey, later Princeton University, the leading Presbyterian college.
12 The OED dates 'anti-semitism' from 1881.
13 See e.g. P. Edwards (1981). T.L. Busby (1820) has an illustration and description of the celebrated street musician (and apparent previous incarnation of Jimi Hendrix) Billy Waters, the latter of which is highly sympathetic and makes no reference to his colour at all.
14 See the account in Chapter 4 of the 'Negro education' issue, which rather bears this suggestion out.
15 Even this perhaps defines some of its current usages too narrowly – any negative reference to someone's nationality, even their being Welsh, may be seen as racist in some quarters. My personal reaction to this is mixed, for the very extension of the term in this way paradoxically suggests that the grounds of the issue are shifting away from physical traits alone to a broader appreciation of the injustice of using ascribed group memberships of *any* kind as a basis for discriminatory treatment. Racism, sexism, ageism, and healthism are thus becoming seen as aspects of a more overriding general error. This is surely to be welcomed. On the other hand an extension of the meaning of 'racism' in this way also renders it harder to stay focused on the central issue. This might be a price worth paying, but I would have thought that winding up a Welsh workmate by accusing him of indecency with sheep is in quite a different category from insults based on colour.
16 'The Little Black Boy'. The opening verse runs: My mother bore me in the southern wild,/And I am black, but O! my soul is white;/White as an angel is the English child,/But I am black, as if bereav'd of light. The poem as a whole though defies quite such a simplistic reading and may in fact be taken as aimed against taking such colour symbolism literally. The negative symbolism of blackness is the cross which the black boy has to bear, but it is the English boy, not he, who is actually misled by it (for the

black boy's mother has already explained to him its spiritual meaning). In any event it is hardly likely that Blake's real view of race was any more conventional than his view of anything else, though it barely figures anywhere else in his work.

17 As e.g. in the sarcastically overeuphemistic usage of a phrase like 'dusky brethren' – 'Needless to say the other driver was one of our dusky brethren.'

18 Howitt and Owusu-Bempah (1994, pp. 133–4) claim that consulting 'the dictionary' they found 'black' had 55 negative connotations to 9 positive and 'white' 21 negative and 19 positive (none given for 'neutral' connotations). While suggesting that 'black' does have overwhelmingly negative connotations this excludes positive and neutral synonyms such as 'ebon', 'sable', 'jet' etc. and suggests that 'white' is also slightly negative. Rather than offering clearcut support for Kovel, as they imply, these figures surely signify a more ambivalent situation such as that being proposed here.

19 I thus leave in abeyance here the further psychodynamic twists and turns of the argument, such as the possibility that negative characterisations of black skin mask a repressed attraction towards it and so forth. I am also aware that I have here merely raised, rather than explored, some problems with the logic of the 'projection' metaphor. The argument sketched here is akin to that made by Klineberg (1940) against Dollard (1957) mentioned below p. 138.

20 Major English-language polygenist texts include: James Hunt's paper 'On the Negro's Place in Nature' (1863), Robert Knox's *Races of Man* (1862), and in the USA, where the doctrine was most popular, S.G. Morton's *Crania Americana* (1839) and *Crania Aegyptica* (1844), Nott and Gliddon's *Types of Mankind* (1854) and John Campbell's *Negro-Mania* (1851). The eminent Harvard zoologist Louis Agassiz, a Swiss emigré, was also a powerful voice in the polygenist camp. The phrenologists got in on the act in J.W. Jackson's *Ethnology and Phrenology* (1863) (the leading British phrenologist G. Combe also wrote a supportive appendix to *Crania Americana*). The irreconcilability of polygenism with Christianity was the theme of Rev. T. Price (1829) who roundly attacks the polygenist views being aired by J. Pinkerton and J. Macculloch (which had appeared, curiously enough, in books on Scotland and pertained to the differences between Celts and 'Goths'). See also n. 34.

21 It should be noted that S.L. Gilman (1992), drawing almost exclusively on French material, gives the impression of a broader acceptance of polygenism than is warranted.

22 S.J. Gould (1984) has an excellent account of US polygenism and suggests that it was most influential in scientific circles. He also notes that the polygenists were far from all being supporters of slavery. Louis Agassiz was the last major US-based exponent of the doctrine. J.C. Prichard (1831) observes that polygenism 'now seems to be gaining proselytes among the French naturalists and physiologists, and among some writers on history and antiquities in Germany' (p. 2). It persisted in Britain until the 1930s as a minority position, being espoused by the eugenicist Ruggles Gates for example.

23 Interestingly S.J. Gould's quote from a letter by Agassiz indicates that his own polygenism was rooted in precisely such an emotional revulsion to being served food by 'negroes' (Gould, 1984, p. 45).

24 S.L. Gilman (1992), for example, tends to be unclear about this issue, implying both that Europeans cast Hottentots on the lowest rung of the Scale of (human) Nature and that they saw them as non-human. That being the lowest form of humanity entails being more animal-*like* is of course true but, as he shows, women were thought more animal-like than men, and the same is true of children.

25 For example, Argyll (1869).

26 The German *Untermensch* is earlier, but does not mean quite the same thing, referring to 'men' who are naturally subordinate or an inferior underclass, not to those who are hardly 'men' at all.

27 Physiognomy's relatively greater stress on external form compared with phrenology's emphasis on the brain rendered it rather more supportive of racialism. See M. Staum (1995) for some discussion of this, particularly with reference to Camper's 'facial

angle' and the acceptance of the significance of this by early 19th century French writers such as J.-J. Sue and Moreau de la Salhe. After Gall and Spurzheim phrenologists such as F.-J.-V. Broussais also accepted this, however, and in popular British phrenology racialist/racist engravings comparing head-shapes were commonplace throughout the century.

28 See Lorimer (1978).

29 J.P. Rushton (1989) still touts the idea that: 'if individuals are biased to learn or produce patterns of culture maximally compatible with their genotypes, then dissimilarities in cultural patterns among the populations may be as much a result as the cause of any differences' (p. 138).

30 See, for example, the discussion of Galton in the next chapter.

31 Carothers (1972) seems to be the last writer in English seriously advocating these within academia. See below pp. 258–61.

32 For example, the quote from Pruner Bey given below p. 16.

33 'Occasional discourse on the Negro question' (1849) in *Fraser's Magazine*, reprinted as a pamphlet in 1853 with 'Negro' changed to 'Nigger' in the title.

34 Regarding the Celts, however, there was an earlier strand of thought which cast them as quite distinct from all other Europeans. J.C. Prichard (1831) quotes Pinkerton: 'The mythology of the Celtae resembled, in all probability, that of the Hottentots, or others the rudest savages, as the Celtae anciently were, and are little better at present, being incapable of any progress in society' (p. 21). Prichard strongly opposed such opinions.

35 See Chapter 4 for more on this.

Chapter 2

Psychology and 'Scientific Racism' 1860–1910

INTRODUCTION

From the mid-1850s, and especially following the publication of Darwin's *Origin of Species* in 1859, evolutionary thought supplied an overarching integrating framework for fields of Psychological enquiry hitherto relatively distinct.[1] Animal behaviour, child development, individual differences, physiological psychology, social psychology, psychopathology, emotion and the very nature of 'Mind' itself – all could be cast as facets of the single task of studying human psychology from an evolutionary perspective. Other cultural factors greatly facilitated this, notably growing governmental needs for techniques of 'managing individuality' in the expanding urban and industrialised societies.[2] Also, as Morawski (1992a,b) points out, US culture was, at this time, psychologically confused at many levels, creating a situation in which Psychology both expressed and exploited the wide-felt need for guidance in construing 'subjectivity' and what 'human nature' was *really* (i.e., *scientifically*) like.

This evolutionary orientation profoundly affected scientific views of race,[3] at one stroke moving matters beyond the earlier 'monogenism' versus 'polygenism' debate. In the now extended, albeit still very hazy, time-scale, a common human ancestry could be conceded while retaining much of the thrust of the polygenist case. Different 'racial stocks' could be understood as diverging from a main stem at various times in the long distant past, with some subsequently failing to evolve as far as others.[4] Tree diagrams of this became commonplace.[5] The 'biologisation' of human diversity was thus consolidated; not only physical appearance but temperament and culture reflected a people's innate evolutionary status.[6] It was easy to draw up the rankings; white Europeans at the top, Chinese, Indians and perhaps Arabs jostling for silver and bronze medal placings and at the bottom Australian Aborigines, Bushmen, Hottentots and Tierra del Fuegans, lapped so often it was hardly worth considering them as any longer participating in the event. In the last twenty years the rise of this 'Scientific Racism' has received much historical attention and it will not be rehearsed again here in any detail.[7] Nevertheless some observations on it are relevant to our current concerns.

ASPECTS OF SCIENTIFIC RACISM

The legacy of earlier time-perspectives proved inescapable even though intellectually acknowledged as erroneous. Perceptions were automatically 'presentist'.

The current situation represented time's final verdict on the respective evolutionary merits of the 'races' of 'mankind'. White imperial global domination quite
simply proved the objective evolutionary superiority of whites – they had actually
won the age-long struggle, had proved themselves 'the fittest'. 'Man's' evolutionary marathon was over. Early front-runners (Babylonians, Egyptians, Chinese,
and Indians) had dropped out or been overtaken by the late-sprinting white
Europeans.[8] Few could grasp that, even accepting their simple unilinear image of
social evolution, the two and a half millennia lag separating modern Europeans
from ancestors as savage as any contemporary 'savages' was but a moment in the
new time-scale, entirely explicable by fortuitous geographical and historical circumstance.[9] (Nor, very often, do they even appear to appreciate that, for example,
metal technology cannot arise in the absence of metal deposits – for example, on
a Pacific atoll – rather such failures signified social evolutionary retardation.)
Associated, if not entirely consistent, with this was another image: races and civilisations had life cycles, they were born, flourished and eventually decayed, stag-
nated or disappeared altogether.[10] White Europeans must therefore avoid this trap
by finding means to maintain their racial virility indefinitely. Other races faced
varied fates: some were on the verge of extinction before the 'o'ermastering white
invaders';[11] some, notably 'the Negro', were ever-destined to be humble labourers,
especially in climates unsuitable for large-scale white settlement; some might in
time prove redeemable under white tutelage (the Chinese perhaps). But, barring
some folly which their own efforts aimed to avert, European global hegemony was
seemingly guaranteed in perpetuity. However potentially liberating the evolutionary vision, it was thus immediately interpreted by white scientists and intellectuals
within the constraining terms of their own historically situated consciousness.
This was a form of consciousness, a 'psychology', which the first generation of
psychologists shared, if not always, as we shall see, in quite such strong terms.

As Nancy Stepan (1982) shows, there were some profound, but unconfronted,
contradictions in Scientific Racism.[12] Most significantly, a belief in the immutability of racial characteristics and existence of underlying racial 'essences' of
some sort was smuggled, unaltered, across the boundary between pre- and post-
Darwinian thought. Yet this actually contradicted the central doctrines of both
Darwinian and rival neo-Lamarckian evolutionary theories, in which immutability
was the very illusion to be overthrown. This contradiction was perhaps obscured
by a further, fairly widespread, assumption: at the biological level human evolution had stopped.[13] Physiologically, humans had attained a state nigh on per-
fection and natural selection now took the form of competition between groups,
most importantly between races.[14] 'Primitive' peoples were thus seen as irreversibly stuck in evolutionary *culs de sac*, stymied by innate psychological traits of
declining adaptational value in the face of white civilisation, or suffering from
'arrested mental development'.[15] Continued biological natural selection served
primarily to eliminate the physically and behaviourally unfit rather than to
improve the fit.

This last point was seen as a potential Achilles' heel for Europeans: the high
sensitivity, compassion and moral ideals typifying their exalted evolutionary level
were ironically misleading them into helping the unfit in their societies to survive

and breed. This created an exquisitely painful demand on 'fit' middle and upper-class whites – they must bow to the verdict of scientific Reason and override, however sorrowfully, the imperatives of their uniquely refined feelings. If the white race ever lost its supremacy it would be because it had weak-mindedly let sentiment or a misplaced moral and 'philanthropic' consciousness prevail over Reason. Such thinking provided the rationale for Galton's Eugenics, of which more later, and deeply affected the terms in which Psychology's social and managerial tasks were first couched.[16]

While Galton and Spencer played a major role in developing Scientific Racism, ponderings on psychological differences between races were in any case commonplace.[17] Nonetheless, the running was made primarily not by psychologists but physical anthropologists and philologists, backed up by the grandiose politico–philosophical treatises of figures such as Gobineau.[18] While overtly accepting the evolutionary framework (in one or another of its many forms), physical anthropologists remained especially attached to the 'essentialist' notion of race. While grand theorists depicted race conflict as the great engine of history, physical anthropologists sought to flesh out the details by an obsession with anatomical measurement, above all of the skull. Little genuine consensus emerged as to the number of races, even less as to their character. European races were subject to unceasing analysis: Nordic, Aryan, Teutonic, Anglo-Saxon, Alpine, Mediterranean, Slav, Celt, Semite, Gaul, Ligurian, Dinaric, Phalic . . . the list of racial names and categories was endless, and endlessly reshuffled – as were the plots of the speculative evolutionary histories (often with direct nationalistic implications) of the prehistoric movements and transactions between them. Again, this side of the story has received much attention and will be left largely to one side here.[19] Suffice to say that by 1900 races – especially European ones – were already becoming increasingly elusive entities, existing only as hypothetical original 'stocks' underlying heterogeneous modern-day populations.[20] This only spurred those studying them to ever mightier anthropometric labours. Regarding the broader categories however, particularly 'the Negro' as a catchall term for virtually all sub-Saharan Africans except South African 'Bushmen', the reality of distinct 'races' was little challenged. As regards Europe, a vague agreement emerged that three major racial groups underlay the present confusion: Nordics (or Aryans), Alpines and Mediterraneans.

The 'evidence' of fundamental differences between white 'Caucasian' and 'Negro' was seemingly overwhelming, and all to the latter's detriment. One aspect of this was the previously mentioned endurance of 'physiognomical' (including phrenological) thinking.[21] A sense that physical form reflected underlying psychological character endowed physical anthropological descriptions with a powerful racist rhetorical force. To measure 'facial angle', prognathousness, blackness, and brain size was to quantify proximity to a European aesthetic-cum-psychological ideal, which was tantamount to measuring degree of evolutionary advancement. While this occasionally backfired (e.g. greater European hairiness), the implications could usually be evaded by special adaptational pleading (hair was retained in the colder northern climate). A low brow, a protruding jaw, and small skull possessed psychological meanings which were felt to be self-evident, almost matters of direct perception.[22] The Eurocentric character of physical description could also extend below the surface, as in this early passage on 'Negro' anatomy:

> The intestinal mucus is very thick, viscid, and fatty in appearance. All the abdominal glands are of large size, especially the liver and the supra renal capsules; a venous hyperæmia seems the ordinary condition of these organs. The position of the bladder is higher than in the European. I find the seminal vesicles very large, always gorged with a turbid liquid of a slightly greyish colour, even in cases where the autopsy took place shortly after death. The penis is always of unusually large size, and I found in all bodies a small conical gland on each side at the base of the fraenum.
>
> (from the French Doctor Pruner-Bey, quoted by Hunt, 1863, p. 21)

A converse African description of European male anatomy might of course note its very thin and runny intestinal mucus, peculiarly small abdominal glands, low-slung bladder, undersized penis and lack of conical glands at the base of the fraenum, and so on.[23] This may be obvious to us, but few white readers of the day would have been entirely immune to the appeal of this rhetoric of disgust.[24]

By the time Psychology is cohering as a discipline much is already apparently 'known' about African inferiority. Aside from a clearly (to 19th century whites) more simian appearance,[25] numerous specific characteristics signified their lower evolutionary level: 'Negroes' (a) matured earlier than whites, (b) were less individually varied than whites, (c) were rigid and unadaptable in habit and lifestyle, (d) were, on average, smaller-brained, especially the frontal lobes, (e) were more impulsive and emotional than whites and (f) performed best on 'lower' level functions such as sensory acuity and imitation, in which they usually excelled whites. Only a few unusually cussed and perceptive European writers (like Jean Finot (1969, 1st edn 1906) or W.D. Babington (1895)) challenged all this.

This entire episode has implications beyond the race issue, bearing directly on current debates about the social construction of science. There is a continuing desire to see science as containing some transcendental core immune to the impact of 'external' factors such as funding and ideological interests. It may now be grudgingly admitted that the appeal of evolutionary theory as a metaphor and rationale for capitalism contributed to its acceptance and cultural impact but *beneath* that, it will be said, exists some 'pure' ahistorical scientific nucleus of objective knowledge. In the case of the extensive scientific work on race, however, this certainly seems highly dubious. To put it bluntly, all this research was on something which *was not there*. All that exists is a vast range of human morphological diversity. The very concept of 'race' was entirely a product of non-scientific forces, and no core of objective scientific knowledge about it, no enduring gains in scientific understanding, were obtained.[26] That this diversity *per se* can be partly explained in evolutionary terms may be admitted, but the 'race' concept and its hierarchical progressivist interpretation prevented any permanent 'scientific progress' in understanding it. If this is so, 'Scientific Racism' provides a clear case where apparently normal natural science can be conducted in terms bearing little relationship to any existing 'transfactual' (as Bhaskar would say) natural phenomenon, and is only explicable in strong social constructionist terms.[27]

EARLY PSYCHOLOGY AND RACE

To illustrate how early Psychology tackled race we may consider (a) Francis Galton, (b) Herbert Spencer, (c) G.S. Hall, (d) Gustav Le Bon, and (e) W.I. Thomas. Some general interpretations of this material are then offered before we look, in the last part of this chapter, at two early pieces of empirical research on 'race differences'.

Francis Galton (1822–1911)

Galton's role in Psychology's history is indisputably a major one, ranging from the theoretical (e.g. largely initiating the 'nature–nurture' controversy in its modern form)[28] to the methodological (most significantly in pioneering parametric statistical techniques) to the first empirical studies of several specific topics (imagery being the best remembered). As a candidate for 'founder of Psychology' Galton closely rivals Wundt.[29] The unifying theme in his diverse Psychological work is that this is all presented as an exploration of the implications of Darwinian evolutionary theory for human affairs. In two now classic works he sought to establish the pre-eminent role of heredity in determining intelligence and 'genius' (by which he meant superior ability generally). He then founded a discipline he called 'Eugenics', aimed at promoting the improvement, or at least averting the decline, of the quality of the human, and especially British, 'stock'. His importance for us is twofold. First, while devoting only two relatively short chapters explicitly to 'race',[30] a clearly 'Scientific Racist' position emerges from these and his travel writings, and, moreover, was intrinsic to his wider Eugenic project. Secondly, the statistical psychometric methodology he and his colleague Karl Pearson pioneered in studying 'individual differences' became a central feature of the 'Race Psychology' research to be dealt with in Chapter 4.

Galton's attitudes to race were determined in his twenties, long prior to his Psychological and Eugenic careers, during a trip to Syria and Egypt (1845–6) and an expedition sponsored by the Royal Geographical Society to South West Africa (Namibia) (1850–52). These provided the material for his first major books: *Narrative of an Explorer in Tropical South Africa* (1889, 1st edn 1853) and *The Art of Travel; or Shifts and Contrivances Available in Wild Countries* (1855). Now reading as a caricature of the arrogant, utterly unself-critical, British colonialist, he is especially contemptuous of the South West African Damara,[31] and as Forrest (1974) notes, seemingly devoid of any curiosity about their customs, dismissing them all as savage superstitions beneath Anglo-Saxon contempt. His more mature writings display little softening of this attitude.

Recouched in evolutionary terms, Galton's vision was that the advent of civilisation had rendered numerous traits which evolved to serve the needs of savage, barbaric and nomadic life useless or a positive hindrance to further progress. Only Europeans, of whom the British had advanced furthest, had succeeded in replacing or supplementing these with others conducive to moral, civilised life. 'Civilisation', typically for evolutionary writers of the period, figures as an autonomous 'natural' progressive development, the highest 'stage' in a universal process of social evolution. Peoples unable to adapt to civilisation are doomed to extinction, as happened to past species unable to adapt to climatic changes. The civilisation he represents is thus, for Galton, not essentially a specifically European cultural product, rather the 'white man' has elevated the species as a whole to this new evolutionary height, albeit by virtue of his (no 'her' about it) peculiar evolutionary merits. Being in a sense a natural phenomenon, any reflexive critique of contemporary white civilisation becomes impossible. This view of white civilisation as civilisation *per se* persists, if increasingly contested, down to the present (still underpinning the policies of international financial institutions) and its importance can hardly be overstated. The immediate point is that it is grounded in unilinear 19th century images of social evolution and was at that time hardly contested at all.

Towards the end of *Hereditary Genius* (1962, 1st edn 1869) Galton offers a brief chapter 'The Comparative Worth of Different Races'. On what amounts to a 15-point scale of 'grades of ability' ascending from A (minimally above average) to G and thence to X, and descending from 'a' (minimally below average) to 'g', he calculates in a rough and ready *a priori* fashion that the 'Negro race' is on average two grades below the Anglo-Saxon. The 'Australian type' is a further grade lower. His experience in the USA confirms his confidence in this:

> The mistakes the negroes made in their own matters were so childish, stupid, and simpleton-like, as frequently to make me ashamed of my own species. I do not think it any exaggeration to say that their c is as low as our e, which would be a difference of two grades, as before. (1962, p. 395)

The Athenians of the period 530 BC–430 BC he rates as two grades above modern Anglo-Saxons. Stepan (1982) rightly observes that Galton never spells out quite what he means by 'race', shifting from very broad labels (the 'Negro') to national ones ('Spanish'). His image is less essentialist than that of many contemporaries; the various human stocks are continually mixing and separating, rising to prominence and falling into extinction, and he does not consider higher grade representatives of the lower races (their E's, F's and G's) as irredeemable. His racism is thus slightly mitigated at the theoretical level. This speculative exercise was repeatedly cited and praised by subsequent writers into the 1920s. Forrest (1974) tends to let Galton's racism off rather lightly, ascribing his callous accounts of the Damara people to a lack of modern understanding of the difficulties of anthropological and ethnographic observation. Given that more sympathetic (if not non-racialist) perceptions of African peoples may be found in the vast contemporary genre of writings on colonial experience, this is to acquit him too readily. Its roots surely lay also in Galton's own conflicted temperament as a young man desperate to make a mark congruent with his own high opinion of himself after several early academic set-backs. Modern socio-biologists might well explain his entire career as an attempt to compensate for his own infertility by promoting the inclusive fitness of the genes of his own social class – but then he is one of their heroes, so they don't.

Galton's calculations were the first attempt at quantifying racial differences of a psychological kind. The aim of the exercise is obviously, if not quite explicitly, to canvass the possibility of evaluating the relative suitabilities of the peoples of the European empires for 'civilisation'. The impulsiveness, lack of foresight, erratic oscillations between hard work and laziness and the like, which he believes characterise all 'lower races', represent a serious barrier to their further social evolution. And while the restless adventuring nomadic spirit is still present to a small degree among modern Europeans, and has in part enabled them to create their empires, he sees it as a trait to be discouraged in future as ill-suited to the needs of modern civilisation.[32] Africa is climatically uncongenial to whites, and in *Inquiries into Human Faculty* (1919, 1st edn 1883) he envisages that Arabs and Chinese 'when certain of their peculiar religious fancies shall have fallen into decay' will 'extrude the coarse and lazy Negro from at least the metalliferous regions of tropical Africa' (1919, p. 206).

It should be stressed, since the point is rarely made, that psychometric methodology is rooted in Galton's eugenic project, and that while in Britain most of Eugenics' energies were subsequently directed towards 'degenerate' or 'superior' white groups (criminals, the mentally ill, 'idiots', geniuses and the like) the race issue was an intrinsic part of this. If not immediately, a time was approaching when the 'comparative worth of races' would be among eugenic psychologists' central concerns. As we will see this is exactly what happened, albeit fairly briefly, in the USA. Studying race differences is thus but an extension of the study of individual differences.

Mainland European eugenicists, especially in Italy, turned their attentions to the racial dimension in criminal psychology. In Lombroso and Ferrero's *The Female Offender* (1895) this fuses with the gender issue.[33] Having argued that 'the primitive type of a species is more clearly represented in the female' (p. 109), they proceed, only half-disapprovingly, to an anecdote about aboriginal Australians eating old women. They assert that 'the primitive woman was rarely a murderess; but she was always a prostitute, and such she remained until semi-civilised epochs' (p. 111). 'In female animals, in aboriginal women, and in the women of our time, the cerebral cortex, particularly in the psychic centres, is less active than in the male' (ibid.). Furthermore 'virility' was:

> one of the special features of the savage woman. In proof I have but to refer the reader to the Plates opposite . . . where we have the portraits of Red Indian and Negro beauties, whom it is difficult to recognise for women, so huge are their jaws and cheek-bones, so hard and coarse their features. And the same is often the case in their crania and brains. (p. 112)

(Unfortunately the pictures in question cannot be reproduced here.) The entire text is peppered with physical anthropological observations with established racial connotations: prostitutes tend to be 'brachycephalic' (short-headed), heavy 'Mongolian' features are constantly noted, while 'The maxima and minima [in cranial capacity] among prostitutes more nearly resemble those of Papuan women than of normal females' (p. 22). The English edition was glowingly introduced by W. Douglas Morrison of Her Majesty's Prison Wandsworth (presumably the Governor rather than an inmate).

Racial images could therefore be deployed in characterising 'degenerate' European groups, resemblances between a European physiognomy and a known 'primitive' one demonstrating that the former was 'atavistic' or 'degenerate' – both physically and psychologically. The eugenic, 'degenerationist', strand in late 19th century Psychology was thus virtually premised on the evolutionary hierarchy of races.[34] While Galton had his differences with Lombroso, his own commitment to Scientific Racism is inseparable from the rest of his *oeuvre*, no mere embarrassing blind-spot irrelevant to his other Psychological work. His early experiences firmly convinced him of the superiority of his own racial position, and of the threat potentially posed by the seething masses of lesser breeds. As Billig (1981) observes, Galton's racialist and eugenic convictions were fully formed from the outset, prior to any 'scientific' data having been obtained. Both were articles of his scientific faith, not scientific theories faithfully derived from research.[35] Galton is, indeed, intriguing – an entertaining Victorian eccentric of the highest order, Darwin's cousin, creator of psychometrics, and inventor of a pocket device for recording the beauty of women. Psychologists have found it easy simultaneously to revere and excuse him. But this is a man whose diary entry on what Forrest calls the 'African servant problem' included such punishments as flogging and pouring boiling water and hot sand on their naked bodies (Forrest, 1974, p. 64 n.), measures daily meted out to Damara members of his expedition in his 'little court of justice'. His prolonged enjoyment of such an appreciative academic press itself testifies to how far the discipline has been prepared to condone, forgive or explain away the fundamentally racist (not simply racialist) character of his work – a matter to be mentioned only in passing or in occasional footnotes.[36]

Was Galton not simply displaying himself as a child of his times? One should indeed be wary of judging previous generations' attitudes towards race, or any other issue, in anachronistic terms. But this is to ignore the extent to which he was also a 'father' of his times, and the degree to which his racism possesses a relish beyond anything found in Darwin himself or his contemporary loyal Darwinist and acquaintance Sir John Lubbock,[37] for example. Nor had his position ameliorated one jot by 1908 when he published his *Memories of My Life*.[38] His first statements about race, published in the wake of Darwin's *Origin of Species*, carried considerable authority and were undoubtedly widely known informally before 1869. This is not a proposal that we henceforth demonise him, rather a suggestion that the full weight and moral seriousness of his legacy be confronted, something his admittedly attractive buffoonery has until now enabled us to avoid.

Herbert Spencer (1820–1903)

Central, and ultimately more enduring, though Galton's historical role within Psychology was, it was Herbert Spencer who provided the more immediately influential theoretical rationale for Scientific Racism. His 'Synthetic Philosophy' was a far grander cosmic vision than Darwin's, and had an equal, if not greater, contemporary cultural impact, particularly in the USA. While largely consistent with Darwinism (Spencer, after all, coined the phrase 'survival of the fittest'), it was unashamedly progressivist and extended beyond the strictly biological realm.

His hefty and now largely unread volumes expounding this are, at heart, elaborations of a simple central tenet to which he adhered unwaveringly for half a century: the universe evolves by a process of increasingly heterogeneous organisation of matter. Spencer launched his project with *The Principles of Psychology* (1st edn 1855) which expanded to two volumes with the second edition in 1870.[39] This integrated the environmentalist associationist model of the mind expounded by James Mill with the new hereditarian orientation being developed by contemporary physiologists and neurologists. One central doctrine is that, if sufficiently strong, associative connections established in an individual's lifetime bring about neurological changes, especially in the brain, which are then transmitted to offspring. The internal organisation of organisms therefore evolved to reflect and represent with ever higher fidelity the organisation of their external environments. In humans, especially Europeans, this has reached an extraordinarily high degree of sophistication. The hierarchy from senses via reflexes, instincts, habit, memory and imagination to reason was continuous, these terms being arbitrary distinctions in the spectrum of organic assimilation of learned experience.[40] Finally, the burgeoning role of reason as the latest and most effective route for achieving this assimilation entailed a changed balance in energy distribution. Energy was progressively withdrawn from the 'lower' and reallocated to the 'higher' levels.

As Haller (1971) says, 'Spencer's schema of evolution tolled a note of pessimism for the less civilized peoples of mankind.'[41] Quite simply, Spencer believed the 'primitive' brain incapable of handling the complex associations required for civilised life. The 'primitive's' widely vouched-for superiority in sensory acuity and other lower functions directly reflected the continued commitment of greater amounts of energy to these more animalistic levels: 'The dominant races overrun the inferior races mainly in virtue of the greater quantity of energy in which [the] greater mental mass shows itself' (1876 pp. 258–9/190).[42] (The energy of gunpowder presumably not coming into it.) Spencer can thus provide an ostensibly scientific explanation for all the usual canards against 'lower races': their simpler mental powers and inability to handle generalities; their shorter and more rapid period of mental development ('Travellers from all regions comment, now on the great precocity of children among savage and semi-civilized peoples, and now on the early arrest of their mental progress' (ibid., pp. 259/192)); their lack of plasticity and adaptiveness ('Many travellers comment on the unchangeable habits of savages' ibid., pp. 260/192); their greater homogeneity; their impulsiveness – reflecting the greater role of reflexes – and emotional simplicity (see ibid., pp. 261–2/194–5); their imitativeness ('One of the characteristics in which the lower types of men show us a smaller departure from reflex action than do the higher types, their strong tendency to mimic the motions and sounds made by others . . .' ibid., pp. 265/199); their lack of curiosity and so on *ad nauseam*. Interbreeding between higher and lower races is to be condemned.

Spencer's elaborate Psychological analysis gave the traditional deficiencies of 'lower races' a fresh and quite formidable scientific gloss, and certain US thinkers were highly receptive, as Haller documents in some detail. Youmans, Spencer's leading disciple, accepted his views wholeheartedly and John Fiske (a member of the Immigration Restriction League),[43] 'forever anxious to carry the history of

Anglo-Saxon peoples to higher and higher plateaus of veneration',[44] was especially ardent. Numerous other influential US figures also rallied to the Spencerian banner.[45] The hidden (and sometimes only barely) agenda of this line of thought was that the Negro, in the USA anyway, was doomed to extinction – and demographic data on mortality rates appeared consistent with this. Haller unmasks the double-thinking at work: the Negro race can only improve its lot by its own endeavours, but its innate and ineradicable inferiority condemns it to failure and eventual demise.

There is a further significant twist to the story in relation to the culture vs. biology issue. It was easy to invoke physical and physiognomic traits to argue for the primitiveness of the 'Negro' but such criteria were harder to apply to Chinese, American Indians and other 'less civilised' peoples. The logic is therefore reversed: a lower cultural level signifies biological-level deficiencies unamenable to direct scientific inspection. This is an especially important move, marking the advent of an argument, versions of which remained commonplace into the 1930s: environmentalist accounts are flawed because social environmental conditions are a direct product of the hereditary qualities of those living in them.[46]

Spencer's reputation was declining rapidly even by the time of his death. His system was a vast *aprioristic* construction into which all evidence could be twisted to fit. His 'race' data were, in any case, virtually all second-hand and he had little contact with any of the 'lower races' (his views thus appear less personally motivated than Galton's, being more or less entailed by his system as a whole, and hence more racialist than racist). The 'Spencer hypothesis' (as I will call it) of superior primitive performance on basic functions also, we will see, shared the fate of his system as a whole.

G. Stanley Hall (1844–1924)

Stanley Hall was one of the most eminent of Psychology's US father figures, co-founder of the American Psychological Association, pioneer of child development studies and founder of various university departments and journals from the 1880s onwards.[47] His views on race are best gauged from the 100-page final chapter 'Ethnic psychology and pedagogy, or adolescent races and their treatment' of his two-volume *Adolescence* (1904). While shot through with Scientific Racism, it diverges from Galton and Spencer on certain fundamental matters. In his own mind, Hall was clearly aiming to combat racial bigotry. His departures from the British line stem at the theoretical level from the central roles of recapitulationism and the 'life cycle of peoples' image in his thinking and his deeply held ecumenical Christian faith. From his recapitulationist perspective, 'lower races' are to be considered as still at an 'adolescent' phase, they are 'the world's children and adolescents' (p. 748), 'Natural races are nations in the process of development' (p. 719).

The psychological qualities of the 'adolescent races' are innate but Hall vehemently rejects their essential inferiority, and while accepting the current superiority and global dominance of white Christian civilisation he denies whites any monopoly of the virtues, and doubts the permanence of their commanding position. 'Adolescent races' are not in a state of 'arrested development', but at an earlier stage in their life cycle. It is striking how far, within the constraints of an inescapably racialist conceptual framework, Hall moves beyond this. The situation remains one in which all peoples are being challenged to adapt to the imperially expanding white order, but his paternalism, as we would now see it, is genuine and heartfelt. Our moral duty is to understand and ultimately Christianise all the Earth's races, but by building on, not destroying, existing cultures and social structures. We must approach them with humility rather than arrogance, and learn from the new ethnologists who take the time to live among and understand those whom they are studying, without preconceptions. He revels in our species' genetic diversity (as we would put it) and mourns the loss of the potential legacies of the now extinct Tasmanians and Beothuk tribe of Newfoundland. He is even unhappy about our supposed prehistoric extermination of our ancestral 'missing links', as having opened up a gulf between us and all other species.

It would be hard to find a more thoroughgoing condemnation of white imperial practice than the first part of this chapter, from US policy in the Philippines (then a US possession) to the British Raj, from the treatment of native Americans and Hawaiians to the fates of the Russian Samoyeds and Australians, Hall remorselessly documents the iniquities which Europeans have inflicted on everyone else. The vanishing of the Aztec religion moves him to write:

> The new solutions of so many of our own problems, dimly seen here, should suggest how many more things than our philosophy dreams of or our history records have been in and vanished from the world, and wring our hearts with pity not only for vanished races but for ourselves. (p. 683)

Hall has done his homework and can quote extensively from anthropologists and travellers about the virtues of his 'adolescent' races: their sense of community, complex justice systems, high moral standards, beauty and spiritual sensitivity. The lowest forms of humanity are found in the back streets of white cities. Extinction, decline or degradation is not due to the moral superiority of white culture, quite the reverse, it is due to white greed, ignorance and hypocrisy, to confronting 'their best' with 'our worst'. Nor does he have problems regarding racial mixing, actually suggesting that it has the best results if not confined to white male–non-white female crosses but also includes the reverse.

For Hall, the task is to redress the situation by devising careful civilising programmes of an extended and graduated kind, tailored to the specific needs of the people in question, and with a preparedness to learn from them. While the conversion of adolescent races to Christianity is the desired end-goal, this must have low initial priority, and be shown as a logical development of the best elements in existing religious beliefs. (He believes, on the basis of studies of the development of religion in children, that it is best to begin with the Old Testament.)[48] He is highly conscious of the negative role missionaries have hitherto played, opposing rabid fundamentalism and indiscriminate hostility to all non-Christian beliefs. The last section of the chapter addresses the need to provide missionaries with a proper education and extended training in ethnic psychology, anthropology and cross-cultural respect.

Hall's position here is perhaps as enlightened as anyone could get within the typically American episteme of Christian evolutionism. In this particular text any inherent racism in his belief in innately determined race differences is off-set, as far as it is possible to do so, by a devout Christian paternalism in which these differences represent developmental stages analogous to those of individual maturation. This partly recoups the early 19th century Christian anti-slavery position which had been undermined by the evolutionary image. The idea of the racial hierarchy as a scale of essential evolutionary advancement is reconstrued as representing the current, but impermanent, relative positions of races in their developmental cycles. It is an error to mistake immaturity for decay. Humanity's future rests on the coming maturation of peoples currently 'adolescent'.

But we should not get carried away by Hall's virtues. His logic leads him to argue that US Negroes and Indians actually require quite different modes of education and should not be taught together, and his other writings are altogether less rosy. As is evident in his 1905 paper 'The Negro in Africa and America', while expressing support for the American 'Negro' cause, he cannot escape a stereotyped view of the dire depravity of indigenous West African cultures. Indeed in several papers during the century's first decade, Hall aired views which, if not inconsistent with those of the *Adolescence* chapter, show that in practice he accepted most of Scientific Racism's psychological characterisations of 'the Negro' and native Americans.[49] He felt the Reconstruction experiment to have been mistaken[50] and saw native Americans as less advanced than Africans, as well as endorsing segregated education and limitation of the non-white franchise. Yet Hall views with horror the widely hailed prospect of an impending universalisation and homogenisation of human culture, and his account of imperial practice would not have been out of place in the anti-Columbus literature which greeted the 1992 Quincentenary.[51]

Hall's somewhat complex position played a major role in determining psychologists' orientations towards 'Negro education', the context in which, as we will see, empirical race differences research first flourished.[52] Howard Odum (discussed in Chapter 4), for example, was one of his students, while his journal *The Pedagogical Seminary* was later among those which most often published papers on the topic. Being US Psychology's single most eminent figure in the immediate post-1900 years Hall's ambivalent attitude to race tended to reinforce the discipline's identification with the paternalistic pro-segregationist moderate conservative camp (again, see Chapter 4). His relatively enlightened theory glaringly failed to translate into an equally enlightened position regarding contemporary US 'race problems', but is significant as marking a divergence from some traditional Scientific Racism orthodoxies on the part of a major early psychologist.

There is a lurking tension here, which Psychology has never entirely resolved, regarding the nature–nurture issue: if Psychology is to be an effectively *interventionist* discipline then it must in principle be claiming that environmental ('nurture') factors are of primary importance, but if it is to be an effective *descriptive* or *evaluative* discipline then the phenomena it claims to assess must usually be conceived of as basically fixed ('nature'). Hall, as we saw, argued for an interventionist role for Psychology in regard to race; it would supply techniques by which to nurture the adolescent races – this alleviates the tension by adopting a developmental perspective in which the task is nurturing the innate. In the USA this was soon swamped by the nativist Galtonian psychometric tradition concerned with description and evaluation, which by 1920 had gained the ascendency.

Hall's position must be set in the context of the long-established 'moral project' of academic US Psychological thought, which the 'New Psychology' of the 1880s and 1890s, for all its revolutionary stance, largely took over and extended.[53] This project was deeply imbued with religion, stemming from its early 19th century origin in mainly Protestant colleges and universities as a presidentially taught 'Moral and Mental Philosophy' course. Many of Hall's generation of often quite pious US psychologists would have found difficulty in accepting unmodified the complacent proto-racism of European agnostics and free-thinkers such as Galton, even while feeling bound to adopt an evolutionary framework.[54] It is important to bear these nuances in mind if we are to understand the forms which psychologists' race thinking has taken. 'Racism' is not one thing but many. Hall, by choosing child development and education as his primary fields, had already identified himself as a scientific extension of father-figure. Unsurprisingly then, his attitude to race differences was root and branch paternalism of a most sincere and thorough-going kind. Patronising and mistaken though it now appears, this was far less malevolent than the hypocritical and exploitative attitude usually now associated with the term 'paternalism'. Even so, the practical consequences he derived from his theory were extremely conservative and supportive of what we can now see as blatantly racist policies.

Gustav Le Bon (1841–1931)[55]

In Europe, meanwhile, evolution's supermen continued to reign supreme. Gustav Le Bon, scientific populariser, publisher, gourmet and adviser to the great, is best remembered for his *The Crowd: A Study of the Popular Mind* (1896). Often considered the first book on 'social Psychology', this explained crowd behaviour in terms of atavistic regression to earlier primitive modes of mass-consciousness (akin to the hypnotic trance) which rendered people highly susceptible to 'suggestion' by orators and group leaders. Contemporary French fascinations with hypnotism, 'suggestion', 'the subconscious' and even, post-Pasteur, 'contagion',[56] were thus fused with evolutionary ideas. Le Bon's aims were explicitly political. The Third Republic was threatened by revolutionary socialist and communist internationalism and he believed the appeal of such subversive doctrines could be sapped by evoking a deeper rooted national spirit or 'soul'. *The Crowd* was thus in part to serve as a handbook for society's 'natural' political and military rulers, enabling them to utilise the 'laws' of crowd psychology for their own ends. And so it proved. His influence on French military strategy in the Great War was considerable, and subsequently Hitler, Stalin and Mussolini are all known to have studied the book closely.[57]

For our purposes his previous work, *The Psychology of Peoples* (1899) is more relevant.[58] This presents a third variety of Scientific Racism, distinct from blasé hard-line British evolutionism and fundamentally opposed to Hall's benign paternalism. Le Bon's central tenets were all dubious by the time he was writing the work, but this in no way inhibited his assertions that they carried the full weight of current scientific and historical authority. While distinguishing 'natural races' (now only represented by 'savages') from historical or artificial races (formed over many centuries from the merging of a number of originally distinct peoples), this acknowledgement of the hybridity of most modern 'races' does not temper his position. He sees his culture as still gripped by a naive Enlightenment illusion, egalitarianism, which, in the form of Socialism, threatens to bring all to a horrendous end. He is the proud prophet of a hard-headed inegalitarianism extending to races as well as individuals.

For Le Bon, races are both physiologically and psychologically distinct, all members of a race share a central, immutable, race character or soul. This, rather than intelligence *per se*, distinguishes them and provides the hereditary core of an individual's identity. Heredity is the primary force, second come the individual's parents, and only third environment (other than during the period of historical race creation, when the souls of the source races have been annihilated and a *tabula rasa* situation obtains). 'Natural races' are really different species, although religious etiquette requires that anthropologists call them 'races'. (He is a fairly unreconstructed polygenist on this point.)[59] The psychological gulf between the 'characters' of different races is impassable (comparable to that between the sexes, between whom intellectual communication is also impossible). Superior races are marked by great individual diversity, inferior ones display a total physical and psychological homogeneity.[60] Sex differences are also much larger in superior races. Some quotes are necessary to indicate the tenor of Le Bon's discourse:

> The moral and intellectual characteristics, whose association forms the soul of a people, represent the synthesis of its entire past, the inheritance of all its ancestors, the motives of its conduct. (p. 6)

> The unconscious process by which we arrive at an idea of the physical and mental type of a people [i.e. by travel] is absolutely identical in its essence with the method by which a naturalist classifies species. (p. 8)

(A rather curious methodological doctrine, one would have thought!) The next quotation is especially noteworthy in demonstrating Le Bon's ability to incorporate the latest ideas about the power of the unconscious into what amounts to his own atavistic reversion to ancestor worship.

> A race is to be regarded as a permanent being that is independent of time. This permanent being is composed of a long succession of the dead who were its ancestors, as well as of the living individuals who constitute it at a given moment. To understand the true signification of a race, it must be considered with regard both to its past and its future. The dead, being infinitely more numerous than the living, are infinitely more powerful. They reign over the vast domain of the unconscious, that invisible domain which exerts its sway over all the manifestations of the intelligence and of character. . . . The dead

are the only undisputed masters of the living. We bear the burden of their mistakes, we reap the reward of their virtues. (pp. 10–11)[61]

It is impossible to arrive at any understanding of history unless it be continually
borne in mind that different races cannot feel, think, or act in the same
manner, and that, in consequence, they cannot comprehend one another.
(p. 35)

As these suggest, much in Le Bon verges on 'blood and soil' racial mysticism,
while his 'race soul' concept marks a mid-point between earlier German Idealist
notions and later Psychological ideas of the 'Group Mind' (McDougall)[62] and
the 'collective unconscious' (Jung), as well as those of Nazi theorists like
H.F.K. Günther.[63] He also needs to be understood in the context of contemporary French anthropology's emerging belief in a distinct 'primitive mentality'
(Durkheim, Lévy-Bruhl) – a belief which British and American anthropologists
were soon to de-emphasise or deny.[64] Other than the Nazis, few drew quite such
up-front racist conclusions from this as Le Bon, although Freud certainly took
The Crowd seriously.[65]

The question might be raised as to how far Le Bon should be accepted as a
psychologist, whether his ideas properly belong in its disciplinary history. It is,
alas, now far too late for excommunication. He was accepted as a friend and extra-
mural colleague by leading contemporary French psychologists such as Gabriel
Tarde, Alfred Binet, and Théodule Ribot (with whom he 'formed a monthly ban-
quet association' in 1892 (Nye, 1975)). A major player in the contemporary
French scientific scene, as publisher, populariser and promoter, he was at the hub
of a network linking philosophers like Bergson, physicists such as Poincaré and
politicians such as Clemenceau, as well as senior military figures. He was widely
viewed as drawing the practical political, military and educational implications
from contemporary Psychological thought, and few French psychologists
demurred. And his entire Psychology was underpinned by the racist vision
just sketched. In the long run his influence was greater beyond, than within,
Psychology, but from the mid-1890s to the end of the Great War Le Bon was
accepted as an authoritative psychologist throughout the discipline.

W.I. Thomas (1863–1947)

To adapt an old adage, you cannot judge a paper by its title. Thomas's 1907 paper
'The mind of woman and the lower races' is actually a remarkably insightful rejection of almost the entire Scientific Racism (and Scientific Sexism) position. He
has little truck with brain-size arguments; 'brain efficiency' has probably been
'approximately the same in all races and in both sexes since nature first made up a
good working model' (pp. 438–9). Cultural level has little to do with the brain,
and can be accounted for environmentally and historically. He blames most of the
problem on the 'fixed and instinctive prejudice' of social groups who always take
'an exaggerated view' of their own importance. After a momentary lapse regarding
the 'acuteness of sense perceptions' ('usually better developed in animals and the

lower races than in the civilized' p. 441) he assails the old favourites 'feeble powers of inhibition', 'lack of the power of abstraction' and poor 'mechanical ingenuity'. The extent to which these are manifested is determined entirely by the exigencies of social and cultural life and all races are potentially on a par. As far as lack of inhibition is concerned (Spencer's doctrine) primitive life-styles are more hedged with inhibitions than civilised ones, those making the charge mistake differences from European norms in its forms and direction for its absence. Nor do the civilised and 'the savage' differ in terms of the 'patterns of interest' of everyday life. As far as child development is concerned he also, interestingly, says 'I have no doubt myself that [the] theory of recapitulation is largely a misapprehension' (p. 452).

His view of the cultural diversity of human psychology is summed up as follows: 'The fundamental explanation of the difference in the mental life of two groups is not that the capacity of the brain to do work is different, but that the attention is not in the two cases stimulated and engaged along the same lines' (p. 452). Thus the religious injunction against making 'graven images' inhibited the Hebrews in developing sculpture and the Christian belief that 'man' was made in God's image 'formed an almost insuperable obstacle to the study of human anatomy' (p. 453). 'Western pride in progress' is culturally quite anomalous, and the deep conservatism of Chinese, Indian and Islamic cultures is responsible for their current lack of interest in scientific inquiry. He then, crucially, avers that 'the real variable is the individual, not the race' (p. 456).

His discussion of women is in much the same vein, although he does believe in some innate difference arising from the originally more active, hunting role of males as contrasted with the more sedentary role of women. The former promotes intelligence, the latter 'more cunning' (see pp. 458–9). Nevertheless he is sceptical regarding many of woman's supposed intellectual deficiencies and closes with some surprisingly prescient observations deserving full quotation:

> *The world of modern intellectual life is in reality a white man's world. Few women and perhaps no blacks have ever entered this world in the fullest sense.* To enter it in the fullest sense would be to be in it at every moment from the time of birth to the time of death, and to absorb it unconsciously and consciously, as the child absorbs language. When something like this happens, we shall be in a position to judge of the mental efficiency of women and the lower races. At present we seem justified in inferring that the differences in mental expression are no greater than they should be in view of the existing differences in opportunity.
>
> Whether the characteristic mental life of women and the lower races will prove identical with those of the white man or different in quality is a different question, and problematical. It is certain, at any rate, that our civilization is not of the highest type possible. *In all of our relations there is too much of primitive man's fighting instinct and technique; and it is not impossible that the participation of woman and the lower races will contribute new elements, change the stress of attention, disturb the equilibrium, and force a crisis which will result in the reconstruction of our habits on more sympathetic and equitable principles.* Certain it is

that no civilization can remain the highest if another civilization adds to the intelligence of its men the intelligence of its women. (p. 469, my italics)

Thomas, a sociologist writing in the *American Journal of Sociology*, had little immediate impact on the psychologists, but was, in the long run, a major influence on those sociologists and social psychologists who developed successful critiques of Race Psychology during the 1920s and 1930s (including, in his immediate circle, E.S. Bogardus and E.B. Reuter). And undeniably he has some intuition here that an exclusively white male science is ultimately a limited one.

There is one important contemporary connection with Psychology nonetheless, his close academic relationship with his University of Chicago colleague John Dewey, whose own 1902 *Psychological Review* paper 'Interpretation of the savage mind' was, Dewey notes, 'virtually a joint contribution' with Thomas (p. 223).[66] In this, tackling perhaps the most difficult case, Australian aborigines, Dewey develops an argument very similar to Thomas's, that their psychological character is directly determined by their nomadic hunting lifestyle. (At this time Dewey and Thomas still accepted the evolutionary orthodoxy insofar as both held sex and food, especially the hunting or 'gaming' instinct, to be the basic explanatory principles for social life. Thomas shifted increasingly away from the evolutionary approach after about 1905.) Dewey stresses the positive nature of these traits when understood in this way, and attacks ethnocentrism:

my point here is that present civilized mind is virtually taken as a standard, and savage mind is measured off on this fixed scale. . . .
It is no wonder that the outcome is negative; that primitive mind is described in terms of 'lack', 'absence': its traits are incapacities. (p. 218)

For Dewey the 'savage' hunting mentality underpins much of what we take to be civilised mentality, the latter having 'genetically' developed from it, a theme Thomas also explored elsewhere.[67] Dewey, while to some extent operating within a social evolutionary schema, seems, like Thomas, to see mode of consciousness as, in an almost Marxist way, the product of labour or 'occupational activities'.

Thomas and Dewey, along with the anthropologist Franz Boas, represented voices diametrically opposed to Le Bon's and, while conforming to custom in referring to 'lower races', Thomas rejected virtually every Scientific Racist tenet.[68] In an earlier paper 'The scope and method of folk-psychology' (1896) Thomas was already departing from the orthodox physical anthropological perspectives (including another attack on the brain-size argument), but says little about race as such. It is actually a rather confused text and his position had clarified and hardened up considerably by 1907. In 'Race psychology, standpoint and questionnaire'[69] (1912), Thomas further developed his position, identifying 18 headings under which data relevant to cultural and 'racial' differences ought to be classified, marking a step towards what eventually became the 'Culture and Personality' school. Thomas's major professional achievements came later, first as co-author with F. Znaniecki of the sociology classic *The Polish Peasant in Europe and America* (1918–20) and in 1937 with *Primitive Behavior; an introduction to the social sciences*. In the former of these he completely abandoned his earlier instinct-based position in favour of a cultural-historical one. Thomas is now seen as a founder of 'symbolic interactionism'.

SCIENTIFIC PSYCHOLOGY AND RACE

We may now step back and review the implications of the kinds of approach to race just discussed. They ranged from the, ostensibly at any rate, benignly paternal (Hall) via the blithely imperial (Galton) and elaborately scientistic (Spencer) to the semi-mystical and proto-fascist (Le Bon). Excepting Thomas, each is nevertheless working in the broader framework of what is now called 'Scientific Racism' and two (Galton and Spencer) were major architects of that doctrine. I have also indicated, though not explored, some linkages between attitudes to race and women (especially evident in Lombroso though a universally recurrent theme), which support the claims by contemporary feminist writers such as Sandra Harding, Donna Haraway and Amina Mama that the two are intrinsically linked.[70] Thomas's position by contrast, while jointly considering race and gender, opposes the whole notion of primitive mentalities and his linkage of the two presents, in a way which anticipates current feminist and liberatory thinking, both non-Europeans and women as excluded from a dominant white male culture.

Elaborating on the 'social constructionism' issue raised earlier, what we are getting here is a glimpse of how late Victorian male white 'scientific psychology' (in the subject matter sense) was unable to distinguish between what it saw as a neutral and value-free objective scientific consciousness and the specific gender, class and ethnic consciousness of those who happened to be operating in that mode. Apparently at the pinnacle of the evolutionary, political and social scales they inevitably viewed the rest of the species as from an Olympian height, and, thus centred, could not differentiate this viewpoint from 'scientific objectivity' itself.[71] Only they could have the complete picture. Androcentrism, ethnocentrism, and in the British case, Anglocentrism, were inevitable consequences. Even some black writers failed to withstand the authoritativeness of Scientific Racist perceptions of 'the Negro'.[72]

How this elite then construed those below them was of course affected by more personal factors of temperament and religious belief, but that these others *were* below them could not be doubted. Any lower echelon testimony regarding their 'subjectivity' deserved no more attention than that of artisans and other non-gentlemen regarding natural phenomena during the Scientific Revolution of the 17th century.[73] Interestingly, one of Le Bon's many complaints is about the rise of culturally debilitating 'relativist' thinking, replacing the healthy 'absolutist' mode.[74] That their mode of consciousness might be other than objectively superior to everyone else's would have been a disturbing prospect. That their 'objectivity' might in some fashion have been corrupted by the manner in which their class had achieved its present privileged niche and by its ongoing needs to remain there never seems to have occurred to them (or perhaps to any non-Marxist prior to the 1960s, though Thomas and Dewey nearly see it). And Scientific Racism itself preempted any need to confront such questions. Even less could they ponder on whether their concept of 'objectivity' itself was in any way contestable.[75] The 19th century ideal of 'scientific objectivity' now begins to look like one aspect of the Olympian consciousness of that century's white male elite.[76] This is not intended to 'reduce' it or diminish its effectiveness in the physical sciences, only to stress that as far as the human realm is concerned, genuine 'scientific objectivity' (whatever that means) could *not*, logically, be attained from such a position. It could not do so because their very occupancy of this position precluded the kind of critical self-reflection such a scientific project requires. There is nothing inherently antirational therefore in claiming that Scientific Racism was a straightforward 'social construction'.

Psychology was initiated in this intellectual and social context, but somewhat late in the day. In Hall we see clearly the tensions between the old absolutist and the new relativist thinking. He is, on the one hand, a Christian evolutionist absolutist: white civilisation (though not fault-free) *is* currently the evolutionary high point and Christianity *is* objectively the most advanced religion. On the other hand he has read widely in the relevant literature and understands that Psychology requires those in it to be able to 'see things as the natives do' – this is, after all, Psychological research in its own right. He has a sort of gut-level appreciation of 'genetic diversity', and can admire some non-European achievements.

Eugenic's 'degeneration' spectre loomed large as the century turned and global developments rendered the white male elite rather less secure. Racial attitudes began to become problematised on a scale not seen since the Abolitionist days and across Europe anti-semitism and other forms of 'race consciousness' were increasingly permeating political life. In 1910 a mainstream publishing house like Macmillan could publish the portentous racist musings of B.L. Putnam Weale's *The Conflict of Colour*, written from Peking. The extended anti-black passages of his chapter 'The Black Problem' are even more virulent than Galton's casual throw-away slurs.[77] 'The black man has given nothing to the world. He has never made a nation – he belongs to nothing but a subject race. . . . [he is] the world's common slave' (pp. 232–3). 'Miscegenation' produces 'dreadful hybrids' (p. 231). Old favourites like 'simian features' and even 'unalterable odour' are invoked (p. 228). For Weale, race prejudice was a natural universal human attribute and race mixing anathema. The future would unfold in the mutual confrontations of the great racial groups, especially between white and 'yellow' races for control of the temperate regions.[78] This is the Scientific Racist consciousness under acute stress, in a way partly adumbrated in Le Bon, but absent 30 years earlier when rolling imperial expansion and extermination of 'lower races' represented the unstoppable cutting edge of evolution itself.

PRE-1900 PSYCHOLOGICAL RESEARCH ON RACE

Psychological research had been preceded, mainly in the USA, by psychiatric ponderings on the mental health of 'Negroes' dating back to S.A. Cartwright's (1981) now notorious 1851 paper in which '*Drapetomania*' (compulsive running away) and '*Dysoesthesia oethiopeca*' (disregard of property rights, carelessness and breaking of work tools) were identified as ailments to which slaves were especially prone. In the 1890s, and occasionally thereafter, psychiatric authorities argued that slavery had protected 'the Negro' from mental illness, while apparently lower African American mental illness rates were also used to support the Spencer hypothesis – their higher functions were, it seemed, insufficiently developed for them to go mad![79]

An aside is necessary here. The present work is about Psychology, not Psychiatry. Given the intimacy of their connection this presents certain difficulties, since full coverage of the psychiatric side of things would inevitably spill over into medicine and biology in general. As far as the pre-1900 period is concerned I have thus largely ignored Psychiatry. After this date one obviously cannot exclude psychoanalysis and kindred schools from consideration.

The first stirrings of empirical Psychological research into race differences occur in two papers published in *Psychological Review* in the 1890s,[80] both permeated by Scientific Racist assumptions. Meade Bache's 'Reaction time with reference to race' (1895) begins with a rather rambling evolutionary overview and an invocation of a statement by Spencer who 'somewhere' says that the 'savage' is a 'creature of "secondary reflex movements"' (p. 479). The 'automatic' preceded the 'intellectual condition of man'. From this we may infer that 'lower men' will have faster reaction times (RT) than 'higher' ones because the 'law of compensation' tells us that intellectual growth will be accompanied by a diminution in 'automatic' activity. This, of course, is the standard Spencerian party-line. Meade Bache has long pondered this and concluded from everyday observations that 'the Negro' has faster RTs. 'Pride of race' makes (white) people reluctant to admit Negro superiority in any sphere, but on this point Meade Bache is, given his Spencerian rationale, eager to insist on their superiority.

> That the Negro is, in the truest sense, a race inferior to that of the white can be proved by many facts, and among these by the quickness of his automatic movements as compared with those of the white. . . . the Negro is, in brief, more of an automaton than the white man is. (p. 481)

He 'finally determined to submit the matter to the test of experiment' (p. 482) and appears to have approached 'Professor' Lightner Witmer,[81] then at the University of Pennsylvania, to undertake an experiment on differences in RTs between whites, Indians and 'Africans'. There is a typical passing reference to sex differences; females' shorter RTs have been 'long since determined', 'in accordance with the fact that the brain development of men, as compared with that of women, is greater' (p. 482). We are then presented with three tables of results for the 'Caucasian Race' (N = 12), 'Indians' (N = 11) and 'Africans' (N = 10) respectively. Subjects had been administered 30 trials, 10 each on auditory, visual, and electric shock RT tasks.[82] The resulting rank order in terms of speed was Indians, Africans, Caucasians. The Indian performance is slightly at odds with the author's expectations since he considers them a higher race than the African. Nevertheless, this is easily explained away: because of the conditions of slavery, the black RT has declined from its natural original high level, while some special conditions of Indian life required the maintenance of speedy reactions. Even slavery, however, has not adjusted African RTs to Caucasian levels.

Some comments are in order. While RTs are seen as an essentially 'primitive', 'automatic' level of behaviour, faster black RTs thus reinforcing the image of a 'natural' primitiveness, elsewhere in contemporary Psychology RT speed was being thought by Galton and J. McK. Cattell to be *positively* correlated with intelligence. Secondly the N's and trial runs are pitifully small and we are told nothing about the nature of the selection of subjects. It is in any case a no-win situation for the 'Africans' and 'Indians' – had they performed less well than whites the author would have clearly had even further cause for rejoicing, for this would mean that whites had achieved their intellectual superiority in the teeth of the 'law of compensation'. The author was not a professional psychologist and Lightner Witmer did not personally associate himself with the research. There appear to have been no follow-ups to this paper – it was early days for the *Psychological Review* (just founded as a competitor to G.S. Hall's *American Journal of Psychology*) and may have been little more than a space-filler. (As an aside it might be added that the author displays a strange preoccupation with boxing.)

Two years later a paper appears anticipating the kind of research which would later predominate: 'Some memory tests of whites and blacks' by George R. Stetson (1897). The sampling is impressively extensive: 1,000 4th and 5th grade children in the Washington DC area equally divided between black ('the darkest to be found in the schools' p. 288) and white, though the black age range is from 8–18, as compared with 8–14 for the whites. Their task was to memorise four verses by 'Mr Eugene Field' which were rehearsed three or four times by groups of 20–40 children, who were then required to recite them in private individually. They were rated on a four-grade scale: Excellent, Good, Fair, Poor. Lo and behold, there was 'a very remarkable and unexpected correspondence' in the scores of each race (in fact the blacks were marginally better, and would have been even more so if one verse had not been a peculiarly convoluted version of the opening of Psalm 22 on which they blew it even more than the whites). But rescue is at hand: 'In both races, *of course*, the memory is in decadence from primitive conditions, but as the blacks are much nearer those conditions *I naturally expected to find a much greater auditory mnemonic ability* than is possessed by the whites' (p. 288, my italics). It is therefore the *slightness* of their superiority that becomes surprising! The (marginally) better performance of the blacks is explained as due in part to their 'acknowledged deficiency in reasoning power' (p. 289). To this is also ascribed the discrepancy in age between white and black achievement of grade levels (blacks attaining 4th and 5th grades at 12 and 13.4 as opposed to whites attaining them at 10.63 (!) and 11.4). But both groups, it is asserted, 'exhibit a decadence of the observing faculties from earlier conditions' (p. 289).

Like Meade Bache, Stetson was an amateur, though he had also written on race in the *Protestant Episcopalian Review*.[83] While the sampling has improved, there is no indication that Stetson is doing more than seeking empirical confirmation of Scientific Racism. The 'no-win' nature of Stetson's research is identical with that of Meade Bache's. Again we should note that memory tasks figured prominently in Galton's and Cattell's contemporary, pre-Binet, attempts at measuring intelligence. This contradiction between invoking essential 'primitiveness' to explain superior non-white performance on basic psychological tasks and belief that these were also indices of intelligence was never, so far as I know, noticed at the time.[84]

Meanwhile, in Cambridge, England, preparations were afoot for the first fully professional attempt by psychologists to explore race differences deploying the methods which had evolved during the previous two decades of laboratory research: the Cambridge Torres Strait Expedition of 1898. While this did not, as it turned out, initiate a major British 'Race Psychology' tradition, it did serve to demonstrate, especially to US psychologists, that the topic was one worth addressing. It is most commonly, and charitably, seen nowadays as the founding event in 'Cross-cultural Psychology'. Along with studies by R.S. Woodworth and F.G. Bruner which it seems to have inspired, it deserves a chapter to itself, at the conclusion of which I will attempt to pull together the threads of Scientific Racism in pre-1910 Psychology as a whole.

NOTES

1 While Darwin's *Origin of Species* (1859) launched modern biological evolutionary theory it is important to remember that Spencer's somewhat different brand was initiated at the same time, and in some ways had a more powerful popular influence. Other versions rapidly appeared, competing with or supplementing Natural Selection, and as Bowler (1983) shows, classic Darwinism was largely in 'eclipse' from the 1880s to the 1920s. I thus use the general phrase 'evolutionary thought' to refer to the entire range.

2 See N. Rose (1985) for a fuller account of this dimension with regard to British Psychology.

3 I am somewhat oversimplifying the late 19th century scientific debate on race for the purposes of this work. Participants were operating from several different bases, notably linguistics, anthropology and biology in addition to evolutionary theory *per se*. However the linguistic arguments dropped into the background during the latter 19th century while the biological and anthropological arguments were increasingly framed in evolutionary terms.

4 The fate of polygenism is somewhat confused in that many French anthropologists (from G. Pouchet, 1864 to P. Topinard, 1890) continued to use the term, and saw the point of racial divergence as too far back for races to be considered as closer than distinct subspecies, and in some cases not even that. This was Gustav Le Bon's position also. Nonetheless the notion of *some* evolutionary connection was generally accepted, while such older notions as the founding 'protoplasm pair' disappeared. Post-evolutionary 'polygenism' is thus not quite the same thing as the pre-evolutionary version. This is not to say that bizarre polygenist theories ceased, see for example Crookshank (1931), who traced racial origins to indigenous species of primate – 'Mongols' from orang-utans, 'Negroes' from gorillas and whites ultimately from chimpanzees. See also Chapter 7, n. 68.

5 And remained so well into the present century, Seligman, for example, includes one in his contribution to W. Rose (1931), a popularly pitched, but fairly eminently authored compendium (see p. 433).

6 The last serious effort at swinging this argument was Carleton S. Coon (1963).

7 For a representative selection of eminent Victorian statements of the Scientific Racism position see M.D. Biddis (1979).

8 Running pun intended.

9 By present standards time-scales were still, on the whole, too short. This was reinforced by the calculations of authoritative physicists who, prior to the discovery of

radioactivity, seriously underestimated the age of the universe. This presented evolutionists with a serious difficulty since it seemed that there had been insufficient time for Darwinian mechanisms to have wrought their effects. As far as human ancestry was concerned, the time-scale was nevertheless usually into six figures, though varied widely. The error being noted in the main text was thus perhaps less glaring than I imply.

10 This image of course persisted well into the present century among historians, Arnold Toynbee being a prime example, though in relation to civilisations rather than races.

11 Ernst Haeckel's phrase. The title essay of his collection *The Pedigree of Man* (1883), from which it comes, finishes with a quite spine-chilling few paragraphs on the impending doom of the 'lower races' and why this is such a good thing.

12 Her account deals primarily with the physical anthropology/genetics side of the story, although it has some incidental coverage of Psychology. It provides a useful starting point for anyone wishing to explore the issue further.

13 Some Nazi psychologists later absurdly insisted that while species were changeable races were not (see Chapter 6).

14 A.R. Wallace was a particularly strong advocate of this notion.

15 For example, on the Australians: 'the mental faculties, have become so fixed in their degradation, that it is impossible for them to regain their original capacity. On the American continent the same phenomenon presents itself, although there the arrest of mental development has not occurred at so early a stage of the race existence' (Wake, 1868, pp. 146–7).

16 Eugenics has received much attention since the early 1970s. See especially Kevles (1985). While Eugenics and racism are, as I argue here, intimately connected, Eugenics' main field of operation was in regard to 'race hygiene' issues such as subnormality, crime, madness and the like rather than race as such. Only in the USA after the Great War and Nazi Germany did significant connections between the two develop (see Chapters 4, 6). I have therefore not discussed Eugenics directly at any length in this chapter other than in the context of Galton himself.

17 For example, the French polygenist Pouchet (1864) has a chapter on 'Intellectual and Philological Varieties', while Hunt (1863) predictably raves on about this for a page or two after p. 38, beginning:

> The day is not far distant when we shall be able to analyse the character of the Negro far more minutely than we can do in the present infant state of psychological science. In dwelling on the mental character of the Negro we must, therefore, for the present, rely on the general observations of those *unbiased* (italics in original!) travellers and others who have been much associated with the Negro race. In the first place we will see what is the evidence recently published by our English consuls, who have the best opportunities of judging of the character of the people amongst whom they are placed. (pp. 39–41)

Most of these pages are taken up by a mighty footnote from Pruner Bey, including a quote-within-a-quote: 'Let us not, however, forget that these excesses [i.e. of cruelty etc. just cited] do not constitute the rule, and that "the black man is to the white man what woman is to man in general, a loving being and a being of pleasure"'. Or again, Lefèvre (1894, p. 156) on 'the millions of savages who swarm and vegetate on a soil which is nevertheless full of wealth and resource' tells us 'His memory is short, his foresight almost *nil*. Present enjoyment suffices him, poverty or death affect him little. . . . He is animal in the spontaneity of his instincts' and so on.

18 Again, I am not dealing with the now well-covered topic of 19th century European racial philosophising as a whole, except where this is directly related to Psychological work.

19 Among the earlier critics of this I would draw attention to Jean Finot (1969, 1st edn 1906) and J. Barzun (1965, 1st edn 1937). Both pillory the confusions and inconsistencies of the physical anthropologists' attempts at arriving at a 'scientific' racial

classification, and their total failure to reach any consensus. Finot is, however, handicapped by overrelying on contemporary genetics (particularly that of De Vries). He construes the message of this as being a neo-Lamarckian one and grossly exaggerates the rate at which genetic change occurs – even claiming that the skin colour of white Americans is becoming increasingly like that of American Indians. This was, alas, the worst possible time to be trying to rely on state-of-the-art genetics since it was changing very rapidly and highly confused. Finot's criticisms of contemporary racial thinking itself are pretty effective and sound. While occasionally cited, usually dismissively, between the wars, his book appears to have now been largely forgotten despite a 1969 reprint.

20 See Nancy Stepan (1982) p. 93 ff. for further discussion of this. The notion that contemporary 'racial' variation between European 'stocks' was differentiating *out of* an initial more homogeneous 'stock', rather than the increasingly blurred legacy of originally clearly differentiated 'stocks' which had subsequently interbred, never seems to have occurred to anybody. This is perhaps slightly surprising given the influence of Herbert Spencer's 'increasing heterogeneity' model of evolution.

21 The phrenological connection could be quite direct, e.g. J.W. Jackson (1863) and W.E. Marshall (1873).

22 I am not of course intending to imply here that the identification of such physical features by physical anthropologists was in any case accurate. See Gould (1984) Chapters 2–4 for a critique of 19th century anthropometric techniques.

23 Mama (1995) makes a similar observation regarding modern Psychological research in Africa on the apparently precocious psychomotor development of African neonates. 'Few posed the question the other way round, to ask themselves why it was that European infants have slower psychomotor reflexes than the babies from all the other races that were tested' (p. 35).

24 S.L. Gilman (1992) provides an excellent account of the 19th century European obsession with the sexual anatomy of the African woman and its symbolic role as a signifier of the dirty, disease-ridden, sexualised female, which raises the connection between racism and sexism discussed later, and has to be understood also in the context of the contemporary syphilis epidemic.

25 In fact the typical African's full lips, lack of body hair, curly head-hair and pigmented skin are further from the chimpanzee condition than typical European morphology.

26 This, I understand, is also the thesis of the 1996 work by the late Ivan Hannaford *Race: The History of an Idea in the West* – a book 30 years in the writing. Unfortunately this appeared when the present text was already in press.

27 B. Latour (1987) ups the ante even further. As far as Psychology is concerned my own position is somewhat more complex since I believe the essentially reflexive nature of the discipline raises special difficulties. See the Introduction and G. Richards (1992a, 1992b, 1996).

28 Turner (1994) sees the roots of this as lying in the Helmholtz–Hering controversy regarding visual perception, but Galton's role was surely far more influential regarding intelligence and kindred issues.

29 See K. Danziger (1990) for an account of the victory of Galtonian over Wundtian methodology.

30 These chapters in *Hereditary Genius* and *Inquiries into Human Faculty* might though be supplemented by the occasional popular article such as 'Hereditary talent and character' in *Macmillan's Magazine*,1865, reprinted in Biddiss (1979). In this we find, for instance, an early assertion of what was to become a standard canard: that the children of lower races prematurely ceased their mental development (Biddiss, p. 69). Billig (1981) identifies the 1865 paper as the starting point for his account and discusses it at some length.

31 The Damara, 'a nation of thieves and cut-throats' (1889, p. 52), are unfavourably compared by Galton to his dog Dinah in an oft-quoted passage which concludes

'Taking the two as they stood, dog and Damara, the comparison reflected no great honour on the man' (ibid., p. 82).

32 This position is a little odd in view of his own penchant for nomadic and adventurous exploration and his constantly revised *The Art of Travel* which sought to assist those of similar leanings.

33 See also S.L. Gilman (1992) for further discussion of Lombroso's views on the racial significance of prostitution, drawing on the fuller C. Lombroso and G. Ferrero (1893).

34 This particular mode of linkage between Eugenics and Scientific Racism's racial hierarchy has not I think been widely noted, though Gilman (1992) certainly deals with it.

35 Billig (1981) pp. 15–26.

36 An extreme example of this is to be found in C.P. Blacker (1952) Appendix One on 'Galton's views on race'. Written in an attempt to recoup Eugenics' credentials in the wake of World War II this stresses the difference between Galton's views and those of Nazism (which is fair enough) and argues that despite the impression which the 'casual reader' might glean,

> Galton saw the spread of civilization as a painful though inevitable process the tribulations of which civilized man, by the studious exercise of enlightened foresight, could do something to alleviate . . . Could anything be done by foreseeing man to expedite this biological adjustment and to make it painless and humane? The question was asked and (as far as was then possible) answered without animus. It is the absence of animus which distinguishes Galton's attitude from that of the exponents of racism. Galton's views on race as expressed in *Hereditary Genius* are the first tentative efforts of a kindly man to apply to humanity the harsh lessons of biology as then understood' (pp. 327–8).

Alas, the truth is that contempt oozes from almost every reference Galton ever makes to Africans. It is this which makes me inclined to be so fierce about him and prepared to describe him as 'racist' as well as racialist. Virtually all white Britons were racialist at this time, in the sense of believing in innate race differences, but Galton's emotional 'animus' clearly exceeded this.

37 Lubbock's major relevant works, *Prehistoric Times* (1912, 1st edn 1865) and *The Origin of Civilisation* (1870), are thoroughly Darwinian and suffused with uncritical racialist attitudes and assumptions, but he is also genuinely curious about cultural differences and customs and certainly did not relish the prospect of races becoming extinct. Lubbock was much more the paternalistic Liberal, a true believer in the 'White Man's Burden'. It is interesting to note that he argued strongly *against* the racial arguments for Irish Home Rule in Lubbock (1887), on the grounds that the original ethnic stocks of the British Isles had become so mixed up that Celt, Norman and Saxon were now indistinguishable.

38 See the extensive quotes in Billig (1981).

39 This second enlarged edition was formally presented as the first volume of the *Synthetic Philosophy*.

40 For Spencer's more general influence on 19th century physiological Psychology see R.M. Young (1990).

41 p.127. Haller's review of Spencer's impact on Scientific Racist thought is particularly useful and has informed much of what follows here.

42 'The comparative psychology of man', reprinted in Biddiss (1979). Here and in subsequent quotes the second pagination figure refers to reprint.

43 John Fiske (1842–1901) briefly taught at Harvard in the early 1870s and published his Spencerian magnum opus *Cosmic Philosophy* in 1874, subsequently becoming a populariser. See B. Kucklick (1977, p. 80 ff.) and M. Berman (1961).

44 Haller (1971, p. 132).

45 These included the southerner Joseph Le Conte, faintly remembered by psychologists for his work on perception, Edward Drinker Cope with his 23 'structural evidences of

evolution' (on many of which the 'Negro' predictably failed), the sociologist Charles Ellwood and J.A. Tillinghurst, author of the paper 'The Negro in Africa and America' (1902). One should also mention the somewhat earlier Dr John H. Van Evrie (1868) which was particularly vehement.

46 As S.D. Porteus (1937) crudely puts it: 'It would seem for the most part that a racial group has just about the government, religion and education that it deserves' (p. 5). Herrnstein and Murray (1994) revive this yet again.

47 Hall's role receives fairly full treatment in most orthodox histories of Psychology, but see O'Donnell (1985, Chapter 7 and Chapters 8–9 passim) for a more recent and critical account.

48 The major study on which he based this view was probably G.E. Dawson (1900/1) which appeared in *Pedagogical Seminary*. (Acknowledgements to Sandie Lovie for this reference.)

49 See D. Muschinske (1977) for a review of these. Muschinske, it must be admitted, is less charitable to Hall than I am, considering him 'blatantly racist' (p. 328) and uncritically accepting of most prevailing racist orthodoxies, even if not entirely consistent in this. Somewhat remarkably, however, Muschinske actually does not appear to have noticed the *Adolescence* chapter itself – Hall's most extended 'position statement' on the issue. He draws primarily on Hall (1903, 1905a, b). From Muschinske's paper it is evident that on this issue, as in his career generally, Hall always displayed an opportunistic tendency to go with the prevailing wind.

50 Few would *disagree* with the view that the post-Civil War 'Reconstruction' experiment was a *failure*, but the fault hardly lay with the liberated slaves themselves.

51 Hall's position was not unique; see for example Mary A.M. Marks (1900), H.R. Marshall (1901) and W.J. Roberts (1908), all of which appeared in the *International Journal of Ethics*.

52 An early example is Ernest Coffin (1908), quoted in Muschinske (n. 19, p. 336).

53 I have discussed this in G. Richards (1995).

54 This opens up the whole issue of US responses to evolutionary thought, which is beyond the scope of the present work. This has received much recent attention, see in particular J. Moore (1979), D.N. Livingstone (1987) and R.J. Richards (1987).

55 For a thorough contextualised account of Le Bon's Psychological work see R.A. Nye (1975), pp. 49–54 of which deal specifically with his views on race.

56 Graumann (1996) notes this influence in Le Bon's notion of 'psychic contagion'.

57 Graumann and Moscovici (1986).

58 The French original appeared in 1894; in English *The Crowd* appeared first.

59 But see n. 4.

60 He may, as a matter of fact, be right about this, but purely for sampling reasons. 'Civilised' races having far higher populations than his 'inferior' ones, their range of diversity would naturally be greater. This would be compounded by the higher degree of genetic diversity in his civilised 'historic races' as opposed to the smaller gene-pools of isolated tribal peoples. 'Civilisation' as such has, in principle, nothing to do with it of course.

61 One is bound at this point to wonder what exactly Le Bon is admitting, or claiming, here about his own psychology. Does he actually see himself as the living mouthpiece of this vast constituency of the deceased, an obedient puppet of the ancestral will?

62 W. McDougall (1920a). McDougall's concept of the Group Mind is considerably less metaphysical than Le Bon's. McDougall is discussed in Chapter 6.

63 See below Chapter 6 for discussion of Nazi Race Psychology.

64 See below Chapters 6 and 7.

65 Freud opens *Group Psychology* (1922) with a chapter on Le Bon's 'deservedly famous work' (*The Crowd*). Nor does he reject the notion of a racial mind here, merely saying it 'lies outside the scope of psycho-analysis' (p. 7 footnote).

66 Karpf (1972, 1st edn 1932) claims that W.I. Thomas's thinking was 'to a considerable extent grounded' in Dewey's Psychology (p. 353), though B.N. Meltzer et al. (1975)

cite evidence casting doubt on this and suggesting the influence was in the reverse direction – see pp. 124–5, n. 9.

67 In W.I. Thomas (1901)

68 The rejection, after earlier acceptance, of innate racial differences by Boas, the leading US-based anthropologist, was a powerful factor in constraining racialism in the US social sciences from the early years of the century down to the 1930s. Boas, Thomas, and Dewey are thus already laying the groundwork for post-Great War critiques of Race Psychology.

69 His fullest elaboration of his position from this period was his *Source Book of Social Origins* (1909). His concern with methodological issues was to be particularly import-ant in the emergence of American Social Psychology as an empirical research-based discipline (see Karpf, 1972, especially pp. 351 ff., and K. Young (1931)).

70 See D. Haraway (1989), S. Harding (1986), A. Mama (1995). A work which confirms the endurance of the inter-relatedness of race and sex differences is H.H. Plos et al. (1935). This English translation came 50 years after Plos's own first German edition. Much of the classic Scientific Racism package seems to be carried over quite uncriti-cally, while the callous objectification of non-European (and indeed European) women is sometimes quite horrendous. I am surprised no-one has really got their teeth into this text yet. See also S.L. Gilman (1992).

71 There is I feel an interesting connection, awaiting exploration, between what I am suggesting here and what Morawski (1992a, b) has said about the way in which the psychologists of the 1890s and early 1900s were able to evade the reflexivity issue by asserting that they were operating in a specifically 'Psychological' mode of professional subjectivity which enabled them to view all other 'subjectivities' objectively.

72 For example, H.F. Kletzing and W.H. Crogman (1897) (see J.S. Haller, 1971, p. 207) and the Gambian barrister Joseph Renner Maxwell (1891) who argued that Africans could only overcome their innate physical ugliness by marrying whites. A particularly virulent case was William Hannibal Thomas (1901), some quotes from which are given in G.B. Johnson (1944), who comments that:

> his indictment of his race . . . is perhaps the worst which has been penned by any American since the Civil War. Through some combination of social experience and personal idiosyncrasy, he arrived at a feeling of bitterness and despair concerning his people; and then, as if he had completely disowned them, he sat in judgment on them. (p. 15)

73 See S. Shapin (1991).

74 This is curiously ironic because in the early 1920s 'in a near-paranoid moment that surpassed all his wildest previous claims' (Nye, 1975, p. 156) he was to try and initiate a priority dispute with Einstein over the theory of relativity.

75 I must though duck out of any further discussion of the notion of 'objectivity' and its attendant problematics – this would involve far too great a digression. See e.g. Harding (1986), who is also particularly effective on, among other things, the resist-ance of science to submitting to the kind of enquiry and examination which it insists on as appropriate for everything else.

76 See Harding ibid., especially Chapter 6 for a review of current feminist analyses of the gendered and racial nature of science. Much of what is said there has a direct bearing on the point I am making here.

77 Even the title of this chapter is in contrast to the others, which are entitled 'The yellow world', 'The brown world' etc. Blacks do not have a world, they are simply a problem. 'Brown' for Weale refers primarily to Middle Eastern peoples. The author's real name was B.L. Simpson (according to Weatherly 1911). The kind of anxieties behind Weale's work were exacerbated by a contemporary belief that the Anglo-Saxon race, and white races generally, were in demographic decline. See for example Octavius Charles Beale (1911), a massive compendium in which a vast number of extracts from learned authorities and statistics are marshalled as evidence of a looming

'cloud of extinction'. Russia is an exception. He does not, however, believe non-white races are a threat since their figures are no better. Beale was an ex-Royal Commissioner of Australia. He directs much animus against J.S. Mill and Manchester School economists, the perils of birth control, and so on. The dust-wrapper carries a purple endorsement by Theodore Roosevelt.

78 To exhume another forgotten text of the period, however, Theophilus E. Samuel Scholes' (1907, 1908) must be mentioned as an anti-imperialist and anti-racialist blast from the opposite camp. But he had to be satisfied with the far less eminent publisher John Long.

79 See Fernando (1993) and Mama (1995) for brief discussions of this earlier psychiatric work. Both, however, tend to overconflate the histories of Psychiatry and Psychology for rhetorical ends. Cartwright's paper, originally published in the *New Orleans Medical and Surgical Journal*, owes much of its current fame to having been reprinted in A.C. Caplan et al. (1981). See also W.H. Tucker (1994, pp. 13–14), C. Prudhomme and D.F. Musto (1973). B. Malzberg (1944) cites J.W. Babcock (1895), T.O. Powell (1896) and A.H. Witmer (1891) as examples of southern psychiatrists ascribing increased 'Negro' mental illness rates to an inability to handle the pressures of emancipation.

80 C.S. Myers (1903) cites an 1881 study of the reaction times of some Japanese conjurors by Herzen, which showed them slower than Europeans, but was unable to find details of the research. This is a pity; finding a sample of Japanese conjurors in 1881 can have been no small achievement for a start. Garth (1931b) identifies this as the earliest experimental Psychological study of race differences, followed by Bache (1895). One might also note that M. Prince (1885) accepted the usual Scientific Racism view of the 'lower races' possessing less developed brains which hampered their grasp of moral principles (Part 2, Chapter 4). Ann Tolman Smith's 'A study in race psychology' (1896) which appeared in *Popular Science Monthly* might also be mentioned in passing. This was a case study of a single 16-year-old boy Isaiah. The conclusions are in line with Meade Bache's (whom she cites), namely that the case demonstrates the dominance of 'automatic' functions. She used a word association test – which revealed deficiency in associating to abstract terms – and a memory test. Isaiah, we are told, became a drummer, which 'afforded an outlet for his automatism' (p. 360).

81 Witmer was then in his late twenties. He was one of the first generation of professional psychologists and went on to specialise in educational Psychology and subnormality. I put the 'Professor' in inverted commas here since he was in fact a 'lecturer', only becoming a professor, at Bryn Mawr College, in 1896. US usage of the term has, however, long been looser than UK usage.

82 As C.S. Myers subsequently pointed out, the methodology of this study is actually not entirely clear. See below pp. 51–2.

83 He self-references 'The Negro and the Church', *Protestant Episcopalian Review* July 1896. W.H. Tucker (1994, p. 3) wrongly calls Stetson a 'well-known contemporary psychologist'. There seems to be some confusion here with Raymond H. Stetson (who is also credited with this paper in Murchison 1929a). G.O. Ferguson (1916), consistent with the original *Psychological Review* paper, gives G.R. R.H. Stetson was based at Oberlin University in Ohio until 1896 and was from then until 1899 a Professor of Zoology, so is unlikely to have been running experiments in schools in Washington DC.

84 As it transpired, there turned out to be no correlation at all between reaction time and memory span scores and intelligence as measured by Binet-type tests. This was a severe disappointment for J. McK. Cattell who had sought to correlate such measures on a freshman intake with final degree performance.

Chapter 3

An imperial interlude: the Cambridge Torres Straits Expedition and its aftermath

In March 1898 the Australia-bound *S.S. Duke of Westminster* slipped its moorings in London's Royal Albert Docks. Along with a party of clergymen, including the Bishop of North Queensland, Dr Barlow (who would give Sunday sermons throughout the voyage), the passengers included a group of anthropologists and psychologists (whose leader, Arthur C. Haddon, would often follow these with a talk on some ethnographic topic such as the aborigine bull-roarer).[1] This latter group comprised the Cambridge Torres Straits Expedition,[2] its other six members being W.H.R. Rivers (who had only decided to come at the last moment), his students C.S. Myers and William McDougall, the anthropologist C.G. Seligman, the linguist Sidney H. Ray,[3] and A. Wilken, an archaeologist, anthropologist and photographer.[4] This was the most ambitious and scientifically equipped anthropological field expedition yet mounted, and its researches were to include psychological as well as anthropological matters. Its consequences would extend way beyond the five volumes of *Reports* which appeared between 1901 and 1912.[5]

How far did the expedition move beyond the prevailing Scientific Racism orthodoxy? What impact did it have on Psychology's treatment of the race issue? The usual anthropological view of the episode is as a major step towards more rigorous and scientific field-work methodology and, via its conversion of Rivers to a passionate interest in anthropology,[6] a leading factor in the emergence of the British 'functionalist' school of Radcliffe-Brown and Evans-Pritchard.[7] From Psychology's side it is seen as the foundation, or more accurately an anticipation, of what would later be called Cross-cultural Psychology, as well as having ancillary significance both for methodology and within the intellectual biographies of Rivers, McDougall, and Myers. While historians of anthropology (such as Henrika Kuklick, Ian Langham, G.W. Stocking, and James Urry) have frequently discussed the episode, Psychology's historians have been relatively less interested, partly because they have mostly been US-centred,[8] and partly because, since the Psychological research was not subsequently followed up on a signicant scale, it remains somewhat isolated as a one-off event.[9] Haddon, (in whom, being an anthropologist, historians of Psychology have little interest) was the expedition's prime mover and his position on 'race' must be considered first.

A.C. HADDON (1855–1940) AND THE RACE QUESTION[10]

In Kuper's view, 'Haddon perhaps represented the muscular colonial anthropologist at his simplest' (1973, p. 124). He belonged to the generation intermediate between the Victorian evolutionary anthropology of Edward Tylor and the social anthropology of the 20th century. His original evolutionary approach is best exemplified in *Evolution in Art* (1895). Physical anthropology then became his primary, though far from only, interest and in this he was an eager and uncritical participant in the classificatory and anthropometric enterprise.[11] Immediately prior to the expedition, while still a Professor at Dublin, he had embarked on the Anthropological Survey of the British Isles, to which John Beddoe, author of a classic work in this genre, *Races of Britain* (1971, 1st edn 1885), lent his keen support.[12] While this racial orientation may initially suggest that Haddon was a conventional Scientific Racist, he was even so on the milder wing and in *The Races of Man and their Distribution* (1909) admits 'As to the term *race*, it really seems impossible to frame a satisfactory definition' (p. 6) and wishes to confine it to 'the main divisions of mankind which have important physical characters in common' (ibid.). Neither the Jews nor the English or Irish are thus really races. For smaller groups he prefers *people, nation,* and *tribe.* And yet in 1905, responding to a paper by one Miss Pulton Berry condemning higher education of the Negro as 'a source of evil' he reportedly declared 'that the negro should not be educated to a position he could not occupy'.[13]

While remaining publicly silent on the matter, Haddon privately kept track of the US debate and the 'race problem' generally throughout the early years of the century.[14] In 1895 he had, at Flinders Petrie's behest, participated in the BAAS meeting at Ipswich, participating in a session 'On the Contact of European and Native Civilisations' aimed at countering the 'mischief of hasty interference with codes of morals, customs and government'.[15] Here he attacked the British desire 'to crush other peoples into their own procrustean bed of belief and action'.[16] In 1911 he participates in a Race Congress supporting the 'oppressed' and in 1912 is being approached for support by the editor of the *African Times and Orient Review*, an anti-racist campaigning publication which had received Jean Finot's backing.[17] In his brief *History of Anthropology* (1934), his views remain curiously elusive. Notwithstanding summaries of 'Individual and ethnic psychology' and the polygenism controversy, he never unambiguously shows his hand regarding his views on the meaning of race differences, especially psychological ones. When the chips are finally down the following year he apparently enters the lists on the side of the angels by collaborating with Julian Huxley on the highly successful *We Europeans* (1935, reprinted as a Pelican in 1939), aimed at countering Nazi race doctrines. Doubts hover even here though. Barkan (1992) quotes a letter from Haddon to the adamant racist Ruggles Gates in which he clearly, if implicitly, accuses Huxley of using him. 'In this version Haddon is not merely embittered, but also conveys the impression that he was deceived, betrayed, and perhaps even abused. It clearly suggests that he was a figurehead, whose reputation was utilized for political ends in a way and manner to which he opposed [*sic*]' (Barkan, p. 304). Other statements by him, however, adopt a different tone.[18] By this point it is as if the racialist rationale of physical anthropology has self-destructed, the utter complexity of physical variation which the project's researches have disclosed now, itself, undermines the notion of clearly identifiable races as unitary biological entities. By deploying the data to this end in *We Europeans*, Haddon – by then eighty – finally openly committed himself, however hesitantly, to the anti-racist camp. But as Barkan points out, even the most 'anti-racist' of British anthropologists and biologists in the 1930s (including Expedition veteran Seligman) are unable entirely to abandon racial attitudes and assumptions common to their class and culture. Of his *Races of Man* (1925, i.e. 1925 reprint of 1924 2nd edn), Barkan observes 'the disjunction between Haddon's cognitive recognition of the inability to classify a pure race and his acquiescence in cultural prejudices of racial hierarchy led to contradictions' (p. 301). (Julian Huxley's own pre-1928 writings fully espoused many Scientific Racist positions the later rejection of which involved considerable intellectual struggle.)[19]

The nearest we seem to come to a clear, and even then highly hedged, earlier statement is in the Introduction to *The Study of Man* (1898), where, regarding the view 'that the lower races of man are more simian than the higher' Haddon observes, 'This generalization must be accepted with great caution; it is only partially true, and some of the characters on which reliance is placed may prove to have another signification' (p. xxv). Although he goes on to say 'Of course there can be no doubt that on the whole the white race has progressed beyond the black race' (p. xxvi), it is unclear how far he means physical as opposed to cultural progression.

My own impression is that while Haddon was absolutely fascinated by race and the relations between peoples both in the present and in pre-history, prior to the 1930s (if then) he was extremely reluctant to become involved in contemporary controversies. If so, he was far from unique among British and American anthropologists (and geneticists) as Barkan demonstrates in great detail. He is certainly disinclined to pronounce on the merits of different races and rarely if ever invokes the usual authorities dear to Scientific Racists – Galton, Spencer, Gobineau, Topinard, Broca and the like. Lack of inhibition, earlier maturation, even the implications of skull morphology, hardly figure in his writings (though skull morphology *per se* certainly does). He describes, compares, catalogues and relishes physical and cultural diversity, but steers clear of drawing moral lessons from all this. In this he shares with Rivers (and indeed Franz Boas) a shift in mood from armchair theorising to empirical field research.[20] While an evolutionist, he recognises that the unilinear schemes of social evolution proposed by Lubbock, Tylor and L.H. Morgan were oversimplistic, thus although an evolutionary hierarchy of peoples may exist in a broad sense, the notion breaks down when it comes to comparing specific peoples in detail.[21]

Haddon, the expedition's leader, is thus an ambiguous figure regarding race, being both a dyed-in-the-wool physical anthropologist of precisely the kind usually identified with Scientific Racism and someone loath openly to commit himself on any aspect of the race differences issue (even though the archival evidence shows his deep interest in it). The Cape Town story, in which he seems most racist, may suggest the contrary but given the brevity of the account, the unreliability of press reports, and, in fact, the obscurity of what, precisely, his alleged comment meant,[22] not too much weight ought to be placed on it. All of which rather leaves us little more enlightened than when we started as far as his 1898 position is concerned.

What it perhaps suggests, nonetheless, is that the Torres Straits Expedition was *not* a strictly Scientific Racist project, even if its leader shared the physical anthropology enthusiasms of many who avidly supported the doctrine. Haddon's promotion of the expedition actually had its roots in an earlier eight month visit (as a marine biologist) to the region in 1888–9 to study its natural history.[23] During this visit the lifestyle and culture of its 'cheerful, friendly and intelligent folk' (Haddon 1935, p. xi) had come to appear more interesting than the flora and fauna, and in more need of urgent scientific study in view of its probable impending demise (already in train under the impact of missionary and trading activity). The majority of his publications following this earlier trip were indeed on ethnographic topics. His first expedition thus converted Haddon to an interest in anthropology, much as the second converted Rivers. Rather than, as Galton, Spencer and Haeckel would have done, losing no sleep over the coming extinction of a few unfit savages, Haddon, while accepting the grim diagnosis, reacted to the prospect with alarm. This, in conjunction with his shift in methodological attitude, provides sufficient grounds for seeing Haddon as having moved somewhat beyond classic Scientific Racism, even while retaining some of its perspectives.

We may now turn to the Psychological researches of W.H.R. Rivers (1864–1922), C.S. Myers (1873–1947) and William McDougall (1871–1938).

PSYCHOLOGICAL RESEARCH IN THE TORRES STRAITS[24]

Preliminary points

The psychologists set themselves an ambitious programme, presenting many practical problems which they only partly overcame. Standard laboratory equipment was often unsuitable, being too delicate or otherwise inappropriate, for the field-work, 'Politzer's Hörmesser' for measuring auditory acuity, for example, proved unworkable, as did 'Zwaardemaker's olfactometer' for testing smell – the Murray Islanders 'entertained a great objection to inserting the glass tube of the olfactometer within their nostrils' (RCAE 2, p. 170). Over 20 psychological and psycho-physiological phenomena were studied in all, mostly psycho-physical in nature.[25] These included Rivers' studies of visual acuity, discrimination, visual illusions and colour perception, Myers's work on hearing and smell and McDougall's on 'cutaneous sensations' and 'muscular sense'. Their success was variable. Myers in particular seems to have drawn the methodological short straw, finding great difficulty in devising reliable techniques for assessing auditory acuity, pitch threshold, and olfactory discrimination, his research also being affected by the high incidence of aural damage from pearl-shell diving.[26] Rivers' work on perception was more rewarding, the phenomena being more amenable to investigation and Rivers already being highly experienced in perception research, hitherto his primary field and one in which he was a leading figure. Other diffi-culties could arise too. On Murray Island (where the majority of the research was conducted), villagers from the far end of the island were deterred by an 'enthusias-tic native' who told them that Queen Victoria would send a man-of-war to punish them if they were not entirely truthful in their responses (RCAE 2, p. 4).

Before considering the results, a little more needs to be said about the project's rationale and the conditions under which it was conducted. In the first place the expedition provided an intrinsically interesting opportunity: 'The people were sufficiently civilized to enable us to make all our observations, and yet they were sufficiently near their primitive condition to be thoroughly interesting' (RCAE 2 p. 2). This however had an added technical dimension as Rivers explains (ibid., p. 6). German experimentalists had differentiated between subjects who were *wissentlich, halbwissentlich* and *unwissentlich*, that is, between those who under-stood the nature of the research, those who half-understood and those who were completely naive. One difficulty in using Psychology students and colleagues, or even educated lay subjects, was that their responses could be confounded by knowledge of the aims and hypotheses behind the research. This did not apply to Torres Straits islanders: 'in no investigation has the procedure ever been so com-pletely "unwissentlich"' (ibid.). Langham (1981) suggests that Rivers regretted being unable to perform introspective studies (then still a major experimental method) with his subjects, but this was I think more than off-set by their *unwissen-tlich* virtues. Moreover, the scale of the research exceeded any previously underta-ken, even on 'civilised' subjects. Almost the entire male population was involved and the research extended over weeks in contrast to the hour or two per subject typical of laboratory research (ibid., pp. 4–5). While not entirely reliable in atten-dance, and occasionally bored, it seems that the subjects were mostly eager to assist the team. Co-operation was stimulated by an appeal to their vanity;

> The natives were told that some people had said that the black man could see and hear, etc., better than the white man and that we had come to find out how clever they were, and that their performances would all be described in a big book so that everyone would read about them. This appealed to the vanity of the people and put them on their mettle. (ibid., p. 3)

Their 'degree of application' was 'surprising in face of the widespread belief in the difficulty of keeping the attention of the savage concentrated on any one thing for any length of time' (ibid.).[27] The subjects were primarily male adults or children (mostly boys) who had had some European-style education in a missionary school (whose principal, Jack Bruce, assisted and co-operated fully with the expedition, being Haddon's primary contact). In the long run, as Schaffer (1994) shows, the whole experience made Rivers, at least, reflexively aware of how they were in effect imposing their own 'scientific' culture on their subjects. This adumbrated the later separation between Anthropological and Psychological orientations towards race differences. Such anxieties regarding the viability of transferring Western laboratory techniques to the field were later reinforced by Titchener's 1916 critique of the expedition's Psychological work.

Regarding Rivers, Langham (1981) identifies a rather more profound level of motivation linking the older Spencerian framework and the Torres Straits research. His physiological work on perception had suggested to Rivers the existence of two levels of neurological functioning which he and his colleague Henry Head termed 'protopathic' and 'epicritic'.[28] The former, characterised by all-or-nothing responses of an indiscriminate kind, came to be identified in his thinking with the instinctive and emotional. The 'epicritic' level, by contrast, was marked by fine discrimination and more sophisticated rational judgment. 'Protopathic' thinking tended, Rivers believed, to be visual and highly concrete, while 'epicritic' thinking was verbal and abstract. This is, let me stress, a considerable simplification. The relevant point for us is that Rivers had concluded that 'primitive' thinking was more markedly 'protopathic' than that of civilised people. This has clear Spencerian echoes (and his teacher, the neurologist Hughlings Jackson, was indeed a Spencerian) but it is markedly different in the terms in which it is couched, and not spelled out explicitly in the *Reports*.

While centred on Murray Island, additional psychological research was undertaken on Mubuiag Island (Rivers and Seligman), Kiwai and the Fly River district of New Guinea (Seligman). Aboriginal Australian data from the neighbouring mainland is also occasionally included, as is data obtained subsequently in Sarawak.

The Psychological research was just part of a much wider ranging project, occupying only one of the six volumes of reports. Rivers additionally contributed to vols 5 (1904) and 6 (1908) dealing with 'Sociology, magic and religion of the eastern islanders' and 'western islanders' respectively. In these he tackles genealogy and kinship (his most influential area of contribution to Anthropology, and for anthropologists *the* single most important outcome of the entire exercise), totemism, personal names, regulation of marriage, funeral ceremonies (with Myers, vol. 6) and, with Haddon, the 'Cult of Bomai and Malu', a major religious cult of the western islands. Other volumes concerned Linguistics (vol. 3 by Ray, 1907), arts and crafts (Haddon and others vol. 4, 1911) – in which Rivers contributed on Astronomy, and general ethnography (vol. 1, Haddon, 1935). Myers supplied the 'Music' section to volume 4. Gluttons for punishment, most of the expedition's members (though not Rivers) moved on to Sarawak in 1899 at the invitation of Charles Hose, and McDougall includes data from Sea Dayaks in his report on cutaneous sensations. Psychological research was thus embedded in extensive anthropological enquiries regarding religion, social structure, language, customs, and artefact collection. The amount of work which the expedition achieved during its stay is in truth quite staggering.

Rivers, Myers and McDougall all understood the need for European control groups, each, on their return, replicating their studies on a British sample. Rivers chose students and people (including children) from the village of Girton, Myers 'a small village' near Aberdeen, and McDougall, somewhat oddly, the 'mostly working class' inmates of a 'Cheadle convalescent home', though only those who had regained their health.

Findings

As already noted, the research basically concerned sensory and psychophysical phenomena. While the researchers adopt a resolutely empirical and ostensibly supposition-free approach, virtually every report is introduced by a discussion of the prevailing opinions of travellers and scientists regarding 'primitive' performance on the topic in question. Almost invariably this is, predictably, that such people are unusually adept and discriminating whether it be in relation to vision, hearing, smell or reaction times. Dissenters are also noted. (These literature overviews remain highly useful.) If, as claimed earlier, the expedition was not overtly Scientific Racist in its orientation or agenda, the Psychological research was inevitably framed by traditional Scientific Racist assumptions about 'savage' psychophysical performance. The participants do not appear to have had strong personal investments in the validity of these assumptions, but they provided their only available 'scientific' starting point. As we will see, they also tend to construe their findings in terms of this framework even as they are eroding it.

Rivers' studies of perception

Rivers begins with visual acuity, not an easy concept to define (in fact three different definitions had been used) but usually taken as the smallest visual angle at which two points can be distinguished. This posed some methodological difficulties we will leave aside here. While, on the face of it, it transpired that Mabuiag Islanders were two to three times superior to the supposed European norm, the Murray Islanders ($N = 115$) were 'normal'. Problems of comparison with European studies are discussed and Rivers asserts that European islanders 'living an outdoor, seafaring life do not differ very greatly in visual acuity from Papuan islanders' (RCAE 2, p. 28). In general he concludes that 'the visual acuity of savages and half-civilized people, though superior to that of the normal European, is not so in any marked degree'. He believes the superiority is due to the higher incidence of 'refraction errors', notably myopia, in 'civilized people'. Taking this into account it is far less than travellers' tales would lead one to expect. He conscientiously confirms that his subjects are capable of the kind of discriminatory feats which generated the myth – seeing birds in dense foliage and craft far out at sea for example.[29]

At this point we seem to have a straight refutation of race differences, the apparently high discriminatory skills of 'savages' simply result from learned habits of attention. But some compatibility with conventional wisdom can be salvaged. Invoking the experience of the German Ranke who had lived with the Bakaïri of South America, Rivers argues that the primitive lifestyle requires minute attention to detail.

> Minute distinctions of this sort are only possible if the attention is predominantly devoted to objects of sense. and I think there can be little doubt that such exclusive attention is a distinct hindrance to higher mental development. If too much energy is expended on the sensory foundations, it is natural that

the intellectual superstructure should suffer. . . . (this) may help to account for another characteristic of the savage mind. There is I think little doubt that the uncivilized man does not take the same aesthetic interest in nature which is found among civilized peoples. (ibid., pp. 44–5)

Although psychophysiological level differences in acuity are minimal, the situation can thus be recouped by shifting to the practical behavioural level where traditional tales of visual virtuosity may still stand as evidence. The explanatory level shifts from physical to psychological, but this move in itself enables the notion of psychological-level differences to be reinforced, with a quite Spencerian conclusion: savages devote too much energy to their (protopathic) senses at the expense of their reason. If no longer physiological in nature, a Spencerian mechanism is retained as the favoured hypothesis.

He next tackles colour vision, an especially rich topic since it had been hypothesised by several people, including William Gladstone (on the basis of his studies of Homeric language),[30] that colour perception had changed over historical time, perception of blue in particular having improved. By the 1890s the prevailing view was that colour language had no necessary connection with colour perception, but it remained a live controversy. Rivers' studies of this were to become among the most frequently cited.

Using both a supplemented set of 'Holmgren's wools', the standard equipment for studying the topic, which required subjects to match strands of wool, and Lovibond's tintometer (a new device), Rivers set to work. His 107 Murray Island subjects comprised 56 adult males, 7 adult women, 31 boys and 13 girls. In addition Seligman obtained data for him from Fly River in New Guinea and he was also able to use linguistic data from aborigines of the Seven Rivers district of Queensland. While by and large the results differed little from European norms, there was one exception: Murray Islanders seemed to be relatively more sensitive to red and less sensitive to blue. This, he speculated, may be due to the greater amount of yellow pigmentation in the macula of the eye in black-skinned people, resulting in greater absorption of green and blue than in the European and therefore relatively less sensitivity to blues (see ibid., pp. 78–9). He also felt that colour contrasts appeared less vivid than to Europeans. With the exception of one island (Lifu) red–green colour blindness was virtually absent.[31] Rivers was not, though, entirely happy with the research. It had presented numerous practical difficulties which may have only been partly solved, most notably frequent linguistically rooted misunderstandings of what was required. He accepted that the linguistic evidence for colour-sense differences was dubious but felt that 'One cannot, however, wholly ignore the fact that intelligent natives should regard it as perfectly natural to apply the same name to the brilliant blue of the sky and sea which they give to the deepest black' (ibid., p. 94). Blue did seem to be a darker or duller colour to the islanders than to 'us'. While physiological insensitivity may be one factor, Rivers felt that others of a cultural nature, such as absence of blue pigments, were also implicated. Regarding these findings Berlin and Kay (1969) concluded that the central source of error was confusion between colour and brightness distinctions, a point also made by Titchener (1916). (Titchener also suggested that discrimination of blue is affected by illumination level and that while Rivers' subjects were apparently tested in an unlit 'disused missionary house', the control group were tested in a brightly lit laboratory.)[32] They claim that 'In the light of modern knowledge . . . one suspects that what Rivers took to be informants' confusion in perception of blue was in fact the result of his inability to effectively communicate, through interpreters, the distinction between the perceptual and naming tasks' (Berlin and Kay, 1969, p. 148). In other words, lacking a specific name for blue, subjects called it something like 'dark', using a word assumed to be equivalent to 'black'. As for his physiological explanation: 'This explanation is almost certainly wrong, despite the considerable ingenuity it displays' (ibid.). They also comment that the extensive discussion of colour vocabulary contained in the report (RCAE 2, p. 53 ff.) 'was the last attempt to discuss the evolution of color nomenclature until the present study nearly seventy years later' (ibid., p. 149).[33]

An experiment on binocular visual space perception (N = 17) showed no differences from 'normal' results, although the opportunity arose to study a three to four-hour-old neonate who apparently displayed binocular vision, a result rare, though not unknown, in Europeans.[34] Another experiment on the ability to divide lines into various numbers of equal lengths, again with small N's, also showed no major differences from the control group, aside from a tendency when dividing into two for Murray Islanders to overestimate the left and English subjects the right.

Finally, Rivers reports a group of studies on visual illusions. These included three forms of the vertical–horizontal illusion, the Müller–Lyer illusion, some Zöllner illusions, the moon illusion[35] and several others. The vertical–horizontal illusion seemed particularly marked in Murray Islanders, their results being comparable to European children. Taken overall, the findings were varied. There was less susceptibility to the Müller–Lyer illusion than among Europeans, for example, but particular sensitivity to, and excitement by, figures generating spiral after-effects and perception of movement. Sensitivity to illusions based on 'irradiation' effects (for example, a black square on a white background usually appears larger than a white square of the same size on a black background) was apparently lower.[36] This last led Rivers to wonder if it was related to superior acuity. From drawings of the moon and sun in various positions in the sky, Rivers also concluded that the moon illusion occured as for Europeans.

What messages did these findings convey regarding race differences in visual perception? The major message for Rivers' contemporaries was that while such differences might exist (and in the case of deficient perception of blue almost certainly did), they were much smaller than traditional views would have predicted. The second message was of a different kind; Rivers and his colleagues had vindicated the new Psychology's scientific value in clarifying and advancing understanding in an area hitherto dominated by aprioristic assumptions. Thirdly, however, it at best modified rather than fundamentally challenged Scientific Racist positions, notably by offering a compromise solution to the 'superior primitive acuity' question which merely shifted the explanatory level from the neurological to the psychological. While opening the door to more radical environmentalist accounts, the hints at residual physiological factors left the nativist door ajar. In spite of this, Rivers' results were nonetheless soon being widely read as actually falsifying the notion of primitive superiority and (along with some of the expedition's other findings) played a major historical role in the subsequent removal of psychophysical phenomena from the agenda of race-differences research.

Myers' studies of hearing, smell, taste and reaction time

The youngest member of the team, Myers, was a skilled musician and highly interested in the sense of hearing. It was clear from the outset that things were not going to go smoothly: as already mentioned there was the problem of aural damage caused by pearl fishing and there was also the possibility that a measles epidemic 'many years ago' had affected older subjects (RCAE 2, p. 141). Abandoning Politzer's Hörmesser as unsuitable for open-air experiments on acuity, with background noises of the 'rustle of palm-leaves and the breaking of the surf' (ibid., p. 145) he fell back on the ticking of a stop watch and another piece of equipment he had devised. Even so, variation in background noise necessitated a constant control, which meant himself or Rivers – who to compound things further was 'certainly suffering from partial deafness when these estimations [i.e. on Murray Island girls] were made' (ibid., p. 148). For upper pitch limit measures difficulties arose with the widely used Galton whistle, applying even to those, like his, supplied by Hawksley of Oxford Street. His measures were thus given in pipe-length terms rather than frequency. With perhaps more hope than conviction he affirms of his data: 'Their value rests on the supposition that after considerable practice with the instrument I am able again and again to produce the same force of blast . . . I have no doubt as to the general reliability of the figures given' (ibid., p. 150). As far as discriminating differences between tones was concerned, he knew this was very much affected by practice. No similar studies had ever been attempted. Undaunted, and armed with specially adapted tuning forks, he forged ahead even though the subjects found the task 'certainly' the 'most distasteful' of all the experiments (ibid., p. 159). The results showed that (a) compared with the Aberdeen group, the Murray Islanders were somewhat poorer in general auditory acuity, (b) Murray Island children were marginally inferior to Aberdeen children regarding upper limit of hearing range but taking ear damage into account the difference disappeared, and (c) Aberdeen subjects discriminated intervals half as great as the Murray Islanders could.[37]

While the raw figures on pitch discrimination were impressive, Myers was well aware that they were far from conclusive. His subjects were ignorant of European notes, intervals and instruments, and pitch discrimination is susceptible to learning (the children had a slight familiarity with hymn tunes, but no musical training, while six of the Aberdeen adults played musical instruments and four had experience in tuning them). His conclusions were so highly hedged that all the questions really remained open. The main lesson was little more than that methodology and equipment needed radical improvement before reliable findings could be obtained. Even so, the kind of 'primitive superiority' which travellers' lore predicted was most definitely not in evidence.

Studying smell sense was even harder. Again the prevailing wisdom was that 'savage races approach the animal world' (Ribot, cited in ibid., p. 169). For Myers, the Torres Straits research was intended primarily to discover methods suitable for future experiments on this underdeveloped research topic (ibid., p. 170). Regarding acuity he tentatively does conclude that it is slightly higher among his subjects than in the Aberdeen control group. A smaller proportion had 'obtuse' 'smell-power' and a greater number were hyper-acute. Children were better than adults in both communities. This finding is again highly qualified due to the small subject numbers, and ubiquitous methodological problems relating to equipment.[38] Memory and discrimination of odours was investigated using a range of 14 odours supplied in solid form by Messrs Plesse and Lubin of New Bond Street, including camphor, thyme, jasmine, benzaldehyde, asafoetida and civet. This experiment the islanders greatly enjoyed. The usual 'primitive superiority' assumptions lie in the background: their mode of life made them 'more aware of and attentive to the majority of external stimuli than we ourselves are' (ibid., p. 181). Myers also thought that 'there can be little doubt' that 'most coloured people' emit a skin-odour 'sufficiently distinct from that of Europeans to be generally recognizeable' (ibid.). While the experiments showed little more than that his subjects had 'much the same liking and disliking for various odours as obtains among ourselves' (ibid., p. 185) he gives a spin to the findings similar to Rivers' earlier construal of visual acuity.

> My impression was that the old associations and new thoughts which the . . .
> odours awakened were more numerous and more vivid and were more rapidly
> evoked than they would have been in the case of Europeans tested under simi-
> lar circumstances. If this is so, it is yet another expression of the high degree to
> which the sensory side of mental life is elaborated among primitive peoples.
> (ibid., pp. 184–5)

He does not seem to have taken his scent range to Scotland. His studies of taste are of a mainly philological nature and find only that, unlike sweet, salt and acid, 'bitter' is a problematic notion in many cultures – even apparently in Aberdeen. He treated this more fully in Myers (1904).

Myers was on more familiar ground with reaction times (RTs), but again relying on relatively crude equipment involving an electrically driven tuning fork and a 'Deprez' signal upon the smoked surface of a hand-rotated drum'. For auditory RTs he used a one-off piece of apparatus 'devised for us by Captain E.T. Dixon' (ibid., p. 206).

Incorporating data later obtained in Sarawak, he found that on auditory RTs Murray Islanders and English subjects did not differ, on visual RTs the English were better, but Sarawak Sea Dayaks were the best in both conditions. On choice RTs[39] Murray Islanders were notably slower than an educated English control group, but he suspects they 'would have compared more favourably with an English villager' (ibid., p. 216). In discussing the Murray Islanders' relatively poorer performance on visual and choice RTs, he argues that 'the attendant psychical conditions were more complex than in the auditory reactions' (ibid., p. 220). He adds a discussion of previous work, including a critique of the Meade

Bache study (see Chapter 2) about which he is highly dubious, suspecting that the 10 highest RTs for each subject were selected under each condition and that the analysis was not of 10 consecutive trials. He ends by observing that 'racial differences in reaction times, if actually established by further research, may turn out to be merely the expression of racial differences in temperament' (ibid., p. 223).

While numerous methodological lessons were learned, the overall implications of Myers' findings were far from clear-cut. Again, the principal message was that the expected 'primitive superiority' could not easily be demonstrated, and insofar as it was evident, was at a fairly modest level. The biggest differences were often found in the studies which were most methodologically suspect (for example, the RT findings were based on very small N's – 17 Murray Islanders, 24 Europeans and 18 Sarawak Dayaks).

McDougall's studies of cutaneous sensations and blood pressure

McDougall studied five main topics: the 'two-point threshold' as a measure of tactile discrimination, sensitivity to pain, 'muscular sense' – basically the ability to discriminate weights, the 'size–weight illusion' (larger objects seem heavier than small ones of the same weight) and variations in blood pressure in relation to mental activity. Methodologically he faced fewer problems than either of his colleagues, excepting an attempted study of temperature spots which was sabotaged by the fact that the skin-markings involved always got washed off by his inveterately swimming subjects.

The two-point threshold results were remarkable, revealing powers 'about double that of Englishmen' (ibid., p. 192). 'It should be noted that the skin of these islanders is of a very fine glossy texture' (ibid., p. 193). Sarawak findings showed far less superiority. Sensitivity to pain, however, was, in adults at least, only half that of Englishmen (though Murray Island boys were only slightly less sensitive than the English controls). Again the Sarawak findings were intermediate. On weight discrimination the islanders proved 'rather more delicate' than Europeans, a surprising finding, McDougall felt, as this was a judgment 'with which they are totally unfamiliar', even lacking an abstract word for 'weight' (ibid., p. 198). Curiously however, in view of this superior 'delicacy' of judgment, they were also more susceptible to the weight–size illusion, a finding which McDougall immediately speculates may be due to their higher degree of 'suggestibility'.

The apparent robustness of these findings was soon called into question. The pain sensitivity finding was most likely due not to differences in sensation *per se* but to cultural norms regarding the level of intensity at which it is appropriate to use the 'pain' word. Given the appeal to the islanders' vanity which initiated the programme it is also likely that they would wish to display fortitude, not realising that this would be construed as evidence of primitive insensitivity! The two-point threshold findings are also difficult to interpret. A *wissenlicht* European subject might, for example, tend to report 'two points' only when aware of two distinct sensations; the more naive Murray Islanders, by contrast, treated the task rather as a guessing game and used stimulus magnitude as such as a basis for their responses –

McDougall, without more ado, therefore simply lowered the criterion for success to the point of correct guessing (p. 190). It was a finding about which Titchener (1916) was particularly scathing. The interpretation of these results was especially important because the pain and tactile discrimination findings were quite clearly in the direction orthodox wisdom predicted: both greater sensory acuity *and* more animal-like insensitivity to pain being held to characterise the 'primitive'. Although I am unaware of any subsequent discussion of the weight discrimination results, McDougall is surely wrong in assuming this to be an unfamiliar task. Lack of an abstract word for 'weight' proves nothing, even if true; weight judgments are surely pretty ubiquitous in connection with food-sharing, use of spears and the like.

The blood pressure study may be dealt with briefly. The rationale for this was the belief that

> inferiority of the black races is due to a cessation of the growth of the brain at an earlier age than in the white races, and it may be that this is in part, or wholly, due to a less active response of the blood-pressure to mental activity. *I may say at once that I did not succeed in discovering any evidence to this effect.*
>
> (ibid., pp. 201–2, my italics)

McDougall was subsequently the only expedition member to maintain a strong Scientific Racist position, especially after emigrating to the USA. This is discussed in a later chapter, but it is worth remarking here that McDougall's findings were those which, excepting the blood pressure research, were most consistent with racialist expectations, and he always accepted their validity despite the criticisms they later attracted.

Some follow-up work by Rivers and Myers

In 1905 Rivers published a 76-page paper in volume one of the *British Journal of Psychology*: 'Observations on the senses of the Todas'.[40] He reports a number of Torres Straits type psychophysical studies with the 800-strong hill-dwelling Todas. As far as visual perception was concerned, he again failed to find systematic differences from European norms and with visual illusions the differences, such as they were, varied in direction. The Todas' sense of smell may have been marginally poorer than that of the English. On hearing he was only able to study two subjects, thereby ruling out any general conclusions. This report served to reinforce the message of the Torres Straits findings – the Spencer hypothesis remained unconfirmed. The next paper in the journal, incidentally, was 'A study of rhythm in primitive music' by Myers, drawing attention to the rhythmic complexity of the music of Borneo (his own study) and other 'primitive' people (drawing on secondary sources). He argues that whereas in Western music complexity has been developed most in the elaboration of harmony, in these other cultures it has taken place in elaboration of rhythm. This paper too served to shift the emphasis from crude evaluative judgments of musical ability according to Western criteria to appreciation of cultural differences.

Myers' only other paper explicitly on race appeared in 1911, having been pre-sented to the First Universal Races Congress at the University of London in June that year. This had been convened by Gustav Spiller to encourage fuller under-standing, 'friendly feelings' and 'greater co-operation' between races. Others attending included Franz Boas and W.E.B. DuBois. No further such Congress appears to have ever taken place. The central argument of Myers' paper 'On the permanence of racial mental differences' is that there is no difference between the 'mental characteristics' of the European 'peasant class' and those of 'primitive communities'. His experiences in the Torres Straits, and subsequently in Borneo, Egypt and Sudan, had convinced him there were no sensory differences, that reli-ance on mechanical rote learning was common to both peasants and 'primitives', and that variations in temperament were the same. The European peasant was not superior in 'logical and abstract thought' to 'his primitive brother' and, far from being less inhibited, the 'savage' was 'probably more hide-bound than we are by social regulations' (p. 74). There was perhaps more variability overall in 'advanced people' due to 'racial admixture' and their more complex social environment. He adds an attack on Lévy-Bruhl's 'primitive mentality' theory, which he had just read.[41] So far well and good, but we are faced with a rather baffling final sentence in the main text. Here he asserts that Negro–white differences may be reversed 'if the environments to which they are respectively exposed be gradually, *in the course of many hundreds of thousand of years*, reversed' (p. 78, my italics). Probably this should have read 'hundreds *or* thousands', but even so an unexpected gulf suddenly opens up between us and Myers here regarding the time-scale in which he is operating, at the end of what has hitherto read as a perfectly sound anti-racist statement. Otherwise the tone and position of this paper quite closely anticipates that of Bartlett's *Psychology and Primitive Culture* (1923) (see Chapter 7).[42]

THE TORRES STRAITS EXPEDITION AND RACE

We may now return to our opening questions. First, how far was the expedition racist in character? As we have seen, neither the motivation behind the research nor the explicit agenda were overtly racist. On the other hand, Scientific Racism provided its intellectual framework, no other being in fact available. 'Primitive' superiority in basic sensory and psychophysical functioning is generally the initial hypothesis. We have also seen that regardless of the direction of the results, the researchers tend to try and reconcile them with this hypothesis, even while stress-ing the minimal or weak nature of the differences identified. In at least one instance, Rivers' discussion of colour perception, there is a shift back towards a harder physiological view from a current trend towards cultural explanations.

At a perhaps deeper level, there is no indication that any of them were at this stage inclined to rebel against what was, by then, the well-established role of the educated Englishman among his colonial subjects, with its attendant attitudes. The subjects are, for instance, frequently identified by nicknames such as 'Tom Tom' and 'Smoke', but what forcefully strikes a present-day reader is the quite uninhibited use of 'primitive', 'savage' and 'uncivilised' to refer to the people among whom the researchers are living, seemingly on highly cordial terms. How seriously should we take this? The use of 'savage' even by anthropologists as anti-racist as Malinowski continued into the 1930s (for example, in Malinowski's titles *The Sexual Life of Savages*, *Sex and Repression in Savage Society*, and *Crime and Custom in Savage Society*), and W.I. Thomas, as we saw, was happy to use 'lower races' in 1907 even though as radically opposed to nativist racism as anybody.[43] While it is correct to see such usages as indices of racism, this needs qualifying: at the period under consideration here they are indices of the racist nature of the culture producing the discourse rather than that of individual writers. The language, in this case, eventually, but belatedly, shifted to reflect changed attitudes which had already been articulated in the older terms.[44] As young sons of Empire (and Myers and McDougall were still in their twenties), the expedition members were certainly well socialised into the mores of imperial travel, and had mastered those skills of 'managing the natives' in a paternal fashion, eliciting co-operation while maintaining social distance, which had evolved over the previous half-century. The expedition was clearly in one sense a thoroughly establishment imperial adventure (it emanated from Cambridge University after all).

Cloaked in this role (and pragmatically adopting the appropriate attitudes) though they may have been, this is not the whole story. Their professional identities as scientists, and psychologists at that, rendered them somewhat less conformist. They were scientific pioneers in a discipline itself new, and established wisdom was far from sacrosanct. If the whole enterprise was somewhat suffused by contemporary cultural racist norms, Rivers and Myers at least appear to have few personal psychological needs to maintain racialist positions even if these cultural norms rendered it difficult to escape them completely. Regarding how far Scientific Racism was superseded, we can at least say they muddied the waters. With their apparently authoritative findings on record, later writers were unable to trot out many of the old clichés in unqualified form. The reports themselves do not address the general Scientific Racist thesis, but are content to nibble at the edges of a variety of its subsidiary hypotheses. Perhaps the greatest effect the work had was towards shifting the nature of the debate from a matter of evolutionary theorising to one of empirical evidence. One might also remark that both Rivers and Myers (but not McDougall) later became clearly identified with a left-of-centre political ideological position (at the time of his premature death Rivers had been adopted as a Labour parliamentary candidate for London University).

What of the impact on Psychology itself? The most immediate was to inspire R.S. Woodworth, then still in the early stages of his career, to attempt to carry out similar work, albeit on a smaller scale but with a wider range of 'racial' groups, at the St Louis Exposition of 1904. Rivers personally advised him with respect to the visual perception experiments and, although his findings were not published until 1910, he sent a brief report to Rivers in October 1906 apologising 'for this excessively tardy acknowledgement of your kindness in writing me so fully and suggestively from your experience in Torres Straits'.[45] We will return to this in due course. Myers' work on hearing was followed up on the same occasion by F.G. Bruner (1908), to which we will also return. Aside from the previously mentioned papers by Rivers and Myers themselves, however, there is little evidence that further Psychological work beyond Woodworth's and Bruner's was directly stimulated, even if the studies were widely cited. Furthermore, Titchener's 1916 critique went a long way towards discrediting the findings on methodological grounds. The absence of clear-cut findings on psychophysical level differences seems in fact to have had an inhibiting effect, since it suggested that any important differences would exist at a higher level than these commonly shared basic functions. There is thus something of a hiatus for several years in the USA, ending around 1910 with the advent of intelligence testing, which promised to address these 'higher functions'.

If the research itself long remained a somewhat isolated one-off exercise, it played a central part in the development of British Psychology. Rivers, Myers and McDougall constituted a core group within the discipline until the 1920s. While this may have happened in any case, perhaps the 'male bonding' established in the Torres Straits reinforced their collective influence, and facilitated their involvements in the treatment of shell-shock during World War I – itself a central episode in the discipline's British history. (As by then seasoned globetrotters they would also have acquired a level of credibility with the military which college-bound academics would not have enjoyed.) Rivers impressively managed to straddle Psychology and Anthropology for the remainder of his career and the ethnographic study of music became a lifelong interest for Myers, if only as a relaxation from his labours at the National Institute of Industrial Psychology. McDougall enjoyed a less distinguished post-war career in the USA, lapsing into neo-Galtonian eugenic concerns for the quality of the national racial stock.[46]

In the absence of chat-shows, the returnees still found venues at which to dine out on their experiences. Let us close the topic pondering the scene at a Royal Society 'Conversazione' in Burlington House on 20 June 1900. Haddon is holding forth on the Native Dances of the Torres Straits, but more is to come, the lights are lowered, 'the sacred masked dance of the *zoyole* (sacred men) will be shown by the cinematograph. Mr A. Wilkin, a member of Dr Haddon's expedition, will at the same time chant some of the appropriate sacred Malu songs.'[47] The expedition was surely as much a founding Modernist event as it was a terminal Victorian one.

MEETING WOODWORTH IN ST LOUIS

The 1904 St Louis Exposition celebrating the centenary of the 'Louisiana Purchase', provided Woodworth and his assistant Bruner with an opportunity for attempting to extend the Torres Straits research.[48] Besides a 'Model Indian School', about 200 young Filipino policemen, plus a handful each of Japanese Ainu, Congolese 'Pigmies', some 'Negritos' and representatives of various American Indian tribes (ranging from Patagonia to Vancouver) were in attendance. The many visitors provided an ample 'white' sample.

Woodworth's findings, never fully published, were summarised in an address to Section H (Anthropology and Psychology) of the American Association for the Advancement of Science in 1909, appearing the following year in *Science* as 'Racial differences in mental traits'.[49] He begins on a general note, warning of the illusory nature of classifying groups of 'men' into types when the internal variability of groups usually exceeds the difference between their averages. He is very insistent on this, and cites brain size as a case in point; from a small average difference between the 'Negro' and white brain sizes, 'we straightway seize upon it as the important result, and announce that the Negro has a smaller brain than the white. We go a step further, and class the white as a large-brained race, the Negro as a small-brained' (1910a, p. 172). A variety of other difficulties with such studies are also discussed, including the problem of culture-fairness of tests and the role of environmental or historical circumstance in determining which abilities are called upon and in which areas of life demands on intelligence will be made. This opening section of the paper is fundamentally sceptical in tone and dismissive of 'statements . . . denying to the savage powers of reasoning, or abstraction, or inhibition, or foresight' (p. 174).

As far as the St Louis results are concerned, while a variety of differences between certain subject groups and others are found regarding perceptual phenomena and form-board performance Woodworth quickly downplays the significance of any of these, which in any case display no systematic pattern. Small sample size or unrepresentative sampling, and different understandings of the task or familiarity with it, are usually implicated. He repeatedly observes that 'people of widely different cultures are subject to the same errors, and in about the same degree', 'the races are essentially equal in keenness of vision', 'the keenness of the senses seems to be about on a par in the various races of mankind' and the like. He also stresses the scantiness of Psychological knowledge about non-visual senses and higher mental functions. The only exception is that on the form-board tests the Pigmy and Negrito groups did perform extremely badly – even here though 'the fairness of the test is not, however, beyond question' (p. 181). 'This crumb is . . . about all the testing psychologist has yet to offer on the question of racial differences in intelligence' (ibid.). Given this paucity of Psychological evidence why not simply compare races according to their 'civilisations and achievements'? Woodworth answers with a lengthy, thorough and insightful deconstruction of the rationale of such a procedure.

Only at the very end of the paper is there a straw in this enlightened wind. This is the problem of 'selective migration'.

> Wisdom would dictate that the nation which is in progress of formation should exert some influence on its own account, but, from all the facts in hand, the part of wisdom would be to select the best individuals from every available source, rather than, trusting to the illusory appearance of great racial differences in mental and moral traits, to make the selection in terms of races or nations. (ibid., p. 186)

Within a decade the dictates of Woodworth's wisdom on this point would have been quite forgotten.

The St Louis findings only occupy about a third of the paper, but they plainly firmed up the central messages of the Torres Straits research. No clear-cut supporting empirical evidence for the Spencer hypothesis is forthcoming and, both methodologically and conceptually, studying race differences in psychological performance presents many recalcitrant problems. Even so, while more or less writing off the existence of differences at the psychophysical level, Woodworth does hold out that 'it might still be that great differences in mental efficiency existed between different groups of men', and '[a] good test of intelligence would be much appreciated by the comparative psychologist' (p. 180).

For all his scepticism Woodworth does not quite reject the whole exercise of race-differences research as intrinsically mistaken. This would have been premature; regarding the higher processes Psychology has not even begun to investigate the issue. His 1916 *Psychological Bulletin* report on the current state of the topic somewhat unexpectedly adopts an uncritically deadpan stance in summarising the findings of the new wave of 'Negro'–white studies on children and other work, even letting Gobineau (who had just been translated into English) off the hook very lightly. Returning only rarely to the topic in his own subsequent work, Woodworth continued to play an ambiguous background role until the 1930s.

Playing Myers to Woodworth's Rivers, Bruner set about studying differences in upper limit of pitch and auditory acuity. Much of his 1908 report concerns methodological problems related to the calibration of measuring equipment. These were still considerable in the study of hearing, involving reliance on tuning forks, whistles and the like which were difficult to calibrate and often unreliable. Some slight improvements on what had been available to Myers had, though, been made. For the upper limit of pitch audibility Bruner used the more advanced Edelmann whistle rather than the Galton whistle, carefully calibrating it using the technique of Kundt dust figures.[50] For acuity he devised an *ad hoc* instrument utilising a telephone receiver which presented a 'metallic click noise' of directly measurable intensity.

Bruner's results may be fairly briefly summarised. Upper limits of pitch audibility in the various 'races' sampled were, in descending order: Pigmies, whites, Cocopa Indians, Indians (Model School group), Filipinos, Patagonians, Ainu, Vancouver Indians (Filipino, Patagonian and Ainu rankings were different for right and left ears however). The reported average limits ranged from over 33,000 c.p.s. (cycles per second) down to under 28,000 c.p.s. – well above the currently accepted figure of $c.\,20,000$ c.p.s. The superiority of the Pigmies (N = 6!) gives him some difficulty, but he suggests that 'the Pigmy is a motor individual. His reactions to incoming stimuli likewise are direct and excessively overt' (1908, p. 45). The range of hearing of the 'primitive' groups also appeared to be less than that of the whites. As far as acuity is concerned the order obtained, with some difficulty in interpretation of the results, showed whites superior, Indians (Model School group) third and Filipinos last, but other rankings were different for right and left ears! It is perhaps clearer to us than it was to Bruner that only the most tentative of conclusions could legitimately be drawn from this study; the samples are hardly comparable in how they represent the 'racial' groups, and four number 10 or less. The Ainu and Pigmies in particular were also in what must have been a highly disturbing alien environment.

Bruner's attitude to his subjects may be judged from the following: 'the Pigmy is stupid and dense and apprehends meanings slowly and often incompletely' (p. 10),[51] the Cocopa or Seri Indians (from Tiburon Island, North West Mexico) were 'of so low a grade of culture that they may be classed as just entering the stone age'[52] and were 'dull and stupid in the face of an untried problem' (pp. 6–7), while Ainu were 'very immature in their mental conceptions and aptitudes' as well as very timid (p. 8).

Nothing daunted, Bruner proceeds to draw one quite firm conclusion:

> the clearly evident superiority of Whites over all other races, both in keenness and in the range of the hearing sense. The evidence is so clear as to silence effectually the contention that the hearing function, inasmuch as it is of relatively less utility in the pursuits attending modern social conditions than those surrounding the life of the savage, has deteriorated and is degenerating. (ibid., pp. 111–2)

On the contrary, he argues that the greater the 'complexity and variety of reactions to elements in their respective environments', races will 'be gifted with keener and more acute sensory mechanisms' (p. 112). He expands on this with speculations about the 'startling auditory inferiority on the part of some of the natives of tropical lands' (pressing Myers' findings into service). These are 'regions where lack of thrift and indolence are fostered by nature's bounty', 'adaptive activities are found at their lowest ebb'. While reinforcing the notion of white superiority, his conclusions actually therefore ran counter to Spencerian assumptions. He also suggests that the complexity of the acuity test was such that differences in 'mental alertness' or 'intelligence' might be responsible for the relatively poor showing of some groups, but is frankly puzzled by the poor showing of the Filipinos (who came last). He ends with a programmatic plea for the value of Psychology in future scientific studies of race differences.

CONCLUSIONS: SCIENTIFIC RACISM'S LEGACY IN PSYCHOLOGY

These two chapters have demonstrated how Scientific Racism set the terms in which Psychology began addressing the race-differences issue. Psychology itself was at this period thoroughly infused with the evolutionary thinking underlying Scientific Racism, indeed it had provided the discipline with its initial integrative theoretical framework. Along with child development, animal behaviour, psychophysiology, social deviancy and crowd behaviour, race differences fitted into the wider project of studying 'man's place in nature' from an evolutionary perspective. While few rejected white superiority, and the blasé use of terms such as 'savage', 'inferior', 'lower', 'primitive' would continue for several decades, the Torres Straits and St Louis Exposition findings nevertheless discredited one central tenet of Scientific Racism – the 'Spencer hypothesis' of marked primitive superiority in basic functions. Yet they were not quite the enlightening events sometimes suggested: the Torres Straits reports themselves contain no explicit abandonment of Scientific Racism in general, and there are frequent attempts at rendering the findings consistent with it, although cultural and environmental options are also admitted. Similarly, Bruner's overall attitude was hardly a step towards emancipation from stereotyping and dogma. Woodworth on the other hand, in 1910 at any rate, is more radical and verges on dismissing the whole enterprise, though he later backtracked. While the 'Spencer hypothesis' had, it was widely felt, been refuted by these two bodies of research, the notion of a hierarchical ranking of racial quality had hardly been dented. If anything it had been reinforced, for it now appeared that white superiority might exist at *all* levels of functioning. Some findings, like Bruner's, did point in this direction, and where no significant differences were found (as in much Torres Straits work) there were frequently *in*significant levels of white superiority that could easily be read as 'suggestive'.

The total non-white sample size on which such conclusions had been drawn was, let us remind ourselves, probably under 500.[53] The only Asians were six Ainu and about 200 Filipino policemen (Woodworth appears to have studied more of these than Bruner) and the six Pigmies were the only Africans (no African Americans participated in the St Louis research). It was a very oddly assorted sample, selected primarily by fortuitous circumstance. The groups also totally differed from one another in gender and age composition. By far the majority of the findings were open to a variety of interpretations, and none of course generalisable from the specific groups studied to all 'tropical' or 'primitive' people. The inference that Spencer's hypothesis was probably wrong was reasonable, and from our position welcome, but strictly speaking the research hardly amounted to a definitive refutation. Had the hypothesis not, like its author's reputation, been falling from favour anyway, claiming its refutation on this data alone could have been far more controversial than it actually was.

The result was that attention shifted from basic processes to the higher 'cognitive' level. This move reflected that occurring in psychometry at large. By 1910 the number of psychological tests potentially available had expanded dramatically from that available in 1900, and unlike the methods required for studying psychophysical phenomena they were *technologically* unproblematic.[54] The change did not happen immediately. Aside from Bruner (1908) and Rivers (1905), between 1901 and 1910 virtually no new empirical research of any note (and little Psychological discussion of any kind) on race-related topics was published. The reason for this was primarily that Psychology in both the USA and elsewhere had more urgent and promising matters to tackle. These related to both disciplinary organisation and professionalisation and the forging of new research methodologies appropriate for the experimental study of the expanding range of topics Psychology now sought to encompass. Race differences were necessarily, for the moment at least, a peripheral concern. As we will see in the next chapter, when the topic revived from 1910 onwards Scientific Racism's assumptions and attitudes continued to be much in evidence in the new Race Psychology.

The subsequent story is, I will argue, a curious one of how, via the Race Psychology project itself, US Psychology came to shuffle off the coil of Scientific Racism. But that reflexive point must wait until we have examined this strangely neglected episode.

NOTES

1 See Cambridge University Library Haddon Collection (HC henceforth) 1030 (Haddon's journal) and 1055 (Haddon's diary), the former of which is far more substantial. Both begin with the expedition's departure.

2 There is some confusion as to whether 'Strait' or 'Straits' is correct. While 'Strait' is now, as it were, 'geographically correct', the plural form was used in the expedition's official title and by writers up to L. Hearnshaw (1964). To avoid constant switching I have thus adopted the plural form throughout.

3 Ray had co-published 'A study of the languages of Torres Straits, with vocabularies and grammatical notes' in two parts with A.C. Haddon in Haddon and Ray (1893, 1897).

4 Wilkin died prematurely in May 1901 in Cairo.

5 These were volumes 2–5, volume 1, on the ethnography of the region, did not appear until 1935. To further complicate things, volume 2, in which we are interested, originally appeared in two parts, in 1901 (Rivers on perception) and 1903 (the other Psychological research) respectively.

6 Ironically Rivers was a nephew of the polygenist James Hunt, but prior to the expedition he 'cared so little for anthropology . . . that he had turned down the offer of the anthropological library left by his uncle' (Slobodin, 1978, p. 21, citing G. Elliot Smith). Slobodin provides a fairly detailed account of the origins of, and preparations for, the expedition.

7 For its anthropological significance and its crucial role in turning Rivers' interests towards the genealogy and kinship issues which became the cornerstone of British social anthropology see Langham (1981). Other relevant studies include Urry (1982), Gathercole (1976), Stocking (1986) and H. Kuklick (1991, in press), which are essential 'further reading'.

8 But even Hearnshaw (1964, 1987) gives it relatively little direct attention. In 1964 it receives about a page but its importance is seen as lying primarily in its impact on Rivers' and Myers' later careers. In 1987 it receives only a seven-line footnote.

9 While Rivers and Myers both published a few further studies of a similar kind in the first decade of the century no other British Psychologists followed their lead and after 1914 more pressing matters such as shell-shock and fatigue became their main priority.

10 See Barkan (1992, pp. 26–30, 296–304) for a fuller review of Haddon's views on race, which does not radically depart from mine in its conclusions. His coverage of the expedition itself however is minimal as well as misleadingly referring to its members as 'six anthropologists' and failing to get Myers' name right even in the index. For Haddon's career in general see Quiggin (1942), Urry (1982), Kuklick (1996).

11 This interest never abated. HC 4039–47 contain detailed notes, offprints and diagrams relating to the physical anthropology of various European peoples dating from the 1920s, still lovingly enumerating and mapping the skull-shapes, hair and eye colours etc. of Turks, Finns, Moravians, Basques, Swedes et al.

12 Beddoe helped particularly with the Irish material, lending Haddon some of his notes. See letters from Beddoe in HC 4046. As Simon Schaffer points out, the charts used for classifying skin and hair colour were adopted by Haddon from Beddoe who in turn got them from the French doyen Paul Broca, a party-line Scientific Racist (Schaffer, 1994, p. 16). Prior to the expedition Haddon had been involved in studies of 'Irish craniology' and ethnology (with C.R. Browne) in the Aran Islands, and Inishboffin (both Co. Galway) and a neolithic cist burial in Oldbridge, Co. Meath. This resulted in four publications in the *Proceedings of the Royal Irish Academy* 1893–8.

13 This was at the 1905 Cape Town meeting of the British Association for the Advancement of Science. The report was in the *New York Tribune* 18th August under the headline 'Evil in education of Negro', see clipping in HC 5368.

14 See HC 5368, 5406, 5408, which contain extensive newspaper clippings, ephemera and offprints on the issue.

15 Flinders Petrie to Haddon 24.4.1895, HC 5408, which also contains a printed pamphlet report of the session and some hostile contemporary newspaper clippings.

16 See pamphlet in HC 5408.

17 See HC 5406 for two letters, one to Haddon and the other from Finot.

18 E.S. Fegan and J.D. Pickles (1978) also list two letters to *The Times*, 7.8.34 and 16.7.36 on 'the Aryan race' and 'the German race' respectively, plus two 1935 papers co-authored with J. Huxley in *Antiquity* and *Discovery* on the racial question and racial myths. This hardly suggests much resistance on his part to Huxley's alleged arm-twisting.

19 See Barkan (1992), especially pp. 234–48.

20 See S. Schaffer (1994) for a detailed account and interpretation of this.

21 See Haddon (1898, p. xxi).

22 One would certainly like to know more about this episode. It is, in one sense, a truism to say that somebody should not be educated to a position they could not occupy, and the statement could be taken as subtly leaving this open. Given that the meeting was in Cape Town shortly after the Boer War it is at least possible that the muscular colonial anthropologist was not keen on rocking his hosts' racist boat and gave a suitably oracular reply. Alternatively one could read the statement as being compatible with the opposition to hasty interference in native cultures expressed at the same organisation's Ipswich meeting in 1895 (recollections of which would have been in the air too). On balance we should, I feel, suspend judgment.

23 In addition to the papers with S.H. Ray (see n. 3) this had generated *The Decorative Art of British New Guinea: a study in Papuan ethnography* (1894), 'The Actinaria of Torres Straits' (1898), 'The geology of Torres Straits' (1894, with W.J. Sollas and G. Cole), plus numerous brief notes and articles in *Nature*, the *Journal of the Anthropological Institute*, and elsewhere between 1889–1897 (see Fegan and Pickles, 1978 for full listing).

24 These are reported in detail in vol. 2 ('Physiology and Psychology') of Haddon (1901–35) *Reports* (1901, 1903), the first volume to be published (RCAE 2 henceforth). Rivers also published a popular spin-off article (Rivers,1900), while C.S. Myers (1902, 1904) also expanded on work done during the expedition. Text quotes are from Rivers except where relating to hearing, smell and reaction times (Myers) or cutaneous sensation and blood pressure (McDougall). Much of Rivers' field-note material is preserved in HC 12070–75, including physical anthropological data on record cards developed from those designed for Haddon's earlier British survey (see blank form in HC 4046). The black notebook in HC 12071 has, in addition to data, some notes on attention problems. One handicap for the Rivers researcher is that his handwriting, though neat, is often virtually indecipherable. HC 12034 contains Rivers' notes on colour names.

25 See RCAE 2 pp. 1–2 for listing. There is another dimension to this, which cannot be discussed here, which pertains to the broader methodological question of the late 19th century creation of the scientific (not just Psychological) laboratory and the problems of transferring this to the field. S. Schaffer (1994) offers a preliminary exploration of the episode from this perspective.

26 RCAE 2, p. 141 and pp. 152 ff. passim.

27 This was in effect the first myth which the research challenged. Rivers later strongly reiterated the point in the light of his subsequent anthropological work on genealogy (Rivers, 1926, pp. 51–3 'Intellectual Concentration in Primitive Man'), when this was written is unclear but it post-dated most of his field-work in Melanesia and India.

28 This was subsequently explored in more detail in the famous study of nerve regeneration in which the nerves in Head's forearm were severed and the returning sensations recorded over five years by Rivers. I cannot do justice here to Langham's remarkable,

if controversial, diagnosis of Rivers' psychological motivation and its relationship to his theoretical orientations. See Langham (1981, Chapter 2).

29 RCAE 2, pp. 42–7.

30 W. Gladstone (1858).

31 The variability of incidence of colour blindness in different peoples was later confirmed in numerous studies, some of which are mentioned in Chapter 4.

32 See also Segall *et al.* (1966, pp. 37–48) for a discussion of the colour perception issue from Gladstone onwards, including Rivers' findings and Titchener's critique, the latter of which they rate highly.

33 Since 1969 the topic has received further study by ethnolinguists, but the views of Rivers offered by Berlin and Kay have not, I believe, been substantially challenged.

34 This finding may have had an implicit significance in relation to the common 'earlier maturation' argument, but this is not articulated in the text.

35 Most psychologists will know these. For those readers who do not they are, briefly: (a) the tendency to see a vertical line as longer than a horizontal one of the same length, thus when subjects are required to draw a vertical line equal in length to a horizontal they generally draw it shorter: three versions of this are to draw a vertical from the centre, at the end, or make a cross; (b) the Müller–Lyer illusion is the tendency to see a < bisecting a >→ line as falling to the right of centre; (c) in Zöllner illusions parallel lines overlaid by patterns of angular lines appear bent or converging; (d) the moon (and sun) appear larger on the horizon than when high in the sky.

36 The study of cross-cultural differences in sensitivity to the Müller–Lyer illusion later became a major research area for post-World War II perception theorists. See Segall et al. (1966) for an extensive discussion.

37 Using C. as the comparison note (256 cycles per second), the Aberdeen subjects were able to discriminate a difference of 7.6 c.p.s. as against Murray Islanders who could only manage 15.4 c.p.s.; the children performed better than the adults in both cases but the difference was maintained: 4.7 c.p.s. against 12.5 c.p.s. (RCAE 2, pp. 167–8).

38 Zwaardemaker's olfactometer proving unsatisfactory, he had to resort to various strength dilutions of Japanese camphor (familiar to the islanders), but olfactory strength of solution is not directly proportional to strength of dilution and because his distillation equipment left a smell from the metal condenser he had to use rainwater.

39 In a choice reaction-time experiment the subject has to identify a target stimulus among several presented, the simplest version being to identify one of two.

40 In 1901 Rivers also published two papers on the colour vision of Eskimos (1901b) and 'the natives of Upper Egypt' (1901c), followed by 'Observations on the vision of the Uralis and Shologas' (1903).

41 See Chapter 6 for discussion of Lévy-Bruhl.

42 Space precludes fuller discussion of this Congress here. The only other paper specifically Psychological in character was J. Gray (1911), a rather batty scientistic exercise in estimating the 'intellectual standing of different races and their respective opportunities for culture' on the basis of such things as university education rates, etc. Boas aired his views on the impermanence of human physical types; E. Finch was generally positive about 'The effects of racial miscegenation'; Sir Harry H. Johnston attempted a survey of 'The world position of the negro and negroid', which DuBois must have listened to with some bemusement before telling it like it was for 'The Negro race in the USA'. Most of the other presentations were on political and economic issues with regard to specific 'races' and nationalities.

43 The first ironisations of the term 'savage' I have come across are Tom Harrisson's title *Savage Civilisation* (1937) and Julius Lips's title *The Savage Hits Back* (1937).

44 For example, it would hardly be fair to accuse a writer of around 1900 who wrote 'The savage is in no way inferior to the civilised white man' of racism. This is the only way the thought could have been put. 'Savage' at this time seems in any case to refer primarily to a cultural level rather than psychological character, a usage introduced by

post-Darwinian social evolutionary theorists (such as L.H. Morgan) who identified the three stages of savagery, barbarism and civilisation.

45 Woodworth to Rivers 10.1.06 in HC 12034. I am assuming this is US style dating in which month precedes day. I have published this in G. Richards (1994).

46 Most notably in McDougall (1921). See below Chapter 6 for McDougall's later racism. More immediately McDougall, like Rivers, ventured into anthropology (notably C. Hose and W. McDougall, 1912).

47 See Royal Society item in HC 1021. A few minutes of the film survive.

48 Officially Woodworth was Superintendent of the Sections of Anthropometry and Psychometry under the Division of Anthropology, and Bruner his Assistant Superintendent.

49 In the same year he published a paper (Woodworth, 1910b) summarising the St Louis findings on colour perception which found no special inferiority in 'primitive' ability with regard to blues, although a general inferiority in colour discrimination across the spectrum. He argued against Rivers' physiological explanation for lack of names for blue, arguing that it was due to lack of need for such names (p. 333).

50 Boring (1942) makes no mention of Bruner's research. This is a little curious given the work's thoroughness, but it is possible that Boring was by then inclined to censor out race-differences research – as F. Samelson (1978) noticed, in the 1950 2nd edition of his *A History of Experimental Psychology* he dropped all reference to Yerkes's post-Great War race-differences interests, stressing instead his primate studies.

51 He describes the Pigmies as essentially parasitic scavengers on 'Kaffir' neighbours, on a par with dogs. If so they were not drawn from the Ituri forest dwelling Pigmies (generally known as BaMbuti) described by e.g. Colin Turnbull (1961), although the seasonally symbiotic relationship between these and neighbouring peoples may have been misinterpreted. He gives their tribal affiliations as three Batwas, two Batsubas and one Cheri Cheri, none of which are mentioned by Turnbull. Both Woodworth and Bruner are careful to refer to them on occasion as 'so-called Pigmies'. They were allegedly the first Pigmies to cross the Atlantic, and were brought from the Congo by a missionary.

52 This is especially ludicrous; as agriculturalists they must have been at least in the Mesolithic according to the contemporary social evolution scheme of things.

53 In his entry in Murchison (1932) Woodworth states of the St Louis research 'We examined about eleven hundred individuals . . .', this does not square with the published N's. The 'eleven hundred' may, however, include whites or subjects on tasks which were never reported.

54 That they were problematic in many other respects is undeniable, but they did not involve the high-tech electrical devices and the like which psychophysical studies required, being by and large paper-and-pencil tests.

Chapter 4

'Race' in US Psychology to 1945: I. The rise and nature of 'Race Psychology'

INTRODUCTION

The most intense exploration of psychological race differences, known as Race (or Racial) Psychology, was undertaken by US psychologists between 1910 and 1940. Historical coverage of this has so far been highly selective. In the following two chapters I attempt to unravel the unexpectedly complex nature and meaning of this episode.

Race Psychology's origins lie in a very specific historical context which largely determined its nature and fate. All knowledge is 'situated' in specific times and places – and none more so than racial 'knowledge'. If today, many believe such knowledge to be in principle impossible, it was otherwise in, for example, New York and Virginia in 1917. In these sites two issues had arisen which enabled psychologists to muster the resources (economic, ideological, scientific) to embark on the empirical investigation of 'race differences'. Taking slight chronological precedence was the 'Negro Education' question. Second was the immigration issue – settlement in the USA during the decade 1900–10 amounting to the largest voluntary migration in history.[1] The first of these was the longer lasting and has, in various guises, continued to dominate, if not monopolise, US Psychology's orientation to the issue. Some initial historical elucidation of this is especially necessary.[2]

During the post-Civil War 'Reconstruction' period, which lasted until about 1883, considerable governmental and philanthropic support had been forthcoming for the education of the African American population in the South towards full participation in the nation's socio-economic life. This aspiration proved vain. With the fall of the Hayes Presidency and mounting legal chicanery, white hegemony was firmly re-established, which the North acceded to with few qualms.[3] In the new circumstances black leadership had little option but to adapt as best it could. Under Booker T. Washington, the goal of socio-economic and political parity was abandoned and hopes pinned on a programme of separate, complementary, development. 'Negro' education was to focus on inculcating values of hard-work and self-respect and be vocationally oriented towards agricultural, domestic and industrial skills fitting pupils for the only modes of life open to them. A handful of all-black universities would supply the doctors and lawyers needed to service the southern African American community, while Booker T.

Washington's Tuskegee Institute and the older Hampton Institute became the leading sites for the new vocationally oriented education.

This policy was eagerly supported by religious philanthropic organisations, wary of identifying with more radical schemes. As funding sources, these charitable organisations became increasingly important, state funding for black education declining as segregationism entrenched itself. In comparison with white education every indicator, from per capita expenditure and teacher salaries to term lengths, shows a dramatic gulf between the two by 1910, a point we return to later. Two factors now sabotaged the ambitions of these educationists. In the background lay the rising scientific authority of the Scientific Racist image of the 'Negro'. At the end of the Civil War this was still hazily formulated, and the relevant literature primarily European. Support for the older US polygenist tradition had never been widespread, religion proving a major cultural stumbling block. By the 1880s however, Spencer's US disciples had succeeded in swinging the scientific argument. Extreme anti-'Negro' publications were numerous. Whites involved in educational fund-raising and policy making now tended to accept, even if reluctantly, that the average African American was incapable of benefiting from the kind of education normally provided for white children.

The second factor was more immediate: the economic context. At the time of liberation there were substantial numbers of skilled ex-slaves. Slave owners were never reluctant to exploit the economic value of their chattels – a high-grade carpenter or mechanic for example could be profitably hired out and also enhanced his owner's status. By the 1880s this group had all but disappeared, unable to withstand white competition in a free marketplace. This was exacerbated by the new modes of industrial mass production and the difficulty facing southern African Americans in gaining employment other than menial in factories where the white workforce was jealously guarding its interests. Taken alongside the sharecropping system under which most black farmers lived, maintained in permanent debt, this added up to a situation where there was little market for the skills of vocationally educated 'Negroes'. Those qualified in 'scientific farming' were unlikely to be able to acquire their own farms and could often end up merely teaching the subject again to a new, equally doomed, generation. The proportion of the workforce engaged in agriculture was in any case declining.

The broad effect of all this on African American morale was understandably extremely negative. It is perhaps arguable that the betrayal of the hopes raised by Reconstruction was actually more traumatic than the slavery experience itself – which by 1910 was already history to the under-45s. The recalcitrant 'Negro Education' problem would not go away, and constituted a major component in the so-called 'Negro Question'. How the 'question' was to be answered was a matter which defied consensus. In his *Through Afro-America* (1910) the English traveller William Archer, claiming to adopt a detached and unprejudiced perspective, identified four options: extinction of the Negro, tolerant co-existence without mingling (the 'Atlanta compromise' proposed by Booker Washington in 1895), obliteration of the 'colour line' by inter-marriage ('miscegenation') and geographical segregation into a separate state. The first was both immoral and unfeasible; the second, if temporarily achievable, unsustainable; and the third justifiably unacceptable to white race pride (his horror of a 'piebald' nation, amounting to a deterioration of the superior white stock, rather belying his claim of unprejudiced detachment). Archer advised the last. The 'back to Africa' option also had supporters in both communities.

Prior to World War I the problems intensified in the face of the early stirrings of a number of further changes. A few more radical voices were beginning to become audible (e.g. W.T. DuBois), migration to the North was rendering the topic of more genuinely national concern, while a small educated middle-class elite within the black community (often of house-slave origins and eager to differentiate itself from the rest) was starting to emerge. For all their efforts Southern whites could not halt the wider dynamics of economic and social forces affecting the nation as a whole. But they tried. A large literature of mainly Southern authored social commentary appeared as the 20th century got under way, variously alarmist, meliorative, defensive and desperate in tone. Demoralisation was not confined to the black community, but had extended, by the time we are considering, to their sympathisers and patrons in the white community too.

When psychologists began to research 'race differences' among children after 1910 they were thus entering a situation in which deep frustration and pessimism had become endemic. They initially aligned themselves with what may be described as a paternalistic, pro-segregationist, moderate conservative camp of white educators and philanthropists simultaneously wishing to improve the 'Negro' lot but unable to countenance challenging the established political and social order. This camp was effectively paralysed, caught between well-intentioned sympathy and fear of political radicalism, between its horror at the failure of the South to make proper use of the black labour force and its underlying convictions of general 'Negro' inferiority and belief in the validity of eugenics.[4] Psychology offered an ideologically 'neutral', respectably scientific, route for readdressing the intractable difficulties from a new angle – one which located the source of the problem safely at the individual psychological level.

One upshot of this was that after about 1917 US Psychologists came to devote relatively little time to openly elaborating any Scientific Racism rationale in research reports, adopting instead a more strictly empirical approach, attempting to identify race differences using experimental or psychometric methods. One might call it 'Empirical Racism'. Scientific Racism more often surfaces in occasional book-length monographs (such as Porteus and Babcock's *Temperament and Race*, 1926). Most of these would-be scientific early psychologists were in fact critical of the older physical anthropological and anecdotal approaches to the study of 'racial mental differences'.[5] Their own work however, while rejecting some earlier conclusions regarding specific traits, initially presented this as a scientific rectification of detail, rather than a departure from the entire doctrine. After all, any scientific project worth its salt has to refute *some* previous 'knowledge' in the field. Rivers' and Woodworth's work thus fell into place as a kind of ground-clearing exercise.

The second factor, immigration, is more straightforward. From 1913, and especially from about 1917, the 'Negro education' issue was supplemented, and for a time overshadowed, by eugenic anxieties regarding immigration, boosted by the

Nordicist doctrines of Madison Grant's highly successful *The Passing of the Great Race* (1916), with its concluding peroration against the 'maudlin sentimentalism' that has made America an 'asylum for the oppressed' and is 'sweeping the nation toward a racial abyss' (p. 228). This represents a much closer translation of contemporary European concerns across the Atlantic. In Europe the 'race' question had been couched in terms of national interests rather than migration – but the emanating messages of Nordic superiority over Slavs and 'Mediterraneans' raised alarm in the New World melting pot.[6] Now free Germans, Russians, Swedes, Irish, Scots and Poles, acquainted with the latest European race thinking, viewed with alarm the huddled masses of Sicilians, Italians, Portuguese, Jews and Slavs whose yearnings in this direction were as yet ungratified. Only in Britain, somewhat earlier, had similar fears surfaced over East European Jewish immigrants, but with one exception[7] this inspired no Psychological work. More explicit Scientific Racism thus resurfaced (e.g. in Brigham, 1923). H.H. Goddard, America's leading eugenicist psychologist, had tackled the topic as early as 1913, testing immigrants on Ellis Island,[8] but after 1918 the issue escalated, culminating in the 1924 Immigration Restriction Act. Among leading psychologists Terman, Yerkes and Thorndike may be noted as active in eugenic circles such as the Galton Society endorsing, though contributing little of their own to, Race Psychological research.[9]

White America thus saw itself beset on two racial fronts. On the one hand the legacy of slavery had laid upon it the responsibility of somehow managing a huge minority population of 'Negroes' – whom it now believed to be truly inferior in evolutionary terms. The fact that these included substantial numbers of 'mulattoes' and 'mixed race' people only made things worse – for these represented a route by which this inferior breed could irreversibly contaminate the pure white stock. On the other hand the land now also seemed imperilled by a flood of inferior European stock – inferior either racially or on eugenic grounds as being drawn from the 'dregs' of its source populations. Such a situation had not been foreseen by the Union's Enlightenment founders with their combination of blind egalitarianism (for whites) and insousiance about slavery's durability as an institution able to keep whites and 'Negroes' forever separated, notwithstanding the consequences of white male sexual peccadilloes. America's Manifest Destiny was being manifestly soured. We may now return to Race Psychology itself as it expresses and engages these collective psychological concerns.

AN OVERVIEW OF RACE-RELATED GENRES

Prior to 1910, Psychology's relative neglect of race partly reflects the discipline's nature during its US founding phase. Primarily interested in general psychological processes (such as memory or perception), it had no immediately obvious place for questions pertaining either to race differences or, even less, race prejudice. The topic lacked even a title. Various entries in Baldwin (1902–5) indicate that 'Race Psychology' initially designated 'the science of the evolution of mind in animals and man' – a usage ascribed to Spencer. Race differences were usually considered a minor aspect of 'Folk Psychology', a group of enquiries on the

Table 4.1 Summary of English language publication data 1909–40

	A	B	C	D	E	F	G	H	N
1909/10	8							1	9
	89							**11**	
1911/12	4	3						2	9
	44	**33**						**22**	
1913/14	16	2						2	20
	80	**10**						**10**	
1915/16	16	2			2			3	23
	70	**9**			**9**			**13**	
1917/18	19			2	1			4	26
	73			**8**	**4**			**15**	
1919/20	19	1					1	3	24
	79	**4**					**4**	**12.5**	
1921/22	35	1						2	38
	92	**3**						**5**	
1923/24	26	13	1		1			5	46
	57	**29**	**2**		**2**			**11**	
1925/26	53	12	6	3	3		2	5	84
	63	**14**	**7**	**4**	**4**		**2**	**6**	
1927/28	33	21	13	13	2		1	10	93
	35	**22.5**	**14**	**14**	**2**		**1**	**11**	
1929/30	23	14	10	11	2	3	2	8	73
	31.5	**19**	**14**	**15**	**3**	**4**	**3**	**11**	
1931/32	22	22	14	36	5	4	1	11	115
	19	**19**	**12**	**31**	**4**	**3**	**1**	**10**	
1933/34	22	21	16	29	8	4		10	110
	20	**19**	**14.5**	**26**	**7**	**4**		**9**	
1935/36	10	22	20	35	4	5		9	105
	9.5	**21**	**19**	**33**	**4**	**5**		**9**	
1937/38	14	20	20	35	21	3	1	17	130
	11	**15**	**15**	**21**	**16**	**2**	**0.8**	**13**	
1939/40	11	22	28	51	39	2	1	11	165
	6.5	**13.3**	**17**	**31**	**23.6**	**1.2**	**0.6**	**6.6**	
Total	331	176	128	215	88	21	9	103	1071
	30.9	**16.4**	**12**	**20**	**8.2**	**2.0**	**0.8**	**9.6**	

Notes: A – Race Psychology. B – Anti-race psychology. C – Prejudice/Attitudes. D – Applied/Intra-racial. E – Culture and Personality. F – Genetics of colour blindness etc. G – Non-white autobiographies etc. H – Other: mostly sociological or historical receiving citations in Psychological literature and *Psychological Abstracts*. This does not include physical anthropology/genetics except where bearing on psychological issues.

Bold figures: %.

Anthropology/Psychology boundary, but occasionally appear as part of 'Comparative Psychology', referring then, as now, primarily to animal psychology. In Rand's 1905 Bibliography (Baldwin, 1905, Vol. 3), such few entries as there are on 'race' are under 'Individual and Social' or 'Comparative', and the entries in Vol. 2 under 'Race' comprise a general entry (by Jastrow and Baldwin) on the history of the concept in anthropology and an extremely brief one on 'Race Psychology', in the aforementioned Spencerian sense. Only in the increasingly highly charged context just described did Race Psychology gather momentum.

Between 1909 and 1940 a vast amount of English language discourse on race was published by psychologists, and in neighbouring disciplines such as anthropology and sociology, which is relevant to our present concerns. In order to obtain a clearer overview of the nature of this material well over 1,000 titles of books, journal papers and articles were identified. For the period 1909–40 they may be classified into seven broad camps (though the boundaries are not entirely clear-cut on occasion).[10] (See Table 4.1.)

Psychology

This aimed at empirical identification of innate race differences in psychology. These ranged from intelligence (the most salient and best remembered) to, for example, personality traits, colour preferences, psychopathology, memory and musical ability. The themes of child development and sex differences were also often incorporated. Subjects were usually infants, children and adolescents up to college student age, though criminals, psychiatric patients and other adult groups sometimes figured. Some of the earlier texts classified here are of a more orthodox Scientific Racist and less empirical character. Three underlying projects may be identified.

The earliest, as we have seen, is educational. Understanding innate racial differences can, it is argued, guide educational policy regarding the curricula and teaching modes appropriate to different racial groups, and the wisdom or otherwise of multi-racial education. This is adumbrated in the work by G.S. Hall discussed previously, African Americans sometimes being viewed as representatives of an 'adolescent race', especially in earlier papers.

The second, which flourished during the years 1917–26, is the more explicitly eugenic project of informing immigration policy by identifying which European and Asian races are undesirable and need to be restricted or excluded. Sometimes eugenicists also considered racial proclivities towards psychopathology and crime, but (unlike in Germany in the 1930s) this had little *overt* impact in terms of racist legislation (although eugenics did affect the policies adopted on such topics generally). Existing historical accounts of Race Psychology invariably concentrate almost exclusively on this eugenics dimension.

A third underlying project is to render Scientific Racism itself more scientific and sophisticated by mapping race differences in greater detail, offering more physiologically and genetically advanced explanations for them and developing methodologies to eliminate environmental sources of variance. This gave added significance to studies of 'race-mixing', particularly in connection with the 'mulatto hypothesis' that abilities of those of mixed race were intermediate between those of parental stocks. (An earlier, and frankly rather bizarre, example is F.H. Giddings' (1901) analysis of the US population into psychological classes.)[11]

Race Psychology research utilised the full range of psychometric and psychological tests currently available, from the Porteus Maze test to the Seashore music ability tests, from the Downey Will-Temperament scale to various forms of the Binet intelligence test itself, plus school achievement measures. It goes into decline (both relative and absolute) after 1930[12] (Table 4.1). Race Psychology was dominated by US psychologists but the Chinese and Japanese produced a number of papers on Asian racial differences during the 1920s using translated adaptations of US intelligence tests. I have largely ignored these in the discussions which follow. A handful of British and Indian papers also belong in the Race Psychology genre. Post-1930 texts classified here tend to differ from the earlier ones (a) in containing a higher proportion of non-US authored work, (b) in the lower level, in US work, of experimental empirical research, and (c) a frequently more cautious or moderate attitude to the interpretation of empirical findings. The US decline of what we might term the 'strong Race Psychology programme' is thus if anything somewhat more rapid than the data indicate.[13]

Anti-race differences, anti-racism

From early in the century some, like W.I. Thomas, John Dewey and Franz Boas, were disputing the race-difference hypothesis (including Harvard's Josiah Royce, William James's close friend).[14] During the 1920s this opposition mounts. Their arguments are of four basic kinds. First, that any differences can be accounted for environmentally. Secondly, outside Psychology, there is the occasional philosophical or ideological argument that egalitarianism is a moral imperative unaffected by empirical evidence. Thirdly, there are those arguing on methodological grounds that innate race differences either have not been, or cannot in principle be, demonstrated. Fourthly, and in the end most profoundly, there is the argument that 'race' is an unscientific category, a myth for rationalising oppression and injustice. This last line, though voiced by some earlier writers (such as Finot) becomes prominent in the late 1930s, bolstered both by the spectre of the rise of Nazism and by invocation of contemporary developments in genetics. Leading anti-racist figures are the social psychologist Otto Klineberg and the anthropologist Margaret Mead.[15] Not all in this camp were equal in their degree of hostility, they varied from those as yet simply unconvinced to those whose opposition was extremely intense.[16] The heatedness of the debate gradually increased from the mid-1920s onwards. This opposition camp is explored in Chapter 5.

Publications in this category first exceed Race Psychology ones in 1931 and consistently do so after 1934. These two camps represent, if you want to be Kuhnian about it (but see below p. 123), the 'Race Psychology paradigm' and those seeking its overthrow. On this model Race Psychology's phase of 'normal science' spanned, roughly, 1910–33.

Prejudice and attitude research

The first alternative 'paradigm', slowly expanding from the late 1920s, radically redefined the problem. Instead of the innate psychological character of races, it was individuals' difficulties in overcoming their 'race prejudices' which lay at the heart of racial conflict and tension, thus turning the issue on its head.[17] Whereas Race Psychology arose in the psychometric and experimental wings of the discipline, this new approach emerged in Social Psychology and Sociology (and often among non-Anglo-Saxons).[18] Scales for measuring race attitudes were devised, and developmental studies undertaken into the child's acquisition of 'race consciousness'. Both the nature of race prejudice and its impact on its target groups were investigated. This camp, discussed in Chapter 5, was fairly diverse in orientation both theoretically and methodologically, but unified in rejecting the pragmatic value of research on innate race differences, the existence of which its members, by and large, rejected. The primary task was ameliorating 'race relations', a social and educational task to which race difference research could make no discernible positive contribution and some only too discernible negative ones.

Texts classified here begin appearing in significant numbers around 1927, maintaining a consistent if variable presence until the mid-1930s when they increase and usually outnumber those on Race Psychology. They did not though rise much further during the 1930s, the hey-day coming in post-war Social Psychology.

Applied, comparative and intra-race research

Behind all this during the 1930s was a burgeoning of practical down-to-earth research in applied fields such as education, social work and clinical Psychology addressing the problems confronting specific ethnic groups. This research was primarily (though not exclusively) 'intra-racial' rather than 'inter-racial' in character and appeared mostly in journals such as *Journal of Negro Education*, *Smith College Studies in Social Work*, and *The Journal of Criminal Law and Criminology*. While such work sometimes carries titles ostensibly of a Race Psychology kind, the results invariably report failure to find statistically significant race differences (if any at all) or, if found, they are interpreted in environmentalist terms (e.g. Sukuo and Williamson, 1938). (Occasionally though one comes across intra-racial papers the rationale for which is quite enigmatic, for example Eagleson and Taylor's 1940 'A study of chord preference in a group of Negro women'.) Also included here are some psychiatric studies which, while focusing on 'the Negro' are purely descriptive, drawing no explicit conclusions regarding innate racial causes (for example, Greene and DuPree, 1939 and Parker et al., 1939).

The proliferation of work in this category (which has received little historical attention) reflects how far US Psychology had, by the 1930s, penetrated the culture's everyday social management functions. Race Psychology was simply irrelevant to the problems that applied psychologists were being required to tackle at this grass-roots level. As noted before, interventionist roles naturally tend to be associated with environmentalist perspectives. Also of course the psychologists themselves were no longer an entirely ethnically homogeneous group. This too will be discussed further in Chapter 5.

This category rose from being virtually unknown pre-1925 to exceeding all others (and accounting for at least 25% of the titles) from 1931 onwards except in 1934 (when it is second to Anti-Race Psychology papers), nearly doubling from

1939 (18) to 1940 (33), at which point it accounted for almost 40% of the identified texts.

Anthropological Psychology and 'Culture and Personality' approaches

US cultural and social anthropologists such as Franz Boas, Edward Sapir, Margaret Mead, Ruth Benedict and M.F. Ashley Montagu were in the forefront of academic anti-racism. Their own anthropological work was used to support this position and during the 1930s increasingly informed the work of psychologists in the personality and child development fields. The psychoanalytically based anthropology of writers such as Geza Róheim and George Devereux was also influential. By the end of the 1930s the 'Culture and Personality' school of Kardiner, Kluckhohn, and Henry Murray was beginning to coalesce, incorporating anthropologists like Mead and Benedict. This contrasts with the British situation (see Chapter 7) where relationships between Psychology and Anthropology had atrophied following the death of W.H.R. Rivers. Anglophone social and cultural anthropology was, by the 1930s, theoretically at least, anti-racist, although when working in the field, British anthropologists were certainly inclined to compromise with the racist assumptions and agendas of colonial administrators.[19] French anthropologists such as Durkheim and Lévy-Bruhl who were more inclined towards inherently racialist theories of 'primitive mentality' were translated into English but had little contemporary impact on US Psychology (see Chapter 6).[20]

The crux of the matter is that the new cross-cultural approach to ethnic psychological diversity, fusing Anthropology and Psychology, was offering a far richer, better informed, more humane and ideologically congenial way of dealing with the 'race' issue than anything Race Psychology could offer. From this perspective, psychological diversity emerged from culture and social structure and was explicable in historical and environmentalist terms (although the Marxist implications of this were discreetly ignored and the individual generally remained the unit of analysis). New developments in genetics were also being increasingly noted by physical anthropologists, although Nancy Stepan suggests that each camp was inhibiting the other in making the final move of abandoning the race concept altogether.

While occasional earlier papers in the Boasian spirit occur, this category only begins making headway around 1930, overtaking Race Psychology in 1938 but rising to second place in 1940. Again we reserve this genre for the next chapter.

Physiological Psychology

One area where race difference research persisted was the study of the epidemiology of three specific conditions: colour blindness, PTC (phenyl-thio-carbamide) -taste blindness and, to a lesser extent, Down's syndrome ('Mongolism' or 'Mongolianism' as it was still being called). This cannot I think be classified as racist *per se*, being indeed one aspect of the broader programme of global investigation into

the distribution of genetically determined traits (such as blood group) which ultimately subverted the notion of races as genetically unitary entities. In the case of
Down's syndrome it was found to be extremely rare among blacks, W.H. Thompson (1939) locating only 21 'colored' cases from 1,777 inmates of 45 institutions
nation-wide. Nor, on either of the other traits, were differences found which could
conceivably denote racial inferiority.[21] Garth (1931c) did, however, suggest that
colour blindness was relevant to the notion of an evolutionary hierarchy of races
since it arises when 'the genesis of color vision is incomplete' (p. 2) and therefore
its incidence should, if that notion was correct, be higher among the 'lower' races.
Neither his, nor anybody else's, colour-blindness research confirmed this, among
Fijians and American Indians it was if anything rarer than among whites. This
category begins appearing in 1930, contributing one to five publications a year
thereafter.

Black-authored autobiographies and anti-racist journalism

Although not academic in character, a number of non-fictional black-authored
and pro-black texts were published during the period, of which white psychologists took some cognisance and which affected the prevailing attitudes of liberal
white intellectuals. Not all are included in the figures given here; for example
H.L. Mencken's *American Mercury* included articles such as J.W. Johnson's
'A Negro looks at Prejudice' (1928) and A. Holsey's 'Learning how to be black'
(1929). R.R. Moton's *What the Negro Thinks* (1929) and H. Odum's fictional
Rainbow Round My Shoulder (1928) clearly impressed T.R. Garth, the most prolific Race Psychologist.[22] Also included here are the occasional native American
autobiographies which appeared in anthropological journals or books (e.g. Dyk's
Son of Old Man Hat of 1938). The black journals *Crisis* and *Messenger*, as well as
the radical *Opportunity*, provided the principal popular media for African American aspirations throughout most of this period. Even so, black voices were barely
audible within Psychology at this time, far less so than white female voices. After
1932 the *Journal of Negro Education* partially broke the silence, but primarily
addressed an intra-racial professional audience of black educators and its editorial
policy was initially against desegregating education. American Indian autobiographies were typically mediated by white anthropologists (e.g. P.Radin's *Crashing
Thunder: the autobiography of an American Indian*, 1926, and Dyk, 1938, just
cited). While white anti-racists keenly and effectively spoke on their behalf,
African Americans and native Americans were practically excluded from academic
discourse, and we are still dealing with an essentially white male discipline. Even
when black authors get into academic print (as in *The Journal of Negro Education*)
this is at the price of conforming to a white mode of discourse. By contrast, in the
study of Jewish problems and, after 1939, anti-semitism, researchers did tend to
be Jewish.

Since no systematic sampling of popular journalism and autobiography was
undertaken texts in this category are seriously underrepresented in Table 4.1. It is
though worth noting that the earlier (1923–26) texts classified under B in the table
contain a relatively high proportion from *Opportunity* and *Crisis*, rather than

academic journals, even though the authors are often academics (e.g. H.A. Miller, 1923).[23]

Miscellaneous

This includes various non-Psychological texts cited in Psychological works or noticed by *Psychological Abstracts*. Many are sociological and historical studies of African American life and culture, including works by Melville Herskovits, E.B. Reuter and the black sociologist E.F. Frazier. The frequency of these 'fringe' texts oscillates around 15% throughout the period.

Psychology's engagements with race therefore took several forms during this period, and only Race Psychology itself pursued an approach immediately recognisable as racialist. The relationships between these camps may be summarised fairly simply. Race Psychology constitutes a starting point against which there had, from the beginning, been various 'anti-race differences' reactions. Two alternative 'paradigms' then emerge in the late 1920s: first, in Social Psychology, the study of race prejudice and attitudes and then among child psychologists and personality theorists a cross-cultural, anthropologically oriented, 'Culture and Personality' approach. Meanwhile, as Applied Psychology expands and black voices become more audible beyond academia, a large corpus of studies pragmatically addressing the practical problems of ethnic minority groups is produced (in which the Psychology/Sociology borderline is often blurred). Distinct from any of these, but in the end fuelling anti-racist arguments, is a small body of psychophysiological studies addressing colour blindness, PTC taste-blindness and Down's syndrome rates, these constituting the Psychological end of a spectrum of studies of the global distribution of genetically determined physiological traits.

This classification is more of texts than of authors, since many writers contributed to more than one and others shifted their allegiance over time, particularly away from Race Psychology. Within most camps, writings range from specialist research reports to methodological, theoretical and popular review papers, magazine articles and books. There are of course texts which cross boundaries and others which are difficult to place. Nonetheless, given the sample size, the validity of the overall picture provided by the figures is unlikely to be seriously affected by misclassifications.

We now turn in more depth to Race Psychology, in which English-speaking modern Psychology took its most racist form.

RACE PSYCHOLOGY

In outline, the plot of the story is as follows: around 1910–14 the advent of intelligence testing triggers an immediate flurry of interest in comparing 'Negro' and white scores among schoolchildren, thus hooking Psychology firmly into the, by then stalled, 'Negro Education' debate. The subsequent rapid expansion in the number of psychological tests and the advent of group tests consolidates this. This rise is reinforced by eugenic concerns about the quality of south European and Asian immigrants. By 1925, at least 13 different 'races' (rising to over 30 by 1930) have been studied, as well as various 'mulatto', 'mixed blood' or 'mixed race' groups. Confidence was boosted by the Army Alpha and Beta test results (discussed below). Research peaks around 1925–8, by which time race psychologists are facing growing criticism (Category B in Table 4.1). They initially respond by striving for ever tighter methodological rigour, but ultimately this only exacerbates their difficulties. There was also, from the beginning, a minor strand of clinical work on race differences in psychopathology.[24] As the emancipationist struggle intensifies, a number of psychologists and sociologists turn their attention to 'race prejudice', attitudes and inter-race perception (Category C). Initially this is seen as a subdivision within Race Psychology[25] but their mutual incompatibility becomes increasingly clear: the supposed, highly evaluatively loaded, psychological differences between races cannot be studied except as part of an intrinsically racist project, promoting the very social pathology which researchers on attitudes and prejudice seek to combat. In the early 1930s interest in the plight of African Americans and other minority groups increases (Categories D and G). By 1934 firm belief in innate differences is declining rapidly among psychologists. By 1940 classic 'race differences' research has dwindled to minor occasional papers – and as mentioned earlier many 1930s papers with titles suggesting that they are of the orthodox kind report findings of 'no differences', a rare result indeed during the 1920s.[26] In 1935 Klineberg (1935a, b) publishes two highly effective critiques of Race Psychology and soon the anthropologists Ashley Montagu and Ruth Benedict are attacking the concept of 'race' as devoid of scientific validity (as are many geneticists and biologists), proposing alternative terms such as 'ethnic group' and 'caste'. Meanwhile an environmentalist 'Culture and Personality' project is emerging at the Psychology–Anthropology boundary (Category E).

Race Psychology also faced difficulties within the discipline as too dogmatic an insistence on the innateness of race differences ran counter to the prevailing environmentalist behaviourist trend (ironically, South Carolina-born J.B. Watson, Behaviourism's founder, was personally quite unselfconsciously racist).[27]

Who were the 'Race psychologists'? While Woodworth (1910a) was the first major American psychologist to take an empirical interest in the issue, aside from a review paper in 1916 he rarely returned to it in print during his post-Great War years of eminence.[28] F.G. Bruner's 1908 monograph on primitive hearing was the only important pre-1910 US text. H.W. Odum's 'Social and mental traits of the negro: Research into the conditions of the negro in Southern towns' (1910) may be taken as the subdiscipline's starting point, and by 1916 numerous papers had set the pattern for subsequent work, those by Alice Strong (1913), Marion Mayo (1913), and G.O. Ferguson Jr (1916) being particularly important. Its leading figure during Race Psychology's prime, publishing over 40 papers on race issues between 1919 and 1939, as well as a book, *Race Psychology* (1931b), was Woodworth's protegé Thomas R. Garth of the University of Denver, though his later work can no longer be considered Race Psychology. A second major figure was Australian-born S.D. Porteus of the University of Hawaii. His position was at heart a fairly hard-line Scientific Racism, and though forever hedged with qualifications and gestures towards moderation, his position never wavered. J. Peterson (George Peabody College for Teachers, Nashville) was considered the leading researcher on 'Negro'–white differences.[29] Numerous psychologists published one or two 'race differences' papers, while C. Murchison, later one of the most important organisational figures in US Psychology, published extensively on race differences among, and racial traits of, criminals in 1925–6 but never returned to the topic again. C.C. Brigham's *American Intelligence* (1923) was a key text in promoting the race-differences case, both regarding African Americans and south vs. north European 'races' in the context of immigration policy. Another monograph which attracted attention for a while was D. M. Hirsch's 'A study of natio-racial mental differences' (1926) in which he sought to replace the traditional concept of 'race' by the notion of 'natio-racial' differences which, while innately based, evolve and develop over time as various 'racial' groups in a population merge, as well as by natural selection and mutation. The institutional affiliations of the Race Psychologists were rarely with the high prestige elite universities.

Defining 'Race Psychology' as Psychological research and theorising committed to belief in innate race differences in psychology of whatever kind, I have identified 331 publications between 1909 and 1940 (Table 4.1) While US-centred this research was not, as noted earlier, entirely confined to North America. As well as the Japanese and Chinese work previously alluded to, isolated papers are published originating from South Africa (e.g. M.L. Fick, 1929), East Africa (e.g. R.A.C. Oliver 1932a, b, c, 1933–4), India (e.g. Das Gupta and Basu, 1936), the West Indies (where the eugenicist C.B. Davenport was particularly active) and Britain (but see Chapter 7 on the complexities of the British scene).

My impression is that until about 1930 the tone of the academic opposition was relatively unheated and concentrated on methodology, with few critics actually challenging the good faith in which race-difference research was being conducted or outrightly accusing researchers of 'race prejudice'. Only after 1930 do white critics really start becoming conscious of the inherent racism of their colleagues' approach.

Let us now examine the major Race Psychology research in more detail.

The beginnings of Race or 'Racial' Psychology: 1910–16

Howard W. Odum (1884–1954)

We may start with the 1910 monograph by G.S. Hall's student, Howard W. Odum, published in the series *Studies in History, Economics and Public Law*; 'Social and mental traits of the negro. Research into the conditions of the negro race in Southern towns. A study in race traits, tendencies and prospects'. Much of this 300-page work concerns social issues of no direct relevance here, but his initial discussion of Negro[30] education and Chapter 7, 'The emotions of the negro and their relation to conduct', mark an apt beginning to the story. On initial reading this is a pretty offensive text – almost devoid of academic references it seemingly consists of an unremitting, uninhibited and relentless outpouring of racial bile.

The chapter on education paints a dire picture: less than a third of the Negro children in the Southern states are enrolled, most attending less than six months of the year (p. 25). Their schools 'are not producing and have not produced results which were expected of them' (p. 23). He then launches into a tirade against the quality of both teachers ('The negro teacher has little reasoning power or depth of originality', p. 33, 'lack of moral strength on the part of women teachers', p. 40) and children (their 'minds are so dense that they can learn scarcely anything', p. 37). There is, incidentally, a passing remark that 'experiments with negro children seem to show that the age of brightness is later than that of greatest ability' (p. 38), though to which experiments he is referring is unclear – I have identified none in the Psychological literature at this date.[31] Imitativeness, propensity for rote-learning, early maturation and cessation of development, 'vivid but general and vague imaginations' (p. 37) and the like are predictably reeled off. Odum lowers his locks yet further:

> The negro has little home conscience or love of home, no local attachment of the better sort.
>   He has no pride of ancestry, and he is not influenced by the lives of great men. The negro has few ideals and perhaps no lasting adherence to an aspiration toward real worth. He has little conception of the meaning of virtue, truth, honor, manhood, integrity. He is shiftless, untidy, and indolent; he would live 'coolly in the shadow of his skin'.
>   He does not know the value of his word or the meaning of words in general.
>   (p. 39)

Older Negroes, he ruefully observes, are less cheerful than formerly and 'a spirit of moroseness and sullenness is developing' (p. 40). If this is not bad enough, educated Negroes are 'not a force for good in the community but for evil' (p. 41), their 'moral natures are miserably perverted' (p. 42).

The only redeeming feature is that Odum does have an eye for double-binds: 'It is complained that they learn too much, and it is complained that they cannot learn at all . . .' (p. 45), and they are encouraged to imitate whites then condemned for doing so (p. 47). He also understands that white-oriented textbooks, especially elementary readers, alienate black children and need to be replaced. Odum's treatment of 'Negro education' clearly reflects the strong contemporary feeling of disappointment, impatience and even despair with the whole topic. His account of the abysmal quality of all facets of black education should be kept in mind when considering the studies of Strong and Ferguson.

In the 'Emotions of the negro' chapter Odum becomes, if anything, more extreme, even allowing for his qualification that the 'statements are only tentative pending the final results of experimental studies' (p. 238). After detailed accounts of the 'negro's' fear, anger, and 'unreasonable abuse of sexual license' (p. 260), Odum identifies six chief characteristics (pp. 274–5). These are: (a) . . . 'easily *responds to stimuli*' and thus is '*controlled by present impulses*' resulting in '*lack of restraint*', (b) 'this free response *tends always to pleasure*', (c) 'the Negro *tends to carry all responses to an extreme*', which 'exhausts and degenerates his vital powers', (d) '*little capacity for sustained control*', (e) 'he does not, therefore, lend himself to the *development of deep and permanent qualities through the working out of essential processes*', (f) 'he is therefore *superficial and irresponsible*' (all italics in original). And then, after this unrelenting catalogue of flaws he suddenly switches tack and begins praising 'the negro' for his 'great plasticity and much promise' (p. 275), his 'flowing consciousness', 'mental imagery of unusual vividness', 'wonderful spontaneity', 'quick response in repartee', 'richness of folk-songs' and so forth. Odum does in fact realise that much of the situation has arisen from the 'confusions and inconsistencies of the way [the 'negro' race] has been treated' (p. 262) and professes to believe that there is 'no need for pessimism' (p. 265), actually ending on a fairly up-beat note regarding the possibility of American civilisation's potential ability to cope with 'the adjustment of the relations between different races' (p. 297).

Additional mention must be made of the Appendix by Thomas P. Bailey, Superintendent of Schools in Memphis, who seems to be that strange creature, an anti-hereditarian segregationist. What is interesting for us is his plea for scientific study of the whole issue: 'Let us have this Negro Question studied' (p. 301, in capitals in original), 'Let us take the Negro Question out of politics. Let us put the Negro question into science, and science into the Negro question' (ibid.).

> It is science and science alone . . . that can prepare us for the doing of this Nation's greatest duty – the solution of this problem, so as to free two unallied peoples and make the states of this union *United States* indeed and in truth! (p. 302, italics in original)

It is to such voices that Race Psychology is initially in large part a response.

What are we to make of Odum's treatise? While painting a monstrous picture of the contemporary US 'Negro' and 'his' lot, it is far too detailed to be dismissed as pure fantasy. My initial reading was that Odum had failed to recognise that he was describing something rather worse than he could appreciate. Perhaps what he saw as typical racial traits were symptoms of a kind of collective 'post-traumatic stress disorder', and the 'double-binds' he identified had had repercussions more far-reaching than he knew. This reading, I subsequently suspected, was to fall into the trap of opting for the 'damaged Negro' stereotype. Perhaps an alternative reading would be that he was Eurocentrically describing what was in fact a fairly vigorous alternative culture whose departures from white cultural norms he could only view negatively. On the other hand, as discussed earlier, the years 1900–10 represented a nadir in the fortunes of the African American population. While, taken in isolation, this text appears to be the product of a pathological Negro-phobe, Odum's subsequent career strongly belies this impression. A third reading thus suggests itself – that Odum was deliberately, and provocatively, painting as negative a picture as possible in order to communicate the seriousness of the current African American situation. He subsequently published numerous socio-logical works on the South of an increasingly moderate nature, as well as the fic-tional *Rainbow Round My Shoulder* which attempted to communicate the African American plight at a popular level. In the mid-1930s he is writing that one of the errors of sociology is the 'assumption that races are inherently different rather than group products of differentials due to the cumulative power of Folk-regional and cultural development', and became actively involved in promoting the anti-racist cause.[32] He and Paul Green created a centre for 'racial studies' at the University of North Carolina, highly praised by, for example, Weatherford and Johnson (1934) for its work on 'Negro' 'folk life, folk music and . . . drama' (p. 511).[33]

While Odum's position thus remains somewhat unresolved, the amount of attention given to psychological issues, its frequent citation and his acknowledgements to G.S. Hall and Giddings justify us in identifying this as the first, if not unanticipated, US Race Psychology text, along perhaps with Woodworth (1910a). It was however non-experimental, and while wide-ranging drew primarily on the author's personal experience and discussions.

Three studies of race differences among children

Three pieces of research on race differences in children now appear, referred to throughout Race Psychology's career as among its founding texts: Mayo (1913), Strong (1913) and Ferguson (1916). We must examine these in a little detail since they display, with unself-conscious clarity, several features which became typical of Race Psychology discourse. I will say relatively little about their actual results, although Mayo's require some attention, since they conform to the general pattern, maintained thereafter, of 'Negro' (or 'colored') underperformance in relation to whites. Of more interest to us now are the kinds of argument and rhetoric used by the authors, the implicit and explicit attitudes they display, and the significance they ascribe to their findings. Several similar pieces of research had been done by 1916 (notably by Pyle) to which reference will be made en route.

Marion J. Mayo (1913) 'The mental capacity of the American Negro'

This 70-page monograph falls into three sections: an introductory review of the issue to date, a research report on school performance in integrated New York schools, and a lengthy conclusion on the nature of race differences. Methodologically it is fairly rigorous, with no immediately glaring design flaws (although the statistics are all descriptive, with no probability levels being calculated). Since the schools are integrated and education compulsory, performance differences cannot, Mayo argues, be ascribed to environmental factors. The data are performance marks on various courses over four years (eight terms) of high school. (One feature of this does deserve immediate comment: the pass mark is 60, and Mayo does not notice that (white) teachers may well be more reluctant to fail white pupils.) While differences vary considerably between courses, black children never outperform white ones. In the event he concludes that black scholastic efficiency is 76% that of whites – a far better figure than those reported from segregated Southern schools, but nonetheless sufficiently poor for him to assert that the research confirms their innate inferiority. He was unable to test the 'mulatto hypothesis' for practical reasons. The difference is insufficient to warrant separate schooling, but only just.

Several points must be made about the severity of Mayo's avowedly 'moderate' conclusions. First, like other contemporary white researchers, he cannot grasp the scale of the black handicap. This general blinkeredness occurs *even though the problem is acknowledged in relation to specific issues*. Thus poor performance on 'commercial' subjects 'may be' due to 'present social conditions or to differences in race experience, or both' (p. 40). 'Very likely, too, the practical value of such training appeals less strongly to the colored pupil, so that his interest and effort are, in consequence, less actively aroused' (ibid.). This complacency is captured in the following:

> But in as much as everything in the power of educator, philanthropist, and law giver has been done for the equalization of opportunity, it is hard to escape the conclusion that the fundamental explanation of the difference in scholastic standing is to be found mainly in the factor of race heredity. (p. 67)

The assumption that the educational arena can be considered in isolation from the total cultural situation of the African American typifies such research at this period. Even so, overall, 'the median mark of the 150 cases of white pupils in all subjects combined is 66; and of the 150 cases of colored pupils 62, a difference of 4 points, or 4 per cent' (p. 28). To our eyes this difference cannot sensibly be ascribed to any sources other than cultural ones – including lower identification with, and engagement of, black pupils by white teachers.[34] In short, the data are actually highly ambiguous in their implications, and hardly legitimise the strong line taken in the paper's other sections, to which we turn next.

Mayo's position is not entirely without confusion, although clear enough at the end of the day. He scorns earlier physiognomic views of relative racial standing, recognises the power of some of the opposition's arguments and accepts those findings of Rivers and Woodworth which refute older assumptions: racial differences in mental traits do not 'now appear so striking and obvious as they were formerly supposed to be' (p. 6). But 'the estimates hitherto made of racial differences in mental traits have always proceeded on a very slender basis of relevant and carefully ascertained fact' (p. 7). This is where Psychology comes in – 'carefully devised mental tests' and 'comparison of the relative attainment and efficiency of different racial groups . . . under like conditions' are what is required (ibid.), 'it is confidently to be expected that racial differences in mental traits will eventually submit themselves to exact description and measurement' (p. 8). (The notion of 'racial differences' 'submitting themselves' is an interesting one!) In this context he can claim 'that the conclusions derived from this study are, for the most part, coincident with views that have long been of general acceptance. They differ widely . . . however, in the way in which they have been obtained . . . They are based upon numerical data – upon measured facts' (p. 9).

How though does he counter sociological and anthropological arguments that all may be explained culturally? Here we encounter what at first glance seems a remarkable piece of back-handed logic. For this case to hold its proponents must 'also give some positive evidence that mental inequality actually does not exist among them' (p. 55).

It seems quite clear, then, that the fact that different rates of human progress and different degrees of civilization may be explained without the assumption of the mental inequality of different races and peoples does not prove such inequality not to exist. (ibid.)

This became a popular line of argument. What it signifies is a profound disagreement on the default explanation. For egalitarians the ball is in the inegalitarians' court – race differences need be invoked only when all other options have been exhausted. For Mayo and the inegalitarians it is the reverse, that until the contrary is *positively* proved we must assume race differences as a significant factor in addition to obvious cultural and historical ones. Mayo devotes much of his 'Conclusion' to elaborating on this. He musters all the traditional arguments about the brain, concluding that although the evidence is equivocal the balance lies with those who argue for innate brain differences. Earlier closure of African skull sutures, the occipital lengthening of the dolichocephalic (long-headed) Negro skull (unlike that of long-headed Europeans) indicating a 'preponderance of the lower mental powers' (according to Brinton, 1901), and findings that in 'civilized boys and girls' there is a growth in the 'association fibres' after 18 years of age, are all summoned up. While they must be 'subjected to the more rigid tests of present-day scientific methods', '. . . it is hard to escape the conclusion that they are not without some basis in fact'.[35] 'That such differences, which have been so often asserted and reiterated by numerous investigators should be absolutely without foundation seems hardly credible' (p. 58). The key statement is really the following:

Not only then does it seem admissible to assume the existence of mental inequality between the races to account for the various facts in our human relationships, but it would seem that apriori considerations, in view of our knowledge of human evolution,[36] would make no other assumption tenable. (p. 62)

Another vein he enthusiastically mines is the 'great man' theory of history. This too was a commonplace. Even if the 'coloured races' overlap substantially with the white in ability, it is their inability to produce the rare genius which in the end dooms them (along with women) to cultural inferiority. 'It is by the production of these highly gifted individuals that social progress and racial supremacy are assured' (p. 70). The assumption that races are distinct entities with different destinies is thus absolutely fundamental to Mayo's world-view.

Finally, the more immediate objectives of Mayo's labours are explicitly economic. 'The facts make it plain that the burden of education falls much more heavily upon those communities having a large proportion of colored population' (p. 46). Expenditure 'would probably be on an average not less than a fourth or fifth greater per unit of colored population' (ibid.). Even here, he can suddenly out of the blue say, 'Another great drawback to the teacher's work, it may here be pointed out, is that the social and economic ideals of the colored race are not such as to inspire effort and perseverance in the acquisition of knowledge' (p. 50).

Mayo's monograph is thus noteworthy in several respects. First in its clear spelling out of Race Psychology's aspirations, namely to refine rather than controvert the Scientific Racism orthodoxy. Secondly in his deployment of a number of arguments which become engrained in Race Psychology, particularly the assumption of race differences as the default explanation, and the belief that environmental factors are, methodologically, easily eliminable. Thirdly, his pose of moderation in relation to earlier views lacking clear empirical scientific bases. Fourthly the claim that such research has immediate value for those determining educational and economic policy. He accepts at the outset that the white feeling of racial superiority 'is a feeling "bred in the bone," and so strong that it can hardly be eradicated' (pp. 1–2). But there *is* a measurable degree of mental difference – and he closes by saying, 'And this is believed to be the view that will be ultimately gained from a purely scientific study of the question, stripped, on the one hand, of philanthropic considerations, and, on the other, *of racial bias*' (p. 70, my italics). Clearly Race Psychologists can eradicate their 'bred in the bone' feeling of white superiority even while failing to see that this underpins the entire exercise!

Alice C. Strong (1913) 'Three hundred fifty white and colored children measured by the Binet–Simon measuring scale of intelligence: a comparative study'[37]

This appears to be the first paper to apply the Binet–Simon scale (or any other psychometric instrument) in the context of race differences, certainly the first to do so on a large scale. Written against the background of work by Goddard (on 'mental defectives') and Terman,[38] it is more modest in tone than Mayo's, being 'offered as a slight contribution to the widespread experimentation now being made' (p. 486), and while studying race differences, is equally intended to shed light on the reliability and arrangement of the test itself. (Strong uses Goddard's 1911 revision of the test, slightly modified for practical reasons.) Her South Carolina subjects were 225 white children (6–12 years) (from three schools, two in Columbia, one in a poorer cotton mill village) and 125 'colored' children from the Howard School, Columbia, of a similar age range, though including some older than 12. The first part of the paper, concerning technical discussion of the test, may be left aside. In her account, as in Mayo's, environment is, if less wholeheartedly, discounted:

> The course of study in the colored school is practically the same as that in the white schools. To what extent this difference is due to racial inferiority, to what extent to difference in the home environment, cannot be said. *It is certainly not due to difference in school training.* (p. 501, my italics)

This is an astonishing statement. South Carolina expenditure per head on education 1916–17 was reportedly $14.79 for whites and $1.68 for blacks, in Columbia teacher salaries per child were, for white teachers $19.18, for black teachers $5.06. In Howard School itself 'the elementary classrooms are crowded', while the 1910 staff–child ratio appears to be 34:1 and 78.5:1 for white and black respectively (per child in the Columbia population).[39] Her results cannot then be taken at face value. Such as they are they show a quarter of the colored children more than one year backward compared to 15% for city whites (18% at the mill school), and none more than a year advanced (compared to 10% of city whites). The figures are analysed descriptively by age in some detail. The general conclusion is that 'colored' children are mentally younger than white children of the same age and 'test more irregularly'. (One right-on 11-year-old 'colored' boy passed all six-year tests, failed all seven-year tests, and passed four eight-year tests – his results were discarded.)

If the results themselves warrant little attention there is one further point worth noting in the discourse itself; the author's descriptions of the responses of the city white and 'colored' groups. On the whites:

> There was no difficulty in securing cordial relations with the children. They were always encouraged, and apparently exerted themselves to do their best. They invariably responded with interest, if not with eagerness. (p. 487)

On the 'colored' group:

> So far as the examiner could judge, the children felt at ease and did their best. *It is quite possible, however, that an examiner of their own race might have obtained different results.* (p. 500, my italics)

This last insight subsequently fell from view until the late 1920s when the 'rapport' factor began receiving attention (Klineberg, 1928; Peterson and Lanier, 1929). Clearly rapport between child and tester was lower with the African American group. Touching on the 'mulatto hypothesis', Strong compares 'dark', 'medium' and 'light' Howard School children, though admits 'this may be entirely worthless'. As it turned out, the 34 darkest children were the best (14.4% below age – better than the whites in fact) and the lightest worst (44.2%), as well as most varied – a deviant finding never mentioned by later researchers!

Though hard to pin down textually, one senses a certain level of uneasiness about the race issue in this paper. It is not explicitly embedded in a Scientific Racism framework and in any case is as much concerned with the test itself as with race differences. Historically however it came to be identified as a pioneering contribution and the main results were regularly cited.[40] Strong's usage of the Binet–Simon Scale inevitably marks the paper as a turning point in the methodology of race-difference research, regardless of any ambivalence we may fancy we detect in her own attitude.

The next year it was the American Indians' turn. E.C. Rowe's 'Five hundred forty-seven white and two-hundred sixty-eight Indian children tested by the Binet–Simon tests' (1914) reported even greater Indian underperformance. Rowe is once again sanguine about environmental causes and believes 'inferior racial ability' to be 'the only satisfactory explanation' (p. 456). The practical lesson is spelled out: 'it seems clear that the type of education suited to the one is not suited to the other' (p. 456). This paper, in G.S. Hall's *Pedagogical Seminary*, may reasonably be seen as reflecting Hall's own position.

George Oscar Ferguson Jr. (1916) 'The psychology of the negro:
an experimental study'

Ferguson begins typically by reviewing previous work. He also takes Le Bon
seriously and spends time on the brain-size issue. By 1916 he has rather more to
discuss than Mayo had done. In addition to Strong and Mayo, there are studies by
B.T. Baldwin (1913), J. Bardin (1913), B.A. Phillips (1912, 1914) and Pyle (1913,
1915a, b). All showed 'colored' or 'Negro' performance to be inferior to that of
whites.[41] One of the largest discrepancies emerged from Baldwin's study of
37 white and 30 'colored' delinquent adolescent girls (13-21 years) involving a
'substitution test'. The latter 'accomplished 62.4 per cent as much work as the
white girls and made 245.3% as many errors' (Ferguson, 1916, p. 19). This was,
we rapidly realise, among the more ludicrous pieces of research.

> The negroes . . . were slow to warm up, quick to lose interest, difficult to stimu-
> late except through flattery, irregular, moody, vacillating in attention, in-
> accurate, envious of each other's progress, given to mumbling, grumbling,
> humming, saying funny things while at work. . . . *the very fact that the negroes
> were not interested as were the whites possibly points to a deficiency in the colored
> group.* (pp. 20-21, my italics)

One is inclined to riposte that it possibly points to all kinds of other things as well!
The 'colored' delinquent girls were, I think we can assume, patently winding up a
white male experimenter psychologically incapable of accepting that black girls,
however delinquent, would dare to deliberately subvert white male authority.

Ferguson almost completely ignores egalitarian arguments, and while critical of
the deficiencies of earlier work (such as Stetson's and Bache's), concludes:

> it is clear that by far the greater number of writers who have dealt with the
> problem of the relative mental ability of the white and the negro take the view
> that the negro is inferior. This is particularly true of those investigators who
> have used quantitative methods. The negro has not shown the same capacity as
> the white when put to the test of psychological or educational experiment, and
> the racial differences revealed have been considerable. (p. 25)

This is especially so regarding the 'higher mental processes that go to make up the
capacities necessary to a successful conduct of civilized life' (ibid.), though as far
as 'the elementary traits which man has in common with the lower animals' are
concerned there is no difference.

His own research was conducted in various towns in Virginia, the subjects
being 486 white and 421 'colored' pupils in the 6th and 7th grades of various
segregated high schools. He claims: 'That the schools themselves were comparable
as between the two races there is no valid reason to doubt. All of them pursued the
same general course of study' (p. 33). As in Strong's case this is belied by the
1916-17 Department of the Interior, Bureau of Education Report and data in
Bullock (1967). Salaries of white teachers exceed those of black teachers, staff–
student ratios in black schools are worse (with one exception – Armstrong High in
Richmond) than those in white schools, and Virginia as a whole is criticised for

'very limited provision for high school education' for black children.[42] He tells us also that '(n)o difference could be perceived in the attitude of the two races toward the tests: both white and colored seemed to enjoy the work rather than the reverse, and both worked with vigor' (p. 34). Five performance tests of various kinds were used.[43] As ever, with a few exceptions (e.g. 17-year-old black girls beat white girls on Mixed Relations Tests), black underperformance was found. Further analysis in terms of amount of 'white blood' (visually assessed from skin colour) indicated that 'the subjects with the greater amount of white blood were superior' (p. 110), 'it is a native ability and not an acquired capacity that differentiates the mixed and the pure negroes, and . . . skin color is its outward sign' (p. 111).[44]

Ferguson reports his data extremely fully, with tables by test, grade, school and sex. The immediate lesson he draws is to argue for segregated education with differing curricular emphases, 'no expenditure of time or of money' is likely to raise Negro scholastic attainment to that of whites (p. 125). 'The movement toward industrial education for the negro finds sanction in the studies of his psychology . . . economy would indicate that training should be concentrated upon those capacities which promise the best return for the educative effort expended' (ibid.). (Implementing such a policy would, one might remark, have prevented any replication of his research.) Ferguson's 'Conclusion' also holds forth on matters way beyond his empirical research, returning to Scientific Racist stereotyping of the 'negro's' lack of foresight, improvidence, emotional volatility, and sexual immorality. Galton-style estimates of the incidence of 'eminent men' we might expect in the 'negro' and 'mulatto' sections of the population are also made.[45] Some consolation is at hand nonetheless: demographic data suggest the 'colored' death rate is higher than that of whites, partly for reasons to do with their 'natural constitution', while race mixing will partially improve their standard.

Ferguson returned to the issue in three subsequent publications: 'The intelligence of negroes at Camp Lee, Virginia' (1919), a study of army draftees, 'White and colored school children of Virginia as measured by the Ayers Index' (1920) and 'The mental status of the American Negro' (1921), an overview paper. The first is a preliminary report of the Army tests to be discussed later. The last is of some interest as his final published statement on the matter. Beginning in somewhat milder tone, Ferguson poses as a moderate who accepts that individual 'Negroes' can be of high ability and concedes that 'As yet comparatively little of a scientific nature has been accomplished in investigating the mind of the Negro' (p. 533). He explains the meaning of the overlapping in performance revealed by studies to date (including the Army tests) which leads him to adopt a slightly more circumspect view of intelligence differences. He is also a smidgen more cautious regarding non-intellectual differences, though still views 'Negroes' as generally more impulsive, emotional and the like. The superior performance of 'mulattos' is reiterated, repeating a warning that while this may raise the black race's level it might also cause race friction since the 'mulatto' is less submissive. He also rejects the notions of less variability and cessation of development at adolescence (both commonplace ideas a few years earlier). Nevertheless he re-affirms the desirability of segregated education. While the 'Negro' will never equal the white, Ferguson expresses optimism that beneficial effects of contact with the white 'man' in the USA will raise him above his fellow 'Negroes' elsewhere (women not of course figuring). While his conclusion is much the same as in 1916 (including some textual recycling) it is perhaps noteworthy that the overall tone has marginally softened.

What do these samples of the first wave of Race Psychology tell us? First they confirm the central role of the 'Negro education' debate. Two messages may be discerned: (a) African Americans really are innately inferior, (b) segregationist policies and industrial education are probably the wisest policy. If pessimistic, this at least alleviates white guilt about poorer educational provision (while often simultaneously actually denying this deficit). By focusing on individual level performance, and casuistically discounting context, Psychology can at least give the impression of scientifically homing in on the crux of the matter. This work remains highly infused with Scientific Racist assumptions and attitudes, the authors continually invoking people like Galton and Le Bon, along with racial physical anthropology and craniology, when interpreting and explaining their findings. Though willingly abandoning specific doctrines (such as superior primitive sensory acuity or physiognomic arguments based on Eurocentric aesthetic standards), they basically aim to refine Scientific Racism's fundamentally sound intuitions and insights. Secondly we note the presence already of a number of arguments which became routine: (a) the 'status is correlated with intelligence' argument against environmental explanations of black underperformance; (b) the assumption of innate race differences as the default explanation, placing an onus of *disproof* on their opponents; (c) the 'mulatto hypothesis' that high performing blacks have more 'white blood' (long commonplace); and (d) use of 'great man' arguments to offset the implications of racial overlap in scores. The notion that 'Negroes' are less variable in general, thus more homogeneous in character, is also common (if rejected by Ferguson), implying a relative lack of that individualism so prized by US white males. By 1916 the Boasian cultural anthropology opposition is being largely ignored.

Most obviously in Mayo's case but also in fact in Ferguson's, the actual data are far less clear-cut than is claimed, and they are sometimes driven to quite convoluted *ad hoc* arguments to explain away better than expected black performance (for example, as resulting from more selective sampling or specific, discrete, environmental effects on motivation). Finally, the glaring disparity between the expenditure data (much of it already available) and the claims for educational comparability between white and black subjects made by Strong and Ferguson signifies an almost reckless degree of disciplinary insularity, to say the least.

Immigration and the impact of the Army intelligence tests

The next major development came with the famous Army Alpha and Army Beta group tests devised, on US entry into the Great War in 1917, to assess draftees.

These have attracted much historical attention on several counts.[46] For intelligence testing this marked the advent of 'group tests' administrable to large groups (earlier Binet-type tests had to be given individually). Psychology's historians often cast the episode as something of a 'coming of age', US psychologists establishing their professional credibility with fellow scientists, the military and politicians for the first time.[47] Those involved included many eminent psychologists including Yerkes (who headed the programme) and Thorndike. For Race Psychology it proved a godsend, promising scientific quantification of race differences in a vast, unbiased, sample from across the Union, including a large number (12,492) of immigrants. The Army Beta test, designed for illiterates, ostensibly eliminated even the distorting effects of poor education. As things transpired the results triggered a controversy which ran until the 1940s, when Ashley Montagu and the fiercely racist H.E. Garrett were still battling out their meaning, and it rumbles on yet.[48] While attracting wide attention from the outset, it was C.C. Brigham's *A Study of American Intelligence* (1923), with a foreword by Yerkes, which provided the most authoritative support for the Race Psychology project.[49] Its appearance coincided with the height of the immigration panic. The leading eugenicist expert on 'feeble-mindedness', H.H. Goddard, had already explored the use of Binet tests on immigrants arriving at Ellis Island, reporting that 40% were 'feeble-minded'.[50] Brigham himself was, at the time, under the spell of Madison Grant, W.Z. Ripley's *Races of Europe* and most directly Charles W. Gould, eugenicist author of *America, A Family Matter* (1920) who had argued for 'pure-bred races'. In Yerkes's view, 'no one of us as a citizen can afford to ignore the menace of race deterioration or the evident relations of immigration to national progress and welfare' (p. vii). While immigration is the work's dominant theme, Brigham's analysis and interpretation of the 'Negro' data had a longer-lasting impact. We will consider these in turn.

Immigration

Preliminary examination of the data on the European immigrant sample revealed a large difference in mean scores between most north European groups and those of the Irish, southern and eastern Europeans. An important proviso appears at one point which is elsewhere overridden, Brigham explicitly stating that these immigrants '*can not themselves be taken as representative of the country* [i.e. of origin] *as a whole*' (p. 156, my italics). Nevertheless the figures 'suggest immediately that the race factor may underlie the large differences found'. To explore this further Brigham utilises contemporary estimates of the racial composition of each nationality, adopting the three-fold Nordic, Alpine and Mediterranean classification. By weighting the national immigrant samples he derives general figures for each of these three 'races', revealing that Nordics are superior to Alpines and Mediterraneans (the lowest), even when allowing for their higher English-speaking abilities. There was also a correlation between scores and years resident in the USA – more recent immigrants scoring lower. Examination of immigration records since 1841 reveals that proportionately more recent immigrants are of Mediterranean and Alpine race. He can thus argue that while length of residency is not without effect, the difference between old and recent immigrant scores is partly at least due to the racial factor: the quality of immigrants has deteriorated. This inference was particularly influential, bolstering the immigration control campaign and the role of Psychology in monitoring and managing this. Throughout this chapter (Section VIII 'The racial hypothesis'), the previously noted proviso is forgotten,[51] and constant reference made to 'the superiority of the Nordic race', not 'the superiority of Nordic immigrants'.

There are, patently, numerous *prima facie* reasons why European immigrants during this period would differentially sample their source populations. Southern immigrants were primarily driven by poverty from traditional rural peasant environments while northern immigrants were more likely to be urban, higher social classes would be better represented, and possibly more were driven by choice rather than necessity.[52] In short, northern immigrants would be both more *au fait* with modernist culture as represented by Psychological tests, and from environments more congenial to the development of intelligence as measured by such tests.

Brigham next discusses the relationship between his results and the views of other writers. He attacks T.R. Garth's views on the merits of Mediterraneans, saying they cannot be judged on past achievements (p. 184). This implicitly concedes the entire case, since it implies what Garth later called 'race mobility', thereby undercutting the assumption of a *necessary* and permanent connection between 'race' and intelligence. Brigham appears oblivious of this, preferring Madison Grant's Nordicism: 'The entire book [i.e. *The Passing of the Great Race*] should be read to appreciate the soundness of Mr Grant's position and the compelling force of his arguments' (p. 184). The Irish are of unstable temperament and 'lack . . . coordinating and reasoning power', their culture is marked by 'Pre-Neolithic survivals' and 'aloofness from the general trend of European culture'. (He does not say how, with an oppressive Britain interposed between them and the mainland, they could, even in principle, have fully participated in this 'general trend'!) He finds his results fairly supportive of McDougall's views,[53] though difficult to compare in detail and concludes:

> The intellectual superiority of our Nordic group over the Alpine, Mediterranean and negro groups has been demonstrated. If a person is unwilling to accept the race hypothesis as developed here, he may go back to the original nationality groups, and he cannot deny the fact that differences exist. (p. 192)

Furthermore he robustly attacks environmental arguments, taking the usual line that such differences are themselves a reflection of innate differences in ability.

> Particularly misleading and unsound is the theory that disregards all differences found between racial groups unless the groups have had the same educational and environmental opportunities. . . . to select individuals who have fallen behind in the struggle to adjust themselves to the civilization this race has built as typical of that race is an error, for their position itself shows that they are, for the most part, individuals with an inferior hereditary endowment. (pp. 193–4)

Conklin (1921) is also gloomily cited on the effects of hybridisation and the un-avoidable impending 'commingling' of peoples. On immigration his conclusions were unambiguous, ominous, and evidently ratified by an empirical 'scientific' methodology which endowed them with an authority absent from more theoretical works. Nordics were best, immigrants were getting worse, and the cultural welfare of the Union under threat. Yerkes urged Brigham's publisher to bring the book out in time for the immigration-restriction hearings and generally lobbied the chairmen of relevant Congress committees regarding the importance of the Army Alpha findings.[54]

Negro intelligence

The crux of the matter is really contained in the graph on p. 81 of Brigham's text (Fig. 4.1 here). Quantifying this a little more clearly it showed 99.97% of white officers and 86.31% of the total white draft exceeding the Negro mean score. Even 70.44% of the 'foreign born draft' (immigrants) exceeded this figure. Since the white draft sample was 93,973, the Negro draft sample 23,604 and white officer sample 15,544 the picture was so clear-cut that relatively little further discussion seemed to be required.

Brigham argues later that since educational institutions are part of 'our own race heritage', 'The average negro child can not advance through an educational curriculum adapted to the Anglo-Saxon child in step with that child' (p. 194). Any sampling controlling for age would necessarily sample either superior Negroes or inferior whites.[55] Northern black superiority to Southern blacks he ascribes without much ado to: (a) better educational opportunity in the North,

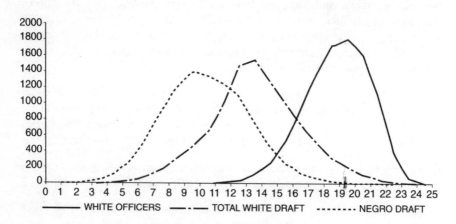

Figure 4.1 Overall 'Negro' vs. White intelligence scores

Note: Distributions of scores of white officers, white draft and Negro draft on the combined scale. The horizontal scale from 0 to 25 represents combined scale measurements, reading from left to right according to increasing intelligence. The vertical scale represents the number in each ten thousand.
Source: Brigham (1923), p. 81.

(b) greater amount of 'white blood', (c) tendency for the more intelligent to migrate northwards (pp. 191–2). (These last two arguments were, we will see, convincingly refuted by the mid-1930s.) What is most revealing is the degree to which Brigham's fears of race-mixing intensify when he turns to the 'negro'. There are, he says, already 264 'mulattoes' per 1,000 of the black population.[56]

> We must face a possibility of racial admixture here that is infinitely worse than that faced by any European country today, for we are incorporating the negro into our racial stock, while all of Europe is comparatively free from this taint. (p. 209)

There are 10 million Negroes and the proportion of mulattoes has risen with 'alarming rapidity' since 1850 (p. 210).

A Study of American Intelligence provided a warrant for drastic eugenic measures both on the immigration front and domestically.[57] Immigration should be restructured and 'highly selective' while measures should be taken for the 'prevention of propagation of defective strains' (p. 210). (These last actually included native Americans, but as he viewed their decline as inevitable they were no cause for concern.) Domestically Brigham clearly supports segregation and banning of mixed marriages. The work as a whole is far more explicitly Nordicist and Negrophobic in tone than I suspect many present day psychologists, knowing only the broad trend of the data, realise. R.M. Yerkes wholeheartedly supported Brigham (whom he recruited from the Canadian army into the US Army Sanitary Corps in 1917); his foreword greets the book in glowing terms, and refers to 'my intense interest in the practical problems of immigration and my conviction that the psychological data obtained by the Army have important bearing on some of them' (p. v).

Seven years later Brigham no longer saw things in the same light. His 1930 paper 'Intelligence tests of immigrant groups' amounted to a total recantation. (Yerkes too dropped the topic in due course, but never, to my knowledge, explicitly recanted.)[58] Brigham now argues that 'current studies' (particularly those of T.L. Kelley)[59] reveal that the meaning of test scores is unclear, and that what they are measuring is not unitary: 'test scores may not represent unitary things' (p. 160). The British psychologist Spearman's notion of general intelligence (g) is unsupported. One especially fallacious procedure is adding the scores of subtests, '(a) case in point is the army alpha test' in which components were added to form a 'so-called combined scale'. He now considers this 'absurd' (p. 164). Kelley's statistical studies show that these do not yield a comprehensive g factor (Kelley, 1928). He then spells it out:

> As this method was used by the writer in his earlier analysis of the army tests as applied to samples of foreign born in the draft, that survey with its entire hypothetical superstructure of racial differences collapses completely. (p. 164)

Furthermore, the use of 'tests in the vernacular' is unacceptable for comparative studies 'of individuals brought up in homes where the vernacular is not used, or in which two vernaculars are used' (p. 165). This effectively rules out using any existing tests for such studies, and shows 'that one of the most pretentious of these comparative racial studies – the writer's own – was without foundation' (ibid.).

There can be few scientific instances of quite such deadpan and laconic back-tracking. It was too late though. In 1924 the Immigration Restriction Law drastic-ally reduced the quota of South East European immigrants, legislation brought about in some part at least by these 'pretentious' conclusions. As Samelson (1978) notes, European-oriented race–difference research declined considerably after this date.

The material discussed so far illustrates our opening observation that Race Psy-chology was rooted in the 'Negro Education' and immigration issues. In both cases it served to support particular parties in the related debates. In the first instance it bolstered the segregationist, 'industrial training' camp while locating the cause of the problem firmly in the innate deficiencies of the 'Negro', thus alle-viating in some measure the guilt of white philanthropists and others who had been unsuccessfully striving to ameliorate the African American situation via educational programmes. Regarding immigration, Psychologists placed them-selves in the service of the immigration restriction camp, providing both theoreti-cal eugenic justification and monitoring technology. L. Terman, the leading US authority on intelligence testing, though undertaking no race–differences research himself, wholeheartedly endorsed their existence: 'The writer predicts that . . . there will be discovered enormously significant racial differences in general intelli-gence, differences which cannot be wiped out by any scheme of mental culture' (Terman, 1919, p. 92).[60] During the 1920s, however, Race Psychology broadened its concerns. The two most productive researchers, whom we consider next, diverged – albeit in different ways – from these initial preoccupations.

Garth and Porteus: Race Psychology's forgotten leaders

Thomas Russell Garth (1872–1939) and Race Psychology 1919–31

Woodworth's student, T.R. Garth, devoted the heart of his professional career to the promotion of a scientific Race Psychology. As the most prolific writer in the field, author of the only book specifically entitled *Race Psychology* (1931b), and the *Psychological Bulletin*'s choice of commentator on the field in 1925 and 1930, no other figure identified so totally with the field. Yet, after 12 years of intense effort, he conceded that the race-differences case remained unproven and con-fessed himself sceptical. By 1934 he was an adamant environmentalist and, though often not immediately apparent from their titles, his 1930s researches were pri-marily focused on uncovering the environmental factors determining group underperformance. Just about his last paper (1939) concluded that 'Negro' hand-writing was indistinguishable from any other group's, while a newspaper interview accompanying an obituary in 1939 was headlined 'Superiority Bunk Denver

University Scientist, Held That Any Differences Are Only Skin Deep, After 20 Years Study'.[61]

I discuss Garth's case at length elsewhere and believe it is especially significant.[62] Essentially, he came to recognise (a) the methodological impossibility of demonstrating the existence of race differences 'objectively' and (b) the unscientific nature of the concept 'race' itself. By the end of his career what began as a quest for profound differences in 'racial' character had transformed into a more practically oriented study of differences in performance between specific ethnic subgroups with an eye to rectifying underperformance. In terms of the categories outlined in Table 4.1 he moved from Race Psychology to Anti-Race Psychology (and occasionally Physiological Psychology). From 1919 to 1930 the majority of his research was with Mexican and Indian children, including 'mixed blood' subjects, mostly on intelligence, achievement, fatigue or colour preferences. Early on he apparently decided not to study African Americans since he felt that as a Southerner he could not do so in an unbiased fashion.[63] Underpinning his approach was a formula which he devised right at the outset to express formally what was required for the demonstration of race differences. He eventually saw that it was methodologically virtually impossible to meet this criterion.

While there are indications of tension almost from the outset, particularly his concerns about what he called 'racial mobility' – the idea that a race's performance may change over time – he was still trying to hold the field together in his 1930 overview paper, striving to include the rising genres of prejudice research and cultural anthropology in Race Psychology. It is, additionally, a particularly significant paper for the historian in identifying a dozen contemporary trends in research which are often incompatible. The following year however his *Race Psychology* virtually threw in the towel, concluding:

> Much of the difference found in the results of studies of racial differences in mental traits is due to differences in nurtural factors and the rest is due to racial mobility, so that one race has a temporary advantage over another. *What we call races are merely temporary eddies in the history of human kind.* (p. 221, my italics)

His 1934 *Journal of Negro Education* paper is even more up-front, invoking the Black Hawk War and the Battle of Wounded Knee and arguing:

> What effect did this slaughter of the braves have upon the surviving Indian generation? It is not doubted that some of the best blood of the Indian race has gone to enrich the soil, rather than propagate the race.
>
> A like picture could be given of the slaves who refused to be transferred to America in the early days of the slave trade. In many instances, the bravest jumped to a watery grave off a slave vessel rather than submit to slavery in the New World.
>
> (1934a, p. 323)

This turns the Darwinian argument against the racists: African Americans and native Americans have both been the objects of European predations in such a way that the best have been disproportionately selected against. The long-standing

Darwinian suggestion that altruistic self-sacrifice in battle is a paradox in selecting against the 'fittest' is in these cases realised. From henceforth his research falls primarily in the category of applied intra-racial research, being concerned with practical issues relating to native American and African American education. He also undertakes the research on colour blindness cited earlier.

Garth's slow and somewhat disguised conversion involved several interacting factors. First, as an aspiring scientific psychologist of the mainstream Woodworthian functionalist 'dynamic' school he was especially sensitive to methodological difficulties, which he came to see as insuperable; secondly he was increasingly attracted to contemporary anthropology as well as conversant with relevant developments in genetics; thirdly both from his own writings and such biographical material as is available,[64] it is apparent that Garth came to identify with the plights of the native American and Mexican, his main subject groups. Temperamentally Garth was not fundamentally racist, and his original choice of research specialty clearly owed much to Woodworth's influence. His diligence in empirical data gathering was remarked on by his academic eulogist.[65] While not an original theorist, Garth had an eye for 'unscientific' racialist speculations which went beyond the empirical evidence, and hence was seduced neither by Lévy-Bruhl's conjectures on primitive mind nor M. Grant's and L. Stoddard's Nordicism. When, in the 1930s, the chips were down, Garth was in no doubt where his sympathies really lay. His joined that rare group of scientists who end up rejecting the central hypothesis on which they have built their professional career.

Garth's Race Psychology work may be read as an attempt at rendering the topic a more 'purely' scientific one, decoupled to some extent from the heated contexts in which it had previously been conducted, his own geographical location in the South West facilitating this. He displays little ideological partisanship prior to 1930, and his subsequent anti-racist partisanship appears to stem from his scientific experience, rather than being its determinant.

Stanley David Porteus (1883–1972) and Hawaii as a racial Galapagos

Australian-born S.D. Porteus is a complete contrast. His 1969 autobiography describes his early interests as being in 'the effect of environment on mental and cultural evolution'.[66] This, we will see, is revisionism of the grossest kind – his interest was actually in proving that such effects were minimal.

Having graduated from Melbourne in 1912, Porteus spent several years working with 'mental defectives' before emigrating to the USA in 1919 to succeed Goddard as head of the Vineland Training School.[67] With the first version of his Maze Test already under his belt he implemented a major programme of research into factors affecting the social adjustment of 'mental defectives'. Realising the inadequacies of intelligence measures for predicting 'social adaptability' he developed two tests for measuring more relevant factors.[68] One was his 'Porteus Maze Test' which he claimed tested foresight, prudence, planning abilities and 'to a certain extent, emotional stability' better than Binet-type intelligence tests (Porteus 1930, p. 129). Being untimed this placed subjects under no time pressure. The other, the Social Rating Scale[69] measured seven traits: planning capacity, suggestibility, prudence, resolution, self-control, stability of interest and 'conciliatory attitude, tact' (Porteus and Babcock 1926, p. 88). He also assembled a battery of performance tests for predicting 'social sufficiency' (comprising the Maze Test, Kohs Blocks, Form and Assembling Test and Pintner-Paterson scales).[70] The Social Rating Scale and performance test battery provided the basis for his race differences research in Hawaii, following his 1922 appointment as Professor of Clinical Psychology at the University of Hawaii.[71] The former underpinned *Temperament and Race* (1926) (co-authored with Babcock) and the latter 'Race and social differences in performance tests' (1930). Along with a book on Australian aborigines[72] these constitute the core of Porteus's Race Psychology. From 1927 he was largely funded by the Rockefeller Foundation 'for the purpose of continuing and extending studies already begun on the subject of racial differences' (1930, p. 95),[73] the same agency backing his Australian aborigine work via the Australian National Research Council.

For Porteus, Hawaii presented itself as Race Psychology's potential Galapagos. But while the Galapagos Islands provided Darwin with a variety of isolated environmental niches in which the process of speciation could be seen, Hawaii, conversely, offered Porteus an apparently uniform social environment in which innate racial differences could be identified uncontaminated with environmental variables.

> The advantage of the studies in Hawaii has been that one of these [environmental] variables – viz. social status, has been eliminated so that differences in achievement are due entirely to inherent capacity for progressive adaptations.
>
> (Porteus and Babcock, 1926, p. 310)

Discovered, or perhaps rediscovered, by Europeans (Captain Cook) in 1778, Hawaii remained an autonomous kingdom until 1894 when it became a republic, only to be annexed by the USA in 1898. Under the impact of Western culture, Hawaiians had become Christianised by the end of the 1820s. White-owned sugar and pineapple plantations multiplied thereafter, but the Hawaiians had little interest in becoming plantation labourers, resulting in an influx of South Chinese from the 1860s to 1880s. Many of these soon rose to more profitable occupations, a process repeated with each cohort of immigrant labourers in turn. After 1885 it was the turn of the Japanese, although most returned home when their contracts ended, but from 1900 to 1907 around 40,000 Japanese immigrated permanently, again initially as plantation labourers. During the 1880s, a considerable number of Portuguese from the Azores were also recruited. Finally, when Japanese immigration was halted (1908) 'Filipinos' were attracted to refill the constantly depleting labouring ranks (the USA assumed control of the Philippines in 1899, US possession ending in 1945).[74] Small numbers of Spanish, 'Porto Rican' and Pacific Islanders were also present. People of African descent were largely absent (although Porteus suspected some of the 'Portuguese' of having a significant proportion of 'African blood').

Excepting a few 'Caucasians' in the governing class, it appeared to Porteus that each racial group had started from the same point, each (the Hawaiians aside) beginning at the bottom of the ladder as plantation labourers. Any differentials in achievement and economic status were thus due to innate racial psychological characteristics. There was, additionally, much inter-marriage except with regard to the Japanese, among whom exogamy was inhibited (if not entirely prevented) by, he says, 'racial pride'. Tolerance towards 'race-mixture' appears to have prevailed from early on.[75]

Porteus's first extended offering was *Temperament and Race* (1926), an oddly conflicted text. Befitting the inventor of a maze test, he constantly oscillates between hard-line and soft-line statements, often rendering his arguments quite tortuous. One root of his difficulty, as I read him, is his anxiety to convey the impression of occupying a moderate position between 'race-levellers' and 'race-dogmatists' while really being committed to Scientific Racism. The dust-wrapper displays two attractive photographs of a Spanish-Hawaiian girl and a Portuguese-Hawaiian girl, and we are, throughout, periodically presented with group portraits of families and children representing different racial groups, including even a Russian family (although Russians figure nowhere in his written text). Their function is unclear. With one exception (depicting head shapes of Japanese boys) they are not, like typical 'races of Man' text mugshots or Lombroso's galleries of degenerate rogues, being used to stress the alienness and otherness of their subjects. On the contrary, one depicts the 13-year-old Chinese winner of the American Legion National Essay Competition, a boy called Ah Sing Ching, feeding chickens, under the caption 'Environment or Heredity?'.[76] Yet people of 'mixed race' who figure frequently in these pictures receive scant mention elsewhere. These images seem to serve only the rhetorical purpose of conveying the author's humane and tolerant character.[77] His final pages however are permeated by anxieties over Japan, backed up by quotes from Madison Grant. And he accepts that 'there is going on a ceaseless racial struggle for dominance that no number of platitudes about brotherly love will obviate' (p. 327). How his cover-girls are implicated in this strife is obscure.

There are several strands in Porteus's agenda: the ostensibly dominant project of scientifically exploring the nature of racial differences *per se*, a social management strand relating to local issues of education and social policy, and a deeper political message concerning the long-term fortunes of the USA, Canada and Australia in relation to Japan. Negotiating the intrinsic tensions between all these adds to his expository headaches.

Establishing a 'Racial Efficiency Index' is the first positive task undertaken after a historical introduction. This is based on a direct extension of the Social Rating Scale from the individual to the group level. He now ascertains the relative strengths of the seven traits measured by this (adding an eighth, 'dependability') among the six major racial groups: Japanese, Chinese, Hawaiian, Portuguese, 'Porto Ricans' and Filipinos. His method was to obtain ratings from

> twenty-five people of long experience in the islands, observers whose work brought them very intimately into contact with the various racial groups. Sixteen of the judges were plantation managers while among the remainder of the group were head workers in social settlements, plantation doctors, and several educationists. (p. 90)

(He defends the high proportion of plantation managers at some length.) The scale comprised two counterbalanced questions regarding each trait, one scoring 5 and the other 1. Average scores for each group are then calculated (p. 97).[78] The Chinese came first or second on all traits, the Japanese first or second on all except 'Tact' where they fell last (on Planning Capacity they obtained the maximum possible score). Conversely Filipinos were last or penultimate on all except Tact where they rose to third place while 'Porto Ricans' also fared rather badly throughout but managed fourth on Self Determination (i.e. low suggestibility) and Tact. These results were mulled over at length and found consistent with informal assessments written prior to the research. He next weighted each trait between 6 (e.g. Planning Capacity) and 1 (e.g. Stability of Interest) as a contributor to overall social efficiency (as had in fact been done with the original scale) and derives a group 'social efficiency' score. And now . . .

> Multiplying each of these population quotas[79] by the average social efficiency index for each race, and assuming 100 per cent efficiency for the Caucasian (!) other than Portuguese, the total of the products works out as 181,099. This is 73.3 per cent of the total possible rating. (p. 111, my exclamation)

His social managerial agenda now surfaces, Hawaii, with a 'social efficiency index' of only 73.3% is likely to be more burdened with 'all kinds of social and medical relief work' than 'mainland communities of similar size'. High Filipino and 'Porto Rican' crime and 'mental retardation' rates therefore come under scrutiny. Starting from a quite reasonable argument that intelligence tests cannot assess 'social efficiency', Porteus thus arrives at a population analysis in terms of the social worth of each racially defined group. And at no point has a single member of any of these 'races' been directly studied! He can thereby cast himself as playing a professional expert role in informing social policy in general, especially, as we will see, in relation to immigration.

Moving on to discuss the brain, Porteus reverts completely to Scientific Racist type. He quotes Brinton (1901)

> 'We are accustomed familiarly to speak of higher and lower races, and we are justified in this even from merely physical considerations. These indeed bear intimate relation to mental capacity and where the body presents many points of arrested or retarded development we may be sure that the mind will also.' *In substance this view is correct.* (p. 137, my italics)

Eschewing such features as prognathous jaws as indices of mental capacity, Porteus holds that the brain is the crucial organ to consider.[80] He also accepts Mayo's verdict on the innate incapacity of the 'Negro' for scholastic achievement and cites Kaes[81] to implicate an early cessation of brain development as responsible for the most important differences.

An utterly classic passage (pp. 158–67) on sex differences, female inferiority and feminine psychology is included, albeit (equally classically) diplomatically larded with compliments. 'Feminine charm is in part undoubtedly due to the fact that as far as emotional tone and expression goes a woman is never wholly grown up' (p. 162). We are then treated to a study of the heads of 4,000 Honolulu schoolchildren. The apparent Japanese superiority it discloses (a typically bright brachycephalic morphology) feeds into the covert (at this point) message he is building up regarding them. Later in the book Porteus accepts that the physical basis of racial temperamental variation lies in differential patterns of hormone production, as proposed by the eminent Scottish anatomist Sir Arthur Keith.[82]

The Psychological content is completed by a critical review of intelligence tests which, interestingly, he begins by rejecting Brigham's analysis of the racial implications of the US Army tests as statistically and conceptually flawed. We may forgo further consideration of this section other than to note that in his view 'The absolute inferiority of the negro we may assume to be fairly established' (p. 210).

He now turns to 'Racial Theory', doggedly posing as steering that middle path between 'race-levellers' and 'race-dogmatists' mentioned earlier while simultaneously arguing a position essentially, to our eyes, of the latter sort. Environment is perhaps important, but he believes the Hawaiian evidence clearly demonstrates that its effects are constrained by hereditary endowment. In attacking the egalitarians he also smites 'sex levellers', as well as ending with an extended though critical excursus on the superiority of brachycephalic races (despite the fact it was well known that long and short-headed individuals may occur in the same family and that Swedes, for example, are particularly dolichocephalic).[83] Broad-headedness probably signifies superior brain development, which may correlate with brachycephaly. In any case the Japanese subjects notably tended towards short-headedness.

At last turning to 'Racial Futures', his political agenda finally emerges in an undiluted form. This extraordinary finale deserves a fairly full examination. The evident superiority of the Japanese over all other non-Anglo-Saxon groups and the poor Portuguese is no cause for optimism. Their disinclination to inter-marry, their 'policy of watchful waiting' (p. 322), their planning ability, resolution, superior brain size over the Chinese and so forth – all are grounds for anxiety regarding the 'ceaseless racial struggle'. 'While we are not alarmists we recognise that a serious situation confronts the dominant white race' (p. 329).

> America alone has fought two great wars [i.e. the Civil War and World War I] of principle at immense cost to the flower of her people. Japan during all this time did not raise a hand nor strike a blow in these great causes [i.e. liberty and religious tolerance]. She has become the inheritor of all of the ideals of our time without any greater cost than the labour of understanding them.
>
> But perhaps the heaviest handicap that western civilization still carries is the humanitarian impulse. (pp. 330–31)

Porteus hugely resents Japan's current fortunes, it is all so *unfair* on the noble white races:

> During the centuries when the white races were exploring the furthermost seas and territories of the earth, and paying tribute with valuable lives to the spirit of wonder and adventure; while their blood was being poured out without stint in the causes of religious or political freedom; while capital and industry together were being spent with prodigality to make transportation safe, and communication easy, . . . while the deadly scourges of earth were being

combatted at infinite cost . . . during all this time Japan remained dormant and unexpressive. Knowing nothing of all this much vaunted progress, she was conserving her national strength through the elimination of her unfit by natural eugenics. Now at one stride she steps forward into the front rank of nations, inheritor of all the fruits of the efforts and wisdom of the Western mind. (p. 334)

G.S. Hall would surely have hooted with derision at this.

Yet it is all suspicion – he constantly concedes that the Japanese are honest in trade and that while representing 40% of the population they have made no political capital out of this. But there are 'deep laid schemes for ultimate advantage' and 'Despite all of Japan's protestations we believe that her ambition is by no means dormant, and that her policies are shrewdly shaped and hidden behind a mask of [wait for it!] inscrutability' (p. 334). He thus advocates their rigid exclusion from North America and Australia, not 'from the standpoint of an unfounded racial superiority complex' but because 'these lands have been pioneered and developed through the determination of the men who pressed forward into their silent places, and by the devotion of the women who followed them. These lands belong to the white race by right of peaceful [*sic*] conquest' (pp. 335–6). If, regarding long-term Japanese national ambitions, Porteus's worries may not have been unfounded, the Hawaiian and West Coast immigrant Japanese population were mostly happily upwardly mobile descendants of imported contract labourers from the lowest stratum of Japanese society, hardly a lurking potential fifth column of enemies within.[84] It would be interesting to know something of the book's impact in Hawaii itself, especially among the Japanese.

The Porteus case indicates how our view of the linkage between Race Psychology and US immigration concerns has so far been European-centred. On Ellis Island the task was to weed out inferior European 'stocks', in Hawaii the psychologist is playing the reverse role of arguing that it is the *superior* Japanese race against whom the barriers must be set.

While on occasion insightful regarding technical issues, Porteus's acumen fails in two fundamental respects. First, like all Race Psychologists, he accepts 'races' as coherent entities with specific psychological characteristics, this being exacerbated by his Scientific Racism. Secondly he is irredeemably ethnocentric, uncritically accepting the categories by which he identifies his 'traits' as culturally neutral and objective. And how much more interesting, for example, his Racial Efficiency study would have been had he recruited 25 people from each 'race' to evaluate all the others (including the 'Anglo-Saxons'). We now look, more briefly, at his 1930 monograph.

This is a far more focused study of the performance of children on the Porteus Maze Test and the Form and Assembling Test. His subjects include 'mixed race' as well as 'pure' racial groups, and he considers sex differences as well as 'racial' ones. Mainland samples are incorporated for purposes of comparison. The opening tone has softened a little since 1926, notably in stressing that 'we are entirely in the wrong in debating the matter as one of racial superiority or inferiority, . . . the question is truly one of racial *differences*' (p. 100, italics in original). He has also taken on board Hirsch's 'natio-racial' concept. Nonetheless he is adamant that sociologists and cultural anthropologists have overstated the environmentalist case, criticising Yoder and Herskovits at some length.[85] The unique advantages of the Hawaiian situation and inappropriateness of intelligence tests for studying race differences are repeated. We may overlook the earlier part of the paper, an account of the development and standardisation of the tests.

It must be conceded that Porteus leans over backwards to ensure representative sampling, using a variety of schools of different kinds. While the detailed results require little discussion, there are a number of passages which are significant in demonstrating what can happen in Porteus's form of racial discourse. The first relates to the argument that social status reflects intelligence: 'There seems to be no adequate reason for ignoring the very obvious relation between intelligence and social status' (p. 173). But five pages later, deep in a discussion of the Portuguese (of which more shortly) he has to explain why 'their present social and industrial status in the Territory hardly matches their low standing in the tests' (p. 177). At this point he has to reverse the whole argument. The tests do not show them at their best. There are capacities not being assessed. We are then treated to a brief purple passage about the shrewdness and mother-wit of country-dwellers, their dogged determination and grit and so forth (p. 178). The initial proposition thus becomes irrefutable: if people of high social status perform well then this confirms a correlation between social status and intelligence, if they do not then this simply indicates that the tests are missing something.

Secondly though, the whole section on the Portuguese deserves comment. His problem is that somewhat embarrassingly the Portuguese have come bottom on all the tests. 'The low position of the Portuguese, in comparison with the Oriental, would seem to merit an attempt at an explanation' (p. 175). This he proceeds to do, arguing (probably correctly) that the Portuguese in Hawaii are not representative of the European Portuguese in general. Since they came from the Azores and Madeira there are strong grounds for believing that there has been an infusion of 'African Negroid' strains (p. 177). They were in any case those who had been least successful at home in the first place. There then follows the aforementioned paean to unassessed rural mother-wit. Porteus is, we realise, deploying the kind of arguments (e.g. the cultural bias of tests and unrepresentative sampling) usually used by the opposing camp to, in his case, excuse the inconveniently poor showing of an ostensibly white European racial group, while elsewhere denying their validity in relation to the 'American Negro'.

Later, in addressing the 'causes of natio-racial differences' (p. 183) he raises, without realising it, a central difficulty in maintaining the heredity–environment distinction on which racial discourse depends: from an evolutionary viewpoint the current 'character of peoples' is the product of environmentally located selection pressures. This being so it follows that current 'character' is never fixed *even if you are accepting a hereditarian position*. (This is in fact the 'race mobility' phenomenon which Garth found so troubling.) But Porteus can assert that 'the Australian aborigine has become entirely unadaptable to the changes in environmental conditions which white occupation has effected' (p. 183). The differences 'become biological' (p. 184). This has obvious Spencerian echoes. The problem of differentiating the cultural from the biological is never fully confronted. Even if Hawaiian 'racial' groups began at the same economic level, each imported pre-existing culturally engendered values and attitudes pertaining to the factors relevant to 'social efficiency' (i.e. efficiency in white American industrial culture). While attempting to counter some of the more specific points being made by contemporary critics such as Herskovits, Porteus never really addresses the 'social constructionist' case put forward by, for example, W.I. Thomas, merely asserting that 'sociologists, absorbed in their studies of the effect of various environmental factors, are rather prone to overestimate the influence of culture contacts, education, etc., and thus lean heavily towards the idea of racial equality' (p. 99) (forgetting his earlier shift from 'superiority' to 'difference'!).

Porteus's Race Psychology was erected on a false premise: Hawaii was a 'level playing field'. Ignoring their varied cultural legacies, all current differences between its ethnic groups become, for Porteus, reflections of their biologically based racial characters. We might speculate about why this Australian émigré was personally quite so passionate about racial identity, and his autobiography gives some clues.[86] His attitude towards the Japanese is perhaps much as one might predict of a romantic white racist Australian in Hawaii at this time. Porteus continued to write on Australian aborigines into the 1960s, often in *Mankind Quarterly*, the only anthropology journal continuing to espouse Scientific Racism.[87] In this later work he paternalistically tries to promote the Australian Aborigines, whom he had held in some affection since childhood, from their traditional Scientific Racist ranking as the lowest of the races, although he never challenged such ranking exercises as such.

Porteus thus extends Race Psychology from its opening base in three ways. First he transfers the immigration issue from East Coast to West Coast, bringing Asian groups, especially the Japanese, into the picture. Secondly, methodologically, he replaces conventional psychometric tests of intelligence with alternatives having more face validity. Thirdly he attempts to globalise hard-line Race Psychology research by incorporating Australian, and in fact, South African Kalahari, subjects (though space considerations prevent discussion of this final foray into the field). No other psychologists were as professionally identified with the field as Garth and Porteus, and ironically none have sunk deeper into oblivion. The cultural centre of gravity remained unchanged. Race Psychology's fate ultimately revolved around its treatment of African Americans, who attracted more attention than any other single group besides white Americans (although Garth's summaries of 1925 and 1930 indicate they comprised only a fifth to a third of the groups studied, white Americans aside).[88] We now turn to the more familiar genres of routine Race Psychology research.[89]

Other Race Psychologists and influential research

J. Peterson (1878–1936) and the study of white–black differences

The leading authority on white–'Negro' differences was J. Peterson of George Peabody College for Teachers, Nashville who, between 1921 and 1934, published about a dozen papers on racial differences between American whites and African Americans, mostly on children. While enjoying a high reputation in this field, it was a relatively minor strand in Peterson's Psychological work. Hearing and learning were among his major interests and he developed a somewhat distinctive, more wholistic, variation of learning theory with some affinities to Gestalt approaches, although never published a formal theoretical statement (Lanier, 1936). Now largely forgotten, during his life Peterson was a major figure in US Psychology, holding 'almost every important office in psychological associations' (ibid., p. 3).[90]

From the outset Peterson's position (and that of co-authors such as L.H. Lanier) was fairly moderate, if less so than Garth's. In 1923 for example, while accepting that US 'Negro' IQ as so far assessed is in the 75–80 range, he is cautious about the meaning of this, rejecting the custom of 'reading the percentage of the Negro median of the white median as percentage of ability' on the grounds that nobody knows where the zero figure is (Peterson 1923b, p. 425).[91] He also opposes segregated education: 'in each race education must be fitted to the individual abilities' (ibid.) and counsels understating rather than overstating differences because of the harm the latter may do to 'the race already seriously handicapped'. In Peterson, Lanier and Walker (1925) the reservations are clearly spelled out, particularly failure to deal with the effects of 'group attitudes':

> In a college or normal school group of Negroes, for instance, you (with your tests) at once fall under a cloud of suspicion. Are these tests like the Army tests? What are the objectives of your testing? These questions, occasionally asked, stand out in the countenances of many who do not ask them verbally. Coöperation can hardly be more than passive acquiescence. Yet under the circumstances of underpaid negro teachers, poor roads to their schools, a relatively stingy allowance for parks and other natural comforts, you are surprised that the attitude is as favorable as it is. (p. 271).

In view of this they prefer using individual over group tests in their research on 12-year-olds, using rational learning, mental maze and disc transfer tasks (N = 69 white, 46 'Negro' subjects). They find no support for Spearman's 'general intelligence' and the results vary, if usually showing some white superiority.

Peterson's first major study of race differences was 'Comparative abilities of white and negro children' (1923a).[92] The numbers of subjects were, for most tests, substantial (e.g. on the Pressey Test, 734 'Negro', 641 white). Although the results showed typical white superiority the differences again varied considerably, ranging from a 'Negro' IQ of 58 on one test to a possible 92 on another.[93] This, like Peterson and Lanier (1929), added substantially to the bank of race differences data, but maintained caution regarding both the degree to which differences were hereditary and the reliability of the measuring instruments.

Peterson and Telford (1930) reported a large-scale study on the South Carolina island of St Helena,[94] conducted in 1928. The research team included J.L. Whiting of the Tuskegee Institute 'himself a negro' (p. 116). This island had been occupied by African Americans for three centuries, being populated by 'pureblood' slaves bought in Charleston Market. After the Civil War the plantation owners quit, leaving a virtually completely black population, the community being self-managed thereafter. In 1927 a bridge to the mainland was built, thus the situation was likely to change rapidly in the near future.

Numerous tests were administered to a high proportion of the island's children, some attending the higher status Penn Normal and Industrial School, others one of nine 'public schools', only three of which were in good repair. Tests included the Otis Group Intelligence Test, a self-administration version of this, the Haggerty Intelligence Examination Delta 1, the Goodenough 'Draw-a-Man' Test and a Digit–Symbol/Symbol–Digit substitution test. The results were dreadful. The group tests were 'enormously deficient', even 12-year-olds failed to reach the standardised 7-year-old median on the Otis. Substitution test scores were so bad ($c.$ 40% of 6–16-year-olds obtaining zero scores) that it was concluded that they were not successfully given and the scores had no scientific value (p. 130). It was obvious to Peterson that the basic cause was lack of school training, a conclusion reinforced by the Goodenough Test results. This test, it was argued, was relatively unaffected by school training and the scores obtained equalled those of other 'Negro' groups, although IQ as assessed by this test tended to decline with age. By contrast, on an individually administered Rational Learning test (RLT) the St Helena median was exceeded by 82% of Nashville blacks (and 95% of Nashville whites). Only children attending the Penn Normal School approached mainland levels of performance.

Interpretation of the St Helena findings was less straightforward than might be assumed. Even if the more enterprising had left the island in disproportionate numbers, the cause of the shortfall in performance was manifestly educational. Here was a case where a difference in performance *within* the African American community, *and one greater than that usually found between members of that community and whites*, could only be explained in terms of an environmental factor – gross pedagogic deprivation. This reinforced findings made by Peterson's associate Lyle H. Lanier (1930), reported in the previous issue of the same journal. Lanier compared differences in RLT performance in three cities: Nashville, Chicago and New York. The RLT requires the subject to learn by trial and error an arbitrarily assigned connection between the numbers 1–7 and the letters A–G. This yields numerous measures: total time, trials, logical errors, perseverative errors, total responses and rate of response (as well as 'unclassified', or total, errors). This is an individual test, and Lanier reiterates that race differences on group tests are greater than on individual tests.

In contrast to white subjects, black performance varied considerably between the three cities. In Nashville 80% of whites exceeded 'Negro' averages on time taken, perseveration errors and rate of response. No difference was found on number of trials. In Chicago, with a rather small sample, no reliable race differences were found although whites were slightly superior on all except rate of response. In New York the blacks were *markedly* superior to the whites on number of trials, unclassified and logical errors. Whites were only markedly superior in rate of response, and slightly superior on time taken. Overall, white superiority was most evident in total time, perseveration errors (although not in New York) and response rate. The last was most marked and Lanier concludes that there are perhaps grounds for believing this to be a real race difference (p. 217). Skin colour and other 'anthropological traits' showed no reliable relationship with performance – contrary to findings previously reported in Peterson and Lanier (1929), which were otherwise somewhat similar in showing Northern 'Negro' parity with whites on the RLT (against white superiority on most other measures). Again then, obviously environmentally determined differences *within* the performance of African American groups were found, ranging from gross inferiority (Nashville) to parity or superiority to whites (New York).

While conforming to the usual Race Psychology methodology and conceptual framework, the work of Peterson and his associates during the late 1920s was inadvertently raising two central questions. First the role of 'group attitudes' in exacerbating race differences in group test scores challenged Race Psychologists' growing reliance on these (reinforcing Garth's increasing doubts on the same issue). Secondly if the great variation in performance *within* the black population arose, as it evidently did, from environmental factors then the case for a hereditarian explanation of sometimes quite minor white–black differences was greatly weakened. Notwithstanding this, Peterson's contribution to the 1934 *Journal of Negro Education* special issue, 'Basic considerations of methodology in race testing', is some way from being an explicit recantation. He identifies such methodological flaws in previous research as difficulty of controlling for age, the problem of 'fair sampling' and 'purity of race' – the latter two of which appear to be insuperable although he does not quite admit it. The group versus individual tests issue is also discussed. He nonetheless maintains that the race differences question is valid and asserts that 'the difficulty that environmental factors influence intelligence-test scores is probably not harder to handle scientifically than the control of malaria or yellow fever' (p. 408).[95] The concept of 'intelligence' itself may of course turn out to be flawed, which will mean that racial differences will pertain to differences 'in *emphasis only* of various capacities common to both races compared' (ibid., emphasis in original).

Given the methodological brief of this final paper it may be unfair to expect any clear evaluation of the topic as a whole, and Peterson certainly implies that he does not believe race differences to have been firmly proven. But despite his evident reservations regarding the methodological calibre of most Race Psychology and his awareness of 'group attitude' factors, he did *not* (as some other contributors did) take the opportunity of actually rejecting the 'race differences' project. He was, however, in his mid-fifties by then and perhaps saw this as one of those 'futile controversies' with which he had, according to his obituarist Lanier, such impatience. What *is* curious though is that nowhere in his eight-page obituary of 1936 does Lanier discuss Peterson's race-differences work – in which he himself played a major collaborative role. Even by 1936, involvement in such research was perhaps becoming somewhat *de trop*.

Other frequently cited papers

While the number of psychologists specialising in Race Psychology was small, a great many ventured briefly into the topic. The following somewhat arbitrary selection of often-cited papers will serve to indicate the character of this extensive background material.

In three papers, typical of the founding phase, W.H. Pyle (1915a, b, 1916) reported results of several studies of Missouri children using such tests as 'a free association test calling for speed in continued association', logical memory, a cancellation task, rote memory, motor co-ordination and 'word building' (creating words from six letters).[96] While white superiority was evident throughout, higher social class Negroes performed better than poor ones and race differences somewhat reduced with age (black scores rising from 50% white score at age 8–10 to 73% at age 14–16). In motor co-ordination, which Pyle believed eliminated environmental factors, Negroes scored 80% of the white score. Superior performance of higher social class Negroes might, Pyle suggested, be due to 'more white blood'. Girls surpassed boys throughout, more so among Negro children according to Woodworth (1916) although the relevant graph in Pyle (1915a) hardly bears this out except for 13- and 14-year-olds. In a later (1918) paper he reported intelligence differences between white and Chinese children.

K. Murdoch's work (1920, 1925, 1926) typifies Race Psychology's early 1920s immigration-oriented strand. The 1920 paper compared the Pressey group Intelligence test performances of native whites, 'Hebrews', 'Negroes' and Italians in two poor districts of New York. The results were notable primarily because, while showing no difference between the first two, Negroes outperformed Italians (30% as opposed to 15% Italians achieving the white/'Hebrew' mean). This finding was critically followed up in Margaret Mead (1927). The 1925 and 1926 papers attempted to incorporate 'moral traits', and expanded the number of races with a study conducted in Honolulu (Hawaii). This latter may be seen as a prelude to Porteus's work, although Porteus (1930) only cites her 1920 paper. Her ranking of Hawaiian 'races' much resembled his.

D. Sunne (1917) is notable as being the first Race Psychology paper to report no clear black–white differences. The children studied (112 white, 126 'Negro') were drawn from the poorest districts of New Orleans in order to control for environmental effects. Binet and Yerkes Point Scale intelligence tests were used.[97] The results were very mixed with whites inferior on some traits. Individual variability was noted as the greatest source of variation. Regarding sex differences, girls were superior to boys throughout, more so in the black sample. Despite the improved sampling, the sceptic could reasonably argue that inferior whites were overrepresented in her poor white group by comparison with inferior blacks in the black group (i.e. that the black group was the more representative.). This 'no difference' result was not maintained in her two subsequent papers (1924, 1925a) and Garth (1925) summarises the results of the 1917 paper as showing whites '1 year older mentally', which is certainly not the tenor of the original.[98] The far larger scale 1924 study (nearly 7,000 subjects, 5,834 white) using the National Intelligence Test and Myers Mental Measurement produced more conventional results: whites 1–1.5 years mentally older (on the former test) and 'Negro' scores overlapping only 21% (on the latter).

M.L. Darsie's 1926 study of 658 American-born Japanese children attracted considerable attention as the first study of the Japanese in the USA. Using Binet and the non-verbal Army Beta tests Darsie found no difference from whites on the latter, and an average Binet IQ of 91, which, with allowance made for language handicap, was, the author estimated, probably equivalent to a normal white score.

R. Pintner, one of the last US psychologists to have studied under Wundt, was a leading authority on intelligence testing and published or co-authored six relevant works during the period 1922–37, one being his successful text-book *Intelligence Testing: Methods and Results* (1923b, 2nd revised edn 1931). The majority of his research was on European groups. Pintner and Keller (1922) looked at Italians, Slavs and Hungarians as well as African Americans, using the Binet test. While the black IQ reported was 88, this was superior to Italians and Slavs (84, 85) and nearly as good as the Hungarians (89).[99] The 'white' (i.e. white American) average score was 95. In Pintner (1927), using a non-language test, Belgians were found to be the same as normal (i.e. white) Americans, which was perhaps reassuring to the citizens of Brussels. In 1934 he contributed to the *Journal of Negro Education* special issue and it is this paper which is of most interest. It is a somewhat tight-lipped text addressing the two issues he sees as the crux of the matter: fair sampling and fair measuring instruments in relation to intelligence. As far as American 'Negroes' and whites are concerned, he does not consider sampling to be a major difficulty even if no research has yet fully met the criteria.

Fairness of measuring instruments is somewhat more complex and Pintner rejects the use of verbal group intelligence tests as well as conceding that tests involving speed measures might be dropped.[100] He does not believe environmental factors can fully account for the differences generally reported since even the Binet – the most susceptible to improvement – has shown gains of at most 10 points. On other tests, especially performance tests, environmental influence is likely to be less. A 'less tangible' criticism which 'the present writer has never quite been able to understand' (p. 517) holds that 'there is some subtle psychological difference between the Negro and the white, which handicaps the Negro when attempting the white man's test' (ibid.). If this is so then he suggests a group of tests should be constructed by Negro psychologists ('there are several competent Negro psychologists who could undertake this task').[101] These could then be given to both racial groups. Since all results so far are in the same direction (white superiority) 'it would look as if the intelligence of the Negroes may turn out to be somewhat below that of the whites' (p. 518). By how much 'we have no idea at present'. Nonetheless, the overlap probably exceeds 25% which means there are 'vast sources of Negro intelligence lying dormant, intelligence that should be utilized for the benefit of the whole nation. . . . We must rid ourselves of prejudice, if we would arrive at a scientific solution of our problem'[102] (ibid.). In the light of the calibre of the opposition case being mounted by 1934 one is struck by Pintner's sheer simplicity and lack of sophistication, particularly regarding environmentalist arguments. He had, though, marginally softened since 1923: then he had held 25% to be 'the most liberal estimate' (Garth, 1925, p. 352), whereas now he considers it the most conservative. He continues to accept the Army test scores as valid indices of race differences in intelligence. Pintner to a large extent typifies the mainstream psychometric tradition, endorsing the findings of Race Psychologists and construing the problems as basically matters of methodology.

C. Murchison, Professor of Psychology at Clark University, is remembered mostly as the editor of major reference works such as the *Psychological Register*, the *History of Psychology in Autobiography* series (1930, 1936) and a number of handbooks. In 1925 and 1926 however he published, alone or with associates, 13 papers reporting a study of the intelligence and other traits of criminals, the majority of which pertained to black and foreign-born prisoners, primarily in Ohio, Maryland, Illinois and New Jersey.[103] Sex differences, analysis by type of crime, differences between home state and out-of-state subjects and between first offenders and recidivists were all examined. While intelligence (as assessed by the Army Alpha test) was his primary interest, other factors such as religion, literacy, marital status and occupation were also encompassed. Although revealing a variety of curious facts, such as the superior intelligence of recidivists (Murchison and Nafe, 1925) and that the most literate Negro religious group were the Catholics who were the least literate among whites (Murchison and Gilbert, 1925a),[104] the study appears, in retrospect, stunningly inconsequential. This is because Murchison nowhere attempts to identify any clear theoretical implications of his findings beyond noting that 'the so-called superior races and nationalities give us still more superior criminals, while so-called inferior races and nationalities give us still more inferior criminals' (Murchison and Burfield, 1925a, p. 36). He does, it is true, draw attention to the geographical variation in the 'Negro' army draft scores, which his own study confirms and which he uses throughout as a point of reference (ibid.), and concludes his study of foreign-born criminals by observing that 'more monarchical forms of government are associated with nationalities that show great mental differences between types of crime' (Murchison, 1925a, p. 25). Otherwise, the papers are little more than robustly empirical reports of the data with scant interpretation.

His agenda, if hidden, is not entirely invisible. The work coincided with the height of the immigration scare and the papers on foreign-born criminals would have been read as bearing on this even though the relevant legislation had been passed prior to publication. The Army test findings also provide the framework for the papers on intelligence, and Murchison still accepts these fairly uncritically, while comparisons of home state versus out-of-state black criminals might have been read as relevant to the 'migration hypothesis'. Murchison never returned to the race issue and barely mentions it in his *Social Psychology: The Psychology of Political Domination* (1929b).[105] Indeed he refers to the very existence of 'groups' in any objective sense as 'one of the greatest illusions of social science' (p. 9), and one can only assume that 'races' are included in this. The *Handbook of Social Psychology* (1935) which he edited is usually taken as marking the full arrival of attitude study-centred US Social Psychology, and includes G.W. Allport's seminal paper on this.

Some subsidiary themes in Race Psychology

Race Psychological research covered many more topics than intelligence. We can usefully conclude this survey by briefly identifying representative studies of some of these.

First one is struck by the number of studies of colour preferences, which it was felt might disclose racial differences in aesthetic appreciation. This was first addressed by Sunne (1917) and Garth published four papers on the topic (the last, in 1938, coming in his post-Race Psychology phase). A typical, if as it happened unsuccessful, piece of research is Elizabeth B. Hurlock's 'Color preferences of white and negro children' (1927), undertaken with 400 children (194 white) of both sexes in a New York public school. The white subjects' average IQ score was 9 points above the black score, but the latter was still in Terman's 'average' range. Subjects were given a list of 13 colours and required, without time limit, simply to underline their favourite. This method eliminated 'any association or thought of its suitability for a specific purpose' (p. 392), as well as the complicating factor of 'shades' present when coloured slips, and so on, were used. Relationships of colour preference to age, sex, IQ and race were all analysed. The differences found were marginal – blue and pink emerged as first and second preferences overall, with the black boys preferring blue somewhat more strongly, younger children showed slightly more variation, white children conformed more to certain choices, nobody chose black as their favourite while other dull colours also ranked low. 'The facts brought out by this study do not confirm the popular belief that negro children have a far greater tendency towards bright colors than do white children' (p. 404). She ends by suggesting that racial differences in aesthetics must be looked for elsewhere than in colour preferences, though does not countenance the possibilities that they do not exist or are culturally determined. Garth (1931c) incidentally found that American Indians had the longest (i.e. most differentiated) colour preference scale of those groups studied, with Mexicans least, and noted the strong white and 'Negro' favouring of blue. Since there were changes during schooling and apparent racial differences increased with age and amount of education, he concluded that any differences were due to 'nurtural' factors.

Personality traits such as 'will-temperament', fatigue, and musical ability (another aspect of the 'aesthetic appreciation' issue) received occasional attention. McFadden and Dashiell (1923) in a study of 154 subjects (77 white, 77 Negro) using the Downey Will-Temperament scale claimed to find that whites had 15.4% stronger personalities, a finding which (using the same test) Sunne (1925b) failed to replicate, but which Garth and Barnard (1927) found seemed to be also true of American Indians. A late study by Steggerda and Macomber (1939) attempting to compare 'mental and social characteristics of Maya and Navajo Indians' reveals the straits in which some Race Psychology researchers were, by this time, finding themselves. Accepting that direct testing was unsatisfactory for all the reasons critics had suggested (biased tests, different motivations of subjects etc.) they seem to hark back to Porteus's earlier approach, enlisting a large number of 'people qualified to judge them' (p. 51) such as 'missionaries, traders, school teachers, government officials, nurses . . .' (p. 52). This motley body were required to rate the tribe they knew on 61 traits using a five-point scale (as far as I can discern). The upshot was an extraordinary muddle. Raters found the task extremely difficult, reporting themselves unable to (a) avoid generalising from a few individuals they knew to the group as a whole and (b) overcome subjective opinion and be 'objective'. They explain that while a group may not be courteous (for instance) by our standards, they are by their own, and so on. The researchers, we realise, simply cannot really hear what they are, apologetically, being told: (a) that their trait categories may lack any transcultural reality or meaning and (b) that the notion that groups 'as a whole' can manifest personality traits which are 'objectively' knowable independently of their possession by individual members known to the rater is absurd – philosophers would recognise it as a nice example of a 'category mistake'.

The studies of musical ability mostly used Seashore's Musical Talent Test (Seashore himself publishing an overview paper in 1928).[106] The ethnocentricity of this test soon, however, became apparent, while it often lacked face validity, with patently accomplished non-European musicians scoring poorly. Aside from the limits of pitch audibility most other variables, (pitch and intensity discrimination, rhythm, tonal memory and experience of note combinations as dissonant) were increasingly recognised as culturally or educationally determined.

Other topics included eidetic imagery (Peck and Hodges, 1937a, b), comparisons of Negro and white infants and neonates (most notably McGraw, 1931), and psychopathology (for example, Bevis, 1921). A persistent *leitmotif* was, as we have seen, the race mixture question. Despite widespread belief in the 'mulatto hypothesis', 'miscegenation' and 'hybridisation' were often strongly opposed, especially by eugenicists. The leading US eugenicist C.B. Davenport gave his alarmism full rein in Davenport and Steggerda (1928) *Race Crossing in Jamaica*, a 516-page Carnegie Institute monograph.[107] Among other things this claimed that 'brown' (as opposed to black) Jamaicans were inferior to either whites or blacks and that race mixing would have 'disharmonious' physiological consequences – a notion authoritatively refuted in a *Science* paper by Castle (1930).[108] The book contained numerous internal inconsistencies and methodological flaws which opponents quickly seized on.[109] In retrospect it was something of a final fling for classic Scientific Racism.[110] Basic psychophysical level studies remained few in number, though Harmon (1937) on reaction times is a late exception. Several writers have noticed A.L. Crane (1923), a study of race differences in inhibition, primarily because of the astonishingly frank account of how he obtained his 'Southern darkie' [*sic*] subjects.[111]

A few broader studies might finally be mentioned: J.W. Dunlap (1930) argued for racial differences in the way intellectual abilities were organised, J.L. Graham (1930a, b) reported research on differences between white and Negro students regarding a variety of 'mental traits' and 'rational responses', while Eells (1933a, b, c) produced a comprehensive study of Alaskan Eskimoes, which was followed in 1935 by Anderson and Eells' *Alaskan Natives: a survey of their sociological and educational status.*

CONCLUSION: INTERPRETING RACE PSYCHOLOGY

While initially relatively narrowly focused on the 'Negro education' and European immigration questions from a Scientific Racism/Eugenics perspective Race Psychology's agenda rapidly broadened during the 1920s. Pressures from within Psychology itself were one factor in this: the widespread theoretical abandonment of instinct models in favour of an environmentalist behaviourist approach, the continued concern with methodological rigour and establishing Psychology's good scientific credentials, and the emergence of Social Psychology all contributed to this. By the end of the 1920s the papers of leading figures such as Garth and Peterson contrast strongly with those of, for example, Mayo and Ferguson a decade or more earlier. Classic Scientific Racist authorities are rarely invoked, environmental determinants are no longer simply swept aside or viewed as easily eliminable, and the deeper conceptual difficulties of, for example, the definition of race are beginning to be admitted. Post-Great War radical Civil Rights agitation and the 'Harlem Renaissance' were also undermining the previous alignment of psychologists with the paternalistic conservative segregationist camp. In the next chapter we will explore the process whereby Race Psychology had collapsed by the mid-1930s. In the meantime I would like to raise some more specific problems about how Race Psychology is to be read and evaluated.

First, the honesty of the research. We have seen for example the gross disparity between the economic data, mostly available at the time, on 'Negro education' funding and assertions of comparability of black and white subjects in Strong's and Ferguson's papers. We have also seen the extraordinary bootstrapping operation by which Porteus, without even directly assessing a single 'non-Caucasian' subject, was able to arrive at purported measures of racial social efficiency purely on the basis of the subjective ratings of 25 white 'experts'. In many of the more extended texts we do not have to hunt very hard to find inconsistencies and double standards operating between the interpretation of white and African American (or other 'race') data (e.g. large within-race differences are environmental but small between-race differences are evidence of hereditary difference). Relatively minor differences in performance can, by statistical juggling, be given the most pessimistic spin possible (e.g. Mayo, 1913). The 'status reflects intelligence' and 'difference as default assumption' arguments now read as spurious or implausible sophistry. These flaws, which seem to the present-day reader so glaring, were presumably largely invisible to most contemporaries, and certainly to the authors. Are we dealing here with genuine dishonesty, intellectual naivety, a defunct but internally consistent 'paradigm' into the spirit of which we can no longer enter, or unthinking conformity to implicit culturally racist assumptions and modes of thinking? Although no single answer is likely to be universally applicable, my feeling is that the last of these is the most common. Race Psychologists were trapped within culturally pervasive racist modes of thought which rendered them either unable to see such failings or unable to grasp their seriousness (e.g. Pintner, 1934). Eventually, under persistent and mounting pressure, most were forced into a series of adjustments and concessions which finally eroded the credibility of the entire race–differences approach. This is not to say that their opponents did not remain similarly trapped in some important respects, but at least the first layer of the onion had, so to speak, been stripped away.

Secondly we may ask how coherent Race Psychology was as a 'school'. This will be addressed further in the next chapter, but the material reviewed here suggests that it was in fact quite heterogeneous, although a core tradition of research on black–white differences in the intelligence of school children persisted throughout. Theoretically Porteus was at odds with Brigham's original position and both were distinct from Garth. After the early 1920s the explicit classic Scientific Racism of the eugenicists (e.g. Davenport and Porteus) contrasts with the dourly empiricist and more pragmatic, even atheoretical, approaches of Peterson and Garth.

Thirdly, reading Race Psychology presents the historian with something of a challenge. One is faced with performing a balancing act between hermeneutic identification and retrospective diagnosis, between treating the authors as 'children of their time' and criticism which may become unfairly anachronistic. The fact that oppositional voices *were* present in the cultural arena to some extent mitigates this anxiety. One is forced to conclude that many Race Psychologists (especially earlier ones) were indeed defiantly blinkering themselves from the full range of contemporary analysis and commentary, particularly choosing to ignore Chicago School sociology and Boasian anthropology, as well as the growing body of African American-authored sociology and history.

One should additionally emphasise that from very early on Race Psychologists were aware of the majority of the arguments against race differences which dominated the 'race and IQ' controversy of the late 1960s and 1970s (and continue to figure whenever the issue enjoys a fitful resurrection). While we examine the opposition in detail in the next chapter these may usefully be enumerated here.

1 Differences may be accounted for by non-hereditary factors.
2 Tests may be biased towards white culture in their content.
3 Overlap in distribution of scores demonstrates that there is no essential connection between 'race' and ability (or any other psychological trait).
4 The tester's own 'race' will have an 'experimenter effect' (as we would now say) on subjects' performances.
5 Sampling of racial groups may, or even must, be unrepresentative.
6 The very concept of 'race' is scientifically problematic.
7 'Racial' levels of performance may change over time ('race mobility'), therefore current underperformance may be transient.
8 The entire project is really racist, not scientific, in motivation.

To each of these Race Psychology developed standard responses, which in turn elicited fairly standardised ripostes from their opponents. These last gradually eroded Race Psychology's credibility but, as already indicated, the ritualised nature of the debate has persisted ever since – radically new angles only beginning to emerge in the late 1980s. Many of these responses and counters have been mentioned already, others will be discussed in Chapters 5 and 9.

This review has important implications for Psychology's prevailing historical image of the period. For a start it is quite remarkable that the three most prolific race-differences researchers – Garth, Porteus and J. Peterson – are virtually *never* discussed or even cited in current historical texts.[112] Coverage is also invariably limited to studies of US white–African American differences and the early 1920s immigration panic (e.g. Fancher 1985).[113] Even this is generally limited to Goddard, sometimes Ferguson and Strong, and, occupying centre-stage, the Army Alpha results followed by mention of Brigham's recantation and perhaps Klineberg's criticisms. 'Enlightened' studies of prejudice then take centre stage in the 1930s with the rise of Nazism. This picture is inadequate in several ways.

- It exaggerates the dominance of African American subjects. Although the largest single subject group (excepting white Americans) these only account for about a fifth to a third of all subjects (with the same proviso). For 73 pieces of research 1925–9 Garth calculates a total of 7,185 'American Negro' subjects in a total of 36,882, or 25 groups from a total of 132 (Garth, 1930a, p. 341). Furthermore, while this was not discussed in any detail, Race Psychology was successfully exported to Japan and China and, though less successfully, to Britain, India and South Africa.[114]
- The existing picture, while rightly stressing US immigration fears as a contextual factor, ignores the West Coast dimension to this, typified by Porteus's work but including several West Coast studies of Asian intelligence and temperament. It also overlooks the interest in native Americans and Mexicans.
- Preoccupation with intelligence has resulted in a failure to appreciate the breadth of Race Psychology's concerns. Intelligence was only the most important in a list including personality, social efficiency, fatigue, inhibition, aesthetic taste, eidetic imagery, psychopathology and neonate behaviour.
- The more extreme wing has understandably hogged such historical limelight as exists with the effect that less racialistically motivated and less dogmatic researchers such, notably, as Garth have been completely forgotten.[115]

This is not to deny that Race Psychology was by current lights racist – of course it was – it does however suggest that engaging in the project was itself on occasion a route by which psychologists came to *discover* their own white racism for what it was. While this holds overtly for only a handful of individuals, at another level it applies to the discipline as a whole: I would argue that in the USA it was the experience of the failure of Race Psychology, and the associated insights into *why* it failed, that actually enabled contemporary US psychologists to really begin to *see* racism (a term only dating from 1936)[116] as a phenomenon. I will explore this further in the next chapter; for the moment I only wish to insist on this reflexive aspect of the situation: the criticising and defending of Race Psychology was the very psychological process by which 'racism' itself came to be recognised and articulated as a problem within and for Psychology. Race Psychology was not so much consciously motivated by racism as the route by which unconscious racist motivations were forced to the surface.

Other historiographic lessons are better held in reserve for the moment. In the meantime I will close this chapter on a minor, querulous, note. In 1930

J.E.W. Wallin published a little paper in the journal *School and Society*: 'The ratio of candidates for sight conservation classes'. The gist of this was that undiagnosed visual impairment was far more common among black children than white ones.[117] Given the now widely recognised deleterious effect of even quite minor visual impairment (especially short-sightedness) on school performance one cannot help wondering whether, with one modest stroke, Wallin had not subverted the findings of the entire edifice of Race Psychology research conducted on children of African ancestry. Possibly not – things are rarely that simple – but it's an interesting thought.

NOTES

1 The number of immigrants 1900–14 was *c*. 13 million.
2 For a general background account relevant to much of what follows see H.A. Bullock (1967). See also: W.E.B. Du Bois (1911a). Bullock argues that the all-black Southern educational institutions inadvertently provided a training ground for future black activists.
3 Historical analysis of this phase has been controversial. One bone of contention has been how far the 'slavocracy' was re-established. Camejo (1994, 1st edn 1976), in an avowedly Marxist account, argues that the evidence now points to Eastern business and railroad interests rather than the old planter agricultural interests gaining economic control after Reconstruction's collapse. White supremacy was now accepted in almost all white camps, including, I was amazed to discover, by an elderly Harriet Beecher Stowe!
4 This camp is typified by e.g. the University Commission in Southern Race Questions which met from 1912–17 and comprised a dozen eminent southern university presidents etc. plus representatives of leading philanthropic organisations such as the Jeanes Fund.
5 They could of course cite the work discussed in the previous chapter in support of this critical stance.
6 See W.H. Tucker (1994, Chapter 3) for fuller discussion of US Nordicist eugenics.
7 Pearson and Moul (1925–8), see Chapter 7.
8 The first tests designed specifically for use with immigrants were the 1914 'Knox Immigration Tests' for identifying 'mental defect' and devised for the US Public Health Service at Ellis Island. These were published by C.H. Stoelting, the major US publisher and manufacturer of Psychological tests. See H.G. Knox (1914).
9 Excepting Yerkes's leading role in the Army testing programme of 1917 discussed below.
10 On occasion it is hard to classify a paper which is highly hedged with qualifications, and I have tended in these cases to classify according to whether it is basically Race Psychological in spirit or not. The 'Other' category includes a variety of texts ranging from Otis (1913–14) about lesbian relationships between black and white inmates of a home for delinquent girls to Grundlach (1932) on Indian music. Most frequently however they tended to be broad sociological or political level overviews of the 'Race Problem', histories, or sociological monographs on specific cities. For the 1909–40 period I felt able to classify 1071 of 1138 (94%), the unclassified 6% were generally journal papers unavailable in the UK.
11 Giddings, of Columbia University, identified four temperamental types and then classified the various US regions, immigrant groups, 'coloreds' and religious denominations accordingly, calculating populations of each using Census data. 'Coloreds' are predominantly 'Ideo-Motor' and 'Ideo-Emotional' (like the Irish) by contrast with 'Dogmatic-Emotional' and 'Critical-Intellectual' New Englanders and 'Scotch'.

Also 'the chronic emotional insanity of the Kansans in their law and politics indicates a strong lean of their mental type towards the ideo-emotional' (1901, p. 343).

12 In fact the peak appears to be as early as 1926: the number of publications in that year (29) was never approached again and although this category accounts for over 40% of publications every year until 1926 (50% or over excepting 2 years), it only exceeds 40% once subsequently (1928). Until 1930 it is always the major category (bar 1912), after 1930 it never is.

13 Pre-1930 non-US publications account for about 3.5% of Category A, 1930–40 they account for about 26% (19/72).

14 J. Royce (1906, 1908).

15 The British biologist Julian Huxley was also prominent in this, see J. Huxley and A.C. Haddon (1935) and J. Huxley (1936).

16 On occasion, as noted in n. 10, it can become somewhat difficult to classify highly hedged papers; this is especially so in the 1930s. This can mean that papers by the same author can be classified differently (e.g. C.W. Telford 1930 and 1932 were coded Anti-Race Differences and Race Psychology respectively).

17 In this respect the shift is similar to that adopted towards homosexuality and women after c. 1970 – in each case the issue is redefined from one of the 'psychology' of the group in question to the nature of hostile attitudes towards it.

18 Samelson (1978). He deduces this from researchers' surnames.

19 See Kuper (1973, Chapter 4) for a brief review of the rather tangled relationships between British anthropology and British colonialism during this period. Langham (1981) is somewhat fiercer: 'An anthropology with the avowed aim of uncovering the factors which kept societies in smoothly-functioning harmony, and a national colonial policy which imposed its will on distant peoples by plugging into the indigenous political organization, could not have been innocent playmates' (p. xv). For a more recent discussion see Shanklin (1994). See also p. 181 n. 1, p. 216, p. 223, n. 74 below.

20 For example, Garth (1925) devotes some space to Lévy-Bruhl, though is somewhat sceptical.

21 For example, Beaglehole (1939) on 'Tongan color vision'; Parr (1934) on 'Taste blindness and race'.

22 In his review article in *Psychological Bulletin* (1930a) he describes Moton's work as 'a very intelligent presentation of the Negro's reaction to his American social, economic, and intellectual environment. It may well be regarded as a true picture of what the educated Negro thinks as well as an account of his aspirations' (p. 335). He also refers to Odum (1928) as a 'remarkable contribution' and in Garth (1931b) as 'redolent of flavor and flaming with color' (p.174).

23 Professor at Olivet College, Michigan, who figures in a footnote to H.E. Jordan's 1913 paper on the 'mulatto'.

24 Some of this was psychoanalytic, some of a more orthodox psychiatric character. Depending on their approach texts on psychopathology usually fall into categories A, B or D.

25 See, e.g., T.R. Garth (1930a).

26 This incidentally raises an interesting question regarding publication policy. It is widely acknowledged that research failing to yield significant findings does not tend to get published. Only when absence of difference itself becomes a point at issue (as, in this case, happened after c. 1930) is this likely to be overridden. We must therefore wonder how far the pre-1930 consistency of 'race-difference' findings was an illusion resulting from the usual unpublishability of 'no significant differences' findings. (This point is elaborated on slightly further in G. Richards, 1995). Two late publications in the genre did however attract considerable post-war attention: Tanser (1939) and Bruce (1940) (see L. Plotkin, 1959; Garrett, 1962; Klineberg, 1963; M.S. Smart, 1963).

27 See, for example, his casual references to 'nigger fighting' and 'putting a nigger in uniform' in his autobiographical entry in Murchison (1936, reprinted 1961).

28 Though he did contribute the Introduction to T.R. Garth (1931b), Garth being 'my friend and former pupil' (p. xiii). As editor of *Archives of Psychology* he also oversaw publication of several important monographs on the topic, e.g. Klineberg (1928). By the 1940 12th edition of his highly successful *Psychology. A Study of Mental Life* he is highly sceptical about innate race differences, giving only two pp. to the topic and citing only O. Klineberg.

29 As will be seen later, Garth did most of his work with American Indians and Mexicans, and Porteus focused on the Japanese and other Hawaiian groups.

30 Whether or not the 'n' in 'negro' should be capitalised was a moot point of political correctness throughout the pre-1940 period. Odum's usage varies. During the 1930s capitalisation became customary, being seen as signifying respect.

31 Certainly Ferguson (1916) cites no such work in his fairly detailed introduction. Coffin (1908) contains no such research, being a review of educational practice in different cultures. Clearly in the G.S. Hall tradition, Coffin nevertheless concluded, 'No conclusions as yet reached . . . justify the assumption that they [i.e. 'backward races'] are specifically inferior, or . . . not susceptible to proper educational influences' (p. 56).

32 The quotation is from 'The errors of sociology' (H.W. Odum 1936–7), cited by Klineberg (1944, pp. 95–6). As well as Odum (1928), see his *Race and Rumors of Race* (1943), a monograph on the racial unrest of 1942–3 largely triggered by the increasing recalcitrance of on-leave African American servicemen who had served overseas. This arose from his involvement in a 'University Committee on the Study of Rumors'. He includes Ruth Benedict (1940b) on his 'fine list of books interpreting both the present situation and the new Negro'.

33 C.S. Johnson was an African American. One product of this work was H.W. Odum and G.B. Johnson (1925).

34 C.S. Johnson also notes the subjectivity of the assessments and that many of the 'Negro' children were from migrant families, and thus were previously in 'inferior and backward' Southern schools. (Weatherford and Johnson, 1934, pp. 226–7).

35 See especially pp. 58–61.

36 Substantial knowledge about human evolution, other than the fact that it had happened, was at this time effectively zero. Things are now a little better, but not so much as one might expect – controversy reigns on most issues of psychological relevance. See K.R. Gibson and T. Ingold (1993) for a recent collection of relevant papers.

37 This research was also incorporated into a 1914 paper by her supervisor J. Morse (Morse, 1914).

38 The leading US proponent of intelligence testing and creator of the 'Stanford–Binet' revision of the original Binet–Simon scale.

39 See Department of the Interior, Bureau of Education (1916, 1917) vol. 2, Chapter XVI; on Columbia and Howard (Public) High School see pp. 504–5. Seven elementary grades were taught in the same building as the High School. Given higher black non-attendance the actual discrepancy in staff–child ratios may have been a bit less, but hardly such as to eliminate the disparity! Bullock (1967) gives the average lengths of term in South Carolina for 1909–10 as 125:74 days (white:black) – in 1928–9 it was 173:114, so at the time of Strong's research black terms were probably still less than two-thirds those of white terms (p.177). Bullock gives 1914–15 expenditure per head as $10.70: $1.04 (p.180).

40 Mayo (1913) cites a preliminary report (on 239 subjects, 120 colored) of this research which had appeared earlier the same year in *Journal of Educational Psychology*.

41 Mayo's relatively good figures on black performance are ascribed to more selective sampling and the fact that subjects were children of the more intelligent and enterprising blacks who emigrated from the South. This 'migration hypothesis' to account

for superior Northern black performance subsequently, as we will see, became the standard line. cf. Johnson's contrasting view, n. 34 above.

42 Department of the Interior, Bureau of Education Report vol. 2 p. 609. Some of the schools Ferguson mentions cannot be identified in the report, for example John Marshall school in Newport News and the George Mason elementary school in Richmond. Overall State figures on salary and staffing levels show teacher salaries per child as $9.64 for whites, $2.74 for 'colored' (p.607). See also data in Bullock (1967, pp. 177–81).

43 Woodworth and Wells Mixed Relations I and II, Ebbinghaus Completion Test, 'a Cancellation Test' and 'one of the Columbia Maze Tests' (p.37).

44 It should be reiterated at this point that among African Americans there was a correlation between skin lightness and higher social status. This is discussed at some length by Dollard (1957, 1st edn 1937). Even *within* the African American group, therefore, skin colour and socio-economic circumstance were correlated.

45 This is a leitmotif throughout the earlier work. It is often oddly naive in appealing to current rates of eminence for confirmation, for it assumes (a) that eminence is an objective phenomenon and (b) that all eminence would be equally known to everyone, rather than seeing that white males have defined eminence according to their own values (a genius kayak-maker would not figure!), and will in any case be more acquainted with white than, say, Chinese cases. Since enduring reputations for eminence can only exist in a literate society, it is also hardly surprising that, say, 'great' African thinkers or sculptors of the 4th century BC have, unlike Aristotle or Praxiteles, been forgotten! I guess this is a very obvious point, but apparently it was *not* so to white writers like Ferguson.

46 See S.J. Gould (1984), M.M. Sokal (1987) and J. Carson (1993) for recent comprehensive and critical studies of the episode which have somewhat demythologised the traditional heroic tale. Gould in particular exposes it as a methodological and conceptual débacle of the first order.

47 Psychology's other Great War involvements in shell-shock treatment and industrial fatigue etc. also contributed to this.

48 See H.E. Garrett (1945), and M.F.A. Montagu (1945). The latest instalments of the saga are Rury (1988) and a more elaborated sequel, Galloway (1994), both in the *Journal of Negro Education*. The latter provides a complex statistical analysis of the contribution of 5 educational and 12 economic factors to the inter-state differences between black and white scores using 1900 and 1910 data and the 1916–17 Department of the Interior, Bureau of Education report. The former prove the most significant and he concludes 'the results leave little doubt that the institutionalized racism that pervaded the educational system in this country at the turn of the century was, to a large extent, responsible for the Black–White score differential on the 1917 Army Alpha' (p. 264).

49 In the popular press the most intense attack on the Army Alpha findings was mounted by Walter Lippman in the *New Republic* from October 1921 onwards following the publication of Yerkes's official report *Psychological Examining in the United States Army* (see also Yoakum and Yerkes, 1920 for description of tests and scoring procedure). His arguments concentrated on what he saw as the absurdity of supposing a single test could measure such a complex phenomenon as intelligence. Terman fought back in an acrimonious exchange which lasted until January 1923. This was reprinted in N. Block and G. Dworkin (1976a).

50 H.H. Goddard (1917a, b, c). See also Kevles (1985, pp. 81–3).

51 Since this proviso appeared on the last page of Section VII he presumably forgot it very quickly!

52 Relative inferiority of rural to city IQ performance was well established by this time, not least by the Army tests themselves.

53 As expressed in McDougall (1921).

54 According to Kevles (1985, p. 97). It should be stressed that Davenport, though not a psychologist, was a major force in this entire episode, being the leading US eugenicist/geneticist at the time and an ardent disciple of Galton. The subsequently world famous Cold Spring Harbor genetics institute was created for him in 1904. 'In addition, he established the Eugenics Record Office and the Eugenics Research Association, which became his empire on the Long Island Shore' (Barkan, 1992, p. 70). He was in close cahoots with Madison Grant. See W.H. Tucker (1994, pp. 94–7) for more on the anti-immigration network.

55 That is, 'Negro' children who achieved a given school grade at the same age as the average white child achieved this grade would be the superior ones and conversely white children who achieved the grade at the same age as the average Negro 'child' would be the inferior ones.

56 Obvious though the point may be, there is of course no logical reason why one should not calculate the number of 'mulattoes' in the white population. The term 'white' has always been reserved for those with no apparent non-white ancestry whatsoever. At the time in question especially, any identifiable degree of non-white ancestry was a 'taint' justifying expulsion from the white community. The fact that this classificatory habit persists to the present day signifies quite how deeply engrained the fetishising of 'pure' whiteness remains.

57 In this connection it should be noted that the apparently poor results on the Army tests generally created widespread popular concern, seeming to imply that 45 million Americans had 'mental ages' no greater than 12. This especially boosted the domestic eugenics program in relation to the 'mentally deficient', causing an 'undue alarm' that S.P. Davies (1930), for example, was still anxious to counter (see pp. 368–70). Doubts about 'Negro' mental capacity were also voiced from a eugenics direction in K. Miller (1917).

58 For a long time I assumed that he did and that I had simply lost the relevant reference, but William Tucker (in a personal communication) informs me that he has no knowledge of such a recantation and I now believe I was mistaken.

59 He cites Kelley (1927, 1928).

60 This passage remained unchanged at least up to the 1932 reprint.

61 Clipping in University of Denver Penrose Library Archives, source unidentified.

62 G. Richards (in press). I have taken the present opportunity of providing a full bibliography of Garth's 'race'-related work (which I was unable to do in this paper) following the main bibliography. The reader should refer to this for works cited in the text.

63 'He said that he concentrated on American Indians because, being from the South, he did not feel he could be completely objective when testing Blacks' (personal communication from his daughter-in-law Mrs Thomas R. Garth 26 March 1995).

64 Born in 1872, he was already in his mid-thirties when he graduated from the University of Denver in 1909, having spent his early years as a country school teacher in Kentucky. His move to Colorado came in 1903 for health reasons. He was thus in his forties when he obtained his doctorate under Woodworth at Columbia in 1917. In 1920 he was head of the 'Universal Race Commission' and was also a member of the Eugenical Research Society. His final papers were therefore written when he was in his sixties (see also Murchison, 1929). In addition to *Race Psychology* he published two other books: *Mental Fatigue* (1918) and *Educational Psychology* (1937). The Denver University Penrose Library Archives also contain a eulogy (no author given) and additional bibliographic information on his later years citing various popular magazine articles, plus a small amount of supplementary documentation and photos. I am grateful to Nancy E. Mann (assistant curator) for supplying this material. I have received additional material and personal communications from his surviving daughter Ethel Nadine Jackson and daughter-in-law Mrs T.R. Garth. The above information is variously drawn from these sources.

65 See pp. 1–2 of the anonymous euology 'Thomas Russell Garth (1872–1939)' in Denver University Penrose Library Archives.

66 A phrase lifted, unreferenced, by L. Zusne (1984) in his *Biographical Dictionary of Psychology* entry. Contributors to biographical reference works really should not take their subjects' accounts of themselves at face value – especially if their lives spanned the first half of the 20th century.

67 Though he eventually recanted, Goddard is remembered as one of the foremost US eugenicists, particularly for his book on the 'Kallikak Family' (1913a), perhaps the best known of the family history cases used to argue for the heritability of 'degeneracy'. For Porteus's early career see Murchison (1929a) and Porteus (1969).

68 A point ignored by pro-differences writers in the modern 'race and IQ' controversy right down to Herrnstein and Murray (1994), though I'm reluctant to draw it to their attention.

69 Fully reported in Porteus (1930).

70 See Porteus (1930, pp. 125–49 for a fairly full account. The Pintner-Paterson Performance Scale comprised 14 subtests such as the Knox Cube Test, the Anderson Picture Completion test and other joys.

71 Though he appears to have maintained his Vineland post until 1925.

72 Porteus (1931).

73 It is of some interest that the physical anthropology side of this was undertaken by the English anatomist and evolutionary theorist Frederic Wood Jones. As a result Porteus and he co-authored *The Matrix of the Mind* (Wood Jones and Porteus,1928).

74 This turn-of-the-century Pacific expansion of US rule is little known in Britain. The attendant 'colonial' management problems are obviously a major political background factor as far as Porteus's Hawaiian labours are concerned. Technically the Philippines became independent in 1934, but this remained unimplemented until after World War II.

75 See R. Adams (1934, 1937).

76 Given that the boy is barefoot and a crumbling shack is in the background we are expected to answer in the latter direction.

77 Or, it occurs to me, did *someone else* infiltrate or suggest them, and Porteus just nod them through without thinking about it? Or were they Babcock's idea? I guess we'll never know.

78 Methodologically this scoring procedure seems, on the information provided, rather suspect, since 'races' generally seen as not being extreme on a trait will rarely receive a rating. The average score must therefore be arrived at by dividing their total *not* by 25 (the number of raters) but by the number who rate it at all – otherwise average scores below 1 would be possible. However, although this is the logic of Porteus's account it was obviously not the actual procedure. There is a suggestion that all the 'races' were ranked on each trait: 'The extreme ratings having been allotted the intermediate scores are more easily determined' (p. 93) – but this is not further elaborated and there are six 'races' and only five ranks! (Maybe I'm missing something obvious.)

79 Population figures on the 1920 census.

80 Australian aborigines are invoked extensively here. Porteus had worked with them prior to emigrating and believes they are rarely capable of proceeding beyond 4th grade in schooling, as well as having small brains. He had published a paper on 'Mental tests with delinquents and Australian aborigine children' in 1917, expounding some of these conclusions.

81 I have been unable to locate Kaes's findings (which Mayo also cites) or even his initial(s) – Porteus gives none. Mayo's citation is within a quote from E.J. Swift (1908, p. 221).

82 See Chapter XVII 'Importance of temperament'. Keith's key paper was 'The Differentiation of Mankind into Racial Types' (1919a). Porteus gives Smithsonian Report 1917, but Keith gives *Nature* 104, p. 301, 1919 (Keith, 1950, p. 397). He also published a lecture (1919b), 'The evolution of human races in the light of the hormone

theory' (Keith,1922) and a small book *Ethnos – The Problem of Race* (1931). While attempting to dissociate himself from anti-semitism and race prejudice, Keith never abandoned his belief in races as 'a powerful manifestation of human nature' (see Keith, 1950, pp. 614–15). *Ethnos* is a no doubt well-meant plea for the importance of understanding the evolutionary roots of race differences if 'the Problem of Race' is to be peacefully resolved, but his evolutionary mind-set is too deeply rooted for him to transcend what is ultimately a Scientific Racist orientation to the issue. His endocrine theory was considered as discredited by the 1930s (see Garth, 1934a, pp. 324–5 and Klineberg, 1935b, pp. 46–54). Incidentally, recent research has fingered him, if not too convincingly, for the Piltdown hoax (F. Spencer, 1990). Barkan (1992) has a fairly good and more widely referenced account of Keith's views on race, which he shows to be notably confused, though always racialist and often racist (see especially pp. 41–53). Keith certainly believed in the Aryan race (Keith, 1932).

83 See for example Finot (1969, 1st edn 1906, pp. 62–71) on this latter point and the follies of race-theorists regarding the issue in general. Some in fact had argued that dolichocephaly was the superior condition, notwithstanding exceptions like Kant!

84 How great a role Porteus played in promoting this view I cannot assess, but in the event it led to the internment of thousands of perfectly loyal US Japanese (but no Germans) during World War II.

85 Herskovits (1928) and Yoder (1928).

86 To start with, he was the son of an émigré Ulster Protestant minister and named after David Livingstone and his 'rescuer' Stanley. His autobiography, (Porteus, 1969) is too complex for exegesis here however.

87 This journal was promoted by the International Association for the Advancement of Ethnology and Eugenics (IAAEE) – a cover organisation for pro-racist academics. Its first editor, in place while Porteus was publishing in its pages, was the Scottish self-professed Nazi and IAAEE committee member Robert Gayre of Gayre. See W.H. Tucker (1994) especially pp. 174–7.

88 His data excludes the native white American groups which were being used mainly as control groups.

89 For a full critical review from a contemporary perspective see O. Klineberg (in Klineberg, 1944, Parts II and III). This usefully sets race-related research in the context of other Psychological work of the period on the traits etc. being studied.

90 His low-status college affiliation was due to a high-minded rejection of Chicago to avert ex-colleagues' denigration following resignation on a matter of principle from the University of Utah (Lanier, 1936).

91 This is an important point. It was a common illusion that if someone had an IQ of say 85 this meant they had only 85% of the normal IQ of, by definition, 100. The illusion becomes obvious if you imagine this procedure applied to height: if mean male height of 5'8" = 100 and the SD (= 15 points) is say 4" then 4'4" would equal a 'Height Quotient' of 40 and zero is reached at about 3'6". The convention was based on the notion of the Chronological Age–Mental Age ratio and continued when this was replaced by basing it on standard deviations from the mean, the earlier method obviously being inapplicable to adults. IQ scores denote someone's position relative to the population on which they were standardised, not, like e.g. measures of height, an absolute value.

92 In Peterson (1921) he had however shown 80–95% of whites surpassing 'Negroes' mean score on learning and multiple choice tasks (N = 626, 311 being white).

93 These figures tended to be expressed as '.58' or '.92' rather than straight whole numbers. Scoring techniques were in considerable flux at this time, with Mental Age–Chronological Age ratios still being commonplace.

94 That is, *not* the British mid-Atlantic island where Napoleon died.

95 Malaria and yellow fever being archetypal African diseases there is obviously some unconscious sub-text here.

96 Two six-letter sets were used: aeobmt, aeirlp (Pyle, 1915a).

97 For the Yerkes Point Scale see Yerkes, Bridges and Hardwick (1915).
98 Garth (1925) seems to include the 1924 paper twice here (see Table 1, pp. 354, 355), once dated 1923, although only 1924 appears in his Bibliography.
99 Here and elsewhere I of course report such figures in a deadpan fashion, and should not be read as endorsing the meaningfulness of differentiating between Hungarian average Binet scores of 89 and African American averages of 88!
100 See discussion of Klineberg (1928) in Chapter 5.
101 According to Samelson (1978) only nine black Ph.D.s in Psychology had been gained by 1940, and between 1920 and 1966, of 3,700 produced by 10 leading Psychology departments only 8 were earned by blacks. See Wispé et al. (1971) for a full analysis. One does not have to have a Ph.D. to be a 'competent' psychologist of course, but the 'several' must have been few in number indeed in 1934.
102 'a scientific solution of our problem' is the key phrase: by this point in time the 'our' primarily consists of white psychologists and the 'problem' is really the highly *internal* one of overcoming methodological difficulties of sampling and test fairness which are hampering the progress of Race Psychology. Why the 'several competent Negro psychologists' should be expected to devote their undoubtedly overstrained resources to assisting the resolution of this white obsession heaven knows. Pintner shows no awareness that the entire project is being problematised at a much more fundamental level than that of technical research procedures.
103 See Bibliography for full listing. He also published on 'white criminal intelligence' (Murchison, 1924), and a book on the whole topic (1926b).
104 On this point it also emerged that black recidivists were mostly Baptist and Methodist while white ones were mostly Catholic or agnostic. How he identified 'agnosticism' is not spelled out – one would not have thought the word itself was widely known among US criminals of the early 1920s. (My father had a yarn about telling a sergeant he was agnostic on joining the British Army in 1940 and being told that they didn't have a church nearby.)
105 He has a few pages on slavery as a form of domination, but does not refer to the racial aspect of this.
106 These include Eells (1933a) on Alaskan Eskimoes, Gray and Bingham (1929) on 'colored and white' children, Oliver (1932c) on East Africans, Ross (1936) on Japanese children and Sanderson (1933) (various). Garth too published one paper on the topic (Garth and Isbell, 1929).
107 For a summary see C.B. Davenport (1929).
108 The notion of disharmonious consequences of 'race-mixing' later received a magisterial rejection, as if one were still needed by then, in K.F. Dyer (1974).
109 For example, R.M. Fleming (1929).
110 See Barkan (1992, pp. 162–8).
111 For example, W.H. Tucker (1994, p. 281). Crane merrily admits 'Threats, cajolery, flattery, bribery and every other conceivable ruse within the bounds of reason and the law were resorted to.'
112 For example, S.J. Gould (1984), W.H. Tucker (1994), Howitt and Owusu-Bempah (1994), Mama (1995).
113 I would also query Barkan's statement that 'In none of these areas [i.e. sociology, anthropology, biology and Psychology] was the study of race part of the disciplinary canon' (Barkan, 1992, p.5). While few psychologists devoted their full-time attention to the issue, it was an intrinsic facet of psychometric research prior to 1930 and thus part of psychometrics' 'disciplinary canon'.
114 See Chapter 6 for the British situation.
115 Or, as in A.M. Padilla's brief treatment of Garth, considered as routine racists warranting little further examination (A.M. Padilla, 1988).
116 To amplify a previous footnote: OED (2nd edn) first use of 'racist' is 1932, of 'racism', 1936. The OED definition of 'racism' as a 'theory' is misleading and needs amending. My impression is that while 'racialism' was traditionally used to refer,

often non-pejoratively, to the 'theory' of race differences, 'racism' was always a pejorative term and referred primarily to a quasi-pathological personality trait or *attitude* (generally assumed to be irrational or at any rate immoral). The linguistic issue has moved on considerably and is discussed elsewhere.

117 He found 'negro' children had three times the undiagnosed eye-defect rate of whites.

Chapter 5

'Race' in US Psychology to 1945: II. The rise of anti-racism

By the late 1920s a new civil rights movement was on the move. In 1924 Marcus Garvey had founded the Negro Political Union, journals such as H.L. Mencken's *American Mercury* were publishing pro-'Negro' and black-authored articles, and William DuBois's Pan-Africanist aspirations were being promoted by the NAACP's journal *Crisis* (which he edited until 1934). The general upsurge in African American cultural activity (notably the New York-based 'Harlem Renaissance') generated much discussion of the 'new Negro' in contemporary social commentary.[1] On the academic front the black historian C.G. Woodson had founded the *Journal of Negro History* and African American sociologists were also beginning to publish. Psychology however, its orientation to 'race' still being dominated by eugenics and Race Psychology, lagged about a decade behind in this respect. After 1930 the Depression exacerbated black dissatisfaction, with a major riot in Harlem in 1935, a mood finding eloquent literary expression in Richard Wright's novel *Native Son* (1940),[2] though politically this was somewhat off-set by the dominance of Rooseveltian 'New Deal' liberalism. Lynchings and the continuing, highly publicised, activities of the Ku Klux Klan in the South meanwhile reinforced white liberal anti-racism.[3] It was a climate to which Psychologists, increasingly confronted with the political and moral implications of the 'race' issue, were bound to respond. Nor, in the light of events in Germany, could the matter any longer be construed as an exclusively domestic US concern. Attacks on Race Psychology thus intensified throughout the 1930s, resulting, by 1940, in a victory for the anti-racist camp which lasted until the 1960s. From a 1990s perspective the terms of this overwhelmingly white-authored 'anti-racism' discourse in Psychology often (though not always) appear naive or patronising and occasionally overcompromising. It would though be naive to imagine it could have been otherwise.

BARKAN'S THESIS

Regarding this period, Barkan (1992) proposes a thesis which is particularly relevant to us. In genetics and physical anthropology, the disciplines most centrally concerned with race, the abandonment of Scientific Racism was, he argues, rationalised by, not derived from, changing scientific knowledge. Scientific understanding of race in these disciplines was, he claims, highly confused and ambiguous.

Those politically or ideologically so inclined could offer anti-racial readings of current data, but their opponents could equally easily offer updated versions of Scientific Racism on the same basis. Is this analysis applicable to Psychology? It will be suggested here that it is not. Barkan's relative neglect of Psychology actually leaves a serious hole in the middle of his picture. Geneticists and physical anthropologists were concerned with race primarily at a theoretical (often eugenic) and taxonomic level but to psychologists fell the task of empirically identifying and quantifying those crucial evaluatively loaded psychological differences in intelligence and so on upon which the cultural significance of the issue hinged. Eager and willing to perform this role, the majority nevertheless eventually abandoned the quest partly at least on the grounds of its scientific futility. Secondly, while anthropology and genetics were, as Barkan stresses, geographically located in a few East Coast institutions, Race Psychology's sites ranged from South Carolina to Honolulu, from Denver to New York and Alaska (as well as in scattered places across the globe). For Psychology as a whole it was, moreover, a far less central topic than in genetics and anthropology, and a less salient factor in intra-disciplinary politics. Thirdly, Psychology was far more practically involved than these disciplines with society at large, rendering the ideology–science connection particularly tangled.[4] Aspiring to become, say, an educational psychologist, might well reflect a prior ideological commitment. Certain areas of Applied Psychology may even be considered as expressions of ideological orientation (setting their goals and priorities) however scientifically orthodox their research methods. Race Psychology's role in the demise of Scientific Racism and the emergence of a dominantly non- or anti-racist orthodoxy turns out to be somewhat more complex than can be captured by Barkan's thesis.

CHANGING 'PARADIGMS'

Use of the term 'paradigm' inevitably suggests the adoption of a Kuhnian framework, but the 'paradigm shifts' in question did not occur quite according to Kuhn's model. Race Psychology's internal disenchantments hardly stemmed from anomalous findings within that 'paradigm' generating a phase of revolutionary conceptual confusion. In Kuhnian terms the paradigm defines the meaning of research findings, but Race Psychology never really succeeded in yielding any findings the meanings of which were unambiguous. It would be more accurate to say that it never moved beyond 'pre-paradigmatic' status (the original Scientific Racism paradigm – if such it was – was never universally accepted, and was in decline after about 1925). 'Internally' it was the eventual admission (with varying degrees of reluctance) that the methodological and conceptual difficulties were insuperable which led to the project's abandonment. A handful, like Porteus and Garrett, nevertheless ploughed on. In Barkan's terms their *failure* to shift might indeed be considered ideological, but the willingness to shift of colleagues such as Garth, Woodworth and Brigham appears to have been substantially due to Race Psychology's perceived scientific failure. Contextual factors are of course in play: the cultural demands being made on Psychology had changed while (shifting to Lakatos mode) alternative research programs which had long existed in one form or another alongside Race Psychology were having relatively greater 'scientific' success and could respond more productively to changed cultural conditions. Such external factors were not, though, exclusively ideological, while in Psychology, as previously indicated, the 'ideological' and the 'scientific' are often fused. This may be true of other disciplines too (I'm sure it is) but their intertwining in Psychology is of an especially high order. While a right-wing R.A. Fisher and a left-wing Julian Huxley can collaborate in genetics, such collaboration is harder to envisage in research on race differences in intelligence or on 'race prejudice'. Ideology may indeed determine a scientist's interpretations of the available data, but in Psychology the situation goes further – it determines the very data a scientist seeks to obtain.[5]

Race Psychology also bears on other historiographic debates regarding the nature of scientific change: the 'closure' of controversy, the role of research schools, styles of school leadership and so on, but it would be premature to address these until the narrative has unrolled somewhat further.

Opposition to Race Psychology within the discipline proceeded on the four fronts previously identified. Beyond the discipline – and scope of the present discussion – is the mounting political resistance of blacks and white radicals. As noted earlier, there was already an alliance between certain sections of the discipline (notably among social psychologists) and those fighting racism in the culture at large. That Psychology's scientific engagements with race could be an expression of ideology is quite transparent here.[6] One could go further: once 'race' has overtly become an ideological issue (and prior to about 1930 it is not entirely clear that it had) the ideological dimension is inescapable.

THE DEMISE OF RACE PSYCHOLOGY

Criticisms of Race Psychology

In the previous chapter we saw that many of the criticisms of Race Psychology were present, if not fully developed, virtually from the start, Woodworth (1910a) identifying several of them as difficulties to be faced by future researchers. Much early Race Psychology work was concerned with trying to isolate and control for environmental factors of various kinds, and with testing the 'mulatto hypothesis'. Critics soon began worrying at these vulnerable points. Margaret Mead (1926) for example identified three weaknesses. First she argued that 'there is no conclusive evidence that skin color, *accurately determined*, is a reliable index of racial admixture' (p. 661, italics in original). This was important because the assumption that skin colour *was* a 'reliable index' was fundamental to much early 'mulatto hypothesis' research. Melville Herskovits in the same year published findings on Howard University students showing no correlation between skin lightness and academic performance.[7] Secondly Mead tackled the 'social status' question, citing A.H. Arlitt (1920, 1921) in support. In general, she concludes, research fails to differentiate social class or status differences from racial ones. When social class is controlled for, race differences appear, on available evidence, to be greatly reduced though not eliminated. But focusing on this one factor is in itself 'vitiated by over-emphasis . . . and a failure to deal with other aspects of the case' (p. 663). Finally she turns to 'language disability' (on which she had undertaken some research, as yet unpublished).[8] Effects of this are more pervasive than hitherto assumed, and smaller differences are usually found with non-verbal than verbal tests. Interestingly she cites some British work (D.J. Saer, 1922; F. Smith, 1923) on performance of Welsh monoglot, English-Welsh bilingual and English monoglot speakers, suggesting that monoglots in either language are superior to bilinguals.[9] This was highly relevant to the case of bilingual children of immigrant parents in the USA (and, as we saw, a factor in Brigham's recantation). While not as yet rejecting Race Psychology outright, Mead advises extreme caution in drawing firm conclusions from existing studies, in which none of these difficulties had been overcome.

Two short 1928 papers by G.H. Estabrooks of Colgate University may be taken as representative of the doubts being increasingly aired about race differences in intelligence. While not excluding the possibility of a long-term solution he is adamant that for the moment research 'has virtually arrived at a position of checkmate' (1928a, p. 137). The difficulties are twofold: first 'we cannot measure intelligence under different environmental conditions with any assurity that we are getting comparable results' (ibid.), second, 'practically all work up to the present has been done on groups which were by no means physically homogeneous' (ibid.). A particularly vicious paradox emerges. We can formally spell out the research design requirements which would meet the case, but these would only work on the assumption that the physical criteria by which racial identities have to be defined were themselves normally distributed throughout the population: 'all we demand is that the racial criteria have a normal distribution – or a uniform distribution – in each of the groups from a *cultural* point of view' (ibid., p. 138). But there's the rub – insofar as such physical criteria *do* differentiate between groups with different intelligence levels they will almost certainly *not* be so distributed since the more intelligent would gravitate to higher social status positions. The fact that a group *is* uniformly distributed is itself *prima facie* evidence that membership is not correlated with intelligence. 'All of which simply means a checkmate so far as a scientific attack on the problem goes, given our present techniques' (ibid., p. 139).

In Estabrooks (1928b) he adds another line of argument. Historical evidence is just as valid as present intelligence tests and shows that 'again and again we have the case of a race or nation being the despised outcast or barbarian one generation and demonstrating that it is capable of high culture the next' (1928b, p. 474). This echoes points made by Woodworth in 1910. In general he feels the problem is not one for psychologists alone but must also involve anthropologists. Brief, and focused on methodology, Estabrooks' 1928 papers nevertheless seem, on the evidence of subsequent citation, to have had considerable impact within the discipline – more so than the broader and more fervent attacks which had been appearing in popular journals and radical magazines since the early 1920s.[10]

As we saw, by 1930 Garth was backtracking while Brigham had also abandoned his original position. Odum was another travelling this course, primarily as a sociologist. Some index of the state of opinion in 1929–30 is provided by C.H. Thompson's contribution to the 1934 *Journal of Negro Education* volume. During that school year he circulated a questionnaire to 100 psychologists, 39 educationists and 30 anthropologists and sociologists, with a response rate of over 90%. While 46% felt that race inequality was possible, *only 4% actually accepted 'the hypothesis of race inequality'*. Thirty per cent positively believed in race equality while 20% took positions not covered by these three options and it is reasonable to suppose this included some who rejected the notion of 'race' itself. On the 'mulatto hypothesis' 15% believed the evidence supported it, 70% believed it was inconclusive, and 15% held it had been refuted. Note that this data comes after Davenport and Steggerda's fervently Negrophobic 'Race crossing in Jamaica' but before Garth's *Race Psychology* . Even by 1934 it was considerably out of date. (We are reassured that 'apprehension as to the subjectivity of selecting respondents is partly dispelled by consulting the list of respondents' (Dearborn and Long, 1934). At the turn of the 1930s the discipline was apparently highly confused, the majority hedging their bets and prevaricating and very few prepared to commit themselves.[11]

This 1934 *Journal of Negro Education* volume, already cited several times, was especially significant, not least as the first major 'internal' contribution to the debate produced under an explicitly African American aegis. It contained 14 papers plus a final overview summary by Dearborn and Long. These address various aspects of the race-differences question, including a historical chapter on pre-1910 work and one on physical constitution concluding that 'neither eugenic nor dysgenic effects from Negro–white crossings have been demonstrated' (Dearborn and Long, 1934, p. 532). In addition to the contributions by Thompson, Garth, Peterson and Pintner already discussed: Herskovits pans the mulatto hypothesis; Daniel reviews research on 'non-intellectual traits and special aptitudes', rejecting it all as too inadequate to offer even a starting point; Price, on general intelligence, argues that measuring race differences is in principle futile; Wilkerson assails the methodology of studies of 'scholastic achievement'; Klineberg (of whom more shortly) savages the selective migration hypothesis, previewing the findings of Klineberg (1935a); regarding 'mental abnormality' Rosenthal finds the information flawed and inconclusive;[12] F.N. Freeman, for his part, believes the 'conditions of comparison' cannot be met 'except by a radical change in the social and economic conditions of the Negro' (Dearborn and Long, 1934, p. 542) and finally C.E. Smith offers factor analysis as the only way forward – a conclusion with which Dearborn and Long seem to agree. Dearborn and Long's overview strongly urges researchers to eliminate 'attitudes' and 'marginal motivations' which are 'extremely subtle, often quite unconscious or almost completely overlaid by rationalisations' (p. 544).

Most of the authors, and certainly the editors, desperately strive to maintain an objective 'scientific' stance. The issue remains a scientific one, and the topic one worth investigating. Ideological factors are intrusions on sound scientific practice. The following passage from Dearborn and Long captures some of the hidden ambiguity of this position:

The objectivity of the discussions by the contributors is highly commendable in view of the fact that a number of the contributors of necessity have much to gain or lose according to the turn of the final solution. Negroes and whites have contributed to this volume, yet, so far as bias is concerned, it is highly probably [*sic*] that if the identity of the authors were concealed, observers would be unable to separate the articles on the basis of the two contributing races. (p. 544)

The more one ponders this the more enigmatic it becomes. It is, *prima facie*, merely a rather self-congratulatory affirmation of their success in maintaining a judicious scientific tone. But this can be read two ways: (a) 'Negro' contributors are being praised for hiding *their* potential bias and writing good white scientific texts, (b) white contributors are being commended for overcoming their anti-Negro bias, as evidenced in the fact that, bar Pintner, they reject race differences or feel them to be unproved. And if the former, is there a further twist – that this of itself disproves their inferiority to the white contributors? At any rate, while the ethical character of Race Psychology is questioned at several points in the volume, and while its message is that race differences research is on the rocks bar some radical methodological innovation (factor analysis?), ultimately this must all be packaged in terms of positivist scientific rhetoric. The following year a less inhibited, more lethal, double salvo was fired.

Otto Klineberg, a Columbia University social psychologist whose training had included a spell under Boas, was the most effective of Race Psychology's critics within the discipline. His three major critiques[13] were the monograph 'An experimental study of speed and other factors in "racial" differences' (1928) and two 1935 books: *Negro Intelligence and Selective Migration* and *Race Differences*. He later edited *The Characteristics of the American Negro* (1944), returning to the fray in a UNESCO Pamphlet *Race and Psychology* (1951) as well as being involved in the *Brown vs. Board of Education* case in 1954 which signalled the end of segregated education.[14] Klineberg combined sophisticated empirical research skills with a penetrating grasp of central theoretical issues. The introduction to the 1928 paper proposed seven factors which might jointly account for reported differences: language, schooling, culture, social and economic status, rapport, motivation and speed (to which the remainder of the paper is devoted). The paper originated in his accepting an invitation from the anthropologist Melville Jacobs to join a field trip to the Yakima Indian reservation in Toppenish, Washington, Woodworth supplying Klineberg with some research funding.[15]

So-called racial groups, Klineberg argues, strike different balances between the requirements of speed and accuracy when taking Psychological tests. While this may be 'racial', it might also relate to culture and lifestyle. The research is aimed at untangling this. What ensues is a well-designed study of the performance on four tests by American Indians, African Americans and whites, cross-nested into urban and rural groups. 'Race mixture' is also taken into account. On each test it is possible to measure both time to completion and number of errors (or, in one case, moves to completion). First comparing rural Yakima Indians with white children from a town in the heart of the reservation he discovers that while whites perform faster, the slower Indians make fewer errors or take fewer moves. In terms of overall performance there is no difference but the Indians prioritise accuracy over speed. When repeated with Indians attending 'the largest and most important Indian school in the country' (the nearest he could get to an urban Indian group) they were found to be faster than the Yakima group. A more complex study on New York 'Negroes', taking into account duration of residence in the city, showed little difference from New York whites in speed though a slight tendency on some tasks for speed to increase with length of New York residence. Rural West Virginian 'Negroes' were slower than the New York group, but more accurate than a small rural white group. No clear-cut relationships were found between physical indices of African ancestry (now broadened from pigmentation to include lip-thickness and nose-width) and speed or accuracy, nor was 'mixed blood' correlated with performance among Indians.[16] He then returns to unpublished data on Form Board Test performance which Woodworth had obtained in St Louis. Reanalysing this he finds that while whites were superior on the first trial (bar four Ainu subjects who came out top), their rank subsequently fell dramatically (the Ainu stayed top), thus their learning ability was in no way superior.

The upshot was that Klineberg could conclude that white superiority over 'Indian' and 'Negro' performance on the tests was due primarily to their speed, whites being inferior in terms of accuracy, making more errors before task completion. This speed difference was, moreover, environmentally determined (rural subjects of all 'races' being slower than urban ones). Whites were not superior in learning ability nor did race mixing with whites increase performance for the other 'races'. For the anti-race-differences camp this was a highly successful paper, enumerating and discussing numerous factors which might affect race differences research, and fairly convincingly demonstrating the operation of one.[17] In detaching speed *per se* from intelligence Klineberg was actually breaking with Woodworth's 1910 position in which 'quickness in seizing the key to a novel situation' (1910a, p. 180) is given as the first feature of intelligence; his use of St Louis data to make his point thus has a certain irony.

The widely advanced 'selective migration' argument to explain superior Northern black performance was his target in a later project involving numerous graduate research assistants. In his 1935 book-length report Klineberg first notes that *a priori* arguments can be made in both directions: maybe the brightest and most enterprising migrate, but maybe also the least successful and more marginalised seek their fortunes elsewhere. Two methods are adopted to investigate this: (a) a comparison of the intellectual levels of migrants and non-migrants, using school records in Nashville (Tennessee), Birmingham (Alabama), and Charleston (South Carolina), (b) a study of Southern-born New York African Americans to see if length of residency was related to performance scores on a variety of tests (including the Binet) – if selective migration was operating no such relationship should be found. The findings were clearly inconsistent with the selective migration hypothesis. The first study detected no meaningful difference, migrants were neither better nor worse than stay-at-homes. The second revealed a tendency on most measures for performance to improve with length of New York residency. Just for good measure he includes data on education expenditure per capita since

1910, detailing the gross inequalities between 'Negro' and white funding in the segregated South. Again level of race mixture, insofar as it was ascertainable, did not correlate with scores. Klineberg's concludes:

> There seems to the writer to be no reasonable doubt as to the conclusion of this study. As far as the results go, they show quite definitely that the superiority of the northern over the southern Negroes, and the tendency of northern Negroes to approximate the scores of the Whites, are due to factors in the environment, and not to selective migration. (p. 59)

Simultaneously he published his overview of the entire issue, *Race Differences*, tackling its every aspect from history, via supposed developmental and physiological differences and Psychological approaches to an exposition of the 'cultural approach' he favoured. In traversing this canvas he systematically undermines virtually all the evidence for 'race differences' on offer. While most of his arguments are not essentially new, they are more thoroughly formulated than before, and presented as a complete package for the first time. As far as physiology is concerned the criteria for differentiating races are incoherent and inconsistent, brain-size differences are minimal and no clear-cut relationship between brain size and intelligence has been established anyway. Contrary to popular belief there is no early suture closure among Negroes, nor are puberty and mental growth related. The data on earlier Negro puberty are inconsistent, while these phenomena are in any case affected by socio-economic factors. And while

> there are interesting and significant group differences in physiological activity . . . there is no adequate proof that these are determined by heredity. . . . The available material suggests, though it does not prove that [these] can be adequately explained without recourse to the racial hypothesis. (pp. 130–31)

Moving to Psychology, he cites the evidence from Rivers onwards to refute differences in psychophysical performance and reaction times and elaborates on the seven factors identified in his 1928 paper, now invoking Garth in support. Although we have already encountered most of these arguments, several points are worth noting. In connection with intelligence he introduces an interesting argument that the 'nature–nurture' controversy only refers to overall group-level variation, not to individual differences as such. Nor, he claims, can heredity apply to *between*-group differences. As I understand him, he means by this (a) that the two factors cannot be sensibly differentiated at the individual level, (b) that, as we would now say, the gene frequencies in a group may be due to heredity, but differences *between* groups in gene frequency are not themselves hereditary – they can in principle be altered (basically this is Garth's 'race mobility' again). This second point was subsequently lost sight of during the post-war 'race and IQ' controversy. As we will see, the 'heritability' of IQ is, from this perspective, really a red herring.[18]

His discussion of the cultural factor contains some interesting cases, such as Australian aborigine children losing marks on the Goodenough Draw-A-Man test for not depicting clothes. He attacks the 'status reflects intelligence' argument as only applicable under conditions of equal opportunity and free competition, neither of which are realised in the USA.

While some of Klineberg's arguments and evidence would require updating and refinement, and while the 'culture-fair' test problem has moved beyond docking marks for nudes on the Goodenough Test in an unclad culture, the case Klineberg mounts remains, in my view, remarkably solid. It came as near to closing the door on the whole race-differences business as any 1935 text could be expected to. Klineberg's initial ideological motivation appears to have been minimal. Although informally influenced by Boas and Mead, prior to his Yakima Reservation trip he 'had no special interest in race or race problems. . . . On the contrary, before coming to Columbia I had read William McDougall's *Is America Safe for Democracy?*, and I thought he had made a pretty good case for qualitative genetic differences between ethnic groups.'[19] At most one can say his Canadian Jewish background would have predisposed him towards a liberal position.

At the centre of Race Psychology's demise as a sensible scientific project lay a genuinely 'scientific' failure. Methodologically it proved impossible to eliminate or control for the non-genetic variables determining group performance. Lumping these together as 'environment' oversimplifies: the issues ranged from sampling to linguistic disability, socio-economic status to 'rapport', differing cultural assumptions and attitudes to clearly establishing the 'racial' identity of subjects. The opposition was quite simply more effective in positively demonstrating the role of these, and in seemingly refuting pro-race differences hypotheses (e.g. selective migration), than Race Psychology was at controlling for them or defending its hypotheses. Of course not every US psychologist personally abandoned racist attitudes. J.B. Watson, as noted earlier, was quite unself-consciously racist and recent research has found Karl Lashley signing off letters to friends 'Heil Hitler and Apartheit!' with defiant jocularity as late as the mid-1950s.[20] The prevalence of racism among psychologists whose work, like Lashley's, was in areas ostensibly unrelated to the issue is unknowable.[21] As far as US Psychology's public 'party-line' is concerned, however, the abandonment of racism by 1940 is quite clear. Insofar as Race Psychology-type research continued, it was (aside from a handful of psychometricians like Garrett) sanitised as a purely scientific issue with little political significance.

By the early 1930s Race Psychology's failure was, if somewhat implicitly, calling into question the motivation of those persisting in it. Garth quite openly 'discovered' the racism behind the project. If Race Psychology had failed, what then was Psychology's role in relation to 'race'? Answers were already in place elsewhere in the discipline, and Race Psychology's mounting difficulties reinforced their credibility. Three final observations may be made.

First, as proposed at the end of the previous chapter, the Race Psychology episode may be seen as the very process by which Psychology came to *discover* 'racism' as a psychological phenomenon to be studied in its own right. Precisely because its collapse took a substantially 'internal' scientific rather than ideological form this lesson was assimilable by the majority of the discipline as a whole. This differentiates it from the course of events in genetics and physical anthropology in a fundamental way.

Secondly, Psychology's failure to substantiate Scientific Racism provided a major source of supporting data and arguments for anti-racists in those other disciplines which, as Barkan demonstrates, could not provide unambiguous refutations of the same 'scientific' order.

Thirdly, the evidence considered here suggests that Race Psychology never achieved sufficient theoretical or organisational coherence to be considered a 'school' in any strict sense. Its research was geographically diffused, and even Garth was not a 'leader' in the way that Watson was a leader of Behaviourism or Hering and Helmholtz led rival schools in the field of perception in the previous century.[22] It remained 'pre-paradigmatic' – never, for example, evolving its own technical vocabulary. Moreover it flourished at the intersections of a number of concerns – first 'Negro education' and immigration, then theories of intelligence, psychometric methodology, experimental design and eugenics – the differing priorities of which exacerbated the task of integration.

The role of 'external' or 'contextual' factors was, nonetheless, also crucial, although their differentiation from the 'internal' is, as already explained, highly problematic. Before turning to the two principal rival 'paradigms' we should therefore look further at this aspect of the issue, as evidenced in our earlier 'Applied and Intra-racial' category.

Applied Psychology in the field

US universities had, from the late 1890s, been producing growing numbers of Psychology graduates. It was a central assumption of those advancing US culture's utopian modernist ambitions that human behaviour and character – in a word, human *psychology* – could and should be scientifically understood and managed. Education, child-rearing, delinquency, mental health, advertising, personnel selection and industrial Psychology are all, by the 1920s, offering opportunities for graduates to deploy their professional expertise. In this context of rapidly expanding demand for, and supply of, psychologists (unmatched by anything happening in physical anthropology or genetics) an increasing amount of research was published addressing and emanating from, these professional groups. The Depression hugely intensified the level of social problems after 1930 (incidentally, as we noted, burying the 'status reflects intelligence' argument, at least until the 1990s.) Sociologists and applied psychologists became the leading experts in those fields just listed.

Responsible for practical, interventionist, engagement, the attention of such professionals was inevitably drawn to specific problems facing their client groups – including those of seemingly distinct ethnic or racial identities. African Americans, Italians, native Americans and Jews (both German and Russian) were the most prominent, although in some regions Chinese or Mexicans were more to the fore. During the latter 1930s the amount of literature relating to these ethnically linked problems rose more steeply than any other (Table 4.1), becoming the largest single genre of race-related Psychological work by 1940. In character it is primarily atheoretical, descriptive and/or problem-focused. Perhaps because of this it is barely acknowledged by historians. While dominantly WASP, a growing number of African Americans (often graduates from Howard or Fisk Universities) and Jews had entered Applied Psychology's ranks.[23] This genre includes an expanding proportion of intra-racial studies, often undertaken by members of the 'race' in question, especially in the Jewish case – but Beckham (1929) is an early African American example. Easy summarising is difficult since the material is so heterogeneous in content, but may be crudely gauged from a sample of titles appearing in journals such as *The Journal of Negro Education*, *Mental Hygiene*, *Smith College Studies in Social Work*, *Journal of Social Psychology*,[24] *Teachers College Contributions to Education*, and *Social Forces* catering to this section of the discipline:

- Anderson, F.N. (1936) 'A mental-hygiene survey of problem Indian children in Oklahoma';
- Baumgarter, H.W. (1935) 'Measuring Negro self-respect';
- Beckham, A.S. (1933) 'A study of the intelligence of colored adolescents of differing social-economic status in typical metropolitan areas';
- Brenman, M. (1940a) 'Minority group membership and religious, psycho-sexual, and social patterns in a group of middle-class Negro girls';
- Caliver, A. (1931) 'A personnel study of Negro college students';
- Cohen, E. (1939) 'Cultural and personality factors in the attitudes of Russian Jewish clients toward relief';
- Du Vinage, T.C. (1939) 'Accommodation attitudes of Negroes to white case workers and their influence on case work';
- Frazier, E.F. (1925) 'Psychological factors in Negro health'.

Several particularly active authors can be identified. Aspects of African American life were addressed by A. Caliver and H.H. Long (education), H.G. Canady (the Negro student, also one paper on Psychology teaching in black colleges), E.F. Frazier (the most prolific sociological writer on the African American family and related issues such as delinquency), and A.P. Smith (psychiatric service provision). Leading writers on Jewish issues included J.B. Maller (especially Jewish students) and B. Malzberg (mental illness). H.C. Hansen specialised (as did Garth after 1935) in native American education. The number of authors with one or two publications is considerable. As an early African American psychologist A.S. Beckham is additionally important as the founder of the Psychology laboratory at Howard University.

The interests of such people partially overlapped with those working more academically, notably regarding attitudes and prejudice, and although their immediate concerns varied the pressure they generated was consistent in its direction. Liberal and non-WASP applied psychologists wanted a Psychology which could guide their interventionist practice in enhancing their clients' well-being. They were more interested in the effects of racism on the self-images and attitudes of those on the receiving end than in seeking the innate roots of race differences. They sought to ameliorate mental illness problems by identifying the socio-economic conditions exacerbating them, rather than smugly assert that high Negro manic-depression rates were only to be expected in such an innately emotional race.[25] This pressure both stimulated attitudes and prejudice research and ensured that, from early on, those academically working in this area represented, as it were, an 'intellectual wing' of the anti-racism movement, inchoate and diverse though this still was. Race Psychology in its traditional form had little of relevance to offer them. Interestingly the fairly hard-line eugenicist M. Steggerda, Davenport's erstwhile colleague, can be found contributing papers loosely belonging in this applied category after the mid-1930s, striving to develop a version of McAdory's 'art test' for use with Navaho Indian children for example (Steggerda and Macomber, 1938). If applied psychologists' needs were feeding back to the academics providing their initial Psychological training, the motivational roots of Race Psychology were being to some degree sapped at source. And such needs are directly 'external' in origin.

In historical retrospect this genre is not quite so ideologically unambiguous as it appears on the surface. It helped create what Mama (1995) terms a 'damaged Negro' image, replacing the biologically racist image of 'Negro' identity. This still (a) ascribes a non-differentiated universal psychological character to all African Americans, (b) sees this as determined by white behaviour, disregarding the existence of any genuinely autonomous African American culture and (c) focuses almost exclusively on African American males.[26] On the other hand it is from this direction that African American psychologists such as, notably, Beckham, Long, Canady, Caliver, F.C. Sumner and Kenneth and Mamie Clark were able to begin developing a 'Black Psychology' with their work on black self-identity and attitudes. Most of this story, however, belongs to the post-1945 phase and will be resumed later. We may now consider the rise of 'prejudice' and 'race-attitudes' research.

Prejudice and race attitudes

The study of attitudes is widely seen as the topic around which experimental Social Psychology crystallised in the USA during the inter-war period. Research on prejudice and race attitudes was a major element in this development.[27] In addition to its intrinsic importance, the wider theoretical and methodological issues it raised were considered both crucial and challenging. Experimental work in this field dates from Emory Bogardus's research on 'social distance' in the early 1920s, his first two papers appearing in 1925. The first research reported (1925a) required (white) subjects to classify 39 national or racial groups into one of three categories depending on their attitude towards them (friendly, neutral, hostile), and then to rank those in each category. The second study (1925b) required 100 'businessmen and school teachers' to rate 23 'races' on the degree of intimacy to which they would admit them, using a scale from 'close kinship through marriage' to 'exclusion from the country'. The field's methodology developed rapidly thereafter but Bogardus's original rankings proved surprisingly resilient until the late 1930s, when historical circumstance shifted some ratings. Precise numbers of race and nationality labels employed vary, but the Scots, English, Irish, German, French and Scandinavian categories invariably comprised the top group, while Mexicans, Chinese, Hindus, Negroes and Turks always competed for bottom position. (The 'cruel, sensual, dirty' Turk is frequently rated lowest of all, a result almost exclusively of World War I media images and stereotypes, since there were few Turkish immigrants.) Prior to Bogardus the problem of 'racial prejudice' had of course been frequently aired (e.g. by Josiah Royce (1906) and W.I. Thomas (1904) before World War I), but received little attention from psychologists other than in routine protestations of personal immunity to it. One influential earlier work must though be noted, Walter Lippmann's *Public Opinion* (1922),[28] which introduced the concept of the 'stereotype'.

Research techniques were refined in a succession of papers, most importantly Thurstone (1928) and Guilford (1931). At the same time the theoretical framework for the field was evolving. Lippmann's 'stereotype' notion received attention from S.A. Rice (1929) who confirmed that reactions to race are 'stereotypical' in nature, arising from previously fixed impressions unrelated to the facts of the present situation. The effectiveness of college courses in reducing prejudice was being studied before the 1920s were out, D. Young (1927) passing a pessimistic verdict on the University of Pennsylvania's 20-hour 1st year elective 'Sociology 3B. American Race Problems'. The first developmental study of the origins of prejudice was Lasker's *Race Attitudes in Children* (1929). The 'Hinckley Scale of attitude toward the Negro' appeared in Thurstone's compendium *Scales for the Measurement of Social Attitudes* (1930, 1931) along with R.C. Peterson's scales for measuring attitudes towards Chinese and Germans. By the mid-1930s D. Katz, F.H. Allport and K.W. Braly were in the midst of a quite complex research programme on racial stereotyping among Princeton students. The 'liberal' character of this genre should not, though, be taken for granted. Two papers by Euri Belle Bolton of the Georgia State College for Women (1935, 1937), for example, consider opposition to desegregation consistent with a 'neutral' position on the social rights of the 'Negro' and she classifies as 'liberal' the statement 'The Negro should have the advantages of all social benefits of the white man but be limited to his own race in the practice thereof' (1935, p. 34). 'Liberal' attitudes towards economic, cultural and political rights are consistent with opposition to social 'intermixture' (1937). Her research goal appears to be to deconstruct the notion of anti-'Negro' prejudice by differentiating the economic, cultural, political and social arenas, as well as separating public and private attitudes.

Theoretically the topic was in flux throughout the pre-1940 period. A widespread initial assumption that prejudice reflected fear of the alien was abandoned as clearly inapplicable to Southern anti-black attitudes. In the early 1930s D. Katz[29] and F.H. Allport proposed the more behaviourist theory that 'we have conditioned responses of varying degrees of aversion or acceptance toward racial labels' (Katz and Braly, 1933, p. 280). In the case of the 'Negro' we respond to 'a personification of the symbol we have learned to despise' (ibid.). Like Bolton, Katz wanted to differentiate between public and private attitudes, but had difficulty in establishing this empirically, finding the differences between the two conditions 'not as great as expected' and suggesting that use of race names evokes public attitudes regardless of experimental design (Katz and Braly, 1935, pp. 186–7). Incorporating the 'stereotype' concept they have to shift away from the simpler behaviourist formula. 'Racial prejudice is part of a general set of stereotypes of a high degree of consistency, and not a single specific reaction to a race name', prejudice is not against 'an empty race name, but towards a race name which represents an imaginary individual of nasty character' (ibid., p. 190). This generalised attitude is nevertheless 'built up and determined by an accumulation of specific responses' (ibid., p. 191). One of the major texts from this period was, however, the least typical, straddling the sociology/Psychology borderline and adopting a basically psychoanalytic theoretical perspective and a qualitative rather than psychometric methodology. This was John Dollard's 1937 *Class and Caste in a Southern Town* (subsequent editions in 1949 and 1957) and it warrants a digression.

A practising psychoanalyst who had studied in the Berlin Psychoanalytic Institute and been trained by, among others, Karen Horney, Dollard was also influenced by the anthropologist Edward Sapir and contemporary US sociologists such as the pioneer symbolic interactionist Robert Park. *Class and Caste in a Southern Town* attempted to synthesise these perspectives into an account of Deep South culture which was simultaneously sociological and Psychological. While offering a more or less functionalist account of the economic, sexual and prestige 'gains' which white middle-class Southerners derive from segregation, he also analyses the emotional causes and consequences of the complex social dynamics by which racial caste roles and attitudes were sustained. In this it verged on the culture and personality school's approach. It was a rather courageous study – a self-consciously archetypal Northern liberal academic immersing himself in a typical small Deep South town whose white inhabitants were deeply hostile to the culture he represented.[30] His initial intention of simply obtaining life-history accounts from Southern 'Negroes', was quickly expanded as he realised this would be meaningless without a broader understanding of the 'class and caste' structure. We are conscious throughout of the tightrope he is having to walk in maintaining the co-operation of his African American informants while remaining *persona grata* with the whites.

The range of material covered defies easy summarisation here. Of particular interest is his concern with the psychological processes compelling each caste to reproduce its psychological character – the multifarious ways in which the ever-present threat of white aggression both maintains the lower-class 'Negro' in an infantilised (as he sees it) state and prevents the emergence of stable domestic and social relations, the strategies and 'accommodations' adopted in response to this, the defensive projections (with a high sexual component) by which whites rationalise their situation, and so forth. For Dollard the roots of prejudice lay in the 'Negro' providing a visible target upon whom whites could discharge the 'latent hostility' universally accumulated due to developmental frustrations but normally held in check. The operation of these psychological mechanisms, notably those related to emotion, is comprehensible only within the complex socio-economic context of Deep South plantation culture, with its fraught historical and cultural heritage. The binds in which the small emergent middle-class African American group find themselves are also dealt with at length. Behind all this lies the tension between the official American egalitarian ideology and the caste culture of the South in which the African American's under-caste position has to be sustained.

A number of observations can be made about the character of this text and Dollard's authorial position. First, reading it in the 1990s, one is struck by how his efforts towards objective even-handed treatment of the two 'castes' occasionally curiously backfire. In striving to compensate for his liberal anti-Southern white bias he is led once or twice into a Pilate-like failure of moral nerve. Having exhaustively examined the collective psychopathological underpinnings of lynching, for example, he suddenly springs the following on us:

> No one should judge even the most incredible of these acts of violence. We should attempt to identify and understand rather than deplore them. No one is justified in pointing with scorn at mob behavior in the South unless he is disposed to have a personal share in any trouble and sacrifices necessary to revising the basic social situation which generates it. It might be, for example, that a government which could effectually stamp out lynching would have to be far more ruthless against the southern white caste than the white caste is today against the Negroes. One should consider well and be certain of thorough understanding before taking sides; can we be so sure that we would do differently if the problem of dealing with masses of Negroes were to come home to us locally? (p. 335)

This is, I must stress, unrepresentative of the text as a whole. I cite it rather as evidence for the psychological limits within which even the most diligently 'objective' liberal white social scientists of this period were as yet operating. (And the implicit assumption that he is addressing an exclusively white readership is among these.)

A second observation is that 'Negro' progress is perceived as simply a matter of full acculturation into white middle-class American virtues. Dollard makes no genuinely positive references to African American culture. Middle-class Negroes are commended for abandoning 'superstitious' beliefs. Even the easy-flowing and relaxed gregariousness of black social life, though appealing, results from a quasi-infantile failure to develop the emotional inhibitions, and sacrifices of libidinal expression, characteristic of white middle-class culture (a failure admittedly stemming directly from exclusion from that culture's goals of personal and economic achievement). In all this he can certainly be read as promoting a 'damaged Negro' image. This unidimensionality, which in retrospect appears so blinkered, gives the book a somewhat pessimistic air. Full 'Negro' participation in American life, we gather, entails acquiring a white middle-class psychology with its particular pattern of repressions and deferred libidinal gratification. He cannot even reflect that anti-black prejudice is itself a component in that very psychology! There is no reference to African American music except in the context of religious services. American culture is synonymous with white middle-class culture, even as black culture of one kind or another (especially music) is determining much of its popular tone. By today's standards Dollard's discourse remains blindly ethnocentric.

Finally, Dollard is remarkably uncritical in his usage and citation of pre-World War I works such as Odum (1910), Page (1904) and A.H. Stone (1908) as acceptable academic authorities alongside Herskovits, Moton and other more recent writers. He fails, in essence, to see that much of this earlier 'academic' discourse on 'the Negro' was itself (wittingly or not) contributing to those very dynamics of oppression which he is elucidating; the Deep South culture he is analysing *included* the books it produced about 'the Negro'. This being so, the testimony of such texts cannot be used, as he tends to do, as a data-source on its own terms.

Since *Caste and Class in a Southern Town* is widely acknowledged as a landmark in the Social Psychological understanding of prejudice, the preceding discussion may seem overly harsh. It is not intended to be. The book remains valuable as a sophisticated and penetrating examination of 'race relations' in the American Deep South, a brave and ambitious book applying a range of psychoanalytic and sociological concepts to the issue for the first time. For example, the sexual fear and envy of the African American male among white males, the need to repress sexual attraction to them among white females, and the numerous psychological and behavioural consequences of these, are elaborated with unprecedented clarity. While not ruling out innate biological differences, Dollard's analysis is entirely in terms of culture and psychodynamics. What I have tried to indicate is how even someone espousing the new 'anti-racist' prejudice-oriented approach was operating within tight, but to them invisible, conceptual constraints. The scale and approach of Dollard's text only renders them more visible than they are in the typical attitude-measurement journal paper. If the eclectic, psychoanalytically sensitised, Dollard is so patently constrained, how much more so his psychometrically focused, lab-bound colleagues?

His Preface to the 1957 edition does not suggest that Dollard's position had significantly changed in the intervening years, although he would now adopt more of a learning theory perspective.[31] Though he had done no further work on the issue in the meantime[32] and felt out of touch with the field, he was conscious that the problem, and the underlying disjunction between ideology and reality, were more acute than ever, and anxious to promote peaceful 'Emancipation'. The most significant comment perhaps is: 'As defenders of an alternate mode of life to that proposed by the Communists we are under additional compulsion to make our mode one which can integrate men of every color and culture' (1957, p. xii). We may now return to the more orthodox work.

As well as white attitudes towards 'the Negro', a sizeable body of research is undertaken on 'Negro' attitudes towards themselves and, more rarely, others,[33] as well as on the developmental origins of racial attitudes.[34] More sociologically oriented writers begin considering the presence of racial stereotyping in the media.[35] J.H. Criswell (1937, 1939) adopted a sociometric approach in studying the dynamics of 'racial cleavage' within 'Negro–white' groups. Nor was attention focused on African Americans alone. H.L. Kingsley and M. Carbone (1938) looked at Italian-American attitudes towards race prejudice and C.W. Luh and R.C. Sailer (1933) considered the 'self-estimation' of Chinese students. The presence of prejudice in educational settings was also a common theme.[36] Studies of anti-semitism had, however, barely begun, no English language Psychological texts on this appearing prior to Fenichel (1940), the first version, in English at least, of the psychoanalytic theory of anti-semitism.[37] (Jews were, though, routinely included in the lists of 'races' and nationalities employed in attitude research, as well as being a frequent subject group in race-differences work.) The majority of papers explicitly relating to Jews fell in the 'Applied' category.[38]

This prejudice work shared the theoretically eclectic character of contemporary attitude research as a whole. After 1935 the most influential approach was Gordon Allport's, expounded in his contribution on 'Attitudes' to C. Murchison's widely used *Handbook of Social Psychology* (1935). An attitude is here defined as 'a mental and neural state of readiness, organised through experience, exerting a directive or dynamic influence upon the individual's response to all objects and situations with which it is related' (p. 810). Nonetheless, by 1940, Klineberg is considering the possibility raised by Dollard of a more psychoanalytic account centred on family dynamics. Regarding Dollard's study Klineberg was concerned that his psychoanalytic interpretation presented a circular argument, since it left unexplained the origin of race prejudice itself – even accepting the existence of 'latent hostility', why is *race* selected as the channel for its expression?[39] From this he moves on to critique the notion that prejudice is purely an individual psychological flaw (see below). Even so he believes Dollard's account may explain variations in the intensity of race prejudice. Later psychoanalytic theorising of course moved beyond Dollard's relatively simple 'displaced aggression' model.

The further convolutions of 1930s attitude theorising must be left aside, but it should be reiterated that it was widely accepted in the US as *the* core field of Social Psychological study. Racial attitudes, although but one sector of this,[40] were a major one, and, unlike the situation of Race Psychology *vis-à-vis* experimental Psychology, fully integrated into mainstream concerns. The outcome was that racism became widely seen as a variety of individual psychopathology, a psychological flaw arising from inappropriate conditioning, reliance on 'stereotyping' or psychodynamic development according to theoretical taste. Although some recognised the limitations of this conceptualisation, and Dollard was, notwithstanding Klineberg's criticisms, to some extent an exception, there seems to be a general consensus that this remained the orthodox position in US Social Psychology until the 1960s. Klineberg, by contrast, was led 'to an interpretation of race prejudice not in terms of the psychological mechanisms operative in the individual so much as in the political and socio-economic conditions prevailing in the community or region' (1940, p. 381).

Samelson (1978) reads the 'prejudice' paradigm's rise as a cunning move by psychologists to retain intellectual authority by moving as it were from one foot to the other. Unable to be experts on now non-existent race differences, they will become experts on the cognitive psychopathology underlying the (now) irrational belief in such differences. Even if having some validity from a retrospectively lofty perspective, this is hardly sustainable as an accurate description of what took place on the ground. Those most central in promoting the prejudice paradigm were a quite different set of people to those working in Race Psychology. (As Samelson himself observes, inspection of their surnames reveals a far higher number of non-Anglo-Saxon names among prejudice researchers than among Race Psychologists.) They included recent Jewish exiles from Germany such as Katz, who can hardly be accused of consciously engaging in this sort of power-game. By choosing to locate the source of racism within individual minds, US Psychology was nonetheless able to avoid having to formulate any serious critique of US culture. In distracting attention from racism's social systemic roots it is, in hindsight, clearly open to the charge that its faulty diagnosis helped sustain racism by misdirecting anti-racist energies. It would be excessively paranoid to claim that this was in any sense deliberate.[41]

A more fundamental, though related, flaw has only become visible in the last decade or so. This is that the discourse of the entire approach remained locked within an implicitly racialist framework. First, the reality of 'racial groups' as such is nowhere contested. Secondly, by aspiring towards 'racial tolerance' as the ultimate goal the deep ambiguities of the concept 'tolerance' have been occluded. 'Tolerance' implies enduring the unpleasant, it takes as given that 'races' will somehow naturally (albeit irrationally perhaps) find one another to varying degrees objectionable, and, as an aspiration, is really an exhortation to those *with* social power to suppress these feelings on moral grounds. This subtly leaves the social power dimension unexamined. Recalling Dollard's position, we can also see that there is no space for consideration of genuine ethnic cultural differences. The assumption is that there is one ideal standard of behaviour or lifestyle – the white US one – divergences from which white Americans must learn to 'tolerate' (pending perhaps some future convergence). This failing should, again, be seen as a perhaps inevitable phase in what has amounted to a long-drawn out exposure of the profundity of the 'race' issue. Nobody in 1940 (even radical African Americans) was talking about 'racial discourse', nor could they.

By the early 1940s the situation in the attitudes/prejudice field was actually fairly chaotic. E.L. Horowitz's 1944 review gives the impression of researchers running hither and thither in all directions seeking angles from which to tackle the topic. While it is a reasonable generalisation to say that they tended to view prejudice as an individual-level quasi-pathology, arising from failure rationally to control lower level irrational impulses, this somewhat oversimplifies the picture. As indicated previously, their concerns included, among others, the development of 'race attitudes' and 'race consciousness' in children, the effects of attitudes on the recipients, private vs. public attitudes, whether or not a single 'attitude to the Negro' could really be identified or was analysable into subsidiary components, and how well attitudes predicted behaviour.[42] Somewhat contrary to the generalisation, it must also be pointed out that Horowitz, by 1944, is tracing race attitudes to the 'interiorization' of social or cultural norms, and finding, in line with this, that they tend to become more integrated and coherent as the child grows older.[43] The 'prejudice' paradigm, while offering explanations of prejudice, could not, as just indicated, address those apparent 'racial differences' which underlay the whole problem. If innate differences were illusory, some other approach to human cultural and psychological diversity was required. Although deep-rooted, the 'culture and personality' paradigm which served this complementary role was somewhat slow to gain momentum, only making serious headway after around 1936. It is to this we turn next.

The 'Culture and Personality school'[44]

This title belongs, strictly speaking, to the work on cultural determinants of personality associated with people such as Kardiner, Kluckhohn and Linton which, beginning in the late 1930s, enjoyed its greatest popularity in the late 1940s and 1950s. Its emergence had nonetheless long been brewing.[45] Embroiled in conceptual controversy with anthropology, its popularity declined in the late 1950s, but productivity was sustained and it metamorphosed into a broader approach termed 'Psychological Anthropology', overlapping substantially with Cross-cultural Psychology.[46] Here it is used more loosely to include all those studies prior to 1940 which attempted to explain human psychological diversity in cultural terms. As we have seen, its roots lay in Franz Boas's cultural anthropology and W.I. Thomas's 'Chicago School' of sociology. It was primarily, though not exclusively, under the tutelage of one or other of these that its leading figures were trained, including Margaret Mead, Melville Herskovits, Ruth Benedict, and E.B. Reuter[47] (though Reuter's texts have not been classified here, being sociology, and most of Herskovits's were also more appropriately placed elsewhere). Also influential was the ethnolinguist E. Sapir who died in 1939.[48] During the 1930s psychoanalysis began casting its spell on those working in this area, who additionally included J.S. Lincoln, G. Devereux, Jules and Zunia Henry, Ruth Landes, Cora Du Bois and, perhaps arguably, the South African psychiatrist B.J.F. Laubscher. The prolific Freudian Géza Róheim had been promoting a psychoanalytic anthropology since the 1920s (e.g. Róheim, 1925) and Erik Erikson's first foray in this direction appeared in 1939.

Psychoanalysis provided a rich new theoretical framework, ideal for analysing the psychological effects of cultural phenomena such as child-rearing customs, domestic arrangements and attitudes towards property. Each culture was perceived as producing a small range of modal character types with a common underlying psychological structure, which its mode of child-rearing succeeded in reproducing and maintaining. For example Devereux, later a major figure in the school, began with an extensive study of Mohave Indians, providing a succinct overview in 'Mohave culture and personality' (1939a).[49] There is a hint of a Gestaltist orientation in his opening statement that 'the life history of any individual can be described in terms of that individual's notions of his deformations in a structured field' (p. 91), though he ascribes this perspective to the sociologist J.F. Brown. The account which follows is, however, totally Freudian in orientation. The Mohave lifestyle results in a 'diffusion of libido over many individuals', creating a deep sense of communal loyalty and social solidarity. The Mohave are 'unbridled oral optimists'; although early swaddling renders them aware of external constraints, there is little sexual repression and the 'primal scene' is apparently not traumatic. Their 'libidinal diffusion' results in a low level of 'individualized object-cathexis', and while there is much affection there is little care-taking behaviour. He suggests that 'gastro-intestinal repression' rather than 'sexual repression' is the primary cultural control. They have a 'naturally cycloid temperament and physique' (the only mention of a possible biological dimension to Mohave character). He also discusses how the variant outcomes of male and female homosexuality and shamanism emerge and are satisfactorily socially integrated. He concludes with an evocation of (male) Mohave personality as 'impulsive, with moods as inconsistent as the sea, intelligently sensitive to the moods of their interlocutors . . . now indolent, now immersed in hectic activity, dreaming and boisterous . . .' with 'a thread of very genuine trustworthiness and of fundamental decency' (p. 109). Devereux subsequently went on to develop a form of 'transcultural' or 'metacultural' psychotherapy, his major work on which was *Reality and Dream: Psychotherapy of a Plains Indian* (1969, 2nd edn).

Ruth Landes' 'Personality of the Ojibwa' (1937a) and 'The abnormal among the Ojibwa Indians' (1938a), if less saturated with Freudian terminology, are clearly psychodynamic in orientation. The Canadian Ojibwa Indian family typically spends half the year in virtual isolation in its woodland hunting ground, a larger, relatively short, social gathering occurring in the summer. This lifestyle has psychological consequences very different from those Devereux found among the Mohave:

> The Ojibwa training in lonely, self-determining living produces an extremely self-conscious ego which is characterised on the one hand by . . . vulnerability and desperate hostility . . . and on the other by a desire for supremacy that assumes some startling forms.
>
> (1937a, p. 57)

Jealous of property, highly superstitious, disregarding of rules and laws when it suits him, the Ojibwa male typically displays an unfortunately negative constellation of personality traits. While superficially explicable in terms of the exaggeratedly individualistic lifestyle necessary for survival in a harsh and relatively unproductive environment, these traits are not shared by neighbouring peoples living in comparably difficult circumstances. Landes argues that they are primarily the result of a 'culturally inculcated masculine pursuit of power' (1938a, p. 32). At the same time the underlying obsession with food, manifested most dramatically in the cannibalistic symptoms of windigo possession (in which relatives appear to be succulent beavers) is clearly related to early inculcation of ascetic self-denial in males.[51] J. and Z. Henry (like Landes, based at Columbia University) studied the Pilagá Indians of the Argentinian Gran Chaco region. They were particularly interested in child-rearing and published two papers in 1940 relating to this: 'Some cultural determinants of hostility in Pilagá Indian children' and 'Speech disturbances in Pilagá Indian children'. Pilagá children are apparently 'hungry for attention and extremely violent and quarrelsome' (J. Henry, 1940, pp. 11–12). This is related to: (a) the fact that food scarcity has, among the Pilagá, somewhat untypically led to a reluctance regarding food-sharing, which in turn heightens hostility 'to an unusual degree'; (b) the very inferior position of women (and high level of female infanticide until 10 years prior to the research), partly because they believe that, reproductively, women are the receptacles of a fully formed homunculus produced by the male. While the child receives affection in early infancy this rapidly attenuates with long periods of maternal absence and ceases peremptorily on the arrival of a new baby. Children are left to their own devices from an early age and largely ignored. There is a 'general atmosphere of insecurity and tension'

(p. 117). 'There are few Pilagá children who do not show symptoms of personality disturbance' (J. and Z. Henry, 1940, p. 362). Again their account is readily translated into (and, albeit somewhat covertly, derived from) the theoretical framework of psychoanalysis.

Aside from Róheim's party-line Freudian writings, the most explicitly psychoanalytic work was Erikson's 'Observations on Sioux education' (1939), a report of work done as a 'mental hygienist' on the Oglala reservation at Pine Ridge, South Dakota in 1937. After presenting much general material on the history of Sioux culture, Erikson attempts to reconstruct the nature of traditional education from interviews with older members of the community and observations on current practice. Using the notion of 'epigenesis' he characterises the educational environment as

> choosing a focus for its interference with the unfolding set of given human elements, by timing this interference, and by regulating its intensity, [this] inhibits the child's impulse rhythms in such a way that the final outcome represents what is felt to be – and often is temporarily – the optimum configuration of given human impulses under certain natural and historic conditions. (pp. 132–3)

The extremely permissive Sioux education reverses the Western way of proceeding. A growing child is gradually guided into cultural norms, progressively shaped by the behaviour of those around it to which it naturally wants to conform, finally emerging as a self-confident integrated individual. Western child-rearing attempts at the outset to constrain the child, gradually releasing the constraints as it approaches adulthood. This results in two quite different modes of psychological individualism. The inner self-sufficiency of the Sioux child results in a remarkable 'strange inner serenity and inner personal harmony which makes it possible for the Indian to submit to white suppression without surrendering to it' (p. 128). Erikson finds their ability to 'live for years, without open rebellion or any signs of conflict' between the Indian and white worlds 'astounding' (p. 124).

Erikson's 'epigenetic' Psychoanalytic framework anticipates his later eight-stage developmental model, and gives a more Freudian gloss to the picture expounded by Margaret Mead, which we will discuss shortly. Despite his evident knowledge of, and sympathy with, the Sioux, Erikson cannot escape a degree of patronisation:

> [the tribe] acts, it seems, somewhat in the same stubborn way as does a patient of long standing who clings querulously and even threateningly to the psychotherapist instead of rewarding his work with recovery. (p. 106)

This is to some extent off-set by frequent passages of what one might call 'moral discourse' on the effects of prejudice and ethnocentric assumptions, to which scientists are not immune.

This late 1930s work built on the foundations Margaret Mead had laid in her studies of Samoan and New Guinea societies, which she claimed were devoid of both sexual repression and serious social conflict. If their mores and customs were often bizarre by American standards who, in the face of the numerous ills besetting contemporary US society, could really say they were worse? And if her message of cultural relativism was not new it had never been so effectively propagated, and came with the 'scientific' authority of a trained field anthropologist. In 1935 her *Sex and Temperament in Three Primitive Societies* spelled out the relativist case in more balanced terms. Based on further field work in New Guinea during 1931–3 this compared three cultures: the Arapesh (mountain-dwellers), the Mundugumor (river-dwelling) and the Tchambuli (lake-dwelling). It became the single most influential text in promoting the notion that personality (including gender-roles) was culturally determined, being cited even today in standard Social Psychology and gender-studies textbooks. Mead's theoretical position was complex. Having initially studied Psychology under Hollingworth (her 1927 paper on the linguistic factor in Italian children's performance originating as her M.A. thesis), she shifted to anthropology, nonetheless continuing to maintain strong links with Psychology and ever seeking to promote inter-disciplinary integration. Her brief autobiographical entry in *History of Psychology in Autobiography* (1974) presents a picture of almost reckless incorporation of nearly every contemporary Psychological theory and methodology bar behaviourism – Piaget, Gestalt Psychology (via contacts with Kohler and Lewin), the Rorschach Ink-Blot and other projective testing techniques, and Gordon Allport's Social Psychology being among the most salient.[52] Freud and Jung she had read early on (tracing the roots of her approach to personality to Jung's *Psychological Types*). In the 1950s she added ethology and Bowlbian attachment theory to her repertoire.

Not all the work classified here was psychoanalytically pitched. At the very end of the period under consideration Wayne Dennis published a clutch of works on native American child-rearing adopting a loosely Piagetian approach.[53] Mead herself largely eschews psychoanalytic concepts in 1935, indeed part of the message of her earlier studies was to cast some doubt on the universality of standard Freudian (and Piagetian) accounts. Instead she offers a model of her own in which each culture stresses and reinforces a particular fraction of the universal spectrum of personality possibilities. In every culture there are nonetheless non-conformers, and these 'deviants' she suggests are actually important sources of social stability (e.g. the non-aggressive individual among the violent Mundugumor). It follows too that the 'deviant' temperament in one society may be the norm in another. She strongly argues that the classification of personality traits along lines of their gender-appropriateness is both arbitrary (the Tchambuli reversing Western norms, with submissive males and aggressive females) and not universal (among the Arapesh and Mundugumor both sexes are either typically 'female' or 'male' respectively in Western terms). The exaggerated tendency to 'specialise' personality types by sex is a major source of the maladjustments afflicting Western culture.[54] This bore little immediate relationship to the psychoanalytic account. Psychoanalysis nonetheless exerted a powerful theoretical hold on culture and personality research. In the 1940s Kluckhohn and Kardiner shifted to a post-Freudian perspective, abandoning the biological component in Freudian theory and such tenets as the universality of the Oedipus complex. The school's continued involvement with psychoanalytic thought contributed to its vulnerability in the late 1950s when psychoanalysis began to fall from favour. Ironically, by challenging its universal applicability, this research itself played a role in the decline of psychoanalysis.

The 'culture and personality' school operated very much on the Psychology/ Cultural Anthropology borderline, cross-disciplinary co-operation being an explicit aspiration of those concerned (in contrast to Britain where the boundary had become almost impermeable). We will be considering post-1945 developments in this genre at a later stage, but a summary of its implications for the 'race' issue and the questions it raised is necessary if its ultimately ambiguous legacy is to be understood.

'National character'

While explicitly rejecting racism, the school's approach entailed a retention of the notion of 'national character'. Indeed Ruth Benedict viewed culture as 'personality writ large'.[55] This national character was a kind of shared personality type resulting from a culture's child-rearing practices, and the received values, beliefs and so forth comprising a culture were usually viewed as cumulative expressions of the attitudes characteristic of such a personality type. While it was recognised that ultimately this was a 'chicken-and-egg' situation, the explanatory mode opted for took the individual psychological level as its starting point. Even though received culture determined a person's personality, this culture was ultimately psychological in origin.

By accepting the reality of 'national character' and attempting to decouple this from belief in innate 'racial' character, advocates of the approach could be accused of leaving the door ajar for views which were racist in all but name. Thus both German and Japanese 'national character' would later be interpreted as in some sense pathologised as a way of explaining their wartime behaviour. Although their explanation had changed, this legitimisation of the 'national character' notion left traditional national stereotypes fundamentally unchallenged. As noted elsewhere, the 'national character' notion is highly suspect; fairly rapid changes in the way national characters are stereotyped are quite common historically (and at this end of the 20th century we might be inclined to consider generational character as being an equally salient reality). As it turned out, the work on national character which flourished in the 1940s provided the school's critics in the 1950s with much ammunition.

Tangentially the question ought to be raised as to whether 'national character' refers to the most profound or most superficial aspect of personality. While the former is the commonest assumption, the opposite could well be argued: we tend to adopt a 'national character' style when dealing with foreign strangers, typically when abroad. Playing the 'national stereotype' game is a way of initiating and managing social contact abandoned when a genuine personal relationship is established. The distinction between 'national character' as a kind of optional social role and 'national character' as a quasi-ancestral identification at the core of someone's identity has never been clarified.

Cultural relativism

The ideological ambiguities of cultural relativism, the doctrine most generally associated with the school, present a difficult knot to unravel. The perennial dilemma is the choice between celebrating differences and denying them. If we adopt the position of basic psychological uniformity among all humans we are certainly offering no crumbs of comfort to racialism, but in countering ethno-centrism, affirmation of diversity may be more effective. One consequence of the school's work was that various theoretical assumptions regarding the universality of psychological phenomena (such as the Oedipus conflict or Piagetian stages) became highly insecure. At what level then was the desired universality to be found? As the pervasiveness of the cultural construction of the psychological was unveiled, the inescapable reflexive corollary – that the researchers' own 'scientific'-cum-humanistic 'psychologies' had no claims to special status – would become inescapable. In 1940 however, this had not been confronted or clearly articulated. The paradox then was that while the basic universality of human nature was a fundamental anti-racist tenet, exchanging genetic explanations of its apparent variety for Psychological ones rendered the universal features of human nature ever more elusive and difficult to specify. Further shifting the explanatory level to 'culture' itself could not solve the problem because this itself was seen as Psychological in origin. In this context the universal applicability of Western Psychological theoretical frameworks offered the only solid ground for researchers to stand on, even as their application beyond Western Psychology disclosed their own cultural specificities – thereby forcing amendments to such source theories themselves – 'amendments' which often verged on outright falsification.

Pragmatically it is undoubtedly necessary for any oppressed people to reclaim and assert their *difference* – self-respect, dignity and a real sense of identity can be acquired in no other way. 'Scientifically' it is equally necessary to affirm that such differences are positive human historical and cultural achievements, not expressions of innate qualities possessed by specific 'races'. But negotiating in detail how these apparently opposing demands for affirmation of differences and their denial are to be integrated remained a task more arduous and complex than anyone appreciated in 1940.

The relationship between culture, society and the individual was a particular concern of Ralph Linton, whose 1939 paper 'Culture, society and the individual' may be taken as a pertinent position-statement.[56] Problems arise most acutely with the concept of 'culture' as a technical term. In a sense 'cultures' are constructs of the anthropological investigator and may not exist 'objectively', but 'whether cultures exist or not, things happen as though they existed. The anthropologist's concept of culture is thus on a par with the physicist's concept of the atom' (p. 427). Linton defines 'culture' in exclusively psychological terms as the 'sum total of the behavior patterns, attitudes and values shared and transmitted by the members of a given society' (p. 425), as opposed to 'society' which is an organised aggregate of persons. The irony is that *within* a society no individual is exposed to the totality of the culture, 'never becomes familiar with its total content'. This rather curiously implies that only the anthropologist, as outsider, can really know a culture completely. Failure to appreciate that exposure to their culture is partial and varies between individuals has, Linton claims, 'been one of the main bars to the successful application of the concept of culture to personality studies' (p. 434). This in itself is a highly effective argument, but one background difficulty US liberal intellectuals such as Linton were having at this time was avoiding being labelled as Marxist. This seriously weakens some of his formulations. Consider the following passage:

> the pattern for the interactions of individuals in different categories will be *adjusted to* the culture's techniques for economic production, its concepts of the supernatural, its system of interests and values and so on. (p. 432, my emphasis)

The 'interactions of individuals' are somehow logically prior to the 'techniques of economic production' and so forth to which they 'adjust'. It would be easy for a Marxist to argue that it is these 'techniques of economic production' which determine the patterns for the interactions of individuals, even the categories of individuality themselves. Forms of economic life are excluded from Linton's definition of 'culture', thereby exacerbating the cultural relativism paradox by excluding *a priori* an explanatory level beyond the psychological in which the true human universal is the necessity of creating a viable form of economic life. From this perspective its culture, and the modes of consciousness this determines, may be apprehended as consequences of a society's 'techniques of economic production'. While dogmatically prioritising the economic may be unwise, avoiding any consideration of the extent to which it is fundamental left the culture–psychology relationship fundamentally mystified. It was to be around the status of the 'culture' concept that the most heated theoretical debates subsequently arose, both within the school and with its mainstream anthropological critics.

Psychological reductionism

Was the culture and personality approach psychologically reductionist? Or perhaps 'culturally reductionist'? From what we have already said, and in the light of the 'mystification' just mentioned, this clearly eludes a simple answer. In that all variability is in the end placed at the door of 'child-rearing', one is inclined to answer in the affirmative. Off-setting this is the deployment of the category 'culture' as an overarching, superordinate, framework factor – but in Linton (a major theoretician in the area) 'culture' itself is defined in psychological terms, as we just saw. The theoretical relationship between these two factors is ambiguous, each being used to explain the other – according, one might add, to the rhetorical requirements of the context. George Spindler, sticking out for culture, later defensively puts it thus:

> The very challenge – that culture was mediated, reinterpreted, individualized, projected in social institutions, only to be recycled through child training (varying from culture to culture of course) to adult personality and belief systems, in an infinite regression of personality upon culture and culture upon

personality – is a complex but not too subtle acknowledgement of the *primary determinism of culture*, largely free of material or biological input.

(1978, p. 16, my emphases)

But with a little bit of rephrasing this passage could surely equally well end up referring to a 'subtle acknowledgement of the primary determinism of psychology'. The majority of those involved certainly saw their work as complementing prejudice, attitude and race relations research[57] which were, as we saw, frequently psychologically reductionist. Failure to confront the issue at the outset was perhaps partly because the power of the school rested substantially on the Boas legacy at Columbia University with which so many of its exponents were identified, Columbia University Press publishing much of its work. If this meant that, field work aside, they were less geographically diffused than the Race Psychologists, this was more than compensated for by their integrated sense of unity as a school and high intellectual calibre. But the kind of radical theoretical critique which would expose the weaknesses of the 'culture' concept was, if not entirely absent, difficult to mount effectively in the late 1930s US political climate and in the face of the Columbia school's academic clout.

Such difficulties thus remained largely latent until the 1950s. In the 1930s the culture and personality approach offered those psychologists concerned with the race issue an exciting alternative to discredited Scientific Racism. Drawing on contemporary Psychological theories and methods it provided intrinsically interesting and plausible accounts of the sources of human variability, while its leading figures were generally politically liberal and philosophically humanistic. Nor was their influence confined to the discipline: the appeal of their anthropological travellers' tales extended to a broad popular readership in a way which psychometrics could not rival. Events in Germany added urgency to the message, reinforced by books such as Julius Lips's *The Savage Hits Back* (1937), a survey of non-European artistic depictions of the European with a moving Preface detailing the author's persecution by the Nazis from his post as Director of the Cologne Rautenstrauch-Joest Museum and Cologne University professorship. This Preface was written while Lips was sojourning with the Canadian Algonquian Indians, which sealed his own self-identification as a 'savage', ironising the 'savage' of the title to mean also himself. At the time of writing he was the only gentile German anthropologist to have opted for exile.

While in some sense complementary, the prejudice and culture and personality approaches each drifted away from the earlier W.I. Thomas and Boas tradition in which the focus was on group differences.[58] As J.M. Jones (1983) argues, the prejudice paradigm reduces the problem to one of individual level psychological processes and a quasi-bureaucratic assumption that all one is aiming for is a kind of numerical egalitarianism between 'racial' groups regarding their representation in the various areas of US social life. Additionally, 'The rising emphasis on methodology inadvertently discouraged a sophisticated analysis of race-related issues' (Jones, 1983, p. 122). This is in line with our earlier remarks on the limitations of prejudice and attitude research. The existence of genuine cultural differences becomes invisible from this perspective, and thus it can shed no light on the cultural level roots of racism itself. The culture and personality paradigm, on the other hand, became, as has been indicated, increasingly concerned with identifying psychological universals, again leaving the cultural sources of racism to one side. It is in its inabilities directly to address these cultural sources, and positively address cultural *difference*, that the ultimate weaknesses of the first wave of anti-racist US Psychology lie. What should also be evident from the culture and personality work mentioned here is that researchers were *not* tackling the domestic situation except in relation to native Americans, African Americans being largely unrepresented in this school's research. This school could not therefore redress the previously identified gaps in the prejudice paradigm's approach.

1940–45: 'RACE' AND US PSYCHOLOGY IN WORLD WAR II

For Psychology, the state of play in 1940 was that the mutually complementary anti-racist camps had all but eradicated nativist race-differences research from the discipline's agenda. Inevitably, this predominantly identified the discipline with the anti-racist forces in US culture at large. With the onset of the war the race issue intensified for a variety of reasons, all centred on that profound contradiction, discussed by Dollard and many others, between the official egalitarian ideology in the name of which a war was now being fought, and the deeply engrained segregationist strand in US culture, North as well as South. Conscription of African Americans into the (still segregated) armed forces, the need for increased propaganda and public education generated by the war itself (plus the involvement of German Jewish exiles in this), the internment of Japanese (but not German) Americans, and the internal dynamics of the African American civil rights movement combined to render an eventual showdown on domestic 'race problems' inevitable. If this had to be postponed until hostilities ended, that very postponement provided an opportunity for highlighting the logical and moral contradictions of the existing order. The early 1940s saw the continued appearance of anti-racist and anti-race differences papers such as J.H. Rohrer (1942) in the Garth tradition (showing that among Osage Indians level of white ancestry had no effect on Goodenough and Otis tests) and H.G. Canady (1943) on the impossibility of equating Negro and white environments in comparative studies of IQ performance – invoking Ruth Benedict and Margaret Mead *en route*.

Whatever the anti-racist consensus within US Psychology by the 1940s, things were never going to be easy in the world at large. In 1943 Ruth Benedict and Gene Weltfish published a Public Affairs Committee pamphlet *The Races of Mankind*. Its 31 pages began by rhetorically invoking the common cause – 'the military destruction of fascism' – and how 'White men, yellow men, black men, and the so-called "red men" of America, peoples of the East and the West, of the tropics and the arctic, are fighting together against one enemy' (p. 1). It then proceeded, in quite elementary terms, to make the case against racial superiority, explain the unity of humanity and irrationality of race prejudice, and assert that 'science' had found no race differences in intelligence that could not be attributed to environmental circumstance. In passing they threw in a little of the old US Army test data showing mean Negro IQ in New York, Illinois and Ohio to be higher than that of whites in Mississippi, Kentucky and Arkansas (drawn from Klineberg, 1935b, in fact). It was liberal certainly, but hardly scientifically contentious stuff – except perhaps in being overaccepting of the race concept itself. Nonetheless it was all too much for the Committee on Military Affairs of the House of Representatives, who ordered it to be withdrawn as 'unfit for US soldiers', the Army test figures apparently being the main cause of apoplexy. Alper and Boring (1944) responded to the row, essentially endorsing Benedict and Weltfish: 'few [psychologists] will assert that any unalterable race differences in intelligence have ever been established, so great is the effect of culture upon intelligence' (p. 471) – though they mildly slapped the authors' wrists for not presenting more complete data (p. 474).

Despite this spat, and the deep-rooted military suspicion of the liberal intellectual establishment which it signified, the liberal anti-racist strands in US Psychology continued making headway in the war years. One factor in this was a seeming shift in policy on the part of the Carnegie Foundation which, in 1938, had solicited the eminent Swedish sociologist Karl Gunnar Myrdal to take leave of absence from the University of Stockholm to oversee, in an impartial manner, 'a general study of the Negro in the United States'.[59] Myrdal obtained 'memoranda' on various aspects of the topic from 20 'American students of the Negro'. Following his return to Stockholm in 1940 his role was taken over by Samuel A. Stouffer of the University of Chicago (subsequently leading author of the massive *American Soldier*, 1949–50). Five books, each important in its own way, resulted from this, being published by Harper as *The Negro in American Life Series*. The largest was Myrdal's own two-volume *An American Dilemma. The Negro Problem and Modern Democracy* (1944). Most relevant to us is Klineberg (ed.) *Characteristics of the American Negro* (1944). Also included was Herskovits' extremely influential *Myth of the Negro Past* (1941) which was in its fourth reprinting in 1967 at the height of the Civil Rights struggle. The only African American authored work in the series was Charles S. Johnson's *Patterns of Negro Segregation* (1943) (Johnson being Dean of Social Science at Fisk University). Myrdal's fellow countryman Richard Sterner authored the fifth work, *The Negro's Share* (1943). Manuscripts of all the memoranda were deposited in the Schomburg Collection of the New York Public Library, authors including, among others, Ashley Montagu, Ruth Landes, Ralph Bunche (an African American who later became a prominent diplomat), and E. Franklin Frazier (the eminent black sociologist), their topics ranging from 'The Church and the Race Problem in the United States' to 'The Negro Press' – covering in fact most economic, educational and cultural issues of relevance, in addition to psychological ones. All these fed into Myrdal's own *magnum opus*. The research and memoranda-writing programme was effectively completed in 1940, but editing and rendering publishable the material under war-time conditions inevitably resulted in some delay in the public appearance of the full series.

Klineberg (1944) may serve as a convenient point of reference for us since it represents the state of play of the field in US Psychology immediately prior to the post-war authoritarianism studies. The variously authored chapters comprise, for the most part, overviews of Psychological work covering much of the material we have already discussed. Klineberg's two chapters on 'Tests of Negro intelligence' and 'Experimental studies of Negro personality' are, as we would expect, detailed and updated reiterations of his 1935 position.[60] There are a few signs of what might be taken as diplomatic compromise, most remarkably that Klineberg frequently refers to the Nordic, Alpine and Mediterranean groups in the European population despite his message that they do not differ psychologically. His conclusion to the 'personality' chapter also seems to be holding it open that, while not yet demonstrated, 'Negro and white' personality differences may occur. On intelligence he remains, however, adamantly anti-difference. While Klineberg's own chapters require little further discussion it should be noted therefore that despite his earlier challenges to the meaningfulness of the 'race' concept he is, in 1944, apparently reluctant to press the point.

Guy B. Johnson's opening chapter, 'The stereotype of the American Negro', has a certain curiosity value. Distilled from a vast body of archival material it first presents representative quotations from both 'Negro' and white authors as to the 'Negro' character, then briefly discusses and summarises them. His primary message is that there is actually a surprising degree of consensus between African Americans and US whites, although the former tend to supplement the fundamentally negative trait catalogue with a few positives.[61] From this he suggests that when all due allowance is made for bigotry and prejudice there may still be a core of truth in this stereotype – though 'In so far as it has any validity, it is of course more applicable to the Negro masses than to the minority of highly sophisticated and *acculturated* Negroes' (p. 18, my italics). He is also keen to leave aside the questions of 'blood versus environment, or race versus culture'. The traits he ends up with, under a dozen headings, are much as we might predict, including, under 'mental' 'relatively low intellectual interests; good memory; facile associations of ideas' and under various other headings 'gregariousness', 'love of music and dance', 'higher interest in sex', 'high interest in superstition', 'high incidence of social disorder', 'role of mother strong', and so on. On 'race pride' he refers to 'acceptance of white standards of physical beauty to a large extent' and, under 'race consciousness', 'high intragroup conflict and cleavage', 'lack of strong race-wide leadership'.[62] On all of these he finds 'Negroes' as likely to agree as whites. Quite how are we to read Johnson's contribution at this remove? One difficulty is that his sources temporally range from 1851 to 1939 and thus any shift in stereotyping (by either 'race') cannot be identified. In view of the publicity given to the 'New Negro' over the 1920s and 1930s one would have expected this to be mentioned at least. Leaving aside all the qualifying statements it is clear that Johnson is holding open the possibility, indeed strong likelihood, that these traits are indeed *real* and possibly that many of them are enduring. There is no discussion of how the stereotypical traits were generated, why 'Negroes' accept them as well as whites, how far they are in flux, or whether their cultural meanings for 'Negroes' and whites differ (which, if true, would render the apparent cross-group consensus to some degree illusory). This chapter reinforces our earlier observations on the inherent limitations on anti-racist white Psychological discourse at this time.

Most valuable is E.L. Horowitz's chapter '"Race" attitudes', to which allusion has already been made. As previously noted, the impression given by this is less of consensus than of confusion. Numerous theoretical positions and distinctions are in play: Are attitudes motivational or adaptational? Are 'race' attitudes unitary or of various kinds? Are they best explained in terms of individual psychological processes (G. Allport, Dollard, Katz) or social ones (Moreno, Criswell, Horowitz)? Should we differentiate between common and individual attitudes? And between private and public ones? Behind all this there are, additionally, a number of methodological difficulties regarding questionnaire and research design. The material presented ranges from gender, regional and social class differences in 'race attitudes' to the development of 'race consciousness' in the child and the effectiveness of college courses in reducing race prejudice among students. If anything, Horowitz's survey is rather more concerned with sociological and social process aspects of the topic than the more strictly individual psychological ones. One underlying message he seeks to convey partly echoes one of Johnson's points, namely that the various minority groups within the US share common evaluations of, and attitudes towards, one another and nationality labels, excepting that each tends to see itself in more favourable terms. This reinforces his own position that race attitudes are acquired by a process of internalising social norms – which of course pushes the question of their ultimate origin back one stage further, but clearly departs from what most writers have depicted as a consensus among early attitude theorists that 'prejudice' was an irrational, individual-level, quasi-psychopathology. The question is thus raised of how far this image itself needs general revaluation. While provisionally accepting the received version here, I return to it more critically in Chapter 8.

It is pertinent here to mention that current black psychologists such as Mama (1995) and Cross (1991) view the work by Horowitz and Kenneth and Mamie Clark on African American self-attitudes during this period (and by others subsequently) as a major contribution to the creation of the 'damaged Negro' stereotype. The 'Negro', they claim, was now depicted as possessing a particular self-hating personality-type formed primarily by being the target of white racism. This was simply to shift from the older biological stereotype to another, social, one – the actual content of which had changed relatively little even if the cause had. The possibilities of African Americans (a) having any autonomous cultural life of their own and (b) being as diverse in personality as anyone else, are thereby excluded from the picture. Cross identifies numerous methodological flaws in their research which biased the results in the desired direction. These observations are clearly consistent with the approach of the Johnson chapter, shed light on Klineberg's acceptance of the possibility of a distinct 'Negro' personality and are confirmed by Horowitz's 'internalisation of social norms' model.

This new image cannot, though, be laid entirely at the door of white psychologists. It was in many respects an inevitable spin-off from the cross-ethnic antiracist position at the time. This involved exploring and articulating the effects of white racism on African Americans, and was undertaken, frequently to more direct effect, by black novelists and social scientists as much as by white ones. In interpreting events as they do, contemporary black writers such as Cross and

Mama are in the difficult position of having to challenge the testimony of black writers of the 1930s–1940s. It does seem that insofar as African American voices could become generally audible in US culture during this period it was primarily by articulating the plight of the 'Negro' as damaged victim, while work such as Bayton's, cited earlier, confirms that African Americans tended, if selectively, to accept much of the 'Negro' stereotype as accurate. To the extent that there was a genuine autonomous black culture, what was being said therein would, almost by definition, *not* be so audible. Clearly the present author is in no position to consider how far such an autonomous culture had existed all along and how far it was positively re-created anew from about 1910 onwards. The possibility is surely open that, the Harlem Renaissance and Jelly Roll Morton notwithstanding, a genuinely live autonomous African American culture in which the majority of US blacks could consciously and satisfyingly exist was still in its infancy in the 1930s? Between the traditional rural folkways and beliefs being lovingly salvaged and preserved on the one hand and the big-city bohemian jazz culture on the other there was surely a vast oppressed, still deculturated, middle ground?

The fifth part of the work is L. Wirth and H. Goldhamer's 'The hybrid and the problem of miscegenation'. While not Psychological, this contains a wealth of information on marriage laws, inter-racial marriage rates, the special problems facing those of 'mixed race', and so forth. There is some relatively brief discussion of the 'mulatto hypothesis', but as the authors conclude, the burden of proof had by then fallen on the pro-differences camp. The conceptual framework of the paper seems somewhat confused, with the authors accepting the racial terms of the discourse within which the issue arises fairly uncritically. Much of the burden of their discussion, however, concerns the social status/skin lightness correlation, which they see as weakening. They conclude that the 'mulatto as a distinct group will play a decreasingly important role in Negro society'. The paper now looks like something of a swan-song for the entire topic. Post-World War II research has virtually never bothered differentiating 'hybrid' and 'pure blood' black subjects, even in race-differences work. Why it disappears is actually an interesting question. It does so, in part at least, because among African Americans themselves the distinction came to be seen as of less and less significance, and sustaining it a divisive – even paradoxical – self-handicapping in the Civil Rights struggle. On the other side, geneticists had ceased to find the 'hybridity' concept useful, at least in this context, with the abandonment of typological theories of race in favour of population genetics' 'gene-pool' models. And as time goes on of course 'pure-bloodedness' becomes ever rarer.

B. Malzberg ended the volume with a brief statistical survey of American 'Negro' mental illness rates, espousing a thoroughly environmentalist view of such differences as appeared to exist. Klineberg's own three-page closing 'Summary' finishes with what might be read as an intellectually frustrated stamp of the foot:

As a part of the American people, Negroes partake of the psychological quality of all Americans. What differences there are appear to depend on existing discrepancies in the opportunities offered to the two groups. When these discrepancies will have been completely eliminated, there will probably be no further reason to write a psychological volume on THE CHARACTER-ISTICS OF THE AMERICAN NEGRO. (p. 402, capitals in original).

Klineberg's volume, along with others emanating from Gunnar Myrdal's programme, was setting the terms on which, it was expected, the issue would be reopened after the war. Intellectually, the anti-racists obviously had the field largely to themselves while the war against racist Nazism lasted. That the US armed forces remained segregated was half ignored as an accepted practice which could not be altered in war-time, and half admitted as an embarrassment which would one day have to be rectified. But on the ground, as the US Army rolled across Germany, its racism did not abate. White American soldiers and their white German POWs caroused together in the chaos while their black comrades sat outside, and Lena Horne stomped out of a forces concert in Arkansas because German POWs were given better seats than African American soldiers.

CONCLUSION

The 1930s witnessed a major reversal in US Psychology's mode of relating to 'race', brought about by a somewhat fortuitous combination of circumstances. 'Internally' Race Psychology had indeed failed 'scientifically' in its own terms, but the rise of the three alternative approaches we have discussed was more complex. Prejudice studies emerged from the increasing centrality of attitude research to Social Psychology. While not in itself a response to 'race' questions, their cultural salience rendered them a natural focus for the new attitude-measuring and attitude-theorising 'paradigm'. In the applied area, the shift is brought about by the sheer numbers of graduate psychologists working in the various applied fields, whose needs and interests Race Psychology simply could not meet, and whose identifications with clients of all ethnicities were heightened by the Great Depression. Only the culture and personality school was motivated from the start by a desire to combat racialist thinking, though its growing theoretical concerns with psychological universals and 'national character' eventually distracted it from this. Its impact was also limited by its relative neglect of the domestic US scene in favour of Pacific, South American and reservation-bound native American sites. In the mid-1930s Psychology is nevertheless clearly an arena where broader ideological debates on 'race' are being fought out. It then becomes futile to try to differentiate 'internal' and 'external'. Psychology is never separate from its host culture, the psychological concerns of which it shares, articulates and reflects, and in the US of the 1930s it was as visibly embroiled in collective cultural life and public affairs as it has ever been. If I choose to research anti-semitism following discussions with a newly arrived Jewish academic colleague, fleeing from Nazi Germany, is this decision 'internally' or 'externally' determined? The question obviously makes no sense.

Notwithstanding these developments, the fact remains that Psychological discourse on 'race' was overwhelmingly white in authorship and, we can now see, oversanguine regarding the issue's depth. However benign in intent, white psychologists simply could not (and cannot) directly articulate and analyse the experience of people of other ethnicities; they could only work as best they could on their behalf. Thus they inevitably ended up creating further *white* images or stereotypes of them, especially the African American, as 'damaged' or as 'victims' (although as we saw, African Americans tended to endorse this at the time). They were also blind to the ambiguities of the 'tolerance' aspiration which underlay the prejudice paradigm. In these deeper senses Psychology retained its place in the cultural system by which white control over black identity and 'subjectivity' (to adopt Mama's term) was exercised. The handful of black psychologists, such as Kenneth and Mamie Clark, Beckham and Canady were in no position to challenge this (even had a challenge been thinkable), their professional credibility and survival depending on their ability to collaborate in the discipline's white liberal projects. In addition, as explained above, the direct study of racism's cultural dimension remained largely neglected – though perhaps less so than some current writers allege. For US Psychology anybody who was not white remained an 'other', albeit a transformed one.

Meanwhile the scene was set to shift from domestic US 'race relations' problems to Europe and the most traumatically evil episode in modern human history, the Holocaust. Before proceeding to this next phase we must turn to European Psychology's pre-war handling of the topic.

NOTES

1 NAACP – the National Association for the Advancement of Colored People. A central text on the 'New Negro' was A. Locke (1925) – who is sometimes credited with coining the phrase. The 'Harlem' or 'Negro' Renaissance is a collective term for the work of numerous African American writers and artists, leading figures being Countee Cullen, Paul Lawrence Dunbar, Jessie Redmon Fauset, Langston Hughes, Claude McKay and Dorothy West. The concept of the 'New Negro' seems to have served a dissonance-reducing function for some white writers (e.g. Odum) by suggesting that the 'Negro' had changed rather than that earlier negative characterisations were mistaken.
2 Rapidly dramatised by Paul Green and produced on Broadway in 1941 by Orson Welles. During the 1920s and 1930s Paul Green, a white from North Carolina, wrote several plays exploring the African American experience including his Pulitzer Prize-winning debut play *In Abraham's Bosom* (1926). See W.D. Sievers (1955, pp. 311–21) for a not altogether satisfactory summary of his work.
3 A major study of lynching at this time was A.F. Raper (1933), on which Dollard (1957, 1st edn 1937) drew heavily.
4 I am using the term 'ideology' somewhat narrowly here to refer to explicit political beliefs and doctrines. Historians often use it more widely to argue that some implicit cultural ideological beliefs are necessary to provide the conditions in which particular research problems can arise at all. In this wider sense any research on 'race' subsumes an 'ideology' in which such a category is both meaningful and salient. I am not disputing this. How racialist 'ideology' in this broad sense is to be transcended is indeed what the current work is ultimately about.
5 Which is not to claim that Psychology is unique in this.
6 Here the extent to which 'Science' is itself a modern white male ideology, a point raised in Chapter 2, should of course be borne in mind.

7 Both Mead and Herskovits were at this point studying under Boas. Herskovits also cites Mead's unpublished work and the two were clearly working on the issue in tandem to some degree. Herskovits was criticised because his subjects were all students and therefore had all been selected for high intelligence in the first place. This criticism does not though meet the case – if skin colour and intelligence are correlated this correlation should be maintained across samples drawn from limited sectors of the total spectrum – in this case it should show that lighter skinned 'negroes' should obtain proportionately more top grade degrees and dark-skinned ones more lower grade 'passes' – which is not what Herskovits found. Any weakness would lie at the level of the initial admissions procedures over which he had no control. It would be necessary to show that the admissions policy was more lenient towards lighter skinned than to darker skinned applicants, thereby artificially raising the average intelligence level of those in the latter group gaining admittance, and *vice versa*. There are no *a priori* grounds for assuming this to have been the case. Technically, Mead's and Herskovits's arguments actually cancel one another out and leave the mulatto hypothesis open.

8 This research, on the role of language disability in the poor IQ performance of Italian children, appeared in Mead (1927).

9 See below p. 202.

10 Although the 1921–3 *New Republic* spat between Walter Lippmann and Terman had been instrumental in raising public awareness of the issue. See Chapter 4, n. 49.

11 The data additionally confirm this confusion in an intriguing fashion: only 4% believe in race differences in intelligence but more, 15%, apparently accept the mulatto hypothesis which is premised on the existence of these differences!

12 See also S.P. Rosenthal (1933) for his full version of this highly effective demolition job.

13 I am leaving aside here his important 1931 monograph on European 'race' and national differences. His conclusions on their existence were equally negative, scotching Brigham's Nordic-Alpine-Mediterranean hierarchy (in France the order was actually reversed). Subjects were male schoolboys in Germany, France and Italy. Urban–rural differences were the most apparent. Data from this is incorporated in *Race Differences*, and summarised in L.W. Crafts et al. (1938). For most American psychologists the European 'race differences' issue was, by 1931, no longer of primary interest, but Klineberg's monograph reinforced the case against.

14 He also devotes Chapter XI of his 1940 textbook *Social Psychology* to 'Racial differences', but this is basically a reprise and summary of the arguments he had presented earlier. It is particularly good on the lack of necessary correlation between physical and psychological characteristics. Klineberg's later career was dominated by his concerns to promote international understanding and as well as his involvements with UNESCO he taught in Paris, Rome and São Paulo. For an outline of his career and the background to his early 'race' research see his entry in G. Lindzey (1974). See also Chapter 8 below.

15 Klineberg (1974). Woodworth's persisting background role would be worth further research. His own position seems to have long remained equivocal (see also Winston, 1996). The contrast between his 1910 and 1916 papers noted earlier seems to continue in his willingness to support both Garth and Klineberg. In Woodworth (1946) he only cites two of Klineberg's works in the two pages (of over 600) devoted to the issue, concluding that 'From an individual's race or nationality you can infer practically nothing as to his intelligence' (p. 129).

16 He also introduces, I believe for the first time, a version of a speculative point which I made at the end of Richards (1984). 'It might very well be that the white stock which united with the Negro was inferior to the Negro stock, even though the average white stock was superior' (p. 55). As it stands, it should be stressed that this is a relatively weak point arising *within* the hereditarian framework of discourse. But we should be wary of applying to poor Southern rural whites the very hereditarian arguments we

are denying are applicable to African Americans. The way to strengthen this point is to link it to the broader arguments about the impermanence of the current pattern of gene-frequencies in any human gene-pool and the fact that such frequencies themselves reflect the environmental selection vectors which have historically operated on the group. My later point was that it was at least possible, given that Southern white rapists have reportedly lower than average intelligence, that a disproportionate influx of their genes would have had a deleterious effect on the African American gene-pool. This was offered somewhat sarcastically as an argument which could be made even within the hereditarian framework's terms – a framework which, as I argued elsewhere in the paper, was fundamentally flawed anyway.

17 Lambeth and Lanier (1933) did however subsequently mount a rearguard critique of this research which claimed to show that the difference only occurred with more complex tasks and that 'negro' performance was poorer on these in any case. Despite its title this paper did not study RTs but mostly reviewed existing data on performance on various tasks such as paper tapping, 'cancellation of As' etc.

18 Contributors to S. Fraser (1995) like S.J. Gould, are still trying to get this point across. Gould also points out that inter-group differences on a highly heritable trait (e.g. height) may be due to environment (e.g. diet). See below Chapter 9 for fuller discussion of this.

19 Klineberg (1974, p. 167).

20 Quoted by Nadine Weidman (1994). This salutation occurs in two 1955 letters sent from Jamaica, another to J.B. Watson himself included the comment 'I could not quite stomach dining in the best hotel as the only Caucasion [sic] with 26 Negros' [sic] – he obviously knew Watson was a kindred spirit; in 1957 he confides in him his willingness 'to go to any lengths to stop integration'. The originals are in Boxes 1 and 2 of the Lashley papers held by the University of Florida, Gainesville. Weidman does in fact show how Lashley's neuropsychology covertly supported his racism.

21 Within academia generally, informal and covert racism in the selection of students, especially Jewish ones, remained widespread. In addition to the well-known situation at Harvard, numerous other universities were operating anti-semitic policies with respect to staff and/or student recruitment (Bernard Spilka, personal communication; see also McWilliams (1948), pp. 134–40, for a contemporary account). The anecdotal and manuscript evidence on this is in fact legion. As A.S.Winston (1996) has shown, during the 1930s anti-semitism in US academia was at a high level and Woodworth's correspondence often shows him, when providing references for Jewish academics, explicitly spelling out that they do not display 'typical' Jewish traits. This suggests that Woodworth either accepted the stereotype in general or at least felt bound to pose as if he did.

22 See R. Turner (1994) for an illuminating study of the Helmholtz–Hering controversy and the factors involved in determining its fate.

23 The number of African American psychologists remained low until well into the 1960s. Only 93 African American Ph.D.s were awarded between 1920 and 1966 by the 25 largest university Psychology departments, about half from New York, Columbia, Indiana and Chicago. Wispé et al. (1971) elicited questionnaire data from 166 Ph.D.s and 173 M.A.s working in 1966, a response rate of just over 80%. Allowing for mortality etc. it would seem unlikely that the number of post-graduate qualified African American psychologists 1920–66 much exceeded 600. See also Chapter 4, n. 101.

24 As a sign of linguistic inertia it is worth noting that *The Journal of Social Psychology* (begun in 1929) retained its subtitle '*Political, Racial, and Differential Psychology*' until 1948, by which time virtually all three had long ceased accurately to characterise the sub-discipline, while hardly any of its post-1934 papers were Race Psychology in the sense we are using it (Steggarda and Macomber, 1939 is an exception).

25 See S.P. Rosenthal (1933, pp. 312–13) for a sound critique of this notion, which had been proposed by W.M. Bevis (1921).

26 Mama's two historical chapters are seriously flawed in numerous respects, being somewhat selectively researched and overly determined by a desire to cast Psychology's role
in a comprehensively negative light. This is nevertheless compensated for by the
insights which her position as a post-modern black feminist enables her to achieve.
We will return to her important theoretical moves in Chapter 10.

27 See, for example, C.F. Graumann in M. Hewstone et al. (1996, p. 15); G.W. Allport
in G. Lindzey (1954, p. 45); and O. Klineberg (1940, p. 356). The programmatic view
that the study of attitudes should be the core task of Social Psychology is generally
ascribed to W.I. Thomas and F. Znaniecki (1918).

28 Lippmann became one of the most eminent liberal American pundits of the mid-
century period. See also Chapter 4, n. 49.

29 David Katz was a German exile. Previously Professor of Pedagogy and Experimental
Psychology at Rostock University, he was 'relieved of his duties' in April 1933 under
the 'Aryanisation' paragraph 3 of the Law for the Restoration of the Professional Civil
Service proclaimed on 7 April. See Geuter (1992, pp. 42, 53).

30 He renders both town and state anonymous in order to protect informants. My suspicion is that the town was in either Arkansas, northern Louisiana or Mississippi. He
mentions the influence of the Louisiana populist demagogue Huey Long on some of
the lower-class African Americans, and also that the classic slave plantation culture
developed somewhat late in the state (hence there are fairly few old-style mansions).
Someone sufficiently motivated and with access to the sources could probably identify
the state from the data provided on various demographic and economic topics.

31 Dollard's move away from the psychoanalytic position to learning theory came in
N.E. Miller and J. Dollard (1941) in which the 'frustration-aggression hypothesis' is
articulated. It also includes (Chapter XV) a behaviouristically couched 'Analysis of a
lynching'.

32 He did in fact subsequently co-author one quite important study of African American
children: A. Davis and J. Dollard (1940). See below p. 251.

33 For example, A.S. Beckham (1934), K.B. and M.P. Clark (1939a, b, 1940), T.E.
Davis (1937), E.A. Ferguson (1938), C.S. Johnson (1931), C.T. Taylor (1936).

34 For example, E.L. Horowitz (1935, 1936), R.E. Horowitz (1939), B. Lasker (1930),
H. Meltzer (1939a, b, c), R.D. Minard (1931), R. Zeligs and G. Hendrickson (1935),
R. Zeligs (1937, 1938), K.B. and M.P. Clark (1939a, b, 1940). The Horowitz and
Clark and Clark papers attempted to identify the point at which children acquired
'race-consciousness' of their identity. R.E. Horowitz found this to be earlier among
the black than white male children (c. 4 yrs), but her sample of subjects was very
small. The Clarks, modifying Horowitz's technique with a much larger sample of
black children, again found boys to have acquired racial self-consciousness around 4–
5 yrs, but girls showed no change in performance 3–5 yrs, their results being at chance
throughout. Methodological criticisms may of course now be made about both these
pieces of research. Mama (1995) discusses this work at some length, including its
methodological flaws, as crucial in creating the new 'damaged Negro' stereotype. The
Horovitzes changed their Jewish surname to Hartley during World War II, which
Mama rightly sees as significant in relation to their view of the psychological conditions of minorities.

35 For example, N.P. Gist (1932), S.S. Sargent (1939, on stereotyping in the *Chicago
Tribune*), A.L. Severson (1939, on advertisements).

36 For example, W.P. Chase (1940, on North Carolina women students' attitudes
towards the negro), D.D. Droba (1932), K.C. Garrison and U.S. Burch (1933),
J.P. Guilford (1931), D. Peregrine (1936), G.A. West (1936, on attitudes of teachers
in the South West).

37 A.M. Meerloo (1935, Dutch) was the only precursor identified in any language.

38 The pattern of distribution of titles with 'Jew', 'Jewish' or 'Anti-semitism' in their
titles was:

	A	B	C	D
1918	2			2
1926	1	1		
1928	1			1
1929	1			1
1930	4		1	3
1931	6		1	5
1932	2			2
1933	2			2
1935	3	1		2
1936	4	1		3
1938	1			1
1939	3		1	2
1940	4		1	3
Total	34	–	3	4	27

pre-1930 N = 5.   %D: 79

Categories refer to those used in Table 4.1 The four C items are Fenichel (1940), S.H. Markowitz (1931) 'Gentile–Jewish relationships in a small city in the middle west', B. Lasker (1930) and Gerard H. Singer (1939) which deals with anti-semitism's effects on German Jews rather than its causes.

39 See Klineberg (1940, pp. 380–81).
40 Thurstone (1930,1931) already included God, war, evolution, prohibition, birth control, censorship and criminals among the topics for which attitude measuring scales had been devised.
41 The author's reservations regarding the extent to which this widely levelled charge is actually valid are discussed later.
42 This particular issue vexed attitude studies well into the 1970s. At the period in question there was also great dispute as to whether attitudes were to be thought of as determinants of behaviour or products of behaviour. By the late 1960s people such as M. Fishbein were, I think rightly, shifting to seeing 'attitude' as essentially an affective phenomenon, with relatively little predictive value.
43 See E.L. Horowitz (1944, pp. 183–4). Horowitz makes an interesting criticism of Dollard. Dollard, he claims, assumes 'tolerance' as the norm in US culture and thus explains 'intolerance' as a trait of those suffering some special frustration. On the contrary 'our national culture has an intolerant norm and the rebellious people are tolerant, while the compliant are intolerant conformists.' (p. 157) By 'rebellious' he clearly has in mind primarily radicals such as communists, bohemian outsiders etc. – those generally scoring high on 'radicalism' scales on other issues.
44 All the characterisations of ethnic groups in this section are reported as in the original literature and should be understood as 'bracketed'. Current and recent accounts may well provide a quite different picture.
45 In addition to the work of Boas and W.I. Thomas already mentioned, G. Spindler sees Sapir (1917) and Goldenweiser (1917) as significant adumbrations of the issues which concerned the culture and personality school (G. Spindler, 1978, p. 15).
46 See the introduction to G. Spindler (1978) for a reprise of this.
47 While Reuter's approach was cultural and sociological his liberalism was hardly radical and he continued to share many of the anxieties regarding 'miscegenation' etc. of the more racialist camp. See his introduction to E.B. Reuter (1934) for example.
48 See the editorial introduction to Spier, Hallowell and Newman (1941) in which papers by many of the culture and personality school are included.

49 Though he had long been hostile to Freudianism, having been put off by an unspecified work of Róheim's. See G. Spindler (1978, Chapter 11) for Devereux's retrospective review of his work.

50 He had provided a more extensive account of the male 'Alyha' and female 'Hwame' institutionalised homosexual roles in Mohave culture in G. Devereux (1937).

51 Landes published more extensive monographs on *Ojibwa Sociology* (1937b) and 'The Ojibwa woman' (1938b) and a general account in 'The Ojibwa of Canada', (1937c, pp. 87–126). The 'windigo' was conceived as a cannibalistic skeleton of ice, the most powerful force in the Ojibwa cosmology it seems. Shamanistic battles in which each party set a windigo on the other were common, the lay (generally male) victim of windigo possession might insist, in lucid moments, on being killed by his relatives for fear of killing them. Bodies of those possessed would be cremated and thoroughly burned over a period of days in order to destroy the windigo by melting.

52 For her remarkable childhood see M. Mead (1972). See also her contribution to G. Spindler (1978), comprising Chapter 3.

53 W. Dennis (1940a, b, c), W. and M.G. Dennis (1940), W. Dennis and R.W. Russell (1940).

54 See M. Mead (1935, Part 4) for the full elaboration of her 'Psychological' model.

55 Benedict (1961, 1st edn 1934) quoted by M. Mead (1974, p. 314).

56 For a fuller later statement of his position see R. Linton (1947).

57 Weatherford and Johnson (1934) is an important general text on this.

58 Arguing for a reinstatement of cultural level analysis in addition to individual and institutional level analyses, Jones (1983) identifies two traditions, one from Thomas via the sociologist Robert Park to Gunnar Myrdal ('group focus') and one from Bogardus to the authoritarian personality researchers ('individual focus'). As markers of the two positions in Social Psychology he compares Murchison (1935) (group) with Gardner Lindzey's 1954 edition of the same work (individual).

59 Statement by the President of the Carnegie Corporation (Frederick P. Keppel) cited in O. Klineberg (1944, p. vii).

60 Having read these after Chapter 4 was completed I was struck by the frequent convergence between our accounts and passages selected for quotation. They would serve the interested reader as a useful first port of call for further reading.

61 See J.A. Bayton (1941) for a study of 'racial stereotypes of Negro college students' which partially confirmed the position Johnson takes that 'Negroes' accepted much of the 'Negro' stereotype.

62 G.B. Johnson (1944, pp.18–19).

Chapter 6

'Race' in European Psychology to 1940: I. Primitive minds and Aryan supermen

INTRODUCTION

Prior to the 1930s, such explicit attention as post-Victorian European academic Psychology paid to race issues was scattered and disparate. Even after 1930 only the Nazi psychologists – plus a few Italian, Dutch and East European sympathisers – tackled it systematically. In this chapter we consider two mainland European developments in the Psychological treatment of race, first examining a significant transformation of the terms in which 'primitive' psychology was conceptualised, notably by the French anthropologist-philosopher Lévy-Bruhl, and by Carl Jung and Freud. Secondly the most extreme manifestation of racist thought in Psychology, its treatment by avowedly Nazi psychologists, will be tackled.

Regarding non-Europeans, concern with 'race' took the form of a heightened anthropological interest in the subject cultures of Europe's colonies, but was of little domestic interest. The new professional anthropologists' role in this was ambiguous. Theoretically they had abandoned Scientific Racism, and more extended contact with the peoples they studied enhanced their ability to identify with them and appreciate both the complexities of their cultures and the difficulties (theoretical, linguistic and methodological) faced in doing them justice. But they were also representatives and agents of the ruling white authorities, with whose broad interests they also largely identified, and with which they had to collaborate. For these authorities the anthropologist's role was primarily to facilitate relationships between the 'natives' and themselves. An understanding of traditional 'native' institutions, ways of thinking and motivation, such as they could provide, would hopefully enhance both the efficiency and the efficacy of paternalistic colonial administration.[1]

EXPLORING THE 'PRIMITIVE MIND'

If the new generation of anthropologists no longer framed their projects in evolutionary terms, no longer saw their subjects as occupying lower rungs on the ladder of a unidirectional social evolution, they entertained few doubts about the objective superiority and 'advanced' status of European culture.

In this context some mainland-based thinkers began reformulating the nature of the psychological difference between themselves and 'primitive people'. Hitherto, as we saw, this was couched in recapitulationist terms. The 'savage' was a child, in a state of arrested development or passing through an adolescent phase, 'savage' thought was fundamentally similar to that of the European child. Such simple formulae were soon unsustainable in the face of the wealth of field data emerging in the first decades of the new century. Among the French, interest began to focus on the precise nature of 'primitive thought', an enterprise effectively initiated by the '*Année Sociologique* school' of Durkheim and Mauss (influenced by Saussurean linguistics).[2] While a discussion of Durkheim is beyond our present remit, it should be noted that his central tenet was that classification systems and religious beliefs could not be explained in terms of individual psychological processes, but existed at the collective level as 'collective representations'. As such they could be studied in their own right as quasi-natural phenomena disregarding the psychological level. The individual mind, Durkheim argued, 'lacks the innate capacity to construct complex systems of classification'. Since every culture does possess such systems, they must originate at the cultural level as, initially, social categories: the 'first logical categories were social categories'. Thus belief systems and logical categories are ultimately expressions of social structure: 'the unity of knowledge is nothing less than the very unity of the social collectivity extended to the universe'.[3] This represented a claim for the autonomy of the sociological level of analysis from the Psychological. While Durkheim soon began to influence anthropologists such as Arthur Radcliffe Brown (then still plain Arthur Brown), his work signalled the beginning of the split between Anthropology and Psychology in European academia which came to fruition in the 1920s.

Lucien Lévy-Bruhl (1857–1939)[4]

Of more direct relevance to us is the work of Lévy-Bruhl. Following a number of philosophical works (including, interestingly, one on Comte), Lévy-Bruhl turned to armchair anthropology with *Les fonctions mentales dans les sociétés inférieures* (1922a, 1st edn 1910),[5] followed by *La mentalité primitive* (1922b), *L'âme primitive* (1927), *Le surnaturel et le nature dans la mentalité primitive* (1931)[6] and several other works. In these he developed a detailed account of 'primitive mentality' with an interesting bearing on our present concerns.[7]

If, in the 1990s, we are inclined to assume that the *dramatis personae* of our story are easily classifiable as tending towards or away from racism, reading Lévy-Bruhl is an odd experience. While occasional relics of classic Scientific Racism slip through (such as a passing reference to earlier maturation) he explicitly rejects the notion that 'primitives' are innately inferior to the 'civilised'. He could, at a pinch, be read as advocating a version of radical cultural relativism akin to that of the Culture and Personality School. At the same time he dramatically exaggerates the gulf between his primitive and civilised 'mentalities', while terms like 'lower', 'inferior' and 'undeveloped' pepper his texts, suggesting implicit acceptance of some kind of social evolutionary orientation. For Lévy-Bruhl, possession of 'the primitive mentality' apparently unifies all non-literate 'tribal' peoples. He culture-hops in quite Victorian fashion between Australians, Bantus, Huron Indians, Melanesians and the Ashanti. But again, he construes his endeavours as enabling Europeans to bridge the very gulf he sees so widely yawning, rendering the humanity of the 'primitive' more accessible to the civilised. Rejecting any inherent stupidity and incompetence he strives to explain how 'primitive' behaviour is quite comprehensible once we have grasped the 'primitive' world-view, one which in its own terms is complex and sophisticated.

Lévy-Bruhl's 'primitive' is apparently uninterested in, even incapable of, abstract logical thought, and little concerned with seeking the causes of phenomena in a deterministic fashion. He calls this mentality 'prelogical'. In practical affairs such as setting traps, making artefacts, and so forth the primitive's grasp of cause–effect relations is as adequate as anybody's – often startlingly ingenious and subtle to European eyes. But this does not extend to a general logical understanding of the universe as a whole. Beyond practical technology their relationship to the world is fundamentally different from the European's. Lévy-Bruhl's central and most influential conceptual principle is 'mystical participation' (*participation mystique*). Primitives experience no boundary between self and world, and view the determining factors behind all life events (and indeed death) as invisible quasi-human agencies of various kinds (which we may very inadequately call 'spirits') with which they are engaged in constant transactions.

Attempting a coherent account of this mentality is extremely difficult precisely because the primitive does not accept the principle of logical contradiction, thus whether an omen bird is a messenger from a higher deity/spirit or itself an embodiment of that deity/spirit might be quite unclear. This realm of invisible agencies is directly apprehended, no secondary inference from overt events – the occult 'meaning' of an event is as immediately known as the meanings of words. If somebody is killed by a crocodile this is not evidence of their carelessness in avoiding crocodiles but because the crocodile is the agent of a witch or sorcerer – crocodiles, being harmless, need not themselves be avoided. All deaths are due to witchcraft (another problematic term) or some other invisible agency, there is no such thing as a 'natural death'. Witches, wizards, ancestors and the recently dead, animal spirits, deities of rocks and trees – it is these which really govern events. Communication with such entities is constant and direct, not least in dreams – which are invariably taken extremely seriously. Life in this cosmos is a constant round of efforts to avert sorcery, placating ancestors, obtaining good omens (no mere signs of what is to come but the very guarantee of their coming), hunting down evil wizards and conversing with the dead.

For Lévy-Bruhl, following Durkheim (though Durkheim himself disputed Lévy-Bruhl's general position), this reality consists of 'cultural representations' which directly frame the world of primitive experience. Challenging this world-view is extremely difficult, since it resists European logical critique. Explaining that a tree fell on somebody by accident because it was rotten and the wind was blowing leaves unanswered the *real* questions – why it fell on *this* particular person at *that* particular time. There are no 'accidents'. The weak tree and the wind merely provided the occasion of which a hostile power took advantage. Secondary causes are thus not so much denied as considered irrelevant. Our problem lies in our difficulty in fully apprehending the internal comprehensiveness of such a world-view. Spirits, magic and omens are, for this mentality, in every sense as real as the physical world perceived by our waking senses. Primitive 'lack of foresight' is laid at the door of their lack of a Western sense of unidirectional time and abstract space, as evidenced by the belief that events foretold in dreams have in some sense already happened even though they must be subsequently enacted, and the ready acceptance that the souls of the dead can exist in two places at once.

The above is, of course, an inadequate condensation of the vision Lévy-Bruhl expounded through a succession of book-length treatises. It is, nonetheless, hopefully sufficient to provide the basis of a number of observations.

In the first place Lévy-Bruhl seems unwilling or unable to reflect on the extent to which Europeans share this 'primitive mentality', thereby overstating the psychological distance between Europeans and his 'primitive' peoples. How ironic that in *Primitive Mentality*, for example, he draws heavily on the testimony of missionaries, often Jesuits at that. Indifference to 'secondary causes' is a well-established tactic in Christian, especially Catholic, argument. If the blood-weeping Virgin turns out to be directly underneath a rusty dripping pipe, the priest will nevertheless turn a twinkling eye on the sceptic and say 'so what?' – God (like the crocodile-commanding witch) is providentially using the physical circumstance – why is the pipe rusting at just this point and the drips falling on just this spot on the statue? The 'simple faith' of the awe-struck peasant is, we are then to understand, somehow wiser than the scepticism of the sophisticate with an eye for dodgy plumbing. And 'evolution is God's way of doing things' was a standard argument of pro-evolution 19th century Christians. Whereas indifference to the 'law of contradiction' is seen as a failing among 'primitives', in Western theology and mysticism such indifference is seen as necessary to signify truths beyond human comprehension. No wonder the American Indians gave the Jesuits such a hard time! Anthropologists now generally acknowledge that Lévy-Bruhl's characterisation of the primitive mentality seriously overplayed its difference (even assuming it exists) from that of Europeans. In his last years Lévy-Bruhl himself shifted his ground significantly, no longer seeing the 'prelogical' and 'mystical' as uniquely primitive but as 'more marked and more easily observable among 'primitive peoples' than in our societies'.[8]

This apparent lack of reflection raises a second point: who are the 'we' with whom Lévy-Bruhl is authorially identifying? Superficially it includes all Western people, but actually it is far narrower. 'We' are those sharing his own rational 'scientific' psychology. 'We' are logical, analytic, assume things to be explicable by material cause–effect sequences, can accept 'chance' and 'accident' as sufficient explanations for events (thereby denying them any further 'meaning'), never experience events as omens, do not take our dreams very seriously, and so forth. Projecting this *'mentalité scientifique'* (so to speak) onto European culture as a whole he can avoid confronting the extent to which European and 'primitive' mentalities overlap. F.C. Bartlett (1923), in a critique we will return to elsewhere, made the same point:

Lévy-Bruhl's antithesis is not between the primitive man and the ordinary member of a modern social group, but between the former and the scientific expert at work within his own field. This ignoring of 'secondary causes' . . . is a common enough response, to be observed by anybody who cares to look for it in modern life almost any day he wishes. The error here, as in much recent social and abnormal psychology, is not that the primitive or the abnormal have been wrongly observed, but that the modern and normal are hardly observed at all. (p. 284)

Thirdly, his use of the global term 'primitive' clearly obscures the diversity of the cultures he is dealing with. More recent anthropologists have shown that so-called 'primitive' cultures range as widely across the spectrum from down-to-earth hard-headed materialism to religious–cum–mystical as so-called 'advanced' ones.[9] American-based anthropologists such as Mead, Benedict, Landes and Devereux[10] were, as we saw, soon discovering a rich diversity in the cultures and beliefs of the peoples they studied.

Fourthly, as W.H.R. Rivers soon pointed out, apparent failure to adhere to the principle of logical contradiction and similar lapses of rationality (including perhaps mystical participation itself) may prove illusory on closer examination.[11] More specifically they may arise from translation of a key concept into a supposed Western equivalent, when the meanings of the two terms differ to some degree. Rivers used the Melanesian term *mate* to illustrate this. *Mate* is generally translated as 'dead', so if used to describe somebody who is alive there is an apparent breach of the 'principle of contradiction' – the person is being thought of as alive and dead at the same time. But *mate* does *not* mean 'dead' in precisely the Western sense – as I understand Rivers' account it is more akin to loss of a will to live or departure of some spiritual life-force. It is thus quite rational to use it for the severely ill or extremely aged. Once declared *mate* the funeral rites might be enacted, and somebody buried who is still alive by Western criteria. The whole meaning of 'death' for these Melanesians differs significantly from its meaning for Europeans. Once the Melanesian conceptual system is understood their seemingly contradictory and irrational behaviour, so typical of Lévy-Bruhl's primitive mentality, turns out to be nothing of the kind. Rivers was in fact far from sympathetic to the general position taken by Durkheim and Lévy-Bruhl.

Never having done any field work, Lévy-Bruhl, like his British contemporary Sir James Frazer, was utterly dependent on secondary sources and initially able to retain his own intellectual '*mentalité*' secure from the challenges facing contemporary field anthropologists.[12] While his own theory is now primarily of historical interest, it nevertheless provided a point of departure for people like Evans Pritchard (who held him in fairly high esteem), whose own *Witchcraft, Oracles and Magic Among the Azande* (1937) in particular may be seen as translating his insights into more sophisticated terms.[13] His distinction between the atemporal 'primitive' mentality and the sequential Western one also laid a basis for the arch-structuralist Lévi-Strauss's subsequent 'synchronic' vs. 'diachronic' polarity.[14]

Jung and Freud

While Lévy-Bruhl is discovering the primitive mentality in the subjects of Europe's colonial empires, others are making similar discoveries closer to home. We cannot now read him without immediately recognising how closely the features ascribed to the primitive mind resemble those which Freud and, even more so, Jung, are ascribing to the unconscious. And one can only imagine how avidly they would have read his chapter on dreams in *Primitive Mentality*, as Jung certainly did.[15] This similarity is, again, ambiguous in its implications. Once more it both bridges and broadens the perceived gap between European and 'primitive'. Several similarities may be noted:

1 In psychoanalysis there are precious few real 'accidents', the overt event signifies some unconscious wish, which is its real cause. Wandering unguardedly into a river full of crocodiles and getting grabbed results not from witchcraft but, perhaps, from an unconscious death wish. The difference is that for the 'primitive' the death wish is someone else's, for Freud the victim's.
2 The Freudian/Jungian unconscious is atemporal and can defy the 'law of contradiction'.
3 The Freudian dream is about wish-fulfilment and Lévy-Bruhl cites numerous examples of cultures where this is the case. The differences are that in some of these the authority of the dream is such that the dreamer's peers must enact a literal fulfilment, and that the wishes are not exclusively sexual. The Jungian dream may, like many of those described by Lévy-Bruhl, involve encounters with authoritative archetype and ancestor figures who provide guidance to the dreamer. In this latter respect the difference is minimal.
4 Jung argued with considerable passion for the authenticity and seriousness of 'synchronous' and omen-like phenomena, and the entire metaphysical system elaborated in works such as *Structure and Dynamics of the Psyche* is virtually a sophisticated version of the 'primitive' cosmological vision as Lévy-Bruhl expounds it. The *psyche* is ubiquitous and the ground for all human experience, it is transpersonal, it defies time and space (which are in a sense its own products), it contains all human experience, fuses all contradictions.
5 The primitive's alleged failure to differentiate self and world, the *participation mystique*, is readily translatable into psychodynamic terms as lack of ego-strength and, echoing recapitulationism, fixation at some infantile level of psychological development. Jung interprets it in terms of projection of unconscious psychic contents, and stresses the occurrence of essentially similar phenomena in European cultures.[16]

Despite the similarities, the net effect of this was, especially in Jung's case, to reinforce the view that the non-Western *psyche* was qualitatively different from the Western one, somehow less evolved, still in a state of more child-like timeless mystical harmony with the universe, but less 'individuated' and, indeed, less conscious[17] – an image with a distant affinity to the Rousseauian 'Noble Savage'. For Jung, unlike Freud, reconnecting with this was among the most urgent *desiderata* for Western 'Man' if psychological health was to be re-established, but it would be a reconnection from the vantage point of a wiser scientific ego. Freud himself only seriously tackled anthropological concerns once, in *Totem and Taboo* (1950, 1st edn 1918), in which he was primarily concerned with establishing the universality of the incest-taboo and developing his notion of the 'primal horde'. Jung's position requires further attention, however, since it sheds a crucial light on the broader psychological relationship between Europeans and their 'primitive' subjects during the inter-war period, as well as providing a cautionary tale.

Jung's concept of the archaic or primitive mentality, while owing a certain amount to Lévy-Bruhl, is more radical in character and more self-consciously ambivalent.[18] This is no place to try to evoke Jung's personality or expound his entire psychodynamic system, but in order to understand his position a little needs to be said about both. Jung was, without question, extraordinarily sensitive to what is called 'the spirit of place' or '*Ortgeist*'. Travel to novel locations and encounters with representatives of other cultures forever seem to place his psyche at risk of being flooded with streams of intuitive insights, images and emotions. Awaking on a train on the third morning of a trip to East Africa he looks out of the window.

> On a jagged rock above us a slim brownish-black figure stood motionless, leaning on a long spear, looking down at the train. Behind him towered a gigantic candelabrum cactus.
>
> I was enchanted by this sight – it was a picture of something utterly alien and outside my experience, but on the other hand a most intense *sentiment du déjà vu*. I had the feeling that I had already experienced this moment and had always known this world which was separated from me only by distance in time. It was as if I knew that dark-skinned man who had been waiting for me for five thousand years.
>
> The feeling-tone of this curious experience accompanied me throughout my whole journey through savage Africa.
>
> (1967, p. 283)

In India, visiting the stupas of Sanchi ('where Buddha delivered his fire sermon') he is 'submerg[ing] myself in the overpowering mood of the place' (ibid., p. 308) when a procession of chanting, gong-striking Japanese make their appearance.

> As I watched them, my mind and spirit were with them, and something within me silently thanked them for having so wonderfully come to the aid of my inarticulate feelings.
>
> The intensity of my emotion showed that the hill of Sanchi meant something central to me. A new side of Buddhism was revealed to me there. I grasped the life of the Buddha as the reality of the self which had broken through and laid claim to a personal life. (ibid., p. 309)

Jung's journeys are as much psychological as physical, as much concerned with exploring the psyche's geography as the world's.[19] Thus visiting the Masai Elgonyi people in Kenya, and subsequently the Pueblo Indians in Taos, New Mexico, become at the same time trips into an archaic mode of consciousness, a level of the psyche which – we soon realise – both fascinates and frightens him.

He senses a constant danger of 'going black' or 'going native', of becoming possessed or swamped by these exotic modes of consciousness which professionally he is ambitiously driven to master. This is especially evident in his reactions in the USA, where he concluded that whites had been somehow dragged down by contact with the more primitive 'Negro'.[20] We will further consider what is, or might be, happening here in a moment.

Concerning his Psychology, his fundamental difference from Freud was, as is well known, his view of the unconscious as (a) having a positive value rather than being simply the repository of negative desires and repressed memories and (b) extending beyond the personal to a collective level (the 'collective unconscious'), containing ancestral wisdoms which, mediated via archetypal symbols, could make themselves known to consciousness. At its deepest the collective unconscious unites all humanity, but subsidiary collectivities of an ethnic and national character exist at intermediate levels between this and the personal unconscious. This eventually raised metaphysical questions about the nature of the *psyche* and led Jung into what I, at any rate, am inclined to read as an updated Transcendental Idealism: the *psyche* is the very source of reality and of all our concepts regarding the world of experience, it therefore forever eludes our attempts to scientifically pin it down and circumscribe it, we can never escape from the bubble. At the end of the day we are its agents.

What then seems to happen, construing events reflexively in, as it were, a 'meta-Jungian' fashion, is that by the 1930s Jung is viewing himself as a key cultural agent of the West's collective *psyche*, increasingly adopting the archetypal mantles of Wise Old Man and Shaman/Trickster. His various exotic trips have reconnected him to the archaic 'primitive mentality', revealed the rationality behind what Lévy-Bruhl saw as the 'prelogical', heightened his own capacity for *participation mystique*. His grandiose task then becomes to rectify the current distortions in the Western *psyche*, resulting from its overemphasis on the thinking function and exaggerated materialism, by reinstalling the legitimacy of the 'spiritual' dimension and resurrecting the valuable elements in this archaic mentality. It is nothing less than to help 'modern man' refind his 'soul', as the title of one of his most popular books, *Modern Man in Search of a Soul* (1989, 1st edn 1933) makes clear.[21] One significant epiphany appears to have been in 1925 while talking with the Taos Pueblo Indian, Ochway Biano (Mountain Lake), who enlightens Jung as to how whites look from the outside, something he had never previously managed to achieve.

> 'See', Ochway Biano said, 'how cruel the whites look. Their lips are thin, their noses sharp, their faces furrowed and distorted by folds. Their eyes have a staring expression; they are always seeking something. What are they seeking? The whites always want something; they are always uneasy and restless. We do not know what they want. We do not understand them. We think that they are mad.'
>
> I asked him why he thought the whites were all mad.
>
> 'They say that they think with their heads,' he replied.
>
> 'Why of course. What do you think with?' I asked him in surprise.

'We think here,' he said, indicating his heart.

I fell into a long meditation. For the first time in my life, so it seemed to me, someone had drawn for me a picture of the real white man.

(1989, p. 276)

And again he is swept away by 'image upon image' from bloodthirsty white history, Julius Caesar, Charlemagne, the Crusades, Columbus . . . until he could take no more. 'All the eagles and other predatory creatures that adorn our coats of arms seem to me apt psychological representatives of our true nature' (ibid., p. 277).

Is he not though falling into a trap here? Is he not, to mix his and Lévy-Bruhl's terms, directly experiencing the non-European via his own culture's 'collective representations', its own repertoire of 'archetypal' images, its own split off psychic projections of what it cannot admit in itself? What he experiences so directly as emanating from the places and peoples he encounters is itself amenable to exactly the same analysis he offers in 'Archaic Man', as a projected part of his own *psyche*, albeit the 'collective' European part of it.[22] Like Lévy-Bruhl he has a blanket conception of the 'primitive', and automatically equates 'archaic' (i.e. from the earliest stage of human psychological evolution) with 'primitive' and both with 'African' or 'Negro' and American Indian. (It should be noted that his researches into alchemy had drawn his attention to the *nigredo* – the 'initial state', the 'chaos' from which the aspirant began the alchemical quest. In alchemical literature this was sometimes symbolised by an 'Ethiopian'.[23] Given that he equates this chaos with the 'shadow', the African clearly possesses an archetypal 'Shadow' meaning for Jung.[24]) He thus somewhat resembles a rich youth sequestered all his life in a luxurious library poring uncritically over exotic images and travellers' tales of strange and primitive peoples, who is then snatched from this setting and deposited in their midst. All he can see is how true it all was.[25] And he is swept away by a feeling of real-life immersion in all the images he has long gazed upon in the library.[26]

Of course he is not entirely *wrong*, there is no doubt *some* correspondence between the 'collective representation' and the reality, but he is, it seems to me, chronicly unable to get beyond received Western 'archetypal' or 'collective' representations and see the immediate down-to-earth details of the actual situation. His spear-leaning African was as likely wondering why the train was late, not in some timeless communion with the universe at all. It is interesting to contrast his mode of relating to a native American culture to that of, for example, Margaret Mead in Polynesia or New Guinea. Apparently lacking Jung's archetypal baggage, she can appreciate the subtleties and individuality of Polynesian and New Guinea cultures and the modes of personality they produce, she is not immediately bounced into reveries about the archaic meaning of the Sun or the differences between European and 'primitive' *psyches*, nor is she haunted by a fear of 'going native'. She rolls up her sleeves and joins in the gossip round the very cooking pot into which Jung, we suspect, fears he might yet be plunged. For American whites the African, the native American and, to some extent, the Polynesian, were part of the domestic landscape, the British and French had long been having direct dealings with non-European imperial subjects, but Jung, we should perhaps remind ourselves, was an empireless Swiss.

In trying to understand Jung I am helped by an experience I had when about 17 or 18 (c.1958). I had never personally met anyone visibly of African ancestry before getting a summer night-job in a small factory. At about 2 a.m. during my first shift the work ran out and a West Indian said we could go and have a nap in a rest room. What ensued was that lying there I felt overcome with a sense of being in the presence of 'archetypal' 'African-ness' which was quite frightening. My point is that this 'African-ness' belonged to *my* 'psyche' not my workmate's (who had in all probability never been to Africa anyway). My experience, in short, was *nothing to do with my workmate at all*. It was simply that his proximity triggered off an 'archetypal' reaction in my own 'psyche'.[27] The value of this experience for me was to reveal to me the psychological profundity of the roots of white racism (which I had already intellectually rejected). Had I reacted like Jung, however, I would have seen it as providing an intuitive insight into the African psyche – accepting the so-called 'archetypal' reaction in its own terms.

Events in the mid-1930s now played disastrously to Jung's self-appointed role as cultural psychotherapist-cum-Wise Old Man (or *mzee* as he delightedly tells us he was called by the Egonyi, in gratifying primitive confirmation of his spiritual rank). His theoretical position inevitably led him to accept the existence of a collective ethnic unconscious, and he veers dangerously close to the Le Bon notion of a racial soul. There followed, in 1933–4, an episode which remains controversial. In what can most charitably be considered an appalling failure of moral judgment he remained in the German Society of Psychotherapy in 1933 following its Nazification and Kretschmer's resignation, took over editorship of the freshly Aryanised journal *Zentralblatt für Psychotherapie* in 1934 and published a paper on the differences between the psychotherapeutic methods appropriate for treating Gentiles and Jews.[28] This episode is entirely absent from his autobiographical *Memories, Dreams, Reflections* (1967), although it does contain the rueful, and in some ways enigmatic, statement: 'Touching evil brings with it the grave peril of succumbing to it. We must, therefore, no longer succumb to anything at all, not even good' (pp. 360–61). While he stoutly defended his actions as motivated by a desire to protect and assist colleagues, and while there is no suggestion of any genuine collaboration with the Nazis on his part, one cannot help feeling (especially in the light of the preceding quote) that there was more to it than meets the eye. His conviction of his own deep rapport with the Germanic collective unconscious, and belief in ethnic levels of psychological difference, would have rendered it all too easy for him to respond empathically, if not sympathetically, to the advent of the Third Reich. Though clearly not consciously an anti-semite, any articulation of what he believed to be genuine Jewish–Gentile differences at this historical moment could not avoid laying him open to the charge. Jung had long been troubled by the problem of evil, and a year later, on his 1935 India trip, was impressed by what he saw as the success of oriental religions in incorporating and integrating evil as a necessary component of their cosmologies. Perhaps his ruminations had addled his capacity for clear moral judgment; perhaps his own psychological identification with German-speaking peoples at a collective level was too profound to allow him to separate; perhaps the situation, as just suggested, simply played too strongly to his vanity and led him to believe himself powerful enough to effect a cure for Germany's collective distress. Whatever the truth, the moral of the story for us is fairly clear: the structure of Jung's new psychodynamic image of the mind, in allowing for the possibility of profound racial differences, gave the charges of anti-semitism levelled against him a *prima facie* plausibility. In short, the 'collective unconscious' and its 'archetypal' contents could only too easily be given a racist spin, regardless of whether Jung himself really did so in this instance. Some Nazi psychologists did indeed interpret his work in this light, E. Moritz (1939), for instance, defended him as an opponent of materialism and rationalism who had discovered an Aryan spirit.[29]

Both Jungian and Freudian theories encouraged a too facile equation between the 'unconscious' and the 'primitive' – an equation which it was easy to render plausible by indiscriminately mustering appropriate examples from the mass of anthropological and anecdotal information on peoples whom one had, in advance, classified as 'primitive'. If Jungian Analytical Psychology was the most prone to this, with its concept of the 'collective unconscious', Freudian psychoanalysis could sometimes be deployed to the same end. Rivers, for example, readily mapped Freudian dream processes onto 'the rites and customs of savage peoples'.[30] On balance however the Freudian focus on individual psychological development and the role of child-rearing served, as we have already seen, more as an initial conceptual resource for those challenging racism, facilitating the formulation of non-nativist explanations for cultural differences.

In the USA a handful of papers by A.B. Evarts (1913, 1916) and J.E. Lind appeared in the *Psychoanalytic Review* between 1913 and 1917. Evarts (1916) presents a case study showing that 'ontogenetic' (i.e. developmental and cultural) as well as 'phylogenetic' elements contribute to 'Negro' psychoses. It is hardly a psychoanalytic paper, however; Freud is not mentioned and virtually all the citations are of J.G. Frazer's *The Golden Bough*. Lind (1913–14b) purported to have discovered a 'Negro complex' in which desire for white skin and belief that God was white played a central role in all 'Negro' mental illness.[31] In Lind (1917) he stresses 'phylogenetic elements' and proposes the Scientific Racist argument that 'The [Negro is] only one degree removed from extremely primitive levels [and] reverts very easily under stress' (p. 330). Again, Lind's papers are hardly very psychoanalytic despite the journal in which they appeared, which subsequently never seems to have returned to the issue. He too fails to cite Freud in the 1917 paper, all his references, aside from Evarts , being to 19th century works on African ethnography and travel. In truth it is hard to see what any of these papers were doing in a psychoanalytic journal; perhaps, especially after 1914, the *Psychoanalytic Review* was hard up for contributors.

While rarely confronting the issue of race differences head-on, it is clear that during the 1920s and early 1930s the work of Lévy-Bruhl and the new psychodynamic schools was engineering a reconceptualisation of the psychological character of 'primitive' people. This retained a number of Scientific Racism's assumptions, albeit in a new form: most importantly it assumed that there *was* indeed a radical difference in 'mentality' between those it cast as 'primitive' and 'civilised'. Secondly its account of primitive mentality sustained such stereotyped notions as primitive lack of abstract logical thought, lack of foresight and general 'child-like' qualities. At the same time it reformulated the meanings of these, abandoning 'innate' biological explanations and seeing them instead as due to prevailing 'cultural representations' which perhaps left those in such cultures fixated at a quasi-infantile level of psychological development (a level which Jungians could view in quite romantic terms). Thirdly, however, it located the 'primitive' within ₁he Western mentality not, as hitherto, as a 'beast within', but as the 'unconscious' (Freudian and Jungian versions of which were on offer). The messages of this were: (a) that the 'primitive' actually retained its hold over the Western *psyche* to a largely unappreciated extent and (b) that this primitive mentality actually had a kind of legitimacy which mental health demands we acknowledge, without being seduced or 'possessed' by it ('going black' as Jung saw it). In a sense the 'discovery' of this unconscious entailed a re-adoption of 'primitive thinking' by its 'discoverers' (for example, re-instatement of the meaningfulness of the apparently accidental), most patently in the case of Jung.

Two crucial illusions remained in play throughout this period. First, the assumption that 'primitive' and 'savage' peoples represent a social condition ancestral to that of the 'civilised'. While no longer couched in the unilinear terms of Victorian social evolution theory this continues to pervade anthropological and European Psychological discourse. Few can see that whatever the common ancestral condition was, current cultures have been evolving away from it for more or less the same length of time, and that current diversity may be construed as reflecting the variety of directions in which they have headed. For those outside advanced anthropological circles this diversity itself was, however, largely masked by the very notion of a common 'primitive mentality' shared by all 'primitive' peoples. A second illusion exacerbated this: 'primitive' societies were static. Lack of historical records apparently meant lack of history. Such peoples are living lifestyles unchanged for many millenia, creating a corresponding psychological inertia. They passively accept the way things are, are unreflecting on their own psychological nature, and lack any notion of time in the Western sense. This assumption of stasis is entirely without foundation, there is ample secondary evidence that lifestyles and cultures of all kinds are constantly changing (if at varying rates and in varying ways), that peoples have frequently migrated, conquered, retreated, coalesced, and so forth, that climatic or other geographical changes have required adaptational changes and so on.[32] Cultures may occasionally seem to remain static for several thousand years (ancient Egyptian and traditional Chinese civilisations for example, or the prehistoric Magdalenian European culture which produced the cave paintings of the Dordogne and Pyrennees). Even in these cases closer scrutiny reveals at least some changes over time in terms of political organisation, the vigour of particular belief-systems, phases of creativity and decline, and so forth. Both these illusions sustained the kind of European 'cultural representations' of the 'primitive' being promoted by Lévy-Bruhl, Jung and their followers.

Two recent writers on Jung's 'racism' (Dalal, 1988; Bagby, 1995) tend to see the issue more or less as a simple question of whether or not he was a 'racist' –

Dalal arguing that he was (a view accepted by Fernando, 1993), Bagby that while naively susceptible to stereotyping (especially of Africans and African Americans) he was not, and that his theories actually provide insight into racism. But this is not really the interesting issue. If 'racism' is too strong (which on balance I suspect it is), it is harder to dispute that his thinking was 'racial' in the sense of viewing Africans, native Americans, Asians, and so on as possessed of distinct collective racial modes of consciousness (albeit ones with features which the European would be advised to adopt, or readopt, alongside others to be avoided) some of which are 'archaic' (even if, again, that is in some respects more healthy than modern European consciousness).

But more interesting than adjudicating on Jung's personal racism, I suggest, is that we are again bound to see a reflexive dimension in this widespread twin fascination with 'primitive mentality' and 'the unconscious': the exploration of 'primitive mentality' was a route for its collective reinstatement in the Western *psyche* itself *qua* reconnection with the 'unconscious'. *But such a reinstatement could not be achieved without, in the long run, undermining its 'primitive' character.* Eventually it would have to be recouched in more positive terms as complementing rather than challenging the 'rational' and 'scientific' mentality, its reinstatement would, after the 1960s, be seen as a reconnection with an intuitive, holistic, 'ecological', mode of consciousness. The 'primitive's' perception of the world as inhabited by a host of discarnate spirits and forces would be reframed as a technique for embodying traditional wisdoms regarding the inter-connectedness of life. The foolish savage bathing with crocodiles would yield to Crocodile Dundee. But all this as yet lay in the post-Freudian and post-Jungian future, leaving Jung himself firmly on the hook as a once-promising scientist who had, essentially, gone native in his own culture ('gone white'?). Worse than that, someone who was then tricked or seduced (if only temporarily) by his own ethnic ancestors into apparent complicity with anti-semitism and the primal Nazi horde. *What we must finally admit however is that 'the primitive mentality' itself was never more than a Western 'collective representation', and that the characteristics ascribed to it actually belonged from the start to the Western mentality which 'discovered' them.*[33] This is not to deny that non-Western 'mentalities' may share them, or that their doing so helped render them visible to Western eyes. It is, though, to deny both that they are essentially 'primitive', and that they add up to a coherent ensemble that can be treated as a genuinely unitary 'mentality'. Perhaps indeed the 'primitive mentality' was no more than an *omnium gatherum* of all the multiplicity of modes of thought and relating to the world which self-consciously rational 'scientific' white male intellects had been striving to cast aside for the previous three centuries. And if that is the case, its 'discovery' would represent an as yet disguised (even to some extent to Jung himself) intuition that maybe this had been a mistake.

While British psychologists and anthropologists were by and large sceptical of the 'primitive mentality' notion we will see in the next chapter that a few of the older generation such as Carveth Read and G.F. Stout were exceptions.

Before leaving the topic of psychoanalysis, there is one further work which demands attention. Wulf Sachs's *Black Hamlet* (1937, reprinted in 1996) possesses a multi-faceted significance which is well brought out in the two introductions to the 1996 edition by Saul Dubow and Jacqueline Rose. A revised version entitled *Black Anger* appeared in 1957, in which the story was updated and the tone of the discourse adjusted in some important respects, adding a further layer of complexity to an already complex text. Lithuanian-Jewish in origin, Sachs, now an exile in South Africa, sought to introduce psychoanalysis there, co-founding the Psycho-Analytic Institute of South Africa in 1935 with another exile, Fritz Perls (later creator of Gestalt Therapy). *Black Hamlet* is the story of a Zimbabwean (then Rhodesian) Manyika healer, John Chavafambira, who had emigrated to South Africa. Sachs's initiation of the relationship was hardly straightforward in motivation. While Sachs wanted to explore how far psychoanalysis could be used with an African, the encounter was also framed as a reciprocal exchange of knowledge between representatives of Western and African medical traditions. The original title was chosen because Chavafambira's case appeared to Sachs to bear close parallels with Hamlet's – he suspected his uncle, who married his widowed mother, of killing his father and displayed paralysing inability to return home and resolve the situation. In the 1937 version the story ends optimistically with him doing so. Subsequent events proved this neat resolution to have been mistaken. Chavafambira returned to South Africa and became increasingly disturbed by the life he was having to lead in the racially oppressed Witwatersrand. In the 1957 version Sachs's therapeutic victory has radically altered in nature. The solution to Chavafambira's problems is no longer psycho-analytic, it rests rather in his recognition and understanding of their socio-political source and the awakening or creation of his political consciousness.

As the 1996 editors demonstrate, with considerable acuity, the text raises numerous questions. Most fundamentally, while claiming to be a mediated auto-biography largely in Chavafambira's own (substantially translated) words, the story is as much Sachs's as his. Sachs has to move from seeing Chavafambira simply as a representative 'African mind' to knowing him as an individual person, but also, ironically, from believing that Chavafambira's problems are amenable to individualistic psychoanalysis to seeing them as inextricably bound up with the oppressive socio-economic conditions of South African township life. Less con-sciously, Sachs has to grasp the fundamentally power-ridden nature of the rela-tionship between the two men (though it is not clear that he ever fully does) – and the interaction between the (reportedly quite charismatic) exiled white Jewish intellectual and the exiled African healer inevitably generates a forest of transfer-ences and counter-transferences. There are simply too many grounds on which Sachs identifies with Chavafambira for a separation of their respective presences in the narrative to be possible. Sachs is resolutely liberal and anti-racist, he rejects the notion of a distinct primitive African mind, he indefatigably wants to help Chavafambira. But the power relationship is such that Chavafambira has no option. He cannot get this incessantly questioning, interrogating, white man off his back, though he clearly often wants to do so. Sachs is, in the final analysis, demanding from Chavafambira a ratification and endorsement of his own multi-racial values, a recognition on Chavafambira's part that 'the black and the white people must work together' (the very note on which he closes the 1937 version). The result is that while Sachs can come to acknowledge Chavafambira's individual autonomy he cannot let go of him. As Jacqueline Rose puts it: 'His dilemma captures the ambiguity of fostered, nurtured autonomy: "Go forward. Take my hand."' And this dilemma, we might add has, in a thousand forms, been the liberal white's bind ever since the anti-slavery campaign days.

Theoretically it is clear that Sachs cannot escape the psychoanalytic doctrine that the 'primitive' is in some sense immature psychologically, locked into a narcissistic phase of development by reason of the prolonged suckling period typical of African child-rearing and the subsequently traumatic nature of the eventual weaning. Thus psychoanalysis can provide a rationale for simultaneously denying essential race differences (since the theory is universally applicable) and identifying and explaining them as pathological, consequences of inadequate primitive child-rearing. The Scientific Racist 'primitive as child' image can thus be preserved.

The richness of Jacqueline Rose's 1996 introductory essay, on which I have been drawing, can be done scant justice here. While focused on Sachs's text it has a much wider relevance, not least in her efforts to redeem Chavafambira's maligned (by both parties) wife Maggie as a pivotal, though marginalised figure.

For our present purposes there is another facet to the text which both Saul Dubow and Rose are at pains to stress: the need to read it in context. Written at a time when anti-semitism was rising in South Africa and proto-apartheid legislation entering the statute book it documents a particularly significant episode in modern 'race' relations and Psychology's response to this. South African 'racism' and the task facing its opponents were very different from those obtaining in the USA. The 'racism' was both more confident and old-fashioned, white South Africans were generally convinced of the 'naturalness' of black subordination and Scientific Racism clichés passed largely unchallenged. Neither Psychology nor psychoanalysis were well-established, and the former – as exemplified in the work of, for example, M.L. Fick – seems to have adhered to the US psychometrics approach in studying 'race differences'. (That Dr Hendrik Verwoerd, later, as Prime Minister, the architect of apartheid, was for some years a Professor of Applied Psychology was also ominous.) The psychoanalytic perspective was, as we have seen, ambiguous with regard to race differences, even if overtly opposed to them. Psychiatry, as exemplified in B.J.F. Laubscher (1937), was especially susceptible to racialist readings and construals of contemporary ethnographic and psychiatric work. Sachs's attempted in-depth encounter with a 'native' was, in this setting, courageous and fraught with difficulties and risks for both parties. The result is a text pervaded by the character and dynamics of the setting. Could an exiled Jew on the eve of the Holocaust and a migrant black healer in Johannesburg on the eve of full-blooded apartheid really effect a meeting of minds? That the former tried is to his enduring credit. That the latter endured the exercise is to his. But who learned most from whom, and what, we cannot really ascertain, since only the former is audible.

'RACE' IN NAZI PSYCHOLOGY

The intention in this section is to clarify the views on race of avowedly Nazi, or Nazi-sympathising, German-speaking psychologists. This task is rendered difficult both by the paucity of secondary English-language accounts and the unavailability of primary texts. What follows is thus a rather schematic and provisional account, much reliant on *Psychological Abstracts* entries, pending more in-depth studies by German scholars.

Nazi race doctrines themselves were developed largely independently of any direct input from Psychology. While numerous psychologists opportunistically jumped on the bandwagon and strove to place these doctrines on a more scientifically respectable basis, their efforts, especially after about 1936, were not particularly welcomed by Nazi Party ideologues anxious to maintain total control over the party line.[34] The government considered psychologists to be most usefully employed in practical applied areas such as personnel selection, testing and training, for which racial typology soon proved useless.[35] As Geuter's (1992) masterly study has shown, it was in these fields, particularly in the form of military *Wehrmachtpsychologie*, that the discipline enjoyed a dramatic expansion at the end of the 1930s, continuing to prosper under the Third Reich until about 1943 when everything began to fall apart. Nonetheless, while in no way challenging Geuter's thesis that the race issue played little part in the discipline's professionalisation, the number of German Race Psychology publications published during 1932–40 is well over a hundred, and it was thus by no means a marginal topic.[36]

German-speaking Psychology had several traditional strands congenial to racialist thinking even if not necessarily entailing it. They are traceable as far back as the late 18th century revival of physiognomy by J.C. Lavater (a Swiss pastor) and J.G. Herder's ideas on linguistics. The former's promotion of the doctrine that form expresses essence fuelled the development of the 19th century tendency to see physiognomic traits as direct signifiers of psychological character. The latter argued that language reflected the deep collective spiritual nature of a kind of national soul. During the early 19th century the concept of the collective national soul became commonplace in post-Kantian Romantic *Naturphilosophie* receiving its fullest formulation in the work of Hegel. Despite the positivist turn of German science and philosophy after the mid-century the deep-rooted appeal of this Romantic idea remained, lending force to German nationalism and receiving additional impetus from post-evolutionary Scientific Racism (especially in the case of Ernst Haeckel). Most obviously, it underlay Jungian thought. Another influential German exponent of racism at this time was J.F.K. Zöllner, an astronomer and keen spiritualist, remembered by psychologists for the visual illusions he devised.[37] In the early years of the present century English writers were already scorning German racial glorification of the Nordic 'blond beast'. German, unlike British, Eugenics (and its applied face, 'race hygiene') maintained a deep preoccupation with race which provided Nazism with a pre-adapted 'scientific' rationale. If the word 'race' in the phrase 'race hygiene' tended, in British usage, to mean 'the human race' or, more narrowly, 'the national stock', in Germany it increasingly connoted the Nordic German race as such. Writers such as Paul Weindling have provided us with extensive analyses of the role of German Eugenics and *Rassenhygiene* in Nazi race-theory and the interested reader is referred to these.[38] German Psychology was relatively marginal to the Eugenics story, which is perhaps only to be expected given that Eugenics and race hygiene were quite explicitly biologically, rather than psychologically, focused. If Psychology had any role to play it would be an ancillary one: developing theories of the connection between racial physiology and psychological character, and methods of diagnosing and exploring the latter.

For mainstream German Psychology the legacy of the earlier tradition was especially marked in its approach to personality. Writers as varied as Spranger, the graphological theorist Klages, the clinical psychologist Kretschmer and Rorschach, inventor of the ink-blot test, all espoused different forms of the typological approach. While not necessarily racialist, typological approaches to personality are especially susceptible to this kind of interpretation. In the first place they frequently propose a direct connection between physiology and temperament (e.g. in Kretschmer's typology). Coupled with the previous labours of Scientific Racist physical anthropologists this could readily bolster a belief in innate racial temperaments correlated with 'racial' morphology and physiognomy. Secondly, the relative underdevelopment in German Psychology of either a strong environmentalist school or trait-oriented psychometrics reinforced this tendency. German psychologists, as a result of their 19th century philosophical legacy, were more holistic and nativist in approach, less inclined to embark on analytical projects of the kind which marked anglophone Psychology.[39] Wundt (who was quite explicitly anti-racist)[40] may appear to be an exception to this, especially where psychophysics was concerned, but his post-Great War heirs, under Kreuger, were anxious to espouse what they called *Ganzheit* Psychology in rivalry with the more renowned holistic Gestalt school, *Ganz* meaning 'whole' or 'entire'.[41] The word *Gestalt* (roughly meaning 'form') was itself co-opted by the Nazis to mean 'ideal type'.[42] All this immediately suggests that when someone like Fernando (1993) says 'the arguments of Jensen and Eysenck may have helped the revival of a "scientific racism" of the type that thrived in Germany in the 1930s' (p. 51) they are quite simply wrong as a matter of fact. Although the Nordicist ideologues Madison Grant and Lothrop Stoddard were eagerly adopted by Nazi racist writers, Nazi Psychology was coming at race from a fundamentally different direction from the psychometric empiricism of today's 'race and IQ' research and inter-war US Race Psychology. While underpinned by a version of 'Scientific Racism', this had acquired a rather distinct character of its own compared to the positivist empiricist Galton/Pearson variety. Nothing in current Psychology that I am aware of remotely resembles the doctrines we will be encountering in this section, although, as with the famous case of E.R. Jaensch's typology presenting a mirror image of the later authoritarianism vs. democratic dimension with the evaluative loading reversed, we occasionally find apparent partial anticipations of later ideas of both the pro- and anti- race-differences camps.[43] Let's not get *too* paranoid.

Philosophical tradition, political and cultural climate, heightened eugenic anxieties and theoretical inclination therefore combined to render early 20th century German Psychology especially vulnerable to racialism. (This lineage continues, in effect, unbroken from the European degenerationist tradition of Lombroso et al.) Not that all German-speaking psychologists took this route: besides Jewish psychologists, those ideologically committed to the left or to humanistic concepts of science strongly resisted such a move.[44] Nonetheless those sympathetic to Nazism were sufficiently numerous to provide disciplinary support for its racist doctrines when the opportunity finally arose. An influential pre-Nazi period work which was adopted as the quasi-official position was H.F.K. Günther's *Rassenkunde des deutschen Volkes*, first published in Munich in 1926. Günther espoused Nazism long before it became widely popular.[45] Another of his works was published in English as *The Racial Elements of European History* in 1927. During the late 1920s the Munich publishing house Lehmann's issued a stream of further works by Günther and others promoting racial doctrines. Günther became the single most influential Nazi race psychologist, and his work underpinned E. Zilian's later (unsuccessful) *Wehrmachtpsychologie* efforts at racial diagnostics (e.g. 1938, 1939). The other most ardent early exponent of racial doctrines within Psychology appears to be L.F. Clauss whose *Rasse und Seele* also first appeared in 1926 (reaching a 7th edition in 1941), followed by *Von Seele und Antlitz der Rassen und Völker* in 1929. Clauss's theoretical position was, however, an odd one, and his texts rarely contain any explicit anti-semitism, even in their later editions.

Although the issue was clearly intensifying from the mid-1920s, aside from Günther's and Clauss's works and a handful of other earlier anticipatory papers, German Psychology paid little explicit attention to race until 1931, after which the number of publications rose rapidly, to peak in 1938–9 (over 70 identified in these two years).[46] In 1932 the journal *Zeitschrift für Rassenkunde* was founded, followed in 1934 by the more extreme *Rasse*. While both of these, along with the older *Archiv für Rassen- und Gesellschaftbiologie*, provided the major outlets for *'Rassenpsychologie'*,[47] it also found space across the range of more orthodox Psychology journals such as the *Zeitschrift für angewandte Psychologie, Zeitschrift für Psychologie, Zeitschrift für pädagogische Psychologie* and the *Archiv für die gesamte Psychologie*.[48] Of these the *Zeitschrift für angewandte Psychologie* and *Zeitschrift für pädagogische Psychologie* were most frequently represented among the publications identified. The latter's prominence is unsurprising, for as Wohlwill (1987) observes, after the Nazification of its editorship in 1933, by the appointment of Oswald Kroh,[49] it 'soon became a virtual mouthpiece for Nazi propaganda directed at those encharged with the education of German youth' (p. 176). The former's is somewhat less expected in the light of Wohlwill's account since he views it as one of the journals more resistant to political pressure, continuing to cite Jewish psychologists for example. Both E. Fischer (the leading Nazi eugenicist) and E.R. Jaensch managed to get into its pages in the late 1930s nonetheless (Fischer, 1939; Jaensch 1938a, b). The *Zeitschrift für Psychologie*, edited by Jaensch, was, as Wohlwill shows, among the most pro-Nazi journals, but figures relatively less frequently in our sample.[50] The *Archiv für die gesamte Psychologie* managed, in general, to avoid ideological papers, but published two Race Psychology papers by Bruno Petermann plus his attack on Garth (in 1936 and 1937). While clustering in those journals most in sympathy with Nazi ideology, *Rassenpsychologie* papers could occasionally crop up almost anywhere, from the *Archiv für Musikforschung* to the *Zentralblatt für Graphologie*. From 1940 onwards *Psychological Abstracts* entries on German *Rassenpsychologie* collapse dramatically, leading exponents such as Petermann, Pfahler, Zilian and Jaensch ceasing to figure.

This probably exaggerates the rate of the collapse, though not its occurrence, since *Psychological Abstracts* ceased comprehensive monitoring of German journals in the late 1930s.[51] By 1943 even the most ardently racist psychologists, such as Pfahler, were finding it hard to keep the Party happy and a general atmosphere of paranoid mayhem began to prevail, in academia as well as everywhere else.

Exponents of a Nazified Race Psychology were numerous, the most important being, besides Günther, E.R. Jaensch, G. Pfahler, B. Petermann and E. Zilian. While these were all especially ardent in their efforts to support Nazi race doctrines, many others, in their writings, teaching and research practice, sought to provide their work with an acceptable racist veneer. Others, again, seem to be naively cautioning against too facile an acceptance of the predominance of biology over culture even in the late 1930s.[52] Far more of course compromised with the regime without venturing into print on this particular issue. We may now turn to the Psychological views promulgated by some of those so far mentioned.

Perhaps the most anomalous, and least overtly racist, was L.F. Clauss.[53] The theoretical framework for his ideas was supplied less by orthodox Scientific Racism than by the phenomenology of his teacher, Edmund Husserl. Indeed he rejects crude physiognomic criteria for classifying races, even while liberally sprinkling his books with photo-portraits of members of various European and Middle Eastern 'races' (gathered during extended travels early in his career). Employing an empathetic phenomenological method (having some affinities perhaps with the James–Lange theory of emotion) it seems that one can, in Clauss's view, tune into distinct racial modes of being. This provides one with an insight into the specific characters of the various 'racial souls'. 'The real Nordic is not known by his hair, but by the tenor of his soul.'[54] Even a cursory glance at his texts, however, reveals some confusions, for example, he compares German and Italian driving behaviour to show how the former, with their planning and overall sense of form, take bends differently from the more spontaneous Italians – but elsewhere northern Italians are said to be primarily Germanic. Although numerous, Clauss's texts display a high degree of recycling and are pitched at a fairly popular level. The most interesting thing about him from our point of view is surely the discovery that even Husserlian phenomenology can be co-opted as a basis for racial theorising, a possibility I am unaware anyone has noticed hitherto. This reinforces Goldberg's (1993) argument regarding the parasitic nature of race thinking, as able to attach itself to almost any theoretical system. Secondly, however, Clauss's texts would appear to have served the broader function of popularising the general notion that racial theorising was a respectable scientific enterprise rather than promoting Nordicism and Nazi racism as such.

Clauss aside, German Race Psychology appears to have fallen into two broad camps. Pfahler, Petermann, L. Krieger and Günther adopted a physiological level explanation for the supremacy of the Nordic race. Unlike Clauss, Günther claimed of the Nordic that 'his soul is as fair as his eyes'.[55] Petermann (1935) claimed

A new theory can be founded on the evidence of biopsychic nuclear layers, from which will be derived the different varieties of psyche, i.e. the concrete substance of the doctrine of racial soul.[56]

Krieger (1937) goes further, claiming that his studies of writing show 'there is a special development of the extrapyramidal center common to all Nordics and found only in them'.[57] By 1939 Pfahler is proclaiming that a 'a pure Nordic soul can inhabit only a Nordic body' (as well as asserting that 'All educational measures of the Reich are fanatically devoted to getting rid of all non-German, international and intellectualistic elements').[58] The other position, of which E.R. Jaensch was the leading exponent, supported by Kroh, adopted a more Psychological position invoking psychological 'integration types'. An initial account of Jaensch's typological approach, rooted in his work on eidetic imagery, may be found in Jaensch (1930), in which the racial aspect is alluded to but treated in a neutral fashion. In this he differentiates between two fundamental 'integrate' and 'disintegrate' types (of which subvarieties may be further identified) which are 'true fundamental forms of human existence' (Jaensch, 1930, p. 105). In the former the 'psychic functions' 'mutually interpenetrate', in the latter they 'act separately' (ibid., p. 106). The 'modes of existence' signified by these differentiate youth from age, male from female and 'northern and southern types as described by race biologists' while reflecting, at heart, the difference between organic and inorganic processes (ibid.). Nevertheless, he seems, at this stage, to be viewing these types as complementary. In 1934 he introduced his 'Gegentypus' or 'anti-type' which, as Baker (1936) has it:

> can neither form a whole nor subordinate himself to a whole. . . . liberalistic, egocentric, individualistic, the representative of a free-floating isolated intellect. This is a phenomenon of degeneration which becomes most apparent in race mixture, where it is also most dangerous. (p. 153)

Even Jaensch's theory was underpinned by a notion of fundamental differences in psychophysical structure and organisation, a notion he developed in collaboration with his twin brother W. Jaensch, a physiologist.

While Jaensch was widely respected as a psychologist until around 1930, his Nazism put him increasingly beyond the pale on the international scene thereafter and any residual credibility he had retained was blown by one of the most hilariously ridiculous pieces of Psychology ever to have appeared: his 1939 paper, the title of which translates as 'The poultry-yard as a medium of research and clarification in problems of human race differences'. The *Psychological Abstracts* summary of this, slightly abbreviated, is as follows:

> The superiority of Nordic races is reflected in race differences among chickens. The Nordic chick is better-behaved and more efficient in feeding than the Mediterranean chick, and less apt to over-eat by suggestion. The poultry-yard confutes the liberal-bolshevik claim that race differences are really cultural differences, because race difference among chicks cannot be accounted for by culture.[59]

This was also pursued by his acolyte S. Arnhold (1938) and felt of sufficient weight to be worthy of reissuing separately as a pamphlet.[60]

Even if bolstered by a variety of ostensibly scientific theories, Nazi Race Psychology never achieved much intellectual coherence. As Baker (1936) observed, the criteria for 'Nordic' were continually 'amended or replaced, as the need may be, by certain vague philosophic concepts' (p. 153). H. Böker (1934) argued in the journal *Rasse* that while species were mutable, races were immutable, a doctrine which while patently contradictory (since any species must presumably be comprised of 'races') was necessary to preserve the essentialist notion of Nordic superiority. Baker (1936) concluded that recent efforts by Nordicists had brought their doctrine no nearer to consolidation; they offered no experimental proof, not even logical unity, remaining riven by contradictions. Nordic doctrine 'remains a scientific failure' (p. 158).

The value of this work, insofar as it possesses any, rests in whatever light it may shed on Nazi period German psychology. Although I baulk at entering on this here, numerous texts would seem to be worth further exploration. Stölting (1938) for example:

> The Germans and a few millions of related peoples are the last reserve of creative humanity, and the influence of uncreative modern man must be kept away from their youth.[61]

While on Nazi education, F. Berger (1939) in the *Zeitschrift für pädagogische Psychologie* is positively raving:

> The symbol of this education is not the racially and psychologically alien cross, but the swastika, which is identified with the strenuousness, accomplishment and racial superiority of the Nordic soul. The strengthening of this is the deepest religion.[62]

Petermann meanwhile appears to have declined into a kind of scientistic babbling:

> According to the law of totality, the presence of definite concerns implies a peculiarity of racial soul. . . . a total relationship which corresponds, with no exceptions, to the racially specific basic direction.[63]

An associated concern was the fate of German emigrés (especially in the USA) who, it was feared, were becoming 'de-Germanized'. Melching (1938) reports on the first meeting of 'the German institute for the racial study of "non-resident" Germans' set up specifically to consider this.[64] The Berlin Olympics of 1936 appears to have inspired L.G. Tirala's *Sport und Rasse* (1936) in which, for example, the endurance of non-European runners is ascribed to the lower sensitivity of their nervous systems to fatigue and fatigue products rather than to their special training.[65] This has echoes of the Spencer hypothesis.

The impression I have derived from *Psychological Abstracts* summaries (mostly authored by M.E. Morse), Baker (1936) and such other primary and secondary material as has been available, is that Nazi race psychologists were scrabbling around eclectically in all directions for ideas which might be co-opted to support Nordic supremacy and essential race differences. In particular they draw on elements in the German-speaking typological tradition and German idealist philosophy, anchoring these in speculative physiology and eugenics. Non-Psychological notions of 'purity', 'race destiny' and 'racial soul' clearly underpin much of their discourse, while as the 1930s proceed their self-critical faculties evidently enter an ever-steeper tailspin as contact with the rest of the discipline is lost. Initially, as previously noted, they also drew inspiration from Madison Grant, Lowthrop Stoddard and other latter-day anglophone Nordicist racial theorists. Aside from the Pfahler et al. versus Jaensch division, and Clauss's anomalous position, I have been unable to identify theoretical doctrines in any detail. Further enquiry would undoubtedly clarify this, while we need to know far more about the personal relationships, internal politics and organisational dynamics of the situation. For present purposes it is perhaps of most relevance to observe that German Race Psychology was (a) non-psychometric, (b) only fitfully experimental, (c) showed high levels of internal contradiction, (d) veered over time ever further away from orthodox scientific discourse into hysterical polemic and such bizarreries as Jaensch's chickens, even in ostensibly academic journals. For all the literature it generated, it became the least professional branch of German Psychology.

How far Nazi race doctrines affected Psychology teaching courses is unclear. M.G. Ash (1995) comments, in relation to the Kaiser Wilhelm Institute for Anthropology in Berlin (arch-Nazi eugenicist Ernst Fischer's domain) that 'A former student professed to have heard "not a single Nazi sound" in the institute's regular psychology lectures, and the dissertations of the period appear to support his claim' (p. 340).[66]

A final poignant curiosity emerging from the literature search may be mentioned, a 1937 paper in the *Zentralblatt für Psychotherapie* by E. Stransky. Identifying himself as a 'pure' Jew 'rooted in Germany' Stransky appears to accept Jung's views on the differences between the Aryan and Jewish unconscious and offers the solution that Jews should have Aryan therapists and Aryans Jewish ones.[67]

If Germany was obsessed with race, on the surface at least British Psychology between the wars inclined more towards a diplomatic indifference, as we will see in the next chapter.

NOTES

1 See e.g. E.N. Fallaize (1925). Regarding the current rising aspirations of colonial subjects he writes 'These aspirations it will fall upon the white races, and particularly upon ourselves, to guide into right channels in accordance with the ideals of tutelage which it is now generally recognised should inspire the administration of the affairs of backward races' (p. 77), and proceeds to stress the importance of anthropology's role in ascertaining the good and bad elements in traditional culture. Grimshaw and Hart (1993) argue that this role seriously compromised the intellectual independence of British anthropologists (typified by Rivers), a compromise exacerbated by their aspirations towards respectability within the academic system. While personally I am persuaded, their position remains controversial. If true it has ramifications for the human sciences in general.

2 The key texts are: E. Durkheim and M. Mauss (1903, Eng. trans. and intro. R. Needham 1963) *Primitive Classification*, and E. Durkheim (1912, Eng. trans. 1915) *The Elementary Forms of Religious Life: A Study in Religious Sociology*.

3 These quotes from R. Needham, intro. to Durkheim and Mauss (1963, pp. xi–xii).

4 One year younger than Freud and dying in the same year, thus virtually an exact contemporary.

5 Eng. trans. (1926) as *How Natives Think*.
6 These were published in English as, respectively, *Primitive Mentality* (1923), *The Soul of the Primitive* (1928) and *Primitives and the Supernatural* (1936). Three further works were *La mythologie primitive* (1935), *L'expérience mystique et les symbols chez les primitifs* (1938) and a posthumous selection from his notebooks *Les Carnets de Lucein Lévy-Bruhl* (1949) – these last 'would seem to some degree to reverse his earlier position' (E.E. Evans Pritchard, foreword to 1965 edn of *The Soul of the Primitive*, p. 5), a point we return to.
7 For a succinct sympathetic summary of Lévy-Bruhl's ideas see J. Cazeneuve (1972, pp. 1–23). This also contains an introductory biographical sketch and representative extracts from his works.
8 See extract from the posthumously published notebooks *Les Carnets* (1949) in Cazeneuve (1972, pp. 86–7).
9 For example, Roy Willis (1974) contrasting the Lele and Fipa notes that while the Lele universe is a 'static universe, in which the relation between the component parts – human, animal and the mediating world of spirits – remains unchanged', which would roughly fit with Lévy-Bruhl's image, the Fipa one 'posits a state of constant change as man transforms his environment and, in so doing, changes himself' (p. 75), which very obviously does not. (The Lele live in central Africa, the Fipa to the East of Lake Tanganyika.)
10 Devereux was a Hungarian-born emigré.
11 'The primitive conception of death' in Rivers (1926).
12 During the 1920s in particular Lévy-Bruhl was nonetheless a veritable globetrotter addressing academic audiences across North and South America as well as in Britain, and certainly had closer contacts with field anthropologists than Frazer. This exposure to informed anthropological criticism led to his eventual back-tracking. See the introductory chapter of Cazeneuve (1972).
13 To complete a nice paradoxical loop, this work was, in turn, subsequently invoked by Paul Feyerabend (1975) in arguing for the radical incommensurability of different theoretical and philosophical belief systems, and the culturally determined nature even of logic itself – thereby subverting the very 'objective' *mentalité scientifique* in the name of which Lévy-Bruhl was working.
14 Most comprehensibly elaborated in *Le pensée sauvage* (1963) (Eng. trans. *The Savage Mind*, 1966).
15 In his essay 'Archaic Man' (in Jung, 1969, 1st edn 1933) he uses Lévy-Bruhl's *Primitive Mentality* extensively as a source of material, though interpreting it somewhat differently (see ensuing discussion of Jung).
16 Ibid.
17 See the passages in Jung (1967) dealing with his East African trip.
18 See Bagby (1995) for a fairly generous and sympathetic account of this. I believe she is right to stress this ambivalence as against Farhad Dalal's (1988) argument that Jung held a simple evaluative hierarchical view of 'primitive' vs. 'civilised' mentalities. Jung's views on race are scattered throughout his writings, the most notorious being Jung (1930) (Jung, 1970, being a retitled version which was 'slightly revised stylistically').
19 Bagby (1995) quotes James Hillman ('1986' but unreferenced) as noting that Jung described 'the vast lands and dark peoples he encountered [in Africa] in language he applies as well to the immemorial unconscious psyche' (Bagby, p. 294).
20 See Jung (1930) from which Fernando (1993, p. 50) quotes the following:

> Now what is more contagious than to live side by side with a rather primitive people? Go to Africa and see what happens. When the effect is so very obvious that you stumble over it, then you call it "going black" . . . the inferior man exercises a tremendous pull upon civilised beings who are forced to live with him, because he

fascinates the inferior layers of our psyche, which has lived through untold ages of similar conditions.

21 This is basically Bagby's reading also.
22 On this point I would agree with Dalal (1988): 'His error is in not recognizing the "primitive" and "prehistoric" aspects that he sees in the black as his own projection' (p. 21).
23 See Jung (1980, 1st edn 1944, figs 219, 286). This work was based on two papers published in the mid-1930s.
24 Ibid., p. 317. It is perhaps spelled out more clearly elsewhere in Jung's *Collected Works*, but this should be sufficient to establish the point.
25 I recall on arriving in the USA for the first time, at Seattle, being overwhelmed by how 'archetypally' American everything was, how literally expectations I was not even conscious of having possessed were being freshly confirmed every minute. This is surely a common enough experience.
26 This perhaps relates to Mannoni's point: 'The observer is repelled by the thoughts he encounters in his own mind, and it *seems* to him that they are the thoughts of the people he is observing. In any such act of projection the subject's purpose is to recover his own innocence' (O. Mannoni, 1990, cited in Jacqueline Rose's introduction to 1996 reprint of W. Sachs, pp. 53–4), though 'repelled' is hardly applicable in Jung's case.
27 In putting it this way I should not be understood as endorsing the Jungian notion that this was innate, rather it was the product of hours looking at Arthur Mee's *Children's Encyclopedia*, the memory of the terrifying statue of a larger-than-life-size wide-eyed Zulu warrior waving a spear which used to stand in the entrance of the Imperial War Institute in Whitehall, and a thousand similar images, folk myths and so on current in 1940s and early 1950s Britain.
28 C.G. Jung (1934). See Ellenberger (1970, pp. 675–8) for a brief account of this episode. G. Wahr (1988, p. 324 ff.) has a fuller account, noting that Jung's efforts were to internationalise the society and the journal, so that only the German section was bound by Aryanisation laws, and German Jews could join the society without being members of the German section itself. Ellenberger seems to give him the benefit of the doubt, and indeed his books were all blacklisted by the Nazis. Wahr is clearly pro-Jung but acknowledges Jung's own subsequent acceptance that he had made errors of judgment – after the war he also mended his bridges with alienated Jewish colleagues. Clearly I am in no better position to judge the truth of the matter than anyone else, nevertheless there can be little disputing that Jung's actions over 1933–5 reflect a surprising degree of confusion on his part as to how to react to events. The controversy rumbles on. My concern here is to suggest that in both his psychology and his Psychology we can see reasons why he got landed in this fix.
29 According to the abstract entry 6234 in *Psychological Abstracts* (13) 'Those who oppose [Jung's] psychology of complexes unwittingly advance materialism and rationalism and discredit the great discovery of an Aryan spirit.' See Wahr (1988) for additional material on Nazi perceptions and treatment of Jung and his initial failure to deal with these adequately.
30 Rivers (1918).
31 Mama (1995) discusses Lind (1913–14b) briefly, as well as Jung's suspicion that living alongside 'Negroes' might have a deleterious effect on US whites. To select Lind as in any way typical of US Psychology or psychoanalysis seems to me to be stretching it somewhat. US Psychiatry in the 19th century had of course supported Scientific Racism, as mentioned in Chapter 2. Mama makes much of this as evidence of Psychology's ubiquitously oppressive role, but since the discipline did not really emerge until the mid-1880s this is also rather hard to swallow. Lind's papers are 1913–14a, b; 1914, 1917. Mama refers to 'Evarts (in 1913)' but does not include anything in her bibliography, this must be Evarts (1913) on 'dementia praecox'. She

lumps him together with Lind but they actually seem to be adopting somewhat different positions and Evarts (1916) does not mention the 'Negro complex'.

32 Rivers was smarter, initiating a 'historical' approach in vol. 2 of Rivers (1914). In Rivers (1926) he astutely suggests that an apparent contradiction in beliefs regarding the location of the dead as both on a distant island and in a cave on the home island (the kind of evidence Lévy-Bruhl cited to support 'pre-logicality') was historically due to a fusion of two original belief systems, one held by the indigenous inhabitants and one by an invading group. Where, incidently, do Christians really believe the dead to be? Are they 'only sleeping', awaiting the final trump, or are they already in Heaven or Hell? They certainly act as if they believe both to be true.

33 See J. Rose's introduction in 1966 reprint of W. Sachs (1937, pp. 51–4) for a more psychoanalytically technical elaboration of what is essentially the same point, but with the added twist that the allegedly ubiquitous 'primitive' tendency to 'project' in infantile fashion is itself a projection: 'On what is the belief in the infantile nature of the primitive founded if not on a moment of projection?' (p. 53).

34 See Geuter (1992, pp. 169–70). For general coverage of German Psychology during the 1930s see Geuter and also M.G. Ash (1995, Part IV, 1996).

35 See Geuter (1992, pp. 121–4).

36 These are by over 70 different authors. During most of this period the number of members of the German Society for Psychology was around 250–300 (Geuter, 1992, p. 41). How many of these authors were members of this, and conversely how many German Psychologists were members, I have not ascertained, but the figures suggest, *prima facie*, that we may perhaps infer that around a fifth of German psychologists published papers explicitly espousing Nazi racist doctrines. This is far higher than the proportion of US psychologists publishing on Race Psychology during the 1920s and early 1930s.

37 I am unaware of any English language discussion of Zöllner, I owe this point to Simon Schaffer and Richard Noakes.

38 See e.g. P. Weindling (1989).

39 Geuter (1992).

40 See e.g. W. Wundt (1916).

41 The leading exponent of *Ganzheit* Psychology was Wundt's successor at Leipzig, Felix Kreuger, appointed in 1917. While *Ganzheit* Psychology later became co-opted by the Nazis, Kreuger himself, despite sympathies with much of the National Socialist agenda, balked at its anti-semitism. Nevertheless he retained his post until 1937 and was prominent among those active in promoting a discipline of service to the regime (see Geuter, 1992, passim).

42 According to Cassell's *German and English Dictionary* (12th edn 1969).

43 For example, rejection of the notion that intelligence is a single unilinear trait (F. Becker, 1938a; E.R. Jaensch, 1938b). One complaint was that orthodox intelligence tests were biased in favour of 'Jewish intelligence' – oddly echoing the 'cultural bias' argument against race differences findings!

44 *Psychological Abstracts* includes several pre-Nazi anti-racism German papers such as S. Weissenberg (1927, denying the racial and biological unity of Jews), R. Müller-Freienfels (1931, opposing anti-semitism), J. Loewenthal (1931, denying biological unity of Jews), J. Rotislav (1932, no racial differences among schoolchildren in Limburg), as well as a few in the opposite direction, e.g. E. Schutz-Ewerth (1925, 'Die farbige Gefahr' – 'The coloured peril'), D. Wolberg (1927, Jewish inferiority in recognising geometrical figures etc.), F. Noltenius (1930, 'Character study as a means to race study') and H. Rosenthal (1931) who claims Jewish musical ability is a compensation for a Jewish racial tendency towards defective hearing!

45 See W.H. Tucker (1994, p. 115 and passim throughout the rest of the chapter) for more on Günther, who he states 'provided the theoretical foundation for Nazi racial theory and was widely regarded as its official spokesman' (p. 115). He does not,

however, discuss the content of Günther's theory, although he notes the close affinity with Madison Grant's position.

46 The author's data show this growth to be uneven, with no German authored work for 1933 being included. The reason for this is unclear. These data must be assumed to be far from complete.

Distribution of German publications on, or relevant to, Race Psychology by year*:

n.d.	8
1924	1
1925	1
1926	1
1927	6
1928	0
1929	3
1930	1
1931	7
1932	6
1933	1
1934	10
1935	14
1936	18
1937	22
1938	32
1939	29
1940	2
1941	2
1942	1
Total	165

*Figures include a handful of Dutch, Italian and East European language papers. Some papers are on typology rather than race as such. Not all are pro-Nazi. The 1933 paper is Italian.

47 The term *Rassenpsychologie* was commonly used, but others such as *Rassenseelenlehre* and *Rassenkunde* (covering race studies as a whole) were also used. Words using the root *Volk* (e.g. *Volkscharakter*) also typically denote a racial concern from c.1934 and often earlier, although *Völkerpsychologie* is, albeit very loosely, more equivalent to 'Social Psychology' prior to the 1930s (e.g. in Wundt's usage).

48 The total number of journals identified as publishing at least one paper on the topic was 43, including one in Dutch (in *Mensch en Maatsch*). Italian fascist journal papers have not been included.

49 Kroh was an especially ardent pro-Nazi, but published little directly on race himself, though he favoured Jaensch's position.

50 As Wohlwill indicates, however, much of the Nazi message in this, as in other journals, was mediated via the book review pages, both in terms of books selected for review and stances taken by reviewers. The one major journal which does not figure is, unsurprisingly, the *Psychologische Forschung*, the major mouthpiece of the Gestalt School. Köhler continued to edit this from exile after 1935 until 1938 (see Wohlwill,1987, pp. 177–9).

51 Pfahler was, I imagine, working on his three-volume opus which appeared in 1942. In 1944 he had to become actively engaged in the fighting. Surprisingly he was allowed to return to teaching in Tübingen after the war (Geuter, 1992, pp. 257, 274). Zilian's productivity declined when Race Psychology lost favour in *Wehrmachtpsychologie* as of no practical use, turning to medicine in 1943 (see Geuter, 1992, p. 243). L.F. Clauss fell from favour with the party in 1942, having been instructor in Race Psychology at

Berlin since 1936 (Geuter, 1992, p. 81). Jaensch died in 1941. I have no information on Petermann's fate.

52 For example, T.W. Danzel (1936) and W. Mühlmann (1938).

53 I am grateful to Dr Colin Berry for perusing the available Clauss works and clarifying their character.

54 Clauss (1934) cited by A. Baker (1936, p. 152). Baker's is a useful, if brief, contemporary review of German Race Psychology, which is fairly damning.

55 Cited by Baker (1936, p. 152).

56 *Psychological Abstracts*, vol. 10, 3123.

57 *Psychological Abstracts*, vol. 11, 2229.

58 *Psychological Abstracts*, vol. 14, 1013.

59 *Psychological Abstracts*, vol. 13, 5290.

60 See ibid., 5833.

61 *Psychological Abstracts*, vol. 12, 5460 summary. He also claims here that 'Mixed races are static, without purpose or future, but they clamour for any regime offering them a foothold.'

62 *Psychological Abstracts*, vol. 13, 3283 extract from summary.

63 *Psychological Abstracts*, vol. 11, 5260 extract from summary.

64 *Psychological Abstracts*, vol. 12, 5444.

65 See *Psychological Abstracts*, vol. 11, 4115.

66 As in Geuter's case, Nazi Race Psychology is not really part of Ash's brief and is barely discussed aside from incidental references to Clauss, Pfahler and Jaensch. That neither of the two major English-language historical monographs covering German Psychology during this period addresses the topic in depth is regrettable, albeit reasonable given the specific issues they are concerned with.

67 *Psychological Abstracts*, vol. 11, 5758 summary.

Chapter 7

'Race' in European Psychology to 1940: II. Its presence and absence in British Psychology

INTRODUCTION

In the received historical image, such as it is, British Psychology from 1913 to 1940 is pervasively racist,[1] primarily because of the deep Galtonian roots and eugenic connections of its strong psychometric tradition. With Britain as the world's greatest imperial power, it is also perhaps taken for granted that most British Psychology must have been implicitly racist. Since the 1898 Cambridge Torres Straits Expedition, which initiated professional Psychological race-difference research, was also British we might again expect a continuing interest in the topic. In this chapter I examine how far the evidence justifies this image. First the presence of racial topics of a psychological kind in the eugenics literature is assessed. Secondly the positions of the Cambridge School psychologists (W.H.R. Rivers, Frederic Bartlett and C.S. Myers) are discussed. Thirdly the positions of William McDougall and R.B. Cattell are considered. Fourthly I identify the main race-related themes tackled in British Psychological journals, text-books and other genres before, finally, addressing the implications of all this.

PSYCHOLOGICAL RACE DIFFERENCES IN BRITISH EUGENICS

That Galton, the founder of eugenics, and his successor Karl Pearson were racist is indisputable. The existence of profound race differences was a central dogma of 19th and early 20th century eugenic and degenerationist thought and Galton himself one of the main architects of Scientific Racism. As we have seen, US eugenics under C.B. Davenport and H.H. Laughlin was adamantly racist and a major force in promoting Race Psychology. Moreover, Galton and Pearson virtually founded the psychometric tradition. By 1913 the value of the eugenic approach to social problems was accepted across the ideological spectrum[2] and the utility of psychometric techniques as an adjunct to this was fast gaining credibility. All this being conceded we might well expect racial issues to maintain a constant, if not necessarily large, presence in British eugenics discourse at least until the mid to late 1930s when Nazism put the topic beyond the pale. Let us then examine the two principal eugenics journals: *The Eugenics Review* (founded 1909) and Pearson's *Annals of Eugenics* (founded 1925).

From 1913 to 1924, when US Race Psychology was expanding rapidly, the *Eugenics Review* contains very few papers of a relevant kind, and these were mainly US-authored (e.g. Yerkes in 1922 on the US Army tests flagging the imminent publication of C.C. Brigham's *A Study of American Intelligence* in 1923). The three British authored exceptions are McDougall's 1913 invited address to the Eugenics Society 'Psychology in the Service of Eugenics' (McDougall 1914, to which we return later), A.T. Bryant's 'Mental Development of the South African Native' (1917) and G.P. Mudge's 'The Menace to the English Race and to its Traditions by Present-day Immigration and Emigration' (1919). In 1921 the geneticist William Bateson's invited address 'Commonsense in Racial Problems' took an explicitly anti-racialist (and courteously anti-eugenics) line.

Bryant's paper, 'adapted' for publication by the anthropologist and Torres Straits veteran C.G. Seligman, is the closest we get to US-style Race Psychology, although not based on empirical research. Based on '33 years intimate intercourse with . . . the Zulu-Kaffir tribes' (p. 42) as a teacher, it is an anecdotal and impressionistic account of the respective capacities of 'South African native' and European children. Its position may be classified as 'moderate scientific racism'. Bryant repeats the traditional view that African boys are relatively precocious in their intellectual development until puberty and then stagnate,[3] but has observed no similar difference from Europeans among girls. He also believes there is some innate difference between European and African adult males, but immediately qualifies this as 'transient and accidental' (p. 43). The most old-fashioned aspect of the paper is his continued acceptance of some tenets of the Spencer hypothesis:

> The African, in company with the lower animals, is still possessed of certain instincts or senses which in us, perhaps by atrophy, through disuse, have entirely disappeared. (p. 44)

This includes the usual list of 'sense of direction', 'keen eyesight' etc. Furthermore, curiously adumbrating L. Lévy-Bruhl's concept of *participation mystique*,[4] 'He is endowed with some peculiar sense of sympathy or telepathy, existent between himself and other living beings, animals no less than man' (ibid.). Superiority in memory and imitation are also cited. Even so, the few who have had a European or American university education were well able to hold their own – 'extraordinary specimens of their race, exceptions to the rule' (p. 49).

Seligman clearly did not acquaint Bryant with the doubts about 'primitive' superiority in basic functions raised by the Torres Straits data. Bryant knows little of the academic work and the paper must really be considered a late provincial example of an approach already obsolete. Even in South Africa things had moved on – H.R. Loades and S.G. Rich (1917) reported 'attempts to apply the ordinary Binet tests to Zulus' starting in 1914. This was cautious but concluded 'It appears from our tests that the disposition to rely on verbal memory, without much attention to meanings, and the absence of systems of association groups, are characteristic features of the native mind' (p. 383). (This typical Race Psychology approach, published in G.S. Hall's *Pedagogical Seminary*, was not however followed up until M.L. Fick's 1929 *South African Journal of Science* paper on racial differences in intelligence in South Africa and R.A.C. Oliver's Kenyan work – discussed below – in the 1930s.) It is somewhat unclear how far Bryant holds the differences he observes to be innate or is simply reporting his observations and conclusions at the end of a career which must have begun in the early 1880s, when a non-racialist orientation would have been virtually unthinkable to one in his position.

Mudge's 1919 paper is very different. Dedicated to the 'memory of English boys who have fallen in the War', it is a virulent and alarmist jeremiad on the impending contamination of the English stock by immigrant 'orientals', 'a silent supplantation of our race by other races, largely of Eastern origin is relentlessly proceeding' (p. 208). This is argued using calculations of rates of net immigration and immigrant reproduction, plus outrageously xenophobic descriptions of the 'orientals' of East London and Manchester with their 'strange garb' and facial features: 'they are not among the jewels of the denizens of the earth' (p. 206).

> The immigrants are not gametically or somatically constituted as our people are. There is little sportsmanship about them. They do not love manly games and exercises as the Englishman does. . . . It is innate in the gametic constitution to do these things. (p. 211)

They are also accused of selfish and undisciplined panic behaviour during Zeppelin air-raids on the East End, and, in effect, of hampering the war effort. He ends with references to the 'Nordic type of Englishman and Englishwoman'. After some initial bafflement as to what he is talking about we realise that 'oriental' is code for Jewish. Have we uncovered the racist face of British eugenics? Turning to the next volume, we find an apologetic 'Editorial Comment' on the paper which 'has been regarded as an attack on the Jewish race in certain quarters' (p. 38). While slightly prevaricating on whether this was the correct reading they proceed to defend the Jewish war record in the strongest possible terms, argue that immigration laws should be based on the present qualities of individuals, not on race, and point out that neither the Jews nor the English are racially homogeneous. Statements made by Mudge 'are not endorsed by the Society' (ibid.). Seligman, in a supplementary attack, says Mudge makes it clear that by 'oriental' he means Jewish and disputes the Nordic-Alpine-Mediterranean definition of 'Caucasian' he had used.[5] Ethnically Jews must, in any case, be members of the 'Caucasic' group. Mudge comes close to 'Prussian glorification of the "blonde beast"' (p. 40). The paper thus turns out to be a genuine rule-proving exception.

From 1925 the presence of 'race' issues slightly increases. The major preoccupation is not, however, with race differences but with the possibly 'disharmonious' or 'dysgenic' effects of race crossing or 'miscegenation'. In a 1926 report of studies on Chinese and Anglo-'Negro' children in Liverpool R.M. Fleming investigates 'how far and in what way racial type affected development, if it affected it at all' (p. 294). Her findings regarding the 'psychological traits' of the former are basically positive, while any shortcomings of the latter are ascribed to social, rather than racial, factors. Fleming was an assistant to H.P. Fleure, Professor in the Department of Geography and Anthropology at the University of Wales, Aberystwyth, an avowed socialist unsympathetic to the Eugenics Society. His own position combined acceptance of innate racial characteristics and racial classification with strong opposition to using this for ideological ends or to bolster racist policies. He was also wary of US-style IQ testing and psychometrics, discouraging Fleming from adopting them in her research.[6] In 1929 Fleming published a further paper on 'human hybrids' which, while conceding the possibility that race mixing may have deleterious results, opposes anti-mixture policies as likely to cause more problems than they prevent. Regarding 'disharmony', she has only noticed it with regard to the jaws (citing the case of the daughter of a small European woman and a robust African). Modern humanity results from a long period of racial crossing and the notion of racial purity is highly dubious. She vehemently, even sarcastically, criticises Davenport and Steggerda's *Race Crossing in Jamaica*,[7] which would appear, on the information provided, to have required obtaining 63 measurements in 20 minutes on each subject (p. 261). She strongly opposes 'racial megalomania' and 'white self-glorification'.

Not all contributors were of her opinion. The Norwegian J.A. Mjöen (1931), reporting studies of Norwegian–Lapp race crossing, adopts an extreme position, claiming that crossing results in 'glandular disturbance'.

> In full agreement with this suggestion of glandular disturbance is the general opinion of biologists that the human hybrid shows a typical instability in mental and moral respects – a want of balance. His motives and actions are incalculable, his impulse stronger than his self-control. (p. 36)

He ends by proclaiming that 'race-hygiene' shall not be used 'to persecute other races, but only to safeguard our own. We shall love our own race, just as a man loves his father and mother, not because it is better than other races, but because it is *our* race' (p. 39). A short editorial comment notes the affinities between Mjöen's position and A. Keith's 'endocrine theory',[8] further suggesting that anthropologists have gone too far in reaction against earlier racial theories. While conceding that no techniques are available for measuring racial differences the editors feel it is 'highly unscientific to assume that these differences do not exist' (p. 5). They do not explain why, in principle, this is less scientific than assuming that they do, but this echoes the now familiar 'differences as default assumption'.

K.B. Aikman (1933) also asserts that 'the best eugenic opinion is definitely against' race crossing (p. 161) and urges 'some form of mass-segregation'. In the same volume the editors welcome the new Nazi eugenics measures which will 'command the assent of all experienced eugenists', but immediately deride their racist and anti-semitic element: 'we have not for many years had so disturbing an example of a great nation making itself ridiculous as the whole German campaign against the Jews' (p. 77). In 1934 an 'Aims and Objects of the Eugenics Society' statement deals with race only in relation to race crossing, on which it may be quoted in its entirety:

> In certain circumstances, race mixture is known to be bad. Further knowledge of its biological effects is needed in order to frame a particular eugenic policy. Meanwhile, since the process of race mixture cannot be reversed, great caution is advocated.

(Eugenics Society, 1934, p. 134)

In 1930 and 1938 H.J. Fleure and Julian Huxley, respectively, opposed Nordicism and Huxley (in the 1936 Galton Lecture) now went so far as to reject the application of the 'race' idea to 'man', opting for 'ethnic group' instead,[9] 'the very term race disintegrates when subjected to modern genetic analysis' (p. 18), 'so-called racial problems on analysis invariably turn out to be problems of culture contact' (ibid.). Thereafter the issue rumbles on at a low level in the occasional anthropological paper[10] and correspondence, but, by and large, heads are kept below the parapet.

Aside from race crossing, only one relevant paper is published; A.G. Hughes' 1928 'Jews and Gentiles. Their intellectual and temperamental differences'.[11] This is the sole paper appearing in the journal during the inter-war period closely approaching US-style 'Race Psychology', but Hughes immediately notes that he is using the term 'race' 'in a very loose sense' (p. 89, n.) and assures us that 'the aim of the psychologist is not to prove that one race is more valuable than another, but to measure as accurately as possible specific differences between them' (ibid.). From what he accepts as differential physical and mental disease rates between Jews and Gentiles[12] he infers that Jews probably have a 'somewhat distinct physical constitution' (p. 89), likely 'to carry with it mental qualities of a particular kind' (p. 90). Jews are generally believed to be better at music, mathematics and languages and inferior at handwork, drawing and painting. These abilities can now be Psychologically tested and 'some data on drawing which have already been obtained, seem to confirm popular impressions' (ibid.). Four of eight 'previous American' studies have also found Jews superior in the appropriate abilities (the remainder finding no difference).[13] He then criticises the study by K. Pearson and M. Moul (1925–8), to be discussed shortly. The remainder of the paper reports research on children using the Northumberland Standardised Tests in General Intelligence,[14] conducted by Hughes and M. Davis under Cyril Burt, *and funded by a Jewish Health Organisation of Great Britain grant*. Four London schools were involved, one for the 'better class', two for the poor and 'very poor' and one identified as attended by the poorest Jewish children. In the first three the Jews, both boys and girls, performed better than non-Jews, while in the last the poorest Jewish children out-performed the poorest non-Jews. Gentile children were superior in only two of 126 age-groups tested (p. 91). The results, he stressed, ought not to be generalised beyond London. If classifiable on methodological grounds as Race Psychology, this paper was thus hardly promoting anti-semitic racism, on the contrary it was Jewish-funded and its findings flattering.

Coverage of race issues by the Eugenics Society's main journal from 1913 to 1940 is thus both marginal and inconsistent. The primary concern is with effects of race crossing, and while the Society eventually plumps for a cautiously negative official line the papers vary from Fleming's two highly moderate contributions to Mjöen's alarmism. Bryant's early reprise of a somewhat moderate Scientific Racist position is not followed up. Mudge's anti-semitism is vigorously stamped on in the next issue, nor does Hughes's paper offer any comfort to anti-semitism, even if uncritical regarding some traditional stereotyping. By the late 1930s the concept of 'race' is visibly under attack, but its known defenders, such as Ruggles Gates, barely figure in the journal's pages. Race crossing was, we should remember, not an anxiety of the ideological right alone, J.B.S. Haldane (1938) expressing concern about the 'extraordinary importance of a scientific study of effects of race-crossing' in *Heredity and Politics* and, like the Eugenics Society, worrying about its irreversibility. It is true that readers were kept briefed on developments across the Atlantic and US concerns over immigration, but the fact remains that whatever the broad racialist, or racist, sympathies of the Society's members, its journal devoted very little space to discussing them, eschewed anti-semitism, and was prepared to publish papers from opposing camps on the race-crossing question. The topic was hardly prominent in other official British eugenics literature: of 80 post-1909 publications under the aegis of the University College Eugenics Laboratory none were on race.[15]

Rather than 'race', by 1913 British eugenics was concentrating on measures (such as, notoriously, sterilisation) for controlling individual level pathology and deviance (commonplace terms such as 'racial health' referred primarily to the human race or the national population in general). The 'feeble-minded', insane, carriers of genetically transmitted diseases and such might occur in all 'races', but so could the brilliant and healthy. Regarding immigration it was the individual, not the ethnic or 'racial', level that mattered.[16]

In 1925 Karl Pearson launched his weightier *Annals of Eugenics*, his opening editorial adamantly asserting the inequality of races. It was in this that the most notorious British piece of eugenic research on race differences appeared in five parts between 1925 and 1928: Pearson and Margaret Moul's 'The problem of alien immigration into Great Britain, illustrated by an examination of Russian and Polish Jewish children', the first part being concerned with psychological differences. Ironically this, like Hughes and Davies's later work, was supported by Jewish funding. The conclusion is summed up in the following passage from the first paper:

> What is definitely clear . . . is that our alien Jewish boys do *not* form, from the standpoint of intelligence a group markedly superior to the natives. But that is the sole condition under which we are prepared to admit that immigration should be allowed. . . . Taken *on the average*, and regarding both sexes, this alien Jewish population is somewhat inferior physically and mentally to the native population. (p. 126, italics in original)

Sex differences are also greater in Jews, girls being markedly inferior. The subjects were, however, from the post-1906 immigrant group of Russian and Polish Jews, data-gathering being completed by 1913.[17] As Hughes (1928) later stressed, being recent immigrants they were linguistically handicapped, and he summarily dismissed the findings as unreliable.[18] If monumental, by the time of publication, the research was also, patently, a monumental waste of time. US debates between Race Psychology and its critics had moved the whole topic beyond the pre-1914 framework within which the authors were operating. While Michael Billig and others have played up the significance of this work, particularly its anti-semitism (though this was hardly of a stereotyped kind), there is scant evidence that British psychologists took it seriously, especially in view of the Hughes and Davies research, with its very different results. Even US Race Psychologists would, by then, have found it methodologically and conceptually naive.

Despite Pearson's editorial affirmation of race differences on its launch, the *Annals of Eugenics* carried *no* other papers on race differences, or even race crossing, in any of its first 10 volumes up to 1940, other than one on sexual and racial variation in PTC tasting (W.C. and L.G. Boyd, 1937). Again, then, there is no evidence that 'race differences' was high on the British eugenics research agenda – indeed precious little evidence for it figuring on it at all after the mid-1920s. Moreover, such publications as do appear are rarely by psychologists, Hughes and, arguably, Fleming and, even more arguably, Pearson[19] being the only exceptions. McDougall, who might have added his weight, emigrated to the USA in 1920, (presumably finding Ellis Island no problem). None of this is meant to deny that British eugenicists adopted an underlying attitude to race issues deeply coloured by Galtonian Scientific Racism. It does though suggest that, unlike US eugenics, such issues were low in its priorities and that, especially from the late 1920s, a clear-cut party-line proved elusive, while its impact on British Psychology's treatment of the topic was very limited.

THE CAMBRIDGE SCHOOL

The well-known rivalry between the London and Cambridge schools of Anthropology was, if less fervently, echoed in a difference between their Psychologies. Until the 1930s Cambridge Psychology maintained a closer connection with Anthropology, but also became more experimentally than psychometrically oriented (and has remained so). Its leading figures were C.S. Myers (who initially financed the Cambridge Psychology Laboratory) and the young F.C. Bartlett. W.H.R. Rivers played somewhat the role of father-figure and we will consider his position first.

Rivers' premature death in 1922 deprived the British human sciences of the one person who might have averted the imminent splits between Psychology, Anthropology and Sociology. He had successfully straddled these disciplines, especially the first two, for two decades and regularly insisted on their complementarity. His friend, the Australian Grafton Elliot Smith, sharing his aspirations, vainly strove to establish a unified 'Human Biology' programme of studies at University College (where he was Professor of Anatomy) spanning the range from Sociology to Anatomy. But Elliot Smith was no diplomat and his own diffusionist anthropology strongly alienated other anthropologists, nor did he forge productive links with University College's psychologists, such as C. Spearman and J.C. Flügel. While Rivers joined the diffusionist camp during the last decade of his life, he, in contrast, remained *persona grata* in all quarters. How, during his latter years, did Rivers view the race issue?

The truth is that Rivers never addresses the matter directly in any of his later works[20] and it would be a Procrustean endeavour to attempt to extract any clear-cut answer from them. After about 1912 his views evolved in two directions, neither congenial to direct consideration of 'race'. The first was an adoption, and modification, of psychoanalytic ideas, following his World War I psychiatric work with shell-shock victims. While accepting, often in a qualified fashion, many of Freud's concepts regarding the mechanisms operative in dreams and psychological life (wish-fulfilment, condensation, repression, censorship etc.) he rejected both the need to invoke infantile origins for dreams and neuroses and their exclusively sexual character. Rivers applied these concepts to the understanding of 'primitive' cultures, particularly to magic and mythology, but again refused to follow Freud[21] (even less, Jung) in seeing a common universal unconscious symbolism and rejected Lévy-Bruhl's notion of a distinct 'primitive' mentality. His reluctance in this respect is related to the second development, a growing acceptance of Elliot Smith's diffusionism. (Elliot Smith opposed the ethnological application of psychoanalytic ideas undertaken by Freud and his disciples, and argued that Rivers would have modified one of his texts further in the anti-Freudian direction had he lived.[22]) Rivers had abandoned the older 'evolutionary' approach in favour of a 'historical' orientation in *History of Melanesian Society* (1914). While initially continuing to pursue the methodological innovations in kinship studies and analysis of social organisation which anthropologists now consider his major achievement, by the end of World War I he was firmly in the diffusionist camp.[23] For our purposes diffusionism's most significant tenet was its rejection of a common, inherent, human capacity for creating similar cultural forms. A high proportion of customs, beliefs and artefacts had diffused from a common source (ultimately, in Elliot Smith's strong version of the theory, ancient Egypt). Such a doctrine thus had no place for the orthodox Scientific Racist tenet that culture somehow directly expressed the innate biological-cum-psychological racial character of peoples.[24]

Rivers' combination of qualified Freudianism as a framework for understanding individual psychology and ethnological diffusionism in relation to cultural variation left little room for considering psychological differences between 'races'. It also, as we saw in the previous chapter, precluded the kind of speculations about 'primitive mentality' being developed by Lévy-Bruhl and Jung; Rivers' own extensive field experience had alerted him to the many ways in which ethnocentrism and mistranslation could create fundamental misunderstandings of 'primitive' world-views and thought-processes.[25] The nearest we come to any 'Race Psychology' topic is a three-page note in Rivers (1926) on 'Intellectual concentration in primitive man' in which he refutes the view that 'The chief intellectual difficulty of primitive man is concentration. He cannot keep his mind on one problem for more than a minute or two' (p. 51). His experience in Melanesia was quite the contrary:

> in intellectual concentration, as well as in many other psychological processes, I have been able to detect no essential difference between Melanesian or Toda and those with whom I have been accustomed to mix in the life of our own society. (p. 53)

His final position might perhaps be best classified as an incipient social constructionism, eschewing both the revisionist evolutionary notion of 'primitive mentality' becoming common in mainland Europe and the older Scientific Racist assumptions still underlying US Race Psychology at the time of his death.

In 1923 Bartlett, Rivers' one-time tutee, published his first book *Psychology and Primitive Culture*. This, now largely neglected, work deserves attention for a number of reasons. While a full account cannot be given here, Bartlett essentially co-opts and supplements McDougall's list of instincts, as expounded in *Introduction to Social Psychology*[26] as the basis for a proto-social constructionist theory of social behaviour. Social behaviour is not the sum total of individual responses, but determined by the dynamic interplay of social instincts and 'group tendencies' as a whole. The contribution of 'individual subtleties of attitude' is 'I think, not the first, but the last question of social psychology' (pp. 279–80). This theoretical scheme is then applied successively to the Folk Story, social management of conflicting tendencies, culture contact and borrowing, diffusion of culture and the nature of 'special groups' within culture, before some general conclusions. Despite its title, the work is actually intended as a kind of prolegomenon to a scientific Social Psychology, as Bartlett states at the end:

> It will now be clear that these studies in the application of psychology to certain problems of primitive culture are to be regarded as introductory to further studies in the psychological treatment of modern culture. (p. 287)

'Primitive' cultures are the focus of attention essentially because basic social psychological processes are more readily visible, not because they are in principle different from 'advanced' ones. Had they indeed been different, they could not have served Bartlett's purpose.

The book may also be read as attempting to maintain the unity of the human sciences to which Rivers had been so committed, but which was by then rapidly dissipating in Britain. It does this in two ways: first by portraying Social Psychology as a necessary facet of any functionalist understanding of society of the kind being developed by the new generation of British anthropologists, second by attempting to keep the diffusionists on board while recouching their central question. Rather than challenging the notion of cultural diffusion he focuses on the mechanisms by which it operates and the conditions for its occurrence. Cultures will borrow or assimilate features from alien cultures only insofar as these correspond to features already existing in their own, and often, in doing so, will radically change them. This is demonstrated by cases such as the origin and spread of the North American Indian Winnebago peyote cult and Rivers' work in Melanesia. Diffusionism and functionalism are thus reconciled, while a scientific Social Psychology is a necessary complement to both.

Like Rivers, Bartlett opposes the 'primitive mentality' notion. Lévy-Bruhl has conflated two different issues: 'There is the question of how primitive man reacts, and the further question of what he reacts to' (p. 283). It is with respect to the latter that the 'primitive man' seems to differ so greatly from 'ourselves', but regarding *how* 'he' reacts there is actually no difference. The apparent gulf arises from differing interests and priorities, not a fundamental difference in 'mentality'. This is all totally incompatible with the orthodox view that culture directly expresses or realises a pre-existing collectively shared mentality. On the contrary, an individual's mentality is largely determined by the social psychological dynamics of the culture into which she or he is born. This, he admits, actually brings him close to behaviourism but he firmly rejects US behaviourism's reductionism:

> Not one of the general conditions of human behaviour in the group which we have dealt with can, it seems to me, be reduced without remainder to contractions of muscles, secretions of glands, and the passage of nerve impulses. (p. 269)

One might speculate that, from this basis, Bartlett could have developed an autonomous British Social Psychology tradition within which the nature of prejudice and inter-group attitudes could have been tackled in a less individual-centred way than that which US Social Psychology adopted. This did not occur. While Bartlett's 'constructionist' orientation pervaded his influential *Remembering* (1932) (a fact often overlooked by the cognitivists who 'rediscovered' it in the 1970s), his subsequent career as Professor of Psychology at Cambridge saw him heading the most scientifically 'hard' experimental Psychology department in Britain – a paradox of which he remained ruefully aware.[27]

The word 'race' hardly appears in *Psychology and Primitive Culture*, while, as we have seen, its entire tenor is anti-racialist. On the other hand, unlike Bartlett's later work, it appears to have enjoyed little influence among the social psychologists or anthropologists at whom it was directed. Although heir to the Rivers and Myers Cambridge tradition Bartlett failed to pursue much further its anthropological and cross-cultural Psychology strands and 'race' questions fell from its agenda.[28] 'Primitive society' would henceforth be a matter for the anthropologists, and while Malinowski incorporated some of Freud's and McDougall's ideas into his functional anthropology,[29] after the early 1920s there was little productive contact between British psychologists and anthropologists until the post-World War II period (S.F. Nadel is, as we will see, the main exception).

For his part, C.S. Myers was soon fully occupied with promoting industrial and applied Psychology at the National Institute of Industrial Psychology. The principal legacy of his Torres Straits experience was a lifelong side interest in ethno-musicology. In 1933 he also re-published a 1904 paper on 'The taste names of primitive people', a spin-off from the expedition research which had first appeared in volume 1 of the *British Journal of Psychology*.[30] His sympathies were clearly with the left-of-centre anti-racist camp, but this yielded nothing in the way of Psychological work beyond the 1911 paper (see above p. 54).

Its prevailing theoretical orientation thus ruled out much interest in race differences among the Cambridge School. But neither were they inclined to adopt the psychometric approaches to race prejudice and attitudes being developed in the USA, these being incompatible with Bartlett's social constructionist view of Social Psychology, while Myers was too busy testing occupational aptitudes and identifying the causes of accidents to railwaymen.

Malinowski does not really come within our orbit, but it is perhaps worth noting that despite the salacious titles of some of his major works – *The Sexual Life of Savages in North Western Melanesia* and *Sex and Repression in Savage*

Society[31] – he was no defender of racism. In introducing J. Lips (1937) he says of the anthropologist:

He has to break down the barriers of race and of cultural diversity; he has to find the human in the savage; he has to discover the primitive in the highly sophisticated Westerner of to-day, and, perhaps, to see that the animal, and the divine as well, are to be found everywhere in man. (p. vii)

He later reprimands 'England' for

regarding . . . the Africans, educated and tribal, Christian and heathen, as though they were mere chattels whose lives, welfare, and happiness can be sold for some imaginary diplomatic advantage in Europe. (p. ix)

How far Malinowski nevertheless accepted some variant of the 'primitive mentality' notion is, however, too complex an issue to consider here.

WILLIAM McDOUGALL (1871–1938) AND R.B. CATTELL

Of all eminent British psychologists the one most in tune with Nordicism was William McDougall, now remembered primarily for his *Introduction to Social Psychology*, a long-influential exposition of the instinctual basis for human behaviour and the relationship between instincts and emotion. His racism emerges in his other writings and was deeply felt. In his 1913 invited address to the Eugenics Society (McDougall, 1914) we find him already picking up on US anxieties about immigration and claiming

healthy political organisms cannot grow up where the population consists of two or more racial stocks that remain persistently averse to intermarriage, and therefore racially distinct. . . . And it seems highly probable that some blends of human subraces are eugenically admirable and others disastrous. (p. 307)

Following his emigration his racial concerns intensified, their fullest statement being *Is America Safe for Democracy?* (1921). McDougall now seems to have bought the entire Scientific Racism package including the racist eugenics of Madison Grant[32] and Davenport. He accepts the Nordic-Alpine-Mediterranean classification including the innate special virtues, such as assertiveness, of the first of these (whose 'restless energy is chiefly responsible for the transformation of the modern world' (p. 97)). He endorses the most nativist interpretation of recent work on 'Negro'–white differences in intelligence as well as the 'mulatto hypothesis' that people of mixed 'Negro' and white ancestry outperform those of exclusively African descent.[33] He also notes (connecting, in doing so, with his theoretical position in *Introduction to Social Psychology*) that in 'Negroes' the 'instinct of submission' is especially well developed. Any residual sympathy we have for him evaporates on examining the photographs following the main text. After Abraham Lincoln and 'my friend Tama Bulan . . . chief of a small village in the heart of Borneo' who had 'brought peace, happiness and prosperity to many thousands of his fellow men' (p. 180), we are faced in true Lombroso style with a rather ugly African from northern Rhodesia (Zimbabwe). The second part of the caption runs:

> We are told nothing of his moral and intellectual qualities; but the most reso-
> lutely optimistic humanitarians will hardly claim him as a 'mute inglorious
> Milton,' or even as a 'village Hampden'. Nor is it easy to suppose that they
> could contemplate with equanimity the substitution of the Anglo-American
> stock with persons of this type. (p. 182)

Presenting a mug-shot of one unattractive individual as a 'type' is propaganda of the crudest type and McDougall – as a psychologist recently involved in a war in which Britain had developed propaganda into an art – surely knew it. (The fourth photo is of all five of McDougall's children sprawled on a lawn to prove that he practises the positive eugenics he preaches.)[34] So much, we might add, for the enlightening effects of the Torres Straits experience!

For his own career the book was a serious misjudgment. 'I did not then realize that in touching, however impartially, the racial question, I was stirring up a hornets' nest. To this raising of the racial question in 1921 is due, I must sup-pose, much of the hostility of the American press that has continued to greet my successive publications.'[35] It certainly identified him thereafter with the Grant–Davenport camp, although he rarely returned to the topic at any length.[36]

Race was central to McDougall's own self-image. The autobiographical sketch just cited opens with his racial lineage: his father 'was a typical dark highlander, that is to say, of the Mediterranean type, small, dark, long-headed, fiery, and markedly extroverted' (1930, p. 191). His mother 'was of pure Saxon type, as were both her parents. . . . Both she and her mother were strikingly beautiful examples of the fair, calm, introverted Nordic' (p. 192). Hence: 'I thus represent that blend of Mediterranean and Nordic races which has produced the British people' (ibid.). Alas, as an 'F_1' cross between the two stocks (unlike most British people in whom crossing took place many generations ago) 'I have never felt myself to be altogether and typically English or altogether at home in the English social atmosphere' (ibid.).

His earlier *Group Mind* (1920a)[37] (written, incidentally, following a brief spell of analysis by Jung in Zurich) also includes a concise but categorical assertion of the existence of innate psychological differences between 'the Negro, the White, and the Yellow' (pp. 155–6), somewhat more on the evil consequences of racial crossing (including 'the inharmonious combination of physical features, character-istic of the mongrel' (p. 332)), and acceptance that 'national character' and culture are direct expressions of innate, hence racial, mental character (p. 162 ff.). Curiously perhaps, given the book's subject, the 'primitive mentality' notion is not addressed.

After his emigration McDougall's position within Psychology became progres-sively marginalised, and as it did so he increasingly devoted his energies to fringe topics such as psychic research and Lamarckian inheritance. (His acceptance of Lamarckism does not seem to have affected his views on race.) By 1930 he is cast-ing himself as a perennial rebel and outsider, possibly the consequence of his own, presumably disharmonious, F_1 hybridity. If he was the most unambiguously racist of the inter-war British psychologists, he was also among the least influential (however prolific) of its major figures, especially after the early 1920s, and was not working in Britain. (His reputation rested primarily on the *Introduction to Social Psychology*, which certainly did remain among the most cited Psychological texts of the inter-war years.)

Raymond B. Cattell's eminence came primarily after World War II when he was well ensconced in the University of Illinois, and later, the University of Hawaii. Prior to the war he had however already begun to make his presence felt in Britain as an educational psychologist (in Leicester) and author of the popular *Your Mind and Mine* (1934), along with other works to be mentioned shortly. For those knowing Cattell only as creator of the widely used 16 Personality Factor test and author of the best-selling Pelican *The Scientific Analysis of Personality* (1965) his views on race may come as something of a shock. Tucker (1994) has a thorough exposé of these (though in truth Cattell never bothered to hide them), revealing him as an almost atavistic throwback to insouciant high Victorian Scientific Racism.[38] They were contained primarily in *Psychology and Social Progress* (1933), *The Fight for Our National Intelligence* (1937) and *Psychology and the Religious Quest* (1938). His Nordicism was unrestrained, and, as Tucker observes, like Galton and Spencer (and with echoes of Le Bon too, one might add) he aspired to the creation of a scientific religion. Races were the evolutionary unit and race mixing disastrous. Anti-semitism was a natural reaction to the 'Jewish practice of living in other nations'.[39] We have more in common with all other members of our own race than we can ever have with a member of another. He eagerly endorsed segregation in the USA, Mussolini's invasion of Abyssinia and the Third Reich. Tucker (1994, p. 243) summarises Cattell's position thus: 'In a generally uninformed world the Nazis and the fascists provided a beacon of moral light, a model of evolutionary progress to be emulated.' He yearns for the advent of a global eugenic scientocracy which will control humanity's evolution on a scale beyond even Galton's wildest dreams (and Galton's could be pretty wild on occasion). Nor did he shrink from advocating that, faced with resistance, these scientific rulers should implement genocide or 'genthanasia'. In 1972 he was still plugging away at the same theme in *A New Morality from Science: Beyondism*, while deriding the current concern with 'prejudice' and backing A.R. Jensen to the hilt.

Cattell's case is somewhat odd. While clearly an unapologetically racist psychologist right from the start, Cattell succeeded in maintaining a respectable, indeed honoured, position within the discipline throughout his career as a leading factor-analytic personality theorist. Yet, as with the present author, one can, if Cattell's personality theory is the sole capacity in which his work is encountered, spend several decades in the discipline entirely oblivious of his extremist ideology and goals.[40] Few of his contemporaries in pre-war British Psychology appear to have taken much notice of his non-technical work, and in *Your Mind and Mine*, his most successful book of the period, his anti-democratic and racist position is but fitfully glimpsed and easily overlooked.[41] While the discipline's preparedness to turn a blind eye to Cattell's racism is certainly disturbing, it must be said that his eminence was gained despite, rather than because of, his views on race.

OTHER RESEARCH AND COVERAGE IN GENERAL TEXTS

A search of the *British Journal of Psychology*, *British Journal of Educational Psychology* (founded in 1931) and *British Journal of Medical Psychology* (founded in 1921), along with the broader inter-war Psychological literature published in Britain, enables us to fill out the picture already given and clarify the prevalent race-related topics and themes. (None of the 24 *British Journal of Psychology Monograph Supplements* published by 1940 concerned a race-related topic.)

'Primitive mentality'

During World War I Carveth Read (Grote Professor of Mind and Logic at University College, London) published several papers on 'primitive mind' which formed the basis for *The Origin of Man and His Superstitions* (1920).[42] These are fairly heavily influenced by James Frazer, although he differs from Frazer regarding the nature of 'animism'. His position somewhat resembles Lévy-Bruhl's but is expounded in more conventional Scientific Racist terms. The following quote is typical:

> The peculiarity of savage beliefs [is due] to the riot of imaginations, unrestrained by criticism and reinforced by the popular consensus. . . . Imaginations spring up in his mind by analogy with experience; but often by remote or absurd analogies; and there is no logic at hand to distinguish the wildest imaginative analogies from trustworthy conclusions.
>
> (1914, p. 308)

The young Bartlett warily and respectfully reviewed Read's book in 1921, but disputed his view that science involves abandonment of reasoning by analogy. Read's work, literary-philosophical rather than empirical, represents the last fling of an older Scientific Racist generation and bears little methodological or theoretical resemblance to the kind of Psychology then emerging.[43] In 1924 H.G. Baynes, a Jungian, published a paper highly supportive of Lévy-Bruhl, explicitly equating the primitive mentality with the civilised unconscious:

> I have used the term 'prelogical psyche' as a comprehensive term covering both the primitive psyche and civilized unconscious mentality. I am unable to discover any essential difference between these two forms of psychic activity. (p. 48)

The 'primitive mentality' theme receives little further attention until 1928 when C.G. Seligman roundly dismisses it. Lévy-Bruhl's theory 'has not been accepted so far as I am aware by anthropologists in this country, and is in my opinion in contradiction to the experience of field workers, who are of all the best to judge' (Seligman, 1928, p. 373). Seligman's position here resembles Bartlett's: 'I hold it true to say that there is no basic difference in mode of thought of savages and of ourselves, but only quantitative differences' (ibid., p. 374) due to their different '*weltanschauung*'. He nevertheless suggests that the 'extravert disposition' of 'savages' may be 'a neuronic, i.e. congenital trait, although it is admitted that most primitive environments are socially favourable to this disposition' (p. 386). Pursuing a Freudian approach, he sees parallels between neurotic fears of castration and ritual circumcision, and between the primitive's 'exaggerated fear of incest' and the incestuous fears of European 'psychoneurotics'. Seligman thus retains a trace of the 'primitive mentality' notion for all his disclaimers.

There continue to be echoes of this theme in the 1930s. The Uganda-based District Officer E. Dauncey Tongue, not a professional psychologist, managed to publish a somewhat old-fashioned paper (lacking any references) in 1935, adopting the well-worn view of the 'native as child'. It is most significant perhaps for the way it embodies the earnest paternalism, typical of the period (a point we will return to later), but he expresses doubts about imposing 'our individualistic civilization *en bloc* upon the African when it has by no means yet fully justified itself in Europe' (p. 364). Careful and patient study is required, it is best to try 'grafting' the most suitable elements onto native culture. A.T. and G.M. Culwick (1935)[44] also claim that everything is explained by ever-present and pervasive supernatural forces (a central doctrine in Lévy-Bruhl). Neither paper can really be considered Psychological, the first is an avowedly amateur offering from the sidelines, the second a report of anthropological field-work. Quite what they were doing in the *British Journal of Psychology* is unclear.

As far as 'primitive mentality' is concerned it would appear that, bar the Jungians, no British psychologists (and few anthropologists) after Carveth Read were very enamoured of the concept. The fullest British-authored Jungian exposition of the concept appears to be C.R. Aldrich (1931). Four other papers: Verrier Elwin (1936), G. Róheim (1937), Ian Suttie (1932) and Seligman (1939), bore more affinities with the emerging 'culture and personality' approach, often with a pronounced Freudian bias.[45]

Jewish intelligence

In addition to the studies discussed earlier, the following may also be noted:

W.H. Winch (1930). Winch finds Jewish children to have a higher average intelligence than 'Christian' children, but the reverse regarding manual ability. Sex differences are greater in the Jewish group, which also shows greater variation generally. Most of these differences are ascribable to social class, but not, he thinks, entirely (see p. 273). His failure to differentiate between ethnic and religious identities certainly tells us something about contemporary assumptions, but is clearly not anti-semitic as such.

J. Rumyaneck (1931). This review paper was written under the auspices of the Jewish Health Organisation. It comprehensively attacks the notion that any biologically based difference in ability between Jews and Gentiles has been demonstrated, and includes a strong critique of Pearson and Moul's paper. The assumption of racial superiority and inferiority 'has hindered the advancement of racial psychology' – but what 'racial psychology' could be without such an assumption is obscure.

C. Rangacher (1932). This simply finds Jewish boys to be somewhat superior to English boys on a perseveration task.

Research on Jewish performance thus continued to be funded by Jewish organisations and none of it replicates the Pearson and Moul findings. One would be very hard put to identify any anti-semitic component in the work, although of course without a wider cultural presence of, and concern with, anti-semitism it is unlikely the research would have been done in the first place.[46]

Welsh bilingualism

One relevant theme, not in itself couched in racial terms, was the effect of bilingualism on test performance, studied by comparing monoglot and bilingual Welsh children in a number of papers spanning 1922–38.[47] Margaret Mead cited the earliest of these in her influential research on the linguistic factor in poor immigrant Italian performance in New York.[48] All concluded that monoglot children (speaking only English or Welsh) performed better on verbal tests than bilinguals. It was also found that the latter had smaller vocabularies. On non-verbal tests the differences disappeared. The importance of this research, as just indicated, was in providing strong evidence that linguistic handicap remained a factor in determining test performance among bilingual children who superficially appeared to be competent. This had added force because clearly no biological difference was involved, nor any additional factor such as the trauma of emigration.

Test construction

Besides those previously noted, three attempts at designing intelligence tests for use in non-European colonial cultures appear to have been undertaken. The first of these was undertaken in Kenya, the others in India, one by an Indian.

Kenya: R.A.C. Oliver

In the early 1930s Oliver was involved in a Carnegie Foundation project to develop a general intelligence test for use in Kenya and other East African British colonies. This yielded the *General Intelligence Test for Africans (with Manual of Directions)* (Oliver, 1932a) officially published in Nairobi, plus three spin-off papers on design and standardisation, interpretation, and 'The musical talent of natives of East Africa'.[49] While the last appeared in the *British Journal of Psychology*, the others appeared in *Oversea Education* and the *East Africa Medical Journal*, rather than Psychology journals The two-part paper on design and standardisation (Oliver 1933–4) is primarily descriptive with little theoretical content. Although he uncritically accepts the need for special tests for East Africans, the 'need for culture-fair tests' argument is barely articulated.

The paper on musical talent reports findings on 90 pupils at the 'Alliance High School, Kikuyu, Kenya Colony' (the primary site where the intelligence test was developed). Using the Seashore Measures of Musical Talent he finds that compared to US norms Africans are superior in 'intensity', time and rhythm, inferior in pitch discrimination, consonance and memory for tones. Administration problems rendered the consonance findings unreliable, and scores on both consonance and memory being correlated with intelligence, Oliver suggests that less intelligent subjects failed to understand the procedure. Poor performance on pitch discrimination puzzles him, given the use of minor pitch changes in African music, and he suggests the test may have been unsuitable. Criticisms of the use of the Seashore Measures in relation to 'race differences' had already been raised by Garth,[50] but Oliver does not cite them, arguing positively that they 'measure functions closely dependent on comparatively simple physiological mechanisms' (p. 333), and hence lack cultural bias. There is no explicit discussion of the innateness or otherwise of African musical talent, or lack of it.

If these papers reasonably belong in the broad 'Race Psychology' category, Oliver hardly comes across as especially fired by racialist zeal, just as a colonial educator doing his job. His more generally interpretive 1932 paper 'The comparison of the abilities of races: with special reference to East Africa' rectifies this image. It opens with a balanced, if rather elementary, review of the race-differences issue, including the unreliability of current cultural level as a guide, difficulties of eliminating cultural and environmental factors from research and so on. But Oliver then rather complacently proceeds as if these need to be no more than 'borne in mind', rather than presenting serious obstacles. In particular he contentedly accepts US findings of an IQ difference of about 20 points between 'Negroes' and whites, even construing this as meaning a 20% shortfall, which most US researchers had by then realised was statistical nonsense.[51] This misinterpretation is crucial in his subsequent analysis of his findings as we will see in a moment.

We proceed to a study using the new General Intelligence Test for Africans comparing 93 Alliance High School subjects with 124 from the European Prince of Wales School in Kabele. This appears to be the only British-authored research on black–white race differences in children's intelligence of the kind which had become typical in US Race Psychology. Very conveniently the African subjects' mean score is 85.3% [sic] that of the white (mostly British) boys. Oliver next reviews the evidence on brain size. Accepting that correlations between brain size and intelligence are modest he now invokes a paper published in the same journal earlier in the year: F.W. Vint (1932). Not only has Vint found the mean weight of African brains to be around 88% of the European brain, the thickness of the pyramidal cell layer in the East African cortex is apparently 84% of that of Europeans.[52] The variation in this latter is also extremely low. This excites Oliver enormously. While the brain size difference is 'definite but not strong evidence of inferiority . . . in intellectual capacity' (p. 198), the latter ties in with Karl Lashley's recent findings of 'equipotentiality',[53] Spearman's general intelligence notion (1927) and the views on brain functioning advanced by the Gestalt psychologist Wolfgang Köhler (1929). All indicate that 'educable capacity' is 'fairly closely proportional to the amount of cortical tissue in [Lashley's] "association areas"' (Oliver, 1932b, p. 201). And the pyramidal layer is more important in this respect than the outer cerebral cortex.

This clustering of figures in the 80–88% range is, Oliver believes, very persuasive: 'the similarity of the histological and psychological conclusions is at once apparent' (ibid., p. 202). The 'East African native' scores '85.3%' of the European mean IQ and has 84% of the European 'association area' capacity as indicated by pyramidal cortex thickness. Q.E.D. It but remains for the educational implications of this to be rationally worked out in paternalistic fashion. While fairly *au fait* with US Race Psychology, Oliver appears unaware of the rapidly shifting climate of opinion on the matter in US Psychology.[54] This paper is the only one I have located in which a British psychologist expounds a *typical* Race Psychology position of the hard-line variety in the US sense. This is no doubt in part due to the fact that the Carnegie Foundation funded his research on the completion of a Commonwealth Fund Fellowship at Stanford University, Terman's base.[55]

Vint's paper itself carries a brief discussion providing an interesting glimpse of that colonial medical preoccupation with the African brain which the South African J.C. Carothers continued to pursue until the early 1970s.[56] Scientific Racist ideas on African physiology and its significance remained alive and kicking in these circles, including earlier maturation and ridges on closed skull sutures.

India: C.H. Rice and V.V. Kamat

In 1929 C.H. Rice published a Hindustani version of the 'Binet-Performance Point Scale'[57] (plus some Pintner-Paterson Performance Tests) designed for use in the Panjab [*sic*] and research comparing the performance of different 'caste' groups. This had begun in 1922 and Rice, of the Forman Christian College in Lahore, was clearly extremely painstaking in his efforts to produce a test viable in an Indian context, standardising it on 929 schoolboys (and again in 1928 with 1,388). While undertaken in British-ruled India this project was fundamentally American in background, Rice's academic acknowledgements being to C.C. Brigham (who helped extensively) and H.C. Warren and their Princeton University Psychology Department (Princeton University Press also co-published the work). I am unable to confirm Rice's nationality but the balance of probabilities is that he was American. As a document the work is valuable for providing a full account of an early attempt at adapting western psychometrics for use in a radically different non-European culture.

Rice attempts no comparisons between his 'Panjabi' subjects' performance and European norms (the changes made to the tests would have rendered this impossible anyway). As to whether there was a racial dimension to the work the answer is unexpectedly complex. The comparison of boys of different 'castes' was primarily between religious groups: 'Chuhras' (the 'depressed' or 'untouchables'), Christian boys of Chuhra origin, Muslims, Sikhs, Brahmins and non-Brahmin Hindus. In the report's closing section Rice concentrates on the performance of the second of these, and is keen to show that it is not significantly different from that of the other groups (excepting the low-performing Chuhras). This finding is used to affirm and support the humanitarian aim of emancipating the untouchable caste from which this group was drawn. The racial twist to this comes with his citation of anthropological work demonstrating that the Chuhras are not racially different from any other groups, being like them 'Indo-Aryan'. Since there are no grounds for ascribing to them any racial inferiority their potential equality is thus not surprising.

Pending further information one can only hypothesise, but the most plausible reading of the situation is that Rice was an American Christian working in a mission school whose agenda was to deploy US psychometric expertise to further the social egalitarian emancipation of the Chuhras, to which caste his pupil converts mainly belonged. Brigham's close involvement suggests that Rice would have accepted his early-1920s belief in innate racial differences in intelligence and therefore been eager to assimilate this caste into the superior Indo-Aryan category. As to whether Rice was using Psychology to promote imperialism, the furthest one can go is to say that, in a sense, any non-Indian seeking to introduce a Western cultural practice (like intelligence testing and Christian education) was participating in the general imperialist enterprise. How, in any stricter sense, he was reinforcing British rule it is difficult to discern. Finally, aside from its being undertaken in the British Empire and published by Oxford University Press, there is no evidence that the work was really British at all – indeed, all the indications are that it was American.

V.V. Kamat more briefly reported a similar revision of the Binet scale, for use with Kanarese and Marathi-speaking children, in the *British Journal of Educational Psychology* in 1934 and 1939. While observing that, for environmental reasons, the female norms among his subjects were lower than those of English girls, Kamat does not go much beyond describing the standardisation and design procedures. He is not interested in race differences, rather he is trying to adapt an apparently useful Western scientific procedure for use in an Indian educational context.

Perception revisited: R.H. Thouless and W.M. Beveridge

In 1933 Thouless briefly reopens the question of innate psychophysical-level differences. His starting point is the absence in Oriental art of shadow and the 'partial or total' absence of perspective. The argument that the images are symbolic rather than representational is insufficient to explain why parallel-sided objects are drawn so as to appear to diverge. Using 20 Indian subjects, he measures 'phenomenal regression to the real characters of objects', that is, how far knowledge of the character of objects overrides perspectival distortion and so on in determining perceptual experience. Two tasks were involved, one requiring the drawing of a circular stimulus presented at an angle so as to appear elliptical, the other, judgment of size. His findings appeared to confirm his initial hypothesis that:

> There is a measurable difference in the perceptions of these races, and this difference is such that they see objects in a manner much further from the

principles of perspective than do the majority of Europeans and also that they tend not to see shadows.

(Thouless, 1933, p. 330)

(This last was not, however, actually studied.)

W.M. Beveridge followed this up with two papers (1935, 1939) on West African subjects attending the Presbyterian Training College at Akropong (Gold Coast, now Ghana). First, replicating Thouless's experiment (although the size-constancy task was a little different) he again finds that the 'West African has a considerably higher index of phenomenal regression than the European. This explains some peculiarities of African drawings which the European tends to regard as mistakes' (1935, p. 61). In the 1939 paper things become more complicated, since phenomenal regression for *brightness* is less among West African subjects than among Scots, but more for *whiteness* (the two measures being negatively correlated −.27). In a picture preference test, European pictures are overwhelmingly preferred to Oriental ones (86.5% : 13.5%), despite the latter's apparently greater fidelity to phenomenal regression. Beveridge ascribes this to greater familiarity with European as opposed to Oriental art. Finally he conducted a rather curious experiment on what he called 'mental compromise in estimating direction' – which turns out to resemble the phenomenon now known as field-dependency. Subjects stood in a sealed box which was then tilted, and were then required to set a pole (extending beyond the box) in as near a horizontal position as they could, deviation being measured on an external indicator set against the end of the pole. Africans proved slightly superior to Europeans, which Beveridge interpreted as consistent with their greater tendency to phenomenal regression. There is perhaps a faint residual hint of Spencer's 'primitive superiority' hypothesis here: superior African 'field independence' signifying lower sensitivity to the phenomenal field than that of Europeans. (Nowadays of course high field-independency is implicitly 'good'.)

Thouless's work attracted immediate criticism from Z. Piotrowski (1935) who argued for a purely cultural explanation (Beveridge ignores this paper). Had Thouless ever looked at pre-Renaissance European art, or pre-18th century popular book illustration, in which lack of perspective, absence of shadows and 'phenomenal regression' are as commonplace as in Oriental art? That question aside, Thouless and Beveridge's views were soon superseded by, for example, J.J. Gibson's work on the psychology of perception and by art historians such as E.H. Gombrich. Perspective is just one of several distance cues artists may use, alongside texture, position and level of blue-saturation, for example. No direct inferences about perception can be drawn from artistic images – the function of the image, cultural customs, artistic skill and how it is allocated and so forth all intervene. The notion of innate differences in phenomenal regression between 'races' was never, to my knowledge, further pursued, although depth perception was taken up by cross-cultural psychologists after the war.[58] One must now assume that cultural factors (or differences in experimental demand characteristics of some sort) underlay their results. Neither appears to have been inclined to draw broader racialist conclusions from the research. Thouless elsewhere accepts on balance that there might be a small deficit in average intelligence in the specific case of the 'Negro', but immediately strongly qualifies this in a footnote, 'it lends no support to the popular view of "race inferiority"'.[59] If the hidden agenda is that Europeans are innately better in perceptual performance (or at least in creating phenomenally accurate images), on the surface at least they seem to have been merely exploring what struck them as a rather discrete perceptual phenomenon.[60] Perhaps another subtext was a routine British middle-class hostility to 'modern art'.

Other

Two papers less easy to classify should also be noted:

S.F. Nadel (1937)

'A field experiment in racial psychology', the title of Nadel's 1937 *British Journal of Psychology* paper,[61] certainly sounds as if it belongs unambiguously in the Race Psychology camp, but proves to be a somewhat problematic text from our point of view. Two 20-strong groups of Nigerian Yoruba and Nupe boys aged 15–18 were compared in an adaptation of Bartlett's memory experiments in which subjects are required to recall stories or pictures – in Nadel's case four hours (or immediately, in the case of the pictures) and a week after presentation. The 'primary aim' of the study was 'to discover "typical" psychological traits among groups of different culture, in other words, to study by means of a psychological experiment what Professor Bartlett calls the "preferred, persistent tendencies of groups"' (1937a, p. 196),[62] rephrased in the Summary as 'to study . . . the correlation between diversity of culture and psychological differentiation' (p. 211). In contrast to the work of the leading US race psychologists, Garth and Porteus, it was intended as a qualitative rather than quantitative study.

Nadel notes at the outset that he is using 'racial' 'simply for want of a better term' (p. 195) and not in any strict sense, it simply refers to cultural groups. 'The term culture-psychology, however, with its philosophic connotation, does not recommend itself' (ibid.). This is somewhat puzzling, the connotations of 'racial' would already, one would have thought, have been somewhat more to be avoided.

Responses were classified under five headings (a different quintet for story and pictures), including such things as 'set phrases and formulae' and 'emotional and moral aspects' (the story), 'imagination' and 'exactness' (the pictures – of which there were six). The Yoruba emerged as dominantly 'rational, logical and intent on meaning-oriented interpretations' and the Nupe as 'combining an enumerative approach to observational data with stress on spatial and temporal arrangement', with a secondary Nupe 'type' 'characterized by an emotional and impressionistic disposition' (p. 210). These appeared to correspond to their broader cultural differences.

Nadel had, in the same year, also published 'The typological approach to culture' in *Character and Personality* and in 1940 followed up with 'New field experiments in racial psychology' in *Advances in Science*.[63] His position is ambiguous, seemingly pointing in opposite directions. First, his continued willingness to accept the 'Racial Psychology' label as late as 1940 suggests an indifference, at the least, to the racist connotations this had now acquired. Regarding Garth and Porteus (the only two researchers cited, aside from Bartlett) he simply expresses lack of interest in the kind of quantitative psychometric work they have done, rather than opposition to it. Secondly however, his own aims appear to have more affinity with those of the Culture and Personality camp, although he is working in the more social constructionist Bartlett tradition rather than the US developmental one of Margaret Mead and her colleagues. If we were to classify Nadel's work it would, on balance, belong in this camp rather than Race Psychology, primarily on the grounds that the actual research, if not its title, seems to be addressing issues more typical of that school and because he never offers a nativist explanation of the differences he finds, speaking only of 'correlation' between culture and psychological traits.

This ambiguity is also present in his contribution to Bartlett et al.'s *The Study of Society* (1939). By this time Nadel was working as a government anthropologist in Sudan. Entitled 'The application of intelligence tests in the anthropological field', this is a finely balanced critique of the methodological pros and cons of the various tests on offer and what can and cannot be achieved by them. His conclusion endorses views expressed by Bartlett (1937) that the quest for universally applicable tests should be postponed and energies devoted to designing culture-specific tests for intra-racial use only. This 'would, in fact, alter the whole meaning of intelligence tests' (Nadel, 1939, p. 197). Any concern with questions of heredity versus environment he eschews as being mistaken, and he cautions against using tests for political purposes or to assess relative 'superiority'. In general Nadel, as an anthropologist, was clearly more concerned with getting to grips with qualitative differences in 'intellectual organisation' than quantifying general intelligence.

H.W. Nissen et al. (1935)

Nissen et al. (1935), in a study of test performance among French Guinea children of the Sousou branch of the Mandingo people, adopt an almost standard Race Psychology methodology, but include discussion of the cultural background and explicitly reject a nativist interpretation of the findings, as well as exploring the cultural biases of the tests.[64] The authors' attitude, if not the methodology, again suggests a 'Culture and Personality' orientation rather than a 'Race Psychology' one.

Textbook coverage

If actual race differences research was scanty, in their textbooks British psychometricians like Burt, Spearman and, of course, R.B. Cattell accepted the findings of US Race Psychology at face value well into the 1930s. Spearman, for example, refers to Nordic vs. South European differences in intelligence in Spearman (1927). Even so, excepting Cattell, most references to the issue are brief passages embedded in works from which the topic is otherwise absent.

We may now sample a few representative general Psychology texts of the period. The Edinburgh-based James Drever's *Instinct in Man* (1921) would certainly have offered him the opportunity of considering the issue of whether or not different 'races' were biologically different in basic psychological character. The index has six entries on 'race'. In three cases the word occurs in a quotation. All refer broadly to the notion of 'preservation of the race' without reference to specific human races (and sometimes without reference specifically to humans). Neither race differences (or their absence), race prejudice nor race crossing are anywhere mentioned. While, as noted above, Spearman (1927) accepted race differences, his actual coverage is a little over four pages (of over 400) and concludes: 'nevertheless such racial differences, even if truly existing, are indubitably very small as compared with those that exist between individuals belonging to one and the same race. Proof of the influence of heredity in the former case can then, after all, carry us but a small way towards estimating its scope in the latter' (p. 380). This hardly sounds like someone fired with concern over the issue.

L. Wynn Jones's *An Introduction to the Theory and Practice of Psychology* (1934) is a London University textbook based on Spearman's 'neogenetic' theory. The chapter on 'The "G" factor and tests of "intelligence"' contains not a single word on race differences (though some research on 164 'crippled children' is discussed), and only one relevant paper (M. Fortes (1932), published in South Africa[65]) is cited in passing in the context of discussion of verbal versus non-verbal tests. There are occasional citations elsewhere such as C. Rangacher (1932) (but only with reference to his method of testing 'perseveration') and Rivers' Torres Straits and Todas work (Rivers, 1905) on the Müller–Lyer illusion. He is also happy to use the phrase 'primitive savage', but 'race', 'Negro', 'prejudice' and 'primitive' do not appear in the index and there is no evidence that Wynn Jones felt it necessary to inform students about race-related issues. Francis Aveling was also a University College colleague of Spearman. His popularly pitched *Psychology: The Changing Outlook* (1937), while covering several applied Psychology topics, is even more devoid of references to either race or race prejudice.

C.K. Ogden's highly popular and much reprinted *The ABC of Psychology* contains three pages on 'primitive mentality'[66] which offer, without acknowledgement, a summary of Lévy-Bruhl's claim that primitives are not interested in 'how' questions, only 'why' ones (he uses Lévy-Bruhl's example of the sorcery explanation for a person being killed by a crocodile).[67] Aside from this there is no mention of race – with one bizarre exception: his apparent sympathy towards F.G. Crookshank's polygenist theory that white, black and yellow races are respectively allied to chimpanzees, gorillas and 'orangs', which he mentions in passing.[68] While obviously accepting that racial differences existed, Ogden does not direct the reader to any relevant Psychological work.

One of the most successful textbooks throughout the period was G.F. Stout's *Manual of Psychology*, a fourth edition of which appeared in 1929[69] (revised by C. Mace of St Andrews University). This has four pages (of over 650) on 'primitive mentality' which again focus on alleged lack of logicality in Lévy-Bruhl fashion, with particular reference to the 'Tshi-speaking tribes of the Gold Coast'. Stout's position closely resembles Carveth Read's, for example, a later reassertion of the classic Scientific Racist canard of 'savage' impulsiveness and lack of self-control. 'The self which determines action is predominantly the present self, not the total self as ideally represented' (p. 649), the 'savage' thus 'wastefully exhausts his present store in riotous indulgence, and is improvident of the future' (ibid.). Elsewhere there are numerous invocations of the intellectual shortcomings of the 'savage', amplifying the 'lack of logicality' argument. But these passages are all unchanged from the 1907 edition. That Mace did not revise them in the light of Bartlett's and Rivers' work certainly suggests a complacent ritualised acceptance of classic Scientific Racist attitudes and beliefs. It also, however, signifies the quite marginal character Stout's approach had assumed in relation to the rest of the discipline by the 1920s. Intelligence is nowhere discussed, for example. Eminent contemporary figures (aside from McDougall and Thorndike) are more notable by their absence than their presence in the index: Burt, Bartlett, Freud, Spearman, Terman, Woodworth and Yerkes – none of them figure. The text's Scientific Racism must be judged an archaic survival, not a manifestation of active current interest.

Two more examples should suffice. Beatrice Edgell, Professor of Psychology at the all-female Bedford College in London published an introductory textbook *Mental Life* in 1926, revising it in 1929. Working from the index there is no way of locating any relevant material whatsoever (race, primitive, savage, Negro, attitude, prejudice, all yield a blank) and the chapter 'Primitive values' is about instinct theories, not 'primitive' people. Finally we may consider W.J.H. Sprott's (1937) *Psychology for Everyone*. This has a page on racial differences in intelligence baldly summarising the results of four US studies (including Brigham regarding European rankings) and ending with a paragraph simply noting that 'a test which may be of use for one cultural background may not be valid for another' (p. 80). The index is again barren of relevant terms. Scanning their works, the overall impression is that British textbook writers have scant interest in race-related questions and actually know very little about contemporary developments in the topic in the USA.[70] In the other genre of Psychology which flourished in Britain from the early 1920s, psychoanalysis, racial questions are rarely touched on, theoretical expositions and discussions of child development predominating. One exception is the India-based psychoanalyst Owen Berkeley-Hill, Medical Superintendent of Ranchi European Mental Hospital, whose work has been discussed by C. Hartnack (1987).

Owen Berkeley-Hill: Psychoanalysis in India

In 1919, in the wake of the Amritsar massacre, Berkeley-Hill wrote a paper which attempted to explain Hinduism in terms of 'sublimations of, or reaction formations against, anal-erotic impulses' (Hartnack, p. 241). This further provided him with a rationale for continued British rule, to quote Hartnack:

> He concluded by implying that British rule is justified, since the Hindus are neither interested in responsible leadership, nor do they have the psychological

disposition for it, since they are, in addition to being obsessive-compulsive, also infantile. (ibid., p. 242)

This paper (Berkeley-Hill, 1921c) was initially proscribed in India by the authorities for fear of exacerbating anti-colonial tensions among the Hindus, but appeared in Berkeley-Hill (1933), published in Calcutta. In Berkeley-Hill (1921b) he turned his attention to the character of Mohammed, arguing that he suffered from 'an all-pervasive father complex' (ibid.). This led him to view Islam as a greater challenge than Hinduism, by virtue of the aggressive character its founder had infused into the religion. The unconscious roots of the conflicts between Muslims and Hindus were also, he believed, illuminated by his analysis (Berkeley-Hill, 1925). As Hartnack shows, Berkeley-Hill's attempt at exporting psychoanalysis to India was less than successful, vitiated by his commitment (as one bearing the rank of Lt. Colonel, after all) to continued British rule and his own inability to enter into meaningful dialogue with either his patients or Indian culture. It is interesting to turn to a further paper overlooked by Hartnack, 'The "color question" from a psychoanalytic standpoint' (1921a).

In some respects this anticipates the line more recently taken by Kovel (1988), since he argues that the association of black with 'witchcraft, devils, sin, bad luck' (1921a, p. 248) is universal, even among black-skinned people. On the other hand he adopts a curiously ambivalent attitude to this, verging on viewing it as in some sense 'natural' or unavoidable, so deep-rooted are its unconscious origins. Thus 'the "white" man is the victim of varying degrees of repulsion when brought into contact with races whose skin is more pigmented than his own, to however slight a degree' (p. 250). He acknowledges, however, that an opposite emotion, a 'powerful attraction' is also present. 'It is a purely sexual attraction. It is a form of sexual perversion' (ibid.). 'It seems to me not unlikely that there probably exists in the Unconscious of most, if not all, of the non-African races, a horror of the Negro which can be traced ultimately to sexual jealousy' (p. 252). Rather than deploying psychoanalytic concepts as a resource for exorcising or unmasking the irrational roots of race prejudice, Berkeley-Hill's tone serves rather to convey the impression that the situation is unrectifiable precisely because such reactions are 'instinctive'. While psychoanalysis has, since the 1920s at least, been used primarily as a theoretical framework for challenging racism (e.g. by Dollard, the culture and personality school or Kovel), when in the hands of a colonially based white military doctor it assumed the very different aspect of a technique for pathologising other cultures and naturalising race prejudice based on skin colour. This also appears to be true of the only other India-based psychoanalytic writer, C. Dangar Daly (son of a New Zealand farmer) also discussed by Hartnack, who again saw Hindu culture in pathologised terms centred on a feminised mother-fixation with 'Mother India'.

R.F.A. Hoernle and others

Staying in the colonies, a paper by the South African R.F. Alfred Hoernle 'Prolegomena to the study of the black man's mind' (1927) comes as an unexpectedly refreshing change. Somewhat philosophical in pitch, this argues that as far as we can currently tell the psychological differences between Bantu and white are social rather than constitutional in origin. Regarding the 'abstract' level of mind in general, he claims of a hypothetical textbook written on studies of Bantus rather than Europeans:

> it is not easy to see that any difference between the black man's mind, as such, and the white man's mind, as such, would have appeared in such a textbook at all, certainly not in one written on behaviouristic lines. (pp. 59–60)

As far as the more 'concrete' level is concerned, this, while it should be the province of Social Psychology, is currently the province of Social Anthropology. He also asserts that 'It is only our evolutionary habit of thought which makes us construe different civilizations as stages in a progression of which our present civilization is the apex' (p. 56). As for Lévy-Bruhl, 'what Lévy-Bruhl calls "prelogical", I would rather call "pre-scientific"' (p. 60). While holding open the possibility that constitutional factors may be involved, Hoernle is provisionally sceptical, 'present knowledge throws only a feeble and uncertain light' (p. 55).

The first volume of the journal in which this paper appeared, the regrettably short-lived *Journal of Philosophical Studies* (1926–8), contained a three-paper Symposium on 'The Problem of Colour in Relation to the Idea of Equality' as well as a Russian-authored paper from a Lévy-Bruhl perspective by N. Lossky 'The primitive and the civilized mind' (which is basically a philosophical excursus on modes of thinking). Two of the Symposium papers, Sir Frederick Lugard's and Morris Ginsberg's, shed a little more light on British orientations to the issue in the 1920s. Lugard (1926) notes that there is no clear physiological demarcation of colour and observes that 'so-called Nordic races' have 'the Colour prejudice' more strongly developed than the 'darker races of Southern Europe' (pp. 211–12). But his final position is significantly ambiguous: on the one hand 'In the *political* sphere the British ideal is that there should be equal opportunity for every man, irrespective of colour or creed' and when this is disregarded the motive is desire to retain power rather than 'crude prejudice' (which may, however, be a reasonable stance!) (p. 212). But while political egalitarianism is acceptable, social and racial separation is necessary to maintain 'race purity and race pride' (p. 213). Ginsberg's (1926) position is, predictably, firmer. The crude heredity versus environment polarity is nonsense, the US findings of Negro–white IQ differences are highly dubious (especially the US Army tests) and, as Rivers and Woodworth showed, sensory differences were non-existent. Changes in tradition or culture are independent of changes in the 'germinal constitution of man'. He strongly attacks US race hatred based on 'pseudo-biology and psychology' (p. 223). While considering wholesale inter-marriage undesirable on sociological grounds pending higher levels of socio-economic equality, he rejects Lugard's notion of social separation. He closes with a fairly contemptuous rejection of McDougall's *Ethics and Some Modern World Problems*, in which the disastrous consequences of global egalitarianism had been aired. (The third paper, by H.A. Wyndham, was political in character, primarily concerning South Africa. He is concerned about the 'fair division of the world's surface between different races' (p. 225).)

G.H. Fox-Lane Pitt-Rivers

The ambivalence present in Lugard also pervades Pitt-Rivers' *The Clash of Culture and the Contact of Races* (1927), a strangely syncretic work combining a genetic approach to races as such with Jungian personality typology. While in some ways rooted in older Scientific Racist assumptions, his treatment of the topic seems largely to evade explicit evaluative racism. He roundly condemns missionary 'endeavour' as 'incapable of achieving any result in the end except to assist in the extermination of the people it professes to assist' (p. 14) and derides White Australia rhetoric (pp. 103-4).

There are two major strands in his thinking. First there is the central, classic Darwinian, notion of the 'adaptability of stocks'. Isolated racial groups become highly specialised and hence unadaptable. These are especially endangered when contact is made with other races, especially those of a radically different cultural level. When this happens they either die out, or are gradually replaced by a mixed blood or 'miscegenated' population which is more adaptable, but at the price of the disappearance of the 'full blood' stock.

Secondly, he uses Jung's extroversion/introversion and fourfold 'functional type' typological classification, which he considers may have ethnic applications. However he dismisses the 'general intelligence' notion: 'a complex of affective and intellective factors interact and condition each other, and are moreover bound up with variation in the type of mental adaptation' (p. 171). Races, he believes, will display similar variations to individuals, thus the Negro is extroverted and adaptable while the American Indian is introverted and unadaptable – hence, in the USA, their differing fates. The sexes also show differences:

> the female being mentally, as she is also anatomically and physiologically, the more generalized, closer to the racial stem, less divergent from and closer to the infantile. (p. 171)

Pitt-Rivers does not, however, make significant use of the standard Scientific Racist evolutionary schema. Race differences pertain, biologically, to the levels of adaptability present in the 'stock' and its degree of specialisation and psychologically to the prevailing personality type or temperament, which also affects adaptability.

Coda on Burt

And what of Cyril Burt's position?[71] Here is the close of a radio broadcast on the topic:

> It is clear that racial intelligence and racial temperament may impose certain minor limitations upon each community; but within those limitations there is no reason why custom and culture should not be reorganized and changed. Just as within the British Isles we have fused together two if not three different stocks and produced a single nation, so within Europe, and perhaps throughout the globe, we may unite the entire population in one commonwealth and give it a character of its own, and thus ultimately evolve, not only a national

consciousness, but a world consciousness, not only an ideal for each country, but an ideal for the whole world.

(C. Burt, 1935, p. 224)

This is hardly consistent with his current image as an apologist for racism. Howitt and Owusu-Bempah (1994, p. 27) finding no explicitly racist Burt text are driven to pressing into service a passage from Burt (1937) describing the physiognomy of the extremely backward child. OK, he does use the word 'negroid' in this, but this is surely just blasé unreflective linguistic cultural racism. It may be hard to excuse but it is nothing to do with his Psychology *per se*. If that's all they could find he was doing pretty well for 1937!

SUMMARY

Inter-war British work thus falls into five categories, although probably only publications in the first reached double figures.

1 Discussion of the 'primitive mentality' notion. Commonest during the early 1920s, by the 1930s few non-Jungian British psychologists and anthropologists are sympathetic to the concept.
2 Research comparing the educational and test performances of Jewish and non-Jewish schoolchildren. Only the earliest, Pearson and Moul's, reported any Jewish deficit, the rest found no difference or Jewish superiority.
3 Studies of differences in intelligence test performance between Welsh monoglot and bilingual schoolchildren. These all found a bilingual deficit on verbal tests, but not on non-verbal tests. Such findings served the anti- rather than pro-race differences camp.
4 At least three attempts at devising intelligence tests for colonial use are published in Britain: Oliver's in Kenya and in India, Rice's and Kamat's. (South African work did not appear in Britain as far as I can determine.) The motivations behind the Indian work were basically practical, but Oliver was clearly pursuing a more Race Psychological agenda.
5 Within eugenics circles there was concern about the effects of 'race crossing', but the few psychologists involved, like Ruth Fleming, were sceptical regarding deleterious consequences.

Otherwise, the Beveridge and Thouless work on perception was atypical and of little real consequence. The researches done by Nadel and Nissen each represent an attempted fusion of anthropology and experimental Psychology with its closest parallels in some of the US Culture and Personality work by Margaret Mead and others in the Columbia school. Extending the net more widely, we find a further medley of approaches: Berkeley-Hill's imperial psychoanalysis, Pitt-Rivers' odd fusion of a sort of old-fashioned Darwinian population genetics and Jungian personality typing, Hoernle's provisional rejection of innate race differences and Lugard's 'separate but equal' aspirations.

DISCUSSION

While much race-related material has been identified here, it should by now be clear that the notion of any homogeneously racist orientation evaporates on systematic inspection. At the most one can say that vestiges of classic Scientific Racism are still present in the early 1920s in the writings of the discipline's elder figures and that conformity to conventional racist expressions like 'savage' is widespread. Even the revisionist Scientific Racism associated with the continental theories of 'primitive mentality' finds little support. The conclusion is inescapable: there was no real interest in racial issues in domestic British Psychology during this period comparable either in extent or approach to the kinds of research present in the USA. Coverage of the topic is too heterogeneous in character and too scattered in provenance to amount to anything like a coherent project. British psychologists were not of course entirely devoid of interest in 'race'. Psychometricians like Burt, Spearman and Cattell happily accepted the pro-race differences findings of their US counterparts at face value. Others, such as Read, Stout (and, by implication, Mace) and Ogden endorsed older Scientific Racist images of 'savage' character and irrationality, but with scant reference to contemporary work. Among the new generation, McDougall endorsed this tradition but with his 1920 emigration ceased to be an active player on the British scene, Cattell's ideological convictions seem to have been successfully segregated from his professional Psychology (and he too had gone to the USA before World War II broke out). Colonially based psychologists paid the topic more attention, but excepting Oliver and the India-based psychoanalysts it would be hard to pin the charge of racism (as opposed to racialism) on any of those discussed here. Their work was also often published in the USA or in the country where they were based rather than in British journals. Finally, the eugenicists who received wisdom suggests were deeply embroiled in the issue also prove to be neither consistent nor very productive, and more concerned with biological race crossing than psychological race differences.

Without for a moment denying that some British psychologists held racist attitudes, that many conformed to the cultural racism of the times, or that eugenics-related psychometrics was implicitly racist throughout, the fact remains that precious little of this is on paper. The close historical connection between Galtonian scientific racist eugenics and the psychometric tradition within Psychology has, I suggest, somewhat confused the current historiographic picture, while the mighty Pearson and Moul monograph is something of a red herring. (Billig's account requires some modification here. British Galtonian psychometrics may well be implicitly racist, and inclined to support race differences findings, from 1913–40 however it rarely engaged race issues directly at all as far as active research was concerned, its implicit racism only resurfacing with the post-1969 Jensen controversy.) Nor however are the anti-racist or 'race prejudice' oriented camps much in evidence either.[72] While battle had been joined among geneticists and anthropologists (e.g. in J. Huxley and A.C. Haddon, 1935), professionally most British psychologists appear to be quite disengaged from the controversy during the 1930s.

If my account is correct we are bound to ask – why the somewhat fitful and dilettante nature of British Psychology's interest in 'race'? Two answers suggest themselves. First, British Psychology was in no position to tackle the issue directly. Immigrant groups were simply too small and localised to present social problems sufficiently great to attract psychologists into looking either at 'race differences' or 'race relations'. Notwithstanding the high level of anti-semitism in some quarters of British society, neither psychologists nor eugenicists were inclined to support it. This is hardly surprising: Myers, one of the discipline's most eminent figures throughout this period, had largely funded the Cambridge Department from his own pocket, and Jewish organisations were among those funding eugenics research. Insofar as the issue was dealt with in British Psychological Society publications, it was certainly from the opposite direction.

The second answer is a little more complex. British contact with non-Europeans across its ever-illuminated empire placed rather different demands on those white Britons dealing with them than were being faced by US whites. After World War I the easy racism of 19th century colonials became difficult to sustain for a variety of reasons. Independence movements were increasingly assertive and ever greater familiarity with indigenous cultures (along with the trauma of World War I) was creating an ambivalence about blanket notions of primitiveness and universal white superiority. Insofar as the British had dutifully discharged their 'white man's burden' civilising mission they were also now confronted with growing numbers of educated, fluent, sometimes even Oxbridge-educated, representatives of the 'savage races' whom they ruled (such as Jomo Kenyatta). The urgent need to inculcate patriotic loyalty to the British Empire in all its subjects could only be successfully met if racist attitudes and beliefs, however deeply felt, were reined in. An often absurd and patronising paternalism became the order of the day.[73] This was of course racist in viewing black people as inferior and childlike, but it was a very different kind of racism to that prevalent before 1914. Nobody any longer proposed that genocide and racial subjugation were simply the way natural selection operated among humans. Just as the domineering Victorian father-role had, by the 1930s, been replaced by a friendly (but still sexist) pipe-smoking 'daddy' on the middle-class home front, so the Great White Father role also changed (but remained racist) in the colonies. And as Britain's imperial grip weakened, the felt need to live up to the official 'civilising mission' ideology intensified.[74] In this political context the development and open formulation of racist ideas could have little place, even if private attitudes and policy were being guided by racist assumptions. Educated Africans and West Indians, let alone Indians, were now capable of reading, and – verbally if not so easily in print – replying to, white-authored discourse. The underlying hypocrisies would come home to roost a quarter century later, but in the meantime, I suggest, the inter-war political climate in the British Empire genuinely inhibited the overt articulation of racist ideas at an intellectual, cultural, level.[75] It would nonetheless be absurd to dispute that an underlying 'cultural racism' remained in place at home and that racism – of a variety of kinds – was rife among expatriates in the colonies.

Indeed the nature of British 'cultural racism' is rather illuminated by this material. Three things in particular are rather striking, which if present in most

US and European writers, become especially visible in the peculiarly conflicted British context just sketched. First the persistence of the use of the language of 'lower races', 'primitive', 'uncivilised' and 'savage' to characterise non-European cultures and peoples. This is true even in discourses wherein the very basis for such evaluative comparisons is being explicitly undermined. There seems to be little consciousness of the need for linguistic-level reform in the anti-racist camp, who appear then to have no other terms available for referring to the people in question. The only glimmer of light comes in the late 1930s with the attempt, by Julian Huxley in particular, to replace 'race' itself with 'ethnic group'. Secondly, related to this, is the continued acceptance of the old Galtonian assumption that European civilisation *is* civilisation *per se*. While anxieties are sometimes expressed about the threat to 'native' cultures posed by unwise attempts at over-hasty imposition of Western civilisation, the notion that white civilisation is in principle the universally applicable most advanced lifestyle is never seriously contested. Even in Pitt-Rivers' work, the task is to facilitate 'adaptation' to, and eventual adoption of, this lifestyle. Again the Galtonian echoes are clear. Nobody spots that a central feature of this civilisation is precisely its colonialist character.

The third aspect is subtler, it is what I would call a 'ground-level' view of things. Nobody remotely foresaw the colossal impacts which technological advances in global mobility, mass media and economic globalisation, were about to exert. It remained a world of basically autonomous, geographically localised, 'races' and cultures slowly having to reach mutual accommodations with one another. The distant end-result was indeed that they would all 'rise' to the European condition, but at the same time they possessed separate 'destinies' regarding how they did this, and to some extent regarding the end-result (some may yet be doomed to extinction). The flaw here is not so much that they were wrong as that events were proceeding at a pace of a far higher order of magnitude, and in far more complicated fashion than they could appreciate. Nor could they see that the very psychological changes these events would universally entail would render many of their central assumptions obsolete. Whatever camp they were in, their perspective was premised on the belief in the psychological continuity of the 'character' of the 'races', ethnic groups, nations or whatever involved. This is true even when, intellectually, they subscribe to some 'social constructionist' theoretical position. In short, they remained Earth-bound. It was a world of sea-lanes, railway tracks, maps and travel, not one of satellite photos, air-line routes, Internet and tourism.

British Psychology's lack of sustained overt engagement with either 'race' or racism during these years appears then to be multi-determined; the discipline itself was preoccupied with issues closer to home, such as industrial psychology, education, and child development, while the cultural and political climate was exerting an inhibiting effect. In the 1930s most discourse on race in Britain was coming from the anti-colonialist, anti-racist political left and its allies within academia, but relatively few among the latter appear to have written on the topic in the capacity of professional psychologist.

A broader concluding point needs also to be made. Despite a general recognition that knowledge is historically and culturally situated, the still sparse historiography of Psychology's involvement with race and racism has invariably lumped the British and US stories together. Most of this work has been directed at uncovering Psychology's racist past and been content to rhetorically cite supporting texts regardless of historical or cultural context. The material presented here makes it clear that British and US psychologists differed fundamentally in their treatment (or non-treatment) of racial questions, and this indeed reflects their differing historical and cultural situations. While British Psychology certainly sought on occasion to serve the imperialist 'civilising mission', the kind of 'racism' this entailed was quite dissimilar to that espoused by hard-line Race Psychologists in the USA. Its goals were patronisingly paternalistic and it even on occasion aspired to protect 'primitive cultures' from disruption and destruction by over-rapid Europeanisation and Eurocentric colonial policies. The 'primitive as child' trope can, we should ponder, be deployed in a variety of ways and to several different ends. (Let us also not forget that throughout the period, both within Psychology and Western cultures at large, a number of often inconsistent images of the meaning of childhood were in play. They remain so.)[76]

One might go further. The situation again seems amenable to a reflexive interpretation in that we might wonder how far the perennial middle-class British inability to consciously admit to racism has its psychological roots in this inter-war era of self-consciously benevolent paternalism, which those on the home-front, like some on the receiving end too, naively took at face value.[77] US debates on racial issues have, if nothing else, always been open and up-front. In Britain, by contrast, when such debates became unavoidable after the 1950s, 'race' was treated with embarrassment, denial and a degree of honest bewilderment that accusations of racism should even be levelled. Racism, Britons had learned, was a foreign vice – of Americans with their 'colour bar' and Germans with their anti-semitism. Thus the present account may be read as signifying how British Psychology reflected a psychological repression of race issues in the culture at large. This was a dramatic reversal of the pre-1914 situation when British scientists were in the forefront of Scientific Racist theorising, but by the 1930s, trying to retain a grip on its gloriously multi-cultural empire and confronted by rampant Nazi racism, Britain was in a very different pickle. A self-consciously 'decent' ethnic ecumenicism invoking images of the Empire as a great multi-racial family seemed to most the only viable psychological option. And it was, by and large, the only viable Psychological option too. What was confessed in the privacy of all-white male clubs and academic common rooms was another matter.

NOTES

1 M. Billig (1981), D. Howitt and J. Owusu-Bempah (1994).
2 See e.g. M. Freeden (1979).
3 Since precocity of development in white children is always considered a sign of high intelligence, its interpretation as signifying the opposite in black children (even if it were true) has always been paradoxical. This has not been widely noticed.
4 See Chapter 6.
5 'Editorial comments on Mr Mudge's Article', *Eugenics Review* (1920) 12, 38–39; 'Notes on the Article by Dr Seligman' ibid., 39–40.

6 See Barkan (1992, pp. 59–65) for a review of Fleure's position. While an important figure in the history of British academic treatment of 'race', Fleure cannot be considered significant for the Psychological side of the story and will not be discussed further here. As an example of an 'anti-racist racialist' his case reinforces the argument that 'racialism' and 'racism' need to be kept distinct.

7 See above p. 109.

8 See above Chapter 4, n. 82.

9 This proposal was eagerly adopted by M.F. Ashley Montagu (1942).

10 Notably J.C. Trevor (1938).

11 Arguably another relevant paper is E.N. Fallaize (1925, see above Chapter 6, n. 1). This however is more anthropological than Psychological and does not pertain to innate race differences.

12 He accepts that Jews have a higher incidence of insanity, particularly 'neurasthenia' and hysteria. This belief was common among Jews, so cannot be dismissed as a racist slur. It was effectively refuted by B. Malzberg in a succession of papers (1930, 1931, 1936c).

13 He does not cite these in full, but they appear to be findings incorporated in broader immigration studies rather than studies specifically on Jews – of which I have not located any from this period. See J. Rumyaneck (1931) for a slightly later full review of this research.

14 This was a group test of 60 items devised by Godfrey Thomson, initially for identifying gifted children. Originally published as G. Thomson (1921) an account may be found in P.B. Ballard (1923, Chapter V). A fuller technical account appeared simultaneously: M. Davis and A.G. Hughes (1927).

15 See Cambridge University Press Catalogue, 1938. Five series of publications are listed: *Eugenics Laboratory Memoirs* (28, including the multi-volume *The Treasury of Human Inheritance*), *Eugenics Laboratory Lectures* (14) (12 by Pearson), *Questions of the Day and of the Fray* (12), *Drapers Company Research Memoirs* (14) (only 11 listed in this source), *Biometric Series* (12).

16 It should be noted however that the 1905 Aliens Act had sought to restrict immigration on racial grounds, and was aimed against Jews in particular. Clearly this was not the result of eugenic concerns alone but reflected broader anxieties of the kind Mudge voices.

17 There had been a substantial immigration scare in Britain during the pre-1914 period aimed primarily at East European Jews fleeing pogroms. Racist attacks on Jews and Chinese also erupted occasionally (notably in Wales), and 1919 saw the first major anti-black 'race riot' in Liverpool. Unlike in the USA, however, psychologists, aside from Pearson in this paper, do not seem ever to have become significantly engaged in the matter. Three Aliens Acts of increasing severity were passed in 1905, 1914 and 1919.

18 In the USA the importance of linguistic handicap in immigrant performance on intelligence tests had been raised the previous year by Margaret Mead in M. Mead, (1927). This, as is discussed later, was a topic first addressed by British psychologists, and Mead drew on their work. Rumyaneck (1931) was also especially scathing about Pearson and Moul's research, enumerating six basic flaws, which all seem to remain valid (see p. 409).

19 Pearson's role in the history of Psychology is primarily as the statistician responsible for inventing some of its most widely used statistics, notably the χ^2 and the correlation coefficient 'r'. His own research centred on genetics and heredity, not on psychological topics *per se*. Even in the research programme in question here non-psychological physiological and morphological traits predominated. I am thus reluctant to call Pearson a psychologist.

20 See Bibliography for principal works by W.H.R. Rivers. All from 1923 were published posthumously, edited and prefaced by G. Elliot Smith, although the contents had

sometimes appeared previously. Rivers (1923a) also includes an 'Appreciation' by C.S. Myers.

21 This view had been advanced in S. Freud's *Totem and Taboo* (1950, 1st edn 1918).

22 See Appendix II to Rivers (1923b) where Elliot Smith seeks to rectify what he believes may be a misunderstanding of Rivers' position in Chapter IX 'Dream and psycho-neurosis'. For a fuller version of Elliot Smith's rejection of the Freud/Jung position see 'Ethnology and psychology. A note on "The aims of ethnology"', a supplementary chapter to Rivers (1923a) in which Rivers' 'The aims of ethnology' appeared. In this Rivers adopts an almost party-line diffusionist position.

23 See I. Langham (1981) for a full account. Quite *how* wholeheartedly he accepted Elliot Smith's 'Egyptian origins' position is a matter of debate, R. Slobodin (1978) for exam-ple suggests that Elliot Smith, in his posthumous editing, distorted Rivers' position. That he *did* become a diffusionist is undeniable.

24 Elliot Smith's own position on race is not entirely clear. He was certainly strongly opposed to Nordicism. He also, consistently with his diffusionism, rejected the exist-ence of psychological universals, but this in itself could be construed in two ways: (a) as meaning that cultural differences had no biological basis and (b) that major innate psychological differences between peoples were highly possible. See R. Slobodin (1978, p. 150, where references refuting an accusation of rabid racism by Glyn Daniel are provided) and G. Elliot Smith (1932).

25 See e.g. his paper 'The primitive conception of death' in Rivers (1926, 36–50).

26 W. McDougall (1908). This had reached its 23rd edition by 1936 and was by far the most successful of his works.

27 For fuller discussions of Bartlett's career and its contradictions see A. Costall (1991, 1992, 1995). Bartlett's entry in C. Murchison (1936) is disappointing for our purposes, being mostly a programmatic statement of his view of Psychology rather than auto-biography. While quite critical regarding contemporary Psychology, his earlier social constructionist tendency is no longer much in evidence and though referring to his initial attraction to anthropology it contains no mention of *Psychology and Primitive Culture*. Incidentally, H. Kuklick (in press) 'Islands in the Pacific: Darwinian bio-geography and British anthropology' notes a resemblance between the 'serial repro-duction' method Bartlett used in his memory research and Haddon's earlier studies of the evolution of artistic style.

28 The only later Bartlett papers on the topic I have identified are F.C. Bartlett (1927, 1937), in the former of which he reasserts more concisely the position taken in *Psychology and Primitive Culture*.

29 See A. Kuper (1973) for a summary of Malinowski's role and theoretical position, insofar as he had one. 'The underlying psychological theory was an ill-considered mix of McDougall's "instincts" and Shand's "sentiments", each searching out an appro-priate expression' (p. 45). This would suggest that he might have found Bartlett's account congenial, but he rarely if ever cites it – perhaps its Cambridge provenance was too much for him.

30 In C.S. Myers (1937, pp. 131–3) he makes a plea for the social psychological study of 'primitive' communities as a protective safe-guarding exercise against 'the present dangers of having a European culture blindly forced upon them' (p. 131).

31 In addition to his well-known major works Malinowski published two short mono-graphs from a Psychological angle: B. Malinowski (1926b, 1927a)

32 M. Grant (1916). For a while this was extremely influential in promoting Nordicism in the USA. Grant was a close associate of Davenport (see Barkan, 1992).

33 The most effective refutation of this was O. Klineberg (1935a).

34 These photos appear to have acquired some notoriety among black psychologists at least, see e.g. L. Hicks (1969).

35 C. Murchison (1930, p. 213).

36 His *Mind* review of Freud's *Totem and Taboo* (W. McDougall, 1920b) is of interest primarily in its scepticism about the primal horde and universality of the Oedipus

complex: 'there are limits to our credulity beyond which the glamour and prestige of the Freudian psychology cannot and should not carry us; and in this matter, I think, those limits have been surpassed' (p. 349). He also contributed to 'Racial mental differences. Joint discussion with the anthropological section of the British Association' in 1924 (McDougall, 1925b). W. McDougall (1925a) has an 11-page chapter on 'The Negro problem' in which he prevaricates as to whether 'Negroes' are less evolved but rejects integration and racial mixing in favour of a territorial solution in the Southern USA, Africa or New Guinea ('occupied by only a few scattered and savage branches of the Negro race' (p. 164)) – this would be a long due act of reparation for the original injustice of slavery. In W. McDougall (1934) he briefly reiterates the existence of racial differences and goes so far as to claim that in the Torres Straits, 'I was able to demonstrate certain large differences between ourselves and the oceanic negroes in respect of sensory endowment' (p. 184). This is a gross exaggeration, and such differences as he found were open to other explanations (see Chapter 3 above).

37 See also Bartlett (1921), a negative review which also contains hints of the ideas soon to appear in *Psychology and Primitive Culture*.

38 See Tucker (1994) especially pp. 239–49, from which the following is largely drawn. Readers suspecting I am overstating the case are referred to this well-documented discussion which is replete with bloodcurdling quotes. See also Billig (1981) for brief coverage of Cattell's racism.

39 See Tucker, 1994, p. 241; the quote is from Cattell (1933).

40 See Tucker, 1994, pp. 248–9. The *Beyondism* book was 'vigorously promoted and distributed by Wilmot Robertson's Howard Allen Press', though 'received little attention in the scientific community'. Robertson lamented Hitler's 'failure', and drew directly on Cattell's work to devise a plan for restricting US minority 'races' to their own enclaves – a plan taken up by leading US Nazi, David Duke's, National Association for the Advancement of White People in the *NAAWP News*.

41 This book was reprinted as late as 1946.

42 C. Read (1914, 1915, 1916, 1917, 1918).

43 Born in 1848, Read was in his mid-sixties when the first of these papers appeared and over seventy when his book was published.

44 No affiliation is provided for these authors.

45 Róheim's paper argues that the apparent ignorance of the male role in procreation among the Australian Aranda is an illusion, Aranda children are aware of it and it becomes suppressed. Seligman argues that 'mental derangement' in Papua New Guinea is primarily caused by contact with whites, although the people are normally extremely excitable.

46 See T. Kushner (1989) on the persistence of British cultural anti-semitism during World War II.

47 Chronologically these are: D.J. Saer (1922), F. Smith (1923), D.J. Saer (1924), E.M. Barke (1933), E.M. Barke and D.E. Parry Williams (1938).

48 See above p. 125.

49 R.A.C. Oliver (1932b, c, 1933–4).

50 See T.R. Garth (1931b, Chapter 9), P.R. Farnsworth (1938) for criticism of the use of the Seashore musical ability tests.

51 This had, for instance, been spelled out in J. Peterson (1923a).

52 The brain size data was obtained from *post mortem* examination of 351 adult males, the pyramidal cell layer data from 35 adult male hospital patients. It should perhaps be stressed that according to S.J. Gould (1984, p. 112) the measurement of brain size and weight is so fraught with methodological difficulties that we still do not know 'as if it mattered' whether African and European brain sizes are significantly different. It is perhaps doubtful whether pyramidal cell layer comparisons are any easier.

53 From extensive research on effects of ablation of rat brains Lashley concluded that brain functioning was not localised except in very broad terms, functioning of removed areas could be taken over by remaining parts. This he called 'equipotentiality'. Subsequent

research has largely refuted the applicability of this to humans except in a very quali-fied fashion. In the early 1930s, however, this work was receiving wide attention and acclaim so Oliver's invocation of it to support his position was a smart rhetorical move. The key text is K.S. Lashley (1929). Most of Lashley's relevant work was in journal paper form, but much of it was reprinted in K.S.Lashley (1960).

54 This is possibly a bit on the generous side – he relies rather heavily on T.R. Garth (1930a) in places, and his referencing is never extensive.

55 The Carnegie Foundation was a major funder of Race Psychology research until the late 1930s, supporting C.B. Davenport and S.D. Porteus for example. In 1937, how-ever, they had a change of heart and provided the financial backing for the massive five-year study overseen by Gunnar Myrdal which adopted an essentially anti-race dif-ferences stance. (See the Foreword and Preface in G. Myrdal, 1944.) Oliver became Professor of Education at the University of Manchester in 1938. His little book on educational research (Oliver, 1946) makes no reference to this African work although he clearly remained wedded to the psychometric approach.

56 See below Chapter 8 for discussion of Carothers.

57 The India Bureau of Education had also published a 'Provisional Series of Mental Tests for Indian Scholars (Binet Revision)' in 1924, and a revised series based on the Stanford Binet in 1930. I have not been able to inspect these or compare them with Rice's scale.

58 Notably by W. Hudson (1960, 1967).

59 R.H. Thouless (1937, p. 447). He devotes one page to the whole issue.

60 See M.H. Segall et al. (1966, pp. 55–60) for further evaluation of the Thouless and Beveridge research.

61 He also undertook some studies of perception in Nigeria, reported in Nadel (1937b). For a brief sketch of Nadel's career and subsequent position see the 'Memoir' by Meyer Fortes in S.F. Nadel (1957). Nadel, an Austrian emigré, had studied under Moritz Schlick and Karl Bühler. The work discussed here represents an early phase in his work. His mature theoretical position as an anthropologist is beyond the remit of the present book.

62 The quote is from Bartlett (1932, p. 255).

63 Nadel (1937b) is really an essay review of Ruth Benedict (1961, 1st edn 1934), Margaret Mead (1935) and Gregory Bateson (1958, 1st edn 1936). It discusses the problems of applying typological approaches to cultures and is generally supportive of these authors.

64 They also note 'It is conceivable that under a culture which would place greater emphasis upon affective performance there might be correspondingly less concern with matters which seem to us of major importance' (p. 352).

65 Fortes, like Nadel, was, although an anthropologist, interested in psychological topics, publishing for example Fortes (1938). Both were thus rebuilding the bridge between the disciplines which had been burned following Rivers' death.

66 This was retained in subsequent editions including the Pelican of 1944.

67 This had appeared in L. Lévy-Bruhl (1927).

68 F.G. Crookshank (1931) (a much briefer first edition appeared in 1924). Crookshank was a leading British Adlerian and had also written a number of medical works for Ogden's *Psyche Miniature* series. His theory was never taken seriously by any of the palaeontologists concerned with human evolution.

69 Stout, born in 1860, was thus nearly seventy when this appeared.

70 Space considerations preclude discussion of more peripheral literature. Two works worth noting, however, are Cynthia Playne's *Neuroses of Nations* (1925) and R.N. Bradley's more popularly pitched *Racial Origins of British Character* (1926). The first is an earnest but somewhat rambling effort at diagnosing the psychological roots of World War I, comparing, as it were, their 'psychohistories'. While drawing on much of the same kind of psychiatric and Psychological work as Le Bon it is, however, couched in entirely non-racial terms. An ambitious, original and well-researched, if

often confused and repetitive, work it deserves fresh attention. The latter, while telling a thoroughly racialist tale, does not seek to set any of the familiar trio of European racial stocks (Nordic, Alpine, Mediterranean) on a pedestal and depicts the British character as a happy fusion of their best features.

71 This image has arisen from the use later made of his data on heritability of IQ by A.R. Jensen etc. (see Chapter 9).

72 The earliest British journal paper I have found on prejudice is S.P. Adinarayaniah (1941).

73 See e.g. A.R. Paterson (1934) (written for Kenyans) among what must be a considerable comparable literature. This work is written in what now sounds like a parody of great-white-father-speak, pitching off with:

> This is a book about health, about healthy children, and healthy houses and healthy cattle, and good crops, and about the real uses of schools and the real uses of cattle. This book is written for the Akikuyu and the Luo, the Akamba and the Waswahili, the Wakisii and the Tiriki, the Maragoli and the Wameru and the Waemu, and the Giriama and the Wadigo and the Waduruma, and the Wateiti and the Wataveta, and for the Masai. It is written for all the people of Africa.

74 J.H. Driberg (1929) represents something of this mentality, as well as presenting what is, in effect, a plea for the value of anthropology. He ends:

> If we persist in the belief that the savage is an irrational creature and that his institutions are valueless because they are unlike our own, no amount of goodwill and sympathy will make our administration acceptable to him. We have to realise what the savage is before we can hope to eliminate friction: we must have a full knowledge, not only of his institutions and beliefs, but of what lies behind his institutions and beliefs. The savage as he really is is not an academic problem, but a very concrete and urgent reality. (p. 76)

75 The South African situation was already far more tangled than this, but most South African Psychological research was published either in South Africa or the USA. Verwoerd, the architect of apartheid was a professional psychologist by training. See Howitt and Owusu-Bempah (1994, pp. 144–6) for more on South African Psychology.

76 See G. Richards (1996, Chapter 13) and J. Cleverley and D. Phillips (1988). Ivan Ward (Kovel, 1988, p. xlvi) also raises the point, from a psychoanalytic perspective, that the black = child equation requires further interrogation.

77 Older West Indian readers, for example, will not need to be reminded of the degree of fervent imperial loyalty exhibited by the British-ruled Caribbean population up to and during World War II. This middle-class inability to recognise racism would surely have been reinforced by the British class system, being comparable to their inability to acknowledge that they were oppressing the maid who still slept in the attic of most middle-class homes into the 1930s, rising at 6 a.m. to black the grate. See A. Dummet (1973) for a fuller treatment of the topic of English racism.

Chapter 8

Racism at bay: Psychology and 'race' 1945–69

The immediate post-war years were dominated by two historical factors which, with a few exceptions, effectively suppressed whatever aspirations towards overtly racialist theorising and research were left within mainstream Psychology: the Holocaust and the US Civil Rights movement. This suppression was reinforced by the continued elaboration of those alternative 'paradigms' identified previously, particularly the culture and personality school and the study of 'race prejudice' in Social Psychology. In the USA moreover, the 'applied and intra-racial' genre had initiated what is today known as 'Black Psychology', albeit small in size and as yet insufficiently intellectually secure to radically challenge orthodox methodologies and conceptual frameworks. Even if somewhat lethargically, professional Psychology's ethnic composition was also diversifying. More generally, the 1940s saw the 'nature–nurture' issue acquire clear-cut ideological connotations, adherence to nativist positions becoming seen as inherently right-wing and racist. During the period under consideration here overt racism was clearly at bay within US Psychology. At the same time, anti-racist Psychology's understanding of the issue can now be seen to have retained a considerable degree of naivety, the erosion of which began in earnest in the 1970s. By the 1990s it is apparent, as we will be seeing, that a host of implicitly racist and ethnocentric assumptions persisted undiagnosed among many of even the most anti-racist psychologists.

The discussion will be organised around five principal topics. First, the meta-morphosis of the Culture and Personality approach into Cross-cultural Psychology will be considered, continuing the story begun in Chapter 5. Secondly, we will look at the continuing 'prejudice' tradition in Social Psychology and the impact of 'authoritarianism' theory, which leads into the third, broader, issues of the role of Social Psychology in the US Civil Rights movement and studies of 'Negro personality'. Fourthly the residual continuation of race-differences work will be considered. Moving to a more general level, the 'nativism = racism' doctrine will be briefly examined before a concluding interpretation of the post-war phase. The date of 1969 is taken as the cut-off date because it (a) sees the publication of Arthur Jensen's work on race differences in IQ which broke the post-1940 anti-racialist consensus and (b) sees the arrival of a more self-consciously 'Black' Psychology in the USA, the Association of Black Psychologists being founded in 1968.

FROM CULTURE AND PERSONALITY TO CROSS-CULTURAL PSYCHOLOGY

The immediate post-war years witnessed a massive expansion in interest in exploring psychological issues in non-European cultures. Initially this primarily took the form of a continued development of the Culture and Personality approach, with its neo-Freudian theoretical orientation predominating. This is especially apparent in the annual *Psychoanalysis and the Social Sciences* founded in 1947. The first volume contains papers by Clyde Kluckhohn and Geza Róheim, as well as one by H.M. Spitzer on the Japanese, which typically deploys a psychoanalytic framework to pathologise Japanese national character. Prior to his death in 1960 Kluckhohn and Abram Kardiner had become the major figures in this (Kluckhohn collaborating with personality theorist Henry Murray), alongside Margaret Mead, Erik Erikson, Cora DuBois, Ralph Linton, and Róheim, a now veteran Freudian anthropologist. Kardiner and Associates (1945) provides a useful starting point for assessing the interests and position of this school at the onset of peace. Subsequent developments may be tracked through, for example, Kluckhohn and Murray (1949), and B.B. Whiting (1963).[1]

The relative decline in the popularity of psychoanalysis during the 1950s, coupled with increasingly problematic relationships between the school and other branches of anthropology, were soon placing the project under strain. Meanwhile other psychologists, both American and British, were extending their more orthodox research fields to include non-European subjects. Gustav Jahoda (1966) and A.C. Mundy-Castle (1966), for example, undertook research on perception (in Ghana), an interest matched in the USA by M.H. Segall et al. (1963, 1966). Field dependence, cognitive development in the child, language and achievement motivation similarly attracted attention from around 1960, while the cross-cultural applicability of tests remained a perennial theme. By the 1960s the field was becoming known as Psychological Anthropology in the US and Cross-cultural Psychology in Britain. These are, nonetheless, not entirely synonymous. The former signifies a much closer inter-disciplinary connection and higher degree of anthropological concern as such than the latter, which typically involved undertaking standard type Psychological experiments in non-European settings – procedures only being changed insofar as practically necessary.

For the most part this work was not being conducted within any explicit racialist framework. The culture and personality school continued to focus on the notion that a society's cultural and child-rearing practices yielded a particular type of core personality structure. The others were concerned with the generalisability of Western theories and models to other cultures and empirically identifying cross-cultural variation in psychological phenomena which had come to prominence in Western experimental Psychology. In some cases (e.g. the perception and field-dependency work) they were taking up where pre-war researchers (e.g. Nadel, Thouless and Beveridge) had left off. The long-term goal was often to discover genuine psychological universals while accepting a broadly culturally relativist perspective. As we have previously discussed, this aim was far from straightforward, for the maintenance of the latter stance tended to render such universals ever more elusive.

If non-racialist, the stance adopted by most cross-cultural researchers during this period thus remained, often unwittingly, Euro-centric. The fact that the new generation of researchers was by and large highly sophisticated regarding issues of cultural bias and so on rendered their Euro-centrism far more opaque than in Torres Straits days. It took two major forms. First, research interests had been determined by Western Psychological concerns. This means that whereas in Europe and North America Psychological research emerges from the psychological preoccupations of the society at large, Psychological research undertaken in other cultures by Europeans and North Americans does not. The very quests for universals and interest in cultural relativism were issues arising within Western p/Psychology. The Psychologists did not, as they did at home, actually *represent* the communities they were studying. Secondly, the habit of taking white performance as the norm could prove difficult to shake off. M. Gerber's widely cited 1958 study of African children's 'psycho-motor' development, for example, has recently attracted attention in this respect.[2] The finding that African children's psycho-motor development is faster than that of white children is construed as displaying their precocity or acceleration, rather than white retardation.

By the end of the 1960s a vast amount of cross-cultural data had fed into certain areas of mainstream Psychology, notably on child-development and gender differences (in which J. and B.B. Whiting were especially productive),[3] perception and linguistics.[4] Social Psychology textbooks now typically discussed cultural influences on perception, the lengthy snow vocabularies of the Inuit and rice vocabularies of Phillipine Islanders, and child-rearing methods ranging from permissive to ferocious. While we cannot explore this in detail here it should be noted that its effect turned out, in the long run, to be double-edged. Part of the intention behind acquainting students with this material was to overcome ethnocentrism and facilitate an ability to distance themselves from their own cultures. Since the target readership for whom the texts were written was primarily a white US undergraduate one, the discourse itself nevertheless remained ethnocentric in that authors identified with the assumptions, values and attitudes of that group. The original intention was thus subverted by the very nature of the genre itself, and the real effect was all too often to exoticise rather than familiarise, to enhance rather than reduce the otherness of the peoples under discussion.[5] This was made worse by the fact that some at least of the accounts of other cultures were already dated or remained affected by the ethnocentrism of the original observers, so that when encountered by people from those cultures (as they increasingly were) they read as inaccurate and bizarre.[6]

A thorough review of cross-cultural Psychology and associated ethnicity issues cannot be provided here. For present purposes the central point to be made is that while cross-cultural psychologists ostensibly identified with the anti-racist cause, the net effect of their work was oddly ambiguous. This was inevitable perhaps as long as those within the subdiscipline remained mostly white North American and European, working to agendas set by US and European Psychology. Secondary mediation of their work via teaching texts only exacerbated the ambiguity. We will be returning to the bearing of the cross-cultural approach on views of the African American later.

THE AUTHORITARIAN PERSONALITY

If, hitherto, European psychologists rarely found cause to consider the nature of racism, the Holocaust dramatically placed the issue centre-stage. The Dutch psychologist Meerloo and a few psychoanalytic writers had begun discussing anti-semitism in the late 1930s and early 1940s, but only when the dust of war had settled was a concerted attack on the problem possible. Following a 1944 conference, the American Jewish Committee sponsored a series of 'Studies in Prejudice' under the general editorship of Max Horkheimer and S. H. Flowerman, of which three works, all published in 1950, were especially influential within Psychology: N.W. Ackerman and Marie Jahoda's[7] *Anti-Semitism and Emotional Disorder: A Psychoanalytic Interpretation*, Bruno Bettelheim and Morris Janovitz's *Dynamics of Prejudice*, and the two-volume *The Authoritarian Personality* by T.W. Adorno, Else Frenkel-Brunswik, Daniel J. Levinson and R. Nevitt Sanford. Of these *The Authoritarian Personality* had the most profound long-term impact. It was arguably these analyses, rather than the earlier prejudice studies, which most firmly consolidated the view of prejudice as an individual level psychopathology. It should, though, be emphasised that this focus was a consciously made decision on the grounds of the need to tackle anti-semitism at an individual educational level. In fact the two other volumes in the series addressed the social dimension and it would be wrong to ascribe indifference to the socio-economic roots of anti-semitism – or racism in general – to the psychologists engaged in this work. Rather, what happened was that within Psychology the comprehensive range of the 'Studies in Prejudice' volumes taken as a whole was later lost sight of, and the essentially complementary nature of the works considered here ignored. We return to this point later. This Psychological work was, of course, only a small proportion of the broader post-war literature on the topic.[8]

Ackerman and Jahoda had begun publishing on anti-semitism from a psychoanalytic perspective in three earlier papers of the late 1940s,[9] along with Arthur Brenner (1948) and R.M. Lowenstein (1947). *Anti-Semitism and Emotional Disorder* was a case-study-based report attempting to identify in broad psychoanalytic terms the personality characteristics of US anti-semites. The cases included 27 reported by 25 New York-based psychoanalysts plus a further 13 from ongoing social service cases which it was felt went some way to balancing the bias in social class sampling, analysands tending to be from the wealthier sector. The authors are fairly frank about the inherent methodological limitations and problems of the study, but the basic consistency of the findings is felt to outweigh these.

The work eventually extends beyond the specific topic under consideration, developing towards the end into a vehement general critique of contemporary US society and culture. How this happens will become clearer as we proceed. In their 'General Foreword' the series editors uninhibitedly identify anti-semitism as a 'social disease',[10] while Carl Binger, in his Preface, spells out that 'The day is now past when the true scientists can be indifferent to ethical values and moral judgments' (p. xi). In the definitional preliminaries 'prejudice' is differentiated from 'prejudgment' and 'stereotyping' on the grounds that it involves 'irrational hostility' rooted in the individual's personality. While rather begging the question, this move serves to identify a specifically psychological component in anti-semitism, as distinct from its social aspects. It is also argued that in the US people have a 'free choice' about whether to be anti-semitic, by contrast with some other societies, which reinforces the relevance of the psychological, more specifically psychodynamic, level of analysis. While prejudice may be the social norm, it can never be normal in the psychiatric sense. The authors accept, in qualified fashion, that some Jewish 'national character' might exist, but stress that invoking this is always a rationalisation for, not a cause of, anti-semitism.[11]

The body of the text is organised around three levels at which attitudes are determined: the function of the attitude, its 'genetic' or developmental history in the individual, and circumstantial factors facilitating its behavioural expression. The first firm finding is that while anti-semites enter psychoanalysis with a wide range of problems, none seem to be suffering from deep depression. This, it is suggested, is because the guilt feelings and hostility towards the self which underly depression are, in the anti-semite's case, directed outward. Following this a whole catalogue of psychodynamic disorders come to light. These include diffuse and pervasive anxiety, confusion of the 'self' concept, difficulty in establishing 'mature and complete' relationships, conformity and fear of the different, 'vague, dull, indefinitely formed' perception of reality (sometimes verging on the psychotic), and lack of a consistent value system.

These in turn stem from almost universal deficiencies in the anti-semites' developmental circumstances: relations between parents are invariably poor with 'superficial respectability' overlying violence, quarrels, desertion, divorce, and so forth – there is little warmth or affection and the parents are mutually incompatible and hostile at basic levels. The anti-semite has usually been rejected by one or both parents and subject to brutal and inconsistent disciplining. The oedipal struggle has been intense, confused and unresolved and anti-semitism demonstrably serves almost the entire range of defence mechanisms. Projection, denial, avoidance of contact, displacement and so on can all be seen in operation but must be understood as interacting with one another as a system rather than working separately. In a few cases where anti-semitic feelings had emerged unexpectedly during analysis of liberal analysands a reaction-formation defence appeared to be operating – one (Gentile) for example with an enduring legacy of childhood polio had devoted his life to defending the 'weak' Jews, thereby sustaining a self-image as 'strong' by identifying with the plight of the 'weak', while unable to accept his own weakness.

The emerging picture therefore is of typical anti-semites as people who are stymied at every psychological turn, unable to see, understand or accept the true inner sources of their problems. Being emotionally isolated they envy the Jew's secure group identity; hankering to belong they despise the Jew's independence; unable to confront their weakness they view the Jew's weakness with contempt, because of their weakness they are paranoid about the Jew's strength and success; sexually frustrated, they see the Jew as libidinous and sexually active; unable to admit this frustration they see the Jew as castrated and puritanical. Traits like 'intelligence', 'self-discipline' and 'ambition' which are virtues in every other group become sinister when ascribed to the Jew. The glaring internal contradictions in the anti-semitic stereotype thus become comprehensible. Anti-semites essentially hate everything about themselves, and thus everything ascribable to the Jew becomes a source of hatred for them: they are dirty *and* obsessionally clean, clannish *and* loners, intrusive *and* seclusive, inferior *and* superior, lustful *and* 'castrated', mean *and* generous, loyal *and* treacherous and so on. (The authors observe that the internal contradictions in the anti-semitic stereotype of the Jew are far greater than those of the 'Negro' stereotype.) The catalogue of their flaws is a direct reflection of the extent of the anti-semite's own inner confusions. And this is applicable as much to Jewish anti-semites as Gentile ones, although the former have certain distinctive traits. While those entering psychoanalysis or coming to the attention of social services may be more extreme than others, some such mechanisms are operative in all cases of anti-semitic prejudice. (And, of course, none of the cases was in analysis or under social services attention because of their anti-semitism as such.)

The degrees and precise nature of anti-semitism do indeed vary, in particular between those whose anti-semitism is centred on a restricted number of stereotypic traits and those who buy the whole package. One should also differentiate between the individual whose anti-semitism is more or less accidental, for whom some other group would have served just as well in different circumstances, and those for whom it is rooted very specifically in the content of the anti-semitic stereotype. In the former case, the processes of social compliance are particularly marked.

The authors are, nonetheless, eventually driven beyond the details of anti-semitism. What the psychoanalytic case-studies reveal to them is a broader cultural situation highly congenial to the development of this 'social disease'. They thus shift from psychoanalytic to almost Marxian tones in launching an attack on the materialism, affectionless greed and emotional superficiality of contemporary life. Family life is crumbling, all human relationships construed in opportunistic and exploitative terms, and self-image has come to depend on monetarily determined social status. In a (Marxist) word, people are becoming increasingly *alienated* – both from others and themselves, and thus from any viable moral value system. We are engaged in a fight for nothing less than the 'survival of civilized mankind' (p. 94). The work thus anticipates and shares in the mood of much of the broader US social commentary of the 1950s concerned with 'status-seeking' and 'conformity'.

The Ackerman and Jahoda portrait of the anti-semite tended broadly to confirm the findings of E. Frenkel-Brunswik and R. Nevitt Sanford (1945), using questionnaire, Thematic Apperception and Rorschach Inkblot tests with 76 women subjects. These had already noted, for example, lack of internalised conscience and strict conventionality, anxiety, poor human relationship skills (these being construed in terms of dominance and submission, and ambivalence towards parental figures) and possibly 'paranoid' trends – all components of, or directly derivable from, Ackerman and Jahoda's model. Frenkel-Brunswik and Sanford identify a further distinction, however, between the 'typical' puritanical form of anti-semitism and that which characterised the Nazi leadership, which was definitely not puritanical. They suggest that whereas typical anti-semites project their id onto Jews, the Nazis by contrast projected the restricting super-ego and 'reasonable relativistic ego' onto them. Incidentally one of their subjects with very low anti-semitism was attracted to Jews precisely because she liked the negative attributes stereotypically ascribed to them.

Bettelheim and Janowitz's *Dynamics of Prejudice*, subtitled *A Psychological and Sociological Study of Veterans* was based on interviews conducted with 150 army veterans from Chicago. This too advanced a psychoanalytic model, though one slightly less elaborated than Ackerman and Jahoda's. The two distinctive features of this work were their classification of attitudes into four main types (Tolerant, Stereotyped, Outspoken, Intense) and a comparison of anti-semitic and anti-'Negro' prejudice. The classification perhaps suggests a dimension of personality, an individual's position being determined by the strength of their ego–defence mechanisms. In comparing the two varieties of prejudice they conclude that in the US anti-semitism differs from the European variety in that it is almost exclusively directed against the oppressive super-ego – the stereotypes of Jewish power, cunning, ambition and so on being most commonly invoked – while defence mechanisms against the id underly anti-Negro stereotypes (sexual promiscuity, dirtiness etc.). In Europe both are projected onto the Jew. This is somewhat at odds with the Frenkel-Brunswik and Sanford view in seeing US (like Nazi) anti-semitism as typically resulting from the oppressive super-ego. The availability of two distinct target groups in the US thus enables prejudiced individuals to divide their stereotypes into two blocs according to whether they are super-ego- or id-related. This mitigates in some degree, though not totally, the intrinsically contradictory contents of classic European anti-semitism previously noted.

The book also relates levels of intolerance to social mobility, socio-economic status and salary. Only regarding mobility did a clear relationship emerge, the upwardly mobile being markedly more tolerant. They thus suggest that social and economic background as such are less important than the current direction of the individual's economic fortunes. This relationship held for both anti-semitism and anti-'Negro' attitudes. The subjects were mostly blue-collar workers and taken overall their intolerance level was extremely high: only 8% being rated tolerant towards 'Negroes' and less than half (41%) tolerant towards Jews.[12] This may account in some part for the divergence from Frenkel-Brunswik and Sanford's findings (with women subjects) regarding the nature of anti-semitism's ego-defensive function.

While these two studies succeeded in elaborating on the psychoanalytic model of prejudice, neither achieved the influence of the third Psychological work in the series, *The Authoritarian Personality*. Recent historical studies on the origin of this research[13] have elucidated its somewhat ambiguous position. The prime motivators of the project (such as Horkheimer and Adorno) were in effect the Frankfurt Institute for Social Research in exile (housed in, but not formally managed by, Columbia University). Another leading figure in this Institute had been Erich Fromm, who had moved across to psychoanalysis and had published his highly successful *Escape from Freedom* (1941a) in which the authoritarian anti-democratic personality had also been identified. Here the plot thickens.

M. Horkheimer had edited a study of authoritarianism in the family in 1936 and Fromm, in 1929–31, had undertaken a partly questionnaire-based study of workers in the Weimar Republic under the Institute's auspices, but it had been rejected by Horkheimer as deviating too far from a Marxist approach towards humanistic psychoanalysis (he advised him to read Lenin). This remained unpublished until 1980 (1984 in English) and was unreferenced in the *Authoritarian Personality*. Even earlier, in 1912, A. Levenstein had published a questionnaire-based social psychological study of workers' attitudes for the Marxist German Social Democratic Party, while an archival search by the Institute's Hilde Weiss, Fromm's collaborator, turned up an 1880s questionnaire by Marx himself designed for circulation among French workers, which failed to come to fruition.[14] The trajectory of this succession of projects was a two-fold shift (a) from being focused on the demographic, economic and living conditions of workers to the almost entirely psychological content of *The Authoritarian Personality*'s battery of scales,[15] and (b) from politically engaged research, in which the very research process served a consciousness-raising function for the subjects, to a more objectified quasi-clinical diagnostic approach.

The members of the exiled Frankfurt School were, in 1950, anxious to cover their Marxist tracks, at least for the time being. This was partly for fear of appearing as a clique of foreign intellectuals interfering in US political questions and partly due to the delicate ideological climate in which they were working at the onset of the Cold War and McCarthyism. Nonetheless at least two of the California-based authors of *The Authoritarian Personality*, R. Nevitt Sanford and, less directly, Daniel Levinson, became embroiled in the notorious oath-taking controversy at Stanford University (led by the neo-behaviourist psychologist E.C. Tolman).[16]

All this helps illuminate the somewhat fuzzy nature of the way in which psychological and social factors are related in the authoritarianism literature. Roiser and Willig (1995) also note that those involved in the project were only partly academy-based (given the American Jewish Committee funding), as well as observing that their multi-disciplinary orientation has been obscured by the discipline- and US-centred nature of historical accounts. Indeed they find a relative neglect of the authoritarianism episode in most post-1970 reviews of Social Psychology's development, which, given its cultural impact and ramifications, is extraordinary.

We are perhaps drifting somewhat from the topic of racism, but it is of paramount importance to grasp the immediate context in which Adorno et al., and the other writers under discussion here, were working and the complex nature of the constraints under which they did so. As emerges from all three texts these, mostly exiled, psychologists were especially apprehensive that conditions were ripe in the USA for an upsurge of anti-semitism and fascism. They remembered from personal experience that anti-semitism had had a fairly low profile in Germany prior to 1930 and were desperate to fathom the psychological factors which rendered people susceptible to fascist and anti-semitic propaganda.[17] That these factors could in turn be explained, in part at least, by socio-economic and cultural ones was implicitly understood but could not easily be overtly articulated without risking the authors' marginalisation as Marxists – a silence which partly subverted the hope that their psychological-level diagnoses might have some genuine effect. Even so, each of the books includes some efforts towards incorporating the socio-economic dimension, Ackerman and Jahoda being the least inhibited about ascribing the deep roots of American anti-semitism to central features of US cultural and economic life. Coincidentally with the book's appearance Horkheimer and Adorno returned to Frankfurt and re-established the Institute, thereby further reducing any neo-Marxist 'critical philosophy' input into the ensuing fray.

As far as race prejudice is concerned, the impact of the authoritarianism work lies primarily in that it firmly consolidated the psychoanalytic model's place alongside, and in rivalry with, the more behaviouristic accounts developed by G.W. Allport and the attitude-measurement school of the pre-war years. They were able to build on and refine the ideas of Fenichel, Simmel and Fromm, and integrate the case-study approach with more US-style questionnaire-based methodologies. The resemblance between their scales and the typical US attitude-measurement variety is nonetheless deceptive, and it was to this that much of the immediate criticism was directed. As we have seen, they were in some respects covertly importing an independent European questionnaire tradition, one less centred on statistical and design issues than the US approach. The heart of the difference lay in a basic divergence in aims. US psychologists had conceptualised attitudes as relatively narrow and discrete factors affecting the individual's responses to specific classes of 'attitude objects'. Adorno et al., by contrast, are more interested in teasing out the individual's general world-view or ideology and discovering unities behind what might appear to be a quite diverse set of surface 'attitudes' in the US sense. Adorno et al. cite Sartre (1946) on the myth that anti-semitism is a discrete attitude, that an individual can be a good parent, generous, honest, hard-working and so on *and* just happen to be an anti-semite.[18] The way in which the authors' aims differ from those of more orthodox attitude research in this respect is clearly spelled out in the work's opening section. The study additionally used the Thematic Apperception Test technique, developed initially by Henry Murray, which lent itself to psychoanalytic interpretation. It would be over-simplistic to view the work as 'European Psychoanalysis meets US Attitude Research' – the authors included American psychoanalytic psychologists and the questionnaire design involved the Europeans.[19]

Why did *The Authoritarian Personality* so overshadow the two companion volumes? In the first place it was on a far larger scale and more methodologically ambitious, thus presenting a distinctively monumental aspect. Secondly, it moved beyond exploration of the psychodynamic roots of anti-semitism and ethno-centrism to proposing a distinct personality type – the authoritarian – in whom these various psychopathological mechanisms were embodied. Introduction of this new label (though the authors did not coin it) facilitated the adoption of the work as a focus of debate in a way which the other works could not match. This effect was reinforced by the new questionnaires themselves, which enabled others to explore the topic further. In inventing both a theory and a method the authors thus initiated a distinct research programme. By 1955 at least 64 further studies had been reported.[20] Of the four scales devised in the course of the study, two were directly relevant to the 'race' question, the A-S (Anti-Semitism) and

E (Ethnocentrism) scales;[21] initially A-S was found to correlate 0.80 with E (although only 0.69 with a 'patriotism' subset within E). The two were then integrated into a single 10-item revised E scale questionnaire.[22] However it was felt that a larger 20-item questionnaire containing three subscales might prove more useful in the long run (Jews – 6 items, 'Negroes' – 6 items, 'Other Minorities and Patriotism' – 8 items).[23] (The most widely used scale originating in the study, the F (for 'Fascism') scale, did *not* include any race or minority related items.) Many subject groups were used in the research and the development of the scales varying from San Quentin prisoners to University of Oregon students, 'Professional' and 'middle-class' women, male psychiatric patients and people taking a 'public speaking class'.

Theoretically *The Authoritarian Personality* perhaps added relatively little to the positions elaborated in its two companion works, but its scale and the richness of its variegated content (which we must pass over), along with the neat 'authoritarian personality' concept itself, enabled it to occupy centre-stage in the ensuing controversy. In the 'authoritarian', white liberal Psychology had produced a demonised image of the white racist as psychopath. This emotionally crippled, repressed, sado-masochistic, quasi-psychotic character threatened us all by its irresponsibly maniacal projections and fundamental amorality. But if the 1950s white Gentile authoritarians are projecting their repressed oedipal conflicts onto the Jew and the 'Negro', one cannot help raising the question as to whether 'liberal' 'democratic' whites are not in part projecting their own racism onto the authoritarian. The scapegoating authoritarian becomes a scapegoat in turn. As Ackerman and M. Jahoda stressed, the truth or falsity of a stereotype is actually irrelevant, it is the psychological function the stereotype serves for the holder which is crucial. The 'authoritarian' personality type may well be predisposed to irrationally rooted racist prejudices of a most malevolent kind. This does not exclude the possibility that a stereotype of 'authoritarians' in general as the source and site of all white racism served to enable non-authoritarians to avoid confronting guilt-inducing racist elements in their own, albeit healthier, psyches.

In the ideological wars of the 1950s there was little space for such reflexive niceties. In the US in particular the situation was also peculiarly fractured. Overtly the ideological conflict was between democratic capitalism and totalitarian communism. For US (and many European) liberals, however, Soviet Communism was seen as a fundamentally benign ideology which had been usurped by Stalin, while the more dangerous enemy ultimately remained fascism, seen as fundamentally evil. Fanatical McCarthyite anti-communism now sought to override the very rights which were the defining feature of the democratic ideology it was claiming to defend. In the case of those it saw as sympathising with left-wing ideologies in any degree, such rights amounted to a loophole via which enemy doctrines could enter and subvert the Union. The House Un-American Activities Committee hearings thus became a bizarre mirror-image of the Stalinist show trials (if with less deadly consequences for those arraigned). McCarthyism therefore presented itself to the liberal camp as sinister proto-fascism.[24] US anti-communism was never as clearly articulated or formulated an ideology as communism itself. It fused old-fashioned American patriotism, the ideals of the founding fathers and commitment to a particular economic system – free market capitalism – within which there lay numerous contradictions. In particular the egalitarian component in which an individual's fate was determined by their own enterprise and the 'little guy', triumphing over the 'system', was hero, conflicted with a socio-economic reality in which individual enterprise and interests were unremittingly squeezed by unregulated monopoly capitalism. A further contradiction was the co-existence of a quasi-official Protestant Christian morality inherited from the Puritan past and the constitutional ideology of 'free speech' and 'free expression'. The first was, and remains, a constant source of attempts at establishing forms of censorship which circumvent the latter (usually in relation to mass media).

In this climate the intellectual and academic communities were under severe strain. The 'scientifically discovered' and intrinsically pathological 'authoritarian' acquires considerable significance in this context. For liberals in particular it can be deployed as a powerful weapon of self-defence.[25] For their opponents and those striving to maintain some sort of ideological middle ground the challenge is to co-opt the concept but purge it of its ideological connotations. In 1954 an influential set of five essays appeared, two of which marked a move in this direction.[26] One, by Frenkel-Brunswik herself, focused on the 'rigid cognitive style' of the authoritarian, a move subsequently further developed by Milton Rokeach.[27] This recouches authoritarianism more neutrally (and consistently with the general 'cognitivist' move in US Psychology) as rooted in a dogmatic or rigid cognitive style. More explicitly E.A. Shils suggested that there was an authoritarianism of the left as well as the right. This involved differentiating between 'humanitarianism, and New Deal interventionism' and 'totalitarian Leninism' and Stalinism (Shils, 1954, p. 30).[28] Such a move had obvious appeal. It differentiated between the 'good' left-wingers and the real 'Stalinist' enemy, thereby affirming the loyal anti-communism of the liberals and challenging the justice of their McCarthyite persecution. But it also had an element of special pleading, accepting that such liberals and left-wingers had naively fallen victim to Communist propaganda in the past and become unintentional fellow-travellers. Having learned their lesson they would not re-offend. In Britain H.J. Eysenck (1954) took a similar tack. Eysenck had the advantage over US researchers in being able to obtain respondents openly identifying with the fascist and communist extremes. His claims to have confirmed that avowed communists were extremely authoritarian were, however, soon revealed as unconvincing – their scores actually being 'egalitarian' in US terms. To circumvent this he devised a scale which differentiated between tough–tender mindedness and radicalism–conservatism.[29] This reached a wide popular readership, being included in his popular best-seller *Sense and Nonsense in Psychology* (1957). The empirical evidence for a distinct variety of left-wing authoritarianism in the USA and Britain eventually proved fruitless. Research on authoritarianism then declined during the 1960s, the imminent threat of fascism having receded, but the intolerant 'authoritarian' stereotype was now well-established in both the discipline and the popular mind.

The authoritarianism episode, while emerging from the anti-semitism issue, was not primarily about explaining racism, and concern with anti-semitism

rapidly declined in the early 1950s. It was an expression of a complex but fundamental set of ideological conflicts being waged within and between industrialised
white cultures: capitalism vs. communism, democracy vs. totalitarianism, liberalism vs. puritanism. Within these conflicts white race attitudes acquired a sympto-
matic function, signifying the holder's ideological allegiance. If negative race
attitudes could be shown to be associated with a distinctive pathological personality type who was in turn likely to espouse the ideology one opposed, then the case
against this ideology was obviously reinforced. In this context those engaged
in the controversy who are not ethnically white European can have little input
into the terms in which racism is being construed. They can only strive to
strengthen the hand of those whites who cast themselves as their allies. I am not,
of course, intending to ascribe bad faith or cynicism to any of the parties involved.
The ideological conflicts in question remain with us yet in altered terms, and the
historical role of the authoritarianism research for those with liberatory goals was
undoubtedly a positive one, for all the ambiguities and shortcomings we can
restrospectively detect.

The indigenous US prejudice-research tradition continued to flourish alongside
the new authoritarianism work. Its fullest statement was perhaps G. W. Allport's
The Nature of Prejudice (1954b), which incorporated some discussion of authoritarianism. Over 500 pages this examined the topic from all angles including in-
group–out-group relations, cognitive processes, stereotyping, the aetiology of
prejudice, its dynamics, personality structure and possible ameliorative measures.
Allport's position is avowedly eclectic, and like the Studies in Prejudice editors he
views this topic as a site for inter-disciplinary communication:

> The author hopes the present volume may be regarded as a reflection of the
> present tendency for specialists to cross boundaries and to borrow methods and
> insights from neighboring disciplines in the interests of a more adequate under-
> standing of a concrete social problem. (pp. 206–7).

Far from ascribing prejudice solely to individual-level factors he identifies six
nested levels at which the phenomenon can be addressed, each yielding its own
insights: 'stimulus object' (object of prejudice), phenomenological, personality
dynamics and structure, situational, socio-cultural, historical. The last three are
clearly transpersonal. A full synopsis of this work would be out of place here. Of
most immediate interest is the brief chapter on 'Racial and ethnic differences',
which provides a useful snapshot of how a representative liberal white US
psychologist was conceptualising 'race' at this time. Allport is sceptical about the
concept 'race', although he does not abandon it, citing Kluckhohn (1949) to the
effect that 'not more than one percent of the genes involved in producing a person's inheritance are racially linked' (p. 108).

> Even a fragment of visibility, however, focuses people's minds on the possi-
> bility that everything may be related to that fragment. A person's character is
> thought to tie in with his slant eyes, or a menacing aggressiveness is thought to
> be linked to dark color. Here is an instance of our common tendency to sharpen

and exaggerate a feature that captures attention and to assimilate as much as possible to the visual category thus created. (pp. 108–9)

The ascription of racial identity to 'Negroes' is 'at least half purely social invention' since it is often applied to people whose racial ancestry is mostly white. Even though 'true racial differences' of a physical kind exist,

> Two points stand out . . . from anthropological work on race. (1) Except in remote parts of the earth very few human beings belong to a pure stock; most men are mongrels (racially speaking); hence the concept has little utility. (2) Most human characteristics ascribed to race are undoubtedly due to cultural diversity and should, therefore, be regarded as ethnic, not racial. (p. 113)

Since it stresses differences, he is worried about cultural relativity, counselling that at the 'present juncture' it would be well to study 'uniformities' and similarities which serve 'to call attention to the common ground upon which cooperation between the various branches of the human family may proceed' (p. 116). National character is also problematic – certainly there are differences in national character, but the realities may not correspond to popular images. 'Objective studies' are needed to correct 'false images'. He then turns to the Jews and critically examines the stereotypes held of the Jew. While arguing that none of these stand up to investigation he is somewhat less sophisticated in his treatment of this topic than the writers previously discussed.

The Nature of Prejudice amounts to a detailed liberal 'position statement'. The position Allport espouses – the irrationality of prejudice, the need to combat it in the interests of global harmony, the need to 'tolerate' differences and the uneasy combination of rejection of an 'essentialist' biological conception of race with practical acceptance of racial discourse – becomes the orthodoxy among post-war US social psychologists. Occasionally a glaring ethnocentrism slips through – for example, at one point he uses the phrase 'people who live in close contact with Negroes' (p. 217) as if Negroes were not people! It would be grossly unfair to hang him for such lapses however, their significance is rather to signify how even those white psychologists most intellectually emancipated from racism – people probably more fully conscious of the issue and its nature than nearly anyone else in the US white community – retained unconscious attitudes and assumptions which constrained how far they could go.

Anti-semitism may have faded as a major concern in the early 1950s but the African American situation was rapidly returning to the fore. As the Civil Rights campaign and school desegregation got under way Kenneth B. Clark, the most prominent African American psychologist, published the first edition of *Prejudice and Your Child* (1955), a 2nd edition appearing in 1963 (reissued 1988), drawing on the 'authoritarian personality' concept. This, however, was an engaged and practical book aimed not just at Psychology, but, as the title indicated, at the wider public audience. Within US Psychology the domestic race relations issue had, from the start, figured centrally on agenda of the newly formed APA group, the Society for the Psychological Study of Social Issues (SPSSI), whose *Journal of Social Issues* was founded in 1945. We may now consider how US Psychology engaged the new Civil Rights campaign, which came to a head coincidentally with the height of the Vietnam War at the end of the 1960s during the Lyndon Johnson Presidency.

US PSYCHOLOGY, CIVIL RIGHTS AND THE 'NEGRO PERSONALITY'

A survey of the *Journal of Social Issues* coverage of race-related issues up to 1969 provides a useful starting point. The APA's house journal, *American Psychologist*'s, parallel coverage helps set the broader disciplinary context.[30] The Civil Rights campaign moved the topic beyond simple 'race prejudice'. Practical questions related to desegregation soon begin to attract the SPSSI's attention. In most of the years 1945–69 the *Journal of Social Issues* (a quarterly) devoted at least one, and sometimes two, of its numbers to race-related topics.[31] Some concerned Cross-cultural Psychology but about two-thirds of them (out of 25) bore in a direct way on the domestic 'prejudice'/civil rights issue. In the *American Psychologist* (a monthly), by contrast, the topic crops up far less frequently, which is not entirely surprising given the discipline-wide range of its concerns. Not until 1954 does Mark Grossack break the ice with a two-page communication on 'Some Negro perceptions of psychologists: an observation on psychology's public relations' and another two-pager on 'Psychology in Negro colleges'.

This intra-disciplinary focus is maintained in the next relevant publication, T.W. Richards (1956), a further two pages on 'Graduate education of Negro psychologists'. S.W. Cook's (1957) lengthier 'Desegregation: a psychological analysis' is the first more substantial treatment. 'Race' remains a mostly dormant topic for *American Psychologist* until the early 1960s when the intelligence issue has a brief resurgence. Garrett, E.S. Lee, Klineberg, Irwin Katz and others contend on this across 1962–4 and the topic again crops up intermittently from 1966–8 until, in 1969, the ordure finally hits the air-conditioning. The APA's policy of striving to remain apolitical now came under severe strain. In 1968, the African American psychologist Gordon Becker, of Howard University had pleaded with the profession to act in the context of the nationwide upheavals asking 'Can we permit psychology to sleep through the present holocaust?' (G.M. Becker, 1968, p. 584). In 1969 E.E. Johnson, another black psychologist, examined 'The Role of the Negro in American Psychology', emphasising that a 'hard reappraisal of past and current approaches to research in the ghetto' was impending and that the 'black psychologist will regard himself more and more as an agent of social change' (pp. 757–8). He queried 'popular theorizing about the "matriarchal society" of the black ghetto' and stressed the need for the 'restoration of the psychological manhood of the black ghetto male' (p. 758). Becker's and Johnson's letters represent, as far as I can determine, the first time that African American psychologists gained a genuine hearing on their own terms in the *American Psychologist*'s pages. Johnson's letter was followed by one from L.H. Hicks on 'Black studies in Psychology', an attempt at opening up the discussion on what the content of Black Psychology courses should be, again signalling the emergence of an autonomous academic agenda. (Incidentally, Hicks recommends including Madison Grant and Stoddard as case-study texts and derides McDougall's 'notorious' family photo.)

While certain sections within US Psychology anxiously sought to constructively engage Civil Rights issues and related questions from 1945 onwards, the APA itself was apparently extremely wary of putting the discipline as a whole on the line. This is unsurprising, Garrett himself had been its President in 1946 and his portrait appeared in the *American Psychologist*'s first issue. In the ensuing turbulent years of McCarthyite harrassment of academics, the California oath-taking episode and the desegregation controversy, the APA might give space to opposing views but, as an organisation, was politically paralysed by the sheer breadth of its members' interests and political attitudes. Any general statement about US Psychology and the Civil Rights movement is thus impossible. The SPSSI at least was involved in such specific issues as desegregation of housing, minorities in trade unions and social psychological dynamics in the Deep South. Length considerations preclude detailed discussion of the numerous papers on these topics which appeared in the *Journal of Social Issues*, but taken together they played a major role in rendering visible many deeper problems of social psychological dynamics which straight 'attitude' research could not handle.[32] For black psychologists this also provided the context in which white Psychology first became amenable to serious critical consideration. In 1967 the SPSSI invited Martin Luther King Jr to deliver its 'Distinguished Address', 'The Role of the Behavioral Scientist in the Civil Rights Movement'. Somewhat flatteringly he opened by saying that, in contrast to the physicists who created nuclear weapons 'Social scientists, in the main, are fortunate to be able to extirpate evil, not to invent it' (Wilcox, 1971, p. 467). While much of the address was inspirational rather than concrete in content he identified four main areas in which research was desperately needed: (a) what he called the 'suicide instinct' emerging among black rioters; (b) the problem of leadership, many successful blacks tending to distance themselves from the 'Negro'[33] community but gaining no acceptance in the white one; (c) the effectiveness of political action, the power to vote perhaps having fewer positive consequences than people hoped, although he himself was optimistic; (d) psychological and ideological changes in 'Negroes'. He later observed that the 'worst aspect' of oppression was the 'inability to question and defy the fundamental percepts [sic] of the larger society' (ibid., p. 473). The *American Psychologist* could hardly omit King's address from its pages, and it duly appeared the following year just prior to his assassination. Much of what King was calling for was undoubtedly already in train, but for African American psychologists his words were certainly still echoing when the Jensen controversy broke in 1969.[34]

The SPSSI group's work during this period was complemented by various studies of African American personality, of a more problematic character. From the Culture and Personality side came Kardiner and Ovesey's *The Mark of Oppression: Explorations in the Personality of the American Negro* (1962, 1st edn 1951), which was followed at some remove by J.K. Rohrer and M.S. Edmonson, *The Eighth Generation Grows Up* (1960) and T.F. Pettigrew's *A Profile of the Negro American* (1964).[35]

The Mark of Oppression was especially influential and represents a paradigm example of the ambiguities into which white liberal Psychology was unwittingly drifting at this time. As the work's title indicates this is very much an exercise in applying the psychodynamic culture and personality approach to the domestic US scene. More specifically, it yielded a picture of 'Negro personality' which fully articulated the pathologised 'damaged Negro' stereotype. This picture had three particularly influential components: (a) the 'Negro' family was 'matriarchal' or 'uterine' (this being construed in a highly negative fashion); (b) the 'Negro' male character was marked by anxieties about his masculinity, often amounting to a kind of psychological emasculation; (c) 'Negro' personality was, it seemed, wholly comprehensible as an adaptational response to white racism. None of this is being proposed in a consciously racist spirit, on the contrary, in an introductory 'Advice to the Reader' Kardiner and Ovesey spell out their anti-racist commitment:

> The authors will give no comfort or support to those who wish to use some part of this work out of its conceptual and sequential context in order to hurt the interests of the Negro people. (p. iv)

It is precisely in these pathologies that the book's very title lies: 'The Negro still bears the psychological scars created by caste and its effects. It is these scars that we have chosen to call "the mark of oppression"' (p. xv). Their position is reinforced by a rejection (endorsed by the black sociologist Frazier) of significant survivals from African culture (contrary to Melville Herskovits's position in *The Myth of the Negro Past* of 1941).[36] Since their African cultural heritage was 'smashed', the African Americans' current situation is therefore one of what came to be called 'cultural deprivation' and '. . . the present state of the Negro family structure is a function of the social adaptation of the Negro in America and not an aboriginal survival' (p. 39). Post-Civil War emancipation has barely changed the psychological situation, indeed ironically made it worse, for the 'passivity' and lack of responsibility which slavery had instilled left the ex-slave more vulnerable than ever. Perceived as a 'racial character' of the 'Negro' this damaged character was now used as an excuse for maintaining the very conditions which created it. The consequences of this are catalogued in detail ('degradation of self-esteem', 'destruction of Negro social cohesion', simultaneous idealisation and hatred of the white 'master', etc.).

On the other hand the introductory sections on black American life do counter some white stereotypes, notably in the sexual sphere, where female fidelity to husbands is 'higher than would be expected from frequency of family disruption' (p. 69) and the black male is 'hardly the abandoned sexual hedonist he is supposed to be' (ibid.) (quite the contrary as it will turn out). The majority of the text consists of 25 case studies of Harlem residents, all either clients, or paid informants, of Ovesey (with one exception seen by someone else who remained anonymous). Ovesey's approach is psychoanalytical and there is much reporting and interpreting of dreams, while his conclusions are couched in psychoanalytic terms. These case histories certainly remain valuable as, often moving, testimony to the nature of immediate post-war urban African American life, and like most case histories stand as human stories in their own right. Whether the conclusions which Ovesey and Kardiner drew from them are justified is another matter. (For a start half the 10 'lower class' cases hardly fit the 'matriarchal family' image.)[37] More fundamentally those subjects who were receiving psychotherapy clearly cannot be taken as representative, even allowing for the argument that abnormal cases reveal the 'normal' personality processes more clearly. Taking Harlem as typical of the US African American's social environment is also, surely, somewhat questionable. Among the male subjects it is certainly true that impotence, stifled (repressed or suppressed) aggression, low self-esteem and problems with their masculinity are prevalent problems. That these are often clearly exacerbated by their racial oppression is indisputable, but how far does the incidence of such symptoms differ from that which would have been yielded by a comparable study of any other group? Lack of some kind of control study was, methodologically, a major weakness of the study.

The upshot of the authors' interpretation is a model of the underlying personality structure of the African American (primarily the male, though women were equally represented in the research). Low esteem and self-hatred ('direct or projected') result from the fact that aggression towards whites generates 'retaliatory fear' and towards fellow blacks retaliatory fear plus guilt, which combine to produce fear of success. Acceptance of white ideas results in disparagement of fellow 'Negroes' (and lack of social cohesion) and overstriving for middle-class white objectives. Since the latter are obstructed, more aggression, anxiety, depression and self-hatred are produced, creating a vicious circle.

African Americans were thus confronted with a comprehensively depressing image of their 'personality', 'character' and way of life, made worse by the fact that it emanated from their white allies. The classic racist stereotype of the sexually potent, happy-go-lucky, amusingly stupid, emotionally expressive Negro with a good sense of rhythm had yielded to an ostensibly anti-racist stereotype of emasculated, over-dependent, emotionally fickle, depressed and self-hating black males and frigid, status-seeking, domineering black females! That it wasn't their fault was hardly much consolation and only reinforced an image of passivity. Any African American women who read it would have felt doubly damned since they are cast as the primary mediators of these dysfunctional 'personality' patterns. With friends like this . . .

It is important to recognise the role played by such supposedly supportive white liberal-authored analyses in laying the ground for the ultimate break with their white academic 'allies' by black Americans. In that sense such work may have had a back-handed positive effect in bringing home to African Americans the necessity of directly articulating and analysing the psychological and social realities of their life. Clearly, with the best will in the world, white psychologists were incapable of doing so and operating within theoretical frameworks in which racism was somehow endemic. Since white Psychology was produced by white psychology, and white psychology was, consciously or not, racist, this was not really surprising. Beneath its veneer of natural scientific objectivity white Psychology, even when produced by doyens of the culture and personality school, remained deeply ethnocentric.

For some white liberal academics the penny was a long time dropping. D. Moynihan's 1965 report on *The Negro Family in the United States: The Case for Action* bought the package wholesale, again identifying the 'emasculating' matriarchal black family as the source of a 'tangle of pathology'.[38] By the mid-1960s a considerable body of research on 'Negro' personality and attitudes had accumulated, including much on attitudes towards civil rights issues and whites generally. The first two chapters of Thomas F. Pettigrew's *A Profile of the Negro American* (1964) provided a summary of much of this. Again the Kardiner and Ovesey image of the dysfunctional matriarchal black family and its deleterious effects (especially on the black male) was accepted fairly uncritically, although in a somewhat more qualified fashion. The view of black personality as primarily developed as a reaction to white racism was also largely retained. Pettigrew's book was, nonetheless, presented as a direct contribution to the on-going Civil Rights struggle, with much discussion of the effectiveness of various anti-racist strategies and how social class differences within the African American population affected these.

Pettigrew's use of attitude data to support his arguments inadvertently discloses some of the technical difficulties associated with the design and meanings of personality and attitude scales at this period. For example, the greater 'feminisation' of the black male is apparently supported by MMPI responses, such as greater black agreement to the item 'I would like to be a singer'.[39] This is surely misleading since the whole meaning of being a singer in African American culture was different to its meaning in white culture, not least since it provided one of the few occupations in which black males could become eminent. Big Bill Broonzy is hardly a 'feminine' role model! A 1963 *Newsweek* poll is cited which included the question 'On the whole do you think most white people want to see Negroes get a better break, or do they want to keep Negroes down, or do you think they don't care one way or the other?' Upper and middle-class blacks were far more generous to white intentions than lower-class blacks in Northern ghettoes (Pettigrew, 1964, pp. 39–40). But this confounds two different factors, attitudes as such and the factual realities of respondent's situations. It is reasonable to assume that the whites with whom higher social class blacks interacted were indeed more favourable towards improving their lot than those with whom impoverished Northern ghetto blacks interacted. Put more technically, the two groups are partly responding to different 'attitude objects'.

Again, if somewhat less starkly and with a good deal more insight and optimism overall, a pathologised image of the Negro at this stage underpinned Pettigrew's view of the issue. Admittedly a somewhat different note was struck in J.H. Rohrer and M.S. Edmonson, *The Eighth Generation Grows Up* (1960), a longitudinal follow-up study of the subjects of A. Davis and J. Dollard (1940). (The title referred to their being the eighth post-slavery generation.) Here much more attention was paid to the role of subjects' primary 'reference groups' in determining their personality, thereby locating the sources of personality formation within the black community rather than simply in individual reactions to the white one.

As suggested elsewhere, the 'damaged' or pathologised image of the African American presents some genuine difficulties. Being the victim of persistent racist oppression certainly has psychological consequences, some of which may be pathological in some sense. (But this is also true, if more subtly, for the oppressor.) What was wrong was not the claim that many African Americans will be so affected, but the deeper, less articulated, creation of an image of the African American as a passive victim who is *invariably* and *necessarily* so pathologised. Even efforts towards active resistance can thus be viewed as handicapped by the insidious effects of an inescapable pathology – a subtext which lurks throughout Pettigrew's 'Reactions to oppression' chapter. Black articulations and analyses of the sufferings resulting from racism can ironically reinforce this. Black psychologists subsequently had to try and turn this round and assert the positive features of 'black personality' and redeem the 'matriarchal' family.[40] What was remarkable was not, in the end, how pathologised African Americans were, but how successful they had by and large been in retaining their psychological health – which was in itself a far healthier (as well as more heroic) version of things.

In some respects this 1950s–60s genre of white-authored studies of 'Negro' personality tells us as much about the US white liberal personality of the period as it does about African Americans. It needs to be read in the light of Kovel's analysis of the development of white racism in the US, particularly his views on the intensely idealised superego phase (see Chapter 10).

Finally, one cannot leave the topic of Psychology's links with anti-racism during this period without considering Franz Fanon. Born in Martinique and a black psychiatrist during the period of the Algerian war of independence against France, Fanon was confronted with racism in its most pernicious forms. His two best known texts – *The Wretched of the Earth* (1965) and *Black Skins, White Masks* (1967) – transcended the genre of 'Psychology' and are among the most influential expressions and articulations of the black person's situation under colonialism, being much excerpted in later anthologies.[41] The majority of *The Wretched of the Earth* is socio-political in character, an evocation and analysis of the nature of colonialism, colonial and anti-colonial violence, anti-colonial national rebellion and the problems faced in creating a post-colonial society. Throughout this, Fanon wove a broadly Marxist political analysis together with an exploration of the experiential psychological realities of colonialism. In Chapter 5 ('Colonial wars and mental disorders) he brings his own psychiatric experience to the fore. The task of 'curing' a 'native' sufferer is problematic to say the least:

> Because it is a systematic negation of the other person and a furious determination to deny the other person all attributes of humanity, colonialism forces the people it dominates to ask themselves the question constantly: 'In reality, who am I?' (p. 200)

The five cases with which Fanon opens this chapter each disclose the embeddedness of the presenting psychopathology within the colonial context: the liberation fighter suffering from impotence after his wife had been raped for refusing to disclose his whereabouts; the massacre survivor who becomes homicidal; a 19-year-old liberation fighter, now suffering from vampiristic persecution delusions, who murdered a settler's wife in a fit of madness because his own mother had been killed by the French; but then also the anxiety-ridden European policeman haunted by screams who turned out to be a torturer (and his encounter with an ex-victim who was a patient in the same hospital and immediately tried to commit suicide on recognising him) and most remarkably of all perhaps the police inspector who has begun violently physically abusing his wife and children and who again turns out to be a torturer. In this last case the patient just wants to be cured so he can return to work. But this is just the beginning, a range of cases and case types, from two Algerian boys who murdered a European playmate to the after-effects of electrical torture and brainwashing are described. Fanon then moves on to criticising contemporary theories of the African and Arab character proposed by Carothers (see below) and the French psychiatrist A. Porot.

In this historically important chapter Fanon achieved two things of immediate relevance here: he (a) exposed the deep psychological effects of colonialism on both victims and perpetrators and (b) demystified the stereotypes of, for example, innate Arab criminality or 'Negro' laziness by explaining such behaviour as a response of the oppressed to their oppressors.

But Fanon too was faced with the question 'In reality, who am I?' In *Black Skins, White Masks* he portrayed his own struggle to find an answer. This is very different in tone to *The Wretched of the Earth*, poetic, personal and autobiographical rather than analytical, expository and social scientific. The anger and despair, hitherto present but kept on a tight rein, are now given their due. Fanon's reference points are the great black Francophone writers such as Leopold Senghor and Aimé Césaire, along with figures such as J.P. Sartre (who wrote an introduction to the earlier work, but who at one point Fanon now feels has betrayed him). It would be utterly foolish to try and summarise, or reduce to Psychological terms, the content of this work. For many African Americans it gave an added dimension, authority and confidence to their own understanding; to radical whites it was in a sense even more challenging since it forced them to *hear* the black man (and I genderise deliberately), not for perhaps the first time, but now disclosing and voicing the depths of his wrath with unprecedented intellectual clarity and force, putting even (perhaps especially) the most self-consciously 'enlightened' on the spot. For African Americans Fanon was voicing what they already knew, for whites it seriously undermined well-meaning liberal self-confidence, subverted their self-image as benign and understanding participants in the anti-racist struggle.

Nonetheless a previous problem returns. In passages such as that included in Donald and Rattansi (1992) (as 'The fact of blackness') the existential challenge Fanon is having to face is that he *is*, once he is outside his own community, being defined by the white world. 'The black man has no ontological resistance in the eyes of the white man.' Under the white gaze 'I burst apart'. And in striving to rediscover or recreate himself he is driven to a succession of resources, each of which proves inadequate. Now we are not talking here about anything as straightforward as the 'damaged Negro' stereotype; we are talking about the raw effects of 'racial' power and the denial of their true humanity on colonial subjects. But how far is Fanon's existential crisis translateable to the US context? African Americans are certainly only present on the continent in the first place as a result of colonial power in the now distant past, and have assuredly been denied their full humanity. But there remains a difference. As we have been seeing, the very notion that

African American identity is entirely comprehensible as a reaction to white racism has been one which African Americans have been striving to overcome as a major blind-spot in white anti-racist discourse. White Americans are not colonisers of African American *territory*, not keeping an African American *nation* in sub-jugation. Fanon's account ought to apply more directly to native Americans than African Americans. The African American situation is both worse and better than the orthodox colonial situation. It is worse in that the baseline, slavery, was even more dehumanising and destructive than that imposed on most colonised cultures. It is better in that the oppressors' own position has always been more internally heterogeneous and conflicted – the African American has always had 'allies' in the white American camp. While I am in no position to explore the matter, I would raise the question then – how far does the situation depicted in Fanon's moving and inspirational text correspond to that of contemporary African Americans? The debate has, of course, moved on since the mid-1960s, and the book may be seen in retrospect as an opening move in the debate on black identity to which Mama (1995) is a recent contribution. In this she disputes Fanon's, admittedly 'sardonic', view that the black 'man' wants to be white, has a desire for 'lactifica-tion', as pathologising black people. But we should surely read *Black Skins, White Masks* as a personal testament, not a Psychological theory.

THE RACE PSYCHOLOGY UNDERGROUND

The 1930s had seen the rise in the USA of a small, but well-funded, pro-Nazi movement. The old-guard Nordicist eugenicists such as Madison Grant and Paul Popenoe were delighted with the advent of the Third Reich, promising as it did to put their 'scientific' eugenic dreams into effect. The American *Eugenical News* hailed Hitler as leading the way 'towards a biological salvation of humanity'.[42] Madison Grant sent copies of his latest offering, *Conquest of a Continent* (1933) to the leading German Nazi ideologues, including Alfred Rosenberg. T. Lothrop Stoddard, author of *The Rising Tide of Color* (1920), undertook a German tour during which he interviewed Goebbels, Himmler and Hitler and returned full of enthusiasm. US Eugenics, now being led by the fanatical racist Harry Hamilton Laughlin (editor of *Eugenical News*), was, by the late 1930s, firmly in the evangeli-cal Nordicist racist pocket.[43] In 1937 Wyckcliffe Draper, a right-wing Massa-chusetts textile millionaire, established the Pioneer Fund, with backing from Laughlin and other racist eugenicists.[44] Few psychologists immediately allied themselves to this movement, with the exceptions of H.E. Garrett and, as yet at a distance, the British psychologist R.B. Cattell. Now the war was ended racists were soon panicking over the gains being made by the anti-segregationist, pro-Civil Rights movement in a post-war cultural climate in which overtly racist doc-trines were, by and large, anathema outside the Deep South. While a network linking various white supremacist organisations, the House Committee on Un-American Activities, a newly established International Association for the Advancement of Ethnology and Eugenics (IAAEE) and a number of Southern academics was soon in place, their backs remained tightly to the wall.

In 1954 the bombshell fell, the Supreme Court sitting on the case of *Brown vs. The Board of Education of Topeka, Kansas*, decided for the plaintiff and desegregation.[45] As Tucker (1994) explains, this event, though epochal, was more complex than appears on the surface. During the hearing anti-segregationist lawyers had called numerous expert witnesses, such as Klineberg, Jerome Bruner and Kenneth B. Clark, to argue for the deleterious effects of segregation, and much of this was appended to the published report in a 'Statement' signed by 35 leading US social scientists. The real point at issue, however, was not a scientific one, but a legal one – whether the plaintiff's constitutional rights had been infringed by not being allowed to attend an all-white school. Technically it was about whether the pro-segregationist Supreme Court ruling in the 1896 *Plessey vs. Ferguson* case (which established the right to enforce segregation on inter-state railcars) could be overturned. By throwing as much supportive scientific evidence into the case as they could, the plaintiff's lawyers had, Tucker argues, conceded a very dangerous point. They had shifted the issue from being a straightforward moral and constitutional one to being a 'scientific' one. And, as the proverb says, what is sauce for the goose is sauce for the gander. While, in point of fact, the Supreme Court, in its judgment, stressed that its decision was taken on purely legal and moral grounds, not scientific ones, the prominence given to the involvement in the case of psychologists and sociologists overshadowed this. Psychology had, apparently, a place in law-making. Aggrieved and embittered racists and pro-segregationists eagerly picked up the gauntlet and sought to demonstrate that the scientific evidence was actually in their favour. They could readily find data suggesting, for example, that 'Negro' children suffered more in integrated than in segregated situations – most embarrassingly perhaps K.B. Clark and N.I. Plotkin (1963) reported students at segregated colleges performing better than those at integrated ones, as C.C. Josey (1966) noted with some glee in a pro-Garrett letter to *American Psychologist*. While much of this reaction originated outside Psychology, perhaps most notably Carleton Putnam's *Race and Reason* (1961), Garrett, hitherto content to publish in academic journals in dispassionately 'objective' style, was especially incensed and spent the rest of his career passionately striving to oppose desegregation and racial egalitarianism in increasingly polemic fashion. But he was not entirely alone in the discipline in attempting to reassert the race differences case.[46]

This post-1954 mini-resurgence of Race Psychology served as a prelude to the events following A.R. Jensen's 1969 papers. In 1963 Klineberg (then in Paris) was prevailed upon by the SPSSI to re-enter the ring in the *American Psychologist*, partly in response to Garrett's attack on the SPSSI the previous year (Garrett, 1962). Others, too, became involved in *American Psychologist* exchanges on the topic at this time, with much wrangling over the Tanser (1939) and Bruce (1940) findings.[47] The most powerful text coming from this direction was Audrey M. Shuey's *The Testing of Negro Intelligence* which first appeared in 1958, an expanded second edition (with an introduction by Garrett) being published in 1966. This demands some attention.

The Testing of Negro Intelligence presents a detailed resumé and interpretation of 380 studies (240 in the first edition) ranging over 50 years. Written in a conciliatory tone and acknowledging many of the flaws in specific pieces of research this may be seen as an overture to the Jensen controversy. The chapters systematically summarise and tabulate the available data on pre-school children, school children, high school and college students, armed forces, various adult groups such as criminals and the gifted, plus the issues of 'racial hybrids' (the old 'mulatto hypothesis'), experimenter effects, and selective migration. She concludes that the findings in all these areas support the race differences interpretation, being 'remarkably consistent' in showing black mean performance at around 13–15 points lower than white performance. The data 'inevitably point to the presence of native differences' (pp. 520–1). The findings regarding 'racial hybrids', experimenter effects and selective migration are less clear-cut, but such as they are, in her opinion they (a) suggest that 'hybrids' have an advantage (but 'these studies make no important contribution to the problem of race differences in intelligence' p. 466), (b) there are experimenter effects but they are neither strong nor consistent in direction, (c) 'have not disproved the selective migration hypothesis' (p. 490) – she guesses that about half the difference between Northern and Southern blacks may be accounted for by this factor (various weaknesses in Klineberg's 1935 study are noted). Taken at face value it is a very effective text, but closer examination reveals a number of features which undermine this.

1 Twenty-two per cent of her references (122 of 555 by my count) are to unpublished material, mostly masters' and doctoral theses. Virtually all of these are among the 380 studies providing the data, thus accounting for almost a third of them, 70 date from the 1941–60 period (16 from 1961–5). Many emanate from Southern colleges and universities, including black universities such as Fisk and Howard. Insofar as they are Southern in origin a question mark must hang over their acceptability. Work emanating from Deep South universities and authored by white post-graduates in their early twenties in, for example, the 1940s was itself a product of that region's racist segregationist culture. In the absence of evidence to the contrary we must assume the young authors' orientation (and mode of relating to African American subjects) still to be deeply pervaded by the prevailing attitudes, values and assumptions of the cultural context in which they lived. Black-authored work from this region (generally intra-racial in character and included insofar as it provided black performance data) will also reflect the realities of this culture (and usually did not claim otherwise). Garrett, in his introduction, praises the recent research which succeeds in 'equating background variables' (p.vii). But how could this be done in a Deep South culture which systematically ensured, as a central matter of cultural principle, precisely that these were kept unequatable?[48]
Given the decline in published research on the topic during the 1930s, Shuey had, however, few alternative sources of recent research to these unpublished theses. Of 76 studies cited for 1941–50 45 (59%) were of this nature.[49] While citation of unpublished theses is not in itself an academic sin – on the contrary, it can boost an author's cloister-credibility – the excessive scale on which Shuey does so and the uncritical use she makes of them as reliable primary data sources is one of the work's major shortcomings.

2 Pursuing this line of bibliographic critique we note that 191 (34%) of the references are to material from 1940 or earlier (but not all to race differences studies as such). While she is neither uncritical nor entirely undiscriminating regarding the quality of these studies, they nevertheless provide Shuey with a substantial proportion of her data and are incorporated without much ado into her various summarising 'meta-analyses'. Yet, as we have already seen, this earlier work had failed to convince the discipline at large by the 1930s and was vitiated by numerous methodological and conceptual flaws.

These two points, taken together, indicate that the calibre of much of the data Shuey is drawing on is very poor or must be assumed to be so.[50] If unpublished and pre-1941 data were excluded from consideration her case would be considerably weakened. Adding bad data to good, even if it is consistent with it, does not strengthen the latter. Nor does the fact that the same findings emerge from repeated use of flawed methods render them less flawed.

3 Shuey overstates the 'remarkable consistency' of the findings. They are consistent to the extent that they invariably show African American underperformance, but certainly not consistent regarding the extent of this.
4 She fails to notice that successive restandardisations of several intelligence tests required setting the mean '100' score at relatively higher levels. She therefore claims that 'Negro' intelligence has remained static throughout the period covered. If, in fact, the gap in scores has been static it must however imply that black performance has improved in parallel with white performance.[51]
5 Finally it must be stressed that Shuey's resolutely empirical approach enabled her to dodge any in-depth consideration of underlying conceptual and theoretical problems. Since these are considered at length in the next chapter it is only necessary here to note that Shuey's position is fully vulnerable to the points which will be raised there.

Much cited and valuable as a reference source, the solidity of Shuey's compendious text is thus none the less illusory. It relies on the cumulative impact of presenting masses of data and findings while largely disregarding the problematic nature of much of this and ignoring conceptual or theoretical questions which cannot be answered by empirical data alone. Historically it was the most comprehensive and forcefully articulated statement of the traditional 'race differences in intelligence' position prior to the Jensen controversy, and served as a primary reference point for succeeding pro-differences researchers. Its wider impact appears to have been relatively limited even so, there was little essentially new in it and many in the anti-differences camp felt disinclined to plough yet again through evidence they believed had long been proved valueless. The presence of Garrett's introduction also probably did more harm than good to Shuey's cause: if he was her ally then the authenticity of her own generally meliorative tone was surely cast into doubt.

Her linkage with the Pioneer Fund network was, in fact, intimate. Two of her closest associates were R. Travis Osborne and Frank C.J. McGurk, who at her request first helped, then brought to completion, a second volume of the work which appeared (after her death) under their editorship in 1982 and covered material from January 1966 to December 1979. McGurk had published one of the few extensive 1940s studies (McGurk, 1943) and was an ardent segregationist. He and Travis Osborne were both members of the IAAEE and co-directors of the Athens, Georgia-based Foundation for Human Understanding (FHU), another Pioneer Fund project. The FHU published the second volume of *The Testing of Negro Intelligence* as well as other works by, or edited by, Travis Osborne, who also contributed to *Mankind Quarterly*.[52] While Tucker (1994) does not mention Shuey (who was based in Randolph-Macon Women's College, Lynchburg, Virginia) there is little doubt that she was in the Pioneer Fund segregationist loop.

Though classic Scientific Racism was now rare outside the USA, an updated version was promoted by the South African born, Kenya-based psychiatrist J.C. Carothers (1947, 1951, 1953, 1954, 1972). Carothers first ventured into the topic in Carothers (1947), a study of 'mental derangement' in Africans which adopted a basically cultural line. In Carothers (1951) he returned to the subject with a new insight: Africans were psychologically indistinguishable from European leucotomy patients. This was, he concluded, because they did not use their frontal lobes. It is an odd text even for 1951, the stereotypical view of 'primitive African' character is unapologetically presented with no more academic support than D. Westermann's *The African Today and Tomorrow* (1939), a semi-popular work.[53] He treats us to a list of 33 illustrative anecdotal examples of the failings of normal seemingly intelligent Africans which amounts to little more than an amusing recital of colonial gripes about servants forgetting to salt the soup and the indifference of menial laboratory and hospital employees to their masters' priorities. They cannot grasp situations as a whole, live for the moment, lack foresight, cannot understand cause–effect relations, learn by rote and have no sense of visual spatial relationships (though their verbal faculties are well-developed and they are good at music). The old Deep South slave-owners would have sympathised deeply. Seeing everything through the framework of contemporary psychiatric discourse, Carothers discovers a profound significance in the new psychosurgery findings being reported in the British journals. Leucotomy, which involves severing the connection between the frontal lobes and the rest of the brain, had been used to treat a number of severe psychotic conditions. It invariably had major consequences for the patients' personalities: 'cheerful self-satisfaction', 'lack of self-criticism and self-consciousness', 'lack of sympathy for the feelings of others', 'lack of sense of right or wrong', and above all *'failure to see an event as an element in a total situation and as having a variety of relevant relationships'* (p. 37, italicised in original). One cannot help commenting that it is surely Carothers who cannot see the total situation. Without more ado Carothers then proclaims that 'except that the African shows no lack of verbal ability or of phantasy, the resemblance of the leucotomized European patients to the primitive African is, in many cases, *complete'* (ibid., emphasis in original).

The distinctive character of African psychopathology and the normal African's pre-eminent psychological traits all fall into place. For whatever reason, Africans do not learn to use their frontal lobes, allegedly necessary for synthesising, reasoning, maintenance of integrity of personality etc.: 'all the observed African peculiarities can be explained as due to a relative idleness of his frontal lobes' (p. 46). This may in part be due to the rote nature of African socialisation and lack of concern with the visual but, in the light of Vint's work on the African cortex (Vint, 1932, 1934)[54] and 'various other bodily differences, it would be rather surprising if the African brain were identical with the European' (p. 46). While still holding the precise nature of the cause of the phenomenon open, Carothers leaves little doubt that he is tending towards an innate anatomical explanation.

Following UNESCO's strong anti-racist statement on race of 1951, Carothers's WHO book *The African Mind in Health and Disease: A Study in Ethnopsychiatry* (1953) struck a rather different note. The 'idle frontal lobe theory' was dropped[55] but Carothers reiterated his belief in the African's lack of psychological integration and argued that Africans typically exhibited 'less cleavage' between the conscious and unconscious elements of the mind (echoes of Jung!). This resulted in their living in a half-awake state of 'monoideic consciousness'. Unlike the earlier paper, this text includes references to contemporary psychologists such as Hebb, Piaget and Gesell as well as to Nadel and Lévy-Bruhl. While insistent that underlying innate physiological differences from the European or 'Caucasoid' must be assumed to be implicated, he feels that the nature of these is currently unknown, being particularly concerned about how far malnutrition is also involved. His generalised depiction of the 'African' character is maintained, invoking Westermann again, although he acknowledges (citing Nadel 1937a) that this is less than entirely homogeneous.

By 1972 his position had, if anything, firmed up, claiming 'it would be astonishing if these two races ['Caucasoid' and 'Congoid'] should have remained identical in the genetic basis of their mental functions' and explicitly condemning the 1951 UNESCO statement. It is nevertheless a somewhat strange amalgam of the hoary and the trendy. He uncritically cites long dubious brain-size difference data (even Bean, 1906 which Mall, 1909 had effectively refuted) and US IQ difference research (plus the pre-war African work by Fick and Oliver), while again rehearsing the stereotyped image of the modal African character. But he has also by now read some Margaret Mead and familiarised himself with Culture and Personality school views on the effects of different kinds of child-rearing (e.g. age of weaning),[56] the Freudian nature of which he goes along with in qualified fashion, and – as we will see in a moment – he adopts the ideas of Marshall McLuhan. His brief account of the genetics of human diversity is actually pretty accurate, but somewhat in thrall to an already obsolete account of human evolution which affects his interpretation of this. He also claims that no genetic selective process occurred during the slave trade and US slavery to differentiate black Americans from Africans. Four factors in particular lead him to remain convinced of a 'constitutional' factor over and above disease, malnutrition and specific climatic or geographical environmental ones: (a) the failure of literacy to become established even though writing had occasionally been autonomously invented, (b) the 'precocity' of African child development, (c) US 'Negro' underperformance on IQ tests and (d) African difficulty with three-dimensional problems. African peculiarities are the product of evolutionary adaptions to the African environment which have become 'constitutionally engrained'.

Yet, as already indicated, he is not entirely oblivious of the cultural dimension. Most originally he now interprets the African's alleged 'ear' dominated culture and lack of visuo-spatial ability in the light of McLuhan's account of the transition to literacy in European cultures. The move from an 'ear', or language and sound, centred culture to an 'eye' culture based on writing and visual images entailed a dramatic psychological change. Africans failed to make this transition, but possibly because of their 'engrained' constitutional character. Given the antiquity of African rock art, the powerful and creative character of much African carving and sculpture, and common cultural relishing of colour, this seems rather hard to take. There are, even so, signs that Carothers is uneasy. His account, he says, is less true of urbanised Africans than those living traditional lifestyles and many Africans have shown themselves perfectly capable of educational and professional success and competence in European terms. While still citing his earlier 33-item list of typical African failings and foibles he is more on the defensive – perhaps the 'inability to see total situations' would apply to Europeans as well if placed in an alien context, although the hilarious irony of this concession eludes him completely. As Fanon (1965) points out:

> And is it not the simple truth that under the colonial regime a *fellah* who is keen on his work or a Negro who refuses to rest are nothing but pathological cases? The native's laziness is the conscious sabotage of the colonial machine; on the biological plane it is a remarkable system of auto-protection; and in any case it is a sure brake upon the seizure of the whole country by the occupying power. (p. 238)

Carothers never escapes what Mama (1995) calls his 'colonial psychiatric paradigm'.[57] She is understandably merciless in her page and a half summary of his position. She rightly notes the deep contradiction between his claim to be discussing a generalised 'African mind' and the qualifications he enters about not being concerned with Christians, Muslims, urban and educated Africans, or groups 'like the Yoruba' who have 'diverged from the usual rural pattern'. 'Non-Negroes' which in traditional European racial classifications included pygmies, Hottentots, 'Hamites, half-Hamites and Semites' are also excluded. Once all these are omitted, who *are* the typical 'Africans' of whom he is speaking? Moreover, he views Africa in typically Eurocentric terms as a 'disease-infested place with a hostile climate, held in check by the persisting legacies of 'tribal' culture' (Mama, p. 31).

As a colonially based psychiatrist, Carothers is relatively marginal to the main story regarding Psychology, but his case has some interesting features. First, the specific form his racism took differs from that of the Shuey–Garrett camp (though he takes their data at face value), he does not see his account as polarised against other branches of Psychology but is happily eclectic. (McGurk would never have co-opted McLuhan.) He is centred in a paternalistic medical role, not as a defender of segregation and psychometrics. Secondly, an intriguing passage in his introduction to the 1971 work ought to be noted. He is ostensibly talking about the notional reader of the book who, he says, sometimes seems to him to be a twin-headed prodigy who, with one of his minds, adheres staunchly to the faith that Africans belong to a different and wholly inferior species of man, and with his other mind holds the equally staunch faith that human groups are mentally identical. (pp. 7–8)

He of course rejects both of these poles and seeks to address a 'reasonable' reader who is only interested in the 'facts'. But this surely signifies his own inner tension by 1971 (which he in effect admits in a displaced fashion). The old colonial era has passed away beneath his feet. He is having to work for and alongside newly independant Africans and, let's be charitable, this is where his own psychological home now is. His position owes most, one feels, to an uncritical acceptance of the objective and universal character of Western Psychiatry and its scientific vocabulary (which he applied in 1954 to the Mau Mau revolutionary independence movement). The most productive use to be made of Carothers' work now would be to explore his discourse further for insights into the specific mode of racialist consciousness it represents, a mode of consciousness clearly bound up with the peculiar socio-historical circumstances of late colonial East Africa.[58] What is most striking, when you think about it, is that nowhere is there any indication that Carothers ever adopted the most obvious elementary procedure in trying to ascertain the reasons why Africans behaved (in the presence of whites) in the way they did – sitting down and talking with them about it. Of course they notoriously only told you what you wanted to hear anyway – but in this case what was that?

In summary then, the Race Psychology 'underground' during this period was certainly not inactive. It included some fairly eminent figures such as, most obviously, Garrett, and in the USA it continued to pump out research on intelligence differences of a somewhat ritualised kind (at the same time co-opting relevant data from black-authored sources). A great deal of this was in the form of unpublished post-graduate theses, often from Southern Universities where the segregationist academic network was strongest. Financially the show was largely kept on the road by the Pioneer Fund and Southern racist organisations which backed the FHU, the IAAEE and *Mankind Quarterly*.

'NATIVISM = RACISM'

It is useful at this point briefly to consider an assumption which became widespread among psychologists in the immediate post-war period and still commonly persists. The so-called 'nature vs. nurture' controversy had of course been running ever since Galton launched it in the 19th century. The issue seemed simple enough – how much of our psychological character is due to heredity and how much due to learning or the environment? This could be asked of everything from perception to sex-roles. To oversimplify, within early 20th century US Psychology two strands came to co-exist: the highly environmentalist 'behaviourist' approach within experimental Psychology and the highly hereditarian approach within psychometrics. Prior to World War II this controversy was seen as primarily an empirical scientific matter. Hereditarian eugenics in particular spanned those of both left and right (especially in Britain, Karl Pearson after all considered himself a socialist), although a strong right-wing strand was already evident, in the USA especially. Nazism changed all that. In the late 1940s and 1950s the dimension became firmly ideologically loaded: 'nativism' was inherently right-wing, environmentalism left-wing. Nazi hereditarian racial theories and broader use of nativist eugenic arguments to support the persecution and extermination of homosexuals and the mentally handicapped as well as Jews and other ethnic minorities were the central factor in this shift. Within Psychology itself the aspiration to turn the discipline into a resource for practical intervention in the solution of individual and social problems additionally heightened the appeal of environmentalism for reasons mentioned earlier.[59]

At the theoretical level the nature vs. nurture controversy supplied an underlying structure for much of the debate within Psychology – one might even claim that since it was applicable to such a wide range of issues it served as a unifying force for the inherently fissiparous discipline. It represented a long-term legacy from the late 19th century heyday of evolutionary thought which had, at the time, served to (almost) integrate Psychology into a single multi-faceted enterprise. For reasons more fully dealt with in the next chapter, the scientific coherence of this polarity began to crumble after 1970, and although it continues to frame much popular thinking on a range of topics, geneticists and, hopefully, most psychologists, no longer see it as a particularly useful schema. The flaw is not so much that the two 'interact' as that the very notion of them being distinguishable, even in principle, has been undermined. One can never know what 'genes' would produce in the absence of an 'environment'. And even more obviously one cannot say what an 'environment' would produce in the absence of 'genes'.

How does this relate to the 'race' issue? During the years being considered here these conceptual difficulties were as yet only partly formulated. Those psychologists espousing strong 'nativist' positions almost inevitably gave some credence to race-differences doctrines, while those with the opposite allegiance opposed them. The major theoretical moves in Psychology were in the latter camp: the shift from behaviourism to cognitivism largely retained the former's environmentalist character in being concerned with formulating a better model of the human as a learning system. While cognitivism left the door open for innate programming (e.g. in Noam Chomsky's psycholinguistics), 'race' as such was not a cognitivist concern (and Chomsky himself was resolutely radical politically).[60] The close linkage between nativism and racialism during this period may perhaps best be seen as a transient phenomenon arising from the still crude way in which the genes–environment relationship was being conceived. While the discovery of the nature of the DNA molecule in 1953 changed the terms of the entire question it inevitably took a considerable time before the implications became fully apparent.[61] Within genetics itself the credibility of the 'race' concept was, as we saw, already in question in the 1930s. This trend gathered momentum, genetics itself progressively cutting the ground from under the hereditarian racialists' feet. By 1968 the game was effectively over. For the contributors to M. Mead et al. (1968), who included the doyen of contemporary geneticists T. Dobzhansky, the concept of race was at best a convenient short-hand term for reproductively isolated populations within a species, and even then of dubious applicability to humans among whom such populations were extremely rare.[62] This only reinforced the message of A. Montagu (1964) which included such papers as F.B. Livingstone's 'On the nonexistence of human races'.[63]

Few eminent geneticists or palaeontologists now endorse the racialism which typified many of their predecessors. We can surely afford to be a bit more relaxed about claims that particular psychological phenomena involve genetic factors. Acknowledging this is in no way fundamentally inconsistent with accepting the socio–culturally determined nature of meanings, values and classification systems in relation to such phenomena, and that it is these which actually render them *psychological*.

'Nativism' owes much of its power to the (erroneously drawn) implication that that which is inherited is immutable. It is therefore seen as legitimating existing gender-roles, hierarchical social structures and so on as direct expressions of an unchangeable 'human nature'. Since it views the possibilities of change as highly constrained, however, it actually provides a less secure rationale for totalitarian schemes of mass social engineering (as opposed to authoritarian regimes of social control) than radical environmentalism. If one is interested in drawing ideological consequences, either right- or left-wing, from these spuriously opposed positions it is fairly easy to invoke elements of each. Their ideological line-up in the post-war years nevertheless seemed clear-cut: nativists to the right, environmentalists to the left (and 'the two interact' compromisers in the middle). My point here is that that is indeed *history*. Even the 'interactionist' position must now be considered too crude a formulation. In the relevant 'hard' scientific disciplines at least, this schema is long obsolete.

CONCLUSION

Developments during the period under consideration were obviously complicated. The liberal wing within white US Psychology devoted an extraordinary amount of effort to the task of investigating the psychological nature of 'race prejudice', deploying a mixture of theoretical frameworks. It also began to become more reflexively conscious of the problems involved in white psychologists undertaking research on African Americans. Notwithstanding this it remained handicapped in several respects. First, despite an early insistence on the multi-disciplinary nature of the issues and the essentially complementary role of Psychological work *vis-à-vis* Sociology and Economics, the effect of its work was to reinforce an image of racism as an individual level psychological phenomenon. Equally seriously, the 'damaged Negro' stereotype, the 'cultural deprivation' hypothesis and the pathologisation of the 'matriarchal' black family were among the products of this white liberal position when it turned to the 'Negro' personality itself. They were unable to create productive links with sociologists such as the Caribbean-born Marxist O.C. Cox, the most eminent black sociologist,[64] and their approach unwittingly served to distract attention from the more structurally fundamental socio-economic sources of racism. This tendency was exacerbated by the prevailing ideological climate of the late 1940s and 1950s in which an embattled liberal intelligentsia were wary of mounting any serious critiques of US society remotely construable as pro–communist or Marxist in character.

Secondly, their own psychological situation was usually such that they were unable fully to acknowledge the ethnocentricities instrinsic to their approaches. They continued to write as if for white readers alone, continued to adopt a basically paternalistic orientation to African Americans as victims or damaged, and persisted in seeing the orthodox white middle–class life–style and culture as the rational universal aspiration. While there are indications of an emerging awareness of these issues as the 1950s progressed, the majority of white liberal psychologists remained seriously blinkered. This should not be misunderstood. Many undoubtedly sensed that some such issues were lurking beneath the surface and would have addressed them if they could, but they were ultimately constrained in what they could think or articulate by the implicit, unspoken, virtually invisible, assumptions and attitudes of their generation, culture and class, as are we all. Such assumptions and attitudes can only be rendered visible by those of different generations, cultures, classes, and so forth – and, although the situation was set to change dramatically, these as yet were in no position to do so.

Thirdly, within American Psychology's institutional structures, notably the APA, the anti–racist camp had relatively little direct power. The SPSSI could be little more than a specific lobby or interest group. With figures such as Garrett and Porteus remaining eminent and respected within the APA, there was little hope of engineering any unambiguous, formal anti–racist commitment from the organisation on behalf of US Psychology as a whole. Instead, a policy of explicit avoidance of political issues was adopted and adhered to. This in turn further alienated the growing number of African American and other non–European psychologists, for whom racism was not simply a 'political' issue but a matter of life and death. Again the Cold War climate may be seen as contributing to the APA's moral paralysis. The situation was further compounded by the persistence of a vociferous, sometimes powerful and influential, segregationist and pro–race differences constituency within the discipline, especially in the South.

If racism was in some sense 'at bay' within post–war US Psychology, it was nevertheless impossible actually to expel it. To have tried to do so would have meant not only condemning some contemporary disciplinary heroes (like Garrett), not only have risked the wrath of the Cold War ideological establishment, but also of course have been seen as breaching fundamental Constitutional and academic rights to free speech. The discipline's dilemmas here only reflected in particularly acute form those of US society at large. There was a patent *prima facie* contradiction between, on the one hand, the aspirations and values of the US Constitution and Declaration of Independence, in the name of which World War II had just been fought, and on the other hand the domestic situation of African Americans and native Americans. Touring black musicians whose records were selling millions still had to eat among the garbage–cans at the back of Texas diners.[65] Within Psychology, as outside, important developments were in train in the understanding of 'race' issues, and the anti–racist position was making significant headway, but the opposing and inhibiting forces remained sufficiently powerful to prevent any genuine resolution. This ensured that, again both inside and outside the discipline, the pressure was building to intolerable levels. By the mid-1960s the lid had blown.

Beyond the US, race differences and 'race prejudice' occupied a relatively low place on Psychology's list of priorities during these years. Fanon, however powerful his work, was operating in virtual isolation as a black Marxist psychiatrist. There was a considerable expansion of colonially sited 'cross-cultural' work being conducted, but this was (South Africa aside) invariably presented as non-racialist in nature, though with ambiguities only now readily apparent. J.C. Carothers' psychiatric racialism, if well-aired, was an isolated effort with no research back-up from others. When black immigration into the UK brought race relations to the forefront in Britain the issue was construed primarily as a sociological one, with British psychologists for the most part rehearsing US 'prejudice' theories rather than conducting further research themselves. Robb (1954) reported a study of working-class anti-semitism in Bethnal Green (East London) but otherwise British Psychology did little at this time other than familiarise itself with US work. Two factors contributed to the sociological emphasis in Britain. First the British resistance to admitting to psychological racism, as noted in the previous chapter, meant that socio-economic explanations for 'race relations' problems were more attractive. Secondly, even after the fall of the radical post-war Labour government the ideological climate remained more congenial to this level of analysis than in the USA. Social engineering remained to some degree an accepted aspect of governmental functioning. The legacy of this has been that within British Psychology 'race'-related topics have subsequently been actively tackled most frequently on the Sociology/field Social Psychology borderline rather than in the experimental Social Psychology and psychometric 'attitude measurement' traditions.[66] Another consequence of this however has been to strengthen 'colour-blind' racism in British political life.[67]

The essential problem facing white anti-racist Psychology during these years was perhaps this; that as reflexive understanding of white racism developed among white psychologists their own confidence in their ability, or even right, to continue acting as if on behalf of a client/victim group was undermined (and Fanon served to drive the message home). Although the word only became used somewhat later, the 'empowerment' of African Americans (including of course African American psychologists) required that white psychologists step aside, or at least take a back seat on the freedom-ride bus. But to do so was psychologically very difficult, it would seem like yielding the field uncontested or moral cowardice masquerading as moral courage. For US Black Psychology one problem was trying to operate within a discipline which explicitly refused to acknowledge that Civil Rights and combating racism were more than 'political' issues. More fundamentally, as we will see in Chapter 10, they were faced with making difficult choices regarding how much of existing Psychology they could accept or co-opt, and how much they would be wiser to abandon. The issues waiting to be addressed by Black Psychology were legion.[68] How could theoretical frameworks be developed directly from their own experience to tackle them? For white pro-race differences psychologists the period largely involved playing a waiting game in the hope that the cultural climate would eventually become more sympathetic, or an opportunity arise to re-open the race differences question. In the meantime they could but conduct a kind of academic guerrilla campaign, firing the odd salvo of new data on IQ score differences, but unable to mount any serious theoretical rebuttals of the seemingly solid case of their opponents (basically Klineberg, 1935b, now buttressed with extended further outworks). Thus marginalised they opportunistically sought support from any quarter they could and (as discussed further in the next chapter) became progressively enmeshed in the neo-Nazi/ Ku Klux Klan network.

We may end by pondering on why, in the light of all this, Jensen's 1969 papers had such a momentous effect. In truth it was only the spark which triggered a well-laid powder keg. By 1969 the Civil Rights movement had achieved its immediate constitutional and legislative aims and, following Martin Luther King's assassination, a new generation of less non-violent and less integrationist radical black activists had emerged as the most publicly visible representatives of African America. In the wider context of the Vietnam War débacle and an un-manageable alternative or 'counter' culture, some attempted backlash was inevit-able. Instead of a white sheet Jensen now rode into town in the white coat of the solid old-fashioned scientist. It was back to psychometric basics. For the first time since 1945 the, by now desperately frustrated, pro-differences camp had a cred-ible, ostensibly purely scientific cause, around which to rally. The widely used counter-culture slogan 'the return of the repressed', was not, after all, hippiedom's monopoly.

NOTES

1 For a general overview see P.K. Bock (1980), and for a collection of personal accounts of work in the area see G.D. Spindler (1978).
2 See Mama (1995, p. 35).
3 See J. and B.B. Whiting (1978) for a useful retrospective account.
4 M.H. Segall et al. (1963, 1966) and R. Brown (1958, Chapter VII) are major examples of the incorporation of this work regarding perception and linguistics respectively.
5 See Howitt and Owusu-Bempah (1994, pp. 69–76) for examples.
6 See ibid. for a critique of R.L. Atkinson et al. (1990) (the 10th edition of a highly suc-cessful textbook) from this angle. This subsequently generated a rather heated exchange in *The Psychologist*.
7 It should perhaps be noted that Marie Jahoda and Gustav Jahoda are unrelated.
8 Of particular relevance is Carey McWilliams (1948), which charts the topic from its apparent emergence in 1877 when Joseph Seligman, a New York banker, was refused accommodation at the Grand Union Hotel in Saratoga Springs – prior to this the record 'had been largely free of overt or significant manifestations of anti-Semitism' (p. 3), although there had been a few incidents.
9 N.W. Ackerman (1947), N.W. Ackerman and Marie Jahoda (1948a, b).
10 This appears in all volumes in the series. Of course the trope of 'prejudice as disease' mirrors the 'alien as parasite' etc. images used by the racist camp.
11 This point was reiterated from a different direction by D.T. Campbell (1968) who argues that orthodox studies of group differences tend to imply that 'were the actual group differences to exist, discrimination would be justified' (p. 827). The context here is an attempt to integrate Hullian learning theory and Asch-type Gestaltist Social Psychology in studying stereotyping and perception of group differences.

12 Bettelheim and Janowitz (1950, pp. 16, 26).
13 Notably M. Roiser and C. Willig (1995, 1996). I am indebted to these papers for much of the content of this section, though my interpretation of the episode should not be assumed to be theirs.
14 See Roiser and Willig (1995) for a full account.
15 Marx's questionnaire was intended to serve as a consciousness-raising exercise in itself, as well as a source of information, and included such items as "Do you have the opportunity to strike or are you allowed merely to be the humble servants of your masters?" and "Has the employer ever paid compensation to those who have met with an accident while working to enrich him?" (ibid., 1995, p. 89). Marx had seen the factory setting as congenial to the development of workers' revolutionary solidarity. By Levenstein's time, however, there was a growing feeling that the psychological effects of modern factory work practices were sufficiently damaging in themselves to off-set this – which his study attempted to address.
16 The University of California's regents had introduced a rule requiring all academic staff to swear an oath of allegiance. R. Nevitt Sanford was among those following Tolman in refusing to do so (Levinson, being a graduate student, was 'probably un-affected'). This resulted in their all being dismissed, but they were subsequently re-instated after agreeing to swear a watered-down compromise oath required of all public employees. See Roiser and Willig (1996). *American Psychologist*, vol. 6 (1951) is a useful primary source, containing extensive correspondence on the controversy, this rumbles on subsequently, especially in vol. 9 (1954).
17 See e.g. Adorno et al. (*AP* henceforth) p. 4.
18 McWilliams (1948, Chapter XI) also drew on Sartre's (1946) account.
19 See Roiser and Willig (1995, pp. 78 ff.) on this.
20 Titus and Hollander (1955). The main journal outlet for this was the fairly radical *Journal of Social Issues*, produced by the Society for the Psychological Study of Social Issues (SPSSI), a group within the APA.
21 The others being 'Political and Economic Conservatism' (PEC) and 'Implicit Anti-Democratic Trends' or 'Potentiality for Fascism' (F). The F-scale tended to be that most widely used subsequently.
22 The final version of this had 10 items, four on Jews, three on 'Negroes', one on general threats to America and one on 'Zootsuiters'. See *AP*, p. 128.
23 ibid., pp. 141–2.
24 Membership of the House Un-American Activities Committee actually overlapped with that of the radical racist right, notably in the case of the Chairman, Francis E. Walter, who was also a member of the Pioneer Fund's grants-distributing committee. See W.H. Tucker (1994, p. 173).
25 This was apparent from the outset in B.M. Smith (1950), a review of *AP* in which McCarthyite attitudes to communists and homosexuals are explicitly identified as con-forming to the authoritarian personality syndrome. (see Roiser and Willig, 1996).
26 R. Christie and M. Jahoda (1954).
27 E. Frenkel-Brunswik (1954); M. Rokeach (1960) is the fullest statement of his position.
28 Shils was a Chicago sociologist and co-editor with Harvard's Talcott Parsons, perhaps the most eminent US sociologist at this point, of *Toward A General Theory of Action* (1962, 1st edn 1951).
29 I have periodically redone this for amusement ever since the 1960s, though many items are now obsolete, and always come off the end of the radicalism scale.
30 *American Psychologist* first appeared in 1946.
31 The gaps are: 1946, 1948, 1960, 1961, 1965. In 1986 the *Journal of Social Issues* sub-stantially devoted one issue, vol. 42(1), to historical recollections and analysis of the SPSSI's founding and the journal's early years. Klineberg added another in 42(4) (containing L.J. Finison, B. Harris, O. Klineberg, J. Morawski, R. Stagner – see D. Howitt and J. Owusu-Bempah, 1994 for full citations).

32 For example, vol. 7 (1 and 2) (ed. R.K. Merton et al.) and vol. 13 (4) (1957) (ed. A.J. Mayer) on housing; vol. 9 (ed. D. Bell and S.M. Lipset) on 'Trade Unions and Minority Problems' and E.T. Prothro (1954) on the Deep South. Japanese–American relations figured relatively frequently in the early years and intermittently thereafter and vol. 9 (3) (ed. E.O. Melby and M. Brewster Smith) tackled 'Academic freedom in a climate of insecurity' at the height of the Stanford oath-taking affair and McCarthyism.

33 In 1967 King was still using the word 'Negro', this changed shortly after of course when Black American was adopted and 'Negro' seen as intrinsically derogatory.

34 William Brazziel's scathing contempt for Jensen's paper (Brazziel, 1969), for example, ought surely to be read in this context.

35 See also B.P. Karon (1958) which I have not been able to discuss here, which further explored the theme of 'Negro' male passivity and repression of aggression.

36 Ironically Herskovits's efforts to identify a continuing African heritage in African American culture (i.e. that it actually *had* a culture) alarmed African American writers such as E. Franklin Frazier and A. Locke in the 1940s because it was thought this would heighten white beliefs that they were unassimilable and reduce white guilt. This perhaps gives some indication of quite how fearful US black intellectuals still were at this point and the psychological distance separating them from the 1950s and 1960s black radicals and activists. See G. Myrdal (1944, vol. 2, p. 1394, n. 32).

37 Cases 1,3,4,7 and 8, and arguably 2 and 10 too. Brutal fathers, bad stepmothers and maternal abandonment figure in these.

38 See Howitt and Owusu-Bempah (1994, pp. 41–6), who cite work into the 1980s which continued to attack the 'pathological' black family. It is perhaps worth noting that a work such as A. Meier and E.M. Rudwick (1970) – 'an interpretive history of American Negroes' – totally ignores Kardiner and Ovesey's book, failing to mention it even in the substantial bibliographic essay. This despite the detailed attention Kardiner and Ovesey give to the 'psychology of slavery'.

39 See p. 19. The MMPI is the Minnesota Multiphasic Personality Inventory, one of the most widely used diagnostic instruments.

40 See Chapter 10 and E.E. Johnson (1969) cited above.

41 For example, P. Brown (1973) and J. Donald and A. Rattansi (1992).

42 See W.H. Tucker (1994) especially pp.110–27 for more on this; the quote from the *Eugenical News* editorial is on p. 124.

43 ibid. pp. 124–7.

44 ibid. p. 173.

45 See Tucker (1994, p. 141 ff.) for a detailed account and analysis of the impact of this and racist responses, on which my coverage here primarily draws.

46 See e.g. E.S. Lee (1951), F.H. Stallings (1960).

47 L. Plotkin (1959), M.S. Smart (1963), C.C. Josey (1966).

48 The impossibility of 'equating background conditions' had long been argued, e.g. F.N. Freeman (1934) and H.G. Canady (1943).

49 Only nine unpublished references predate 1931; the distribution has three main clusters: 1932–8 (19), 1946–51 (44), 1962–5 (15), but 1954 (12), otherwise isolated, is the single most cited year, 1946 and 1947 coming next (11 and 10 respectively). The 1932–8 cluster presumably reflects the decline in published work during this decade, and the relative trough from 1939–45 corresponds to the war years, though begins a little earlier from a US viewpoint. It may be relevant that 1954 was the year of the *Brown vs. Board of Education* case, though it is hard to see quite how. The 1955–61 trough corresponds with the post-war low point for pro–differences doctrines, and the early 1960s cluster presumably reflects the intensifying civil rights struggle and the backlash against it. 1965 is the last year cited.

50 T.F. Pettigrew (1964) additionally notes, regarding the 1st edition, that 'three-fourths of her studies on students' come from 'tightly segregated Southern and border

communities' (p. 102), accuses her of selectivity and notes that she ignored some crucial studies of examiner effects (p. 116, footnote).

51 We return to this point, related to the so-called 'Flynn effect', in the next chapter.

52 See W.H. Tucker (1994) passim and especially pp. 249–55 for more on this duo.

53 D. Westermann, a German anthropologist, signs off his Introduction from the University of Berlin, 1939, which alone raises one's eyebrows.

54 See above pp. 203–4 for discussion of Vint (1932). Carothers only cites Vint (1934).

55 Carothers never seems to have returned to it, in fact, and is never again quite so specific regarding physiological causes of alleged African shortcomings.

56 J.F. Ritchie (1943) had been particularly keen on this theme, claiming that the lateness of African weaning engendered a distinctively conflicted psychological outcome. They are 'driven by two opposing forces: a benevolent force giving them everything for nothing, and a malevolent force depriving them of life itself. The resulting ambivalence and conflict were said to make the African dependent on a mother or mother-surrogate (read European)' (Howitt and Owusu-Bempah, 1994, p. 71).

57 B.J.F. Laubscher (1937) is an earlier example, though with a more 'culture and personality' flavour.

58 Such a study might fruitfully include J.F. Ritchie (1943), M.L. Fick (1939) and S. Biesheuvel (1943) – an attack on Fick's nativism – as examples of South African Psychology's dealings with 'race' and the forms of racism it manifested slightly earlier. See also the discussion of W. Sachs (1937) in the previous chapter. I have been unable to incorporate full discussion of all this work in the present book. A French psychoanalyst in a somewhat similar bind to Carothers was O. Mannoni (O. Mannoni, 1956, 1966), who is critically discussed by both Fanon (1965) and Mama (1995). Mannoni was anti-colonialist but nevertheless saw his Madagascan subjects as suffering from a 'dependency' complex etc. In 1966 he substantially recanted.

59 See above p. 24.

60 Since Chomsky was concerned with linguistic universals, the notion that grammar was deeply programmed would in any case have been of little use to racists. Jerome Bruner, a leading cognitivist, had testified in the *Brown vs. Board of Education* case, as mentioned earlier.

61 Though Pettigrew (1964), for one, has a pretty sound grasp of the genetic situation (see his Chapter 3).

62 Dobzhansky himself (in his late sixties), it should be admitted, did dig his heels in a bit as a self-confessed 'old compromiser'. He cannot see how human differences can be discussed at all without using the 'race' concept. He admits that clear-cut definitions of race are impossible, but this is because if there were we would be dealing with different species, not races. If scientists do not study race then pseudo-scientific race bigots will. As is argued in the next chapter, however, it is indeed possible to discuss differences using the technical concepts of modern population genetics. Dobzhansky could not then conceive of the possibility of non-racialised discourse.

63 Among the papers in M. Mead et al. (1968) Gloria A. Marshall's 'Racial classifications: popular and scientific' and Morton H. Fried's 'The need to end the pseudoscientific investigation of race' are particularly handy. Another influential work from this period was Marvin Harris (1964) in which he coined the term 'hypodescent' for the practice of racially classifying people of mixed parentage as belonging to the group with lower economic status – as happens with African Americans.

64 See O.C. Cox (1970, 1st edn 1948). Cox became Professor of Sociology at Lincoln University, Missouri.

65 According to various Tamla Motown veterans speaking on *Dancing in the Streets*, BBC2, 6 July 1996.

66 An important British figure from this period whose work I have been unable to discuss was, of course, Philip Mason.

67 See Chapter 10 and G. Ben-Tovim et al. (1986).
68 See R. Wilcox (1971) for a representative collection of work by black psychologists concerned with these, mostly dating from this period. Some of course were practising in unrelated areas of mainstream physiological or experimental Psychology.

Chapter 9

Race and IQ 1969–96: An undead controversy

BACKGROUND AND OVERVIEW

It is, I confess, with great weariness that I turn to this topic. Perhaps we may begin on a slightly distanced note. Historians of science have recently been much concerned with the 'closure' of scientific controversies. Bruno Latour's picture is particularly relevant to the present topic.[1] Controversies, he argues, close when one party has marshalled so many 'allies' of various kinds – including already closed controversies – that the cost (both economic and intellectual) of keeping the topic open becomes simply too high for dissenters to meet. An additional, very pertinent, feature of his account is the apparent futility of trying to draw any clear line between an internal purely 'scientific' realm and an external 'social' one. The network of allies extends in intricate fashion beyond the laboratory to sources of funding, political interests, industry and the media. Scientific activity is, in today's world, locked into vast inter-penetrating 'associations' of interests. Let us bear this in mind in what follows.

In Chapter 4, modern Psychology's concern with race differences was traced, if not exclusively, to the early 20th century preoccupation with 'Negro education' in the US. The key question it asked was: Are 'Negroes' inferior to whites in intelligence? Much depended, so it seemed, on the answer. If they were, then their segregated education, concentrating on 'industrial' training, could be justified 'scientifically'. The allies of this first generation of race psychologists were the 'establishment' educational policy makers of the day, especially in the Deep South, and the then powerful eugenics lobby, who extended the topic to their own immigration concerns. During the inter-war period this network of 'external' allies weakened, as did the 'internal' scientific support for Scientific Racism and eugenics doctrines, which had hitherto verged on becoming 'closed', 'Black Boxes' as Latour calls them – that is, findings and theories no longer being contested. The angle of interest in African American education shifted to identifying rectifiable (in principle) environmental factors determining black academic under-performance. By 1940 it looked very much as if the question of race differences in intelligence was settled – there were none, or such as existed were too minimal to worry about and not necessarily permanent. The liberal Rooseveltian 'New Deal' climate, the growing emancipationist movement and events in Germany, 'internal' theoretical challenges to the concept of 'race' and acknowledgement of recalcitrant, probably insoluble, methodological problems – all combined to create a formidable network of allies for the no-difference camp which left their opponents highly marginalised. The switch in tack of the Carnegie Foundation mentioned earlier may be cited as signifying the changed situation.[2]

As we have seen, the 'Negro intelligence' issue had begun simmering again in the wake of the *Brown v. Board of Education of Topeka, Kansas* case in 1954, but it was in 1969 that Jensen's *Harvard Educational Review* monograph 'How much can we boost IQ and scholastic achievement?' signalled what was in effect a reversion to Race Psychology's opening agenda – did race differences cause African American educational underachievement? In doing so it returned the topic from the pro-segregationist ghetto to the mainstream of the discipline's concerns. What had appeared a closed controversy was reopened – or was it? The consequences of this monograph, which continue even yet, present a rather curious case. In essence the situation has been that for the *majority* of psychologists, geneticists and anthropologists the question has remained 'scientifically' closed – it is meaningless and unresearchable. The controversy is not so much alive as undead. On the other hand the minority pro-differences camp, consisting primarily of a small group of, occasionally quite eminent, psychometricians (though not all psychometricians I must stress) has managed to muster enough allies to keep the controversy culturally alive. Just who these allies are we will consider later. A highly controversial reading of the 'socio-biology' approach during the latter 1970s and 1980s reinforced this, leading many to fear a return to Social Darwinism, of which Scientific Racism was a central dogma.[3] At the disciplinary institutional level the pro-differences camp has been able to maintain a certain level of representation in the journals under the 'academic freedom' rubric, and professional associations such as the British Psychological Society have proved chronically incapable of taking an unambiguous stand lest they be seen to be engaged in a witch-hunt. As a discipline Psychology in general has thus, over the last decade and a half, been seen as continuing to collude with racism. This contrasts strongly with the public image of, for example, Sociology. This situation has not arisen solely because of the 'race and IQ' issue, as we will see in the next chapter, but this remains a central factor.

The literature generated around the issue since 1969 is dauntingly vast, and a comprehensive review is impossible here.[4] Instead I offer a specific reading of events from an avowedly anti-race differences perspective. To strive for 'objectivity' in this context is vain. Historians of the English Civil War of the 17th century still remain aligned along pro-monarchist and pro-Cromwellian lines, so one can hardly expect disinterested detachment regarding an ongoing conflict in which any author is bound to be an enlisted participant – even were such disinterestedness to be recommended even in principle, which is debatable to say the least. Anything written while the battle rages is itself a part of the contest.

My reading is as follows. Jensen's paper (Jensen 1969a) defined the issue in terms of the heritability of IQ, ostensibly backing this up with what he, somewhat oversimplistically, presented as a consensus position among population geneticists regarding how races should be defined and their differences construed. This was rhetorically clever in co-opting a discipline widely seen, since the mid-1930s, as having subverted the very notion of 'race'. The dispassionate scientific style of the paper, coupled with the status of the journal in which it appeared, enabled it to reach the parts of the disciplinary and US psyches which Cattell and Garrett could not reach. This opening move ensured that the strictly 'scientific' question concerned relatively arcane issues relating to data analysis and population genetics. The environmentalism of many contemporary social scientists had also reached an intensity and a level of dogmatism which made them easy targets, only the more ripe for attack for having been able to render such attacks taboo for so long. The initial reaction to Jensen's paper involved a recovery and restatement of the arguments which had seemingly settled the matter three decades earlier, with some updating in terminology. Things then got messy. First, the extremely fraught political climate in which the issue was reopened led to the debate being conducted on a very broad front in which psychologists were only one of the interested parties. Jensen was rapidly adopted as a hero by pro-segregationist and neo-Nazi groups, endorsed by Garrett and promoted by W.B. Shockley, a Nobel Prize-winning physicist with ample financial resources to indulge his fascination with the eugenics of intelligence and race differences.[5] In Britain H.J. Eysenck quickly entered the lists on Jensen's side, an interview with him appearing in the first issue of the fascist British National Party's magazine *Beacon*.[6] Secondly the whole topic became dominated by the 'heritability of intelligence' question, involving a maze of conceptual issues and generating a range of highly technical critiques which outsiders had difficulty tracking and evaluating. In contrast to the sprawling Race Psychology phase, the scientific grounds on which debate centred were thus tightly drawn, while its wider moral and ideological ramifications were even greater.

The upshot has been a dreadful muddle in which the anti-racist camp, by mounting so many different kinds of argument, continually trips over its own feet, enabling the smaller, but more internally coherent, pro-differences camp to cast itself as a benighted group of pure scientists assailed by a miscellaneous army of ideologues and political partisans intent on denying the Truth, as revealed by their purely scientific procedures. Incidents such as a physical attack on H.J. Eysenck at the London School of Economics reinforced their image as latter-day Galileos defending scientific honesty against fanatical ideologically blinkered foes even, as we will see, while their own funding was coming primarily from extreme ideological sources. While on balance the outcome is nonetheless a sort of victory for the anti-differences camp(s), 'closure' is never definitively achieved. It constantly remains unclear whether the pro-differences camp's case is wrong as a matter of 'fact', or whether we are to simply reject the entire project as meaningless and/or immoral on other grounds. The controversy assumes an increasingly ritualised character. Periodically a pro-differences text (such as Herrnstein and Murray's, 1994, *The Bell Curve*) appears, repackaging the case though rarely significantly changing its contents, and a replay of the same contest ensues, with the same result – after a couple of years the pro-differences case seems to have evaporated. But, as with Dracula, its allies or hidden offspring retain sufficient resources for a remake in due course and overtly tabooed racist discourse can be covertly produced as 'science'.

The controversy has passed through several phases. Initially the response was a reactivation of many of the well-established counter arguments to race-differences theories developed in the pre-1950 period. This was combined with a heightened level of political attack from African Americans who derided the entire Jensen approach.[7] In California the Bay Area Association of Black Psychologists issued a 'Position statement on use of IQ and ability tests' (1972, 1st edn 1969) in which they demanded that the California State Department of Education declare a moratorium on their use in assessing black children. They also asked that culturally relevant tests be 'secured, authorized and required', to be evaluated by their own association. Additionally, disproportionate representation of minority group children in 'mentally retarded' classes should be monitored and accounted for to the State Board of Education. Meanwhile, both in the USA and Britain Jensen's findings were widely publicised and circulated by racist and neo-Nazi organisations, from which pro-differences psychologists did little to dissociate themselves.[8]

In 1972 events took a new turn. Jensen's argument rested, we saw, on the 'heritability of IQ' question. The central evidence used to justify the assumption of high heritability of IQ included the results of the twin studies of Sir Cyril Burt, who died in 1971. US psychologist Leon Kamin began re-examining these and in April 1972 at a Princeton University Psychology Department colloquium first voiced his opinion that Burt's data were fraudulent, a charge he reiterated at several other meetings and conferences over the next year before including them in his *The Science and Politics of IQ* of 1974.[9] This issue assumed a life of its own quite aside from the race differences question, but it was believed that if the high heritability of IQ figures proposed by Jensen and his allies were refuted the race-differences case would inevitably collapse in turn. Jensen, however, promptly dropped the Burt data, turning to other similar findings. In his official biography of Burt, Leslie Hearnshaw (1979) conceded the fraudulency charge, choosing to diagnose the psychological source and nature of Burt's delinquency rather than dispute it.[10]

Even by 1976, however, it was becoming clear in the more technical literature that the Jensen model was in trouble on rather more profound conceptual grounds than the apparently empirical question of the heritability of intelligence. Nonetheless the more visible face of the controversy continued to be the environment vs. heredity wrangle – Eysenck and Kamin squaring up to one another (not for the first time) in 1981 in *Intelligence: The Battle for the Mind*. By then though the race-differences controversy as such had entered a quiescent phase, partly because many thought the anti-camp had clearly won and partly because the prevailing public mood in the USA was, for the moment, less concerned with race issues. Travis Osborne and McGurk's *The Testing of Negro Intelligence, Volume 2* (1982)[11] failed to reawaken the topic before Gould's popular *The Mismeasure of Man* (1984) hammered a more historical nail into the controversy's coffin. Unfortunately the headstone rightly read 'Not Dead but Only Sleeping'. During the later 1980s the US public mood shifted rightward under the second Reagan Presidency. Welfare and ameliorative publicly funded programmes for deprived groups came under growing attack for creating a 'dependency' mentality.

Problems of drug abuse (especially the new cocaine derivative 'crack'), crime and urban decay were becoming worse, not better. This all provided fertile ground for a backlash. African Americans were effectively accused of failing to take advantage of the bounteous efforts made to improve their lot since the mid-1960s. White America was disinclined to feel guilty any more about African Americans' past treatment. Many whites felt everything possible had been done by way of redress and the time for special measures was over (Mayo had said much the same in 1913 of course).

African American attitudes and perceptions were also changing. Cultural auton-omy rather than integration was seen as the more realistic goal, while regardless of the legal situation everyday racism persisted – even for the most successful middle–class blacks.[12] Nor could they accept that the worsening problems of the ghetto were their fault alone, on the contrary they derived directly from Reaganite free-market economic policies which had led to the collapse of many traditional heavy industries and chronic unemployment. Alienation was exacerbated all the more by the absence of the official racism which had provided the Civil Rights movement with visible targets.

In the early 1990s time was ripe for the coffin-lid to be thrown off and yet another remake launched. This time the main pro-differences figures were the Canadian J.P. Rushton, proponent of a socio-biologically based theory of black deficiency, followed by Charles Murray and the late Richard Herrnstein, whose 1994 *The Bell Curve* was directly in the Jensen tradition. While the ensuing debate largely proceeded along its now ritualised tracks, two additional features were now evident. In the pro-differences camp the eugenic argument that social class differences reflected intelligence differences was resurrected, while in the anti-differences camp much more attention was paid to their opponents' network of allies. This last perhaps reflected the sensitivity to funding and contextual issues in science studies which had evolved over the previous two decades.[13]

Works such as Tucker (1994) make it clear that the controversy must now be addressed as something other than a normal scientific controversy. The interesting question is no longer which side is correct, but why the issue resists closure despite the demonstrable incoherence of the pro-differences case. My argument is that under normal circumstances (whatever they are!) the controversy would have reached closure by about 1980 on the strength of the 'internalist' anti-differences case. We must first, therefore, review this.

THE 'INTERNALIST' CASE AGAINST RACE DIFFERENCES IN INTELLIGENCE

By the early 1980s a range of conceptual difficulties (not all new) had emerged which the pro-differences camp has never systematically refuted.[14] Its usual response is to ignore or down-play them. In the more accessible semi-popular texts their strategy often amounts to asserting the 'Black Box' status (to use Latour's term) of arguments (e.g. the validity of the operational definition of intel-ligence) which had actually been thrown wide open again (e.g. in this instance, by Block and Dworkin 1977b). Taken together these difficulties must, I believe, present an insuperable barrier to the continued pursuit of the question as posed: Do races genetically differ in IQ/intelligence? One feature of the situation is that whereas from Galton onwards intelligence measurement and theorising had been a mainly within-discipline topic, after 1969 it was exposed to external scientific critiques of an intensity against which it had hitherto been largely shielded. These uncovered a variety of shortcomings and problems which psychologists, sharing a common interest in promoting the field, had never faced. (Unsympathetic psychologists had simply worked in other subdisciplines, rather than mounted a full critique.) Let us consider some of these conceptual difficulties.

The meaning of the 'H'-measure

The conceptual kernel of the entire controversy is the so-called 'H' (for 'heritability') score. Of what is 'H' a measure? Its name would reasonably lead the non-specialist to assume it meant the degree to which a trait was genetically determined – which is what 'heritable' appears to mean after all. But, as Jensen himself explained, and as has never been contested, it is actually a measure of the amount of *variance* within a specific population which can be ascribed to genetic variability *within* that population. This implies (and again nobody has disputed this) that such human traits as having two eyes or two legs have an H of zero! The variance in number of eyes or legs is almost entirely due to environmental (perhaps pre-natal) factors – thalidomide or stepping on a land mine. While a non-controversial point technically, this runs completely counter to the non-specialist's assumptions. Such a person naturally assumes that if IQ has an H of 0.8, it is 80% genetically determined, compared to having two legs which is 100% genetically determined. Pro-differences writers typically encourage this image in their popular accounts.

H is then, by definition, a population-specific measure. A trait with high H in one population, at one time, may have a low H at a different time or in another population. The usual example is TB (tuberculosis): at one time almost everyone was exposed to the TB virus, hence sufferers were likely to be those genetically susceptible to the disease. It thus had a high H: genetic predisposition largely determined its occurrence. Environmental changes (in medicine and hygiene) have radically changed this. Nowadays it is exposure to environments in which the virus persists which contributes most of the variance. Its H is therefore much lower. Once again this point in itself is non-controversial. But now, buried in Jensen (1969a), we find the following:

> Any groups which have been geographically or socially isolated from one another for many generations are practically certain to differ in their gene pools, *and consequently are likely to show differences in any phenotypic characteristics having high heritability*. This is practically axiomatic, according to the geneticists with whom I have spoken. (p. 80, my italics)

This is doubly confusing. In the first place we will radically misunderstand it if we forget the technical meaning of 'high heritability'. More seriously, however, it quite clearly suggests that 'high heritability' can be given an absolute 'objective' value, quite disregarding its variability. All he can really say, legitimately, is that the heritability of phenotypic traits might differ between mutually isolated groups. (Thus number of fingers would have a degree of heritability in a population if the polydactyly gene, resulting in a six-fingered hand, was common.) This is practically axiomatic according to the geneticists I have read. The phrase 'geographically or socially isolated' is also misleading, it is *reproductive* isolation which is relevant – and this may be absent even where social isolation occurs if covert inter-group sexual relations are at a high level. The passage cited above is rhetorically quite important because, by illicitly making 'high heritability' (implicitly at this point) of IQ a default assumption, it also predisposes the reader to believe that 'race differences' must be the default assumption (a position which, as we saw, had fallen from sight by the mid-1920s after wide acceptance by the first Race Psychologists).

While Jensen (1969a, p. 43) stresses that 'H' is 'specific to the population sampled, the point in time, how the measurements were made, and the particular test used to obtain the measurements', the central role this measure plays in his thinking is fundamentally insecure even in his own terms. For example, he later asserts that 'the heritability index for a test is probably our best objective criterion of its culture-fairness' (ibid., pp. 109–10). These passages are patently irreconcilable. (The first quote refers to the H of a trait, the second to the H of a test for that trait, but this does not affect the crucial point – H scores are, in general, variable across population and time; '*the* heritability index' of anything is a quite mythical entity.)

But even more crucially we cannot draw any conclusions about the causes of *between*-group variance from knowing the H measure of *within*-group variance. The example generally used – from early in the debate – has been height. Height usually has a very high H: within any population its variance is substantially due to heredity – tall parents have tall offspring (although there is a tendency to regress to the mean). But if we compare two populations of different mean heights this gap may be entirely due to differing dietary conditions. *Within* each population the relative rankings of individuals remain genetically determined – parent height correlates highly with offspring height – but the difference in absolute mean height *between* the groups is environmentally determined. 'Heritability' therefore refers to the *relative* positions of individuals within the population, environment may nevertheless determine the *absolute* value of the phenotypic expression of the trait. Mean height has, we know, changed over time in a number of populations with altered environmental circumstances. Mean IQ scores have, interestingly, also risen in a number of populations since they were first assessed.[15] (Conversely, the difference in upper limb morphology between sparrows having two wings and humans having two arms is quite obviously genetic, though as explained earlier, the H for both of these traits is zero since there is no genetically caused variance *within* the two groups.)

Jensen addressed this in replying to the initial *Harvard Educational Review* commentators (Jensen, 1969b, pp. 227–30). It must be admitted that he made something of a hash of it by getting bogged down in a detailed reanalysis of height-change data and arguing that it was genetic rather than environmental in origin. This missed the point that knowing the within-group heritability of a trait sheds no direct light on the roots of between-group differences, nor does it (as he claims in a footnote and as the wing/arm example just given disproves) render one or other cause more probable. More seriously he proceeded to dismiss the improved 'Negro' IQ since the 1920s on the grounds that the white–Negro difference had not been narrowed (it did actually do so subsequently).[16] But this is irrelevant. If a 'Negro' mean IQ figure equal to a white mean IQ figure is found then the temporal locations of the findings are irrelevant – but so too is whether the difference is 'genetic' or 'environmental'. If it is environmental it shows that the current 'Negro' environment is as conducive to high performance as the 1920 white environment. If it is 'genetic' it shows that the 'Negro' gene-pool has now achieved the quality of the 1920 white one, in which case there is no reason why it could not in time equal the 1969 – or any subsequently attained – white one. Either way all the pessimistic prognoses stemming from a 'genetic' theory become unsustainable. The constancy of the gap only signifies that the white environment, or its gene-pool, has improved at the same rate as the 'Negro' one.

The meaning of 'heritability' and what it legitimately entailed rapidly became a central focus of critical theoretical attention, and underlies many of the other problems. Unfortunately the problems just outlined are difficult to communicate coherently in a popular arena fixated on the 'environment vs. heredity' schema.

The distinction between direct and indirect modes of genetic causation

The notion of 'genetic causation' is not unproblematic. A broad distinction may be drawn between 'direct' and 'indirect' modes of genetic causation. If the phenotype (e.g. eye or hair colour) is a direct result of genetically governed biochemical processes, then we have a case of 'direct' causation. But very often the connections are lengthier. Suppose that in a particular culture those with red hair are stigmatised and systematically undernourished and neglected and those with blonde hair highly esteemed and privileged. In this situation we could say that their poor health is genetically determined – possession of a particular set of genes (those determining hair colour) determines health and social status. In this case however the causation is indirect, being mediated by social environmental factors. *The H score as such cannot differentiate between these.* In the case of IQ/intelligence we have reasonable grounds for supposing that any genetic causation may include a substantial 'indirect' component. It has been pointed out for example that a genotypically bright child might find reading and so forth pleasurable and thus engage in intellectually stimulating activity. In doing so its original 'genetic' superiority over a genetically slightly duller child would be greatly amplified. This would be further potentiated if self-images as bright and dull respectively were socially reinforced by, for example, teachers paying bright pupils more attention. Block and Dworkin (1977b) say 'This sort of effect, in which an initial advantage in a meritorious characteristic is magnified, might be called a *meritocratic* indirect genetic effect.' (p. 481, their italics). The 'H' of intelligence as calculated by the pro-differences camp clearly includes the environmental factors involved in such indirect genetic causation.

The 'norm of reaction' concept and Lewontin's model of epigenesis

During the mid-1970s both J. Hirsch and R.C. Lewontin drew attention to a phenomenon they called 'norm of reaction'. This referred to the fact that two genotypes may have the same or similar phenotypic outcomes under one set of environmental conditions but very different outcomes under another set. This directly relates back to the H score problem – H would be low in the first environment and high in the second. Each genotypic trait has its characteristic 'norm of reaction'. This can be identified under laboratory conditions in relation to single continuous controllable variables such as temperature using 'subjects', such as *drosophila* (fruit flies), of known genotype. In humans, however, each genetically unique and living in bewilderingly complex physical and social environments, establishing norms of reaction relevant to intelligence or IQ performance is virtually impossible. That differential norms of reaction occur is nonetheless fairly obvious. One can easily envisage two genotypes achieving differently under low educational expenditure conditions, but equally under high ones (and *vice versa*). Subtler effects of a similar kind must, one would have thought, be legion. In this debate, the 'norm of reaction' notion may be seen as reinforcing the argument that H may vary with environmental conditions. It also, however, raises difficulties for the possibility of any *general* answer, applicable to all genotypes, to the question of how far intelligence is genetically determined. This 'norm of reaction' concept underlay a further move, made in the early 1980s.

In 1982 R.C. Lewontin, long a critic of Jensen, provided a brief account of the 'heredity–environment' or 'nature–nurture' issue with profound implications. As well as elucidating the impossibility of clearly differentiating the two levels, he challenged a long-implicit feature of the 'unfolding innate potential' metaphor. We customarily imagine there to be a single ideal phenotypic outcome for a given genotype, environmental factors determining how closely the phenotype approaches this ideal. The reality is, however, better captured by a different metaphor. Any given genotype may yield a variety of phenotypes, environmental factors serve to switch development onto a particular track (here the linkage with 'norm of reaction' is fairly obvious). Instead of travelling more or less of the distance from genotype to ideal phenotype – the shortfall being environmentally caused – there are numerous branching 'developmental pathways' onto which the phenotype may be directed, these routes being environmentally determined. Lewontin (1982) sums things up thus:

> the relation between genes, environment, and organism is extraordinarily diverse from one species to another, from one organ or tissue or enzyme to another, from one genotype within a species to another. . . . Some species develop virtually the same morphology in any non-lethal environment, while others are remarkably plastic. There is no model that is not trivially generalized, that can serve as a useful metaphor for psychic development. It all depends. (p. 156).

Although Lewontin does not explore the point, this suggests that there may be no *single* environment which will optimise the expression of every socially desirable genetically determined trait. Maximising intelligence might involve sacrificing, for example, 'emotional sensitivity to others', maximising creativity might involve costs to health (insofar as these traits are directly genetically determined). It is easy to find biographical data in which high achievement is a 'compensative' response to environmental deficits.

In the light of these interventions from genetics, seeking the relative contributions of heredity and environment to intelligence was beginning to look naive. It was becoming difficult to see what such a question actually meant. By 1984 even Jensen had dropped arguments based on the H score, turning instead to the old Spencerian theme, reaction times, retitled 'speed of information processing' to give it a cognitivist air. Now however it was slower black RTs that were being sought – in vain as it turned out.[17]

'Environment' and 'heredity' – independent variables or reciprocal?

The status of the concepts 'heredity' and 'environment' has never been clear, and is in some ways deeply confusing. Heredity determines potential or capacity and in an environmentally ideal world all variance would be due to this alone – the role of environment is to determine the degree to which this capacity is realised. (We have just seen that even this image is oversimplified, but we can assume that one phenotypic outcome will surpass all others on any specific quantitatively variable trait.) As a source of variance, therefore, environmental effects are all negative – they determine the level of shortfall from this ideal. An organism can never exceed its genetically determined capacity (for height, intelligence, athletic ability or anything else). New environmental factors may raise performance beyond that previously achievable of course (e.g. steroids).[18] But it is patently absurd to say that environment was not a factor in determining performance in this ideal situation. This raises a further difficulty regarding how we should construe the heritability measure 'H'. We saw that saying that IQ has a heritability of 0.8 does not mean that it is 80% determined by heredity and 20% by environment but that 80% of the variance is due to heredity. But from this new angle it equally means something like 'the environment of the population sampled was 80% of the level needed for achieving maximum performance'. Since both genes and an environment are necessary conditions for existence in the first place both are 100% implicated in determining a given individual's IQ score.

But this is only the start of our difficulties. 'Environment' has a logically different status to 'heredity'. The latter may be specified in concrete terms as an individual's unique DNA sequence at conception (even this, as just shown, proves not to be quite so clear-cut, but we will leave the difficulties aside here). The former is simply 'everything else'. Moreover, 'intelligence', however defined in detail, must refer to the organism's transactions with its environment. This leads to a bewildering tangle – how can heredity and environment be dealt with as mutually *independent* variables determining a third thing, IQ/intelligence, when one variable is defined as everything which is not the other and IQ/intelligence itself refers, in some fashion, to susceptibility to it?

The logical implication that H must be a negative function of IQ/intelligence

This confusion is exacerbated by the 'capacity' metaphor already invoked, for this entails that potential susceptibility to environment is a function of inherited capacity: there is less room for environmentally induced shortfall for those with low capacity than for those with high capacity. *Heritability of intelligence within any population must thus be an inverse function of capacity.* That being so, even within a single population, any *general* statement of the respective contributions to variance of heredity and environment is ruled out, or at least can only refer to those with around mean capacity.[19] We can go further: the reliability of the IQ score as an index of innate capacity will be a positive function of achieved IQ score. It is unlikely that those with an IQ of 150 are very far from their capacity, but people with an IQ of 80 might be genetic geniuses screwed up by their environment. The situation is thus rather like this: everyone is born on the top of an invisible mountain. They either stay there or subsequently slide down to a greater or less degree. What we are being asked to assess is how far, *in general*, current altitude (IQ) is due to the height of natal mountains (innate capacity) and how much is due to subsequent slippage (environment).[20] If the reader is now addled I sympathise, so am I. One root of the difficulty is a conflation between technical and 'common-sense' meanings of the terms involved (heredity, heritability, IQ, intelligence, environment etc), but this conflation is unavoidable since they have never been rigorously differentiated in the first place, and in interpreting the meanings of their findings and rendering them comprehensible researchers themselves inevitably shift from the former to the latter. Moreover, it is only by exploiting the connotations of the 'common-sense' usages that the question can be infused with the desired level of socio-cultural importance.[21]

The operational definition of intelligence as 'what IQ tests measure'[22]

If 'heritability' and attendant issues constituted one front of conceptual controversy, the concept of 'IQ' and its relationship to 'intelligence' provided another. This operational nostrum, originally coined by E.G. Boring, has been clung to through thick and thin by advocates of IQ testing. It has been called into question on a variety of grounds. To avoid a lengthy excursus the main ones may be enumerated as follows:

1 The unitary nature of intelligence, known as '*g*' (the term introduced by Spearman) is an illusion created by the adoption of statistical and design procedures in which this is actually a built-in assumption. The 'discovery' of *g* by the statistical and design procedures used by IQ test designers is thus a vast begged question. (See also 4 below.)

2 IQ is a concept of a different logical status to, for example, height. It is a measure of a person's standing in relation to the population as a whole (scores representing deviation from the mean of the population on which the test was standardised, this being defined as 100), not an 'absolute' measure of a quasi-physical property.

3 Recently theorists such as Howard Gardner and Robert Sternberg have proposed more sophisticated models and theories in which there are a variety of
relatively independent kinds of intelligence.

4 'Intelligence' as measured by IQ tests has a highly problematic relationship to
its everyday meaning. Abilities which might be included in the everyday sense
(e.g. skill in managing relationships) are excluded at the test-design stage if they
do not 'load highly on *g*'.

A fifth, and more technical, point concerns the commonly invoked analogy
between the evolution of the thermometer (involving successive operational definitions of heat, eventually yielding a 'scientific' meaning via ever more advanced
measuring devices) and IQ tests (as similarly leading to a scientific definition of
'intelligence'). This analogy was effectively undermined in Block and Dworkin
(1977b). They point out that, in one sense of the phrase, intelligence would be *by
definition* what IQ tests measure – but this precludes any possibility of improvement, since there could be no external criterion for evaluating an IQ test's success.
If, however, we take the phrase to mean intelligence is what IQ tests are *supposed*
to measure we are back to square one and the very problem the operational definition was adopted to eliminate – how well do IQ tests actually measure intelligence
(which must now be defined independently of IQ tests themselves)? 'The operationalist dilemma here is that one of the interpretations of Boring's definition is
absurd while the other is *useless* for their purposes.' (p. 416, italics in original). A
third possibility is that it is not the meaning of intelligence which is being defined
but its reference, that is, 'intelligence' would refer to 'that quantity which standard
IQ tests succeed in measuring' (ibid.). But this too is useless because we can still
ask how well IQ tests succeed in measuring anything and if so whether it is what
'intelligence' means in its everyday sense. A little later they observe 'you cannot
measure intelligence by finding items which correlate with it unless you already
have a way of measuring it' (p. 417). Altogether, Block and Dworkin spend seven
pages on deconstructing the thermometer/IQ test analogy, stressing in particular
the fact that the former evolved in interaction with theories of heat, while the
operationalist approach of IQ testers is explicitly atheoretical. Eysenck (Eysenck
vs. Kamin, 1981) repeated the analogy, blithely ignoring the entire critique.

While the nature of IQ tests as such is a little distanced from the specific issue
of 'race differences', the pro-differences position is dependent on the validity of
the IQ concept as traditionally conceived by IQ testers. Few psychologists without
vested interests in using IQ testing technology for this purpose would now consider this concept as unproblematic.

IQ test performance reflects other traits beside 'intelligence'

Several critics observed that over and above the conceptual viability of operation-
ally defining intelligence by IQ scores, IQ performance is determined by factors
other than 'intelligence', however this is conceived. Klineberg's identification of
cultural norms of speed of response as a compounding factor was an early example

of this. Two others may suffice here: perseverance and error checking. The degree to which people persevere or give up easily is a personality trait with no immediately apparent relationship to intelligence in any of its usual senses. Obviously IQ performance will reflect, to some degree, the tenacity with which the test taker sticks to the task. Similarly with error checking. There are plenty of careless bright people and plenty of extremely careful people of no great intelligence (indeed one might hypothesise that careful error checking could be more reinforced among the latter just because they *are* more likely to have learned they are error-prone). Again IQ performance will to some degree be improved by error checking. Both of these factors will operate across all the component scales and insofar as they do so they will reinforce the inter-correlation between them and contribute to *g*.

The redundancy of the 'race' concept in the prevailing population genetics paradigm

If the 'H' concept is the kernel of the debate, the 'race' concept is its shell. As Loehlin et al. (1975) and Bodmer (1972) explained at some length, the typological concept of race had been abandoned by the 1930s. Some proposed an alternative population genetics definition of race as an inter-breeding subpopulation or gene-pool characterised by a distinctive stabilised pattern of distribution of genes. The boundaries of such races were necessarily fuzzy since complete absence of out-breeding was rare and its level subject to change. What now becomes increasingly obscure is how, within the 'gene-pool' paradigm, the concept of race retains any role at all. It had become obvious that mapping the frequencies of different genes carved up the total human gene-pool in different ways. It was also clear that the composition of a 'racial' gene-pool, even its (relatively) distinct existence, could change for a variety of reasons, sometimes quite rapidly. In any case, an increasing percentage of humanity could not be assigned a racial identity on this basis anyway, since global mobility and migration were increasingly reducing the reproductive isolation of all but the smallest and most insulated population groups – which rarely warranted the label 'race', usually being subpopulations within populations already racially labelled (e.g. 'Caucasian' rural valley dwellers in the Appalachians). In their discourse, however, many writers, including those just cited, betray an inability to let go of the concept, even while otherwise demonstrating its redundancy. Bodmer (1972) for example, after explaining the arbitrariness of deciding how different groups must be to warrant being considered 'racially' distinct, at one point writes:

> most people would agree that the differences between the indigenous peoples of the major continents, such as the differences between Africans, Orientals and Caucasians, are obvious enough to merit the label race. (p. 90)

But the concept 'race' as usually understood originated to refer precisely to these 'obvious' differences between African, Oriental and European. There can be no external criterion for 'meriting' the label. If these aren't 'races' we can all go home right away. If you are using the term at all the existence of at least these three 'races' or 'racial groups' becomes analytically true by definition. Yet because they *are* each so vast and have such extended fuzzy 'outbreeding' edges they do *not* fit the new 'stabilised inbreeding gene-pool' definition very readily.

Loehlin et al. continually made statements such as 'The degrees of racial differentiation within species may vary greatly, both within living species at a given moment of time, and within species over time' (p. 25) and 'Any racial classification is to a degree arbitrary. Initially, "racial differences" are those genetic differences that are used to define "races". *It does not automatically follow that the geographic distribution of other genetic traits will be concordant with that of the selected set of morphs used to define racial groupings'* (p. 32, my italics). But later they talk of 'blood groups or other genetic marker variables, physical cues to race such as skin color or facial features' (p. 253), as if a lingering 'real' racial identity lurked somewhere behind the confessedly arbitrary traits by which it was now being 'nominalistically' defined.

It is simply not at all apparent what real work the concept 'race' is doing here. From the 1960s geneticists were discussing human genetic diversity and its evolution quite adequately utilising concepts such as 'gene pool', 'population', 'genetic drift', 'founder effects' and so on.[23] Usage of 'race' with all its broader connotations simply obfuscated the situation. It involved writers finding tortuous ways of translating these new technical concepts back into a 'racial' discourse which the rest of their analyses had shown was obsolete, as if they still felt obliged to talk about 'germ plasm', or as if physicists were bound somehow to retain the concept of 'ether'. Loehlin et al. saw an older 'realist' 'typological' notion of race falling by the wayside to be replaced by a 'nominalist' population genetics one. But 'race' is a 'typological' concept or it is nothing. Once we are into changeable gene-frequencies in differentially isolated gene-pools there is simply nothing left for the concept to do. Moreover, the model of human genetic diversity which has replaced the typological racial paradigm dramatically reduces the significance to be ascribed to group differences in gene distribution. As the global village shrinks we may increasingly find that traits once viewed as racial signifiers have simply become 'varieties' distributed throughout the global population.[24]

Most writers in both camps acknowledge that in practice racial identity is a social, not biological, classification, and spot the arbitrariness of labelling all Americans with any visible African ancestry as 'Negro' or 'black'. But socially defined groups lack even the residual degree of meaningfulness as targets of genetic analysis retained by the 'gene pool' definition. In the long run Jensen's attempted enlistment of population geneticists as allies surely fails because the (now far from universal) use of the concept of 'race' in that discipline appears to be little more than a fossil survival. Even more to the point though, while Jensen invokes it, *none of the 'racial' groups figuring in US research on IQ differences meet even this population genetics criterion for distinct racial identity.* There are, quite simply, no stabilised, isolated, inbreeding gene-pools of any magnitude in the US. This point alone (totally separate from the heritability of IQ issue) surely comes close to being a clinching refutation of the race–differences position.

The falsity of the popular assumption that 'genetic' means 'unchangeable'

It should now be clear that any notion that 'genetic' means 'unchangeable' is unsustainable, and not for any reasons related to genetic engineering. Even if we consider only 'direct' genetic causation, the 'norm of reaction' and 'track-switching' phenomena indicate that phenotypic expression can still be environmentally determined. At the 'gene-pool' level the relative frequencies of different genes are not fixed, indeed they can change fairly rapidly. Even were it possible to identify a distinct population, in the gene-pool of which there was a relative deficit of genes directly inducing high intelligence in the present environment, little of significance would follow. Nothing is static. Internal dynamics may be reducing this deficit, while changed environmental conditions might alter the whole picture via norm of reaction and track-switching mechanisms, and increased gene flow between this population and others (which of course could even lead to its disappearance as a genetically distinct group). Given that few such discrete populations now exist anyway, such speculation is of course actually redundant.[25] It is nevertheless important to stress the point, because in lay thinking the contrast between heredity and environment is equated with the unchangeable vs. changeable polarity. It is from this very assumption that the heat of the topic really stems, for from it so much else seemingly ensues, especially that if intelligence is genetically determined then expenditure on improving performance is by definition wasted.

Intelligence of groups as a category mistake

There is a certain irony in the fact that while mainstream Anglophone Psychology has been widely criticised for its individual-level focus and neglect of the socio-cultural explanatory level, the 'race and IQ' theorists reified the 'group'. The 'genetic' explanation for IQ performance was, it was recognised by all, only meaningful at the group level – it meant that the mean performance of the group was largely determined by the frequencies of the relevant genes in its gene-pool. But what follows from this? In places Jensen (1969a) appears to be raising the ghost of 'Negro industrial education', although he does not put it like that. For once we can legitimately affirm the value of the individual level of analysis. This particular argument has not generally been spelled out in the literature, but is I believe a crucial one. The use of 'intelligence' in relation to groups is what philosophers call a category mistake. Groups as such do not have intelligence, only individuals.[26] Groups ('racial', social, ethnic, sexual) do not take IQ tests. Individuals take them – on specific days, in specific moods, in specific states of health and as administered by specific people at specific sites. 'Group performance' properly refers to the collective performance of a group collaborating on a single project – playing a football match, mounting a production of *Sergeant Musgrave's Dance*, besieging Sarajevo or robbing the vaults of the Chase Manhattan Bank. But IQ tests are not taken by such teams. (Nor, it must be said, at the risk of digressing from the point, is ability to operate successfully in them measured by IQ tests – which is pretty remarkable for an instrument supposedly invaluable for predicting socio-economic success. Porteus knew better on that score at least.) In what sense do the 'Negro' and 'white' groups being 'sampled' in typical 'race and IQ' research even exist? They are not 'teams' in the sense just mentioned. They are not, like socio-economic class groups, definable by income or occupation. They do not, like self-identified ethnic groups, share a common lifestyle and culture (though some such groups exist *within* them). They are, as we have repeatedly pointed out, certainly not stabilised inbreeding gene-pools. Is any criterion at all besides discernible level of skin pigmentation really being used? And if not, where is all the research on hair-colour groups?

If we want to prioritise IQ performance as an educational goal (and even Jensen believes this mistaken) then it is individual performances we have to deal with. Assigning a person to a racial category is irrelevant. In normal circumstances the respective weightings of heredity and environment (assuming the distinction makes sense, which, we have seen, is doubtful) cannot, even in principle, be ascertained for *individual* IQ test performance (or any other performance come to that). If we want to study groups we must be able to define them and we must clarify what kinds of question it is meaningful to address at the group level. There are plenty of ways of doing both, and plenty of people doing so. In the present context what might be interesting, for example, would be to examine the social processes by which a self-contained community came to classify, evaluate and cultivate the various human abilities. This would contribute far more to our understanding of the culturally variable nature of 'intelligence' than swooping in, dishing out Raven's Progressive Matrices and Goodenough Draw-A-Man Tests to the children and comparing their scores with US 'white' norms.

Herrnstein's prediction of the emergence of a genetically stratified 'caste' society

By the time *The Bell Curve* was published, the US cultural climate had again become congenial for a revival of one of the oldest eugenic anxieties: social classes were – or were becoming – genetically distinct. Current social status increasingly reflected innate ability. Despite doubts which had been around ever since Porteus, and in the face of masses of data which were at best ambiguous, the further assumption was made that intelligence as measured by IQ tests was a predictor of social success. Again echoing earlier writers like Ferguson and Mayo, it was claimed that African Americans' relative lack of social advancement was ascribable to innate inability. Social status reflected, did not determine, intelligence.[27] And once more it was the apparent failure of educational projects that provided the most immediate social context for the debate. *The Bell Curve* predicted an intensifying of this trend. Now certainly behind all this is what appears to be a fairly tautologous point: in a truly egalitarian meritocratic society those who will succeed socially are those who most fully display the traits that society considers meritorious. To the extent that such traits are genetically determined within that society one might, over time, expect to see a social stratification along genetic lines emerging. (One such meritorious trait might of course be light – or indeed dark – skin colour.)[28] But in reality it cannot be convincingly argued (a) that US society remotely approaches the conditions necessary for this to operate or (b) why 'intelligence' (especially as measured by IQ tests) should be singled out as the single most relevant 'meritorious' trait in question. It is in any case perhaps only at the more extreme ends of the intelligence spectrum that level of intelligence becomes of paramount importance in determining an individual's career options and success within them.[29]

For the historian there are glaring parallels between, on the one hand, late 19th century British and French ruling class fears of a seething ignorant underclass innately incapable of self-improvement draining the national resources and, on the other hand, late 20th century US white ruling and middle-class fears of a similar nature. The ominous difference is in the latter's 'racial' dimension. What is missing in the present debate, especially in the USA, is an appreciation of the extent to which the appeal of such pessimistic diagnoses of current social ills can be shown to be rooted in broader cultural, socio-economic and historical circumstance. This is made worse in the USA because the kinds of analysis which would disclose this relationship are to a large degree tabooed – involving as they do a critical understanding of the roles of social class and forms of economic life. They can thus be cast as Marxist and hence ideological. This is oddly ironic because the inherently ideological character of the neo-eugenic Herrnstein mode of analysis thus remains largely invisible, or only couchable rather crudely as 'racist'. It is of course (among other things) racist, but acknowledging that can only be a starting point in the pursuit of a genuinely insightful understanding of what is going on. Even without reading Tucker (1994), to a non-American observer the connection between the post-1980 right-wing ideological and economic climate of the USA and the popularity of Herrnstein's neo-eugenics is transparently clear, and entirely subverts its credibility as a purely 'scientific' issue. The truth surely is that *any* analysis of the nature of a society's ills is implicitly ideological. It is not being ideological which is the scientific sin here, but the masquerade of *not* being ideological. In the contest between ideologies the 'facts' are certainly relevant, but in this case the neo-eugenicists have few unambiguous facts at all. Their case is a speculative extrapolation from what would obtain in an 'ideal' scenario remote from current social realities, in contrast to the clearly identifiable socio-economic and historical processes linking their 'science' to their unacknowledged ideological and socio-ethnic class interests (which is less to accuse them of bad faith than of false consciousness). It is highly significant that this particular issue only re-emerged prominently in the late 1980s, after being in abeyance since 1929 at least. This in itself suggests that its re-awakening owed relatively little to 'internal' 'scientific' developments as opposed to ideological climate.

So far this angle of criticism has rarely surfaced beyond more radical textual genres easily sidelined in the main public debate. Opposition has tended to be more empirical in character, with a plethora of research on, for example, correlations between IQ and within-occupation income, social mobility levels, correlations between parent and child income in relation to IQ and so on. These have served a useful function in demonstrating how far US society is from meeting the criteria of an ideal meritocratic level playing field necessary for the Herrnstein vision to work, as well as challenging the crude use of IQ as a predictor of socio-economic success. Even within the psychometric camp some have pointed out that the phenomenon of regression to the mean is actually difficult to square with the emergence of an elite high IQ social class.

Meaning of 'overlap'

Finally, what is really a rhetorical, rather than conceptual, point. The literature frequently describes findings as showing, for example that black scores 'overlap white scores by only 30%'. Klineberg (1963) spotted that this, though strictly speaking accurate, was rhetorically misleading because the perfect overlap would be 50% not 100%, the figure referring to the percentage of blacks exceeding the white mean. A figure of 30% overlap meant that about a third of blacks exceeded the white average – which sounds far less dire! In several pieces of research he finds that the lowest figure in the blacks' overall range is higher than that in the white range – thus *all* blacks exceeded at least one white. And in some research, conversely, at least one black exceeded *all* whites.

These conceptual attacks are matched by criticisms of the pro-differences empirical research and data, either in the form of attempts at discrediting the methodology or by invoking counter-data. This is even more tedious to unravel than the conceptual debate, but a few examples may be cited.

The controversy was widely seen, initially at any rate, as centring on the heritability of intelligence, attention was inevitably drawn to the twin studies which had figured so prominently in research addressing this. As is suggested below this was to some extent a diversion from the main issue. The most influential of such studies had been that of Sir Cyril Burt. The leading figures in criticising this twin studies tradition were Leon Kamin and Christopher Jencks. Leaving aside the question of Burt's fraudulency, the methodological difficulties involved in such work have proved extremely difficult to overcome. Most obviously, finding large enough samples of identical (monozygotic or 'MZ') twins reared apart in significantly different environments has proved a perennial headache, and much of the research has been demonstrably flawed in the respect.[30] Moreover the actual correlations found between the scores of MZ twins reared apart have varied considerably – Kamin (1977, p. 243) gives a table with a range from .62 to .86 for example. More broadly, the vast amount of data on IQ score correlations between MZ twins, dyzygotic (DZ) twins (of both same and opposite sex), parents and children and adoptive parents and children has proved open to a wide range of interpretations, from those who see it as clinching the 'H = 0.8' figure to those who see it as leaving the door open for a heritability of zero.

As an example of findings problematic for the pro-differences camp Jane Mercer (1972) is rather interesting. She compared the IQ score performance of mainly lower-class African Americans, Chicanos and mainly middle-class whites with their performance on a set of behavioural indices of retardedness (e.g. shoelace tying, ability to manage shopping and travel alone). She found that while none of the white subjects with IQs below 70 could pass this behavioural test, 70% of the blacks and 60% of the Chicanos did so. This implies, at the very least, that the meaning of achieving a low IQ score differs substantially between the white group and the others.

James R. Flynn, a New Zealand-based psychologist, has devoted much effort to combating the differences case on its own terms. In numerous publications he has shown that mean IQ scores of various 'racial' groups and national populations have risen or varied since first assessed.[31] This rise had been masked by successive restandardisations of tests at higher levels. In Flynn (1984a) he claims to have found that over 1932–78 US white mean IQ rose by 13.8 points – even if African American mean scores remained 15 short of white ones this implies that in 1978 they were performing at around the 1932 white level. This picture is lent support by the findings of K.R. Vincent (1991) comparing pre- and post-1980 differences among children. Although varying in degree[32] these showed a consistent closing of the black–white gap for the post-1980 period (to as little as 1 point on the 4th Revision of the Stanford-Binet). The black mean was now about 93–94 points with the white mean static. This would imply that African American children were, by the end of the 1980s, actually performing better than whites had in the 1930s. While individually focused schemes to improve performance have often proved of limited success, the 'Flynn effect' suggests that macro-level cultural and environmental factors operating over longer periods of time can have a greater effect. This is consistent with the argument that maximum IQ performance is only possible for those within societies psychologically congenial to such 'modernist' inventions as IQ tests. The Flynn effect might therefore be ascribed partly to the globalisation of this 'psychology'. Other factors such as improved education and health are also probably in play. On the basis of his extensive studies of IQ changes over time Flynn (1987a) concluded that 'IQ tests do not measure intelligence but rather a correlate with a weak causal link to intelligence' (p. 190).

Besides these, the anti-Jensenists were increasingly able to point to successful programmes of IQ or achievement enhancement. From the outset his characterisation of the 'failure' of Head Start programmes was criticised as flawed when the realities of how funds had been used on the ground were examined. In the few cases where sustained and comprehensive programmes had been implemented significant and enduring gains in performance had been achieved. (The majority of the children participating in Head Start programmes were also, it is usually forgotten, poor whites.)

The preceding conceptual and empirical difficulties are so fundamental and wide-ranging that had the issue been an exclusively 'internal' scientific matter, the pro-differences position could hardly have survived within the discipline beyond about 1980. But as Latour explains, the allies of any scientific endeavour extend way beyond what we traditionally think of as the 'internal' 'purely scientific' arena. In every discipline, and every research topic, today's scientists are linked into industrial and economic interests beyond the laboratory. Psychology, like all other disciplines, draws its funds from a variety of funding and granting agencies, both public and private. Funder and funded typically trade off their interests to some extent, while availability of funds for a particular topic will almost certainly result in it being taken up by fund-hungry researchers. This is normal and not in itself sinister. It does nevertheless mean that in order to understand what happens in science, especially 20th century science, we have to take the funding question into account. Moreover, in a case like this, where failure to close an issue is unaccountable for in orthodox terms, it suggests that it is precisely in this direction that an explanation most likely lies. It is to this we turn next.

THE PRO-DIFFERENCES NETWORK

Those arguing for 'race differences' have always been sensitive to the notion that science is supported by a network of allies. Resistance to their message is regularly ascribed to the presence within US academia of a kind of left-wing liberal mafia which systematically traduces and suppresses the scientific truths they have discovered. An unholy alliance of Jews and other non-Nordic minority groups is seeking to mongrelise America. Race-differences supporters have to skulk secretively around the corridors of America's universities, only able to confess their true beliefs in the anonymity of unmonitorable meetings in down-town bars. This pose of scientific martyrdom is unaffected by the fact that no US academics yet have lost their jobs, their APA or National Academy of Sciences membership, or ability to publish, as a result of adopting a pro-differences position. It seems that disagreement is in itself sufficient to be experienced as persecution. But what of their own network?

Since Tucker (1994) has done such a thorough job of uncovering the funders and external supporters of race-differences research I will, in this section, do little beyond offering a resumé of his findings, some of which have already been sketched in the previous chapter. One often publicised key player is the Pioneer Fund which, either directly, or via intermediate organisations, is said to have copiously funded Jensen, Rushton, Lynn and Eysenck. Each is reported to have received six-figure dollar sums.[33] Additionally it has, via Garrett's IAAEE, supported the journal *Mankind Quarterly* under a succession of far right editors or managers such as Roger Pearson, founder of the Northern League, who 'once reportedly boasted of helping to hide Josef Mengele' (Tucker, 1994, p. 256). Cattell has sat on the board and published frequently in its pages. *Mankind Quarterly* has, ever since its founding, been a major outlet for pro-differences writers, including psychologists such as Garrett and Ulster psychologist Richard Lynn (also a sometime editor). The even more right-wing German spin-off *Neue Anthropologie*, having first published a bibliography of Jensen's works then made him a member of its board. Another outlet is the blandly titled *U.S. News and World Report*, ever prompt to publish the latest words of Jensen and Shockley. Leading figures in the Ku Klux Klan and various other extremist and white supremacist organisations seemingly interlock in a complex American and European-wide web. These regularly provide space for racist Psychology in their journals. If Tucker's highly documented account is correct, and I know of no refutation, then the mystery largely dissipates: the pro-differences position owes the artificial prolongation of its life to the continued supply of funds and encouragement from extreme right-wing racist organisations and publications. This however raises a further question: how do the recipients of this funding construe their relationship with their funders?

The existence of a funding relationship does not of itself mean that the funded party is entirely in the funder's pocket. It must though signify that the funded party does not find the funder's ideological interests and character a barrier to collaboration, and that any research funded is unlikely to come to conclusions incompatible with the funder's goals. In reality the most widespread ploy has simply been to retreat behind the argument that a scientist is not responsible for what others may do with his or her findings. Pro-race differences researchers generally display an incongruous mixture of professed political indifference verging on ivory-towered innocence with ready access to (and cordial relationships with) members of organisations of the most extreme kind – characters whom most of their academic colleagues would never encounter in a month of Sundays and would run a mile from if they did. This is coupled with an apparently almost pathological inability to understand why their opponents get so angry, as if the proper reaction to being classified as belonging to inferior stock was to treat it dispassionately as a straight scientific proposition. All opposition is simply portrayed as a bigoted ideological attack on 'pure objective science'.[34] A considerable proportion of what is human is seemingly alien to them. To be quite frank, this combination simply does not add up as a coherent *psychological* position. One is bound to conclude that those psychologists who continue to advocate the pro-differences position are knowingly doing so in bad faith. Their higher loyalty to what they see as the white race's cause in an ongoing racial war overrides any duty of integrity in relation to egalitarian and non-white scientific colleagues and intellectuals – whom they despise. We are not the real audience for whom their texts are intended, these are really meant to serve as rallying points for those sharing their racist ideology, signalling to their fellows that they have a presence on the 'inside' and amusing them by winding up the rest of us. There was a time when race differences seemed a legitimate and meaningful area of scientific enquiry. That time has long passed. What persists is a farce in which scientific etiquette requires that we pretend we are all playing by one set of rules when one party is really only interested in honing its skills in cheating.

The reader may be forgiven for thinking I am going over the top here, but consider: we have two choices (a) pro-differences researchers are naive and insensitive fools who can recognise neither the logical incoherence of their position, nor the moral character of their funders, nor (despite being professional psychologists) the reasons why some people are genuinely upset by what they say; (b) they are people deeply committed to a belief in the world as an arena for ruthless racial struggle, in which all their efforts must be ultimately subordinated to ensuring the interests of a white, preferably Nordic, 'race', identification with which is absolutely central to their personal identities. Only (b) gives their behaviour a semblance of genuine integrity, however deluded or mistaken we may believe it to be. Precisely how far this fairly characterises any individual pro-race-differences psychologist one is, in the very nature of things, unable to ascertain.

Finally we should stress that in terms of Psychology's usual network of allies, largely comprised of national grant-giving agencies and mainstream funding organisations, the pro-differences camp's supporters are distinctly anomalous. No other branch of Psychological research draws on these sources.

POSSIBLE POSITIONS ON THE ISSUE AND CONCLUSION

To sum up we may formally list the various positions which might be held regarding 'race differences' in intelligence.

1 Race differences in IQ are logically impossible on conceptual grounds. This is arguable in various ways. As we have seen, the central concepts of 'race', 'heritability' and 'IQ' are all deeply problematic, to put it mildly. If this kind of argument can be carried it in effect renders all others redundant.

2 Race differences are logically possible but as a matter of empirical fact have not been found to exist. This can be argued on the grounds that all reported differences may plausibly be accounted for by non-genetic factors. This is the standard position of earlier writers such as Klineberg, and still the most prevalent response.

3 Race differences are logically possible and as a matter of empirical fact have been found to exist. This is the standard 'race differences' position.

4 Race differences are logically possible and have as a matter of fact been empirically identified, but this does not prove that they cannot be altered. This first appeared as Garth's 'race mobility' notion. Arguable on the genetic grounds that the current constitution of a gene-pool is alterable over time. This might be extended to explain current underperformance by a 'race' as the legacy of a previous situation in which high intelligence was being selected against in some way (e.g. slavery). 'Races' may also fuse and split over time. This position has some affinities with the first position above in regard to the 'race' concept itself. While accepting the 'race' concept it uses this in a weak sense, not seeing 'race' categories or 'race' characteristics as permanent.

5 Race differences are logically possible but methodologically impossible to empirically identify. Arguable by invoking the 'culture-fair test' paradox for example: if a test is culture-fair it will, by definition, show no difference; if a test shows a difference there is no way of knowing whether it is real or due to the test's cultural unfairness. This position is not entirely satisfactory, most traditional positivist philosophers of science would hold that empirically untestable propositions are not scientifically acceptable in the first place. Those not adhering to a positivist philosophy of science would not be too happy with this either (although the culture-fair paradox itself is rather neat) since they would have various grounds of their own for rejecting the notion that something may be logically possible if its occurrence could not, in principle, be demonstrated.

6 Race differences are logically possible but it is immoral to devote resources to finding them. Here a variety of arguments may be invoked from the simple pragmatic 'use of resources' type to the more elaborated ideological kind in which such research is seen as in the service of forces of racist oppression. While this latter may be true, however, it is insufficiently strong in itself to refute the 'you cannot deny scientific facts' kind of response. This requires a more in-depth critique of the 'episteme' (to be Foucaultian) within which race-differences 'facts' are produced. (See 10 below.) Too vehement a pitching of arguments in moral/ideological terms enables the pro-differences camp to present itself in a scientific-martyr role. What is more illuminating is identifying race-difference research funding sources. If these prove to have clear ideological allegiances or goals the 'neutral scientist' argument loses much of its credibility (see above).

7 Race differences are logically possible and empirically identifiable but so far the evidence is inconclusive. This amounts to a recommendation to suspend judgment until more data are in or new methods of settling the matter have been devised.

8 Race differences are logically possible and have been empirically identified, but this fact is of no great significance or interest. This might be offered in combination with position 4. It might also be argued that the really interesting and important thing is intelligence *per se*, hence what are needed are policies to promote the full development of individual potential intelligence regardless of 'race', even though it might turn out that some 'races' are less well, or better, represented than others at particular levels. This was the position typically adopted by British (but not US and German) eugenicists between the wars (see Chapter 7). The flaw in this general position is not so much that it is wrong (although I believe it is) as that it is rather half-hearted, conceding too much to the pro-differences camp.

9 Race differences are logically possible but it has been empirically shown that findings can be explained in non-genetic terms. This is a stronger version of position 2. Whereas 2 refers to the plausibility of other factors being the explanation, this would positively claim to have demonstrated that this is the case. The difficulty here is that it tends to generate endless wrangles over specific pieces of research, and might even serve to keep the show on the road since the pro-differences camp are stimulated to keep producing new findings.

10 While 'races' between which differences might occur may in some sense exist, in choosing to adopt this conceptual framework rather than others which are equally viable are researchers, wittingly or not, betraying their own racialist *weltanschauung*, ideology or motives. This position might be adopted by those espousing a generally social constructionist viewpoint in which no category – be it race or IQ or anything else – can be taken as directly reflecting the objectively real world. It differs therefore from position 1 in that 1 accepts that had they met certain criteria the concepts of 'race' or 'IQ' would have been acceptable. This position goes further – no 'episteme' or conceptual framework has

final objective status and in the face of a variety of epistemic or conceptual options (such as obtain in the present case) the choice a person makes cannot be justified simply on 'scientific' grounds but reflects their own psychological character, motives, values and socio-cultural location.

Further variant positions on these ten may be possible, but they do, I think, cover the main spectrum of options. It is important to realise that the anti-race-differences positions identified here are not 'additive' in a simple fashion. Some, if true, would render others redundant. Some reflect orientations to the issue fundamentally divergent from others. The author's position is a fusion of 1 and 10. Within the orthodox terms of scientific and philosophical discourse neither 'race', nor 'intelligence', nor the simple 'heredity vs. environment' polarity as deployed by race-difference theorists are logically sustainable concepts, and a category mistake is involved in applying 'intelligence' to groups anyway. More broadly the conceptual critiques outlined above (which do not exhaust those presented in the literature) would, as previously indicated, appear to me to be sufficient to 'close' the controversy. Yet this kind of conceptual argument has clearly been insufficient to settle matters.

In the light of this one must assume one of two things. The first is that the pro-differences camp is now actually operating in bad faith and cynically drawing its funding from racist organisations in order to promote their ideological interests. Tucker (1994) gives this considerable credibility, and after a period of reluctance this hypothesis now seems to me the one which best accounts for the data. For those unconvinced by what they might feel smacks of a conspiracy theory explanation, the other option is to accept that the 'race difference' episteme has a sufficient degree of internal coherence to sustain it as far as its adherents are concerned. The move to position 10 thus has much to recommend it since it shifts the focus of acceptability of race differences findings from its adherents' own episteme to the desirability of choosing this episteme in the first place. Other positions (notably 6) have tried the same move, but are often weakened by simply opting out of engaging the issue within the Psychological arena, their advocates thereby allowing themselves to be marginalised as amateurs who do not really understand it. Position 10 was rarely, if ever, articulated in the immediate post-Jensen phase, only becoming possible over the post-1980 period. The form which position 10 generally takes currently is to identify the underlying task as that of moving beyond 'racial discourse' as such – which, as we will see, also includes among its targets even some areas of Psychology which are, on the face of it, anti-racist.

These positions variously tend towards one of three underlying conclusions: belief or disbelief in race differences, and indifference towards the entire controversy. This last ought not to be ignored or underestimated. In some ways it is the position to which we might most wisely ultimately aspire. It will, after all, only be when we are able to view the controversy as, like that over phlogiston in 18th century chemistry, of no current interest, significance or relevance – except as a historical case study – that we will have really laid it to rest. This though is not achievable simply by ignoring it and hoping it will go away. The immediate task is to spell out, yet again and with hopefully more enduring effect and in less fragmented fashion, the cases against both belief in innate 'race differences' and devoting further energy and resources to the topic. The present author believes the most powerful arguments against race differences are logical and conceptual. There are no 'races', the empirical data are accountable for in a host of alternative ways, the underlying 'nature vs. nurture' assumption proves, on examination, to be incoherent, and advocates of race differences can be so only because they have positively *chosen* the one Psychological 'episteme' or 'paradigm' among the many now available within which this belief makes sense. I personally believe they have deliberately made this choice in order to further racist ideological ends.

What is most depressing is how little the controversy has really moved since the 1930s. We seem forever doomed to a rematch every dozen or so years – *The Bell Curve* has now been answered by S. Fraser *The Bell Curve Wars* (1995), much of which comprises revised versions of the old familiar arguments.[35] Adopting a cinematic metaphor, neither *Race and IQ IV: The Bell Curve* nor J.P. Rushton's bizarre independent Canadian production *Black Men Have Big Ones* (see below) add much at all to the previous versions (indeed the trained eye can spot reels full of recycled footage). What we really need now is not so much an explanation of population differences in mean intelligence, but of America's cultural addiction to this series and the 'studios' which fund it.

SUPPLEMENTARY NOTE ON THE IRRELEVANCE OF THE HERITABILITY OF IQ

The 'heritability of IQ/intelligence' issue must, in the light of what has been said, be considered to be a red herring (or perhaps a red whale). The energy some, such as Kamin, have devoted to critiquing the 'heritability of IQ' research may thus prove to have been, if not wasted, at least not entirely to the point regarding the 'race differences' question itself. Indeed Jensen's real success perhaps lay in conflating the two issues and ensuring that the ensuing controversy seemed to hinge on the heritability of IQ issue *per se*. In retrospect it is perhaps clearer how this could have been fought more effectively by making the underlying conceptual incoherence of his position more publicly visible and accessible, rather than getting side-tracked into Burt's alleged fraudulence. For example, I have found nobody, in the initial phase at least, pointing out that the subjects in the research Jensen cites never meet the population genetics criterion of 'racial group' which he invokes at the outset to justify his position.

If the heritability of IQ question is left aside, what are we left with? Actually not a lot. Both sides have committed so many resources to this issue that its abandonment would be tantamount to a cessation of hostilities. Jensen's attempted withdrawal to a 'speed of information processing' level was notably unsuccessful. Some fairly recent papers suggest that US psychologists are still uncertain about the 'race' concept – unsure whether they should be defining it more clearly or giving it up altogether.[36] But by far the majority of 'race'-related Psychological work now being reported is of a very different kind to that generated by this inertial legacy of the ancient US white-defined 'Negro education' question. And being a white-defined issue it is hard to see how it can continue to be incorporated within an increasingly multi-ethnic discipline for very much longer.

BRIEF NOTE ON RUSHTON'S SOCIO-BIOLOGICAL APPROACH

From the late 1980s onwards the Canadian psychologist J.P. Rushton began publishing a series of journal papers proposing that race differences were explicable in socio-biological evolutionary terms (see Rushton 1994 which elaborates this in more detail). The recency of these texts renders in-depth coverage inappropriate for a historical work.[37] His position may be summed up as a kind of Goldilocks story – Orientals have big brains but small genitalia, Africans have small brains but big genitalia, but Europeans Are Just Right. In expounding this, Rushton co-opted a distinction made in evolutionary biology between what is known as a 'K' breeding strategy (few young, long dependency period) and an 'r' one (many young, rapid maturation). These are generally considered to represent adaptations to different environmental/biological conditions (for example, K-strategies suit long-lived species in stable environments, r-strategies short-lived species in unstable ones). Rushton, however, detects a general evolutionary trend from 'r' to 'K' and, moreover, claims that Europeans have been evolutionarily selected for the 'advanced' K-strategy, 'Mongoloids' even more so, but 'Negroids' remain 'r'-selected and hence allegedly breed more frequently and are more neglectful of their offspring.[38] It is this inveterate African randiness which has supposedly resulted in their allegedly mighty genitalia. Energy resources are thus allocated differentially in almost Spencerian fashion between brain and testes among the three racial groups.[39] From this spring all manner of other differences, such as greater black criminality,[40] which Rushton tabulates to show how on everything from age of first walking to 'intercourse frequencies', brain weight to mental health, the three 'races' are ranked as predicted.[41] Given the reproduction rates in Victorian England and, until recently, Catholic Ireland in which offspring numbers into two figures were commonplace one can only react with incredulity.

The appearance of Rushton (1990c) in the British Psychological Society's house journal *The Psychologist* elicited a flurry of protest and some pretty incompetent spin-doctoring by the Society's president and the editors. While its publication was, on balance, a mistake it perhaps served a useful purpose in giving anti-racist members an opportunity to make it clear where they stood.[42]

Another line of argument Rushton has developed is that there is an innate ability to recognise and be attracted towards others genetically similar to oneself. Correlations between the height and other physical measures of marriage partners are used to support this. This may be true, but aside from possibly offering an updated version of the 'race prejudice is natural' argument it has little clear bearing on the race issue. So far there are few signs that Rushton's theory is gaining much support; it is very much a one-man, Pioneer Fund-backed, business. His credibility would be higher had it received the endorsement of geneticists and human evolution theorists, these being the disciplines most relevant to his thesis, but there is little sign of this being forthcoming. To the historically informed,

Rushton's work appears remarkably old-fashioned, reminiscent of Scientific Racism at its most florid. By the time he had jumped on the radical socio-biology bandwaggon it had already stalled and one suspects that perhaps the very momentum of his landing has now sent it rolling backwards. Certainly most leading sociobiologists appear to have transferred to a more sophisticated, less Social Darwinist, model.

CODA

Having drafted the lengthy preceding critique of the pro-race differences position I remained slightly uneasy. Was I granting it too much power and significance? Was I missing something? 'Intelligence testing . . . testing . . .' I began turning the phrase over in my mind and what should have been blindingly obvious (and for that very reason rarely is) hit me. What the pro–differences camp were doing was indeed *testing* the intelligence of the group they identified with *against* that of an Other group. It was intrinsically adversarial, like arm-wrestling – a 'test' of strength. It was, moreover, virtually the only ostensibly scientific weapon left in the racist armoury. The situation then flipped into focus. They were behaving in the way those autistic or disturbed children do who can only relate to others through one game which they always insist on playing and of which they never tire. Despite its sundry problems, intelligence testing is a game which probably has a valid place among Psychological techniques, being pragmatically useful for certain specific purposes in Psychological assessment and diagnosis of individuals. But for the pro–differences camp it is the *only* game worth playing, and they insist on turning it into an adversarial competition because *that is how they see the world*. Their 'white' subjects are surrogates for themselves, their 'black' subjects the surrogates for an imagined unitary Other, demonstrable superiority to whom is central to their own self-esteem. The fact that subjects are arbitrarily assigned to their respective groups on superficial and scientifically implausible criteria becomes irrelevant so long as they possess features facilitating the projection of Self vs. Other onto them. Equally irrelevant is the fact that those assigned the Other role may not even want to play the game, don't like it, don't know its rules, or are simply uninterested. Refusal to collude elicits a tantrum – in the name of academic freedom they *must* be allowed to play it whenever and with whomsoever they like. And if, as they sometimes do, they lose, an instant replay is demanded; the Other cheated, or it doesn't matter because their past record still shows they are best.

When set in the full context of the vast amount of psychological, anthropological, historical, sociological and philosophical literature on 'race' and racism published over the last 20 years by men and women of all ethnicities, the race-differences genre becomes transparently marginal and hardly relevant. Instead of seeking to discover the rankings of the world's diverse population groups in terms of their intrinsic merit, let alone on their abilities to play just one game, this literature addresses the full range of issues from fundamental and profound questions (often of central theoretical significance for Psychology) regarding the nature of human identity to, at the other end of the spectrum, solving the practical problems of managing community relations (economic, judicial, social etc.) which racism either produces or which produce racism in the first place. Non-adversarial and often complex, this material is of course less media-friendly and thus less culturally visible than the seemingly simple, but spurious, 'race differences' issue, while its conclusions, in any case, are often radically challenging to the system. Nevertheless, in the setting of this total corpus of material, the pro-differences literature (which usually ignores it totally) appears trivial in the extreme. Perhaps when this sinks in the controversy will finally close, but whether or not we are any nearer this devoutly to be wished for consummation, it is with no little relief that I declare the closure of this particular contribution to it.

NOTES

1 The most accessible account of this is B. Latour (1987).
2 See above p. 149.
3 I am refering here to the short-lived wave of right-wing readings of E.O. Wilson's new 'Socio-biology' which found within it a 'scientific' rationale for economic deregulation and insistence on the 'instinctive' basis of traditional sex-roles, heterosexuality, selfishness, aggression and competitiveness.
4 For a fairly comprehensive bibliography with summaries of material listed see S.H. Aby and M.J. McNamara (1990).
5 His shared Nobel Prize was for co-inventing the transistor.
6 It is unlikely that Eysenck actually knew that this was where the interview would appear as it had been conducted some time previously. Tucker (1994, p. 342, n. 330) suggests that the original interviewer was someone associated with the Pioneer Fund supported journal *Mankind Quarterly*. It is perhaps necessary to know that post-war neo-Nazi groups have been perennially at loggerheads, being divided between the fanatical Hitler worshippers (e.g. NF) and the 'Strasserites' (e.g. BNP), who espouse the more socialistic variant of National Socialism promoted by Gregor (murdered 1934) and Otto Strasser, who split with Hitler in 1930. Otto went into exile in 1933, founding the 'Black Front' – a short-lived anti-Hitler, but nonetheless Nazi and anti-semitic, group.
7 See e.g. William F. Brazziel's exasperated 'Letter from the South' (1969) which appeared in the first set of responses published in the *Harvard Educational Review*. Jensen chose virtually to ignore this in his reply (Jensen 1969b), presumably treating it as a piece of vitriolic rhetoric beneath his dignity to acknowledge, rather than the welcome dose of down-to-earth reality it really was.
8 See Tucker (1994) especially pp. 249–64 in which the right-wing ideological network of connections between the pro-differences psychologists and their funders is most fully distentangled.
9 According to Tucker ibid. Jensen tried to pre-empt Kamin by claiming priority for discovering Burt's errors, managing to get into print on the issue first (Jensen, 1974), his paper was accepted by *Behavior Genetics* in 26 days as compared with the average of 119 days. (For details see Tucker, p. 345, n. 25.)
10 See Joynson (1989) for a reappraisal of the case which to some degree salvages Burt's reputation. One effect of the affair, and the debate's focus on the heritability of IQ, has been that Burt has himself been classified as a 'racist' although he himself rarely discussed race differences and, as we saw in Chapter 7, literally broadcast his vision of a harmonious multi-ethnic future to the world in 1935 on the BBC. I do not know that his position in the passage quoted had changed by the time of his death.
11 See also above pp. 247–8. One significant point which might be made in passing is that this volume entirely dropped the topic of 'race hybridity' – perhaps a silent concession to the fact that the genetics side of things was developing, as is described later,

in such an inconvenient direction for the racist camp. Like Shuey they invoke numerous unpublished doctoral dissertations, devoting a separate chapter to 89 of them. Again many are from white (or only recently integrated) Southern universities such as the University of North Carolina, University of Alabama, Georgia State University etc.

12 For a fascinating study of the persistence of everyday racism in the USA see J.R. Feagin and M.P. Sikes (1994).

13 The most thorough work of this type was W.H. Tucker (1994), which appeared at the same time as *The Bell Curve* and thus could not take it into account.

14 The review of conceptual difficulties which follows draws on various sources, notably: N. Block and G. Dworkin (1977b), J.M. Blum (1978), J.R. Flynn (1980), J. Hirsch (1977), R.C. Lewontin (1975, 1977, 1982), J.C. Loehlin et al. (1975), W.F. Bodmer (1972), S.J. Gould (1984), Kamin (1974), H.J. Eysenck vs. L. Kamin (1981), S. Rose et al. (1984), M. Zuckerman (1990), A.H. Yee et al. (1993). It must be said that the principal points had all been made by about 1984, and most of them earlier. Block and Dworkin is an especially effective exposition. An additional radical attack on the whole pro–differences position is E. and H. Mensh (1991) who take issue with Lawler (1978) – an ostensibly Marxist 'critique of Jensenism' – for conceding too much. P.Watson (1973) now seems overcautious. It is perhaps worth noting that the recent general textbook on intelligence, N.Brody (1992), while pretty conventional in approach, concludes that 'there is no convincing direct or indirect evidence in favor of a genetic hypothesis of racial differences in IQ' (p. 309).

15 See discussion of the 'Flynn effect' below p. 279.

16 See K.R. Vincent (1991)

17 P.A. Vernon and A.R. Jensen (1984) was the first Jensen paper on this. It was funded by the Pioneer Fund via Jensen's own Institute for the Study of Educational Differences. See Tucker (1994, pp. 264–8) for a summary of this move and its patent failure, in which the redoubtable Kamin again figures prominently.

18 Developments in genetic engineering are, though, reaching a point where the 'fixity of genetic capacity' becomes a moot point – is the outcome of a direct environmental alteration of genes to be considered as due to environment or due to the genes? The question becomes simply one of stipulatory convention rather than 'fact' – if it retains any meaning at all.

19 This is not so paradoxical as it might seem. What it means is that those with capacities in e.g. the 140–160 range might end up with measured, 'phenotypic' IQs anywhere between 60 and 140–160 (an environmentally determined range of up to 100 points), but those with capacities in e.g. the 60–80 range will nearly always end up in the same 60–80 range or a little below.

20 I will try to refrain from exploring this analogy further, but it clearly has possibilities: e.g. some groups may be born on dry flat-topped mountains and others on icy spikey ones – though mean height may be the same, the latter would clearly tend to be lower than the former when measured.

21 Compare the use of 'altruism' in sociobiology.

22 In this section I have drawn primarily on S.J. Gould (1984), Block and Dworkin (1977b) and D. Layzer (1977).

23 See e.g. G.A. Marshall (1968).

24 This has happened already, for example with traits such as hair colour which, in Britain, would at one time have had 'racial' connotations – black hair identifying the individual as somehow 'Mediterranean'. Such connotations have virtually disappeared in the British white population – some people have black hair, some red hair, some brown hair etc. but this has ceased to signify anything else, they are simply 'varieties'.

25 I understand that such a situation does obtain in the present population of the Paraguayan-based 'pure Aryan' Nueva Germania community established by Elizabeth Nietzsche (Friedrich's widow) earlier this century, 75% of whom are now significantly subnormal due to inbreeding practised to maintain their 'purity'. (G. Midgley, personal communication).

26 The categories of individual psychological traits are all ultimately collective constructions, but this is beside the specific point being made here.

27 Herrnstein had first resurrected this argument in R.J. Herrnstein (1973). B.K.Eckland (1971) made a similar point.

28 This might come down in the end to the old Darwinian issue of 'sexual selection' – the process would only work to the extent that display of socially valued traits also enhanced heterosexual sexual attractiveness, which is probably only partially the case. Social and sexual value are not entirely synonymous!

29 See M. Howe (1988) for a critique of the predictive value of intelligence tests in relation to social success.

30 See Kamin in Eysenck vs. Kamin (1981, pp. 106 ff.).

31 See J.R. Flynn (1984a, 1984b, 1987a, 1987b, 1988, 1990, 1991).

32 Depending on the test the gap was 1–12 points, compared with 14–18 for the pre-1980 period.

33 J. Connolly (1994) gives $325,000 for Lynn and $250,00 for Eysenck (1986–88). This article may be read as supplementary to Tucker (1994) as it contains further details of the far right *dramatis personae* involved, albeit journalistically. Tucker gives 'well over $300,000' for Jensen via his Institute for the Study of Educational Differences (p. 280) and $179,000 for Shockley (p. 251).

34 Opponents are also commonly accused of being doctrinaire egalitarians seeking to deny obvious inequalities. The truth is rather that their opponents understand that human 'inequalities' are of such numerous and uncorrelated kinds that singling just one of them out as the most important cannot do justice to human diversity.

35 It is though perhaps even more internally focused on immediate US social policy issues and cultural problems than the post-Jensen debate was, and the contrast with the global interests of pre-1940 Race Psychology is very marked. An avalanche of critical reviews greeted the book on publication, again generally recycling the standard arguments. Among the most important were Leon Kamin (1995), S.J. Gould (1994), George Johnson (1994), Steven Holmes (1994), Jim Holt (1994), Alan Ryan (1994) and Bob Herbert (1994). The APA's house-journal *Monitor* published a statement by eight psychologists, headed by Howard Gruber, opposing the book. Gruber also introduced a special issue of *Peace and Conflict: Journal of Peace Psychology* containing various critiques of the book and these were circulated by Morton Deutsch, director of the International Center for Cooperation and Conflict Resolution (Teachers College, Columbia University). Length considerations preclude a detailed discussion of this material here, which in any case largely served to reiterate, if more thunderously than ever, the existing arguments. Gould himself observes that the book 'contains no new arguments and presents no compelling data to support its anachronistic Social Darwinism' (1994, p. 139).

36 For example, A.H. Yee et al. (1993) still consider 'the fundamental issue' to be 'the need to define race scientifically and designate how it should be used as a psychological concept' (p. 1137). This begs the entire question, 'race' is not, and never has been, a psychological concept, nor is it any longer a scientific one in any discipline. M. Zuckerman (1990), while critical of the concept, still considers 'The question of whether racial studies are racist largely depends on the quality of the research and the reasonableness of the deductions.' (p. 1302) – again it is surely the 'reasonableness' of adopting the 'racial' framework in the first place which is now in question? Betancourt and López (1993) are more critical but their discussion of the concept is still ambiguous, on the one hand suggesting it is inadequate for scientific purposes but on the other retaining terms such as 'racial grouping' and 'interracial' in their own discourse.

37 See Appendix for some observations regarding his much-published table comparing 'Mongoloid', 'Caucasian' and 'Negroid' traits.

38 Ironically a news story has appeared at the time of writing in which concern has been expressed about the increasing number of very young children being dispatched to

Britain's private preparatory schools by their wealthy (white) parents, some as boarders.

39 Even Richard Lynn (1989) balked at this, since tropical environments have been more stable than Northern one's throughout human evolution and the linkage with reproductive strategy should therefore be the reverse of that claimed by Rushton. (By any zoological criteria humans all in fact adopt a K strategy.) Rushton considers that tendency towards twinning signifies an r strategy, as does lower age at menarche. The latter in particular is highly dubious since it is prone to considerable historical variation in relation to diet and other factors such as tightness of female clothing.

40 See the exchange in *Canadian Journal of Criminology* between Rushton and two Canadian criminologists (J.P. Rushton, 1990a, J.V. Roberts and T. Gabor 1990, T. Gabor and J.V. Roberts, 1990) on the race–crime linkage. Rushton's contribution includes an attempt to rehabilitate Lombroso! On Rushton's claims of race–brain size–intelligence linkage see D.P. Cain and C.H. Wanderwolf (1990) and C.H. Wanderwolf and D.P. Cain (1990).

41 This table has appeared in several places, for example, J. P. Rushton (1989, 1990a, b).

42 See D. Howitt and J. Owusu-Bempah (1994, pp. 154–6) for a scathing account of this episode.

Chapter 10

Bringing it all back home

If the 'race and IQ' controversy has dominated public awareness of Psychology's concerns with 'race' in recent decades, there have been far weightier, if less visible, developments of more long-term significance. In this chapter I will attempt a brief overview of some of these, before offering my closing observations on the present situation. The relative brevity of the coverage here compared with that given to the race and IQ controversy is overdetermined: insofar as these developments break new ground they are not yet amenable to historical consideration, their range is extremely wide thus ruling out any comprehensive treatment and they are readily accessible in a way in which much of the material previously examined is not. The race and IQ controversy, by contrast, represents the latest instalment of a long-running saga and has monopolised public media attention. It thus required a fuller exegesis.

The first such development has been the emergence, primarily in the USA, of the Black Psychology movement, begun in 1968 although with deeper roots. The second is the continuing, indeed mounting, concern with the persistent levels of ethnocentrism and racism within Psychology itself, as manifested in Howitt and Owusu-Bempah (1994). Thirdly, some current theories of racism will be briefly discussed. In addressing the first of these we will also consider links between feminism and anti-racism. One area I will not be explicitly covering, except incidentally, is the extensive genre of cross-cultural Social Psychological work which has appeared since 1970. To do so would involve expanding my task too widely, most of this work not being framed in racial terms. We ought not to be too complacent, however, about how far this continuation of the Cross-cultural Psychology tradition has fully emancipated itself from the problems discussed in Chapters 5 and 8. It certainly bears on the ethnocentrism problem, dealt with in the second section.

BLACK PSYCHOLOGY

As we saw in Chapter 8, by 1970 a distinct Black Psychology school had been created in the USA by radical African American psychologists who recognised the need for any Psychology to be rooted in, and emerge from, the concerns of the community it sought to serve and represent. While F.C. Sumner (the first African

American to obtain a Psychology doctorate) had convened the first Conference of black psychologists at Tuskegee Institute in 1938, it took three decades for the Association of Black Psychologists to be formally established, under Charles W. Thomas, its first president, in 1968. A *Journal of Black Psychology* was later founded as a vehicle of US black Psychological work. R. Wilcox (1971) assembled a collection of papers by black psychologists spanning the years since the late 1930s and dealing with topics such as racial integration, higher education, attitudes, achievement, and Psychology as a profession. This aimed primarily to serve both as an accessible source of relevant Psychological work for black students and as a morale booster for them. Increasingly black psychologists were seeing that their task was not so much to criticise white Psychological research on 'race differences' as to ignore it and create new theories and projects of their own. Hopefully black and white Psychologies might reconnect in the future but it would have to be as equals. In the meantime a genuine professional Black Psychology had to be forged, proactive, not reactive, in character. A first target must be abandonment of the 'damaged Negro' stereotype. This emerges very clearly in the opening papers of the first edition of R.L. Jones *Black Psychology* (1972).

Mosby's 'Toward a new specialty of Black Psychology', for instance, argues that it must be based on the recognition that black experience from infancy onwards is both qualitatively and quantitatively different from the US white experience. Joseph White's 'Toward a Black Psychology' states:

> if social scientists, psychologists, and educators would stop trying to compensate for the so-called short-comings of the black child and try to develop a theory that capitalizes on his strengths, programs could be designed which from the get-go might be more productive and successful. (p. 44)

He additionally attacks the 'matriarchal' dysfunctional family and 'cultural deprivation hypothesis' models. Among the theoretical resources available for this task he identifies existential Psychology and the self-theory approaches being adopted in the Growth Movement.[1] Black psychology is needed to explain 'dynamics of the black home, family, hero, role models, language systems, work and time management, and the nature of suspiciousness' (p. 49). On this last point he observes 'A black person who is not suspicious of the white culture is pathologically denying certain objective realities of the black experience' (ibid.). While clearly attacking the 'damaged Negro' image, White sees Black Psychology as 'facilitating the psychological health' of the African American, initiating a process of 'rational cleansing and meaningful reflection' (p. 50).

A different, atypical, note was struck by William A. Hayes. While acknowledging that Psychology has 'contributed disproportionately to the justification of the personal and institutionalised racism which characterizes America' (p. 51), he goes on to argue that it is both unwise and impossible to develop a unified discipline of knowledge called Black Psychology of more value to black people than American Psychology. Since no internally consistent discipline of Psychology exists anyway it is unlikely that Black Psychology could be so. His own theoretical allegiance is to radical behaviourism. Hayes appears to be almost unique in adopting this position among the new generation of African American psychologists.

Jones also reprinted a 1969 paper by James Comer on 'White racism: its root, form and function' in which he explains white racism in America as emerging from 'the social conditions of sixteenth-century Europe and America and . . . shaped by forces specific to the formation . . . of this country' (p. 311). In some respects elaborating on this, J.H. Howard's 'Toward a social psychology of colonialism' attempted to identify the 'colonized mentality' common to all colonised people. This is marked by both hostility and profound self-hatred or low self-esteem. He talks of the 'severe ego-destruction undergone by colonized man' (p. 329). While this sounds like acceptance of the 'damaged Negro' account this would misrepresent Howard's position, encapsulated best perhaps in the following passage:

> We must end the tradition of what one of my colleagues likes to call the 'victim analysis' type of approach and begin to do reconnaissance research on our colonizer. (p. 331)

Lynching, he suggests, might be a good place to start. Colonisation is not a condition which can be adjusted to, 'like an iron collar it can only be broken' (ibid.). He ends somewhat ironically: 'We must think of black people as a whole because, although we think as individuals, we are treated as a whole' (p. 332).

The papers Jones assembled covered a wide spectrum, from education and counselling to racism and the community role of the psychologist, nor was it entirely African American in focus as Howard's paper indicates. Lloyd Delany's 'The other bodies in the river' drew attention to other targets of racism, such as Japanese Americans. The tone, inevitably at this stage, varied from the semi-polemical to the coolly academic. There was little doubt, however, that the range of issues facing Black Psychology was broad and heterogeneous. It remained an open question whether Hayes's doubts about the possibility of a unified approach could be allayed. This pluralistic character was maintained in the enlarged second edition (1980) which retained most of the original papers. One paper in this demands immediate attention, R.V. Guthrie's 'The psychology of black Americans: an historical perspective'. Guthrie was already well known for his earlier lambasting of the discipline *Even the Rat was White* (1976). It has to be said that as a piece of academic historiography this is extremely dire, although it does convey some useful information in passing. For example, he talks of 'psychology's reliance on the principles of psychoanalysis', apparently oblivious of the fact that mainstream US Psychology has perennially resisted any such reliance; he erroneously claims that Rorschach tests have psychoanalytic underpinnings (Rorschach devised them quite independently of psychoanalytic thought); claims McDougall as the 'father of social psychology' – a gross overstatement especially for the USA where W.I. Thomas would be a far more appropriate candidate, and seeks to blame cognitive dissonance theory on Darwin. The historical image of Psychology created by Guthrie has perhaps had a serious deleterious effect on anti-racist understanding of the topic, given that it has probably served many African American psychologists as a reference-setting point.

It is historically somewhat premature to do more than indicate two of the more salient subsequent developments in this field. Two particularly influential figures are Wade Nobles who has sought to identify a genuine African philosophy tradition on which Black Psychology can build (this was outlined in Jones, 1972), and William E. Cross Jr whose 'nigrescence theory' put into effect Mosby's call for a developmental theory based on African American experience. The nigrescence theory in its original form posited five stages in the development of the black identity: (a) 'pre-encounter', during which the individual remains dominated by the negative white view of him or herself; (b) 'encounter', a 'shocking personal or social event' which shakes this world-view and renders the individual receptive to a new interpretation of his or her 'identity and condition'; (c) 'immersion-emersion', described by Cross as 'the vortex of personal metamorphosis', characterised by 'glorification of African heritage' and denigration of 'white people and culture'; (d) 'internalisation', during which the conflicts are resolved and a new open, non-racist viewpoint emerges; (e) 'internalisation-commitment', when lasting ideological change and, perhaps, social activism ensues, though this is not universal.[2] T. Parham (1989) later took issue with this as being too restricted and finite, and stressed the need to consider the whole life cycle and the never-ending process of identity definition. Mama (1995) is highly critical of the whole approach, though she considers Parham's move an advance. Besides its simplistic unilinearity, she claims it is 'essentialist' in assuming that there *is* such a thing as a natural black identity. While an advance in 'theorising racialised identities' as resulting from interaction between individual and society, the theory remains, for her, 'dualistic' in presuming the internal and external worlds of the person to be separate. 'What has yet to be advanced is a theory of subjectivity as a process that is both individual and socio-historical at the same time.'[3] (More on this point shortly.)

By the end of the 1970s, the impact of feminism was making itself felt among black psychologists, black women psychologists seeking ways of integrating the two struggles. (This leads into the second topic of this chapter, the persistence of ethnocentrism and racism within the discipline.) In Britain the 1980s saw black psychologists, for the first time, gaining a significant presence in the discipline. The integration of feminist and ethnic issues has been particularly notable in the work of British-based black women such as Kum-Kum Bhavnani (1990, 1994), Amina Mama (1995), and Ann Phoenix (1994, 1996) (though not all have remained in the UK). A major theoretical development here, related to similar shifts in post-modern thinking at large, has been to challenge a central shibboleth of Western Psychology – the notion of a fixed enduring 'self' or 'personality'. The position of the black woman in particular has highlighted the extent to which the 'self' is constantly having to be recreated and changed in response to the often excruciatingly conflicted worlds in which she lives and between which she has to move, in addition to the constantly shifting nature of these over time. While partly anticipated in traditional role theory under the rubric of 'role conflict' this new approach goes deeper to contest the universal validity of the existence of a fixed 'personal identity'.[4] This is not to say that one does not have a continuous biography or consciousness, but rather that this can include quite fundamental changes in who and what one is. To quote Mama:

None of the identities taken up are 'false' since they are all derived from the person's experience and imbibed knowledge of the various discourses and styles of being. Being multiple in this way can be pathologised within psychological discourse but can be reconceptualised once we view subjectivity as multiple and dynamic.

(Mama, 1995, p. 121)

While in principle generalisable to all of us, the situation of the black woman, especially the black British woman, rendered this position inescapable for a psychologist honestly striving to address the nature of her black 'subjectivity'. This theme is also present in the background of Tizard and Phoenix's *Black, White or Mixed Race?* (1993), a study of the identity problems facing children of 'mixed parentage'.

The preceding hardly does justice to recent moves in Black Psychology, of which, as someone who is basically a disciplinary historian, the author cannot pretend to have been keeping abreast.[5] I have not even alluded to numerous works which current African American psychologists would consider landmarks of the post-1970 years. With regard to this material I can only plead that it is as yet too early to deal with historically and that the task would, in any case, require an African American author if it were to be done competently. Mama (1995) has a brief account of the rise of Black Psychology (pp. 54–7) which includes a firm rejection of Wade Nobles' claims that an autonomous African philosophy can be identified to serve as a basis for an 'Afrocentric' Psychology (Nobles, 1980): 'there is no single set of principles that can be defined as the essential African philosophy' (p. 57). In effect Nobles' error is a mirror image of Carothers's notion of an 'African mind'.[6]

The danger here is clearly that black psychologists will become ghettoised within the discipline as exclusively concerned with ethnic and 'racial' issues, a tendency that has already manifested itself in relation to feminist Psychology and 'women's issues'. It is of absolutely vital importance that mainstream Psychology incorporate the new insights, understandings, and indeed methodologies, which hitherto excluded sections of the human race have to offer. This is the only way in which the discipline can become genuinely deracialised (and degenderised) in its orientation to its subject matter. Which point brings the next thorn within our grasp.

ETHNOCENTRISM AND RACISM IN PSYCHOLOGY

At the present juncture any discussion of this is perhaps best couched as a critique of Howitt and Owusu-Bempah (1994). Let me stress at the outset that I am in fundamental sympathy with this work. In the present text I have either taken on board, or independently arrived at, many of the points made in the book. The material presented and cited, especially from the post-1970 period, amplifies that which I have been able to provide. But, like David Milner (1996), the author of the (somewhat belated) *Psychologist* review, I have a problem with it. While its rhetorical tone does not get quite so deeply under my skin as it does Milner's, two of his criticisms do strike me as especially important. Rather than seek to prove Psychology's racism, Milner suggests:

> Better, perhaps, to approach the problem from the other end: take as read that racism has entered the interstices of British society over 400 years, has penetrated its cultural productions and institutions and is thus endlessly reproduced, and ask, how exactly is psychology immune from this? Please show me how psychology could *not* be racist. Further, list all the books and articles in the entire history of the discipline that have adopted an anti-racist perspective; you will not need a large sheet of paper. (p. 348)

While Milner is mistaken on the last prediction (Table 4.1 above gives a count of over 600 from the 1909–40 period)[7] his main point is clearly correct. The second important criticism is that the authors have tried to make their case by selectively piling up positive instances with no counterbalancing and often in a decontextualised fashion. I will return to these shortly.

The main difficulty facing Howitt and Owusu-Bempah is that on the one hand they are presenting a very angry text (nothing wrong with that) but on the other hand are deeply aware of the sheer complexity of the issue. In a main text of only 185 pages it is difficult to do justice to the latter in such a way that the former can be rendered fully credible to the unconverted. A further source of difficulty, however, is that they lack a theoretical framework for understanding the psychological nature of the discipline itself. It is this which I wish, for the moment, to pursue further. I have no quarrel with the evidence they offer regarding, for example, the sometimes absurd ethnocentricities into which the discipline falls – finding fault with research on black subjects because there is no 'white control group', or assuming that black people develop their identities solely in relation to white perceptions of them. But construing all this requires a grasp of the *essentially* reflexive nature of Psychology. This necessarily entails locating any Psychological work within the specific historical and cultural contexts, within, that is, the *psychological* conditions, which produce it. So Milner is quite right to wonder how, insofar as Psychology has been produced by white people, in pervasively racist contexts, it could have been other than racist. We have to be careful here, even so. As has become evident in the present text, there are many kinds of 'racism' and the contexts in which Psychological knowledge has been created are rarely uniformly or unmitigatedly 'racist' – at least within the terms of the day. Germany 1930–45 was probably the only exception – even South Africa produced Sachs (1937) and Biesheveul (1943) (even if the latter subsequently blew it, as Howitt and Owusu-Bempah document). If an authentic Psychology can only be produced by the community of subjects it pertains to, then its application outside that community, to subjects who have no place in its production, will be 'centric' in its account of them.

Psychology's problem in this respect rests in large part on its desperate aspirations to the status of a natural science in quest of universal laws, and psychologists' own self-images of themselves as this kind of scientist. Now here we are back in a painful bind we have repeatedly encountered. The quest for 'universals' can now be seen to have been vitiated by the Euro-centric nature of the theories whose putative universality guided the quest, but the articulation and exploration of cultural differences is also stymied (a) by the Euro-centric nature of current Psychological modes of construing, and categories of, difference; (b) the current, though in principle rectifiable, lack of a sufficiently large body of non-white (the term seems unavoidable here) psychologists in a position to generate Psychologies which are authentic in the sense just given; and (c) the constant cultural elision of cultural differences with racial ones and their co-option for racist purposes.

By deploying terms such as 'psychological colonialism' and 'psychological imperialism' Howitt and Owusu-Bempah tend to give the impression of a more conscious, and more consciously perfidious, alliance between Psychology and white ruling-class politics than is often the case, especially after World War I. South Africa aside, the Psychology practised in the British Empire prior to the 1950s was in all honesty pretty minimal, and such as there was was quite heterogeneous as we saw in Chapter 7. Since 1950 'cross-cultural' Psychology has flourished of course, but again, as Howitt and Owusu-Bempah themselves at times acknowledge, it is hardly a consistently racist genre, and it cannot be simply dismissed as 'psychological neo-colonialism'. They give us no grounds for accepting that the post-World War II works they cite as evidence of Psychology's collaboration with agencies of colonial exploitation are typical,[8] and it would be easy enough to ferret out examples of Cross-cultural Psychology and Psychological Anthropology during this period of a quite different kind.[9] Though these latter may often display Euro-centric naiveties it would be quite unjust to accuse their authors of somehow deliberately striving to enable exploitative colonial employers to up the output of their workers.

Liberals are given a hard time in Chapter 3, and quite right too *regarding the examples cited*. But how representative are these? They apparently include McDougall (!) and Ray Honeyford (the sometime headmaster of Drummond School, Bradford, a right-wing opponent of anti-racism who published in the *Salisbury Review*), as well as Henri Tajfel because his social identity theory 'is fuel to an ideology which regards intergroup hostility as inevitable' (p. 49), feminism's failure to deal with black women and a somewhat flawed discourse analysis study by T.A.Van Dijk (1987). This is representative of the 'liberal' tradition? The ambiguities and lapses of the liberal tradition are real enough, as we have frequently observed. But from the 1920s to the 1960s 'white liberals' represented, with whatever degree of naivety, the major bulwark against rampant racism within Psychology, and, what is now more important, contemporary white anti-racist psychologists can only be so because their labours reflexively brought the hidden levels and modes of white racism to the surface. If they failed to emancipate themselves from racism they at least tried, and in their failure demonstrated what more remained to be done. It is their failure to understand the historical psychological *process* that is most frustrating about Howitt and Owusu-Bempah's analysis, exacerbated by the fact that they ironically supply so much good material by which to illustrate it. For me it was here that the work's greatest value lay. Explicitly racist Psychology is easy to see and deal with. What is difficult to evaluate is this constant cycle of 'anti-racist' Psychology falling into a yet more profound or subtle racist pitfall and earning itself only condemnation from the next generation of anti-racists. Of all those I have read only Kovel, to be discussed shortly, seems to have found a position, a disturbing one too, from which to address this.

To return to the second of Milner's criticisms, *The Racism of Psychology* really does fall into what appears to be the classic trap of seeking to carry one's thesis by citing reams of positive evidence and ignoring all the rest. The opening historical pages are little more than an exercise in 'racism spotting', citing, as well as psychologists, a variety of philosophers, psychiatrists and eugenicists with scant consideration of historical context. Too many major figures in the story are absent from the text – Garth, Peterson, Porteus, Klineberg, Margaret Mead, Nadel, Caliver, Gunther . . . some were outright racists, some anti-racists, others somewhere in between, but they are all far more relevant to 'the racism of Psychology' than Cartwright and his '*drapetomania*', Carothers's 1951 'lobotomy' theory and Honeyford, let alone Hume and Malthus, all of whom are included.

On the other hand the book displays a wide and detailed grasp of the recent and current situation on the ground within Psychology, not only in relation to contemporary theories of racism but also in relation to intra-disciplinary politics and problems arising in applied Psychology and 'race relations' literature in general. But it is precisely the depth of their grasp of these which, ironically again, subverts the ostensible simplicity of their case. They *know* that 'there is no simple correct position on racism. It is not possible to present a few 'rules' which, if applied, will eliminate racism' (p. 61). They *know* that racism is not a unitary phenomenon (e.g. they list six varieties, from M. Halstead, 1988, on pp. 106–7). But there are indications that Howitt and Owusu-Bempah do in fact believe in an 'unchanging core' of racism behind its 'superficial aspects' (see e.g. p. 99). The resultant tension appears at times to lead them to verge on recommending that psychologists maintain themselves in a state akin to constant cultural revolutionary self-criticism – we never know from whence racism will strike, for (especially if we are white) it lurks like original sin. None of us is innocent. However emancipated from racism we believe ourselves to be it is ever liable to creep up on us unawares, catch us off-guard, and expose us as secret racists after all. (Enter the party faithful to publicly clobber us with sticks until we are duly mortified.) I am caricaturing here, but I sense a real risk. The very last thing any of us need right now is a lapse into paranoid heresy hunting.

If we are to make a reality of the vision of a non-racist Psychology which Howitt and Owusu-Bempah inspirationally offer (as Milner recognises), then we have to be a little more relaxed about it, even if we do feel angry. I believe the reflexive perspective I have advocated elsewhere, and tried to utilise here, may be of assistance in this. Certainly, if you are a psychologist, you cannot pose, as they occasionally verge on doing, as being outside the discipline attacking it as something other. Yes, we do need to be vigilant about our professional practice, we do need to alert one another to hitherto unspotted forms of racism, and our professional organisations really should be pressurised into acting along lines suggested in the book's closing 10-point recommendations for action. But moralistic condemnation of the logically necessary fact that Psychology in racist cultures tends to be racist is pointless, counter-productive even. Let us turn that round.

Our struggle to create a non-racist Psychology is part of the struggle to create a non-racist culture.

Possibly the most insidiously racist or ethnocentric aspect of contemporary Psychology is one which operates less in a positive fashion than by default. As A. Phoenix (1996) and others have observed, the discipline continues to accept white performance as the norm in research on topics unrelated to race or ethnicity as such (e.g. perception or memory). Non-white subjects thus only figure in research in contexts where 'they are being puzzled over as enigmatic or their taken-for-granted pathology is being analysed' (Phoenix, 1996, p. 6). Their 'absence' thus becomes normalised. (The same point has also been made regarding inclusion/exclusion of women subjects.)

CURRENT THEORIES OF RACISM

So what do psychologists now think 'racism' *is*? Psychological theorising on the nature of racism has moved some way beyond those earlier approaches which explained it in terms of irrational stereotyping, projected oedipal anger, unthinking conformity to racist beliefs or idiosyncracies in the individual's learning history.[10] It is now recognised, for example, that an attitude which simply treats everyone the same and ignores the specific needs of different ethnic groups is in its way racist ('Colour-blind racism' as Halstead, 1988, calls it).[11] It is also accepted that racism operates at different levels, some not being psychological in the strict sense ('institutional racism' and 'cultural racism'). Yet the quest continues for some essentialist definition which can comprehensively wrap the whole thing up: J. Katz (1978) influentially proposed 'Racism = prejudice + power'. None of these has proved satisfactory.[12] Among the many works published over recent years in which attempts have been made to theorise racism, two strike me as demanding particular attention: Kovel's *White Racism* (1988, 1st edn 1970) and Goldberg's (1993) *Racist Culture*.

Joel Kovel: *White Racism: A Psychohistory*

As mentioned in Chapter 1, Kovel offered an extended psychoanalytic-cum-Marxist account of white racism as rooted in the deep-seated negative connotations of blackness for Europeans. These in turn, however, have their source in an 'elementary gesture' of 'Western Civilization': 'splitting the world in the course of domination' (1988, p. lxiii). For Kovel racism therefore 'antecedes the notion of race, *indeed, it generates the races*' (ibid., my italics). Kovel's analysis is particularly worth further consideration, for he fundamentally subverts many of our basic assumptions by placing the source of racism at such a core level. Viewed in this light many of Psychology's efforts at dealing with racism, such as studies of prejudice, are ironically created by racism 'for its purposes' in the first place. In the second edition (1984) Kovel added a new Preface in which he indicated a subsequent shift in his views to incorporate Marxist insights into the situation. While not retracting the original psychoanalytic thesis he now saw it as necessary to incorporate these insights if the mediation between psychological and socio-cultural levels was to be fully understood.

The central structure of Kovel's argument is that the consequences of that 'ele-mentary gesture' have worked themselves out over Western history in a succession of phases. The immediate consequence of the 'gesture' was to facilitate a psycho-logical projection of all that is negative onto people with black skins. Prior to the Western encounter with black people blackness had already become symbolically associated with faeces, dirt, sin, the Devil and death and so on in the Western mind and culture. When encountered, black people were, moreover, immediately identified as the cursed descendents of Noah's son Ham. And Ham's crime was essentially more than just seeing his father naked but 'the castration of the father – the violent rejection of paternal authority and the acquisition of the father's sexual choice' (p. 63). The black man is thus 'the bad son, marked with the sign of the black curse' (p. 64) and banished. Invoking Fanon in support, Kovel insists on the centrality of this black–white symbolism, and its oedipal implications, in the Western mind. This has played itself out in three phases: dominative racism, aver-sive racism and 'metaracism'. These are better understood as successive layers rather than distinct phases, since each co-exists with its predecessors. In domina-tive racism, the form prevailing under slavery, the white has free reign in the exer-cise of power over the African. In doing so the unconscious oedipal symbolism is uninhibitedly played out in real life. The mother is split into an idealised pure white mother and an impure, sensual, black 'mammy'. The black man can play the dual symbolic roles of bad father to be castrated and bad son to be castrated as punishment for castrating his father and as the vessel of projected oedipal desires for the white mother. The black woman is a sexually available outlet for repressed white oedipal desires for the mother while symbolising impure sensual lust. This is not without a serious price for the white psyche itself, depriving the white woman, for example, of full maternal and sexual gratification. The complete psychodynamic picture becomes more complex than this as Kovel illustrates with a diagram of the interactions between the black/white and male/female polarities (p. 75, Fig. 1). The consequences for the black male are much as Kardiner claimed – self-hatred and passivity. Kovel's analysis here ought perhaps to be read as the culmination of the project initiated by Dollard (1957, 1st edn 1937), pre-senting the psychoanalytic theory of slavery in its most fully developed form. The highly sexualised nature of the Southern slavery culture is apparent enough – pre-occupation with the black male rapist of white women, castration as a punishment and sexual exploitation of the black woman being among its most obvious hallmarks.

Following emancipation a new mode of racism, aversive racism, emerges. Where previously the all-powerful Southern white slave-owner had created a situation in which he could revel in playing out his oedipal fantasies and anxieties, the African American now becomes the very symbol of these and something to be avoided. Scientific Racism lends support to this of course. Segregationism is thus understood as a sort of shift from an id-dominated slavery culture to an ego-dominated one. The clean, rational, hard-working and self-controlled white now projects onto African Americans the opposite of all these – they are dirty, emotional, lazy, and lacking in self-control (especially sexual). Kovel depicts the id-controlled slavery culture as an 'anal' one in which the world is divided, in the ruling white male psyche, into good and bad 'faeces' or property.[13] The aversive racism phase sees this anality brought under control in the classic psychoanalytic way by obsessional concern with personal cleanliness, purity, and control. This new form of racism is bound up with the growing involvement of the North in race issues during the post-Civil War period. Aversive racism has become typical, says Kovel, 'wherever the bourgeois-capitalist style of life prevails' (p. 193). While hitherto the black had to be a powerless object in order to receive the physical predations of white masters, now again powerlessness has to be imposed in order to carry the full weight of the projection of white anality:

> he must be made into the affirmation of the excremental body. He must become the double negative of anality, the fantasy of a fantasy – not cold, pure, clean, efficient, industrious, frugal, rational (that is, not the pantheon of anal-negative ego traits which are the *summum bonum* of the bourgeois order) but rather warm, dirty, sloppy, feckless, lazy, improvident and irrational, all those traits that are associated with blackness, odor, and sensuality to make their bearer worthy of aversion. (p. 195)

And he observes that this 'prejudice of race was forced precisely in fleeing from the temptations of slavery, and out of the resulting creation of higher, more abstract, things' (p. 198).

But now we discover, in Kovel's account of things, a cruelly ironic and paradoxical twist. This very process of affirming white purity and rejecting the 'temptations of slavery' creates a peculiarly intense, idealistic and self-righteous super-ego.

> But here a deep paradox intrudes: since in history the grossest wrongs have been committed upon the people who inhabited these black bodies, then the object of Western conscience, the goal of its reformist activity, must be the same as the object from which the self flees in the formation of its idealistic superego. (p. 200)

This dilemma was already present in the early abolitionist movement, and has continued to affect American reformism ever since. We can now see why Kovel's view of anti-racism (at least in its classic prejudice-oriented forms) is so disturbing. The white anti-racist is *still*, it seems, *using* the African American in the service of white psychological interests. But now as the target of the attentions of an overintense super-ego needing to reassure itself of its idealistic moral character.

Relating this to the course of events we have been dealing with in the present work, the cycle, identified earlier, of successive white anti-racisms turning out to remain racist may be seen as reflecting this progressive 'notching up' of the stakes as successively more ground is eroded from under the white anti-racists' feet (to muddle my metaphors rather). And as Kovel puts it in a slightly different context,

'Each racist instance becomes assembled out of the deconstruction of an expired antiracism' (p. lxxv).

One final move remains, the rise of 'metaracism'. Formal official, legal, racism has gone. At the psychological level white denial of personal racism prevails. We have now moved from the psychological to the cultural level. It is the system itself which maintains the oppression of the African American in a structural fashion. There is nothing to stop individuals obtaining wealth and status within certain circumscribed fields (sport, entertainment, literature, and to some degree in academia). But the impersonal operation of market forces and emergence of self-enclosed quasi-autonomous social systems keeps the old racial order effectively intact. Racism is mediated by personal acquiescence in an existing cultural order, not by personal racism as such. 'Metaracism exists wherever bureaucracies exist to reduce people to numbers' (p. 217). (In this sense *The Bell Curve* becomes an exemplary 'metaracist' text.) The only way remaining open is via radical structural change. While the first edition ended somewhat apocalyptically, Kovel's 1984 Preface concedes that events have unrolled in a somewhat more complicated fashion than he foresaw. The extent to which the metaracist system could both tokenistically assimilate African Americans into the political process (e.g. as city mayors etc.) while simultaneously practically recouping virtually all the economic and educational gains made by the early 1970s was remarkable, while, writing in the early 1980s, Kovel fears that anti-racist 'zeal has waned' and no new black leaders have emerged of the stature of Martin Luther King and Malcolm X.

Before offering some comments on Kovel's case I would also draw the reader's attention to Ivan Ward's Introduction to the 1988 British edition. Ward ruminates further on the psychoanalytic nature of racism and in particular the pervasive yet hidden role of phantasy in determining political behaviour. While occasionally rather densely technical, this Introduction is a valuable contribution in its own right.

Comments on Kovel's theory

Exciting, challenging and frequently penetrating though this text is, there are several issues on which this reader, for one, remains unclear or has reservations.

• How far is his account really generalisable from the US situation and to other forms of racism than the anti-black African kind he is almost exclusively concerned with? As indicated in Chapter 1, 18th century British domestic views of race were quite diverse but hardly included the extreme kind of 'dominative' racism which prevailed on the Deep South and Caribbean plantations. Some views anticipated 'aversive' racism, others a sort of blasé Enlightenment intellectual universalism which, if ill-informed and ethnocentric in its perceptions, is hard to match to any of the psychodynamic syndromes Kovel discusses. Nor, coming down to the present century, does British racism display these dynamics in quite such ideal forms as Kovel finds them in the USA. This is not to try and let Britain off the hook, only to suggest that Kovel's schema requires considerable modification or adjustment if it is to adequately explain British racial 'psychohistory'. In particular, neither the uncontrolled anality of the Deep South slavery culture nor the extreme reactive swings which ensued in the ego-dominated 'aversive' phase and idealistic super-ego dominated 'antiracist' camp are nearly so transparently evident in Britain. Similarly, anti-semitism, anti-Irish and anti-Asian racisms, while in principle amenable to Kovel's mode of analysis (as anti-semitism has been, of course) would surely disclose rather different psychodynamic scenarios.

- Also, as noted in Chapter 1, I am not entirely convinced by the simple black vs. white symbolism polarity, Fanon's moving testimony notwithstanding. It is not so much wrong as oversimplified, ignoring the presence of a positive 'black aesthetic' in white culture. It is a bit like the yin–yang symbol without the dots. Worth spelling out, however, is that the skin-colour differences between pinkish Europeans and Africans who were more often than not brown (which is symbolically and aesthetically highly ambiguous) have indeed been forced into this polar schema.

- Acceptance of Kovel's case is obviously conditional on acceptance of the psychoanalytic theoretical apparatus as a whole. While the present author is sympathetic to this, it must be admitted that as an orthodox scientific theory, as opposed to being one mode of psychological discourse among many which are pragmatically available to us, psychoanalysis is in serious trouble.[14]

- While Kovel's downbeat characterisation of anti-racism has its merits, it is something of a counsel of despair. Whatever a white person's deeper psychological motives for becoming an anti-racist, the bottom line is surely that there are only three options: (a) identify with the oppressive use of power, (b) oppose the oppressive use of power – if necessary disempowering those exercising it, (c) wash your hands of the whole business. The only moral option is the second, regardless of the intensity or idealistic nature of your own super-ego. To be effective white anti-racists must indeed critically examine their own motives, but Kovel's position here verges on a kind of psychoanalytic reductionism in which the very fact that white anti-racist motives may be traced to unconscious sources discredits them. This is silly, because all our behaviour is, from a psychoanalytic viewpoint, so traceable. That he captures something of the reasons for the *flaws* in mid-century US white liberal anti-racism, and one of the traps to which all white anti-racists should be alerted, I am happy to concede.

- It is difficult to see how much further psychoanalysis can go in relation to race issues. Kovel (and Ward in his 1988 Introduction) have succeeded in finally wrenching psychoanalysis onto the right tracks after a decidedly ambiguous preceding 80 years, but have they also reached the end of the theoretical line?

It is still premature to offer any assessment of the historical significance or impact of Kovel's work. Its technical psychoanalytic character has perhaps so far prevented it from reaching as wide an audience as it deserves. My personal view is that it is 'essential reading' for anyone seriously studying the nature of racism.

D.T. Goldberg: *Racist Culture: Philosophy and the Politics of Meaning*

If Kovel's account represents one of the most elaborated attempts at providing an 'essentialist' theory of racism, one identifying it as stemming from a single under-lying cause, Goldberg's represents the most elaborated denial of this. It is, as the subtitle indicates, a work of philosophy rather than Psychology, although in places he discusses Psychological work in some detail.

Goldberg exhaustively examines essentialist approaches to 'racism' and finds them all wanting. The notion that racism is always 'irrational', for example, raises fundamental general philosophical issues relating to the very concept of 'rational-ity': if defined in terms of internal consistency of beliefs it fails because racist belief systems may be internally coherent (1993, Chapter 6). This shifts the 'irrationality' to the macrolevel of 'racist ends', but this takes us into very deep water indeed, including the whole contemporary philosophical debate about 'rights' and the relationship between morality and rationality. For Goldberg it transpires that racism is intimately connected with 'modernity's rationalities' and that the social sciences and 'social knowledges' which 'modernization' has pro-duced 'have been crucial to the reproduction and transformation of racialized body politics' (p. 147), 'the social sciences have done much to create, authorize, legitimate, and extend both the figures of racial Otherness and the exclusions of various racisms' (p. 175).

His analysis of the processes by which 'racist culture' sustains and adapts itself leads him to the pragmatic position referred to in my Introduction.

> Racist culture is fluid and often manifests itself in covert and subtle forms. Its transforming natures are deeply connected as cause and manifestation to recon-structed and restructured identities, to changing conditions in social structure and organization, as well as to anxieties about impending changes. I have argued that racial identification and racial exclusion could emerge in or define almost any social formation, though they are less likely to do so for some forms and under certain characteristic conditions than other. (p. 222)

The recognition of what he calls 'the radically antiessentialist fluidity of racialized expressions' (p. 236) commits one, he argues, to an active, indeed pro-active, pragmatic anti-racism directed against all the social roots and bases of 'exclusion-ary power' and the institutions which exercise it. Racialised discourse itself is one of the principal instruments of such power. He is thus very far from ending up in a standard white liberal position, ending rather on a radically revolutionary note.

As in Kovel's case it is premature to adjudicate on Goldberg's position. The task is not rendered easier by the paradoxical fact that his dense 'discursive prac-tice' is full of expressions like 'discursive practice' and hence possesses a kind of exclusionary character of its own for any reader uninitiated into post-modernist stylistics. He has sought to cover every angle, resolutely and tenaciously struggling to formulate a theoretically adequate position, and takes no prisoners *en route*. On balance I am provisionally convinced by his 'pragmatic' anti-essentialist view of racism, but am less sure that its adoption is absolutely necessary for engaging in active 'anti-exclusionary' practice. His perspective might also provide a wider theoretical framework for considering the reflexive nature of the events we have been dealing with in the present book. Like Howitt and Owusu-Bempah's, his account of the role of (in his case) the social sciences (which includes Psychology) in creating and sustaining 'racisms' is damning, and it is on this point that the material discussed in the present work might suggest the need for a more discriminating orientation.

The failure of Psychology and allied disciplines to formulate an adequate essentialist definition of racism must be acknowledged. The value of any continued quest for one must now be considered to be in serious doubt. The terms in which recent writers such as Bhavnani, Goldberg, Mama, Howitt and Owusu-Bempah and Phoenix are beginning to reformulate the problem suggest that other ways of approaching the issue may be more effective and rewarding. In the dialectical scheme of things the racism vs. anti-racism antithesis is perhaps in the process of being transcended by a recognition that both terms depend upon acceptance of racialised discourse itself. 'Races' provide only one of the categories with which Goldberg's 'exclusionary practices' sustain and rationalise themselves. A move to a more generalised 'anti-exclusionary' attack on all such exclusionary categories thus has much to recommend it.

CONCLUSION

In this conclusion we can most usefully begin by attempting to identify the main 'race'-related themes and issues now being addressed by psychologists. The order of discussion does not represent any judgment on their respective importance.

1 An axis of tension which we still have not resolved is that between affirmation and denial of difference. The earlier tendency to see denial of difference and identification of universals as the progressive strategy led, as we have seen, to a kind of 'colour-blind' racism in which white cultural norms were Eurocentrically taken as a basis for comparison, so that when differences were considered they became pathologised as deviant. Exclusive concern with 'difference' may, however, be equally counter-productive if it is allowed to reinforce racist stereotypes and attitudes. Acknowledging the specific cultural needs and priorities of different ethnic groups while affirming some common humanity is the ideal balance, but striking it in a way satisfactory to all parties is difficult to achieve and likely to remain so pending changes in the global historical situation which provides the ultimate context in which Psychology exists. The problem becomes most acute when one culture engages in practices which another culture sees as quite simply morally wrong (such as clitorectomy). These controversial practices often hinge around gender relations and roles and render the sexism and racism issues inextricably interwoven. Here we feel we are reaching the limits of acceptable levels of 'cultural relativism'.

2 Emerging from this is the central theoretical issue of the nature of identity or subjectivity. While this is not in itself a purely 'race'-related question it is in this context that it has become most profoundly problematised. This actually raises an interesting question regarding the 'identity' problems which white liberal academics in the 1950s and 1960s diagnosed as characteristic of the 'Negro'. It could be argued that the African American and colonial situations confronted African Americans and people such as Fanon with what was essentially a universal existential question, also being confronted by contemporary French existentialists and writers such as Samuel Beckett. Most (especially Gentile) whites remained shielded from this by virtue of the congenial social identities their circumstances enabled them to acquire. Subsequent post-modernist moves in relation to the 'identity' question thus include Mama's work. This is closely linked with the next issue.

3 'Racialised discourse' is now widely seen as lying at the heart of the entire issue. It is the very fact that we utilise racial labels for identifying both others and ourselves that is seen as central. While this continues cultural and linguistic racism will persist. This cannot, however, be separated from the 'affirmation or denial of difference' question.

4 A further bone of contention is the conceptualisation of 'racism'. In particular there is a division between pragmatic and essentialist theories. While nobody disputes that racism manifests itself at numerous levels, the issue still remains open as to how far these are levels at which a single identifiable underlying phenomenon manifests itself, or whether 'racism' is simply an umbrella term for a whole variety of phenomena having nothing essential in common other than their exclusionary outcomes. This is not an arcane scholastic issue but has direct bearings on how anti-racist efforts are conducted. It is now becoming inseparable from the 'racialised discourse' issue.

5 The relationship between anti-racism and other liberatory struggles is also high on the contemporary agenda. Most prominent is the link with anti-sexism. This too has important connections with each of the preceding themes. Since, as individuals, we often belong to more than one of the groups in question (we may be black and gay, or 'disabled' and female, or even a 'disabled' black lesbian, to mention just four of them), at the personal level the sources of both our felt 'disempowerment' and of our own 'identity' may be multiple. This naturally leads into Goldberg's demands for a shift to a general 'anti-exclusionary' way of proceeding beyond 'anti-racism'.

6 For the discipline itself there are numerous problems regarding racism within Psychology. Some of these are, in principle, fairly straightforward, such as tackling ethnocentric language and attitudes towards research design. Others are less tractable, such as the question of how the discipline operates in culturally and institutionally racist contexts. Psychology is faced with a variety of tangles in relation to its own racism: cross-cultural data ends up only further exoticising the 'other' and leaves white culture unexamined; prejudice studies merely individualise the nature of the problem in a mystifying and misleading fashion;

ignoring 'race' leads to an ethnocentric assumption of the white as normal, while including black subjects all too often pathologises or exoticises them; the 'enlightened' concept of 'ethnicity' both essentialises 'culture' as static and assumes all black people exist in distinct cultures – whereas 'race', while a pernicious biological fiction, is the 'psychologically real' category actually used in everyday life; ways of studying the effects of racism have to be developed which do not end up either portraying the victims as the source of the problem or pathologising them. For some psychologists in particular subdisciplines there are issues of how the 'race' question is to be tackled in educational contexts or how it is to be countered in organisational settings.[15] 'Race-awareness' and 'anti-racism' programmes have often proved counter-productive in the past. Again one might now question whether progress in this area can be achieved without some more basic theoretical reconceptualisation of the kind Goldberg offers.

7 Since global economic, social and military power has been in white hands for the last three centuries it is quite understandable and legitimate that the forms of white racism which developed in the service of extending and maintaining this power have been the main focus of attention, and other 'racisms' seen as reactive products of this. Anti-semitism has often been segregated off as a peculiar intra-white aberration distinct from racism in general. Nonetheless the issue of other racisms cannot now be dumped quite so peremptorily on white culture (what of anti-Korean racism in Japan?). It is true that white culture invented 'race' in the first place, and thus made the concept universally available, but that is not the whole story in the 1990s. It is also true that so-called 'tribal conflict' in Africa is largely a long-term legacy of colonialism (Fanon had much to say on this in 1965). Even so, 'racial' and 'ethnic' inter-group conflicts are increasingly widespread and Psychology, particularly non-European/North American Psychology surely has a role in investigating and theorising the specific natures of such conflicts. In Europe itself the Bosnian situation, British anti-Irish prejudice and even Fleming–Walloon tensions in Belgium (to cite but three examples) show that intra-white racism also requires attention. Tackling such cases will entail a fuller fusion of the 'race' and 'ethnicity' issue with social Psychological theorising on inter-group conflict generally. Again though, we must beware of overly committing ourselves to specifically Psychological modes of analysis.

8 Last but not least is the problem of how Psychology is to deal with the residual, but highly publicised, strand of racist (or thinly disguised racist) work being done within its ranks. This may of course die a natural death anyway, but more resolute tactics for speeding its demise are surely in order.

While not entirely exhaustive, these eight interlocking themes set the framework for most of the work now being conducted. But there is a ninth of more direct concern to the present author. Where do historical studies fit into all this? This is one aspect of the wider question of the role History of Psychology can or should play in a discipline which is reflexively dealing with, and produced by, its historically constructed subject matter.

In the present book I have attempted to exemplify rather than define this role. It enables us to bring into finer focus the dynamics of the 'race' issue over time, its various nuances and incarnations in different settings and at different times, the various roles Psychology has played in both reinforcing and combating racism, and the reflexive ironies and paradoxes of this. In so doing, it illuminates something of the nature of the discipline as a whole. I do believe it is essential to get the historical story right. The present account is a step towards this, but I am well aware that its coverage contains some serious gaps (mentioned in the Preface) and that the balance of the coverage might well, on occasion, be challenged. Since I have been trying to write an account which exemplifies the value to Psychology of a reflexive historiographic approach, the end product is something of a hybrid of History and Psychology (but not, I trust, too disharmonious). One curious result has been to pluck a Whiggish brand from the general deconstructionist fire, albeit in a somewhat back-handed fashion – in some sense white p/Psychology *has* made progress, if only by a succession of dis-illusionments.

Why, though, is it so important to get the history right – or at least as right as history ever gets? There are several reasons. One is that the topics of 'race' and 'racism' have been more prone than most to mythologisation and rhetorical simplification in the heat of the fray. Since these myths and oversimplifications play a large part in determining our current perceptions and representations of the issues they may seriously mislead us. A second is that such a history as I have tried to provide may give us a more confident *feel* for the longer term processes involved in understanding and resolving the 'race question', and thereby render our own practice as Psychologists that much more sophisticated and informed. A third is that in the final analysis history supplies us with much of the raw material, much of the very subject matter, we are considering. The more we know about the history of Psychology the more we know about the psychological phenomena in question – past Psychology is psychological data in its own right.

To try to summarise the situation: received radical wisdom is that perfidious Psychology has perennially served to promote racism, colonialism and paternalism. While this is not entirely untrue it must now be considered a seriously inadequate description, and not a very helpful one either if we are to make any further advances in our understanding. Psychology may be better seen reflexively as an arena in which the cultural 'racial' preoccupations of Europe and North America have been articulated and played out. There are many such arenas, from the street to the theatre, the school to the concentration camp. What is different about Psychology is that it has, until very recently, seen itself as the site where such issues can be submitted to truly scientific, objective, scrutiny and research. The articulation and playing out of cultural concerns in Psychology thus acquired a rather refined character precisely because it was supposed to be something else – dispassionate objective science. Ironically this rendered the underlying anatomy of the issues peculiarly visible.

In order to wrap things up, though, I will remind the reader, or at least the reader who is also a psychologist, of a question which is implicit in everything I have written here. *Who or what is the psychologist?* In this instance there appear to be five broad possibilities:[16]

1 The representative of a ruling elite concerned with managing and controlling the mass of the population. Psychologists overtly adopting this position are now relatively rare, especially as compared with the pre-1914 period, but the social managerial role remains central to some fields of Psychology such as psychometrics, educational Psychology (in some respects), and contexts where the psychologist is engaged directly in advising governmental agencies on policy making.

2 The 'carer' concerned with assisting individuals in particular client categories who are facing difficulties with a major psychological dimension. This would include, for example, social workers, some educational psychologists, those working with juvenile offenders or people with learning disabilities. The boundary with 1 may become blurred in practice.

3 The clinician dealing with specific cases of mental distress. These will view issues like racism in terms of clinical theoretical frameworks and seek to diagnose them in a quasi–clinical fashion.

4 The representative of a particular group who seeks to articulate and understand the 'psychology' of that group. Examples would be those identifying themselves as feminist, gay or black psychologists. A psychologist may of course belong to one, or a permutation, of these groups without identifying themselves in this way, for example, a black feminist engaged in research on the physiology of perception. A psychologist may also often have dual membership of this and other categories.

5 The quasi-autonomous intellectual academic concerned with formulating theoretical frameworks and critiques. Relatively job-secure academic psychologists may feel themselves to be in a position to offer more thoroughly thought out theoretical critiques and analyses of issues such as 'race' and racism. There may be some fudging of the boundary with 3 here since such work may draw on clinical theories (such as psychoanalysis). This category would include many of the post-World War II US prejudice theorists. The present author is, *faut de mieux*, presumably in this category too – even if 'job security' is rather over-optimistic in his case.

No psychologist is encountering the topics of 'race' and racism simply in the capacity of 'pure scientist'. Every psychologist has to be *some kind of* psychologist, and which kind will seriously affect, if not totally determine, their approach. Aside from some of those in category 1 we are all, I hope, working towards the same underlying ends, and not in competition, but we do have to remain conscious of which kind of psychologist we are, or are trying to be. We must also remember that really we are all human, all unique, and all the same as everyone else.

NOTES

1 This umbrella term refers to the psychotherapeutic work of people like Abraham Maslow, Carl Rogers and Fritz Perls.
2 I am further summarising A. Mama's (1994) summary of Cross (1980) here, from which the expressions in quotes are drawn.
3 See Mama (1994, pp. 58–63) for a fuller discussion and critique of nigrescence theory.
4 It should be stressed that this is quite different from the older proto-social constructionism of the Culture and Personality school. R. Linton (1947) for example saw knowledge of the 'norms of behaviour of a society' as necessary in order to 'penetrate behind the façade of social conformity and cultural uniformity to reach the *authentic individual*' (p. 17, my italics).
5 An excellent overview of the current state of the field was given in A. Phoenix's 'Constructing ethnicities, obscuring racisms: issues for the study of identities' (1996).
6 Interestingly Howitt and Owusu-Bempah (1994), discussed below, take Nobles quite seriously and cite him on numerous occasions.
7 Summing columns B, C, D and E. Of course, if texts in which we can retrospectively discern racism are excluded, the number is far lower, but this seems to me to be naive presentism of the crudest kind.
8 For example, Haward and Roland (1954), Parin and Morgenthaler (1969, 1st edn 1956/7).
9 For example, G. Jahoda (1966) or P.M. Greenfield (1966).
10 It is perhaps worth noting that mainstream Social Psychology has virtually abandoned the topic as such, although social cognition theory continues to deploy concepts such as 'stereotyping'. A currently widely used textbook, M. Hewstone et al. (1996) indexes one solitary page on 'racial attitude'.
11 For a good account of how this operates in practice in British political life see G. Ben-Tovim et al. (1986).
12 See Howitt and Owusu-Bempah (1994, Chapter 5) for a useful overview and critique of some recent theories of racism, including J. Katz's.
13 See Fig. 2, p. 142 for Kovel's diagram of the 'Psychohistorical Matrix – Stressing Anally Rooted Symbolism'.
14 This is a whole other terrain I cannot venture into here, but see G. Richards (1996, pp. 84–8) for a synopsis of my own position.
15 See, e.g. V. Coombe and A. Little (1986) on social work, D. Denney (1992) on the probation service, R. Littlewood and M. Lipsedge (1989) on mental illness, and P.C. Rosenblatt et al. (1995) on 'multiracial couples'.
16 Some readers may spot that there are links between this list and K.O. Apel's (1977) three 'human interests of knowledge': manipulative understanding, communicative understanding, and 'critically emancipatory self-reflection'.

Chapter 11

Résumé

The reader, or skimmer, is owed a final summing up. The approach adopted in this book has been determined by the following underlying premises:

- Psychology as a discipline is a product of the 'psychologies' of those within the discipline. It is therefore necessarily reflexive in character. The Psychological knowledge Psychology produces directly articulates and expresses the psychological character of the psychologists producing it – their ways of thinking, their priorities, attitudes, values, and so on.
- Psychologists represent specific psychological constituencies in the discipline's host societies. Until the mid-20th century these were predominantly white, male, and middle- or upper-class. While constituting a restricted sample of the psychological constituencies in society as a whole, there was always a degree of psychological heterogeneity within this group both within and between the sites where the discipline was practised.

The historical process of change within Psychology has thus been determined by several factors over and above any 'objective' knowledge gains. These include: changes in the psychological character of its practitioners in the light of changed socio-historical circumstance (in the present case this includes changes in the nature of their relationship with the non-white and Jewish constituencies providing their subject groups), and broadening of the range of psychological constituencies represented within the discipline. They also reflexively include the discipline's own previously produced 'knowledge'.

Three things immediately follow from these:

- Psychology is one of the social arenas in which the psychological issues facing Psychology's host societies are formulated, discussed, and putatively resolved. Thus historical changes in the discipline both reflect and help constitute psychological change itself.
- The psychological issues facing a particular psychological constituency can only be addressed within Psychology in a fashion which is satisfactory for members of that constituency insofar as it is itself represented within the discipline.
- Conversely, excluded constituencies can be considered only in terms of their psychological significance for those included.

Applying this framework to the topics of 'race' and racism in the history of Psychology enables us to move beyond simple questions of the 'is or was Psychology racist?' kind to a more fruitful analysis. In the course of the book a number of conclusions (not all new) have been provisionally reached, the most important being the following.

- Insofar as the psychology of Psychology's earlier practitioners was infused by the nearly universal culturally racialist character of its predominant constituency during the late 19th and early 20th centuries (in scientific circles 'Scientific Racism' theories largely prevailing), it was *necessarily* racist. This entailed that its initial agendas related to the identification and evaluative construal of 'race differences'. Among these practitioners the levels of personal 'contingent' 'racism' nonetheless varied.

- In the USA the topic entered Psychology as a direct consequence of white ruling class managerial concerns regarding 'Negro education' and, slightly later, immigration (mainly East and South European and Jewish but also Japanese and Chinese).

- The ensuing 'Race Psychology' phase which lasted until the mid-1930s constituted a collective psychological process in its own right whereby, in the light of its failure to unambiguously identify race differences of a significant kind, US Psychology emancipated itself from eugenicist Scientific Racism as such and turned to the study of 'racism' as a now inherently irrational quasi-psychopathology. This was reinforced by an (albeit slow) expansion of the representation within the discipline of hitherto excluded psychological constituencies, by a change in the broader character of US society's psychological concerns ('race' and 'ethnic' relations coming to the fore), and by the increased direct involvement of an expanding Applied Psychology with excluded groups (with whose interests Applied Psychologists came to identify). More scientifically 'internal' developments within genetics were also eroding the biological concept of 'race'.

- The white liberal constituency within US Psychology was nevertheless necessarily unable to emancipate itself from being centred on its own psychological concerns regarding its relationship with, particularly, African Americans, and eventually fell into the trap of patronisingly pathologising them, creating the 'damaged Negro' stereotype. This was the fate both of the culture and personality approach (in which deep-set conceptual problems had always been present) and the more mainstream post-World War II white social psychologists attempting to study 'race relations' and 'race prejudice'.

- Current versions of two specific issues need rethinking. First, the extent to which US social psychologists conceptualised prejudice and 'racism' as purely individual level quasi-psychopathologies – this does not accord very easily with the positions of, for example, Dollard, Klineberg, E.L. Horowitz or Ackerman and Jahoda (1950). It is perhaps truer of texts from the 1930s and 1960s than from the 1940s and 1950s. Secondly, the 'damaged Negro' stereotype requires further in-depth analysis to unravel such questions as 'how far was it actually *true* during the 1920–60 period?', 'how far did African American psychologists promote and/or resist the creation of this image?', 'how far can Fanon's position be applied to the US situation?'. I am denying neither that the stereotype was created, nor that it had to be overcome, but a satisfactory, reflexively sensitive, account of its rise and fall has yet to be produced.

- In Britain the situation was different. The white British relationship to non-European peoples was determined by the nature of Imperial experience and of little domestic urgency. British psychologists had been among the major architects of Scientific Racism. The Torres Straits Expedition had problematised this doctrine however, and thereafter British Psychology, as yet very small in numbers, paid little direct attention to 'race' questions. Owing to growing independence movements and Britain's own straitened circumstances as a global economic power, this neglect was reinforced after 1918 by the need to promote a kind of Imperial patriotism, in which the Empire was a rainbow alliance or family of peoples. British eugenics, unlike US eugenics, paid little attention to psychological race differences. It was suggested that British Psychology's neglect of the topic between the world wars reflected and facilitated a cultural repression of, and complacency regarding, racism in the UK and that this underlies the post-war inability of the white British (especially the middle class) to admit to racism. Nor is there much evidence of any anti-semitism in inter-war British Psychology, quite the contrary in fact (Pearson's now notorious research being quite untypical). R.B. Cattell's extreme right-wing sympathies during the mid-1930s were ignored or went unnoticed within the discipline while McDougall had relocated to the USA.

- Lévy-Bruhl's concept of the 'primitive mind' and Jung's 'collective uncon-scious' notions, along with some mainstream Psychoanalytic ideas, also possessed a clearly reflexive significance. While luring their exponents into racialist perceptions of so-called 'primitive' people they were serving, in a dis-placed or projectifying fashion, to reconnect the over-rational, objectifying, white (primarily male) psyche with its own repressed contents. Once so re-instated however, their 'primitive' character would, ironically, be undermined. The extreme ambiguity of Jung's position is especially to be noted.

- The eventual re-appearance of the 'race and IQ' controversy after 1969 may be seen as a fall-back attempt by the residual racist constituency within Psychol-ogy at defending and preserving their own 'psychologies' against change. The persistence of this strand owes much, it now seems, to ideologically extreme external funding sources. In the USA the initial re-activation of this research was in many respects a reversion to the original 'Negro education' agenda.

- One further thing we have demonstrated is that Psychology's treatments of 'race' and racism have been highly diverse. Even within Race Psychology itself there are quite clear differences between gung-ho racists (like Porteus) and moderates (such as Garth). Nazi Race Psychology was, despite being influenced by Anglophone writers like Grant and Stoddard, radically different in its theorising and methodology from anything outside. When working in a marginal setting, the psychologist (or psychiatrist) will also produce marginal Psychology, as Carothers' case testifies – but also, in rather different ways, Fanon's and Sachs's. (Their very marginality often renders such texts highly significant, since the tectonics of 'race' issues are frequently acutely visible in the conditions under which they were produced.) The concerns of Mid-West and Californian US psychologists also differed from those in the old Deep South and East Coast regions.

- As the hitherto excluded constituencies (notably blacks and women) have gained an increasing presence within Psychology since the late 1960s, numerous fundamental changes have been forced in the way in which it engages 'race' and 'gender' topics. Blacks, women, and, not least, black women, have begun the task of producing Psychological knowledge which emerges directly from their own 'psychologies'. This has, among other things, highlighted the whole issue of how psychological 'difference' and 'similarity' are to be construed and managed. It has also raised central questions regarding previous Psychological assumptions about the nature of personal and social identity (though these were adumbrated in part in late modernist white literature). The material discussed in this book additionally supports the claim, now commonplace among black and feminist psychologists, that 'race' and gender issues have always been closely linked.

- The cyclical process whereby 'anti-racist' Psychology is repeatedly revealed, in hindsight, to have retained racist assumptions or features should be viewed as a self-emancipatory psychological bootstrapping operation in its own right. It is now clear that an exclusively white (and mainly male) Psychology stands no chance of satisfactorily encompassing all that is human, however fine the intentions of some white male psychologists. And that includes the present author.

Clearly we must now abandon a Manichean view of Psychology's past treatment of 'race'-related issues. Not to do so would after all, as the opening premises imply, signify a continued Manichean view of ourselves. No doubt there are some thoroughly evil people, and some thoroughly saintly ones, but most of us cluster far nearer the centre of the dreaded normal distribution curve. Our moral commitment to combating racism (and any other form of 'exclusionism') is surely in no way compromised by making such an admission.

To my fellow historians I will close by ripping off Philip Roth and simply say 'and now perhaps we may begin'.

Appendix

Comments on J.P. Rushton's table of 'Mongoloid', 'Caucasoid', 'Negroid' rankings

In numerous publications J.P. Rushton reproduces a table purporting to demonstrate that on a variety of physical, psychological and social measures the ranking of these is consistent with the thesis that 'Mongoloids' are 'K' reproductive strategists and 'Negroids' 'r' strategists ('Caucasoids' being intermediate). The former strategy is characterised by few offspring, high degree of parental care, slower maturation, long life, etc.; the latter by the opposites of these. The sources of the data used to arrive at these ratings are not all cited in the three versions I have available but even a cursory consideration is sufficient to raise numerous prima facie doubts about many of them.

1 Cranial capacity and brain weight at autopsy show a range between 1448 cc–1408 cc–1334 cc (capacity) 1351g–1336g–1286g (weight) for Mongoloids, Caucasoids and Negroids respectively. They were arrived at from a review of published literature of absolute scores, but it is claimed (Rushton 1990b) that taking allometry into account (i.e. brain/body size ratio) the differences are increased. S.J. Gould (1984), citing the South African palaeontologist P.V. Tobias argues that the determination of average 'racial' brain size is actually so methodologically complicated that nobody has as yet succeeded. Nevertheless let us assume Rushton's figures are correct. As they stand they are impossible to interpret because no standard deviation figures are supplied. Taking the Caucasoid figure as the base, the ranges are 7% (110cc) and 5% (65g). According to Passingham (1982) the modern *Homo sapiens* brain size ranges from 870 cc–2150 cc (N = 1039) with a mean of 1359.1 (p. 110). Rushton does not provide N's. On the face of it a 110 cc difference in mean scores does not look statistically significant. Given the small degree of difference reported, the variety of methodological problems and the likelihood of unconscious bias among many of those obtaining Rushton's source data these figures cannot be taken seriously. However, even if we take them at face value they cannot really serve the purpose Rushton wishes, namely as indices of intelligence differences. Brain size (actually head size)/IQ score correlations provided in Rushton (1990b) are at most .35 (and this is likely to be deviant), Rushton accepts .3 as the likeliest figure, brain size thus accounts for only 9% of the variance in IQ scores at most. Many of the correlations (e.g. on the largest sample, 26,760 US schoolchildren) are under .2 (less than 4% of variance). So how many IQ points does a difference of 7% in brain size signify?

2 The mean racial IQs he gives as 107, 100, 85 (M, C, N respectively). As we have seen in the main text however, the meanings of these figures are highly debatable to say the least. If, as argued in the main text, the 'race and IQ' issue is so conceptually muddled as to be meaningless, then these figures can be safely ignored. To include them is to beg the question.

3 His 'maturation rate' section includes 'Age of first intercourse', 'Age of first pregnancy' and 'Life-span' – showing the Ms as 'late, late, long', the Ns as 'early, early, short' respectively and Cs as medium throughout. The data sources are not provided. On the

face of it, each of these has been, insofar as they are knowable or inferable, highly variable across time. Life expectancy has certainly changed dramatically in European cultures over this century. Cultural norms and religious beliefs will clearly affect the first two. Teasing out the 'genetic' contribution to variance in any of them verges on the impossible given their temporal and cultural variations and the difficulties in obtaining reliable data covering a sufficiently long period of time for temporal fluctuations to cancel out.

4 The 'Personality and temperament' section includes Activity level, Aggressiveness, Cautiousness, Dominance, Impulsivity, Sociability. Again no data sources are provided in the texts available. The implication is (a) that personality-testing methods are currently available capable of measuring these traits in a culture-fair fashion and (b) that these have, as a matter of fact, been administered by cross-cultural psychologists on a wide enough scale for this data to have been obtained. Interestingly 'Negroids' are given as high on 'dominance' – quite counter to the 19th century stereotype of 'Negro' submissiveness! To say that Ns are higher than Cs on 'aggressiveness' is a historical absurdity – Europeans must, by any criterion, be considered as the most aggressive ethnic group ever, since they effectively conquered the world, launched two of the largest wars on record and have raised military technology to the highest levels of destructiveness conceivable. To say that Ms are 'low' on 'activity level' is also rather strange. This section of the table strikes one, in the absence of supporting data, as quite fanciful.

5 The 'Reproductive effort' section includes 'Multiple birthing rate', Size of genitalia, Secondary sexual characteristics, Intercourse frequencies, Permissive attitudes, Sexually transmitted diseases and Androgen levels. 'Multiple birthing rate' (i.e. twinning) is seen as signifying 'r'-selectedness and found to be highest in Ns. In Rushton (1989) he does provide data for this, apparently showing rates of 4 (M), 8 (C) and 16 (N) per 1,000 births. However a strategy 'adopted' in only 1.6% of pregnancies can hardly be said to signify a collective racial policy! (Especially if offset, as in some traditional African cultures, by infanticide of one of the twins.) Regarding size of genitalia, the key statistic for Rushton is presumably erect penile volume (the erect:flaccid penis size ratio is highly variable). Despite the universal fascination with this topic one wonders whether reliable data exist even yet. However, even if the ratings are broadly correct, and male Ms less genitally endowed than Ns, the significance of this for Rushton is that large penis size supposedly correlates with r-selection. That is to say it signifies high sexual activity, many offspring, and so on. What is the evidence that the Chinese and Japanese are less interested in sexual activity than Africans? And what is one to make of a theory that claims the Chinese (around 25% of the world's population) to be more sexually abstemious than, say, Gambians? Even allowing for the alleged higher infant mortality rate of r-strategists (and leaving aside Chinese female infanticide) there is something profoundly askew with this. Again, given that rates of sexual activity and 'permissive attitudes' are intimately bound up with social and religious factors it is difficult to see how the genetic contribution to the overall massive degrees of historical and cultural variance can be confidently ascertained. In general, one supposes that urban city dwellers will be more sexually permissive and active than those living in small, stable rural communities.

6 Finally he provides a list of three 'Social organisation' traits: Law abidingness, Marital stability, Mental health. The first of these was effectively refuted by the Roberts and Gabor critiques (see main text). The second is so historically and culturally variable – a variability including the very nature of what is meant by 'marriage' – that once more the task of isolating a genetic tendency seems insuperable. Mental health and mental illness are historically and culturally relative concepts. Ns are considered to be 'low' on mental health, which is amusing given the tendency of 19th century US psychiatrists to view them as remarkably resistant to insanity! The ethnocentricity of concepts of mental health/ madness must preclude any confident comparisons of mental illness rates, even aside from the comparability of health data.

So what are we left with? Rushton has a tendency to be impatient with criticisms of the quality of his data, mesmerised by the consistency of their direction when taken in aggregate. But bum data is bum data regardless of whether it supports you or not. One thing we need to know is how far the data are drawn from sources which were already biased towards finding the kind of differences they report. Insofar as they were, the entire exercise is question-begging. Given the very considerable differences between the African, Eastern Asian and Western European environments it would in fact be quite remarkable if there were not, after 20,000 years, some consistent differences between their inhabitants taken as a whole regarding certain features of lifestyle, culture, and the psychological traits associated with these. But given the very considerable differences between the late 20th century global environment and any of those which preceded it, there is no reason to suppose the human species' protean character to have finally settled on a permanent form – and every reason to doubt it. We are, as Americans say, into a whole new ball-game. Rushton's table is little more than a scientistic exercise in rescuing the notion of 'race' from the oblivion into which most of his scientific peers have consigned it. And any tendencies he detects only become manifest at such a macro-level that it is difficult to see what possible practical implications can follow from them – other than providing moral support for the racist camp.

Bibliography

For T.R. Garth publications see additional bibliography.

ABBREVIATIONS

Journal titles

A.J.Orthopsych.	*American Journal of Orthopsychiatry*
A.J.Psy.	*American Journal of Psychology*
A.J.Psychiat.	*American Journal of Psychiatry*
A.J.Sociol.	*American Journal of Sociology*
Am.Anth.	*American Anthropologist*
Am.Psy.	*American Psychologist*
Ann.Am.Ac.P.&SS.	*Annals of the American Academy of Political and Social Science*
Ann.Eug.	*Annals of Eugenics*
Arch.Psy.	*Archives of Psychology* (NY: Columbia University Press)
B.J.Ed.Psy.	*British Journal of Educational Psychology*
B.J.Med.Psy.	*British Journal of Medical Psychology*
B.J.Psy.	*British Journal of Psychology*
Bull.B.P.S.	*Bulletin of the British Psychological Society*
Ch. and Pers.	*Character and Personality*
Child Dev.	*Child Development*
Comp.Psy.Monog.	*Comparative Psychology Monographs*
E.Af.Med.J.	*East African Medical Journal*
Eug.Rev.	*Eugenics Review*
Genet.Psy.Monog.	*Genetic Psychology Monographs*
H.H.Sci.	*History of the Human Sciences*
Hum.Biol.	*Human Biology*
Int.J.Ethics	*International Journal of Ethics*
J.Ab.Psy.	*Journal of Abnormal Psychology*
J.Ab.Soc.Psy.	*Journal of Abnormal and Social Psychology*
J.App.Psy.	*Journal of Applied Psychology*
J.Comp.Psy.	*Journal of Comparative Psychology*
J.Ed.Psy.	*Journal of Educational Psychology*
J.Exp.Psy.	*Journal of Experimental Psychology*
J.Genet.Psy.	*Journal of Genetic Psychology*
JHBS	*Journal of the History of the Behavioral Sciences*
J.Nerv.Ment.Dis.	*Journal of Nervous and Mental Diseases*
J.Psy.	*Journal of Psychology*
J.Soc.Psy.	*Journal of Social Psychology*

JNE	*Journal of Negro Education*
Ped.Sem.	*Pedagogical Seminary*
Pop.Sci.Mo.	*Popular Science Monthly*
Proc.Am.Ass.Ment.Def.	*Proceedings of the American Association of Mental Deficiency*
Proc.APA	*Proceedings of the American Psychological Association*
Psy.Bull.	*Psychological Bulletin*
Psy.Rep.	*Psychological Reports*
Psy.Rev.	*Psychological Review*
Pub.Am.Sociol.Soc.	*Publications of the American Sociological Society*
Sch. & Soc.	*School and Society*
Smith.Coll.Stud.S.W.	*Smith College Studies in Social Work*
Sociol.Soc.Res.	*Sociology and Social Research*
Z.angew.Psy.	*Zeitschrift für angewandte Psychologie*

Other

CUP	Cambridge University Press
NY	New York
OUP	Oxford University Press
RKP	Routledge and Kegan Paul
UP	University Press

Dates in square brackets are for 1st edition or publication date except where otherwise indicated.

Aby, S.H. and McNamara, M.J. (1990) *The IQ Debate. A Selective Guide to the Literature*, NY: Greenwood Press.

Ackerman, N.W. (1947) 'Anti-semitic motivation in a psychopathic personality: A case study', *The Psychoanalytic Review* **34** (1), 76–101.

Ackerman, N. and Jahoda, M. (1948a) 'The dynamic basis of anti-semitic attitudes', *Psychoanalytic Quarterly* **17**, 240–60.

Ackerman, N. and Jahoda, M. (1948b) 'Toward a dynamic interpretation of anti-semitic attitudes', *A.J.Orthopsych.* **18** (1), 163–73.

Ackerman, N. and Jahoda, M. (1950) *Anti-Semitism and Emotional Disorder: A Psychoanalytic Interpretation*, NY: Harper.

Adams, R. (1934) 'The unorthodox character of race doctrine in Hawaii', *Pub.Am.Sociol. Soc.* **28**, 99–100.

Adams, R. (1937) *Interracial Marriage in Hawaii*, NY: Macmillan.

Adinarayaniah, S.P. (1941) 'A research in colour prejudice', *B.J.Psy.* **31** (3), 217–29.

Adorno, T.W., Frenkel-Brunswik, E., Levinson, D. J. and Sanford, R. N. (1964 [1950]) *The Authoritarian Personality*, 2 vols, NY: Science Editions.

Aikman, K.B. (1933) 'Race mixture', *Eug.Rev.* **25**, 161–6.

Aldrich, C.R. (1931) *Primitive Mind and Modern Civilization*, London: Kegan Paul.

Allport, G.W. (1954a) *The Nature of Prejudice*, Reading MA: Addison-Wesley.

Allport, G.W. (1954b) 'The historical background of modern social psychology', in G. Lindzey (ed.) (1954), vol. 1, 3–56.

Alper, T.G. and Boring, E.G. (1944) 'Intelligence-test scores of Northern and Southern white and Negro recruits in 1918', *J.Ab.Soc.Psy.* **39**, 471–4.

Anderson, F.N. (1936) 'A mental-hygiene survey of problem Indian children in Oklahoma', *Mental Hygiene* **20**, 472–6.

Anderson, H.D. and Eells, W.C. (1935) *Alaskan Natives: A Survey of their Sociological and Educational Status*, Stanford: Stanford UP.

Apel, K.O. (1977) 'Types of social science in the light of human interests of knowledge', *Social Research* **44** (3), 425–70.

Archer, W. (1910) *Through Afro-America*, London: Chapman & Hall.
Argyll, Duke of (1869) *Primeval Man: An Examination of Some Recent Speculations*, London: Strahan.
Arlitt, A.H. (1920) 'Further data on the influence of race and social status on the intelligence quotient', *Proc.APA* 7.
Arlitt, A.H. (1921) 'On the need for caution in establishing race norms', *J.App.Psy.* 5 (2), 179–83.
Arlitt, A.H. (1922) 'The relation of age to intelligence in Negro children', *J.App.Psy.* 6, 378–84 (Proc. 30th Ann. Meeting APA 1921 14).
Arnhold, S. (1938) 'Die psychophysiker Struktur bei Hühnen verschiedener Rassen', *Zeitschrift für Psychologie* 144, 1–91.
Ash, M.G. (1995) *Gestalt Psychology in German Culture 1890–1967*, Cambridge: CUP.
Atkinson, R.L., Atkinson, R.C., Smith, E.E., Bem, D.J. and Hilgard, E.R. (1990) *Introduction to Psychology*, 10th edn, San Diego: Harcourt Brace Jovanovich.
Aveling, F. (1937) *Psychology: The Changing Outlook*, London: Watts.
Babcock, J.W. (1895) 'The colored insane', *Alienist and Neurologist* 16, 423–47.
Babington, W. D. (1895) *Fallacies of Race Theories as Applied to National Characteristics*, London: Longmans Green.
Bache, R.M. (1895) 'Reaction time with reference to race', *Psy.Rev.* 2, 475–86.
Bagby, L.M.J (1995) 'The question of Jung and racism reconsidered', *Psychohistory Review* 23 (3), 283–98.
Baker, A. (1936) 'Recent trends in the Nordic doctrine', *J.Psy.* 2, 151–9.
Baldwin, B.T. (1913) 'The learning of delinquent adolescent girls as shown by substitution tests' *J.Ed.Psy.* 4, 317–32.
Baldwin, J.M. (1902–5) *Dictionary of Philosophy and Psychology*, 3 vols, NY and London: Macmillan.
Ballard, P.B. (1923) *Group Tests of Intelligence*, 2nd edn, London: University of London Press.
Banton, M. and Harwood, J. (1975) *The Race Concept*, Newton Abbot: David & Charles.
Bardin, J. (1913) 'The psychological factor in Southern race problems', *Pop.Sci.Mo.* 83, 368–74.
Barkan, E. (1992) *The Retreat of Scientific Racism*, Cambridge: CUP.
Barke, E.M. (1933) 'A study of comparative intelligence of children in certain bilingual and monoglot schools in South Wales', *B.J.Ed.Psy.* 3, 237–50.
Barke, E.M. and Parry Williams, D.E. (1938) 'A further study of the comparative intelligence of children in certain bilingual and monoglot schools in South Wales', *B.J.Ed. Psy.* 8, 63–77.
Bartlett, F.C. (1921) 'Review of W. McDougall, *The Group Mind*', *B.J.Psy.* 11, 344–8.
Bartlett, F.C. (1923) *Psychology and Primitive Culture*, NY: Macmillan.
Bartlett, F.C. (1927 [rep. 1974]) 'The psychology of the lower races' in *VIIIth International Congress of Psychology. Groningen 1926*, Nendeln, Lichtenstein: Kraus.
Bartlett, F.C. (1932) *Remembering*, Cambridge: CUP.
Bartlett, F.C. (1936) Autobiographical entry in C. Murchison (ed.) (1961 [1936]), 39–52.
Bartlett, F.C. (1937) 'Psychological methods and anthropological problems', *Africa* 10 (4), 401–20.
Bartlett, F.C., Ginsberg, M., Lindgren, E.J. and Thouless, R.H. (1939) *The Study of Society. Methods and Problems*, London: Kegan Paul, Trench, Trübner.
Barzun, J. (1965 [1937]) *Race: A Study in Superstition*, NY: Harper & Row.
Bateson, G. (1958 [1936]) *Naven*, Stanford: Stanford UP.
Bateson, W. (1921) 'Commonsense on racial problems', *Eug.Rev.* 13, 325–38.
Baumgarter, H.W. (1935) 'Measuring negro self-respect', *JNE* 4, 490–99.
Bay Area Association of Black Psychologists (1972 [1969]) 'Position statement on use of IQ and ability tests', in R.L. Jones (ed.) (1972) 92–4.
Baynes, H.G. (1924) 'Primitive mentality and the unconscious', *B.J.Med.Psy.* 4, 32–49.

Bayton, J.A. (1941) 'The racial stereotypes of Negro college students', *J.Ab.Soc.Psy.* **36**, 97–102.

Beaglehole, E. (1939) 'Tongan color vision', *Man* **39**, 170–72.

Beale, O. C. (1911) *Racial Decay: A Compilation of Evidence from World Sources*, London: Fifield, Sydney: Angus & Robertson.

Bean, R.B. (1906) 'Some racial peculiarities of the Negro brain', *American Journal of Anatomy* **5**, 353–432.

Becker, F. (1938) 'Die Intelligenzprüfung unter völkischem und typologischem Gesichtspunkt', *Z.angew.Psy.* **55**, 15–111.

Becker, G.W. (1968) 'Riots and re-evaluation', *Am.Psy.* **23**, 584–5.

Beckham, A.S. (1929) 'Is the negro happy? A psychological analysis', *J.Ab.Soc.Psy.* **24**, 186–90.

Beckham, A.S. (1933) 'A study of the intelligence of colored adolescents of differing social–economic status in typical metropolitan areas', *J.Soc.Psy.* **4**, 70–91.

Beckham, A.S. (1934) 'A study of race attitudes in negro children of adolescent age', *J.Ab.Soc.Psy.* **29**, 18–29.

Beddoe, J. (1971 [1885]) *Races of Britain: A Contribution to the Anthropology of Western Europe*, London: Hutchinson.

Belo, J. (1935) 'The Balinese temper', *Ch. & Pers.* **4**, 120–46.

Benedict, R. (1940a) *Race: Science and Politics*, NY: Modern Age.

Benedict, R. (1940b [rep. 1943]) *Race and Racism*, London: Scientific Book Club.

Benedict, R. (1961 [1934]) *Patterns of Culture*, London: RKP.

Benedict, R. and Weltfish, G. (1943) *The Races of Mankind*, Public Affairs Pamphlet 85, NY: Public Affairs Committee Inc.

Ben-Tovim, G., Gabriel, G., Law, I. and Stredder, K. (1986) 'A political analysis of local struggles for racial equality', in J. Rex and D. Mason (eds) (1986) Chapter 6.

Berger, F. (1939) 'Grundzüge einer Psychologie unmittelbarer und musischer Bildung', *Zeitschrift für pädagogische Psychologie* **40**, 18–31.

Berkeley-Hill, O.A.R. (1921a) 'The "colour question" from a psychoanalytic standpoint', *Psychoanalytic Review* **11**, 246–53.

Berkeley-Hill, O.A.R. (1921b) 'A short study of the life and character of Mohammed', *International Journal of Psychoanalysis*, **2**, 31–53.

Berkeley-Hill, O.A.R. (1921c) 'The anal-erotic factor in the religion, philosophy, and character of the Hindus', *International Journal of Psychoanalysis* **2**, 306–38.

Berkeley-Hill, O.A.R. (1925) 'Hindu–Muslim unity', *International Journal of Psychoanalysis* **6**, 282–7.

Berkeley-Hill, O.A.R. (1933) *Collected Papers*, Calcutta: The Book Company.

Berlin, B. and Kay, P. (1969) *Basic Color Terms: Their Universality and Evolution*, Berkeley and Los Angeles: University of California Press.

Berman, M. (1961) *John Fiske: The Evolution of a Populariser*, Cambridge MA: Harvard UP.

Betancourt, H. and López, S.R. (1993) 'The study of culture, ethnicity, and race in American psychology', *Am.Psy.* **48** (6), 629–37.

Bettelheim, B. and Janovitz, M. (1950) *Dynamics of Prejudice: A Psychological and Sociological Study of Veterans*, NY: Harper & Brothers.

Beveridge, W.M. (1935) 'Racial differences in phenomenal regression', *B.J.Psy.* **26**, 59–62.

Beveridge, W.M. (1939) 'Some racial differences in perception', *B.J.Psy.* **30**, 57–64.

Bevis, W.M. (1921) 'Psychological traits of the southern negro with observations as to some of his psychoses', *A.J.Psychiat.* **1**, 69–78.

Bhaskar, R. (1991) *Philosophy and the Idea of Freedom*, Oxford: Blackwell.

Bhavnani, K.-K. (1990) 'What's power got to do with it? Empowerment and social research', in I. Parker and J. Shotter (eds) *Deconstructing Social Psychology*, London: Routledge, 141–52.

Bhavnani, K.-K. and Phoenix, A. (1994) 'Shifting identities shifting racisms', *Feminism and Psychology* 4 (1), 5–18.

Biddiss, M.D. (ed.) (1979) *Images of Race*, Leicester: Leicester UP.

Biesheuvel, S. (1943) *African Intelligence*, Johannesburg: South African Institute of Race Relations.

Billig, M. (1981) *L'internationale raciste. De la psychologie à la 'science' des races*, Paris: Maspero.

Blacker, C.P. (1952) *Eugenics: Galton and After*, London: Duckworth.

Block, N. and Dworkin, G. (eds) (1977a) *The IQ Controversy: Critical Readings*, NY: Pantheon (rep. London: Quartet).

Block, N. and Dworkin, G. (1977b) 'IQ, heritability, and inequality', in N. Block and G. Dworkin (eds) (1977a) 410–540.

Blum, J.M. (1978) *Pseudoscience and Mental Ability: The Origins and Fallacies of the IQ Controversy*, NY: Monthly Review Press.

Blumenbach, J.F. (trans. T. Bendyshe) (1865) *The Anthropological Treatises of Johann Friedrich Blumenbach*, London: Longman, Green, Longman, Roberts, & Green for the Anthropological Society.

Boas, F. (1911) 'Instability of human types', in G. Spiller (ed.) (1911).

Bock, P.K. (1980) *Continuities in Psychological Anthropology: A Historical Introduction*, San Francisco: Freeman.

Bodmer, W.F. (1972) 'Race and IQ: the genetic background', in K. Richardson and D. Spears (eds) *Race, Culture and Intelligence*, Harmondsworth: Penguin, 83–113.

Bogardus, E.S. (1925a) 'Social distance and its origins', *J.App.Sociology*, 9, 216–66.

Bogardus, E.S. (1925b) 'Measuring social distances', *J.App.Sociology*, 9, 299–308.

Bogardus, E.S. (1928) *Immigration and Race Attitudes*, NY: Heath.

Böker, H. (1934) 'Rassenkonstanz-Artenwandel', *Rasse* 1, 250–54.

Bolton, E.B. (1935) 'Effect of knowledge upon attitudes towards the negro', *J.Soc.Psy.* 6, 68–90.

Bolton, E.B. (1937) 'Measuring specific attitudes toward the social rights of the negro', *J.Ab.Soc.Psy.* 31, 384–97.

Boring, E.G. (1942) *Sensation and Perception in the History of Experimental Psychology*, NY: Appleton-Century-Crofts.

Boring, E.G. (1950 [1929]) *A History of Experimental Psychology*, 2nd edn, NY: Appleton-Century-Crofts.

Bowler, P. (1983) *The Eclipse of Darwinism*, Baltimore and London: Johns Hopkins UP.

Boyd, W.C. and Boyd, L.G. (1937) 'Sexual and racial variation in ability to taste phenyl-thio-carbamide with some data on inheritance', *Ann.Eug.* 8, 46–51.

Bradley, R.N. (1926) *Racial Origins of English Character with an Appendix on Language*, London: Allen & Unwin.

Brazziel, W.F. (1969) 'Letter from the South', *Harvard Educational Review* 3 (2), 348–56 (rep. *Harvard Educational Review* (1969) 200–8).

Brenman, M. (1940a) 'Minority group membership and religious, psychosexual, and social patterns in a group of middle-class Negro girls', *J.Soc.Psy.* 12, 179–96.

Brenman, M. (1940b) 'The relationship between minority group membership and group identification in a group of urban middle-class Negro girls', *J.Soc.Psy.* 11, 171–97.

Brenner, A.B. (1948) 'Some psychoanalytic speculations on anti-semitism', *The Psycho-analytic Review*, 35 (1), 20–32.

Brigham, C.C. (1923) *A Study of American Intelligence*, Princeton: Princeton UP.

Brigham, C.C. (1930) 'Intelligence tests of immigrant groups' *Psy.Rev.* 37, 158–65.

Brinton, D.G. (1901) *Races and Peoples*, Philadelphia: McKay.

Brinton, D.G. (1902) *The Basis of Social Relations. A Study in Ethnic Psychology*, NY and London: Albermale.

Brody, N. (1992) *Intelligence*, 2nd edn, San Diego: Academic Press.

Brown, P. (ed.) (1973) *Radical Psychology*, London: Tavistock.

Brown, R. (1958) *Words and Things: An Introduction to Language*, NY: Free Press.

Brown, W.O. (1934) 'Culture contact and race conflict', in E.B. Reuter (ed) (1934), 34–37.

Bruce, M. (1940) 'Factors affecting intelligence test performance of whites and Negroes in the rural South', *Arch.Psy.* **252**, 99.

Bruner, F.G. (1908) 'The hearing of primitive peoples: an experimental study of the auditory acuity and the upper limit of hearing of whites, Indians, Filipinos, Ainu, and African pigmies', *Arch.Psy.* **11**.

Bruner, F.G. (1914) 'Racial differences', *Psy.Bull.* **11**, 384–6.

Bryant, A.T. (1917) 'Mental development in the South African native', *Eug.Rev.* **9**, 42–9.

Bullock, H.A. (1967) *A History of Negro Education in the South from 1619 to the Present*, Cambridge, MA: Harvard UP.

Burt, C. (1935) 'The psychology of nations' in C. Burt (ed.) *How the Mind Works*, London: Allen & Unwin, Chapter x.

Burt, C. (1937) *The Backward Child*, London: University of London Press.

Busby, T.L. (1820) *Costume of the Lower Orders of London*, London: Baldwin, Cradock and Joy.

Cain, D.P. and Wanderwolf, C.H. (1990) 'A critique of Rushton on race, brain size and intelligence', *Personality and Individual Differences* **11** (8), 777–84.

Caliver, A. (1931) 'A personnel study of negro college students', *Teacher's College Contributions to Education* **484**, viii, 146.

Camejo, P. (1994 [1976]) *Racism, Revolution, Reaction 1861–1877. The Rise and Fall of Radical Reconstruction*, NY: Pathfinder.

Campbell, D.T. (1968) 'Stereotypes and the perception of group differences', *Am.Psy.* **22**, 817–29.

Campbell, J. (1851) *Negro-Mania, Being an Examination of the Falsely Assumed Equality of the Various Races of Man*, Philadelphia: Campbell & Powers.

Canady, H.G. (1936) 'The effect of rapport on the "IQ"', *JNE* **5**, 202.

Canady, H.G. (1938) 'Psychology in negro institutions', *JNE* **7**, 165–71.

Canady, H.G. (1943) 'The problem of equating the environment of Negro–White groups for intelligence testing in comparative studies', *J.Soc.Psy.* **17**, 3–15 (rep. in R. Wilcox (ed.) (1971), Chapter 10).

Carlyle, T. (1849) 'Occasional discourse on the Negro question', *Fraser's Magazine* **40** (240), 620–79 (rep. 1853 as *Occasional Discourse on the Nigger Question*, London: Thomas Bosworth).

Carothers, J.C. (1947) 'A study of mental derangement in Africans', *Journal of Mental Science*, July, 548–97.

Carothers, J.C. (1951) 'Frontal lobe function and the African', *Journal of Mental Science*, **97**, 12–48.

Carothers, J.C. (1953) *The African Mind in Health and Disease: A Study in Ethnopsychiatry*, Geneva: World Health Organisation.

Carothers, J.C. (1954) *The Psychology of Mau Mau*, Nairobi: The Government Printer.

Carothers, J.C. (1972) *The Mind of Man in Africa*, London: Tom Stacey.

Carr-Saunders, A.M. (1922) *The Population Problem*, Oxford: Clarendon Press.

Carson, John (1993) 'Army Alpha, army brass, and the search for army intelligence', *Isis* **84**, 278–309.

Cartwright, S.A. (1981 [1851]) 'Report on the diseases and physical peculiarities of the Negro race', *New Orleans Medical and Surgical Journal*, May 1851, 691–715 (rep. in A.C. Caplan, H.T. Englehart and J.J. McCartney (eds) *Concepts of Health and Disease*, Reading, MA: Addison-Wesley).

Castle, W.E. (1930) 'Race mixture and physical disharmonies', *Science* **71**, 603–6.

Cattell, R.B. (1933) *Psychology and Social Progress*, London: C.W. Daniel.

Cattell, R.B. (1934) *Your Mind and Mine: An Account of Psychology for the Inquiring Layman and Prospective Student*, London: Harrap.

Cattell, R.B. (1937) *The Fight for Our National Intelligence*, London: P.S. King.

Cattell, R.B. (1938) *Psychology and the Religious Quest*, London: Thomas Nelson.

Cattell, R.B. (1965) *The Scientific Analysis of Personality*, Harmondsworth: Penguin.
Cattell, R.B. (1972) *A New Morality from Science: Beyondism*, NY: Pergamon.
Cazeneuve, J. (1972) *Lucien Lévy-Bruhl*, NY: Harper & Row.
Chase, W.P. (1940) 'Attitudes of North Carolina students (women) toward the negro', *J.Soc.Psy.* **12**, 367–78.
Christie, R. and Jahoda, M. (eds) (1954) *Studies in the Scope and Method of 'The Authoritarian Personality'*, NY: Free Press.
Clark, K.B. (1988 [rep. of 2nd edn 1963, 1st edn 1955]) Foreword S.W. Cook, *Prejudice and Your Child*, Middletown, CT: Wesleyan UP.
Clark, K.B. and Clark, M.P. (1939a) 'The development of the consciousness of self and the emergence of racial identification in Negro preschool children', *J.Soc.Psy.* **10**, 127–45.
Clark, K.B.and Clark, M.P. (1939b) 'Segregation as a factor in the racial identification of Negro pre-school children', *Journal of Experimental Education* **8**, 161–3.
Clark, K.B.and Clark, M.P. (1940) 'Skin color as a factor in racial identification of Negro preschool children', *J.Soc.Psy.* **11**, 159–69.
Clark, K.B. and Clark, M.P. (1941, unpub.) 'Racial identification and preference in negro children', in E.E. Maccoby, T.M. Newcomb and E.L. Hartley (eds) (1958) *Readings in Social Psychology*, 3rd edn, NY: Holt, 602–11.
Clark, K.B. and Plotkin, I. (1963) *The Negro Student at Integrated Colleges*, NY: National Scholarship Service.
Clauss, L.F. (1926) *Rasse und Seele. Ein Einführung in die Gegenwart*, Munich: J.F. Lehmanns.
Clauss, L.F. (1929) *Von Seele und Antlitz der Rassen und Völker*, Munich: Lehmanns.
Clauss, L.F. (1934) 'The Germanic man. An excursion into race psychology', *Rasse* **1**, 2.
Cleverley, J. and Phillips, D. (1988) *Visions of Childhood: Influential Models from Locke to Spock*, London: Allen & Unwin.
Coffin, E.W. (1908) 'On the education of backward races', *Ped.Sem.* **11** (1), 1–62.
Cohen, E. (1939) 'Cultural and personality factors in the attitudes of Russian Jewish clients toward relief', *Smith.Coll.Stud.S.W.* **10**, 151–2.
Cohen, P. (1992) '"It's racism what dunnit": hidden narratives in theories of racism', in J. Donald and A. Rattansi (eds) (1992), 62–103.
Comer, J.P. (1972 [1969]) 'White racism: its root, form and content', in R.L. Jones (ed.) (1972) 311–17.
Conklin, E.G. (1921) *The Direction of Human Evolution*, NY: Scribner's.
Connolly, J. (1994) 'Of race and right', *Irish Times*, 6 December.
Cook, S.W. (1957) 'Desegregation: a psychological analysis', *Am.Psy.* **12**, 1–13.
Coombe, V. and Little, A. (1986) *Race and Social Work. A Guide to Training*, London: Routledge.
Coon, C.S. (1963 [1962]) *The Origin of Races*, London: Jonathan Cape.
Costall, A. (1991) 'Frederic Bartlett and the rise of prehistoric psychology' in A. Still and A. Costa¹¹ (eds) *Against Cognitivism: Alternative Foundations for Cognitive Psychology*, Hemel Hempstead: Harvester-Wheatsheaf, 39–54.
Costall, A. (1992) 'Why isn't British psychology social? Frederic Bartlett's promotion of the new academic discipline', *Canadian Psychology* **33**, 633–9.
Costall, A. (1995) 'Sir Frederic Bartlett', *The Psychologist* **8** (7), 307–8.
Cox, O.C. (1970 [1948]) *Caste, Class & Race. A Study in Social Dynamics*, NY: Modern Reader.
Crafts, L.W., Schneirla, T.C., Robinson, E.E. and Gilbert, R.W. (eds) (1938) *Recent Experiments in Psychology*, NY and London: McGraw-Hill.
Crane, A.C. (1923) 'Race differences in inhibition', *Arch.Psy.* **9**, 2–84.
Criswell, J.H. (1937) 'Racial cleavage in negro–white groups', *Sociometry*, **1**, 81–9.
Criswell, J.H. (1939) 'A sociometric study of race cleavage', *Arch.Psy.* **235**.
Crookshank, F.G. (1931 [1924]) *The Mongol in Our Midst. A study of man and his three faces*, 3rd edn, London: Kegan Paul, Trench, Trübner.

Cross, W.E. (1980) 'Models of psychological nigrescence', in R.L. Jones (ed.) (1980) 81–98.

Cross, W.E. (1991) *Shades of Black: Diversity in African American Identity*, Madison, WI: University of Wisconsin Press.

Culwick, A.T. and G.M. (1935) 'Religious and economic sanctions in a Bantu tribe', *B.J.Psy.* 26 (2), 183–91.

Curtin, P. D. (1964) *The Image of Africa: British Ideas and Action, 1780-1850*, Madison, WI: University of Wisconsin Press.

Dalal, F. (1988) 'Jung: a racist', *British Journal of Psychotherapy* 4 (3), 263–79 (rep. fr. *Race and Class* 29 (3), 1–22, 1988).

Daniel, R.P. (1934) 'Studies on race differences in non-intellectual traits and special abilities', *JNE* 3, 411–23.

Danzel, T.W. (1936) 'Kulturtradition und Kulturstufen als völkerpsychologische Probleme', *Zeitschrift für Rassenkunde* 4, 23–7.

Danziger, K. (1990) *Constructing the Subject: Historical Origins of Psychological Research*, Cambridge: CUP.

Darsie, M.L. (1926) 'Mental capacity of American-born Japanese children', *Comp.Psy.Monog.* 3 (15), 1–89.

Darwin, C. (1859) *The Origin of Species by Means of Natural Selection*, London: John Murray.

Darwin, C. (1871) *The Descent of Man and Selection in Relation to Sex*, London: John Murray.

Das Gupta, P.C. and Basu, M.N. (1936) 'Possibility of a racial significance of colour preference', *Indian Journal of Psychology* 11, 201–4.

Dauncey Tongue, E. (1935) 'The contact of races in Uganda', *B.J.Psy.* 25 (3), 356–64.

Davenport, C.B. (1929) 'Do races differ in mental capacity?', *Psychological Abstracts* 1, 70–89.

Davenport, C.B. and Steggerda, M. (1928) *Race Crossing in Jamaica*, Washington: Carnegie Institute, Publication 395.

Davies, S.P. (1930) *Social Control of the Mentally Deficient*, NY: Thomas Y. Crowell.

Davis, A. and Dollard, J. (1940) *Children of Bondage*, Washington, DC: American Council on Education.

Davis, D.B. (1966) *The Problem of Slavery in Western Culture*, Ithaca, NY: Cornell UP.

Davis, M. and Hughes, A.G. (1927) 'An investigation into the comparative intelligence and attainments of Jewish and non-Jewish schoolchildren', *B.J.Psy.* 18 (2), 134–46.

Davis, T.E. (1937) 'Some racial attitudes of negro college and grade school students', *JNE* 6, 157–65.

Dawson, G.E. (1900/1) 'Children's interest in the Bible', *Ped.Sem.* 7, 151–78.

Dearborn, W.F. and Long, H.H. (1934) 'The physical and mental abilities of the American negro: a critical survey', *JNE* 3, 530–47.

Delaney, L. (1972) 'The other bodies in the river', in R.L. Jones (ed.) (1972) 335–43.

Denney, D. (1992) *Racism and Anti-Racism in Probation*, London: Routledge.

Dennis, W. (1940a) 'Does culture appreciably affect patterns of infant behavior?', *J.Soc.Psy.* 12, 305–17.

Dennis, W. (1940b) 'Piaget's questions applied to Zuni and Navaho children', *Psy.Bull.* 37, 520.

Dennis, W. (1940c) *The Hopi Child*, NY:Appleton-Century.

Dennis, W. and Dennis, M.G. (1940) 'The effect of cradling practices upon the onset of walking in Hopi children', *J.Genet.Psy.* 56, 77–86.

Dennis, W. and Russell, R.W. (1940) 'Piaget's questions applied to Zuni children', *Child Dev.* 11, 181–7.

Department of the Interior, Bureau of Education (1916–17), *Negro Education: A Study of the Private and Higher Schools for Colored People in the United States, Bureau of Education Bulletin* Numbers 38, 39, Washington, DC: Government Printing Office.

Devereux, G. (1937) 'Institutionalized homosexuality of the Mohave Indians', *Hum.Biol.* 9, 498–527.

Devereux, G. (1939a) 'Mohave culture and personality', *Ch. & Pers.* 8, 91–109.

Devereux, G. (1939b) 'The social and cultural implications of incest among the Mohave Indians', *Psychoanalytic Quarterly* 8, 510–33.

Devereux, G. (1942) 'The mental hygiene of the American Indian', *Mental Hygiene* 26, 71–84.

Devereux, G. (1945) 'The logical foundations of culture and personality studies', *Transactions of the New York Academy of Science* Ser.II 7, 110–30.

Devereux, G. (1969) *Reality and Dream. Psychotherapy of a Plains Indian*, 2nd edn, NY: NYUP.

Dewey, J. (1902) 'Interpretation of the savage mind', *Psy.Rev.* 9, 217–30.

Dollard, J. (1957 [1937]) *Caste and Class in a Southern Town*, NY: Doubleday Anchor.

Donald, J. and Rattansi, A. (eds) (1992) *'Race', Culture & Difference*, London: Sage.

Drever, J. (1921) *Instinct in Man: A Contribution to the Psychology of Education*, 2nd edn, Cambridge: CUP.

Driberg, J.H. (1929) *The Savage as He Really Is*, London: Routledge.

Droba, D.D. (1932) 'Education and negro attitudes', *Sociol.Soc.Res.* 17, 137–41.

DuBois, W.E.B. (1911a) *Common Schools and the Negro American*, Atlanta: Atlanta UP.

DuBois, W.E.B. (1911b) 'The Negro race in the U.S.A.', in G. Spiller (ed.) (1911), 348–64.

Dummet, A. (1973) *A Portrait of English Racism*, Harmondsworth: Penguin.

Dunlap, J.W. (1930) 'Race differences in the organization of numerical and verbal abilities', *Arch.Psy.* 19, 7–71.

Durkheim, E. (1915 [French 1912]) *The Elementary Forms of Religious Life: A Study in Religious Sociology*, London: Allen & Unwin.

Durkheim, E. and Mauss, M. (trans. and intro. R. Needham) (1963 [French 1903]) *Primitive Classification*, London: Cohen & West.

Du Vinage, T.C. (1939) 'Accomodation attitudes of negroes to white case workers and their influence on case work', *Smith.Coll.Stud.S.W.* 9, 264–302.

Dyer, K.F. (1974) *The Biology of Racial Integration*, Bristol: Scientechnica.

Dyk, W. (intro. E. Sapir) (1938) *Son of Old Man Hat; A Navaho Autobiography*, NY: Harcourt.

Eagleson, O.W. and Taylor, L.E. (1940) 'A study of chord preference in a group of Negro women', *J.Exp.Psy.* 26, 619–21.

Eckland, B.K. (1971) 'Social class structure and the genetic basis of intelligence', in R. Cancro (ed.) *Intelligence: Genetic and Environmental Influences*, NY: Grune & Stratton.

Edgell, B. (1929, rev. 2nd edn [1926]) *Mental Life: An Introduction to Psychology*, London: Methuen.

Edwards, P. (1981) 'Black personalities in Georgian Britain', *History Today* 31 (Sept.), 39–44.

Eells, W.C. (1933a) 'Mechanical, physical and musical ability of the native races of Alaska', *J.App.Psy.* 17, 493–506.

Eells, W.C. (1933b) 'Educational achievement of the native races of Alaska', *J.App.Psy.* 17, 646–70.

Eells, W.C. (1933c) 'Mental ability of the native races of Alaska', *J.App.Psy.* 17, 417–38.

Ellenberger, H.F. (1970) *The Discovery of the Unconscious: The History and Evolution of Dynamic Psychiatry*, London: Allen Lane.

Elliot Smith, G. (1932) 'The evolution of intelligence and the thraldom of catch-phrases', in C. MacFie Campbell et al. (eds) *Problems of Personality. Studies Presented to Dr Morton Prince Pioneer in American Psychopathology*, 2nd edn, London: Kegan Paul Trench and Trübner, 1–11.

Elwin, V. (1936) 'A note on the theory and symbolism of dreams among the Baiga', *British Journal of Medical Psychology* 16, 237–54.

Erikson, E.H. (1939) 'Observations on Sioux education', *J.Psy.* **7**, 101–56.

Erikson, E. H. (1950) *Childhood and Society*, Harmondsworth: Penguin.

Estabrooks, G.H. (1928a) 'The enigma of racial intelligence', *J.Genet.Psy.* **35**, 137–9.

Estabrooks, G.H. (1928b) 'That question of racial inferiority', *Am.Anth.* **30**, 470–5.

Eugenics Society (1934) 'Aims and Objectives of the Eugenics Society', *Eug.Rev.* **26**.

Evans Pritchard, E.E. (1937) *Witchcraft, Oracles and Magic Among the Azande*, Oxford: Clarendon Press.

Evarts, A.B. (1913) 'Dementia praecox in the colored race', *Psychoanalytic Review* **1**, 388–403.

Evarts, A.B. (1916) 'The ontogenetic against the phylogenetic elements in the psychoses of the colored race', *Psychoanalytic Review* **3**, 272–87.

Eysenck, H.J. (1954) *Psychology of Politics*, London: RKP.

Eysenck, H.J. (1957) *Sense and Nonsense in Psychology*, Harmondsworth: Penguin.

Eysenck, H.J. (1971) *Race, Intelligence and Education*, London: Temple Smith.

Eysenck, H.J. vs. Kamin, L. (1981) *Intelligence: The Battle for the Mind*, London: Pan.

Fallaize, E.N. (1925) 'The study of primitive races, with special reference to forms of marriage', *Eug.Rev.* **18**, 77–87.

Fancher, R.E. (1985) *The Intelligence Men: Makers of the IQ Controversy*, NY: Norton.

Fanon, F. (1965 [French 1961]) *The Wretched of the Earth*, London: Macgibbon & Kee (rep.: Penguin 1967).

Fanon, F. (1968 [French 1952]) *Black Skins, White Masks*, London: Grafton Books (rep.: Paladin 1970).

Farnsworth, P.R. (1938) 'Further notes on the Seashore music tests', *J.Genet.Psy.* **18**, 429–31.

Feagin, J.R. and Sikes, M.P. (1994) *Living with Racism: The Black Middle-Class Experience*, Boston: Beacon.

Fegan, E.S. (ed.) and Pickles, J.D. (Pref.) (1978) *Bibliography of A.C. Haddon*, Cambridge: Museum of Archaeology and Anthropology.

Fenichel, O. (1940) 'Psychoanalysis of antisemitism', *American Imago* **1** (2), 24–39.

Ferguson, E.A. (1938) 'Race consciousness among American negroes', *JNE* **7**, 32–40.

Ferguson, G.O. (1916) 'The psychology of the negro: an experimental study', *Arch.Psy.* **36** (rep.: 1970 Westport CT: Negro Universities Press).

Ferguson, G.O. (1919) 'The intelligence of negroes at Camp Lee, Virginia', *Sch.&Soc.* **9**, 721–6.

Ferguson, G.O. (1920) 'White and colored school children of Virginia as measured by the Ayers Index', *Sch.&Soc.* **12**, 721–6.

Ferguson, G.O. (1921) 'The mental status of the American Negro', *Science Monthly* **12**, 533–43.

Fernando, S. (1993) 'Psychiatry and racism', *Changes* **11** (1), 46–58.

Feyerabend, P. (1975) *Against Method. Outline of an Anarchistic Theory of Knowledge*, London: NLB.

Fick, M.L. (1929) 'Intelligence tests results for poor white, native (Zulu), coloured and Indian school children and their educational and social implications', *South African Journal of Science* **26**, 904–20.

Fick, M.L. (1939) *The Educability of the South African Native*, Pretoria: South African Council for Educational and Social Research. Research Series pamphlet No. 8.

Finch, E. (1911) 'The effects of racial miscegenation', in G. Spiller (ed.) (1911) 108–12.

Finot, J. (1969 [1906]) *Race Prejudice*, Miami: Mnemosyne Publishing Co.

Fischer, E. (1939) 'Rasse und vererbung geistiger Eigenschaften', *Zeitschrift für Morphologische Anthropologie* **38**, 1–8.

Fiske, J. (1874) *Outlines of Cosmic Philosophy*, Boston: Houghton Mifflin.

Fleming, R.M. (1926) 'Anthropological studies of children', *Eug.Rev.* **18**, 294–301.

Fleming, R.M. (1929) 'Human hybrids', *Eug.Rev.* **21**, 257–63.

Fleure, H.J. (1930) 'The Nordic myth: a critique of current racial theories', *Eug.Rev.* **22**, 117–21.

Flynn, J.R. (1980) *Race, IQ and Jensen*, London: RKP.

Flynn, J.R. (1984a) 'The mean IQ of Americans: massive gains 1932 to 1978', *Psy.Bull.* **95** (1), 29–51.

Flynn, J.R. (1984b) 'IQ gains and Binet decrements', *Journal of Educational Measurement* **21** (3), 283–90.

Flynn, J.R. (1987a) 'Massive IQ gains in 14 nations: what IQ tests really measure', *Psy. Bull.* **101** (2), 171–91.

Flynn, J.R. (1987b) 'The rise and fall of Japanese IQ', *Bull.B.P.S.* **40**, 459–64.

Flynn, J.R. (1988) 'The decline and use of scholastic aptitude scores', *Am.Psy.* **43** (6), 479–81.

Flynn, J.R. (1990) 'Massive IQ gains on the Scottish WISC: evidence against Brand et al.'s hypothesis', *Irish Journal of Psychology* **11** (1), 41–51.

Flynn, J.R. (1991) *Asian Americans: Achievement beyond IQ*, Hillsdale, NJ: Erlbaum.

Forrest, D.W. (1974) *Francis Galton: The Life and Work of a Victorian Genius*, London: Paul Flek.

Fortes, M. (1932) 'Perceptual tests of general intelligence for inter-racial use', *Transactions of the Royal Society of South Africa*, **20** (3).

Fortes, M (1938) 'Social and psychological aspects of education in Taleland', *International Institute of African Languages and Cultures Memorandum XVII*, London: OUP.

Fraser, S. (ed.) (1995) *The Bell Curve Wars. Race, Intelligence, and the Future of America*, NY: Basic Books.

Frazier, E.F. (1925) 'Psychological factors in Negro health', *Social Forces* **3**, 488–90.

Frederick, R. (1927) 'An investigation into some social attitudes of high school pupils', *Sch. & Soc.* **25**, 410–12.

Freeden, M (1979) 'Eugenics and progressive thought: a study in ideological affinity', *History Journal* **22** (3), 645–71.

Freeman, F.N. (1934) 'The interpretation of test results with especial reference to race comparisons', *JNE* **3**, 519–22.

Frenkel-Brunswik, E. (1954) 'Further explorations by a contributor to *Authoritarian Personality*', in R. Christie and M. Jahoda (eds) (1954), 226–75.

Frenkel-Brunswik, E. and Sanford, R.N. (1945) 'Some personality correlates of anti-semitism', *J.Psy.* **20**, 271–91.

Freud, S. (1950 [1st English 1918]) *Totem and Taboo. Some Points of Agreement Between the Mental Lives of Savages and Neurotics*, London: RKP.

Freud, S. (1922 [1921]) *Group Psychology and the Analysis of the Ego*, London: Hogarth Press.

Fried, M.H. (1968) 'The need to end the pseudoscientific investigation of race', in M. Mead et al. (eds) (1968), pp. 122–31.

Fromm, E. (1941) *Escape from Freedom*, NY: Holt, Rinehart & Winston.

Fromm, E. (trans. B. Weinberger) (1984) *The Working Class in Weimar Germany: A Psychological and Sociological Study*, Leamington Spa: Berg.

Gabor, T. and Roberts, J.V. (1990) 'Rushton on race and crime: the evidence remains unconvincing', *Canadian Journal of Criminology* **32**, 335–43.

Galloway, F.J. (1994) 'Inferential fragility and the 1917 Army Alpha: a new look at the robustness of educational quality indices as determinants of interstate black–white score differentials', *JNE* **63** (2), 251–66.

Galton, F. (1855) *The Art of Travel or Shifts and Contrivances Available in Wild Countries*, London: Murray.

Galton, F. (1865) 'Hereditary talent and character', *Macmillan's Magazine* **12**, 318–27 (rep. in M.D. Biddiss (ed.) (1979), 57–71).

Galton, F. (1889 [1853]) *Narrative of an Explorer in Tropical South Africa*, London: Ward, Lock.

Galton, F. (1919 [1883]) *Inquiries into Human Faculty and its Development*, London: Dent.

Galton, F. (1908) *Memories of My Life*, London: Methuen.

Galton, F. (1962 [1869]) *Hereditary Genius. An Inquiry into Its Laws and Consequences*, London: Fontana.

Garrett, H.E. (1945) 'A note on the intelligence scores of Negroes and whites in 1918', *J.Ab.Soc.Psy.* **40**, 344–6.

Garrett, H.E. (1962) 'The SPSSI and racial differences', *Am.Psy.* **17**, 260–63.

Garrison, K.C. and Burch, U.S. (1933) 'A study of racial attitudes of college students', *J.Soc.Psy.* **4**, 230–35.

Garth, T.R. Jr (1953) 'Atsuwegi ethnography', *Anthropological Records* **14** (2), Berkeley and LA: University of California Press.

Gathercole, P. (1976) 'Cambridge and the Torres Straits, 1888-1920', *Cambridge Anthropology* **3** (3), 22–31.

Gerber, M. (1958) 'The psycho-motor development of African children in the first year, and the influence of maternal behavior', *J.Soc.Psy.* **47**, 185–95.

Geuter, U. (1992) *The Professionalization of Psychology in Nazi Germany*, Cambridge: CUP.

Gibson, K.R. and Ingold, T. (eds) (1993) *Tools, Language and Cognition in Human Evolution*, Cambridge: CUP.

Giddings, F.H. (1901) 'A provisional distribution of the population of the United States into psychological classes', *Psy.Rev.* **8**, 337–49.

Gilman, S.L. (1992[1987]) 'Black bodies, white bodies: toward an iconography of female sexuality in late nineteenth-century art, medicine and literature', in J. Donald and A. Rattansi (eds) (1992) Chapter 7. (Reprinted from H.L. Gates Jr (ed.) (1987) *Race, Writing, and Difference*, Chicago: Chicago UP).

Ginsberg, M. (1926) 'The problem of colour in relation to the idea of equality', *Journal of Philosophical Studies*, **I**, 213–24.

Gist, N.P. (1932) 'Racial attitudes in the press', *Sociol.Soc.Res.* **17**, 25–36.

Gladstone, W.E. (1858) *Studies on Homer and the Homeric Age*, London: OUP.

Gobineau, Count A. de (1967 [1853]) *Essay on the Inequality of Human Races*, NY: Howard Fertig.

Goddard, H.H. (1913a) *The Kallikak Family: A Study in the Heredity of Feeble-mindedness*, NY: Macmillan.

Goddard, H.H. (1913b) 'The Binet tests in relation to immigration', *Journal of Psycho-Asthenics* **18**, 105–7.

Goddard, H.H. (1917a) 'Mental tests and the immigrant', *Journal of Delinquency* **2**, 243–77.

Goddard, H.H. (1917b) 'Two immigrants out of five feeble-minded', *Survey* **38**, 528–9.

Goddard, H.H. (1917c) 'Mental level of a group of immigrants', *Psy.Bull.* **14**, 69–70.

Goldberg, D.T. (1993) *Racist Culture: Philosophy and the Politics of Meaning*, Oxford: Blackwell.

Goldenweiser, A. (1917) 'The autonomy of the social', *Am.Anth.* **19**, 447–9.

Gould, C. W. (1920) *America, A Family Matter*, NY: Scribner's.

Gould, S.J. (1984 [1981], rep. 1992) *The Mismeasure of Man*, Harmondsworth: Penguin.

Gould, S.J. (1994) 'Curveball', *New Yorker*, 28 November, 139–49.

Graham, J.L. (1930a) 'A quantitative comparison of certain mental traits of negro and white college students I and II', *J.Soc.Psy.* **1**, 267–85.

Graham, J.L. (1930b) 'A quantitative comparison of rational responses of negro and white college students', *J.Soc.Psy.* **1**, 97–121.

Grant, M. (1916 [rep. 1921]) *The Passing of the Great Race*, NY: Scribner's.

Grant, M. (1933) *Conquest of a Continent*, NY: Scribner's.

Graumann, C.F. (1996 [1988]) 'Introduction to a history of social psychology', in M. Hewstone et al. (eds) (2nd edn 1996), 3–23.

Graumann, C.F. and Moscovici, S. (eds) (1986) *Changing Conceptions of Crowd Mind and Behavior*, NY: Springer-Verlag.

Gray, C.T. and Bingham, C.W. (1929) 'A comparison of certain phases of musical ability of colored and white school pupils', *J.Ed.Psy.* **20**, 501–6.

Gray, J. (1911) 'The intellectual standing of different races and their respective opportunities for culture', in G. Spiller (ed.) (1911), 79–85.

Greene, J.E. and DuPree, J.L. (1939) 'Sex differences in certain mental disorders among
whites and negroes in Georgia during the decade 1923–1932', *J.Psy.* 7, 201–9.

Greenfield, P.M. (1966) 'On culture and conservation', in J.S. Bruner, R.R. Olver and
P.M. Greenfield (eds) *Studies in Cognitive Growth*, NY.: Wiley, 225–56.

Grimshaw, A. and Hart, K. (1993) *Anthropology and the Crisis of the Intellectuals*,
Cambridge: Prickly Pear Press.

Grossack, M. (1954a) 'Some Negro perceptions of psychologists: an observation on psychology's public relations', *Am.Psy.* 1, 188–9.

Grossack, M. (1954b) 'Psychology in Negro colleges', *Am.Psy.* 1, 636–7.

Gruber, H. E. (1995) 'Carving the bell', *Peace and Conflict: Journal of Peace Psychology*
1 (1), 97–8.

Grundlach, R.H. (1932) 'A quantitative study of Indian music', *A.J.Psy.* 44, 133–45.

Guilford, J.P. (1931) 'Racial preferences of a thousand American university students',
J.Soc.Psy. 2, 179–204.

Günther, H.F.K. (1926) *Rassenkunde des deutschen Volkes*, Munich: Lehmanns.

Günther, H.F.K. (trans. G.C.Wheeler) (1927) *The Racial Elements of European History*,
London: Methuen.

Guthrie, R.V. (1976) *Even the Rat was White, A Historical View of Psychology*, NY:
Harper & Row.

Guthrie, R.V. (1980) 'The psychology of black Americans: an historical perspective', in
R.L. Jones (ed.) (1980), 13–22.

Haddon, A.C. (1894) *The Decorative Art of New Guinea: A Study in Papuan Ethnography*,
Dublin: Royal Irish Academy.

Haddon, A.C. (1895) *Evolution in Art as Illustrated by the Life-Histories of Designs*,
London: Walter Scott.

Haddon, A.C. (1898) *The Study of Man*, London: John Murray.

Haddon, A.C. (1901) *Headhunters Black, White and Brown*, London: Methuen.

Haddon, A.C. (ed.) (1901-1935) *Reports of the Cambridge Anthropological Expedition to
Torres Straits* (6 vols), Cambridge: CUP 1935 (vol 1), 1901–1911 (vols 2–6).

Haddon, A.C (1909) *Races of Man and Their Distribution*, Halifax: Milner and Co (2nd
edn 1924, Cambridge: CUP).

Haddon, A.C. (1911) *The Wanderings of Peoples*, Cambridge: CUP.

Haddon, A.C. (1934) *History of Anthropology*, London: Watts.

Haddon, A.C. and Ray, S.H. (1893) 'A study of the language of the Torres Straits, with
vocabularies and grammatical notes Part 1.', *Proceedings of the Royal Irish Academy*
3 (II), 463–616.

Haddon, A.C. and Ray, S.H. (1897) 'A study of the language of the Torres Straits, with
vocabularies and grammatical notes Part 2', *Proceedings of the Royal Irish Academy*
3 (IV), 119–373.

Haeckel, E. (trans. E.B. Aveling) (1883) *The Pedigree of Man and Other Essays*, London:
Freethought Publishing Co.

Haldane, J.B.S. (1938) *Heredity and Politics*, London: Allen & Unwin.

Hall, G.S. (1903) 'Civilization and Savagery', *Proceedings of the Massachusetts Historical
Society*, 2nd ser. 67, 4–13.

Hall, G.S. (1904) *Adolescence: Its Psychology and its Relation to Physiology, Anthropology,
Sociology, Sex, Crime, Religion and Education*, 2 vols, NY: Appleton.

Hall, G.S. (1905a) 'The Negro in Africa and America', *Ped. Sem.* 12, 350–68.

Hall, G.S. (1905b) 'A few results of recent scientific study of the Negro in America',
Proceedings of the Massachusetts Historical Society, 2nd ser. 19, 95–107.

Haller, J. S. Jr (1971) *Outcasts from Evolution: Scientific Attitudes of Racial Inferiority
1859–1900*, Urbana IL: University of Illinois Press.

Halstead, M. (1988) *Education, Justice and Cultural Diversity: An Examination of the
Honeyford Affair, 1984–85*, London: The Falmer Press.

Hannaford, I. (1996) *Race: The History of an Idea in the West*, Baltimore: Johns Hopkins UP.

Hansen, H.C. (1937) 'Scholastic achievement of Indian pupils', *J.Genet.Psy.* **50**, 361–9.

Hansen, H.C. (1939) 'Relationship between sex and school achievement of one thousand Indian children', *J.Soc.Psy.* **10**, 399–406.

Haraway, D. (1989) *Primate Visions: Gender, Race, and Nature in the World of Modern Science*, London: Routledge.

Harding, S. (1986) *The Science Question in Feminism*, Milton Keynes: Open University Press.

Harmon, C. (1937) 'Racial differences in reaction time at the pre-school level', *Child Dev.* **8**, 279–81.

Harris, M. (1964) *Patterns of Race in the Americas*, NY: Walker and Co.

Harrisson, T. (1937) *Savage Civilisation*, London: Gollancz (Left Book Club).

Hartnack, C. (1987) 'British psychoanalysts in India', in M.G. Ash and W.R. Woodword (eds) *Psychology in Twentieth-Century Thought and Society*, Cambridge: CUP, Chapter 10.

Harvard Educational Review (1969) *Environment, Heredity and Intelligence*, Cambridge MA: Harvard Educational Review Reprint Series No. 2.

Haward, L.R.C. and Roland W.A. (1954) 'Some inter-cultural differences in the Draw-a-Person test: part I, Goodenough Scores', *Man* **54**, 86–8.

Haward, L.R.C. and Roland W.A. (1955) 'Some inter-cultural differences in the Draw-a-Person test: part II', *Man* **55**, 27–9.

Hayes, W.A. (1972) 'Radical Black behaviorism', in R.L. Jones (ed.) (1972) 51–9.

Hearnshaw, L.S. (1964) *A Short History of British Psychology*, London: Methuen.

Hearnshaw, L.S. (1979) *Cyril Burt: Psychologist*, London: RKP.

Hearnshaw, L.S. (1987) *The Shaping of Modern Psychology*, London: RKP.

Henry, J. (1940) 'Some cultural determinants of hostility in Pilaga Indian children', *A.J. Orthopsych.* **10**, 111–23.

Henry, J. (1941) 'Rorschach technique in primitive cultures', *A.J.Orthopsych.* **11**, 230–5.

Henry, J. and Henry, Z. (1940) 'Speech disturbances of Pilagá Indian children', *A.J.Orthopsych.* **10**, 362–70.

Herbert, B. (1994) 'Race and intelligence: Mrs Maxwell would put it best', *International Herald Tribune*, 27 October.

Herrnstein, R.J. (1973) *IQ & The Meritocracy*, Boston: Atlantic Monthly Press.

Herrnstein, R.J. and Murray, C. (1994) *The Bell Curve: Intelligence and Class Structure in American Life*, NY: Free Press.

Herskovits, M.J. (1926) 'On the relation between Negro and white mixture and standing in intelligence tests', *Ped.Sem.&J.Genet.Psy.* **33**, 30–42.

Herskovits, M.J. (1928) *The American Negro*, NY: Knopf.

Herskovits, M.J. (1934) 'A critical discussion of the "mulatto hypothesis"', *JNE* **3**, 389–402.

Herskovits, M.J. (1941 [rep. 1967]) *The Myth of the Negro Past*, Boston: Beacon Press.

Hewstone, M., Stroebe, W. and Stephenson, G.M. (eds) (1996) *Introduction to Social Psychology: A European Perspective*, 2nd edn, Oxford: Blackwell.

Hicks, L.H. (1969) 'Black studies in psychology', *Am.Psy.* **24**, 759–61.

Hirsch, D.M. (1926) 'A study of natio-racial mental differences', *Genet.Psy.Monog.* **1**, 233–406.

Hirsch, J. (1977) 'Behavior-genetic analysis and its biosocial consequences', in N. Block and G. Dworkin (eds) (1977a) 156–78.

Hodgen, M.T. (1964) *Early Anthropology in the Sixteenth and Seventeenth Centuries*, Philadelphia: University of Philadelphia Press.

Hoernle, R.F.A. (1927) 'Prolegomena to the study of the black man's mind', *Journal of Philosophical Studies*, **II**, 52–61.

Hoffman, F.L. (1896) *Race Traits and Tendencies of the American Negro*, NY: Macmillan.

Holmes, S.A. (1994) 'You're smart if you know what race you are', *New York Times*, 23 October, 5.

Holsey, A. (1929) 'Learning how to be black', *American Mercury*, April, 421–5.

Holt, J. (1994) 'Anti-social science?', *New York Times OP-ED*, 19 October.

Horkheimer, M. (ed.) (1936) *Studien über Autoritat und Familie*, Paris: Alcan.

Horowitz, E.L. (1935) 'A study of the process of the development of attitudes toward negroes', *Psy.Bull.* 32, 575–6.

Horowitz, E.L. (1936) 'The development of attitude toward the Negro', *Arch.Psy.* 194.

Horowitz, E.L. (1944) '"Race" attitudes', in O. Klineberg (ed.) (1944), 139–247.

Horowitz, R.E. (1939) 'Racial aspects of self-identification in nursery school children' *J.Psy.* 7, 91–9.

Hose, C. and McDougall, W. (1912) *The Pagan Tribes of Borneo, a Description of their Physical, Moral, and Intellectual Condition with Some Discussion of their Ethnic Relations*, 2 vols, London: Macmillan.

Houts, P.L. (ed.) (1977) *The Myth of Measurability*, NY: Hart.

Howard, J.H. (1972) 'Toward a social psychology of colonialism', in R.L. Jones (ed.) (1972), 326–34.

Howe, M. (1988) 'Intelligence as an explanation', *B.J.Psy.* 79 (3), 349–60.

Howitt, D. (1993) 'Racist psychology where?', *The Psychologist* 6 (5), 202–3.

Howitt, D. and Owusu-Bempah, J. (1994) *The Racism of Psychology: Time for a Change*, Hemel Hempstead: Harvester-Wheatsheaf.

Hudson, W. (1960) 'Pictorial depth-perception in sub-cultural groups in Africa', *J.Soc.Psy.* 52, 183–208.

Hudson, W. (1967) 'The study of the problem of pictorial perception among unacculturated groups', *International Journal of Psychology* 2, 90–107 (rep. in D.R. Price-Williams (ed.) 1969, 132–60).

Hughes, A.G. (1928) 'Jews and Gentiles. Their intellectual and temperamental differences', *Eug.Rev.* 20, 89–97.

Humphrey, S.K. (1917) *Mankind: Racial Values and the Racial Prospect*, NY: Scribner's.

Hunt, J. (1863) 'On the Negro's place in nature', *Memoirs Read before the Anthropological Society of London* 1, 1–64.

Hurlock, E.B. (1927) 'Color preferences of white and negro children', *J.Comp.Psy.* 7, 389–404.

Hurlock, E.B. (1930) 'The will-temperament of white and negro children', *J.Genet.Psy.* 38, 91–100.

Huxley, J. (1936) 'Galton lecture: eugenics and society', *Eug.Rev.* 28, 11–31.

Huxley, J. and Haddon, A.C. (1935) *We Europeans*, London: Cape.

Jackson, J.W. (1863) *Ethnology and Phrenology as an Aid to the Historian*, London: Trübner/Edinburgh: Maclachlan & Stewart.

Jackson, T.S. (1940) 'Racial inferiority among negro children', *Crisis* 47, 241–66.

Jaensch, E.R. (1930) *Eidetic Imagery and Typological Methods of Investigation*, London: Kegan Paul, Trench & Trübner.

Jaensch, E.R. (1938a) 'Der Gegentypus. Psychologisch-anthropologische Grundlagen deutscher Kulturphilosophie, ausgehend von dem, was wir überwinden wollen', Beiheft, *Z.angew.Psy.* 75.

Jaensch, E.R. (1938b) 'Grundsätze für Auslese Intelligenzprüfung und ihre praktisch Verwirklichung', *Z.angew.Psy.* 55, 1–14.

Jaensch, E.R. (1939) 'Der Hühnerhof als Forschungs- und Aufklärungsmittel in menschlichen Rassenfragen', *Zeitschrift für Tierpsychologie* 2, 223–58 (rep. Berlin: Verlag Paul Parey).

Jahoda, G. (1966) 'Geometric illusions and environment: a study in Ghana', *B.J.Psy.* 57, 193–9.

Jenkins, M.D. (1936) 'A socio-psychological study of negro children of superior intelligence', *JNE* 5, 175–90.

Jensen, A.R. (1969a) 'How much can we boost IQ and educational achievement?', *Harvard Educational Review* **39**, 1–123 (rep. *Harvard Educational Review*, 1969).

Jensen, A.R. (1969b) 'Reducing the heredity–environment uncertainty', *Harvard Educational Review* **39**, (3) 449–83 (rep. *Harvard Educational Review*, 1969, 209–43).

Jensen, A.R. (1973) *Educability and Group Differences*, London: Methuen.

Jensen, A.R. (1974) 'Kinship correlations reported by Cyril Burt', *Behavior Genetics* **4**, 1–128.

Johnson, C.S. (1931) 'Measurement of racial attitudes', *Publications of the American Sociological Society* **25**, 150–53.

Johnson, C.S. (1943) *Patterns of Negro Segregation*, NY: Harper.

Johnson, E.E. (1969) 'Role of the Negro in American Psychology', *Am.Psy.* **24**, 757–9.

Johnson, G. (1994) 'Learning just how little is known about the brain', *New York Times*, 23 October, 5.

Johnson, G.B. (1931) 'A summary of negro scores on the Seashore musical talent tests', *J.Comp.Psy.* **11**, 383–93.

Johnson, G.B. (1944) 'The stereotype of the American Negro', in O. Klineberg (ed.) (1944) 3–22.

Johnson, J.W. (1928) 'A Negro looks at prejudice', *American Mercury*, May, 52–6.

Johnston, Sir H.H. (1911) 'The world position of the Negro and negroid', in G. Spiller (ed.) (1911), 328–36.

Jones, J.M. (1983) 'The concept of race in social psychology: from color to culture', in L.Wheeler and P. Shaver (eds) *Review of Personality and Social Psychology* **4**, Beverly Hills, CA: Sage, 117–50.

Jones, R.L. (ed.) (1972) *Black Psychology*, NY: Harper.

Jones, R.L. (ed.) (1980) *Black Psychology*, 2nd edn, NY: Harper.

Jordan, H.E. (1913) 'The biological status and social worth of the mulatto', *Pop.Sci.Mo.* **82**, 573–82.

Josey, C.C. (1966) 'Desegregation and the intellectual performance of the Negro', *Am.Psy.* **21**, 810–11.

Joynson, R.B. (1989) *The Burt Affair*, London: RKP.

Jung, C.G. (1930) 'Your negroid and Indian behavior', *Forum*, **83**, 193–9.

Jung, C.G. (1934) 'Zur gegenwärtigen Lage der Psychotherapie', *Zentralblatt für Psychotherapie* **VII**, 1–16.

Jung, C.G. (1964 [1923]) *Psychological Types*, London: RKP.

Jung, C.G. (1967 [1961]) *Memories, Dreams, Reflections*, London: RKP.

Jung, C.G. (1969) *The Structure and Dynamics of the Psyche. Collected Works of Carl Gustav Jung*, 2nd edn, vol. 8. London: RKP.

Jung, C.G. (1970) 'The complications of American psychology', in C.G. Jung, *Collected Works* vol. 10 *Civilization in Transition*, (2nd edn), London: RKP, 502–14.

Jung, C.G. (1980 [1944]) *Psychology and Alchemy* London: RKP.

Jung, C.G. (1989 [1933]) *Modern Man in Search of a Soul*, London: Routledge.

Kamat, V.V. (1934) 'A revision of the Binet scale for Indian children', *B.J.Ed.Psy.* **4**, 296–309.

Kamat, V.V. (1939) 'Sex differences among Indian children on the Binet Simon tests', *B.J.Ed.Psy.* **9**, 187–202.

Kames, Lord (Henry Home) (1774) *Sketches of the History of Man*, Edinburgh: W. Creech, London: W. Strahan & T. Cadell.

Kamin, L.J. (1974) *The Science and Politics of IQ*, Potomac MD: Lawrence Erlbaum Associates.

Kamin, L.J. (1977) 'Heredity, intelligence, politics, and psychology I, II', in N. Block and G. Dworkin (eds) (1977a), 242–64, 374–82.

Kamin, L.J. (1995) 'Behind the curve', *Scientific American*, February, 99–103.

Kardiner, A. and Associates (1945) *The Psychological Frontiers of Society*, NY: Columbia UP.

Kardiner, A. and Ovesey, L. (1962 [1951]) *The Mark of Oppression. Explorations in the Personality of the American Negro*, Chicago and NY: Meridian Books, World Publishing Company.

Karon, B.P. (1958) *The Negro Personality*, NY: Springer.

Karpf, F.B. (1972 [1932]) *American Social Psychology: Its Origins, Development and European Background*, NY: McGraw-Hill (rep. NY: Russell and Russell).

Katz, D. and Braly, K.W. (1933) 'Racial stereotypes of one hundred college students', *J.Ab.Soc.Psy.* **28**, 280–90.

Katz, D. and Braly, K.W. (1935) 'Racial prejudice and racial stereotypes', *J.Ab.Soc.Psy.* **30**,175–93.

Katz, J. (1978) *White Awareness: Handbook for Anti-Racism Training*, Norman: University of Oklahoma.

Keith, Sir A. (1919a) 'The differentiation of mankind into racial types', *Nature* **104**, 301.

Keith, Sir A. (1919b) *Nationality and Race from an Anthropologist's Point of View*, Oxford: Humphrey Milford, OUP.

Keith, Sir A. (1922) 'The evolution of human races in the light of the hormone theory', *Bulletin of Johns Hopkins Hospital* **23**, 155–95.

Keith, Sir A. (1931) *Ethnos – The Problem of Race*, London: Kegan Paul Trench & Trübner.

Keith, Sir A. (1932) 'The Aryan theory as it stands to-day', in W.R. Dawson (ed.) *The Frazer Lectures 1922–1932 by Divers Hands*, London: Macmillan.

Keith, Sir A. (1950) *An Autobiography*, London: Watts.

Kelley, T.L. (1927) *Interpretation of Educational Measurements*, Yonkers-on-Hudson: World Book Co.

Kelley, T.L. (1928) *Cross-roads in the Mind of Man: A Study of Differential Mental Abilities*, Stanford: Stanford UP.

Kevles, D.J. (1985) *In the Name of Eugenics*, Cambridge, MA: Harvard UP.

King, M.L. Jr (1968) 'The role of the behavioral scientist in the civil rights movement', *Am.Psy.* **23**, 180–86 (rep. R. Wilcox (ed.) (1971), Chapter 48).

Kingsley, H.L. and Carbone, M. (1938) 'Attitudes of Italian Americans toward race prejudice', *J.Ab.Soc.Psy.* **33**, 532–7.

Kletzing, H.F. and Crogman, W.H. (1897) *Progress of a Race*, Atlanta: J.L. Nichols & Co.

Klineberg, O. (1928) 'An experimental study of speed and other factors in "racial" differences', *Arch.Psy.* **93**.

Klineberg, O. (1931) 'A study of psychological differences between 'racial' and national groups in Europe', *Arch.Psy.* **132**.

Klineberg, O. (1934) 'Cultural factors in intelligence test performance', *JNE* **3**, 446–60.

Klineberg, O. (1935a) *Negro Intelligence and Selective Migration*, NY: Columbia UP.

Klineberg, O. (1935b) *Race Differences*, NY: Harper.

Klineberg, O. (1940) *Social Psychology*, NY: Holt.

Klineberg, O. (ed.) (1944) *Characteristics of the American Negro*, NY and London: Harper.

Klineberg, O. (1951) *Race and Psychology*, Paris: UNESCO.

Klineberg, O. (1963) 'Negro–white differences in intelligence test performance: a new look at an old problem', *Am.Psy.* **18**, 198–203.

Klineberg, O. (1974) Autobiographical entry in G. Lindzey (ed.) (1974), 161–82.

Kluckhohn, C. (1949) *Mirror for Man*, NY: McGraw-Hill.

Kluckhohn, C. (ed. R. Kluckhohn) (1962) *Culture and Behavior. The Collected Essays of Clyde Kluckhohn*, NY: Free Press of Glencoe.

Kluckhohn, C. and Murray, H. (eds) (1949 [US 1948]) *Personality in Nature, Society and Culture*, London: Jonathan Cape.

Knox, H.G. (1914) 'A scale based on the work at Ellis Island for estimating mental defect', *Journal of the American Medical Association* **62**, 741–7.

Knox, R. (1862 [1850]) *Races of Man: A Philosophical Enquiry into the Influence of Race over the Destinies of Nations*, London: H. Renshaw.

Köhler, W. (1929) *Gestalt Psychology*, NY and London: G. Bell.

Kovel, J. (1988 [1984 2nd edn, 1st edn 1970]) *White Racism: A Psychohistory*, London: Free Association Books.

Krieger, P.L. (1937) 'Rasse, Rhythmus und Schreibinnovation bei Jugendlichen und Erwachsenen', *Zeitschrift für pädagogische Psychologie* 38, 15–31.

Kucklick, B. (1977) *The Rise of American Philosophy: Cambridge Massachusetts, 1860–1930*, New Haven and London: Yale UP.

Kuhn, T.S. (1962 [rev. and enl. 1970]) *The Structure of Scientific Revolutions*, Chicago: Chicago UP.

Kuklick, H. (1991) *The Savage Within. The Social History of British Anthropology, 1885–1945*, NY: CUP.

Kuklick, H. (in press) 'Islands in the Pacific: Darwinian biogeography and British anthropology', *American Ethnologist*.

Kuper, A. (1973) *Anthropologists and Anthropology: The British School 1922–1972*, London: Allen Lane.

Kushner, T. (1989) *The Persistence of Prejudice: Antisemitism in British Society during the Second World War*, Manchester: Manchester UP.

Lambeth, M. and Lanier, L.H. (1933) 'Race differences in speed of reaction', *J.Genet.Psy.* 42, 255–97.

Landes, R. (1937a) 'The personality of the Ojibwa', *Ch. & Pers.* 6, 51–60.

Landes, R. (1937b) *Ojibwa Sociology*, NY: Columbia UP.

Landes, R. (1937c) 'The Ojibwa in Canada' in M. Mead (ed.) (1937), 87–126.

Landes, R. (1938a) 'The abnormal among the Ojibwa Indians', *J.Ab.Soc.Psy.* 33, 14–33.

Landes, R. (1938b) 'The Ojibwa woman', *Columbia University Contributions to Anthropology*, 31.

Langham, I. (1981) *The Building of British Social Anthropology*, Dordrecht: D. Reidel.

Lanier, L.H. (1930) 'An analysis of thinking reactions of white and negro children', *J.Comp.Psy.* 10, 207–11.

Lanier, L.H. (1936) 'Joseph Peterson. Editor of *Psychological Monographs* 1934–5', *Psy.Rev.* 43 (1), 1–8.

Lapiere, R.T. (1928) 'Race prejudice: France and England', *Social Forces* 7, 102–11.

Lashley, K.S. (1929) *Brain Mechanisms and Intelligence*, Chicago: University of Chicago Press.

Lashley, K.S. (ed. F.A. Beach, D.O. Hebb, C.T. Morgan and H.W. Nissen) (1960) *The Neuropsychology of Lashley: Selected Papers of K.S. Lashley*, NY: McGraw-Hill.

Lasker, B. (1929) *Race Attitudes in Children*, NY: Holt.

Lasker, B. (ed.) (1930) *Jewish Experiences in America*, NY: The Inquiry.

Latour, B. (1987) *Science in Action: How to Follow Scientists and Engineers through Society*, Milton Keynes: Open University Press.

Laubscher, B.J.F. (1937 [rep. 1951]) *Sex, Custom and Psychopathology. A Study of South African Pagan Natives*, London: RKP.

Lawler, J.M. (1978) *IQ, Heritability and Racism: A Marxist Critique of Jensenism*, London: Lawrence & Wishart.

Layzer, D. (1977) 'Science or superstition? A physical scientist looks at the IQ controversy', in N. Block and G. Dworkin (eds) (1977a), 194–241.

Le Bon, G. (1896) *The Crowd: A Study of the Popular Mind*, London: T. Fisher Unwin.

Le Bon, G. (1899 [1st French 1894]) *The Psychology of Peoples*, London: T. Fisher Unwin.

Lee, E.S. (1951) 'Negro intelligence and selective migration: A Philadelphia test of Klineberg's hypothesis', *Am.Soc.Rev.* 61, 227–33.

Lefèvre, A. (1894) *Race and Language*, London: Kegan Paul, Trench, Trübner, & Co.

Lévi-Strauss, C. (1966) *The Savage Mind*, London: Weidenfeld & Nicolson.

Lévy-Bruhl , L. (1922a [1910]) *Les fonctions mentales dans les sociétés inférieures*, Paris: Alcan (Eng. trans. 1926 *How Natives Think*).

Lévy-Bruhl, L. (1922b) *La mentalité primitive*, Paris: Alcan (Eng. trans. 1923 *Primitive Mentality*, London: Allen & Unwin).

Lévy-Bruhl, L. (1927) *L'âme primitif*, Paris (Eng. trans. with Foreword E.E. Evans-Pritchard *The 'Soul' of the Primitive* 1965 [1928] London: Allen & Unwin).

Lévy-Bruhl, L. (1931) *Le surnaturel et le nature dans la mentalité primitive*, Paris: Alcan.

Lévy-Bruhl, L. (1935) *La mythologie primitive*, Paris: Alcan.

Lévy-Bruhl, L. (1938) *L'expérience mystique et les symboles chez les primitivs*, Paris: Alcan.

Lévy-Bruhl, L. (1949) *Les carnets de Lévy-Bruhl*, Paris: Presses Universitaires de France.

Lewontin, R.C. (1975) 'Genetic aspects of intelligence', *Annual Review of Genetics* 9, 387–405.

Lewontin, R.C. (1977) 'Race and intelligence', and 'Further remarks on race and the genetics of intelligence', in N. Block and G. Dworkin (eds) (1977a) 78–92, 107–12.

Lewontin, R.C. (1982) 'Organism and environment', in H.C. Plotkin (ed.) (1982), 151–70.

Lind, J.E. (1913–14a) 'The dream as a simple wish-fulfilment in the Negro', *Psychoanalytic Review* 1, 300.

Lind, J.E. (1913–14b) 'The color complex in the Negro', *Psychoanalytic Review* 1, 404–14.

Lind, J.E. (1914) 'Diagnostic pitfalls in the mental examination of Negroes', *New York Medical Journal* 99, 1286.

Lind, J.E. (1917) 'Phylogenetic elements in the psychoses of the negro', *Psychoanalytic Review* 4, 303–32.

Lindzey, G. (ed.) (1954) *Handbook of Social Psychology*, 2 vols, Reading, MA: Addison-Wesley.

Lindzey, G. (ed.) (1974) *History of Psychology in Autobiography*, vol. 6, Englewood Cliffs, NJ: Prentice-Hall.

Linton, R. (1939) 'Culture, society and the individual', *J.Ab.Psy.* 33, 425–36.

Linton, R. (1947) *The Cultural Background of Personality*, London: Routledge.

Lippman, W. (1921–3) 'Correspondence', *New Republic* October-November (rep. in N. Block and G. Dworkin (eds) (1977a) 4–46 as 'The Lippman–Terman Debate').

Lippman, W. (1922) *Public Opinion*, NY: Harcourt Brace.

Lips, Julius (1937) *The Savage Hits Back*, New Haven: Yale UP.

Littlewood, R. and Lipsedge, M. (1989) *Aliens and Alienists: Ethnic Minorities and Psychiatry*, London: Routledge.

Livingstone, D.N. (1987) *Darwin's Forgotten Defenders: The Encounter between Evangelical Theology and Evolutionary Thought*, Grand Rapids, MI: Eerdmans/Edinburgh: Scottish Academic Press.

Livingstone, F.B. (1964) 'On the nonexistence of human races', in M.F.A. Montagu (ed.) (1964), 46–60.

Loades, H.R. and Rich, S.G. (1917) 'Binet tests on South African natives – Zulus', *Ped.Sem.* 24, 373–83.

Locke, A. (ed.) (1925) *The New Negro: An Interpretation*, NY: A. & C. Boni.

Loehlin, J., Lindzey, G. and Spuhler, J.N. (1975) *Race Differences in Intelligence*, San Francisco: Freeman.

Loewenthal, J. (1931) 'Jüdische und unjüdische Mischungen', *Zeitschrift für sexualwissenschaft und sexualpolitik* 18, 23–9.

Lombroso, C. and Ferrero, W. (1893) *La donna delinquente: La prostituta e la donna normale*, Turin: Roux.

Lombroso, C. and Ferrero, W. (1895) *The Female Offender*, London: T. Fisher Unwin (a partial trans. of the preceding work).

Long, E. (1774) *The History of Jamaica*, 3 vols, London: T. Lowndes.

Long, H.H. (1935) 'Some psychogenic hazards of segregated education of the Negroes', *JNE* 4, 336–50.

Lorimer, D.A. (1978) *Colour, Class and the Victorians: English attitudes to the Negro in the Mid-nineteenth century*, Leicester: Leicester UP.

Lossky, N. (1926) 'The primitive and the civilized mind', *Journal of Philosophical Studies*, I, 145–58.

Lowenstein, R.M. (1947) 'The historical and cultural roots of anti-semitism', *Psychoanalysis and the Social Sciences* 1, 313–56.

Lubbock, J. (1870) *The Origin of Civilisation*, London: Williams & Norgate.

Lubbock, J. (1887) *Mr Gladstone and the Nationalities of the United Kingdom*, London: Quaritch.

Lubbock, J. (1912 [1865]) *Prehistoric Times*, London: Williams & Norgate.

Lugard, Sir F. (1926) 'The problem of colour in relation to the idea of equality', *Journal of Philosophical Studies* I, 211–13.

Luh, C.W. and Sailer, R.C. (1933) 'The self-estimation of Chinese students', *J.Soc.Psy.* 4, 245–59.

Lynn, R. (1989) 'Criticisms of an evolutionary hypothesis about race differences: A rebuttal to Rushton's reply', *Journal of Research in Personality* 23, 21–34.

Maccoby, E.E. (ed.) (1967) *The Development of Sex Differences*, London: Tavistock.

Malinowski, B. (1970 [1926a]) *Crime and Custom in Savage Society*, London: RKP.

Malinowski, B. (1926b) *Myth in Primitive Psychology*, London: Basic English Publishing.

Malinowski, B. (1927a) *The Father in Primitive Psychology*, London: Basic English Publishing.

Malinowski, B. (1960 [1927b]) *Sex and Repression in Savage Society*, London: RKP.

Malinowski, B. (1929) *The Sexual Life of Savages in North Western Melanesia*, London: Routledge.

Mall, F.P. (1909) 'On several anatomical characters of the human brain, said to vary according to race and sex, with especial reference to the weight of the frontal lobe', *American Journal of Anatomy* 9, 1–32.

Maller, J.B. (1931a) *Background of Jewish Students. Form A*, NY: Union of American Hebrew Congregations.

Maller, J.B. (1931b) 'Studies in the intelligence of young Jews', *Jewish Education* 3, 29–39.

Maller, J.B. (1931c) 'The personality of Jewish college students', *Jewish Education* 3.

Malzberg, B. (1930) 'The prevalence of mental disease among Jews', *Mental Hygiene* 14, 926–46.

Malzberg, B. (1931) 'Mental disease among Jews: a second study with a note on the relevant prevalence of mental defect and epilepsy', *Mental Hygiene* 15 (4).

Malzberg, B. (1935) 'Race and mental disease in New York State', *Psychiatric Quarterly* 9, 539–69.

Malzberg, B. (1936a) 'Mental disease among native and foreign-born whites in New York State', *A.J. Psychiat.* 93, 127–37.

Malzberg, B. (1936b) 'Migration and mental disease in negroes', *American Journal of Physical Anthropology* 21.

Malzberg, B. (1936c) 'New data relative to incidence of mental disease among Jews', *Mental Hygiene* 20, 280–91.

Malzberg, B. (1944) 'Mental disease among American Negroes: a statistical analysis', in O. Klineberg (ed.) (1944), 371–99.

Mama, A. (1995) *Beyond the Masks: Race, Gender and Subjectivity*, London: Routledge.

Mannoni, O. (1966) 'Towards the decolonisation of myself', *Race and Class* 7 (4), April.

Mannoni, O. (1990 [1st French 1956]) *Prospero and Caliban: The Psychology of Colonisation* (*Psychologie de la colonisation*), Ann Arbor: University of Michigan Press (Paris: Seuil).

Markowitz, S.H. (1931) 'Gentile–Jewish relationships in a small city in the middle west', *Religious Education* 26, 323–7.

Marks, M.A.M. (1900) 'The treatment of subject races', *Int.J.Ethics* 1 (10), 417–39.

Marshall, G.E. (1968) 'Racial classifications: popular and scientific', in M. Mead et al. (eds) (1968), 149–64.

Marshall, H.R. (1901) 'Our relations with the "lower races"', *Int.J.Ethics* 1, 409–24.

Marshall, W.E. (1873) *A Phrenologist Amongst the Todas*, London: Longman's, Green & Co.

Maxwell, J.R. (1891) *The Negro Question or Hints for the Physical Improvement of the Negro Race, with Special Reference to West Africa*, London: Fisher & Unwin.

Mayo, M. J. (1913) 'The mental capacity of the American Negro', *Arch.Psy.* 28.

McDougall, W. (1908) *Introduction to Social Psychology*, London: Methuen.

McDougall, W. (1914) 'Psychology in the service of eugenics', *Eug.Rev.* 5, 295–308.

McDougall, W. (1920a) *The Group Mind: A Sketch of the Principles of Collective Psychology*, NY and London: Putnam's.

McDougall, W. (1920b) 'Review of S. Freud *Totem and Taboo: Resemblances between the Psychic Lives of Savages and Neurotics*', *Mind* 9, 344–50.

McDougall, W. (1921) *Is America Safe for Democracy?* (UK title: *National Welfare and National Decay*), London: Methuen.

McDougall, W. (1924) *Ethics and Some Modern World Problems*, London: Methuen.

McDougall, W. (1925a) *The American Nation: Its Problems and Psychology*, London: Allen & Unwin (US title: *The Indestructible Union*).

McDougall, W. (1925b) '"Racial mental differences". Joint discussion with the anthropological section of the British Association. Prof. W. McDougall's contribution', *Report of the 92nd meeting of the British Association for the Advancement of Science*, London, 439–40.

McDougall, W. (1930) Autobiographical entry in C. Murchison (ed.) (1930 [rep. 1961]) vol. 1, 191–224.

McDougall, W. (1934) *The Frontiers of Psychology*, London: Nisbet and CUP.

McFadden, J.F. and Dashiell, J.F. (1923) 'Racial differences as measured by the Downey will-temperament test', *J.App.Psy.* 7, 30–53.

McGee, W.J. (1897) 'Review of Frederick L. Hoffman *Race Traits and Tendencies of the American Negro*', *Science* 8 January, 65–7.

McGraw, M.B. (1931) 'A comparative study of a group of southern white and negro infants', *Journal of Genetic Psychology Monograph* 10, 1–105.

McGurk, F.C.J. (1943) 'Comparative test scores of Negro and white school children in Richmond, Va', *J.Ed.Psy.* 34, 473–85.

McWilliams, C. (1948) *A Mask for Privilege: Anti-semitism in America*, Boston: Little, Brown.

Mead, M. (1926) 'The methodology of racial testing: its significance for sociology', *Am.J.Sociol.* 31, 657–67.

Mead, M. (1927) 'Group intelligence tests and linguistic disability among Italian children', *Sch. & Soc.* 25, 465–8.

Mead, M. (1928) *Coming of Age in Samoa*, NY: Morrow.

Mead, M. (1930) *Growing Up in New Guinea*, NY: Morrow (rep. Harmondsworth: Penguin 1942).

Mead, M. (1935) *Sex and Temperament in Three Primitive Societies*, London: Routledge.

Mead, M. (ed.) (1937) *Cooperation and Competition among Primitive Peoples*, NY: McGraw-Hill.

Mead, M. (1972) *Blackberry Winter: My Earlier Years*, NY: Morrow.

Mead, M. (1974) Autobiographical entry in G. Lindzey (ed.) (1974), 293–326.

Mead, M. (1978) 'The evocation of psychologically relevant responses in ethnological fieldwork', in G.D. Spindler (ed.) (1978), 89–139.

Mead, M. and Baldwin, J. (1971) *A Rap on Race*, London: Michael Joseph.

Mead, M., Dobzhansky, T., Tobach, E. and Light, R.E. (eds) (1968) *Science and the Race Concept*, NY and London: Columbia UP.

Meerloo, A.M. (1935) 'Individual and collective hatred. An attempt at understanding anti-semitism' (in Dutch), *Mensch en Maatschipij.* 11, 352–64.

Meier, A. and Rudwick, E.M. (1970 rev. edn [1966]) *From Plantation to Ghetto, An Interpretive History of American Negroes*, London: Constable.

Melching, L. (1938) 'Umvolkung als psychologisches Problem', *Z.angew.Psy.* 54 (1), 38–140.

Meltzer, B.N., Petras, J.W. and Reynolds, L.T. (1975) *Symbolic Interactionism: Genesis, Varieties and Criticism*, London: RKP.

Meltzer, H. (1939a) 'Children's thinking about nations and races', *Psy.Bull.* 36, 638.

Meltzer, H. (1939b) 'Group differences in nationality and race preferences of children', *Sociometry* 2, 86–105.

Meltzer, H. (1939c) 'Nationality preferences and stereotypes of colored children', *J.Genet.Psy.* 54, 403–24.

Mensh, E. and H. (1991) *The IQ Mythology. Class, Race, Gender, and Inequality*, Carbondale and Edwardsville: Southern Illinois UP.

Mercer, J. (1972) 'IQ: The lethal label', *Psychology Today*, Sept. 44–7, 95–7.

Miller, H.A. (1923) 'The myth of superiority', *Opportunity* 1, 288–9.

Miller, K. (1917) 'Eugenics of the Negro Race', *Science Monthly* 5, July, 57–9.

Miller, N.E. and Dollard, J. (1941) *Social Learning and Imitation*, New Haven, CT: Yale UP.

Milner, D. (1996) 'Racism in the mirror' (Review of Howitt and Owusu-Bempah, 1994), *The Psychologist* 9 (8), 348–9.

Minard, R.D. (1931) 'Race attitudes of Iowa children', *University of Iowa Studies:Studies of Character* 4 (2).

Mjöen, J.A. (1931) 'Race-crossing and glands. Some human hybrids and their parent stocks', *Eug.Rev.* 23, 31–40.

Monboddo, Lord (James Burnet) (1773–92) *The Origin and Progress of Language*, 6 vols, Edinburgh: A. Kincaid & W. Creech.

Montagu, M.F.A. (1942, [1974 5th edn]) *Man's Most Dangerous Myth: The Fallacy of Race*, Oxford: OUP.

Montagu, M.F.A. (1945) 'Intelligence of northern Negroes and Southern whites in the First World War', *A.J.Psy.* 58, 161–88.

Montagu, M.F.A. (ed.) (1964) *The Concept of Race*, NY: The Free Press.

Moore, J. (1979) *The Post-Darwinian Controversies: A Study of the Protestant Struggle to Come to Terms with Darwin in Britain and America, 1870–1900*, Cambridge: CUP.

Morawski , J. G. (1992a) 'Self-regard and other-regard: reflexive practices in American psychology, 1890–1940', *Science in Context* 5 (2), 281–308.

Morawski, J. G. (1992b) 'There is more to our history of giving: the place of introductory textbooks in American psychology', *Am.Psy.* 47 (2), 161–9.

Moritz, E. (1939) 'Materialismus gegen Logik und Complexe Psychologie', *Zentralblatt für Psychotherapie* 111, 303–17.

Morse, J. (1914) 'Comparison of white and colored children measured by the Binet Scale of Intelligence', *Pop.Sci.Mo.* 84, 75–9.

Morton, S.G. (1839) *Crania Americana or, a Comparative View of the Skulls of Various Aboriginal Nations of North and South America*, Philadelphia: John Pennington.

Morton, S.G. (1844) *Crania Aegyptica. Observations on Egyptian ethnography, derived from anatomy, history, and the monuments*, (1st as *Transactions of the American Philosophical Society*, 9, 93–159 entitled 'Observations on Egyptian. . . .').

Mosby, D.P. (1972) 'Toward a new specialty of Black Psychology', in R.L. Jones (ed.) (1972), 33–42.

Moton, R.R. (1929) *What the Negro Thinks*, Garden City, NY: Doubleday, Dora & Co.

Moynihan, D. (1965) *The Negro Family in the United States: the Case for Action*, Washington, DC: US Government Printing Press.

Mudge, G.P. (1919) 'The menace to the English race and to its traditions by present-day immigration and emigration', *Eug.Rev.* 11, 202–12.

Mühlmann, W. (1938) *Methodik der Völkerkunde*, Stuttgart: Enke.

Müller-Freienfels, R. (1931) 'Beiträge zur Rassenpsychologie', *Zeit.angew.Psy.* 39, 1–31.

Mundy-Castle, A.C. (1966) 'Pictorial depth perception in Ghanaian children', *International Journal of Psychology* 1, 290–300.

Murchison, C. (1924) 'American white criminal intelligence', *Journal of Criminal Law and Criminology* 15, 239–316, 435–94.

Murchison, C. (1925a) 'Intelligence and types of foreign born criminals', *Ped.Sem.* 32, 8–25.

Murchison, C. (1925b) 'Intelligence of foreign born criminal recidivists', *Ped.Sem.* 32, 235–8.

Murchison, C. (1925c) 'Literacy of foreign born white criminals', *Ped.Sem.* 32, 435–9.

Murchison, C. (1925d) 'Literacy of negro men criminals', *Ped.Sem.* 32, 440–6.

Murchison, C. (1926a) 'Mental test and other concomitants of some negro women criminals', *Ped.Sem.* 33, 527–30.

Murchison, C. (1926b) *Criminal Intelligence*, Worcester, MA: Clark UP.

Murchison, C. (ed.) (1929a) *Psychological Register*, vol. II, Worcester, MA: Clark University Press/London: H. Milford, OUP.

Murchison, C. (1929b) *Social Psychology: The Psychology of Political Domination*, Worcester, MA: Clark UP, London: Milford, OUP.

Murchison, C. (ed.) (1930 [rep. 1961]) *History of Psychology in Autobiography*, vol. I, NY: Russell & Russell.

Murchison, C. (ed.) (1932 [rep. 1961]) *History of Psychology in Autobiography*, vol. II, NY: Russell & Russell.

Murchison, C. (ed.) (1935) *Handbook of Social Psychology*, Worcester, MA: Clark UP.

Murchison, C. (ed.) (1936 [rep. 1961]) *History of Psychology in Autobiography*, vol. III, NY: Russell & Russell.

Murchison, C. and Burfield, H. (1925a) 'Geographical concomitants of negro criminal intelligence', *Ped.Sem.* 32, 26–44.

Murchison, C. and Burfield, H. (1925b) 'Types of crime and intelligence of negro criminals', *Ped.Sem.* 32, 239–47.

Murchison, C. and Gilbert, R. (1925a) 'The religion of the negro criminal', *Ped.Sem.* 32, 447–54.

Murchison, C. and Gilbert, R. (1925b) 'Some occupational concomitants of negro men criminals', *Ped.Sem.* 32, 648–51.

Murchison, C. and Gilbert, R. (1925c) 'Some marital concomitants of negro men criminals', *Ped Sem.* 32, 652–6.

Murchison, C. and Nafe, R. (1925) 'Intelligence of negro criminal recidivists', *Ped.Sem.* 32, 248–57.

Murchison, C. and Pooler, P. (1925) 'Length of incarceration and mental test scores of negro men criminals', *Ped.Sem.* 32, 657–8.

Murchison, C. and Pooler, P. (1926) 'The seasonal distribution of negro criminal intelligence', *Ped.Sem.* 33, 138–9.

Murdoch, K. (1920) 'A study of race differences in New York City', *Sch. & Soc.* 11, 147–50.

Murdoch, K. (1925) 'A study of differences between races in intellect and morality I., II.', *Sch. & Soc.* 2, 628–32, 659–64.

Murdoch, K. (1926) 'Racial differences found in two American cities', *Individual Psychology* 1, 99–104.

Muschinske, D. (1977) 'The nonwhite as child: G. Stanley Hall on the education of non-white people', *JHBS* 13, 328–36.

Myers, C.S. (1902) 'The visual acuity of the natives of Sarawak' *Journal of Physiology* 28, 316–18.

Myers, C.S. (1903) Parts 2–4 ('Hearing', 'Smell', 'Taste') of A.C. Haddon (ed.) (1901–1935) vol. 2 (2).

Myers, C.S. (1904) 'The taste names of primitive people', *B.J.Psy.* 1 (rep. in C.S. Myers, 1933, *A Psychologist's Point of View*, London: Heinemann).

Myers, C.S. (1905) 'A study of rhythm in primitive music', *B.J.Psy.* 1, 397–406.

Myers, C.S. (1911) 'On the permanence of racial mental differences', in G. Spiller (ed.) 73–9.

Myers, C.S. (1937) *In the Realm of the Mind*, Cambridge: CUP.

Myrdal, G. (1944) *An American Dilemma: The Negro Problem and Modern Democracy*, 2 vols, NY: Harper.

Nadel, S.F. (1937a) 'A field experiment in racial psychology', *B.J.Psy.* 28, 195–211.

Nadel, S.F. (1937b) 'Experiments on culture psychology', *Africa* 10, 421–35.

Nadel, S.F. (1937c) 'The typological approach to culture', *Ch. & Pers.* 5, 267–84.

Nadel, S.F. (1939) 'The application of intelligence tests in the anthropological field', in F.C. Bartlett et al. (1939), 184–98.

Nadel, S.F. (1940) 'New field experiments in racial psychology', *Advances in Science* 1, 447.

Nadel, S.F. (1957) *The Theory of Social Structure*, London: Cohen & West.

Nissen, H.W., Machover, S. and Kinder, E.F. (1935) 'A study of performance tests given to a group of native African negro children', *B.J.Psy.* 25, 308–55.

Nobles, W.W. (1972) 'African philosophy: foundations for Black Psychology', in R.L. Jones (ed.) (1972), 18–32.

Noltenius, F. (1930) 'Charakterstudium als Mittel Rassenerforschung', *Archiv für Rassen-und-Gesellschaftbiologie* 23, 231–48.

Nott, J.C. and Gliddon, G.R. (1854) *Types of Mankind*, Philadelphia: Lippincott, Grambo & Company.

Nye, R.A. (1975) *The Origins of Crowd Psychology: Gustav Le Bon and the Crisis of Mass Democracy in the Third Republic*, London and Beverly Hills, CA: Sage.

Oakesmith, J. (1919) *Race and Nationality, An Inquiry into the Origin and Growth of Patriotism*, London: Heinemann.

O'Donnell, J.M. (1985) *The Origins of Behaviorism: American Psychology, 1870–1920*, NY and London: NYUP.

Odum, H.W. (1910) 'Social and mental traits of the negro: Research into the conditions of the negro in Southern towns', *Studies in History, Economics & Public Law*, 37 (3), 309–606 (1–302) (rep. NY:Columbia UP, Longmans Green/London: P.S. King).

Odum, H.W. (1928) *Rainbow Round My Shoulder*, Indianapolis: Bobbs Merrill.

Odum, H.W. (1936–7) 'The errors of sociology', *Social Forces*, 15, 327–42.

Odum, H.W. (1943) *Race and Rumors of Race*, Chapel Hill, NC: University of North Carolina Press.

Odum, H.W. and Johnson, G.B. (1925) *The Negro and His Songs*, Chapel Hill, NC: University of North Carolina Press.

Ogden, C.K. (1929) *The ABC of Psychology*, London: KPTT.

Oliver, R.A.C. (1932a) *General Intelligence Test for Africans (with Manual of Directions)*, Nairobi: Gov't Printer.

Oliver, R.A.C. (1932b) 'The comparison of abilities of races: with special reference to East Africa', *E.Af.Med.J.* 9 (6), 160–75, (7) 193–204.

Oliver, R.A.C. (1932c) 'The musical talent of natives of East Africa', *B.J.Psy.* 22, 333–43.

Oliver, R.A.C. (1933-4) 'The adaptation of intelligence tests to Tropical Africa', *Oversea Education* 4, 186–92; 5, 8–12.

Oliver, R.A.C. (1946) *Research in Education*, London: Allen & Unwin.

Otis, M. (1913-4) 'A perversion not commonly noted', *J.Ab.Soc.Psy.* 8, 113–6.

Padilla, A.M. (1988) 'Early psychological assessments of Mexican-American children', *JHBS* 24 (1), 111–16.

Page, T.N. (1904) *The Negro: The Southerner's Problem*, NY: Scribner's.

Parham, T. (1991) 'Cycles of psychological nigrescence', *The Counselling Psychologist*, 17 (2), 187–226.

Parin, P. and Morgenthaler, F. (1969 [1956/7]) 'Character analysis based on the behaviour patterns of "primitive" Africans', in W. Micensterberger (ed.) *Man and his Culture: Psychoanalytic Anthropology after 'Totem and Taboo'* (1969), London: Rapp and Whiting, 187–208.

Park, R.E. (1928) 'The basis of race prejudice', *Ann.Am.Ac.P.&SS.* 140, 11–21.

Parker, S., Schilder, P. and Wortis, H. (1939) 'A specific motility psychosis in Negro alcoholics', *J.Nerv.Ment.Dis.* 90, 1–18.

Parr, L.W. (1934) 'Taste blindness and race', *Journal of Heredity* 25, 186–90.

Parsons, T. and Shils, E. (eds) (1962 [1951]) *Toward a General Theory of Action*, Oxford: Freeman.

Passingham, R. (1982) *The Human Primate*, Oxford: Freeman.

Paterson, A.R. (1934) *The Book of Civilization Part 1. On Cleanliness and Health, the Care of your Children, Food, and How to get Rid of Flies*, London: Longmans Green.

Pearson, K. (1905) *National Life from the Standpoint of Science*, Cambridge: CUP.

Pearson, K. (1912) *Darwinism, Medical Progress and Eugenics. The Cavendish Lecture*, London: Eugenics Laboratory Publications Lecture Series IX.

Pearson, K. (1925) 'Editorial', *Annals of Eugenics* 1, 3.

Pearson, K. and Moul, M. (1925-8) 'The problem of alien immigration into Great Britain, illustrated by an examination of Russian and Polish Jewish children', *Ann.Eug.* 1, 5–127; 2, 11–244, 290–317; 3, 1–178, 201–64.

Peck, L. and Hodges, A.B. (1937a) 'A study of racial differences in eidetic imagery of pre-school children', *J.Genet.Psy.* 51, 141–61.

Peck, L. and Hodges, A.B. (1937b) 'A study of the eidetic imagery of young negro children', *JNE* 6, 601–10.

Peregrine, D. (1936) 'The effect of printed social stimulus material upon the attitudes of high school pupils toward the negro', *Bulletin of Purdue University* 37, 55–69.

Petermann, B. (1935) *Das Problem der Rassenseele*, Leipzig: Barth.

Peterson, J. (1921) 'Comparison of white and negro children in multiple choice learning', *Proceedings of the American Psychological Association*, 97–8.

Peterson, J. (1923a) 'The comparative abilities of white and negro children', *Comp.Psy. Monog.* 1.

Peterson, J. (1923b) 'The use of a common unit in the measurement of race differences' *Psy.Bull.* 20, 424–5.

Peterson, J. (1927) 'Problems, methods and some results in race testing', *Social Science Research Council Proceedings of the Hanover Conference, Dartmouth College, Hanover, NH August 15–30*, 34–60.

Peterson, J. (1928a) 'Methods of investigating comparative abilities in races', *Ann.Am.Ac.P.&SS.* 140, 178–85.

Peterson, J. (1928b) 'Comparison of white and negro children in the rational learning test', *27th Yearbook of the National Society for Studies in Education* Part I, 333–41.

Peterson, J. (1931) 'Some effects of environmental factors and of unreliability on rate and variability in psychological development', *Conference on Individual Differences in the Character and Rate of Individual Development, Iowa City, 28 December 1930* Washington: NRC.

Peterson, J. (1932) *The Comparative Abilities of White and Negro children*, Baltimore: Williams & Wilkins.

Peterson, J. (1934) 'Basic considerations of methodology in race testing', *JNE* 3, 403–10.

Peterson, J. and Lanier, L.H. (1929) 'Studies in the comparative abilities of whites and negroes', *Mental Measurement Monograph* 5.

Peterson J., Lanier, L.H. and Walker, H.M. (1925) 'Comparisons of white and negro children in certain ingenuity and speed tasks', *J.Comp.Psy.* 5, 271–83.

Peterson, J. and Telford, C.W. (1930) 'Results of group and of individual tests applied to practically pure-blood children on St. Helena Island', *J.Comp.Psy.* 11, 115–44.

Pettigrew, T.F. (1964) *A Profile of the Negro American*, NY:Van Nostrand.

Peyrère, I. de la (1655) *A Theological Systeme upon that Presupposition that Men were before Adam*, London and Amsterdam: publisher n.a.

Pfahler, G. (1942) *Rassekerne des Deutschen Volkes*, 3 vols, Munich: publisher n.a.

Phillips, B.A. (1912) 'Retardation in the elementary schools of Philadelphia', *Psychological Clinic* 6, 79–90.

Phillips, B.A. (1914) 'The Binet tests applied to colored children', *Psychological Clinic* 8, 190–6.

Phoenix, A. (1996) 'Constructing identities, obscuring racisms: issues for the study of identities', unpublished paper delivered at the *British Psychological Society Annual Conference* April 1996.

Pintner, R. (1923a) 'Comparison of American and foreign children in intelligence tests', *J.Ed.Psy.* **14**, 292–5.

Pintner, R. (1923b [rev.1931]) *Intelligence Testing: Methods and Results*, NY: Holt.

Pintner, R. (1927) 'Non-language tests in foreign countries', *Sch. & Soc.* **26**, 374–6.

Pintner, R. (1934) 'Intelligence differences between American negroes and whites', *JNE* 3, 513–18.

Pintner, R. and Keller, R. (1922) 'Intelligence tests for foreign children', *J.Ed.Psy.* **13**, 214–22.

Pintner, R. and Maller, J.B. (1937) 'Month of birth and average intelligence among different ethnic groups', *J.Genet.Psy.* **50**, 91–107.

Piotrowski, Z. (1935) 'Racial differences in linear perspective', *J.Soc.Psy.* **6**, 479–85.

Pitt-Rivers, G.H.Lane-Fox (1927) *The Clash of Culture and the Contact of Races*, London: Routledge.

Playne, C.E. (1925) *The Neuroses of Nations*, London: Allen & Unwin.

Plos, H.H., Bartels, M. and Bartels, P. (trans. E.J. Dingwall) (1935) *Woman. A Historical, Gynaecological and Anthropological Compendium*, 3 vols, London: William Heinemann Medical Books.

Plotkin, H.C. (ed.) (1982) *Learning, Development and Culture: Essays in Evolutionary Epistemology*, Chichester and NY: Wiley.

Plotkin, L. (1959) 'Racial differences in intelligence', *Am.Psy.* **14**, 526–7.

Porteus, S.D. (1917) 'Mental tests with delinquents and Australian aborigine children', *Psy.Rev.* **24**, 32–41.

Porteus, S.D. (1925) 'Guide to the Porteus Maze Test', *Training School Research Bulletin* **25**, 1–50.

Porteus, S.D. (1930) 'Race and social differences in performance tests', *Genet.Psy. Monog.* **VIII** (2).

Porteus, S.D. (1931) *The Psychology of a Primitive People; A Study of the Australian Aborigine*, NY: Longmans Green.

Porteus, S.D. (1937) *Primitive Intelligence and Environment*, NY: Macmillan.

Porteus, S.D. (1969) *A Psychologist of Sorts*, Palo Alto, CA: Pacific Books.

Porteus, S.D. and Babcock, M.E. (1926) *Temperament and Race*, Boston: Badger.

Pouchet, G. (1864) *The Plurality of the Human Race*, London: Longman, Green, Longman & Roberts for the Anthropological Society.

Powell, T.O. (1896) 'The increase in insanity and tuberculosis in the Southern negro since 1860, and its alliance and some of the supposed causes', *Journal of the American Medical Association* **27**, 1185–8.

Prichard, J.C. (1831) *The Eastern Origin of the Celtic Nations proved by a comparison of their Dialects with the Sanskrit, Greek, Latin, and Teutonic Languages*, London: Sherwood, Gilbert and Piper; J. and A. Arch.

Prichard, J.C. (1836) *Researches into the Physical History of Mankind*, 2 vols, London: Sherwood, Gilbert and Piper, J. and A. Arch.

Price, J.St.C. (1934) 'Negro–white differences in general intelligence', *JNE* 3, 424–52.

Price, Rev.T. (1829) *An Essay on the Physiognomy and Physiology of the Present Inhabitants of Britain; With Reference to their Origin, as Goths and Celts*, London: J. Rodwell.

Price-Williams, D.R. (ed.) (1969) *Cross-cultural Studies*, Harmondsworth: Penguin.

Prince, M. (1885) *The Nature of Mind and Human Automatism*, Philadelphia: Lippincott.

Prudhomme, C. and Musto, D.F. (1973) 'Historical perspectives on mental health and racism in the United States', in C.V. Willie, B.M. Kramer and B.S. Brown (eds) *Racism and Mental Health: Essays*, Pittsburg, PA: University of Pittsburg Press.

Putnam, C. (1961) *Race and Reason*, Washington, DC: Public Affairs Press.

Pyle, W.H. (1913) 'Mental and physical examination of school children in rural districts', *Psychological Clinic* **6**, 260–62.

Pyle, W.H. (1915a) 'Mentality of the negroes compared with whites', *Psy.Bull.* **12**, 71.

Pyle, W.H. (1915b) 'The mind of the negro child', *Sch. & Soc.* **1**, 357–60.

Pyle, W.H. (1916) 'The learning capacity of negro children', *Psy.Bull.* **13**, 82–3.

Pyle, W.H. (1918) 'A study of the mental and physical characteristics of the Chinese', *Sch. & Soc.* 8, 264–9.

Quiggin, A.H. (1942) *Haddon the Head Hunter*, Cambridge: CUP.

Radin, P. (1926) *Crashing Thunder: The Autobiography of an American Indian*, NY: Appleton.

Radin, P. (1927) *Primitive as Philosopher*, NY: Appleton.

Radin, P. (1934) *The Racial Myth*, NY: Whittlesey (McGraw-Hill).

Raleigh, Sir W. (1614) *History of the World*, London: W. Burre.

Rangacher, C. (1932) 'Differences in perseveration among Jewish and English boys', *B.J.Ed.Psy.* 2, 199–211.

Raper, A.F. (1933) *The Tragedy of Lynching*, Chapel Hill: University of North Carolina Press.

Read, C. (1914) 'The conditions of belief in primitive minds', *B.J.Psy.* 6 (3), 304–20.

Read, C. (1915) 'Psychology of animism', *B.J.Psy.* 8 (1), 1–32.

Read, C. (1916) 'The relations between magic and animism', *B.J.Psy.* 8 (3), 285–316.

Read, C. (1917) 'On the differentiation of the human from the anthropoid mind', *B.J.Psy.* 8 (4), 395–442.

Read. C. (1918) 'The mind of the wizard', *B.J.Psy.* 9(2), 151–80.

Read, C. (1920) *The Origin of Man and His Superstitions*, Cambridge: CUP.

Reuter, E.B. (ed.) (1934) *Race and Culture Contacts*, NY: McGraw Hill.

Rex, J. and Mason, D. (eds) (1986) *Theories of Race and Ethnic Relations*, Cambridge: CUP.

Rice, C.H. (1929) *A Hindustani Binet-Performance Scale*, Oxford and Princeton NJ: Princeton UP. (Two versions of this were issued, one of 196 pp. subtitled '*With a comparison of the intelligence of certain caste groups in the Panjab*' and another of 86 pp. subtitled '*With complete instructions for the administration and scoring of tests*'.)

Rice, S.A. (1926–7) '"Stereotypes": a source of error in judging character', *Journal of Personality Research* 5, 267–76.

Rice, T.B. (1929) *Racial hygiene; A Practical Discussion of Eugenics and Race Culture*, NY: Macmillan.

Richards, G. (1984) 'Getting the intelligence controversy knotted', *Bulletin of the British Psychology Society* 37, 77–9.

Richards, G. (1992a) *Mental Machinery: The Origins and Consequences of Psychological Ideas. Part One: 1600–1850*, London: Athlone Press.

Richards, G. (1992b) 'Reflexivity problems in psychology: too embarrassing even to talk about?' *The British Psychological Society History and Philosophy Section Newsletter* 15, 7–22.

Richards, G. (1994) 'A previously unpublished letter from R.S. Woodworth to W.H.R. Rivers', *The British Psychological Society History and Philosophy of Psychology Section Newsletter* 19, 6–9.

Richards, G. (1995) 'Non-reporting of non-significant results: an exception', *The British Psychological Society History and Philosophy of Psychology Section Newsletter* 20, 18.

Richards, G. (1996) *Putting Psychology in its Place: A Critical Historical Overview*, London: Routledge.

Richards, G. (in preparation) 'Thomas Russell Garth: the race psychologist who changed his mind', *JHBS*.

Richards, R. J. (1987) *Darwin and the Emergence of Evolutionary Theories of Mind and Behavior*, Chicago and London: Chicago UP.

Richards, T.W. (1956) 'Graduate education of Negro psychologists', *Am.Psy.* 11, 326–7.

Ripley, W.Z. (1900) *Races of Europe: A Sociological Study*, London: Kegan Paul.

Ritchie, J.F. (1943) *The African as Suckling and as Adult*, Livingstone: Rhodes Livingstone.

Rivers, W.H.R. (1900) 'The senses of primitive man', *Science* N.S. XI, 740–41.

Rivers, W.H.R. (1901a) 'Primitive colour vision', *Pop.Sci.Mo.* 59, 41–58.

Rivers, W.H.R. (1901b) 'The colour vision of the Eskimo', *Proceedings of the Cambridge Philosophical Society* 11, 143–9.

Rivers, W.H.R. (1901c) 'The colour vision of the natives of Upper Egypt', *Journal of the Royal Anthropological Institute*, 31, 229–47.

Rivers, W.H.R. (1903) 'Observations on the vision of the Uralis and Shologas', *Madras Government Museum Bulletin*, 5, 1–16.

Rivers, W.H.R. (1905) 'Observations on the senses of the Todas', *B.J.Psy.* 1, 321–96.

Rivers, W.H.R. (1906) *The Todas*, London: Macmillan.

Rivers, W.H.R. (1914) *History of Melanesian Society*, 2 vols, Cambridge: CUP.

Rivers, W.H.R. (1918) *Dreams and Primitive Culture*, Manchester: Manchester UP.

Rivers, W.H.R. (1921) *Instinct and the Unconscious*, Cambridge: CUP.

Rivers, W.H.R. (1923a) *Psychology and Politics*, London: Kegan Paul, Trench & Trübner.

Rivers, W.H.R. (1923b) *Conflict and Dream*, London: Kegan Paul, Trench & Trübner.

Rivers, W.H.R. (1924) *Medicine, Magic and Religion*, London: Kegan Paul, Trench & Trübner.

Rivers, W.H.R. (1926) *Psychology and Ethnology*, London: Kegan Paul, Trench & Trübner.

Robb, J.H. (1954) *Working-Class Anti-Semite. A Psychological Study in a London Borough*, London: Tavistock.

Roberts, J.V. and Gabor, T. (1990) 'Lombrosian wine in a new bottle: research on crime and race', *Canadian Journal of Criminology* 32, 291–313.

Roberts, W.J. (1908) 'The racial interpretation of history and politics', *Int.J.Ethics* 18, 475–91.

Róheim, G. (1925) *Australian Totemism: A Psycho-analytic Study in Anthropology* London: Allen & Unwin.

Róheim, G. (1937) 'The nescience of the Aranda', *B.J.Med.Psy.* 17, 343–60.

Rohrer, J.H. (1942) 'The test intelligence of Osage Indians', *J.Soc.Psy.* 16, 99–105.

Rohrer, J.H. and Edmonson, M.S. (1960) *The Eighth Generation Grows Up*, NY: Harper.

Roiser, M. and Willig, C. (1995) 'The hidden history of authoritarianism', *H.H.Sci.* 8 (4), 77–97.

Roiser, M. and Willig, C. (1996) 'The strange death of the authoritarian personality', Unpublished manuscript.

Rokeach, M. (1960) *The Open and Closed Mind*, NY: Basic Books.

Rose, N. (1985) *The Psychological Complex*, London: RKP.

Rose, S., Kamin, L.J. and Lewontin, R.C. (1984) *Not in Our Genes. Biology, Ideology and Human Nature*, Harmondsworth: Penguin.

Rose, W. (ed.) (1931) *An Outline of Modern Knowledge*, London: George Newnes.

Rosenblatt, P.C., Karos, T.A. and Powell, R.D. (1995) *Multiracial Couples: Black & White Voices*, London: Sage.

Rosenthal, H. (1931) 'Die Musikalität der Juden', *Internationale Zeitschrift für Individuelle-Psychologie* 9, 122–31.

Rosenthal, S.P. (1933) 'Racial differences in the mental diseases', *J.Ab.Soc.Psy.* 28, 301–18.

Rosenthal, S.P. (1934) 'Racial differences in the incidence of mental disease', *JNE* 3, 484–93.

Ross, V.R. (1936) 'Musical talents of Indian and Japanese children', *Journal of Juvenile Research* 20, 95–113.

Rotislav, J. (1932) 'Anthropological and psychological researches on school children in Limburg' (original title n.a.), *Sammelschrift Physiographische Kommentarien* 4, 5,39–81.

Rowe, E.C. (1914) 'Five hundred forty-seven white and two hundred sixty-eight Indian children tested by the Binet-Simon tests', *Ped.Sem.* 21, 454–68.

Royce, J. (1906) 'Race questions and prejudices', *Int.J.Ethics* April, 265–87.

Royce, J. (1908) *Race Questions, Provincialisms and Other American Problems*, NY and London: Macmillan.

Rumyaneck, J. (1931) 'The comparative psychology of Jews and non-Jews: a survey of the literature', *B.J.Psy.* **21**, 404–26.

Rury, J.L. (1988) 'Race, region, and education: an analysis of black and white scores on the 1917 Army Alpha intelligence test', *JNE* **57** (1), 51–66.

Rushton, J.P. (1989) 'Race differences and r/K theory: a reply to Silverman', *Ethology and Sociobiology* **11**, 131–40.

Rushton, J.P. (1990a) 'Race and crime: a reply to Roberts and Gabor', *Canadian Journal of Criminology* **32**, 315–34.

Rushton, J.P. (1990b) 'Race, brain size, and intelligence: a reply to Cernovsky', *Psy.Rep.* **66**, 659–66.

Rushton, J.P. (1990c) 'Race differences, r/K theory, a reply to Flynn', *The Psychologist*, **5**, 195–98.

Rushton, J.P. (1994) *Race, Evolution and Behavior: A Life History Perspective*, New Brunswick, NJ: Transaction Publishers.

Ryan, A. (1994) 'Apocalypse now?', *New York Review of Books*, 17 Nov., **XLI** (191), 7–11.

Sachs, W. (1937 [rep. 1996, intro. Saul Dubow and Jacqueline Rose]) *Black Hamlet*, Baltimore, Johns Hopkins UP.

Sachs, W. (1957) *Black Anger*, NY: Grove Press.

Saer, D.J. (1922) 'An inquiry into the effect of bilingualism upon the intelligence of young children', *Journal of Experimental Pedagogy*, **6**, 232–40.

Saer, D.J. (1924) 'The effect of bilingualism on intelligence', *B.J.Psy.* **14** (1), 25–38.

Samelson, F. (1978) 'From race psychology to studies of prejudice', *JHBS* **14**, 265–78.

Sanderson, H.E. (1933) 'Differences in musical ability in children of different national and racial origin', *J.Genet.Psy.* **42**, 100–19.

Sapir, E. (1917) 'Do we need a super organic?', *Am.Anth.* **19**, 441–7.

Sargent, S.S. (1939) 'Emotional stereotypes in the Chicago Tribune', *Sociometry* **2** (2), 69–75.

Sartre, J.-P. (1946) 'Portrait of the Antisemite', *Partisan Review* **13**, 163–78.

Schaffer, S. (1994) *From Physics to Anthropology and Back Again*, Cambridge: Prickly Pear Press.

Scholes, T.E.S. (1907,1908) *Glimpses of the Ages or the 'Superior' and 'Inferior' Races, So-called, Discussed in the Light of Science and History*, 2 vols, London: John Long.

Schutz-Ewerth. E. (1925) 'Die farbige Gefahr', *Zeitschrift für Völkerpsychologie und Soziologie* **1**, 337–44.

Seashore, C. (1928) 'Three new approaches to the study of negro music', *Ann.Am.Ac.P.&SS.* **140**, 191–2.

Segall, M.H., Campbell, D.T. and Herskovits, M.J. (1963) 'Cultural differences in the perception of geometric illusions', *Science* **139**, 769–71.

Segall, M.H., Campbell, D.T. and Herskovits, M.J. (1966) *The Influence of Culture on Visual Perception*, Indianapolis and NY: Bobbs-Merrill.

Seligman, C.G. (1920) 'Notes on the article by Dr Seligman', *Eug.Rev.* **12**, 39–40.

Seligman, C.G. (1928) 'The unconscious in relation to anthropology', *B.J.Psy.* **18** (3), 373–87.

Seligman, C.G. (1939) 'Temperament, conflict and psychosis in a Stone Age population', *B.J.Ed.Psy.* **9**, 187–202.

Severson, A.L. (1939) 'Nationality and religious preferences as reflected in newspaper advertisements', *A.J.Sociol.* **44**, 540–45.

Shanklin, E. (1994) *Anthropology and Race*, Belmont CA: Wadsworth Publishing Company.

Shapin, S. (1991) 'A scholar and a gentleman: the Problematic identity of the scientific practitioner in early modern England', *History of Science* **29** (3), 279–327.

Shils, E.A. (1954) ''Authoritarianism, right and left', in R. Christie and M. Jahoda (eds) (1954), 24–49.

Shuey, A.M. (1966 2nd edn [1958]) *The Testing of Negro Intelligence*, NY: Social Science Press.

Shyllon, F.O. (1974) *Black Slaves in Britain*, Oxford: Oxford Institute of Race Relations.

Shyllon, F.O. (1977) *Black People in Britain 1555–1833*, London: OUP.

Sievers, W.D. (1955) *Freud on Broadway. A History of Psychoanalysis and the American Drama*, NY: Hermitage.

Singer, G.H. (1939) 'The influence of sudden oppression on a racial minority', *J.Soc.Psy.* **10**, 127–45.

Slobodin, R. (1978) *W.H.R. Rivers*, NY: Columbia UP.

Smart, M.S. (1963) 'Confirming Klineberg's suspicion', *Am.Psy.* **18**, 621.

Smith, A.P. (1931) 'Mental hygiene and the American negro', *Journal of the National Medical Association* **23**, 1–10.

Smith, B.M. (1950) 'Review of *The Authoritarian Personality*', *J.Ab.Soc.Psy.* **45**, 775–9.

Smith, C.E. (1934) 'A new approach to the problem of racial differences', *JNE* **3**, 523–9.

Smith, F. (1923) 'Bilingualism and mental development', *B.J.Psy.* **13** (3), 271–82.

Sokal, M.M. (1987) *Psychological Testing and American Society 1890–1930*, New Brunswick: Rutgers UP.

Spearman, C. (1927) *The Abilities of Man: Their Nature and Measurement*, London: Macmillan.

Spencer, F. (1990) *Piltdown: A Scientific Forgery*, London: Natural History Museum/OUP.

Spencer, H. (1870 [1855]) *Principles of Psychology*, 2 vols, London: Williams & Norgate.

Spencer, H. (1876) 'The comparative psychology of man', *Pop.Sci.Mo.* **8**, 257–69 (rep. in M.D. Biddis (ed.) (1979), 189–204).

Spier, L., Hallowell, A. I. and Newman, S.S. (eds) (1941) *Language, Culture, and Personality. Essays in Memory of Edward Sapir*, Menasha, Wisconsin: Sapir Memorial Publication Fund.

Spiller, G. (ed.) (1911) *Inter-Racial Problems. Communicated to the First Universal Races Congress held at the University of London July 26–29, 1911*, London: P.S. King.

Spindler, G.D. (ed.) (1978) *The Making of Psychological Anthropology*, Berkeley: University of California Press.

Spitzer, H.M. (1947) 'Psychoanalytic approaches to the Japanese character', *Psychoanalysis and the Social Sciences* **1**, 131–56.

Sprott, W.J.H. (1937) *Psychology for Everyone: An Outline of General Psychology*, London: Longmans Green (also issued as a student textbook as *General Psychology*).

Stallings, F.H. (1960) *Atlanta and Washington: Racial Differences in Academic Achievement*, Atlanta: Southern Regional Council Report No. L-16.

Stanhope Smith, S. (ed. W.D. Jordan) (1965 [1810 2nd edn, 1st edn 1785]) *An Essay on the Causes of the Variety of Complexion and Figure in the Human Species*, Cambridge, MA: Belknap Press Harvard UP.

Staum, M. (1995) 'Physiognomy and phrenology at the Paris Athénée', *Journal of the History of Ideas* **56** (3), 443–62.

Steggerda, M. and Macomber, E. (1938) 'A revision of the McAdory art test applied to American Indians, Dutch whites and college graduates', *J.Comp.Psy.* **26**, 349–53.

Steggerda, M. and Macomber, E. (1939) 'Mental and social characteristics of Maya and Navaho Indians as evidenced by a psychological rating scale', *J.Soc.Psy.* **10**, 51–9.

Stepan, N. (1982) *The Idea of Race in Science: Great Britain 1800–1960*, London: Macmillan.

Sterner, R. (1943) *The Negro's Share*, NY: Harper.

Stetson, G.R. (1896) 'The Negro and the Church', *Protestant Episcopalian Review* July.

Stetson, G.R. (1897) 'Some memory tests of whites and blacks', *Psy.Rev.* **4**, 285–9.

Stocking, G.W. (1986) *Malinowski, Rivers, Benedict and Others: Culture and Personality*, Madison, WI: University of Wisconsin Press.

Stoddard, T.L. (1920) *The Rising Tide of Color Against White World-Supremacy*, NY: Scribner's.

Stölting, H. (1938) 'Blutreinheit und Blutmischungen in ihrer tierferen Bedeutung', *Zeitschrift für pädagogische Psychologie* **39**, 99–105.

Stone, A.H. (ed.) (1908) *Studies in the American Race Problem*, NY:Doubleday, Page.

Stouffer, S.A. et al. (1949–1950) *The American Soldier*, 4 vols, Princeton, NJ: Princeton UP.

Stout, G.F. (1929) *Manual of Psychology*, 4th edn (rev. in collaboration with C.A. Mace), London: University Tutorial Press.

Stransky, E. (1937) 'Rasse und Psychotherapie', *Zentralblatt für Psychotherapie* **10**, 9–28.

Strong, A.M. (1913) 'Three hundred fifty white and colored children measured by the Binet–Simon measuring scale', *Ped.Sem.* **20**, 485–512.

Sukuo, M. and Williamson, E.G. (1938) 'Personality traits and aptitudes of Jewish and non-Jewish students', *J.App.Psy.* **22**, 487–92.

Sunne, D. (1917) 'A comparative study of white and negro children', *J.App.Psy.* **1**, 71–83.

Sunne, D. (1924) 'A comparison of white and negro children in verbal and non-verbal tests', *Sch.&Soc.* **19**, 469–72.

Sunne, D. (1925a) 'Comparisons of white and negro children by the Terman and Yerkes–Bridges revisions of the Binet tests', *J.Comp.Psy.* **5**, 209–19.

Sunne, D. (1925b) 'Personality tests: white and negro adolescents', *J.App.Psy.* **9**, 265–80.

Suttie, I.D. (1932) 'Religion: racial character and mental and social health', *B.J.Med.Psy.* **12**, 289–314.

Swift, E.J. (1908) *Mind in the Making*, NY: Scribner's.

Tanser, H.A. (1939) *The Settlement of Negroes in Kent County, Ontario*, Chatham, Ontario: Shepard.

Taylor, C.T. (1936) 'A study of certain attitudes of negro junior high school pupils', *Bulletin of Purdue University* **37**, 192–202.

Telford, C.W. (1930) 'Differences in responses to colors and their names: some racial comparisons', *J.Genet.Psy.* **37**, 151–9.

Telford, C.W. (1932) 'Test performance of full and mixed blood North Dakota Indians', *J.Comp. Psy.***14**, 123–45.

Terman, L.M. (1919, rep. 1932) *The Measurement of Intelligence*, London: Harrap.

Terman, L.M. (1921-3) 'Correspondence', *New Republic* (rep. in N. Block and G. Dworkin (eds) (1977a) 4–46 as 'The Lippman–Terman Debate)'.

Thomas, W.H. (1901) *The American Negro*, NY: Macmillan.

Thomas, W.I. (1896) 'The scope and method of folk-psychology', *A.J.Sociol.* **1**, 434–45.

Thomas, W.I. (1901) 'The gaming instinct', *A.J.Sociol.* **6**, 750–63.

Thomas, W.I. (1904) 'The psychology of race-prejudice', *A.J.Sociol.* **11**, 593–611.

Thomas, W.I. (1907) 'The mind of woman and the lower races', *A.J.Sociol.* **12**, 435–69.

Thomas, W.I. (1909) *Source Book of Social Origins*, Chicago: University of Chicago Press.

Thomas, W.I. (1912) 'Race psychology, standpoint and questionnaire', *A.J.Sociol.* **17**, 725–75.

Thomas, W.I. (1937) *Primitive Behavior; An Introduction to the Social Sciences*, NY: McGraw-Hill.

Thomas, W.I. and Znaniecki, F. (1918-20) *The Polish Peasant in Europe and America*, 5 vols, Chicago: University of Chicago Press.

Thompson, C.H. (1934) 'The conclusions of scientists relative to racial differences ' *JNE* **3**, 494–512.

Thompson, W.H. (1939) 'A study of the frequency of mongolianism in Negro children in the United States', *Proc.Am.Ass.Ment.Def.* **44** (1), 91–4.

Thomson, G. (1921) 'The Northumberland Mental Tests', *B.J. Psy.* **12** (3), 201–22.

Thorndike, E.B. (1913) *Educational Psychology*, 2 vols, NY: Teacher's College.

Thouless, R.H. (1933) 'A racial difference in perception', *J.Soc.Psy.* **4**, 330–39.

Thouless, R.H. (1937) *General and Social Psychology*, 2nd edn, London: University Tutorial Press.

Thurstone, L.L. (1928) 'An experimental study of national preferences', *J.Genet.Psy.* **1**, 405–25.

Thurstone, L.L. (ed.) (1930,1931) *Scales for the Measurement of Social Attitudes*, Chicago: University of Chicago Press.

Tillinghurst, J.A. (1902) 'The Negro in Africa and America', *American Economics Association Publications* 3, May.

Tirala, L.G. (1936) *Sport und Rasse*, Frankfurt: publisher n.a.

Titchener, E.B. (1916) 'On ethnological tests of sensation and perception with special reference to tests of color vision and tactile discrimination described in the reports of the Cambridge anthropological expedition to Torres Straits', *Proceedings of the American Philosophical Society* 55, 204–36.

Titus, H.E. and Hollander, E.P. (1955) 'The California F-scale in psychological research 1950–1955', *Psy.Bull.* 54 (1), 47–62.

Tizard, B. and Phoenix, A. (1993) *Black, White or Mixed Race? Race and Racism in the Lives of Young People of Mixed Parentage*, London: Routledge.

Tolman Smith, A. (1896) 'A study in race psychology', *Pop.Sci.Mo.* 50, 354–60.

Topinard, P. (1890) *Anthropology*, London: Chapman & Hall.

Travis Osborne, R. and McGurk, F.C.J. (eds) (1982) *The Testing of Negro Intelligence, Volume 2*, Athens, GA: The Foundation for Human Understanding.

Trevor, J.C. (1938) 'Some anthropological characteristics of hybrid populations', *Eug.Rev.* 30, 21–31.

Tucker, W. H. (1994) *The Science and Politics of Racial Research*, Urbana and Chicago: University of Illinois Press.

Turnbull, C.M. (1961) *The Forest People*, London: Chatto & Windus.

Turner, R.S. (1994) *In The Eye's Mind: Vision and the Helmholtz–Hering Controversy*, Princeton NJ: Princeton UP.

UNESCO (1951) *Statement On The Nature Of Race And Race Differences*, Paris: UNESCO.

University Commission on Southern Race Problems (1918) 'Minutes', Lexington, VA: The Commission.

Urry, J. (1982) 'From zoology to ethnology. A.C. Haddon's conversion to anthropology', *Canberra Anthropology* 5, 58–85.

Urry, J. (1992) *Before Social Anthropology: Essays in the History of British Anthropology*, Chur, Switzerland and Philadelphia: Harwood Academic Press.

Van Dijk, T.A. (1987) *Communicating Racism: Ethnic Prejudice in Thought and Talk*, Newbury Park: Sage.

Van Evrie, J.H. (1868) *White Supremacy and Negro Subordination*, NY: Van Evrie, Horton & Co.

Vernon, P.A. and Jensen, A.R. (1984) 'Individual and group differences in intelligence and speed of information processing', *Personality and Individual Differences* 5, 411–23.

Vincent, K.R. (1991) 'Black/white IQ differences: does age make the difference?', *Journal of Clinical Psychology* 47 (2), 266–70.

Vint, F.W. (1932) 'A preliminary note on the cell content of the prefrontal cortex of the East African native', *E.Af.Med.J.* 9 (2), 30–49.

Vint, F.W. (1934) 'The brain of the Kenya native', *Journal of Anatomy*, January.

Wahr, G. (1988) *Jung: A Biography*, Halifax: Shambalah Press.

Wake, C.S. (1868) *Chapters on Man, with the Outlines of Comparative Psychology*, London: Trübner.

Wallin, J.E.W. (1930) 'The ratio of candidates for sight conservation classes', *Sch. & Soc.* 33, 65–8.

Walvin, J. (ed.) (1982) *Slavery and British Society 1776–1846*, London: Macmillan.

Wanderwolf, C.H. and Cain, D.P. (1990) 'The neurobiology of race and Kipling's cat', *Personality and Individual Differences* 12 (1), 97–8.

Watson, J.B. (1936) Autobiographical entry in C. Murchison (ed.) (1936), 271–82.

Watson, P. (1973) 'Race and intelligence through the looking glass', in P. Watson (ed.) *Psychology and Race*, Harmondsworth: Penguin, 360–76.

Weale, B.L.P. (1910) *The Conflict of Colour*, London: Macmillan.

Weatherford, W.D. and Johnson, C.S. (1934) *Race Relations: Adjustment of Whites and Negroes in the United States*, NY: Heath.

Weatherly, U.G. (1911) 'A world-wide color line', *Pop.Sci.Mo.* 79, 474–85.

Weidman, N. (1994) 'Lashley, race and the writing of history', unpublished *Cheiron* conference paper.

Weindling, P. (1989) *Health, Race and German Politics Between National Unification and Nazism, 1870–1945*, Cambridge: CUP.

Weissenberg, S. (1927) 'Zur Sozialbiologie und Sozialhygiene der Juden', *Archiv für Rassen- und Gesellschaftbiologie* 19, 492.

West, G.A. (1936) 'Racial attitudes among teachers in the Southwest', *J.Ab.Soc.Psy.* 31, 331–7.

Westermann, D. (1939) *The African Today and Tomorrow*, London:OUP/ Humphrey Milford for the International Institute for the Study of African Languages and Culture.

White, C. (1799) *Account of the Regular Gradation in Man, and in Different Animals and Vegetables; and from the Former to the Latter*, London: C. Dilly.

White, J. (1972) 'Toward a black psychology', in R.L. Jones (ed.) (1972), 43–50.

Whiting, B.B. (1963) *Six Cultures: Studies in Child Rearing*, NY: Wiley.

Whiting, J.and Whiting, B.B. (1978) 'A strategy for psychocultural research', in G.D. Spindler (ed.) (1978), Chapter 1.

Wilcox, R.C. (ed.) (1971) *The Psychological Consequences of being Black American: A Collection of Research by Black Psychologists*, NY: Wiley.

Wilkerson, D. (1934) 'Racial differences in scholastic achievement', *JNE* 3, 453–77.

Willis, R. (1974) *Man and Beast*, London: Hart-Davis, MacGibbon.

Winch, W.H. (1930) 'Christian and Jewish children in East-End elementary schools', *B.J.Psy.* 20 (3), 261–73.

Winston, A.S. (1996) '"As His Name Indicates": R.S. Woodworth's letters of reference and employment for Jewish psychologists in the 1930s', *JHBS* 32 (1), 30–43.

Wirth, L. and Goldhamer, H. (1944) 'The hybrid and the problem of miscegenation', in O. Klineberg (ed.) (1944), 249–369.

Wispé, L., Awkard, J., Hoffman, M., Hicks, L.H. and Porter, J. (1971) 'The Negro psychologist in America', in Wilcox, R.C. (ed.) (1971), 449–65.

Witmer, A.H. (1891) 'Insanity in the colored race in the United States', *Alienist and Neurologist* 12, 19–30.

Wohlwill, J.F. (1987) 'German psychological journals under National Socialism: a history of contrasting paths', *JHBS* 23, 169–85.

Wolberg, D. (1927) 'Zur differentialen Psychologie der Juden', *Jena Beitrage zür Jugend- und Erziehungspsychologie* 5, Langensalza: Beltz.

Wood Jones, F. and Porteus, S.D. (1928) *The Matrix of the Mind*, Honolulu: University Press Association.

Woodworth, R.S. (1910a) 'Racial differences in mental traits', *Science* N.S. 31, 171–86.

Woodworth, R.S. (1910b) 'The puzzle of color vocabularies', *Psy.Bull.* 7 (10), 325–34.

Woodworth, R.S. (1916) 'Comparative psychology of races', *Psy.Bull.* 13, 388–96.

Woodworth, R.S. (1918) *Dynamic Psychology. The Jessup Lectures 1916–1917*, NY: Columbia UP.

Woodworth, R.S. (1946, 18th edn) *Psychology. A Study of Mental Life*, London: Methuen.

Wright, R. (1940) *Native Son*, NY: Harper.

Wundt, W. (1916) *Elements of Folk Psychology. Outlines of a Psychological History of the Development of Mankind*, London: Allen & Unwin/NY: Macmillan.

Wyndham, H.A. (1926) 'The problem of colour in relation to the idea of equality', *Journal of Philosophical Studies*, I, 224–33.

Wynn Jones, L. (1934) *An Introduction to the Theory and Practice of Psychology*, London: Macmillan.

Yee, A.H., Fairchild, Halford, H., Weizmann, F. and Wyatt, Gail E. (1993) 'Addressing psychology's problems with race', *Am.Psy.* 48 (11), 1132–40.

Yerkes, R.M. (1921) 'Psychological examining in the United States Army', *Memoirs of the National Academy of Science* 15, 1–890.

Yerkes, R.M. (1922) 'Eugenic bearing of measurements of intelligence in the United States Army', *Eug.Rev.* 14, 225–45.

Yerkes, R.M. (1929) 'Testing the human mind', *Atlantic Monthly* 131, 358–70.

Yerkes, R.M., Bridges, J.W. and Hardwick, R.S. (1915) *A Point Scale for Measuring Mental Ability*, Baltimore: Warwick & York.

Yoakum, C. and Yerkes, R.M. (1920) *Mental Tests in the American Army*, London: Sidgwick & Jackson.

Yoder, D. (1928) 'Present status of the question of racial differences', *J.Ed.Psy.* 19, 463–70.

Young, D. (1927) 'Some effects of a course in American race problems on the [*sic*] race prejudice', *J.Ab.Soc.Psy.* 22, 235–42.

Young, K. (ed.) (1931) *Social Psychology: An Analysis of Social Behavior*, NY: Crofts.

Young, R.M. (1990 [1970]) *Mind, Brain and Adaptation in the Nineteenth Century*, NY and Oxford: OUP.

Zeligs, R. (1937) 'Racial attitudes of children', *Sociol.Soc.Res.* 21, 361–71.

Zeligs, R. (1938) 'Tracing racial attitudes through adolescence', *Sociol.Soc.Res.* 23, 45–54.

Zeligs, R. (1941) 'Influencing children's attitudes towards the Chinese', *Sociol.Soc.Res.* 26, 126–38.

Zeligs, R. and Hendrickson, G. (1935) 'Factors regarded by children as the basis of their racial attitudes', *Sociol.Soc.Res.* 19, 225–33.

Zilian, E. (1938) 'Rasse und seelenkundliche Persönlichkeitsauslese in der Wehrmacht', *Rasse* 5, 321–33.

Zilian, E. (1939) 'Zum Rassendiagnostischen Atlas', *Wehrmacht. Mitt* 1 (Heft 7/8), 38–43.

Zuckerman, M. (1990) 'Some dubious premises in research and theory on racial differences. Scientific, social, ethical issues', *Am.Psy.* 45 (12), 1297–303.

Zusne, L. (1984) *Biographical Dictionary of Psychology*, NY: Greenwood Press.

T.R. Garth bibliography
Publications related to race Psychology

Abbreviations as for main bibliography

(1919) 'Racial differences in mental fatigue', *J.App.Psy.* 5, 235–44.
(1920) 'The psychology of the American Indian', *Indian School Journal* 20, 157–60, 220.
(1921a) 'Results of some tests on full and mixed-blood Indians', *J.App.Psy.* 5, 359–72.
(1921b) 'White, Indian and Negro work curves', *J.App.Psy.* 5, 15–25.
(1922a) 'The color preferences of five hundred and fifty-nine full blood Indians', *J.Exp.Psy.* 5, 392–418.
(1922b) 'A comparison of the mental abilities of full and mixed-blood Indians', *Psy. Rev.* 29, 221–36.
(1922c) 'The intelligence of Indians', *Science* 46, 635–7.
(1922d) 'An investigation of the intelligence of Mexican and mixed and full blood Indian children', *Eugenical News* 7, 105.
(1922e) 'Mental fatigue of mixed and full blood Indians', *J.App.Psy.* 6, 331–41.
(1922f) 'The problem of racial psychology', *J.Ab.Soc.Psy.* 17, 215–19.
(1923a) 'Comparison of intelligence of Mexican and mixed and full blood Indian children', *Psy.Rev.* 30, 388–401.
(1923b) 'The mind of the Indian', *Indian School Journal* 22, 132–6.
(1923c) 'Mental fatigue of Indians of nomadic and sedentary tribes', *Proceedings 32nd Annual Meeting APA*, 110–11.
(1923d) 'Mental fatigue of mixed and full-blood Indians', *Proceedings 32nd Annual Meeting APA*, 112–21.
(1924) 'A color preference scale for one thousand white children', *J.Exp.Psy.* 7, 233–41.
(1925) 'A review of racial psychology', *Psy.Bull.* 22, 343–64.
(1926a) 'The industrial psychology of the immigrant Mexican', *Individual Psychology* 1, 183–7.
(1926b) 'Mental fatigue of Indians of nomadic and sedentary tribes, *J.App.Psy.* 10, 437–52.
(1926c) 'Race and psychology', *Science Monthly* 23, 240–45.
(1927a) 'The community of ideas of Indians', *Psy. Rev.* 34, 391–9.
(1927b) 'A comparison of mental abilities of nomadic and sedentary Indians on a basis of education', *Am.Anth.* 29, 206–13.
(1928a) 'The intelligence and achievement of full-blood Indians', *J.App.Psy.* 12, 511–16.
(1928b) 'The intelligence of mexican school children', *Sch. &.Soc.* 27, 791–4.
(1928c) 'Racial minds' *Psyche* 8, 63–70.
(1930a) 'A review of race psychology', *Psy.Bull.* 27, 329–56.
(1930b) 'The color blindness of Indians', *Science* 71 (1844), 462.
(1930c) 'Eugenics, euthenics, ,and race', *Opportunity* 8, 206–7.
(1931a) 'The handwriting of Indians', *J.Ed.Psy.* 22, 705–9.
(1931b) *Race Psychology*, NY: Whittlesey.

(1931c) 'The incidence of color blindness among Indians', *Report to National Research Council and University of Denver.*
(1933a) 'The incidence of color-blindness among races', *Science* 77, 333–4.
(1933b) 'The intelligence and achievement of mixed-blood Indians', *J.Soc.Psy.* 4, 134–7.
(1934) 'The problem of race psychology: a general statement', *JNE* 3, 319–27.
(1935a) 'A study of the foster Indian child in the white home', *Psy.Bull.* 32, 708–9.
(1935b) 'Color blindness in Japan', *Sigma Xi Quarterly.* March.
(1936) 'Colour blindness and race', *Zeitschrift für Rassenkunde* 4, 33–6.
(1937) 'The hypothesis of racial difference', *Journal of Social Philosophy* 2, 224–31.

Joint publications

with Barnard, M.A. (1927) 'The will-temperament of Indians', *J.App.Psy.* 11, 512–18.
with Collado, I.R. (1929) 'The color preferences of Filipino children', *J.Comp.Psy.* 9, 397–404.
with Elson, T.H. and Morton, M.M. (1936) 'The administration of non-language intelligence tests to Mexicans', *J.Ab.Soc.Psy.* 31, 53–8.
with Foote, J. (1939) 'The community of ideas among the Japanese', *J.Soc.Psy.* 10, 179–85.
with Garrett, J.E. (1928) 'A comparative study of the intelligence of Indians in US Indian schools and in the public or common schools', *Sch. & Soc.* 27, 178–84.
with Garth, T.R. Jr (1937) 'The personality of Indians', *J.App.Psy.* 21, 464–7.
with Johnson, H.D. (1934) 'The intelligence and achievement of Mexican children in the United States', *J.Ab.Soc.Psy.* 29, 222–9.
with Ilkeda, K. and Gardner, D.A. (1933) 'Japanese work curves', *J.App.Psy.* 17, 331–6.
with Isbell, S.R. (1929) 'Musical talent of Indians', *Music Supervisors Journal*, Feb.
with Lovelady, B.E. and Smith, H.W. (1930) 'The intelligence and achievement of southern negro children', *Sch. & .Soc,* 32, 431–5.
with Mitchell, M.J. and Anthony, C.N. (1939) 'The handwriting of negroes', *J.Ed.Psy.* 30, 69–73.
with Moses, M.R. and Anthony, C.N. (1938) 'The color preferences of East Indians', *A.J.Psy.* 51, 709–13.
with Schuelke, N. and Abell, W. (1927) 'The intelligence of mixed-blood Indians', *J.App.Psy.* 11, 268–75.
with Serafini, T.J. and Dewey, D. (1925) 'The intelligence of full-blood Indians', *J.App.Psy.* 9, 382–9.
with Smith, O.D. (1937) 'The performances of full-blood Indians on language and non-language intelligence tests', *J.Ab.Soc.Psy.* 32, 376–81.
with Whatley, C.A. (1925) 'Intelligence of southern negro children', *Sch. & Soc.* 22, 501–4.

Name index

Subject index

(The absence of a general entry for 'whites' should be taken as signifying the white-centred nature of the topic, rather than an ethnocentric oversight of the author.)